Real-Time Systems

Jane W.S. Liu

Prentice Hall
Upper Saddle River, New Jersey 07458

Library of Congress Cataloging-in-Publication Data

Liu, Jane W.S.

    Real-time systems / by Jane W.S. Liu.

       p. cm.

    ISBN 0-13-099651-3

    1. Real-time data processing. I. Title.

  QA76.54.L59   2000

  004'.33—dc21   99-051522

                         CIP

Publisher: *Alan R. Apt*
Editorial assistant: *Toni Holm*
Production editor: *Audri Anna Bazlen*
Vice-president and editorial director: *Marcia Horton*
Executive managing editor: *Vince O'Brien*
Managing editor: *David George*
Art director: *Heather Scott*
Assistant to art director: *John Christiana*
Creative director: *Paul Belfanti*
Manufacturing manager: *Trudi Pisciotti*
Manufacturing buyer: *Pat Brown*
Cover image: © *Photodisc*

Prentice Hall   © 2000 by Prentice-Hall, Inc.
Upper Saddle River, New Jersey 07458

The author and publisher of this book have used their best efforts in preparing this book. These efforts include the development, research, and testing of the theories and programs to determine their effectiveness. The author and publisher make no warranty of any kind, expressed or implied, with regard to these programs or the documentation contained in this book. The author and publisher shall not be liable in any event for incidental or consequential damages inconnection with, or arising out of, the furnishing, performance, or use of these programs.

Printed in the United States of America
10 9 8 7 6 5 4 3 2 1

ISBN 0-13-099651-3

Prentice-Hall International (UK) Limited, *London*
Prentice-Hall of Australia Pty. Limited, *Sydney*
Prentice-Hall of Canada Inc., *Toronto*
Prentice-Hall Hispanoamericana, S.A., *Mexico*
Prentice-Hall of India Private Limited, *New Delhi*
Prentice-Hall of Japan, Inc., *Tokyo*
Pearson Education Asia Pte. Ltd., *Singapore*
Editora Prentice-Hall do Brasil, Ltda., *Rio de Janeiro*

To the memory of James N. Snyder

Contents

Preface

This text grew from my lecture notes of a course on real-time systems, which I have been teaching regularly for the past six years. The course is a technical elective for seniors and graduate students in Computer Science and Computer Engineering. It requires as a prerequisite an undergraduate course on operating systems.

Like the course, the book builds on the student's background in operating systems. It covers techniques for scheduling, resource access control, and validation that are, or are likely to be, widely used in real-time computing and communication systems. Each algorithm, protocol, or mechanism is defined by pseudocode or simple rules that can serve as a starting point of implementation. With few exceptions, each scheduling algorithm is accompanied by one or more validation techniques. You can use the techniques to ascertain that your application will meet its real-time requirements when scheduled according to the algorithm.

In addition to information on existing techniques, the book emphasizes basic principles of real-time systems. The foundations of these techniques are presented as theorems and corollaries. (I would like to have avoided this style, but feared that they might be buried in the narratives and details if not thus highlighted. I tried to keep them and their proofs informal.) I cover many of the theorems and proofs in my course in order to give students insight into why and how well the techniques work, and teach them the skills they will need to extend the existing techniques and develop new ones.

While this coverage may make the book a good reference for practitioners, a developer who wants to get information quickly may find its presentation verbose. The summary section at the end of each chapter should help. It gives you either the information you are looking for, or a pointer to the section where you can find the information.

Comments on Contents. The focus of the book is real-time operating systems and networks. It starts with a small part (Chapters 1, 2 and 3) on real-time applications and systems in general. It ends with a part (Chapters 11 and 12) on specific attributes and implementations of network protocols and operating systems. The large part (Chapters 4–10) in the middle covers uniprocessor scheduling, resource access control, and multiprocessor and distributed scheduling. Sections and subsections marked by * are included for the sake of completeness. You can skip over them without loss of continuity.

Chapters 1 and 2. Chapter 1 gives an overview of several sample real-time applications for which the techniques described in the book were developed. I find most computer science and engineering students in my classes are unfamiliar with these applications. The chapter tries to explain for them the characteristics of workloads generated by the applications and the reasons for their timing requirements. Chapter 2 follows by giving the definitions of hard and soft real-time systems and the rationales for this classification.

Chapter 3.   Chapter 3 describes a reference model of real-time systems. Subsequent chapters (e.g., 4–10) characterize the systems we study according to special variants of the model. The reference model has a rich set of features. We can describe a wide spectrum of real-time applications and underlying platforms in a sufficiently faithful manner in terms of the model so that we can analyze, simulate, and even emulate the system based on the description; indeed, some scheduling and validation tools use this kind of description as input. However, many features of the model are not used in later chapters. Sections describing them are marked by *.

Chapters 4–9.   These six chapters describe algorithms and protocols for scheduling and validating real-time systems. In particular, they cover the time-driven approach, the RMA technology, and the dynamic-priority approach.

Chapter 4 gives a brief overview of the three approaches to scheduling: clock-driven, weighted round-robin, and priority-driven, which are treated in depth in later chapters. It also highlights some important facts about priority-driven scheduling. I discuss these facts in the beginning of my course as a way to motivate the techniques to be discussed in the weeks to come. Even if a student drops the course early in the semester, he/she will walk away knowing these facts.

Chapter 5 describes the clock-driven approach in general and cyclic executives in specific. This is the traditional way to schedule more or less deterministic workloads and is still the way used to schedule safety-critical applications.

Chapters 6, 7, and 8 are devoted to algorithms for scheduling and resource access control on one processor (i.e., a CPU, or a network link, I/O bus, a disk, and so on). Most of these algorithms are priority-driven; all of them can be implement easily on modern real-time operating systems and communication networks. The chapters adopt increasingly more complex variants of the periodic-task model: Chapter 6 starts from workloads consisting solely of independent periodic tasks that do not require any resource other than a processor. Chapter 7 adds aperiodic and sporadic tasks, and Chapter 8 adds resource contentions.

Chapter 9 is on multiprocessor and distributed systems. It introduces control and data dependencies among tasks and the end-to-end nature of their timing requirements. It then describes methods for partitioning an application into modules and assigning the modules to processors, controlling their access to resources on multiple processors, and synchronizing the execution of tasks on different processors.

Together, Chapters 6–9 give a comprehensive treatment of the RMA approach, which in essence is synonymous to fixed-priority scheduling. Most algorithms based on this approach allow application components to be added and deleted at run-time and can handle nondeterministic resource demands. The timing behavior of applications scheduled according to the algorithms are nondeterministic. However, the adverse effects of scheduling anomalies are bounded when fluctuations in resource demands are bounded. For most real-time applications, such as those described in Chapter 1, the accompanied validation techniques make it possible for us to predict fairly accurately the worst-case real-time performance of applications thus scheduled. The chapters also describe ways to schedule applications with widely varying resource demands within the deadline-driven framework. As examples, rate-based algorithms can provide timing isolation to sporadic tasks and enables us to predict the real-time performance of a distributed sporadic task independent of other tasks in the system.

Chapter 10.   Chapter 10 introduces the concept of flexible applications. A flexible application contains tasks that can trade off the qualities of their results for their time and resource demands. The flexible computation approach is a means for handling overload and increasing availability. This chapter describes workload models that capture the characteristics and requirements of flexible applications and algorithms that have been developed to schedule them. Another subject of discussion is the temporal distance model. The timing requirements of some real-time tasks can be more conveniently defined in the terms of the maximum length of time between completions of consecutive task instances. The temporal distance model captures this kind of requirement.

Chapter 11.   Chapter 11 focuses on real-time issues in communication networks, specifically, features and capabilities needed to support real-time applications. It starts by describing low-level, real-time flow control, and scheduling schemes for packet switched networks and medium access protocols for broadcast networks. It then describes resource reservation, internet and transport protocols designed for real-time applications.

Chapter 12.   The last chapter examines in depth implementation details that were ignored in earlier chapters. It consists of two parts. The first part discusses how operating systems services and mechanisms should be implemented to enhance the predictability of applications using them. Some services and mechanisms are easy to implement, have low overhead, and can make the implementation of many algorithms described in previous chapters significantly simpler, but are not provided by most commercial operating systems. This part describes examples of them.

The second part gives an overview of several commercial real-time and general purpose operating systems. It highlights good features of real-time operating systems. It explains why Windows NT and Linux, two popular general purpose operating systems, do not work well for real-time applications and how to get better predictability out of them.

Acknowledgments.   Before presenting my thanks to individuals, let me first congratulate the real-time systems community for their accomplishments in recent years. This book tries to document some of these accomplishments. It took me longer than expected to complete it for several reasons (e.g., writing was a background job and keeping up with new advances caused the job to overrun.) The pleasure in writing on the subject is a strong incentive to prolong the project. I admire the algorithms, protocols, and mechanisms developed by the community, not only for their practical merits but also for their good underlying science and engineering. I am grateful for the opportunity to learn and write about them. I regret deeply that both the book and I ran out of space and time to include much excellent work. Most of the work reported in the book began in the late 1980s with the support of the ONR (Office of Naval Research) Real-Time Systems Initiative. The technical leadership provided by Andre Van Tilborg and Gary Koob contributed significantly to the tremendous advances in real-time systems technologies.

I also want to apologize to authors whose work is not cited directly in the bibliography. Rather than providing a comprehensive bibliography to properly acknowledge each contributor, I compiled the bibliography primarily for the readers. It points to where the reader can find further information on topics glossed over in the book. (This is why the deeper and more thoroughly the book treats a topic and, therefore, the lesser the need for further information, the fewer citations on the topic are included in the bibliography.) Because more recent publications in turn provide pointers to earlier work but not vice versa, the bibliography usually cites the most recent work among possible citations and more easily found publications.

I owe my deepest gratitude to Sang L. Min for reading line by line most of the chapters and suggesting ways to correct technical and presentation problems, to Jun Sun, for spending hours helping me understand some of the complex algorithms, and to Michael Gonzalez Harbour and Doug Locke for teaching me POSIX realtime extensions, Jim Anderson, Ted Baker, Sanjoy Baruah, Riccardo Bettati, Greg Morrison, and Hui Zhang pointed out misconceptions and mistakes; I cannot thank them enough. I am deeply indebted to Al Mok, Insup Lee and their students. Al and Insup encouraged me by having students in their real-time systems classes read and presented the chapters in the book. Their students gave me numerous suggestions and pointed out many errors. I also thank my students for their valuable feedback and suggestions, and colleague Lui Sha for his encouragement.

Kimberly Michael drew all the illustrations in the book. I thank her for her excellent work, as well as her patience with me during rounds of revision. Molly Flesner made and sent copy after copy of the manuscript throughout the years. I admire and thank her for her cheerfulness in doing the tiresome chore.

Last, but not least, my husband and colleague C. L. Liu and daughter Kathleen urged me to go on when my patience ran short and confidence low. I thank them for their advice and support and, most of all, for being my best friends.

CHAPTER 1

Typical Real-Time Applications

From its title, you can see that this book is about real-time (computing, communication, and information) systems. Rather than pausing here to define the term precisely, which we will do in Chapter 2, let us just say for now that a real-time system is required to complete its work and deliver its services on a timely basis. Examples of real-time systems include digital control, command and control, signal processing, and telecommunication systems. Every day these systems provide us with important services. When we drive, they control the engine and brakes of our car and regulate traffic lights. When we fly, they schedule and monitor the takeoff and landing of our plane, make it fly, maintain its flight path, and keep it out of harm's way. When we are sick, they may monitor and regulate our blood pressure and heart beats. When we are well, they can entertain us with electronic games and joy rides. Unlike PCs and workstations that run nonreal-time applications such as our editor and network browser, the computers and networks that run real-time applications are often hidden from our view. When real-time systems work correctly and well, they make us forget their existence.

For the most part, this book is devoted to real-time operating systems and communication protocols, in particular, how they should work so that applications running on them can reliably deliver valuable services on time. From the examples above, you can see that malfunctions of some real-time systems can have serious consequences. We not only want such systems to work correctly and responsively but also want to be able to show that they indeed do. For this reason, a major emphasis of the book is on techniques for validating real-time systems. By validation, we mean a rigorous demonstration that the system has the intended timing behavior.

As an introduction, this chapter describes several representative classes of real-time applications: digital control, optimal control, command and control, signal processing, tracking, real-time databases, and multimedia. Their principles are out of the scope of this book. We provide only a brief overview in order to explain the characteristics of the workloads generated by the applications and the relation between their timing and functional requirements. In later chapters, we will work with abstract workload models that supposedly capture the relevant characteristics of these applications. This overview aims at making us better judges of the accuracy of the models.

In this chapter, we start by describing simple digital controllers in Section 1.1. They are the simplest and the most deterministic real-time applications. They also have the most stringent timing requirements. Section 1.2 describes optimal control and command and control applications. These high-level controllers either directly or indirectly guide and coordinate

digital controllers and interact with human operators. High-level controllers may have significantly higher and widely fluctuating resource demands as well as larger and more relaxed
response time requirements. Section 1.3 describes signal processing applications in general
and radar signal processing and tracking in particular. Section 1.4 describes database and
multimedia applications. Section 1.5 summarizes the chapter.

1.1   DIGITAL CONTROL

Many real-time systems are embedded in sensors and actuators and function as digital controllers. Figure 1–1 shows such a system. The term plant in the block diagram refers to a
controlled system, for example, an engine, a brake, an aircraft, a patient. The state of the plant
is monitored by sensors and can be changed by actuators. The real-time (computing) system
estimates from the sensor readings the current state of the plant and computes a control output
based on the difference between the current state and the desired state (called reference input
in the figure). We call this computation the *control-law computation* of the controller. The
output thus generated activates the actuators, which bring the plant closer to the desired state.

1.1.1   Sampled Data Systems

Long before digital computers became cost-effective and widely used, analog (i.e., continuous-
time and continuous-state) controllers were in use, and their principles were well established.
Consequently, a common approach to designing a digital controller is to start with an analog
controller that has the desired behavior. The analog version is then transformed into a digital (i.e., discrete-time and discrete-state) version. The resultant controller is a *sampled data
system*. It typically samples (i.e., reads) and digitizes the analog sensor readings periodically
and carries out its control-law computation every period. The sequence of digital outputs thus
produced is then converted back to an analog form needed to activate the actuators.

A Simple Example.   As an example, we consider an analog single-input/single-output
PID (Proportional, Integral, and Derivative) controller. This simple kind of controller is commonly used in practice. The analog sensor reading $y(t)$ gives the measured state of the plant
at time t. Let $e(t) = r(t) - y(t)$ denote the difference between the desired state $r(t)$ and the
measured state $y(t)$ at time t. The output $u(t)$ of the controller consists of three terms: a term

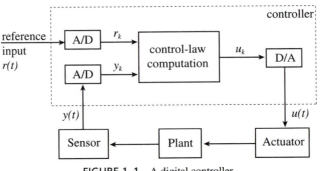

FIGURE 1–1   A digital controller.

that is proportional to $e(t)$, a term that is proportional to the integral of $e(t)$ and a term that is proportional to the derivative of $e(t)$.

In the sampled data version, the inputs to the control-law computation are the *sampled values* y_k and r_k, for $k = 0, 1, 2, \ldots$, which analog-to-digital converters produce by sampling and digitizing $y(t)$ and $r(t)$ periodically every T units of time. $e_k = r_k - y_k$ is the kth sample value of $e(t)$. There are many ways to discretize the derivative and integral of $e(t)$. For example, we can approximate the derivative of $e(t)$ for $(k - 1)T \leq t \leq kT$ by $(e_k - e_{k-1})/T$ and use the trapezoidal rule of numerical integration to transform a continuous integral into a discrete form. The result is the following incremental expression of the kth output u_k:

$$u_k = u_{k-2} + \alpha e_k + \beta e_{k-1} + \gamma e_{k-2} \tag{1.1}$$

α, β, and γ are proportional constants; they are chosen at design time.[1] During the kth sampling period, the real-time system computes the output of the controller according to this expression. You can see that this computation takes no more than 10–20 machine instructions. Different discretization methods may lead to different expressions of u_k, but they all are simple to compute.

From Eq. (1.1), we can see that during any sampling period (say the kth), the control output u_k depends on the current and past measured values y_i for $i \leq k$. The future measured values y_i's for $i > k$ in turn depend on u_k. Such a system is called a *(feedback) control loop* or simply a *loop*. We can implement it as an infinite timed loop:

    set timer to interrupt periodically with period T;
    at each timer interrupt, do
        do analog-to-digital conversion to get y;
        compute control output u;
        output u and do digital-to-analog conversion;
    end do;

Here, we assume that the system provides a timer. Once set by the program, the timer generates an interrupt every T units of time until its setting is cancelled.

Selection of Sampling Period.   The length T of time between any two consecutive instants at which $y(t)$ and $r(t)$ are sampled is called the *sampling period*. T is a key design choice. The behavior of the resultant digital controller critically depends on this parameter. Ideally we want the sampled data version to behave like the analog version. This can be done by making the sampling period small. However, a small sampling period means more frequent control-law computation and higher processor-time demand. We want a sampling period T that achieves a good compromise.

In making this selection, we need to consider two factors. The first is the perceived responsiveness of the overall system (i.e., the plant and the controller). Oftentimes, the system is operated by a person (e.g., a driver or a pilot). The operator may issue a command at any time, say at t. The consequent change in the reference input is read and reacted to by the digital

---

[1]The choice of the proportional constants for the three terms in the analog PID controller and the methods for discretization are topics discussed in almost every elementary book on digital control (e.g., [Leig]).

controller at the next sampling instant. This instant can be as late as $t + T$. Thus, sampling introduces a delay in the system response. The operator will feel the system sluggish when the delay exceeds a tenth of a second. Therefore, the sampling period of any manual input should be under this limit.

The second factor is the dynamic behavior of the plant. We want to keep the oscillation in its response small and the system under control. To illustrate, we consider the disk drive controller described in [AsWi]. The plant in this example is the arm of a disk. The controller is designed to move the arm to the selected track each time when the reference input changes. At each change, the reference input $r(t)$ is a step function from the initial position to the final position. In Figure 1–2, these positions are represented by 0 and 1, respectively, and the time origin is the instant when the step in $r(t)$ occurs. The dashed lines in Figure 1–2(a)

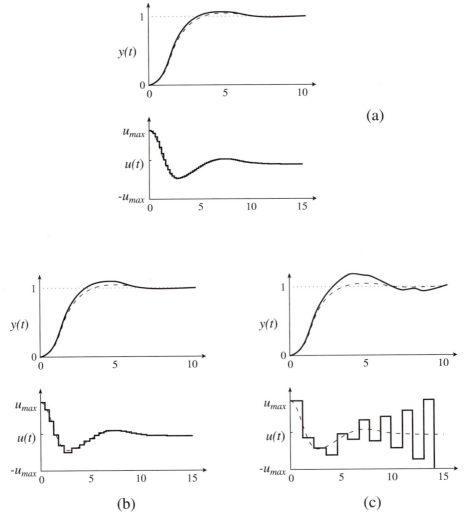

FIGURE 1–2   Effect of sampling period.

give the output $u(t)$ of the analog controller and the observed position $y(t)$ of the arm as a function of time. The solid lines in the lower and upper graphs give, respectively, the analog control signal constructed from the digital outputs of the controller and the resultant observed position $y(t)$ of the arm. At the sampling rate shown here, the analog and digital versions are essentially the same. The solid lines in Figure 1–2(b) give the behavior of the digital version when the sampling period is increased by 2.5 times. The oscillatory motion of the arm is more pronounced but remains small enough to be acceptable. However, when the sampling period is increased by five times, as shown in Figure 1–2(c), the arm requires larger and larger control to stay in the desired position; when this occurs, the system is said to have become unstable.

In general, the faster a plant can and must respond to changes in the reference input, the faster the input to its actuator varies, and the shorter the sampling period should be. We can measure the responsiveness of the overall system by its *rise time R*. This term refers to the amount of time that the plant takes to reach some small neighborhood around the final state in response to a step change in the reference input. In the example in Figure 1–2, a small neighborhood of the final state means the values of $y(t)$ that are within 5 percent of the final value. Hence, the rise time of that system is approximately equal to 2.5.

A good rule of thumb is *the ratio R/T of rise time to sampling period is from 10 to 20* [AsWi, FrPW].[2] In other words, there are 10 to 20 sampling periods within the rise time. A sampling period of $R/10$ should give an acceptably smooth response. However, a shorter sampling period (and hence a faster sampling rate) is likely to reduce the oscillation in the system response even further. For example, the sampling period used to obtain Figure 1–2(b) is around $R/10$, while the sampling period used to obtain Figure 1–2(a) is around $R/20$.

The above rule is also commonly stated in terms of the bandwidth, ω, of the system. The bandwidth of the overall system is approximately equal to $1/2R$ Hz. So the sampling rate (i.e., the inverse of sampling period) recommended above is 20 to 40 times the system bandwidth ω. The theoretical lower limit of sampling rate is dictated by *Nyquist sampling theorem* [Shan]. The theorem says that *any time-continuous signal of bandwidth ω can be reproduced faithfully from its sampled values if and only if the sampling rate is 2ω or higher.* We see that the recommended sampling rate for simple controllers is significantly higher than this lower bound. The high sampling rate makes it possible to keep the control input small and the control-law computation and digital-to-analog conversion of the controller simple.

Multirate Systems.   A plant typically has more than one degree of freedom. Its state is defined by multiple state variables (e.g., the rotation speed, temperature, etc. of an engine or the tension and position of a video tape). Therefore, it is monitored by multiple sensors and controlled by multiple actuators. We can think of a multivariate (i.e., multi-input/multi-output) controller for such a plant as a system of single-output controllers.

Because different state variables may have different dynamics, the sampling periods required to achieve smooth responses from the perspective of different state variables may be different. [For example, because the rotation speed of a engine changes faster than its

---

[2] Sampling periods smaller than this range may have an adverse effect. The reason is that quantization error becomes dominant when the difference in analogy sample readings taken in consecutive sampling periods becomes comparable or even smaller than the quantization granularity.

temperature, the required sampling rate for RPM (Rotation Per Minute) control is higher than that for the temperature control.] Of course, we can use the highest of all required sampling rates. This choice simplifies the controller software since all control laws are computed at the same repetition rate. However, some control-law computations are done more frequently than necessary; some processor time is wasted. To prevent this waste, multivariate digital controllers usually use multiple rates and are therefore called multirate systems.

Oftentimes, the sampling periods used in a multirate system are related in a harmonic way, that is, each longer sampling period is an integer multiple of every shorter period. To explain the control-theoretical reason for this choice,[3] we note that some degree of coupling among individual single-output controllers in a system is inevitable. Consequently, the sampling periods of the controllers cannot be selected independently. A method for the design and analysis of multirate systems is the successive loop closure method [FrPW]. According to this method, the designer begins by selecting the sampling period of the controller that should have the fastest sampling rate among all the controllers. In this selection, the controller is assumed to be independent of the others in the system. After a digital version is designed, it is converted back into an analog form. The analog model is then integrated with the slower portion of the plant and is treated as a part of the plant. This step is then repeated for the controller that should have the fastest sampling rate among the controllers whose sampling periods remain to be selected. The iteration process continues until the slowest digital controller is designed. Each step uses the model obtained during the previous step as the plant. When the chosen sampling periods are harmonic, the analog models of the digital controllers used in this iterative process are exact. The only approximation arises from the assumption made in the first step that the fastest controller is independent, and the error due to this approximation can be corrected to some extent by incorporating the effect of the slower controllers in the plant model and then repeating the entire iterative design process.

An Example of Software Control Structures.   As an example, Figure 1–3 shows the software structure of a flight controller [Elli]. The plant is a helicopter. It has three velocity components; together, they are called "collective" in the figure. It also has three rotational (angular) velocities, referred to as roll, pitch, and yaw.[4] The system uses three sampling rates: 180, 90, and 30 Hz. After initialization, the system executes a do loop at the rate of one iteration every 1/180 second; in the figure a cycle means a 1/180-second cycle, and the term computation means a control-law computation.

Specifically, at the start of each 1/180-second cycle, the controller first checks its own health and reconfigures itself if it detects any failure. It then does either one of the three avionics tasks or computes one of the 30-Hz control laws. We note that the pilot's command (i.e., keyboard input) is checked every 1/30 second. At this sampling rate, the pilot should not perceive the additional delay introduced by sampling. The movement of the aircraft along each of the coordinates is monitored and controlled by an inner and faster loop and an outer and slower loop. The output produced by the outer loop is the reference input to the inner loop. Each inner loop also uses the data produced by the avionics tasks.

---

[3]In later chapters, we will see that harmonic periods also have the advantage over arbitrary periods from the standpoint of achievable processor utilization.

[4]The three velocity components are forward, side-slip, and altitude rates. Roll, pitch, and yaw are the rates of rotation about these axes, respectively.

Do the following in each 1/180-second cycle:
- Validate sensor data and select data source; in the presence of failures, reconfigure the system.
- Do the following 30-Hz avionics tasks, each once every six cycles:
  - keyboard input and mode selection
  - data normalization and coordinate transformation
  - tracking reference update
- Do the following 30-Hz computations, each once every six cycles:
  - control laws of the outer pitch-control loop
  - control laws of the outer roll-control loop
  - control laws of the outer yaw- and collective-control loop
- Do each of the following 90-Hz computations once every two cycles, using outputs produced by 30-Hz computations and avionics tasks as input:
  - control laws of the inner pitch-control loop
  - control laws of the inner roll- and collective-control loop
- Compute the control laws of the inner yaw-control loop, using outputs produced by 90-Hz control-law computations as input.
- Output commands.
- Carry out built-in-test.
- Wait until the beginning of the next cycle.

FIGURE 1–3   An example: Software control structure of a flight controller.

This multirate controller controls only flight dynamics. The control system on board an aircraft is considerably more complex than indicated by the figure. It typically contains many other equally critical subsystems (e.g., air inlet, fuel, hydraulic, brakes, and anti-ice controllers) and many not so critical subsystems (e.g., lighting and environment temperature controllers). So, in addition to the flight control-law computations, the system also computes the control laws of these subsystems.

Timing Characteristics.   To generalize from the above example, we can see that the workload generated by each multivariate, multirate digital controller consists of a few periodic control-law computations. Their periods range from a few milliseconds to a few seconds. A control system may contain numerous digital controllers, each of which deals with some attribute of the plant. Together they demand tens or hundreds of control laws be computed periodically, some of them continuously and others only when requested by the operator or in reaction to some events. The control laws of each multirate controller may have harmonic periods. They typically use the data produced by each other as inputs and are said to be a rate group. On the other hand, there is no control theoretical reason to make sampling periods of different rate groups related in a harmonic way.

Each control-law computation can begin shortly after the beginning of each sampling period when the most recent sensor data become available. (Typically, the time taken by an analog-to-digital converter to produce sampled data and place the data in memory does not vary from period to period and is very small compared with the sampling period.) It is natural to want the computation complete and, hence, the sensor data processed before the data taken in the next period become available. This objective is met when the response time of each control-law computation never exceeds the sampling period. As we will see in later chapters, the response time of the computation can vary from period to period. In some systems, it is necessary to keep this variation small so that the digital control outputs produced by the controller become available at time instants more regularly spaced in time. In this case, we may impose a timing jitter requirement on the control-law computation: the variation in its response time does not exceed some threshold.

1.1.2   More Complex Control-Law Computations

The simplicity of a PID or similar digital controller follows from three assumptions. First, sensor data give accurate estimates of the state-variable values being monitored and controlled. This assumption is not valid when noise and disturbances inside or outside the plant prevent accurate observations of its state. Second, the sensor data give the state of the plant. In general, sensors monitor some observable attributes of the plant. The values of the state variables must be computed from the measured values (i.e., digitized sensor readings). Third, all the parameters representing the dynamics of the plant are known. This assumption is not valid for some plants. (An example is a flexible robot arm. Even the parameters of typical manipulators used in automated factories are not known accurately.)

When any of the simplifying assumptions is not valid, the simple feedback loop in Section 1.1.1 no longer suffices. Since these assumptions are often not valid, you often see digital controllers implemented as follows.

> set timer to interrupt periodically with period T;
> at each clock interrupt, do
> > sample and digitize sensor readings to get measured values;
> > compute control output from measured and state-variable values;
> > convert control output to analog form;
> > estimate and update plant parameters;
> > compute and update state variables;
> end do;

The last two steps in the loop can increase the processor time demand of the controller significantly. We now give two examples where the state update step is needed.

Deadbeat Control.   A discrete-time control scheme that has no continuous-time equivalence is deadbeat control. In response to a step change in the reference input, a deadbeat controller brings the plant to the desired state by exerting on the plant a fixed number (say n) of control commands. A command is generated every T seconds. (T is still called a sampling period.) Hence, the plant reaches its desired state in nT second.

In principle, the control-law computation of a deadbeat controller is also simple. The output produced by the controller during the kth sampling period is given by

$$u_k = \alpha \sum_{i=0}^{k}(r_i - y_i) + \sum_{i=0}^{k}\beta_i x_i$$

[This expression can also be written in an incremental form similar to Eq. (1.1).] Again, the constants α and β_i's are chosen at design time. x_i is the value of the state variable in the ith sampling period. During each sampling period, the controller must compute an estimate of x_k from measured values y_i for $i \leq k$. In other words, the state update step in the above do loop is needed.

Kalman Filter.   Kalman filtering is a commonly used means to improve the accuracy of measurements and to estimate model parameters in the presence of noise and uncertainty. To illustrate, we consider a simple monitor system that takes a measured value y_k every sampling period k in order to estimate the value x_k of a state variable. Suppose that starting from time 0, the value of this state variable is equal to a constant x. Because of noise, the measured value y_k is equal to $x + \varepsilon_k$, where ε_k is a random variable whose average value is 0 and standard deviation is σ_k. The Kalman filter starts with the initial estimate $\tilde{x}_1 = y_1$ and computes a new estimate each sampling period. Specifically, for $k > 1$, the filter computes the estimate $\tilde{x}_k$ as follows:

$$\tilde{x}_k = \tilde{x}_{k-1} + K_k(y_k - \tilde{x}_{k-1}) \tag{1.2a}$$

In this expression,

$$K_k = \frac{P_k}{\sigma_k{}^2 + P_k} \tag{1.2b}$$

is called the Kalman gain and P_k is the variance of the estimation error $\tilde{x}_k - x$; the latter is given by

$$P_k = E[(\tilde{x}_k - x)^2] = (1 - K_{k-1})P_{k-1} \tag{1.2c}$$

This value of the Kalman gain gives the best compromise between the rate at which P_k decreases with k and the steady-state variance, that is, P_k for large k.

In a multivariate system, the state variable $\mathbf{x}_k$ is an n-dimensional vector, where n is the number of variables whose values define the state of the plant. The measured value $\mathbf{y}_k$ is an n'-dimensional vector, if during each sampling period, the readings of n' sensors are taken. We let $\mathbf{A}$ denote the measurement matrix; it is an $n \times n'$ matrix that relates the n' measured variables to the n state variables. In other words,

$$\mathbf{y}_k = \mathbf{A}\mathbf{x}_k + \mathbf{e}_k$$

The vector $\mathbf{e}_k$ gives the additive noise in each of the n' measured values. Eq. (1.2a) becomes an n-dimensional vector equation

$$\tilde{\mathbf{x}}_k = \tilde{\mathbf{x}}_{k-1} + \mathbf{K}_k(\mathbf{y}_k - \mathbf{A}\tilde{\mathbf{x}}_{k-1})$$

Similarly, Kalman gain $\mathbf{K}_k$ and variance $\mathbf{P}_k$ are given by the matrix version of Eqs. (1.2b) and (1.2c). So, the computation in each sampling period involves a few matrix multiplications and additions and one matrix inversion.

1.2 HIGH-LEVEL CONTROLS

Controllers in a complex monitor and control system are typically organized hierarchically. One or more digital controllers at the lowest level directly control the physical plant. Each output of a higher-level controller is a reference input of one or more lower-level controllers. With few exceptions, one or more of the higher-level controllers interfaces with the operator(s).

1.2.1 Examples of Control Hierarchy

For example, a patient care system may consist of microprocessor-based controllers that monitor and control the patient's blood pressure, respiration, glucose, and so forth. There may be a higher-level controller (e.g., an expert system) which interacts with the operator (a nurse or doctor) and chooses the desired values of these health indicators. While the computation done by each digital controller is simple and nearly deterministic, the computation of a high-level controller is likely to be far more complex and variable. While the period of a low-level control-law computation ranges from milliseconds to seconds, the periods of high-level control-law computations may be minutes, even hours.

Figure 1–4 shows a more complex example: the hierarchy of flight control, avionics, and air traffic control systems.[5] The Air Traffic Control (ATC) system is at the highest level. It regulates the flow of flights to each destination airport. It does so by assigning to each aircraft an arrival time at each metering fix[6] (or waypoint) en route to the destination: The aircraft is supposed to arrive at the metering fix at the assigned arrival time. At any time while in flight, the assigned arrival time to the next metering fix is a reference input to the on-board flight management system. The flight management system chooses a time-referenced flight path that brings the aircraft to the next metering fix at the assigned arrival time. The cruise speed, turn radius, decend/accend rates, and so forth required to follow the chosen time-referenced flight path are the reference inputs to the flight controller at the lowest level of the control hierarchy.

In general, there may be several higher levels of control. Take a control system of robots that perform assembly tasks in a factory for example. Path and trajectory planners at the second level determine the trajectory to be followed by each industrial robot. These planners typically take as an input the plan generated by a task planner, which chooses the sequence of assembly steps to be performed. In a space robot control system, there may be a scenario planner, which determines how a repair or rendezvous function should be performed. The plan generated by this planner is an input of the task planner.

1.2.2 Guidance and Control

While a digital controller deals with some dynamical behavior of the physical plant, a second-level controller typically performs guidance and path planning functions to achieve a higher-

---

[5]Figure 1–4 shows that some sensor data to both on-board controllers come from an air-data system. This is a system of sensors and a computer. The computer computes flight and environment parameters (e.g., wind speed, true airspeed, static-air temperature, Mach number, altitude hold and rate) from aerodynamic and thermodynamic sensor data. These parameters are used by the controllers as well as being displayed for the pilot.

[6]A metering fix is a known geographical point. Adjacent metering fixes are 40–60 nautical miles apart.

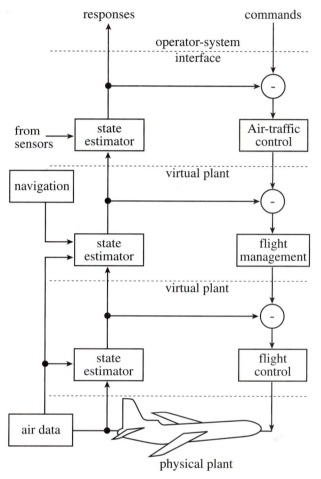

FIGURE 1–4   Air traffic/flight control hierarchy.

level goal. In particular, it tries to find one of the most desirable trajectories among all trajectories that meet the constraints of the system. The trajectory is most desirable because it optimizes some cost function(s). The algorithm(s) used for this purpose is the solution(s) of some constrained optimization problem(s).

As an example, we look again at a flight management system. The constraints that must be satisfied by the chosen flight path include the ones imposed by the characteristics of the aircraft, such as the maximum and minimum allowed cruise speeds and decent/accent rates, as well as constraints imposed by external factors, such as the ground track and altitude profile specified by the ATC system and weather conditions. A cost function is fuel consumption: A most desirable flight path is a most fuel efficient among all paths that meet all the constraints and will bring the aircraft to the next metering fix at the assigned arrival time. This problem is known as the constrained fixed-time, minimum-fuel problem. When the flight is late, the flight management system may try to bring the aircraft to the next metering fix in the shortest time. In that case, it will use an algorithm that solves the time-optimal problem.

Complexity and Timing Requirements. The constrained optimization problems that a guidance (or path planning) system must solve are typically nonlinear. In principle, these problems can be solved using dynamic programming and mathematical programming techniques. In practice, however, optimal algorithms are rarely used because most of them are not only very compute intensive but also do not guarantee to find a usable solution. Heuristic algorithms [GiMW] used for guidance and control purposes typically consider one constraint at a time, rather than all the constraints at the same time. They usually start with an initial condition (e.g., in the case of a flight management systems, the initial condition includes the initial position, speed, and heading of the aircraft) and some initial solution and adjust the value of one solution parameter at a time until a satisfactory solution is found.

Fortunately, a guidance system does not need to compute its control laws as frequently as a digital controller. Often, this computation can be done off-line. In the case of a flight management system, for example, it needs to compute and store a climb speed schedule for use during takeoff, an optimum cruise trajectory for use en route, and a descent trajectory for landing. This computation can be done before takeoff and hence is not time-critical. While in-flight, the system still needs to compute some control laws to monitor and control the transitions between different flight phases (i.e., from climb to cruise and cruise to descent) as well as algorithms for estimating and predicting times to waypoints, and so forth. These time-critical computations tend to be simpler and more deterministic and have periods in order of seconds and minutes. When the precomputed flight plan needs to be updated or a new one computed in-flight, the system has minutes to compute and can accept suboptimal solutions when there is no time.

Other Capabilities. The complexity of a higher-level control system arises for many other reasons in addition to its complicated control algorithms. It often interfaces with the operator and other systems. To interact with the operator, it updates displays and reacts to operator commands. By other systems, we mean those outside the control hierarchy. An example is a voice, telemetry, or multimedia communication system that supports operator interactions. Other examples are radar and navigation devices. The control system may use the information provided by these devices and partially control these devices.

An avionic or flight management system has these capabilities. One of its functions is to update the display of radar, flight path, and air-data information. Like keyboard monitoring, the display updates must done no less frequently than once every 100 milliseconds to achieve a satisfactory performance. Similarly, it periodically updates navigation data provided by inertial and radio navigation aids.[7] An avionics system for a military aircraft also does tracking and ballistic computations and coordinates radar and weapon control systems, and it does them with repetition periods of a few to a few hundred milliseconds. (You can find detailed timing information on this types of avionics system in [LoVM].) The workload due to these functions is demanding even for today's fast processors and data links.

---

[7]The period of navigation updates depends on the speed of the plane. To get within 100-feet position accuracy, this update rate should be as high as 20–30 Hz for a fighter jet flying at Mach 2 but 10 Hz is sufficient for a plane at a subsonic speed.

1.2.3   Real-Time Command and Control

The controller at the highest level of a control hierarchy is a command and control system. An Air Traffic Control (ATC) system is an excellent example. Figure 1–5 shows a possible architecture. The ATC system monitors the aircraft in its coverage area and the environment (e.g, weather condition) and generates and presents the information needed by the operators (i.e., the air traffic controllers). Outputs from the ATC system include the assigned arrival times to metering fixes for individual aircraft. As stated earlier, these outputs are reference inputs to on-board flight management systems. Thus, the ATC system indirectly controls the embedded components in low levels of the control hierarchy. In addition, the ATC system provides voice and telemetry links to on-board avionics. Thus it supports the communication among the operators at both levels (i.e., the pilots and air traffic controllers).

The ATC system gathers information on the "state" of each aircraft via one or more active radars. Such a radar interrogates each aircraft periodically. When interrogated, an air-

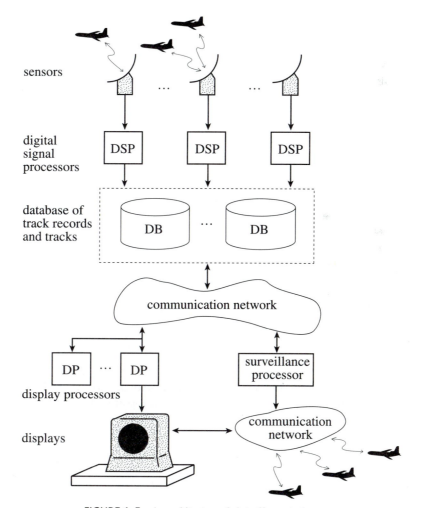

FIGURE 1–5   An architecture of air traffic control system.

craft responds by sending to the ATC system its "state variables": identifier, position, altitude, heading, and so on. (In Figure 1–5, these variables are referred to collectively as a track record, and the current trajectory of the aircraft is a track.) The ATC system processes messages from aircraft and stores the state information thus obtained in a database. This information is picked up and processed by display processors. At the same time, a surveillance system continuously analyzes the scenario and alerts the operators whenever it detects any potential hazard (e.g., a possible collision). Again, the rates at which human interfaces (e.g., keyboards and displays) operate must be at least 10 Hz. The other response times can be considerably larger. For example, the allowed response time from radar inputs is one to two seconds, and the period of weather updates is in the order of ten seconds.

From this example, we can see that a command and control system bears little resemblance to low-level controllers. In contrast to a low-level controller whose workload is either purely or mostly periodic, a command and control system also computes and communicates in response to sporadic events and operators' commands. Furthermore, it may process image and speech, query and update databases, simulate various scenarios, and the like. The resource and processing time demands of these tasks can be large and varied. Fortunately, most of the timing requirements of a command and control system are less stringent. Whereas a low-level control system typically runs on one computer or a few computers connected by a small network or dedicated links, a command and control system is often a large distributed system containing tens and hundreds of computers and many different kinds of networks. In this respect, it resembles interactive, on-line transaction systems (e.g., a stock price quotation system) which are also sometimes called real-time systems.

1.3   SIGNAL PROCESSING

Most signal processing applications have some kind of real-time requirements. We focus here on those whose response times must be under a few milliseconds to a few seconds. Examples are digital filtering, video and voice compressing/decompression, and radar signal processing.

1.3.1   Processing Bandwidth Demands

Typically, a real-time signal processing application computes in each sampling period one or more outputs. Each output $x(k)$ is a weighted sum of n inputs $y(i)$'s:

$$x(k) = \sum_{i=1}^{n} a(k, i) y(i) \tag{1.3}$$

In the simplest case, the weights, $a(k, i)$'s, are known and fixed.[8] In essence, this computation transforms the given representation of an object (e.g., a voice, an image or a radar signal) in terms of the inputs, $y(i)$'s, into another representation in terms of the outputs, $x(k)$'s. Different sets of weights, $a(k, i)$'s, give different kinds of transforms. This expression tells us that the time required to produce an output is $O(n)$.

---

[8]In the case of adaptive filtering applications (e.g., echo suppression), each weight changes with time and must be updated. The update of each weight typically takes one multiplication and one addition each sampling period.

The processor time demand of an application also depends on the number of outputs it is required to produce in each sampling period. At one extreme, a digital filtering application (e.g., a filter that suppresses noise and interferences in speech and audio) produces one output each sampling period. The sampling rates of such applications range from a few kHz to tens of kHz.[9] n ranges from tens to hundreds. Hence, such an application performs 10^4 to 10^7 multiplications and additions per second.

Some other signal processing applications are more computationally intensive. The number of outputs may also be of order n, and the complexity of the computation is $O(n^2)$ in general. An example is image compression. Most image compression methods have a transform step. This step transforms the space representation of each image into a transform representation (e.g., a hologram). To illustrate the computational demand of a compression process, let us consider an $m \times m$ pixel, 30 frames per second video. Suppose that we were to compress each frame by first computing its transform. The number of inputs is $n = m^2$. The transformation of each frame takes m^4 multiplications and additions. If m is 100, the transformation of the video takes 3×10^9 multiplications and additions per second! One way to reduce the computational demand at the expense of the compression ratio is to divide each image into smaller squares and perform the transform on each square. This indeed is what the video compression standard MPEG [ISO94]) does. Each image is divided into squares of 8×8 pixels. In this way, the number of multiplications and additions performed in the transform stage is reduced to $64m^2$ per frame (in the case of our example, to 1.92×10^7). Today, there is a broad spectrum of Digital Signal Processors (DSPs) designed specifically for signal processing applications. Computationally intensive signal processing applications run on one or more DSPs. In this way, the compression process can keep pace with the rate at which video frames are captured.

1.3.2 Radar System

A signal processing application is typically a part of a larger system. As an example, Figure 1–6 shows a block diagram of a (passive) radar signal processing and tracking system. The system consists of an Input/Output (I/O) subsystem that samples and digitizes the echo signal from the radar and places the sampled values in a shared memory. An array of digital signal processors processes these sampled values. The data thus produced are analyzed by one or more data processors, which not only interface with the display system, but also generate commands to control the radar and select parameters to be used by signal processors in the next cycle of data collection and analysis.

Radar Signal Processing.   To search for objects of interest in its coverage area, the radar scans the area by pointing its antenna in one direction at a time. During the time the antenna dwells in a direction, it first sends a short radio frequency pulse. It then collects and examines the echo signal returning to the antenna.

The echo signal consists solely of background noise if the transmitted pulse does not hit any object. On the other hand, if there is a reflective object (e.g., an airplane or storm cloud) at a distance x meters from the antenna, the echo signal reflected by the object returns to the antenna at approximately $2x/c$ seconds after the transmitted pulse, where $c = 3 \times 10^8$ meters

---

[9]The sampling rates of telephone voice, speech in general, and audio are 8 kHz, 8–10 kHz, and 44.1 kHz (compact disc digital audio) or 48 kHz (digital audio tape), respectively.

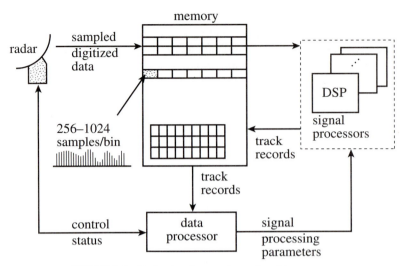

FIGURE 1–6   Radar signal processing and tracking system.

per second is the speed of light. The echo signal collected at this time should be stronger than when there is no reflected signal. If the object is moving, the frequency of the reflected signal is no longer equal to that of the transmitted pulse. The amount of frequency shift (called Doppler shift) is proportional to the velocity of the object. Therefore, by examining the strength and frequency spectrum of the echo signal, the system can determine whether there are objects in the direction pointed at by the antenna and if there are objects, what their positions and velocities are.

Specifically, the system divides the time during which the antenna dwells to collect the echo signal into small disjoint intervals. Each time interval corresponds to a distance range, and the length of the interval is equal to the range resolution divided by c. (For example, if the distance resolution is 300 meters, then the range interval is one microsecond long.) The digital sampled values of the echo signal collected during each range interval are placed in a buffer, called a bin in Figure 1–6. The sampled values in each bin are the inputs used by a digital signal processor to produce outputs of the form given by Eq. (1.3). These outputs represent a discrete Fourier transform of the corresponding segment of the echo signal. Based on the characteristics of the transform, the signal processor decides whether there is an object in that distance range. If there is an object, it generates a *track record* containing the position and velocity of the object and places the record in the shared memory.

The time required for signal processing is dominated by the time required to produce the Fourier transforms, and this time is nearly deterministic. The time complexity of Fast Fourier Transform (FFT) is $O(n \log n)$, where n is the number of sampled values in each range bin. n is typically in the range from 128 to a few thousand. So, it takes roughly 10^3 to 10^5 multiplications and additions to generate a Fourier transform. Suppose that the antenna dwells in each direction for 100 milliseconds and the range of the radar is divided into 1000 range intervals. Then the signal processing system must do 10^7 to 10^9 multiplications and additions per second. This is well within the capability of today's digital signal processors.

However, the 100-millisecond dwell time is a ballpark figure for mechanical radar antennas. This is orders of magnitude larger than that for phase array radars, such as those used in many military applications. A phase array radar can switch the direction of the radar beam electronically, within a millisecond, and may have multiple beams scanning the coverage area and tracking individual objects at the same time. Since the radar can collect data orders of magnitude faster than the rates stated above, the signal processing throughput demand is also considerably higher. This demand is pushing the envelope of digital signal processing technology.

Tracking.   Strong noise and man-made interferences, including electronic counter measure (i.e., jamming), can lead the signal processing and detection process to wrong conclusions about the presence of objects. A track record on a nonexisting object is called a false return. An application that examines all the track records in order to sort out false returns from real ones and update the trajectories of detected objects is called a *tracker*.[10] Using the jargon of the subject area, we say that the tracker assigns each measured value (i.e., the tuple of position and velocity contained in each of the track records generated in a scan) to a trajectory. If the trajectory is an existing one, the measured value assigned to it gives the current position and velocity of the object moving along the trajectory. If the trajectory is new, the measured value gives the position and velocity of a possible new object. In the example in Figure 1–6, the tracker runs on one or more data processors which communicate with the signal processors via the shared memory.

Gating.   Typically, tracking is carried out in two steps: gating and data association [Bogl]. *Gating* is the process of putting each measured value into one of two categories depending on whether it can or cannot be tentatively assigned to one or more established trajectories. The gating process tentatively assigns a measured value to an established trajectory if it is within a threshold distance G away from the predicted current position and velocity of the object moving along the trajectory. (Below, we call the distance between the measured and predicted values the distance of the assignment.) The threshold G is called the track gate. It is chosen so that the probability of a valid measured value falling in the region bounded by a sphere of radius G centered around a predicted value is a desired constant.

Figure 1–7 illustrates this process. At the start, the tracker computes the predicted position (and velocity) of the object on each established trajectory. In this example, there are two established trajectories, L_1 and L_2. We also call the predicted positions of the objects on these tracks L_1 and L_2. X_1, X_2, and X_3 are the measured values given by three track records. X_1 is assigned to L_1 because it is within distance G from L_1. X_3 is assigned to both L_1 and L_2 for the same reason. On the other hand, X_2 is not assigned to any of the trajectories. It represents either a false return or a new object. Since it is not possible to distinguish between these two cases, the tracker hypothesizes that X_2 is the position of a new object. Subsequent radar data will allow the tracker to either validate or invalidate this hypothesis. In the latter case, the tracker will discard this trajectory from further consideration.

---

[10]The term tracking also refers to the process of keeping track of an individual object (e.g., an aircraft under surveillance, a missile, etc.).

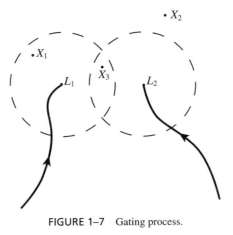

FIGURE 1–7   Gating process.

Data Association.   The tracking process completes if, after gating, every measured value is assigned to at most one trajectory and every trajectory is assigned at most one measured value. This is likely to be case when (1) the radar signal is strong and interference is low (and hence false returns are few) and (2) the density of objects is low. Under adverse conditions, the assignment produced by gating may be ambiguous, that is, some measured value is assigned to more than one trajectory or a trajectory is assigned more than one measured value. The data association step is then carried out to complete the assignments and resolve ambiguities.

There are many data association algorithms. One of the most intuitive is the the nearest neighbor algorithm. This algorithm works as follows:

1. Examine the tentative assignments produced by the gating step.
   a. For each trajectory that is tentatively assigned a single unique measured value, assign the measured value to the trajectory. Discard from further examination the trajectory and the measured value, together with all tentative assignments involving them.
   b. For each measured value that is tentatively assigned to a single trajectory, discard the tentative assignments of those measured values that are tentatively assigned to this trajectory if the values are also assigned to some other trajectories.
2. Sort the remaining tentative assignments in order of nondecreasing distance.
3. Assign the measured value given by the first tentative assignment in the list to the corresponding trajectory and discard the measured value and trajectory.
4. Repeat step (3) until the list of tentative assignments is empty.

In the example in Figure 1–7, the tentative assignment produced by the gating step is ambiguous. Step (1a) does not eliminate any tentative assignment. However, step (1b) finds that X_1 is assigned to only L_1, while X_3 is assigned to both L_1 and L_2. Hence, the assignment of X_3 to L_1 is discarded from further consideration. After step (1), there still are two tentative assignments, X_1 to L_1 and X_3 to L_2. Step (2) leaves them in this order, and the subsequent steps make these assignments. X_2 initiates a new trajectory. If during subsequent scans, no measured values are assigned to the new trajectory, it will be discarded from further consideration.

The nearest neighbor algorithm attempts to minimize a simple local objective function: the distance (between the measured and predicted values) of each assignment. Data association algorithms of higher time complexity are designed to optimize some global, and therefore more complicated, objective functions, for example, the sum of distances of all assignments and probability of errors. The most complex in both time and space is the class of multiple hypothesis tracking algorithms. Often it is impossible to eliminate some assignments from further consideration by looking at the measured values produced in one scan. (An example is when the distances between a measured value to two or more predicted values are essentially equal.) While a single-hypothesis tracking algorithm (e.g., the nearest neighbor algorithm) must choose one assignment from equally good assignments, a multiple-hypothesis tracking algorithm keeps all of them. In other words, a trajectory may be temporally branched into multiple trajectories, each ending at one of many hypothesized current positions. The tracker then uses the data provided in future scans to eliminate some of the branches. The use of this kind of algorithms is confined to where the tracked objects are dense and the number of false returns are large (e.g., for tracking military targets in the presence of decoys and jamming).

Complexity and Timing Requirements.   In contrast to signal processing, the amounts of processor time and memory space required by the tracker are data dependent and can vary widely. When there are n established trajectories and m measured values, the time complexity of gating is $O(nm \log m)$. (This can be done by first sorting the m measured values according to their distances from the predicted value for each of the established trajectories and then comparing the distances with the track gate G.) In the worst case, all m measured values are tentatively assigned to all n trajectories in the gating step. The nearest neighbor algorithm must sort all nm tentative assignments and hence has time complexity $O(nm \log nm)$. The amounts of time and space required by multiple-hypothesis tracking grow exponentially with the maximum number of hypotheses, the exponent being the number of scans required to eliminate each false hypothesis. Without modern fast processors and large memory, multiple-hypothesis tracking would not be feasible.

Figure 1–6 shows that the operation of the radar is controlled by a controller that executes on the data processor. In particular, the controller may alter the search strategy or change the radar operation mode (say from searching to tracking an object) depending on the results found by the tracker. (As we mentioned earlier, a phase-array radar can redirect its beam in any direction in less than a millisecond. This capability makes it possible to dynamically adapt the operation of the radar system to changes in the detected scenario.) Similarly, the controller may alter the signal processing parameters (e.g., detection threshold and transform type) in order to be more effective in rejecting interferences and differentiating objects. The responsiveness and iteration rate of this feedback process increase as the total response time of signal processing and tracking decreases. For this reason, the developers of these applications are primarily concerned with their throughputs and response times.

1.4   OTHER REAL-TIME APPLICATIONS

This section describes the characteristics and requirements of two most common real-time applications. They are real-time databases and multimedia applications.

TABLE 1–1   Requirements of typical real-time databases

Applications	Size	Ave. Resp. Time	Max Resp. Time	Abs. Cons.	Rel. Cons.	Permanence
Air traffic control	20,000	0.50 ms	5.00 ms	3.00 sec.	6.00 sec.	12 hours
Aircraft mission	3,000	0.05 ms	1.00 ms	0.05 sec.	0.20 sec.	4 hours
Spacecraft control	5,000	0.05 ms	1.00 ms	0.20 sec.	1.00 sec.	25 years
Process control		0.80 ms	5.00 sec	1.00 sec.	2.00 sec	24 hours

1.4.1   Real-Time Databases

The term real-time database systems refers to a diverse spectrum of information systems, ranging from stock price quotation systems, to track records databases, to real-time file systems. Table 1–1 lists several examples [Lock96]. What distinguish these databases from nonreal-time databases is the perishable nature of the data maintained by them.

Specifically, a real-time database contains data objects, called *image objects*, that represent real-world objects. The attributes of an image object are those of the represented real-world object. For example, an air traffic control database contains image objects that represent aircraft in the coverage area. The attributes of such an image object include the position and heading of the aircraft. The values of these attributes are updated periodically based on the measured values of the actual position and heading provided by the radar system. Without this update, the stored position and heading will deviate more and more from the actual position and heading. In this sense, the quality of stored data degrades. This is why we say that real-time data are perishable. In contrast, an underlying assumption of nonreal-time databases (e.g., a payroll database) is that in the absence of updates the data contained in them remain good (i.e., the database remains in some consistent state satisfying all the data integrity constraints of the database).

Absolute Temporal Consistency.   The temporal quality of real-time data is often quantified by parameters such as age and temporal dispersion. The age of a data object measures how up-to-date the information provided by the object is. There are many formal definitions of age. Intuitively, the *age of an image object* at any time is the length of time since the instant of the last update, that is, when its value is made equal to that of the real-world object it represents.[11] The age of a data object whose value is computed from the values of other objects is equal to the oldest of the ages of those objects.

A set of data objects is said to be *absolutely (temporally) consistent* if the maximum age of the objects in the set is no greater than a certain threshold. The column labeled "Abs. Cons." in Table 1–1 lists the typical threshold values that define absolute consistency for different applications. As an example, "aircraft mission" listed in the table refers to the kind

---

[11]This intuitive definition of age ignores the rate at which information ages. As examples, we consider two objects: One represents the position of an aircraft, and the other represents the position of a storm cloud. Because the position of the aircraft can change considerably in three seconds, three seconds is a relatively long time and large age. However, for the storm cloud position, three seconds should be a small age since the cloud does not move much in this amount of time. Rigorous definitions of age take the rate of change into account in various ways.

of database used to support combat missions of military aircraft. A fighter jet and the targets it tracks move at supersonic speeds. Hence the information on where they are must be less than 50 milliseconds old. On the other hand, an air traffic control system monitors commercial aircraft at subsonic speeds; this is why the absolute temporal consistency threshold for air traffic control is much larger.

Relative Temporal Consistency.   A set of data objects is said to be *relatively consistent* if the maximum difference in ages of the objects in the set is no greater than the relative consistency threshold used by the application. The column labeled "Rel. Cons." in Table 1–1 gives typical values of this threshold. For some applications the absolute age of data may not be as important as the differences in their ages. An example is a planning system that correlates traffic densities along a highway with the flow rates of vehicles entering and exiting the highway. The system does not require the most up-to-date flow rates at all interchanges and hence can tolerate a relatively large age (e.g., two minutes). However, if the difference in the ages of flow rates is large (e.g., one minute), the flow rates no longer give a valid snapshot of the traffic scenario and can lead the system to wrong conclusions.

Consistency Models.   Concurrency control mechanisms, such as two-phase locking, have traditionally been used to ensure the serializability of read and update transactions and maintain data integrity of nonreal-time databases. These mechanisms often make it more difficult for updates to complete in time. Late updates may cause the data to become temporally inconsistent. Yet temporal consistency of real-time data is often as important as, or even more important than, data integrity. For this reason, several weaker consistency models have been proposed (e.g., [KoSp]). Concurrency control mechanisms required to maintain a weaker sense of consistency tend to improve the timeliness of updates and reads.

As an example, we may only require update transactions to be executed in some serializable order. Read-only transactions are not required to be serializable. Some applications may require some stronger consistency (e.g., all real-only transactions perceive the same serialization order of update transactions) while others are satisfied with view consistency (e.g., each read-only transaction perceives some serialization order of update transactions). Usually, the more relaxed the serialization requirement, the more flexibility the system has in interleaving the read and write operations from different transactions, and the easier it is to schedule the transactions and have them complete in time.

Kuo and Mok [Kuo, KuMo93] proposed the use of *similarity* as a correctness criterion for real-time data. Intuitively, we say that two values of a data object are similar if the difference between the values is within an acceptable threshold from the perspective of every transaction that may read the object. Two views of a transaction are similar if every read operation gets similar values of every data object read by the transaction. Two database states are similar if, in the states, the corresponding values of every data object are similar. Two schedules of a set of transactions are similar if, for any initial state, (1) the transactions transform similar database states to similar final database states and (2) every transaction in the set has similar views in both schedules. Kuo, *et al.* pointed out that the similarity relation provides a formal means for real-time application developers to capture the semantic constraints of real-time data. They also proposed a concurrent control protocol that takes advantage of the relaxed correctness criterion to enhance the temporal consistency of data.

1.4.2   Multimedia Applications

Finally, let us look at one of the most frequently encountered real-time applications: multimedia. A multimedia application may process, store, transmit, and display any number of video streams, audio streams, images, graphics, and text. A video stream is a sequence of data frames which encodes a video. An audio stream encodes a voice, sound, or music.

Without compression, the storage space and transmission bandwidth required by a video are enormous. (As an example, we consider a small 100×100-pixel, 30-frames/second color video. The intensity and color of each pixel is given by the sample values of a luminance and two chrominance signal components,[12] respectively, at the location of the pixel. If uncompressed, the video requires a transmission bandwidth of 2.7 Mbits per second when the value of each component at each pixel is encoded with 3 bits.) Therefore, a video stream, as well as the associated audio stream, is invariably compressed as soon as it is captured.

MPEG Compression/Decompression.   A video compression standard is MPEG-2 [ISO94]. The standard makes use of three techniques. They are motion compensation for reducing temporal redundancy, discrete cosine transform for reducing spatial redundancy, and entropy encoding for reducing the number of bits required to encode all the information. Depending on the application, the compressed bit rate ranges from 1.5 Mbits/sec to 35 Mbits/sec. As you will see from the description below, the achievable compression ratio depends on the content of the video.

Motion Estimation.   The first step of compression is motion analysis and estimation. Because consecutive video frames are not independent, significant compression can be achieved by exploiting interframe dependency. This is the rationale behind the motion estimation step. The motion-compensation techniques used in this step assume that most small pieces of the image in the current frame can be obtained either by translating in space corresponding small pieces of the image in some previous frame or by interpolating some small pieces in some previous and subsequent frames. For this reason, each image is divided into 16×16-pixel square pieces; they are called *major blocks*. The luminance component of each major block consists of four 8×8 pixel blocks. Each of the chrominance components has only a quarter of this resolution. Hence, each chrominance component of a major block is an 8×8 pixel block.

Only frames $1 + \alpha k$, for $k = 0, 1, 2, \ldots$ are encoded independently of other frames, where α is an application-specified integer constant. These frames are called I-frames (i.e., intra-coded frames). The coder treats each I-frame as a still image, and the decoder can decompress each compressed I-frame independently of other frames. Consequently, I-frames are points for random access of the video. The smaller the constant α, the more random accessible is the video and the poorer the compression ratio. A good compromise is $\alpha = 9$.

The frames between consecutive I-frames are called P- and B-frames. When α is equal to 9, the sequence of frames produced by the motion estimation step are I, B, B, P, B, B, P, B, B, I, B, B, P, ... For every $k \geq 0$, frame $1 + 9k + 3$ is a P-frame (i.e., a predictive-coded frame). The coder obtains a P-frame from the previous I-frame (or P-frame) by predicting

---

[12]The luminance signal gives us a black and white video. Linear combinations of this signal and the two chrominance signals give the red, blue, and green components of a color video.

how the image carried by the I-frame changes in the time interval between the times of these frames. Specifically, if a major block in the P-frame closely resembles a major block in the previous I-frame, then the coder represents the P-frame major block by six 8×8 pixel blocks that give the differences between the six P-frame pixel blocks and the corresponding pixel blocks of the best matching (i.e., resembling most closely) major block in the previous I-frame. In addition, the coder generates a motion vector based on which the decoder can identify the best matching I-frame major block. Such a P-frame major block is said to be predictively coded. On the other hand, some P-frame major blocks may be images of newly visible objects and, hence, cannot be obtained from any major block in the previous I-frame. The coder represents them in the same way as I-frame major blocks.

A B-frame is a bidirectionally predicted frame: It is predicted from both the previous I-frame (or P-frame) and the subsequent P-frame (or I-frame). One way is to represent every B-frame major block by the differences between the values of its pixel blocks and the corresponding pixel blocks of the best matching major block in either the previous I-frame or the subsequent P-frame. Alternatively, for each B-frame major block, an interpolation of the best matching major blocks in the I-frame and P-frame is first computed. The B-frame major block is represented by the difference between it and this interpolation. Again, the coder generates the motion vectors that the decoder will need to identify the best matching I-frame and P-frame major blocks. Whereas some P-frame major blocks are encoded independently, none of the B-frame major blocks are.

Discrete Cosine Transform and Encoding.   In the second step, a cosine transform[13] is performed on each of the 8×8 pixel blocks produced by the coder after motion estimation. We let $x(i, j)$, for $i, j = 1, 2, \ldots, 8$, denote the elements of an 8×8 transform matrix obtained from transforming the original matrix that gives the 8×8 values of a pixel block. The transform matrix usually has more zeros than the original matrix. [In the extreme when all the entries of the original matrix are equal, only $x(0, 0)$ is nonzero.] Moreover, if the entries $x(i, j)$'s are ordered in nondecreasing order of $i + j$, zero entries tend to be adjacent, forming sequences of zeros, and adjacent entries tend to have similar values. By quantizing the $x(i, j)$'s to create more zeros, encoding the entries in the transform matrix as 2-tuples (run length, value), and using a combination of variable-length and fixed-length codes to further reduce the bit rate, significant compression is achieved.

Decompression.   During decompression, the decoder first produces a close approximation of the original matrix (i.e., an 8×8 pixel block) by performing an inverse transform on each stored transform matrix. (The computation of an inverse transform is the essentially the same as the cosine transform.) It then reconstruct the images in all the frames from the major blocks in I-frames and difference blocks in P- and B-frames.

Real-Time Characteristics.   As we can see from the above description, video compression is a computational-intensive process. For batch applications such as video on de-

---

[13]We let $y(i, j)$ for $i, j = 1, 2, \ldots, 8$ denote the inputs to the transform. Each of the outputs $x(i, j)$ for $i, j = 1, 2, \ldots, 8$ of the transform is given by a double-weighted sum analogous to the one in Eq. (1.3). The transform is called cosine transform because the weight of each input $y(i, j)$ in the sum is proportional to a product of cosine functions, that is, $[\cos (2i + 1)\pi/k][\cos (2j + 1)l\pi/16]$.

mand, compression is done in batch and off-line, while it must be an on-line process for interactive applications (e.g., teleconferencing). Decompression should be done just before the time the video and audio are presented, in other words, on the just-in-time basis. Today, compression and decompression functions are often handled by an affordable special-purpose processor (e.g., the mmx), rather than by general-purpose processors.

To a great extent, the timing requirements of a multimedia application follow from the required video and audio quality. From the user's point of view, the quality of a video is partially characterized by its frame rate and resolution. A video of standard television quality consists of 30 frames per second. High-definition television uses 60 frames per second to give the picture even less flicker. On the other hand, much lower frame rates (e.g., 10–20) are tolerable for other applications, such as teleconferencing.

The term resolution roughly refers to the number of pixels in each frame (i.e., the size of the frame) and the number of bits used to encode each pixel (i.e., intensity and color resolution). Together, the resolution and frame rate of a video tell us roughly the amount of time required to compress/decompress it and the amounts of storage and transmission bandwidth required to store and transmit it.

Similarly, the quality of an audio component depends on the sampling rate and granularity used to digitize the audio signal. The total bit rate of an audio ranges from 16 Kbits per second for telephone speech quality to 128 Kbits per second for CD quality. Some loss of audio data is unavoidable, because the system may discard data during congestion and some data may arrive too late to be presented to the user, and so on. The quality of speech is usually tolerable when the loss rate is under one percent.

Another dimension of quality of a multimedia application is *lip synchronization*. This term refers to the temporal synchronization of the video frames and related audio data units. In the case where the video is that of a speaker, the speaker's lips should appear to move to make the accompanied speech. Experimental results indicate that the time interval between the display of each frame and the presentation of the corresponding audio segment should ideally be no more than 80 msec and should definitely be no more than 160 msec [StNa] for sake of achieving lip synchronization.

For batch applications, a system can often provide the desired quality by trading between real-time performance and space usage. For example, we want to present the audio to the user without pauses. This can clearly be achieved if there is little or no jitter (i.e., variation) in the delay suffered by audio data packets as they are transmitted over the network. However, the system can nevertheless deliver good audio despite large jitter by providing a sufficiently large amount of buffer to smooth out the jitter.

Finally, our ears are extremely sensitive to glitches and pauses in audio, and an end-to-end delay in the order of a few hundred milliseconds significantly decreases the quality of a conversation. Therefore, both end-to-end response time and response time jitter are important for interactive applications. Now-a-days, news programs often televise live conversations between people who are continents apart. You may have noticed that the interviewee sometimes seems to take forever to react and start to answer a question. The delay is actually only a second or two and is the effect of the large end-to-end propagation delay across a global communication channel.

1.5 SUMMARY

As a summary, we divide real-time applications into the following four types according to their timing attributes.

1. *Purely cyclic:* Every task in a purely cyclic application executes periodically. Even I/O operations are polled. Moreover, its demands in (computing, communication, and storage) resources do not vary significantly from period to period. Most digital controllers, exemplified by the flight control system in Figure 1–3, and real-time monitors are of this type.

2. *Mostly cyclic:* Most tasks in a mostly cyclic system execute periodically. The system must also respond to some external events (fault recovery and external commands) asynchronously. Examples are modern avionics and process control systems.

3. *Asynchronous and somewhat predictable:* In applications such as multimedia communication, radar signal processing, and tracking, most tasks are not periodic. The duration between consecutive executions of a task may vary considerably, or the variations in the amounts of resources demanded in different periods may be large. However, these variations have either bounded ranges or known statistics.

4. *Asynchronous and unpredictable:* Applications that react to asynchronous events and have tasks with high run-time complexity belong to this type. An example is intelligent real-time control systems [SKNL].

An orthogonal dimension is the size of the application. Like nonreal-time applications, some of them run on one or a few microprocessors, even on hand-held devices, while others run on tens and hundreds of computers. They are commonly labeled as uniprocessor, multiprocessor, or distributed systems. As you will see shortly, we will not emphasize this aspect. Of course, a solution suited for a system containing a few microprocessors (e.g., an automotive control system) may not be applicable to a large distributed system (e.g., air traffic control system) and vice versa. The subsequent chapters will try to make which ones are which clear to you.

CHAPTER 2

Hard versus Soft
Real-Time Systems

Now that we have seen several typical real-time applications, we are ready to discuss in depth the characteristics that distinguish them from nonreal-time applications. We begin by discussing exactly what "real time" means.

2.1 JOBS AND PROCESSORS

For the purpose of describing and characterizing different types of real-time systems and methods for scheduling and resource management, it is more convenient for us to speak of all kinds of work done by computing and communication systems in general terms. We call each unit of work that is scheduled and executed by the system a *job* and a set of related jobs which jointly provide some system function a *task*. Hence, the computation of a control law is a job. So is the computation of a FFT (Fast Fourier Transform) of sensor data, or the transmission of a data packet, or the retrieval of a file, and so on. We call them a control-law computation, a FFT computation, a packet transmission, and so on, only when we want to be specific about the kinds of work, that is, the types of jobs.

Similarly, rather than using different verbs (e.g., compute and transmit) for different types of jobs, we say that a job executes or is executed by the (operating) system. Every job executes on some resource. For example, the jobs mentioned above execute on a CPU, a network, and a disk, respectively. These resources are called servers in queuing theory literature and, sometimes, active resources in real-time systems literature. In later chapters, we will use the term server extensively to mean something else. To avoid overloading this term, we call all these resources *processors* except occasionally when we want to be specific about what they are.

26

2.2   RELEASE TIMES, DEADLINES, AND TIMING CONSTRAINTS

In the next chapter we will discuss in detail how jobs and processors are often characterized in order to schedule, manage, and reason about them. For now, we focus on the release times and deadlines of jobs, two parameters that distinguish jobs in real-time systems from those in nonreal-time systems.

The *release time* of a job is the instant of time at which the job becomes available for execution. The job can be scheduled and executed at any time at or after its release time whenever its data and control dependency conditions are met. As an example, we consider a system which monitors and controls several furnaces. After it is initialized and starts execution (say at time 0), the system samples and reads each temperature sensor every 100 msec and places the sampled readings in memory. It also computes the control law of each furnace every 100 msec in order to process the temperature readings and determine flow rates of fuel, air, and coolant. Suppose that the system begins the first control-law computation at time 20 msec. The fact that the control law is computed periodically can be stated in terms of release times of the control-law computation jobs $J_0, J_1, \ldots, J_k, \ldots$. The release time of the job J_k in this job stream is $20 + k \times 100$ msec, for $k = 0, 1, \ldots$. We say that *jobs have no release time* if all the jobs are released when the system begins execution.

The *deadline* of a job is the instant of time by which its execution is required to be completed. Suppose that in the previous example, each control-law computation job must complete by the release time of the subsequent job. Then, their deadlines are 120 msec, 220 msec, and so on, respectively. Alternatively, if the control-law computation jobs must complete sooner, their deadlines may be 70 msec, 170 msec, and so on. We say that a job has no deadline if its deadline is at infinity.

In this example, as in many others, it is more natural to state the timing requirement of a job in terms of its *response time*, that is, the length of time from the release time of the job to the instant when it completes. We call the maximum allowable response time of a job its *relative deadline*. Hence the relative deadline of every control-law computation job mentioned above is 100 or 50 msec. The deadline of a job, sometimes called its *absolute deadline*, is equal to its release time plus its relative deadline.

In general, we call a constraint imposed on the timing behavior of a job a *timing constraint*. In its simplest form, a timing constraint of a job can be specified in terms of its release time and relative or absolute deadlines, as illustrated by the above example. Some complex timing constraints cannot be specified conveniently in terms of release times and deadlines. We will discuss the parameters needed to specify those constraints when they arise, but in most of this book, we are concerned primarily with this simple form.

2.3   HARD AND SOFT TIMING CONSTRAINTS

It is common to divide timing constraints into two types: hard and soft. There are many definitions of hard and soft real-time constraints. Before stating the definition used in this book, let us first look at three frequently encountered definitions so you will be aware of them. They are based on the functional criticality of jobs, usefulness of late results, and deterministic or probabilistic nature of the constraints.

2.3.1 Common Definitions

According to a commonly used definition, a timing constraint or deadline is *hard* if the failure to meet it is considered to be a fatal fault. A hard deadline is imposed on a job because a late result produced by the job after the deadline may have disastrous consequences. (As examples, a late command to stop a train may cause a collision, and a bomb dropped too late may hit a civilian population instead of the intended military target.) In contrast, the late completion of a job that has a *soft deadline* is undesirable. However, a few misses of soft deadlines do no serious harm; only the system's overall performance becomes poorer and poorer when more and more jobs with soft deadlines complete late. This definition of hard and soft deadlines invariably leads to the question of whether the consequence of a missed deadline is indeed serious enough. The question of whether a timing constraint is hard or soft degenerates to that of how serious is serious.

In real-time systems literature, the distinction between hard and soft timing constraints is sometimes stated quantitatively in terms of the usefulness of results (and therefore the overall system performance) as functions of the tardinesses of jobs. The *tardiness* of a job measures how late it completes respective to its deadline. Its tardiness is zero if the job completes at or before its deadline; otherwise, if the job is late, its tardiness is equal to the difference between its *completion time* (i.e., the time instant at which it completes execution) and its deadline. The usefulness of a result produced by a soft real-time job (i.e, a job with a soft deadline) decreases gradually as the tardiness of the job increases, but the usefulness of a result produced by a hard real-time job (i.e., a job with a hard deadline) falls off abruptly and may even become negative when the tardiness of the job becomes larger than zero. The deadline of a job is softer if the usefulness of its result decreases at a slower rate. By this means, we can define a spectrum of hard/soft timing constraints. This quantitative measure of hardness and softness of deadlines is sometimes useful. It is certainly more appealing to computer scientists and engineers who have been trained not to rely on handwaving, qualitative measures. However, there is often no natural choice of usefulness functions. When choices are made, it is difficult to validate that the choices are sound and that different measures of the overall system performance as functions of tardinesses indeed behave as specified by the usefulness functions. Consequently, this kind of quantitative measure is not as rigorous as it appears to be.

Sometimes, we see this distinction made on the basis of whether the timing constraint is expressed in deterministic or probabilistic terms. If a job must never miss its deadline, then the deadline is hard. On the other hand, if its deadline can be missed occasionally with some acceptably low probability, then its timing constraint is soft. An example is that the system recovery job or a point-of-sales transaction completes within one minute 99.999 percent of the time. In other words, the probability of failure to meet the one-minute relative deadline is 10^{-5}. This definition ignores completely the consequence of a timing failure. In our example, if the failure of an on-time recovery could cause loss of life and property, we would require a rigorous demonstration that the timing failure probability is indeed never more than 10^{-5}. However, we would not require a demonstration of nearly the same rigor for a credit validation.

2.3.2 Hard Timing Constraints and Temporal Quality-of-Service Guarantees

In most of this book, we adopt a simple operational definition: The timing constraint of a job is hard, and the job is a hard real-time job, if the user requires the validation that the system always meet the timing constraint. By *validation*, we mean a demonstration by a provably correct, efficient procedure or by exhaustive simulation and testing. A large part of this book is devoted to efficient validation algorithms and methods as well as scheduling and resource management strategies that allow the system to be thus validated.

On the other hand, if no validation is required, or only a demonstration that the job meet some *statistical constraint* (i.e., a timing constraint specified in terms of statistical averages) suffices, then the timing constraint of the job is soft. The satisfaction of statistical constraints (e.g., the average number of missed deadlines per minute is two or less) can usually be demonstrated with a performance profile somewhat more thorough than those used to demonstrate the performance of general interactive systems. Most of the techniques for validation discussed in later chapters are not needed.

This way to differentiate between hard and soft timing constraints is compatible with the distinction between *guaranteed* and *best-effort* services [Lock86, Clar90]. Stated another way, if the user wants the temporal quality (e.g., response time and jitter) of the service provided by a task guaranteed and the satisfaction of the timing constraints defining the temporal quality validated, then the timing constraints are hard. On the other hand, if the user demands the best quality of service the system can provide but allows the system to deliver qualities below what is defined by the timing constraints, then the timing constraints are soft.

We call an application (task) with hard timing constraints a hard real-time application and a system containing mostly hard real-time applications a hard real-time system. For many traditional hard real-time applications (e.g., digital controllers), all the tasks and jobs executed in every operation mode of the system are known a priori. The traditional approach to building and validating such systems is to avoid hardware and software features that may lead to nondeterminism. Therefore, it is possible to verify the satisfaction of all hard timing constraints by exhaustive simulation and testing. Indeed, until recently, this has been the only approach used to build hard real-time systems.

In recent years, several efficient validation methods for a large class of hard real-time applications have been developed. These methods make on-line validation feasible and, thus, make hard real-time applications that dynamically create and destroy tasks feasible. When an application creates a new task with hard timing constraints, it submits an admission request to the scheduler. Upon the receipt of such a request, the scheduler does an acceptance test to determine whether the system can meet the timing constraints of the new task while meeting all the hard timing constraints of tasks previously admitted into the system. The scheduler accepts and admits the new task to the system only when the task passes the acceptance test. This acceptance test is an on-line validation test. Many of the validation algorithms described in Chapters 6–9 are suitable for this purpose.

2.4 HARD REAL-TIME SYSTEMS

The requirement that all hard timing constraints must be validated invariably places many restrictions on the design and implementation of hard real-time applications as well as on the architectures of hardware and system software used to support them. To justify this requirement, this section examines briefly several examples of hard real-time systems and discuss why hard timing constraints are imposed and why users require their satisfaction be validated and guaranteed.

2.4.1 Some Reasons for Requiring Timing Guarantees

Many embedded systems are hard real-time systems. Deadlines of jobs in an embedded system are typically derived from the required responsiveness of the sensors and actuators monitored and controlled by it. As an example, we consider an automatically controlled train. It cannot stop instantaneously. When the signal is red (stop), its braking action must be activated a certain distance away from the signal post at which the train must stop. This braking distance depends on the speed of the train and the safe value of deceleration. From the speed and safe deceleration of the train, the controller can compute the time for the train to travel the braking distance. This time in turn imposes a constraint on the response time of the jobs which sense and process the stop signal and activate the brake. No one would question that this timing constraint should be hard and that its satisfaction must be guaranteed.

Similarly, each control-law computation job of a flight controller must be completed in time so that its command can be issued in time. Otherwise, the plane controlled by it may become oscillatory (and the ride bumpy) or even unstable and uncontrollable. For this reason, we want the timely completion of all control-law computations guaranteed.

Jobs in some nonembedded systems may also have hard deadlines. An example is a critical information system that must be highly available: The system must never be down for more than a minute. Because of this requirement, reconfiguration and recovery of database servers and network connections in the system must complete within a few seconds or tens of seconds, and this relative deadline is hard.

A frequently asked question is how serious is the consequence of a few missed deadlines. A real-time monitor may nevertheless function satisfactorily when some sensor readings are not processed or lost. A single late recovery job may not cause an information system to crash. We surely have more design options and can make the system better in some other respect and make it less costly if some of the hard timing requirements are relaxed, even to a small degree.

In recent years, this observation motivated a variety of approaches to soften hard deadlines. Examples are to allow a few missed deadlines (e.g., [HaRa]) or premature terminations (e.g., [LLSB, LLSC]) as long as they occur in some acceptable way. We will discuss some of these approaches in Chapter 10. Needless to say, these approaches can be applied only when application domain experts know the effects of missed deadlines. Unfortunately, this is sometimes not the case. Even for some simple monitor and control applications, it is difficult to assess the effects of lost sample readings and late commands. In more complex systems, such as the NAVSTAR system,[1] the effect of missed deadlines may be combined with other factors

---

[1]The NAVSTAR Global Positioning System [DoEl] is a distributed system of space-based and ground-based computers and communication links. The system allows users equipped with navigation receivers to determine accurately their own locations. The space subsystem is a constellation of satellites. Together, the satellites provide 24-hour coverage at all locations. On board each satellite, telemetry and track-control subsystems, as well as other subsystems, communicate with each other via the Mission Data Unit (MDU). MDU contains hardware for timing control, modulation control, and navigation. It also interfaces with the intersatellite link and the downlink. The former supports communication among the satellites. The latter allows the satellite to broadcast to the control system on the ground as well as to its users. Each satellite must periodically estimates its own location. The satellites do this in a cooperative manner by exchanging messages with other satellites that are in range. By measuring the differences in the delays severed by messages from other satellites, each satellite can determine its own location with respect to the locations of the satellites whose messages are used for this purpose. This process is called ranging and is an example of functions that require accurate clock and timing signals and has real-time constraints.

in ways impossible to predict. Consequently, the designer makes sure that the system misses no deadline as long as it is in operation. The hard real-time requirement in fact simplifies the process of validating the overall system.

In general, if safety or property loss is involved, the designer/builder of the system has the burden of proof that bad things will never happen. Whenever it is not possible to prove without doubt that a few timing constraint violations will not jeopardize the safety of users or availability of some critical infrastructure, we take the safe approach and insist on the satisfaction of all timing constraints, even though the requirement may be unnecessarily stringent.

2.4.2   More on Hard Timing Constraints

The above examples also show that there may be no advantage in completing a job with a hard deadline early. As long as the job completes by its deadline, its response time is not important. In fact, it is often advantageous, sometimes even essential, to keep jitters in the response times of a stream of jobs small. (Section 1.4.2 gives an example.) In this case, we do not want to complete the jobs too early or too late. In later chapters, you will see that we often choose to delay the start and completion of hard real-time jobs, in favor of soft real-time or background jobs, and this is the reason.

In principle, our definition of hard and soft timing constraints allows a hard timing constraint to be specified in any terms. Examples are

1. deterministic constraints (e.g., the relative deadline of every control-law computation is 50 msec or the response time of at most one out of five consecutive control-law computations exceeds 50 msec);
2. probabilistic constraints, that is, constraints defined in terms of tails of some probability distributions (e.g., the probability of the response time exceeding 50 milliseconds is less than 0.2); and
3. constraints in terms of some usefulness function (e.g., the usefulness of every control-law computation is 0.8 or more).

In practice, hard timing constraints are rarely specified in the latter two ways. We mostly use deterministic hard timing constraints in this book, as in real-time systems literature. A good question is why. The answer is that it is much easier to validate deterministic timing constraints than probabilistic constraints and those expressed in terms of usefulness functions. We will discuss what some of the difficulties are in Chapter 6.

2.5   SOFT REAL-TIME SYSTEMS

A system in which jobs have soft deadlines is a *soft real-time system*. The developer of a soft real-time system is rarely required to prove rigorously that the system surely meet its real-time performance objective. Examples of such systems include on-line transaction systems and telephone switches, as well as electronic games. The less rigorous validation required of the system and, often, more relaxed timing constraints allow the developer to consider other performance metrics equally seriously. Meeting all deadlines is not the only consideration, sometimes, not even the primary consideration. An occasional missed deadline or aborted execution is usually considered tolerable; it may be more important for such a system to have a small average response time and high throughput.

A system may have critical timing requirements but is nevertheless considered to be a soft real-time system. An example is a stock price quotation system. It should update the price of each stock each time the price changes. Here, a late update may be highly undesirable, because the usefulness of a late price quotation decreases rapidly with time. However, in a volatile market when prices fluctuate at unusually high rates, we expect that the system cannot keep up with every price change but does its best according to some criteria. Occasional late or missed updates are tolerated as a trade-off for other factors, such as cost and availability of the system and the number of users the system can serve.

The timing requirements of soft real-time systems are often specified in probabilistic terms. Take a telephone network for example. In response to our dialing a telephone number, a sequence of jobs executes in turn, each routes the control signal from one switch to another in order to set up a connection through the network on our behalf. We expect that our call will be put through in a short time. To ensure that this expectation is met most of the time by the network, a timing constraint may be imposed on this sequence of jobs as a design objective (e.g., the sequence must complete in no more than 10 seconds for 95 percent of the time and in no more than 20 seconds for 99.95 percent of the time). The users are usually satisfied if after extensive simulation and trial use, the system indeed appears to meet this requirement.

As a final example, let us consider multimedia systems that provide the user with services of "guaranteed" quality. For example, a frame of a movie must be delivered every thirtieth of a second, and the difference in the times when each video frame is displayed and when the accompanied speech is presented should be no more than 80 msec. In fact, it is common to subject each new video stream to be transmitted by a network to an acceptance test. If the network cannot guarantee the satisfaction of timing constraints of the stream without violating the constraints of existing streams, the new stream is rejected, and its admission is requested again at some later time. However, the users are often willing to tolerate a few glitches, as long as the glitches occur rarely and for short lengths of time. At the same time, they are not willing to pay the cost of eliminating the glitches completely. For this reason, we often see timing constraints of multimedia systems guaranteed on a statistical basis, (e.g., the average number of late/lost frames per minute is less than 2). Moreover, users of such systems rarely demand any proof that the system indeed honor its guarantees. The quality-of-service guarantee is soft, the validation requirement is soft, and the timing constraints defining the quality are soft.

2.6   SUMMARY

This chapter defines several terms that will be used frequently in subsequent chapters. They are jobs, tasks, and timing constraints. Most of this book focuses on timing constraints that can be expressed in terms of release times and deadlines of jobs. In particular, we say that the scheduler works correctly if it never schedules any job before the release time of the job. A correctly scheduled job meets its timing constraint if it completes by its deadline, or it completes by its deadline with at least a certain probability, and so on.

The timing constraint of a task can be hard or soft, depending on whether a rigorous validation of the timing constraint is required (hard) or not (soft). In practice, a hard real-time system invariably has many soft real-time jobs and vice versa. The division is not always as obvious as we made it out to be here and, moreover, is not always necessary. In subsequent chapters, we will use the simpler terms *real-time system* or *system* whenever we mean either a hard real-time system or a soft real-time system or when there is no ambiguity about which type of system is meant by it.

We will focus on how to design a system so it is possible to validate its timing constraints and how to do validation if validation is required. In general, the process of validating that a system indeed meets its real-time performance objectives involves three major steps. The first step ensures that the timing constraints of each application are consistent with its high-level real-time requirements and that the timing constraints of its individual components are mutually consistent. The second step ensures that every component can meet its timing constraints if it executes alone and has all the required resources. The third and last step ensures that when scheduled together according to the algorithms used by the underlying operating system and networks, the timing constraints of all applications competing for all the available system resources are always met. In other words, the first step verifies that the timing constraints are specified correctly. The second step verifies the feasibility of each component with the underlying hardware and software resources. The last step verifies that the system as a whole behaves as specified by its timing constraints.

You may have noticed that in our discussion thus far the term validation has been used to mean specifically the last step of the validation process. Indeed, the book focuses on the last step of the validation process. We assume that the correct specification of the timing constraints and the feasibility of every individual component have already been verified. Therefore, the timing constraints of the system are given. For methods on specifying timing constraints and verifying their correctness, you need to read books and articles on formal methods (e.g., [Heit, VaKo]). Similarly, you can find algorithms for finding processor time demands of jobs in [AMWH, HeWh, KiMH, LBJR].

CHAPTER 3

A Reference Model of Real-Time Systems

When we study how given applications should be scheduled on a system of processors and resources and how we can determine whether the resultant system meets all its timing requirements, many specific details about each application (e.g., whether it is a Kalman filter computation or a sorting routine, whether it is implemented in Ada or C++) are not relevant. We do not want to keep track of these details and let them cloud relevant issues. Similarly, we do not want to keep track of irrelevant properties of system resources (e.g., whether the processor is by Intel or Motorola or whether the transmission medium is cable or fiber.) A good model abstracts the irrelevant details. It allows us to focus on the timing properties and resource requirements of system components and the way the operating system allocates the available system resources among them. By focusing on the relevant characteristics of the system, we can reason better about the timing behavior of each component and the overall system. By describing the algorithms used to schedule the applications and the methods for validating their timing constraints abstractly, rather than in implementation-specific terms, we can appreciate their general applicability better.

In this chapter, we describe a reference model of real-time systems. According to this model, each system is characterized by three elements: (1) a workload model that describes the applications supported by the system, (2) a resource model that describes the system resources available to the applications, and (3) algorithms that define how the application system uses the resources at all times. The model aims at being good in the sense mentioned above. It has a sufficiently rich set of features in terms of which we can describe the relevant characteristics of a wide spectrum of real-time applications and the properties of the underlying platform. If we choose to do so, we can describe a system in a sufficiently faithful manner in terms of the model so we can analyze, simulate, and even emulate the system based on its description. In particular, analysis and simulation tools (e.g., PERTS [LLRD]) can use such a system description as input to produce accurate estimates of the real-time performance and the associated overhead of the system.

In the following sections, we describe the first two elements of the reference model: the models that describe the applications and resources. In most of this book, we assume that these descriptions are given to us, for some systems, a priori before the execution begins, and for most systems, as new tasks are created and admitted into the system. The third element is the set of scheduling and resource management algorithms. We describe here how this element completes the description of the overall system, but defer the details on how the algorithms work and why they work until the next several chapters. We also introduce here the terminology and notation that we will use later.

Several features of the reference model are not needed to understand the basic scheduling and resource access-control algorithms described in later chapters. However, the models used by some analysis and simulation tools have these features. Sections describing these features are included in this chapter for reference. These sections are marked by "*." You can skip them without loss of continuity.

3.1 PROCESSORS AND RESOURCES

We divide all the system resources into two major types: processors and resources. Again, processors are often called servers and active resources; computers, transmission links, disks, and database server are examples of processors. They carry out machine instructions, move data from one place to another, retrieve files, process queries, and so on. Every job must have one or more processors in order to execute and make progress toward completion.

Sometimes, we will need to distinguish the *types* of processors. Two processors are of the same type if they are functionally identical and can be used interchangeably. Hence two transmission links with the same transmission rate between a pair of sender and receiver are processors of the same type; processors in a Symmetrical Multiprocessor (SMP) system are of the same type, and so on. Processors that are functionally different, or for some other reason cannot be used interchangeably, are of different types. CPUs, transmission links, and disks are of different types, because they are functionally different. A transmission link connecting an on-board flight management system to the ground controller is a different type of processor from the link connecting two air traffic control centers even when the links have the same characteristics, because they cannot be used interchangeably.

We will consistently use the letter P to denote processor(s). When we want focus on how the jobs on each processor are scheduled, how the jobs on different processors are synchronized, and how well the processors are utilized, there is no need to be concerned with whether the processors are identical or different. At these times, we will ignore the types of processors and call the m processors in the system $P_1, P_2, \ldots, P_m$.

By resources, we will specifically mean *passive* resources. Examples of resources are memory, sequence numbers, mutexes, and database locks. A job may need some resources in addition to the processor in order to make progress. One of the attributes of a processor is its speed. Although we will rarely mention this attribute, we will implicitly assume that the rate of progress a job makes toward its completion depends on the speed of the processor on which it executes. We can explicitly model this dependency by making the amount of time a job requires to complete a function of the processor speed. In contrast, we do not associate speed with a resource. In other words, how long a job takes to complete does not depend on the speed of any resource it uses during execution.

For example, a computation job may share data with other computations, and the data may be guarded by semaphores. We model (the lock of) each semaphore as a resource. When a job wants to access the shared data guarded by a semaphore R, it must first lock the semaphore, and then it enters the critical section of the code where it accesses the shared data. In this case, we say that the job requires the resource R for the duration of this critical section.

As another example, we consider a data link that uses the sliding-window scheme to regulate message transmission. Only a maximum number of messages are allowed to be in transit (i.e., they have been transmitted but their reception has not yet been positively acknowledged). One way to implement this scheme is for the sender to maintain a window of valid sequence numbers. The window is moved forward as messages transmitted earlier are acknowledged by the receiver. A message waiting to be transmitted must first be given one of the valid sequence numbers before it can be transmitted. We model the transmission of a message as a job; the job executes when the message is being transmitted. This job needs the data link, as well as a valid sequence number. The data link is a processor. The sequence numbers are units of the sequence-number resource.

Similarly, we usually model transactions that query and update a database as jobs; these jobs execute on a database server. If the database server uses a locking mechanism to ensure data integrity, then a transaction also needs the locks on the data objects it reads or writes in order to proceed. The locks on the data objects are resources.

We will use the letter R to denote resources. The resources in the examples mentioned above are *reusable*, because they are not consumed during use. (In contrast, a message produced by a process and consumed by another process is not reusable because it no longer exists after use.) In our discussion, a "resource" almost always mean a reusable resource. The statement that the system contains ρ resources means that there are ρ types of serially reusable resources, each resource may have one or more units, and each unit is used in a mutually exclusive manner. For example, if the sliding window of a data link has eight valid sequence numbers, then there are eight units of the sequence-number resource (type). The write lock on a file is a resource that has only one unit because only one job can have the lock at a time. A resource that can be shared by a finite number x of jobs is modeled as a resource (type) that has x units, each of which can be used by only one job at a time.

To prevent our model from being cluttered by irrelevant details, we typically omit the resources that are plentiful. A resource is *plentiful* if no job is ever prevented from execution by the lack of this resource. A resource that can be shared by an infinite number of jobs (e.g., a file that is readable simultaneously by all) need not be explicitly modeled and hence never appears in our model. You will notice later that we rarely mention the memory resource. Clearly, memory is an essential type of resource. All computing and communication systems have this resource. We omit it from our model whenever we can account for the speed of the memory by the speed of the processor and memory is not a bottleneck of the system. For example, we can account for the speed of the buffer memory in a packet switch by letting the speed of each input (or output) link equal the transmission rate of the link or the rate at which data can go in (or out of) the buffer, whichever is smaller. Therefore, there is no need to explicitly model this aspect of the memory. By memory not being the bottleneck, we mean that whenever a job is scheduled to execute, it always has a sufficient amount of memory. Many real-time systems are designed so that this assumption is valid. When this assumption is not valid, the timing behavior of the system critically depends on how memory is allocated to jobs. Clearly, the model of the system must include the memory resource in this case.

Another point to keep in mind is that we sometimes model some elements of a system as processors and sometimes as resources, depending on how we will use the model. For example, in a distributed system, a computation job may invoke a server on a remote processor.

When we want to focus on how the response time of this job depends on the way the job is scheduled with other jobs on its local processor, we may model the remote server as a resource. We may also model the remote server (or more precisely the remote processor) as a processor. As you will see that in Chapter 9, we indeed use both of these alternatives to model remote execution in distributed systems. They give us two different points of view and lead to different scheduling and resource management strategies.

As a final example, let us consider the I/O bus. Every computation job must have the I/O bus in addition to the processor to execute. Most of the time, we model the I/O bus as a resource, oftentimes a plentiful and therefore ignored resource. However, when we want to study how long I/O activities may delay the completion of computation jobs that share the I/O bus or when we want to determine the real-time performance of an I/O bus arbitration scheme, we want to model the bus as a resource or a processor.

There are no cookbook rules to guide us in making this and many other modeling choices. A good model can give us better insight into the problem at hand. A bad model can clutter our mind with irrelevant details and may even give us a wrong point of view and lead to a poor design and implementation. For this reason, the skill and art in modeling are essential to a system designer and developer.

3.2   TEMPORAL PARAMETERS OF REAL-TIME WORKLOAD

As stated in Chapter 2, the workload on processors consists of jobs, each of which is a unit of work to be allocated processor time and other resources. A set of related jobs that execute to support a function of the system is a task. We typically assume that many parameters of hard real-time jobs and tasks are known at all times; otherwise, it would not be possible to ensure that the system meet its hard real-time requirements. The number of tasks (or jobs) in the system is one such parameter. In many embedded systems, the number of tasks is fixed as long as the system remains in an operation mode. The number of tasks may change when the system operation mode changes, and the number of tasks in the new mode is also known. Moreover, these numbers are known a priori before the system begins execution. Take the flight control system in Figure 1–3 as an example. During cruise mode, the system has 12 tasks (i.e., 3 30-Hz avionics tasks, 3 30-Hz computations and 2 90-Hz computations, plus 180-Hz computation, validation, output and built-in-test tasks). If the system triply replicates all control-law computations during landing, the number of tasks increases to 24 when it operates in the landing mode.

In some other systems, however, the number of tasks may change as tasks are added and deleted while the system executes. As an example, in an air traffic control system, each surveillance task monitors an aircraft. The number of such tasks changes as tasks are added and deleted when aircraft enter and leave the coverage area. Nevertheless, the number of tasks with hard timing constraints is known at all times. This assumption is valid. When the satisfaction of their timing constraints is to be guaranteed, the admission and deletion of hard real-time tasks are usually done under the control of the run-time system (e.g., by having the application system request admission and deletion of tasks). For this purpose, the system must maintain information on all existing hard real-time tasks, including the number of such tasks.

Each job J_i is characterized by its temporal parameters, functional parameters, resource parameters, and interconnection parameters. Its temporal parameters tell us its timing constraints and behavior. Its interconnection parameters describe how it depends on other jobs and how other jobs depend on it. Its functional parameters specify the intrinsic properties of the job. Finally, its resource parameters give us its resource requirements.

We already defined in Section 2.2 the release time, absolute deadline, and relative deadline of a job J_i; these are temporal parameters. We will use r_i, d_i, and D_i, respectively, to denote them and call the time interval $(r_i, d_i]$[1] between the release time and absolute deadline of the job J_i its *feasible interval*. d_i and D_i are usually derived from the timing requirements of J_i, jobs in the same task as J_i, and the overall system. We consider these parameters to be part of the system specification.

3.2.1   Fixed, Jittered, and Sporadic Release Times

In many systems, we do not know exactly when each job will be released. In other words, we do not know the actual release time r_i of each job J_i; only that r_i is in a range $[r_i^-, r_i^+]$. r_i can be as early as the earliest release time r_i^- and as late as the latest release time r_i^+. Indeed, some models assume that only the range of r_i is known and call this range the *jitter* in r_i, or *release-time jitter*. Sometimes, the jitter is negligibly small compared with the values of other temporal parameters. If, for all practical purposes, we can approximate the actual release time of each job by its earliest or latest release time, then we say that the job has a fixed release time.

Almost every real-time system is required to respond to external events which occur at random instants of time. When such an event occurs, the system executes a set of jobs in response. The release times of these jobs are not known until the event triggering them occurs. These jobs are called *sporadic jobs* or *aperiodic jobs* because they are released at random time instants. (We will return shortly to discuss the difference between these two types of jobs.) For example, the pilot may disengage the autopilot system at any time. When this occurs, the autopilot system changes from cruise mode to standby mode. The jobs that execute to accomplish this mode change are sporadic jobs.

The release times of sporadic and aperiodic jobs are random variables. The model of the system gives the probability distribution $A(x)$ of the release time of such a job, or when there is a stream of similar sporadic or aperiodic jobs, the probability distribution of *interrelease time* (i.e., the length of the time interval between the release times of two consecutive jobs in the stream). $A(x)$ gives us the probability that the release time of the job is at or earlier than x (or the interrelease time of the stream of jobs is equal to or less than x) for all valid values of x. Rather than speaking of release times of aperiodic jobs, we sometimes use the term *arrival times* (or *interarrival time*) which is commonly used in queueing theory. An aperiodic job arrives when it is released. $A(x)$ is the *arrival time distribution* (or *interarrival time distribution*).

3.2.2   Execution Time

Another temporal parameter of a job, J_i, is its *execution time*, e_i. e_i is the amount of time required to complete the execution of J_i when it executes alone and has all the resources it

---

[1]The notation $(r_i, d_i]$ means specifically the interval that begins immediately after r_i and ends at d_i. In general, a square bracket [or] indicates that the interval includes the endpoint next to the bracket, while a round bracket (or) indicates that the endpoint is not included.

requires. Hence, the value of this parameter depends mainly on the complexity of the job and the speed of the processor used to execute the job, not on how the job is scheduled.

The actual amount of time required by a job to complete its execution may vary for many reasons. As examples, a computation may contain conditional branches, and these conditional branches may take different amounts of time to complete. The branches taken during the execution of the computation job depend on the input data. If the underlying system has performance enhancing features (e.g., cache memory and pipeline), the amount of time a computation takes to complete may vary each time it executes even when it has no conditional branches. For these reasons, the actual execution time of a computation job is unknown until it completes. Similarly, the actual amount of time to transmit each frame of a MPEG-compressed video is different from frame to frame because the numbers of bits used to encode different frames are different. The actual execution time of the job modeling the transmission of a frame is unknown a priori. What can be determined a priori through analysis and measurement are the maximum and minimum amounts of time required to complete each job. In other words, we know that the execution time e_i of the job J_i is in the range $[e_i^-, e_i^+]$, where e_i^- and e_i^+ are the *minimum execution time* and the *maximum execution time* of J_i, respectively. We usually assume that we know e_i^- and e_i^+ of every hard real-time job J_i but the actual execution time of the job is unknown.

For the purpose of determining whether each job can always complete by its deadline, knowing the maximum execution time of each job often suffices. For this reason, in most deterministic models used to characterize hard real-time applications, the term execution time e_i of each job J_i specifically means its maximum execution time. We will also use this term in this sense most of the time. However, except where we state otherwise, we never mean that the actual execution time of the job is fixed and known, only that it never exceeds e_i.

You may want to question at this point the accuracy of deterministic models which assume that every job takes its maximum execution time to complete. If we design our system based on this assumption and allocate this much time to each job, the processor(s) will surely be underutilized. This statement is clearly true sometimes. We will encounter applications where the variations in job execution times are so large that working with their maximum values indeed yields unacceptably conservative designs. We should not model such applications deterministically. More importantly, as you will see in Chapter 4, in some systems the response times of some jobs may be larger when the actual execution times of some jobs are smaller than their maximum values. In these cases, we will have to deal with the variations in execution times explicitly.

However, there are two good reasons for the common use of the deterministic approach. Many hard real-time systems are safety-critical. These systems are typically designed and implemented in a such a way that the variations in job execution times are kept as small as possible. The need to have relatively deterministic execution times places many restrictions on implementation choices. (For example, the programs cannot use dynamic structures that can lead to variable execution time and memory usage; performance-enhancing features are not used.) By working with these restrictions and making the execution times of jobs almost deterministic, the designer can model more accurately the application system deterministically. In return, the deterministic approach makes the validation of the resultant system easier.

The other reason for the common use of the deterministic approach is that the hard real-time portion of the system is often small. The timing requirements of the rest of the system are soft. In this case, an option is to design the hard real-time subsystem based on its worst-case processor time and resource requirements even though their actual requirements may be much smaller. We can then use the methods and tools supported by the deterministic models to ensure that the hard timing constraints will surely be met at all times. We also can safely reclaim the time and resources allocated to but not used by hard real-time jobs and make the reclaimed time and resources available to soft real-time jobs and nonreal-time jobs. In this way, the system will not be overdesigned with underutilized resources.

3.3   PERIODIC TASK MODEL

The *periodic task model* is a well-known deterministic workload model [LiLa]. With its various extensions, the model characterizes accurately many traditional hard real-time applications, such as digital control, real-time monitoring, and constant bit-rate voice/video transmission. Many scheduling algorithms based on this model have good performance and well-understood behavior. There are now methods and tools to support the design, analysis, and validation of real-time systems that can be accurately characterized by the model. For these reasons, we want to know it well and be able to use it proficiently.

3.3.1   Periods, Execution Times, and Phases of Periodic Tasks

In the periodic task model, each computation or data transmission that is executed repeatedly at regular or semiregular time intervals in order to provide a function of the system on a continuing basis is modeled as a *period task*. Specifically, each periodic task, denoted by T_i, is a sequence of jobs. The *period* p_i of the periodic task T_i is the minimum length of all time intervals between release times of consecutive jobs in T_i. Its *execution time* is the maximum execution time of all the jobs in it. With a slight abuse of the notation, we use e_i to denote the execution time of the periodic task T_i, as well as that of all the jobs in it. At all times, the period and execution time of every periodic task in the system are known.

This definition of periodic tasks differs from the one often found in real-time systems literature. In many published works, the term periodic task refers to a task that is truly periodic, that is, interrelease times of all jobs in a periodic task are equal to its period. This definition has led to the common misconception that scheduling and validation algorithms based on the periodic task model are applicable only when every periodic task is truly periodic. We will show in Chapter 6 that in fact most existing results remain correct as long as interrelease times of jobs in each task are bounded from below by the period of the task. This is why we adopt our definition. What are called periodic tasks here are sometimes called sporadic tasks in literature. In this book, a sporadic task is one whose interrelease times can be arbitrarily small; we will define this term shortly.

The accuracy of the periodic task model decreases with increasing jitter in release times and variations in execution times. So, a periodic task is an inaccurate model of the transmission of a variable bit-rate video, because of the large variation in the execution times of jobs (i.e., transmission times of individual frames). A periodic task is also an inaccurate model of the transmission of cells on a real-time connection through a switched network that does not do traffic shaping at every switch, because large release-time jitters are possible.

We call the tasks in the system $T_1, T_2, \ldots, T_n$.[2] When it is necessary to refer to the individual jobs in a task T_i, we call them $J_{i,1}, J_{i,2}$ and so on, $J_{i,k}$ being the kth job in T_i. When we want to talk about properties of individual jobs but are not interested in the tasks to which they belong, we also call the jobs J_1, J_2, and so on.

The release time $r_{i,1}$ of the first job $J_{i,1}$ in each task T_i is called the *phase* of T_i. For the sake of convenience, we use ϕ_i to denote the phase of T_i, that is, $\phi_i = r_{i,1}$. In general, different tasks may have different phases. Some tasks are *in phase*, meaning that they have the same phase.

We use H to denote the least common multiple of p_i for $i = 1, 2, \ldots n$. A time interval of length H is called a *hyperperiod* of the periodic tasks. The (maximum) number N of jobs in each hyperperiod is equal to $\sum_{i=1}^{n} H/p_i$. The length of a hyperperiod of three periodic tasks with periods 3, 4, and 10 is 60. The total number N of jobs in the hyperperiod is 41.

We call the ratio $u_i = e_i/p_i$ the *utilization* of the task T_i. u_i is equal to the fraction of time a truly periodic task with period p_i and execution time e_i keeps a processor busy. It is an upper bound to the utilization of any task modeled by T_i. The *total utilization* U of all the tasks in the system is the sum of the utilizations of the individual tasks in it. So, if the execution times of the three periodic tasks are 1, 1, and 3, and their periods are 3, 4, and 10, respectively, then their utilizations are 0.33, 0.25 and 0.3. The total utilization of the tasks is 0.88; these tasks can keep a processor busy at most 88 percent of the time.

A job in T_i that is released at t must complete D_i units of time after t; D_i is the (*relative*) *deadline* of the task T_i. We will omit the word "relative" except where it is unclear whether by deadline, we mean a relative or absolute deadline. We will often assume that for every task a job is released and becomes ready at the beginning of each period and must complete by the end of the period. In other words, D_i is equal to p_i for all n. This requirement is consistent with the throughput requirement that the system can keep up with all the work demanded of it at all times.

However, in general, D_i can have an arbitrary value. In particular, it can be shorter than p_i. Giving a task a short relative deadline is a way to specify that variations in the response times of individual jobs (i.e., jitters in their completion times) of the task must be sufficiently small. Sometimes, each job in a task may not be ready when it is released. (For example, when a computation job is released, its input data are first transferred to memory. Until this operation completes, the computation job is not ready.) The time between the ready time of each job and the end of the period is shorter than the period. Similarly, there may be some operation to perform after the job completes but before the next job is released. Sometimes, a job may be composed of dependent jobs that must be executed in sequence. A way to enforce the dependency relation among them is to delay the release of a job later in the sequence while advancing the deadline of a job earlier in the sequence. The relative deadlines of jobs may be shortened for these reasons as well.

3.3.2   Aperiodic and Sporadic Tasks

Earlier, we pointed out that a real-time system is invariably required to respond to external events, and to respond, it executes aperiodic or sporadic jobs whose release times are not

---

[2]Again, the number n of periodic tasks in the system is known. This number may change when some tasks are deleted from the system and new tasks are added to the system. The amount of time to complete such a change is short compared with the length of time between consecutive changes.

known a priori. An operator's adjustment of the sensitivity setting of a radar surveillance system is an example. The radar system must continue to operate, but in addition, it also must respond to the operator's command. Similarly, when a pilot changes the autopilot from cruise mode to standby mode, the system must respond by reconfiguring itself, while continuing to execute the control tasks that fly the airplane. A command and control system must process sporadic data messages, in addition to the continuous voice and video traffic.

In the periodic task model, the workload generated in response to these unexpected events is captured by aperiodic and sporadic tasks. Each *aperiodic* or *sporadic task* is a stream of aperiodic or sporadic jobs, respectively. The interarrival times between consecutive jobs in such a task may vary widely and, in particular, can be arbitrarily small. The jobs in each task model the work done by the system in response to events of the same type. For example, the jobs that execute to change the detection threshold of the radar system are in one task; the jobs that change the operation mode of the autopilot are in one task; and the jobs that process sporadic data messages are in one task, and so on.

Specifically, the jobs in each aperiodic task are similar in the sense that they have the same statistical behavior and the same timing requirement. Their interarrival times are identically distributed random variables with some probability distribution $A(x)$. Similarly, the execution times of jobs in each aperiodic (or sporadic) task are identically distributed random variables, each distributed according to the probability distribution $B(x)$. These assumptions mean that the statistical behavior of the system and its environment do not change with time, that is, the system is stationary. That the system is stationary is usually valid in time intervals of length on the order of H, in particular, within any hyperperiod of the periodic tasks during which no periodic tasks are added or deleted.

We say that a task is *aperiodic* if the jobs in it have either soft deadlines or no deadlines. The task to adjust radar's sensitivity is an example. We want the system to be responsive, that is, to complete each adjustment as soon as possible. On the other hand, a late response is annoying but tolerable. We therefore want to optimize the responsiveness of the system for the aperiodic jobs, but never at the expense of hard real-time tasks whose deadlines must be met at all times.

In contrast, an autopilot system is required to respond to a pilot's command to disengage the autopilot and take over the control manually within a specific time. Similarly, when a transient fault occurs, a fault-tolerant system may be required to detect the fault and recover from it in time. The jobs that execute in response to these events have hard deadlines. Tasks containing jobs that are released at random time instants and have hard deadlines are *sporadic tasks*. We treat them as hard real-time tasks. Our primary concern is to ensure that their deadlines are always met; minimizing their response times is of secondary importance.

3.4 PRECEDENCE CONSTRAINTS AND DATA DEPENDENCY

Data and control dependencies among jobs may constrain the order in which they can execute. In classical scheduling theory, the jobs are said to have *precedence constraints* if they are constrained to execute in some order. Otherwise, if the jobs can execute in any order, they are said to be *independent*.

For example, in a radar surveillance system, the signal-processing task is the producer of track records, while the tracker task is the consumer. In particular, each tracker job processes the track records generated by a signal-processing job. The designer may choose to synchronize the tasks so that the execution of the kth tracker job does not begin until the kth signal-processing job completes. The tracker job is precedence constrained. In general, a consumer job has this constraint whenever it must synchronize with the corresponding producer job(s) and wait until the latter completes in order to execute.

As another example, we consider queries to an information server. Suppose that before each query is processed and the requested information retrieved, its authorization to access the requested information is first checked. The retrieval job cannot begin execution until the authentication job completes. The communication job that forwards the information to the requester cannot begin until the retrieval job completes. Similarly, in a communication system, the jobs that generate an acknowledgement of a message and transmit the acknowledgement message cannot begin until the job that receives and processes the message completes.

3.4.1 Precedence Graph and Task Graph

We use a partial-order relation $<$, called a *precedence relation*, over the set of jobs to specify the precedence constraints among jobs. A job J_i is a *predecessor* of another job J_k (and J_k a *successor* of J_i) if J_k cannot begin execution until the execution of J_i completes. A shorthand notation to state this fact is $J_i < J_k$. J_i is an *immediate predecessor* of J_k (and J_k is an *immediate successor* of J_i) if $J_i < J_k$ and there is no other job J_j such that $J_i < J_j < J_k$. Two jobs J_i and J_k are independent when neither $J_i < J_k$ nor $J_k < J_i$. A job with predecessors is *ready* for execution when the time is at or after its release time and all of its predecessors are completed.

A classical way to represent the precedence constraints among jobs in a set **J** is by a directed graph $G = (\mathbf{J}, <)$. Each vertex in this graph represents a job in **J**. We will call each vertex by the name of the job represented by it. There is a directed edge from the vertex J_i to the vertex J_k when the job J_i is an immediate predecessor of the job J_k. This graph is called a *precedence graph*.

A *task graph*, which gives us a general way to describe the application system, is an extended precedence graph. Figure 3–1 shows a task graph. As in a precedence graph, the vertices in a task graph represent jobs. They are shown as circles and squares in this figure. (Here, we ignore the difference between the types of jobs represented by them. The need

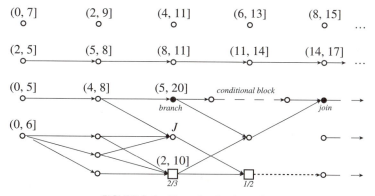

FIGURE 3–1   Example of task graphs.

to differentiate them arises only in the next section.) For simplicity, we show only the job attributes that are of interest to us. The numbers in the bracket above each job give its feasible interval. The edges in the graph represent dependencies among jobs. If all the edges are precedence edges, representing precedence constraints, then the graph is a precedence graph.

Specifically, the system described by the graph in Figure 3–1 includes two periodic tasks. The task whose jobs are represented by the vertices in the top row has phase 0, period 2, and relative deadline 7. The jobs in it are independent; there are no edges to or from these jobs. In other words, the jobs released in later periods are ready for execution as soon as they are released even though some job released earlier is not yet complete. This is the usual assumption about periodic tasks. The vertices in the second row of Figure 3–1 represent jobs in a periodic task with phase 2, period 3, and relative deadline 3. The jobs in it are dependent; the first job is the immediate predecessor of the second job, the second job is the immediate predecessor of the third job, and so on. The precedence graph of (the jobs in) this task is a chain as shown here. A subgraph's being a *chain* indicates that for every pair of jobs J_i and J_k in the subgraph, either $J_i < J_k$ or $J_i > J_k$. Hence the jobs must be executed in serial order.

In the subsequent chapters, we rarely use a task graph to describe a system of periodic tasks. You can see why from the above example: A list of periodic tasks and their parameters suffices. A graph such as the one in Figure 3–1 is necessary only when the system contains components that have complex dependencies as exemplified by the subgraph below the periodic tasks.

Many types of interactions and communication among jobs are not captured by a precedence graph but can be captured by a task graph. Unlike a precedence graph, a task graph may contain different types of edges that represent different types of dependencies. The type(s) of dependency represented by an edge is given by the type(s) of the edge. The types of an edge connecting two vertices and other parameters of the edge are *interconnection parameters* of the jobs represented by the vertices.

3.4.2   Data Dependency

As an example, data dependency cannot be captured by a precedence graph. In many real-time systems, jobs communicate via shared data. Oftentimes, the designer chooses not to synchronize producer and consumer jobs. Rather, each producer places the data generated by it in a shared address space to be used by the consumer at any time. In this case, the classical precedence graph should show that the producer and consumer are independent because they are not explicitly constrained to execute in turn.

As an example, in an avionics system, the navigation job updates the location of the airplane periodically. These data are placed in a shared space. Whenever the flight management job needs navigation data, it reads the most current data produced by the navigation job. There is no precedence constraint between the navigation job and the flight management job.

In a task graph, data dependencies among jobs are represented explicitly by data-dependency edges among jobs. There is a data-dependency edge from a vertex J_i to vertex J_k in the task graph if the job J_k consumes data generated by J_i or the job J_i sends messages to J_k. A parameter of an edge from J_i to J_k is the volume of data from J_i to J_k. In Chapter 9, we will describe algorithms that partition an application system into modules and assign different modules to different processors for execution. Since the cost of communication between jobs on the same processor is usually much lower than that between jobs on different processors, one of the key factors we need to consider in choosing a partition is the amount of data exchanged among jobs. For this purpose, we will make use of the information provided by the *data volume* parameter.

As we will see in later chapters, the scheduler may not be able to schedule the navigation job and the flight management job independently. To ensure data integrity, some locking mechanism may be in place, and this mechanism allows only one job to access the shared data at a time. This leads to resource contention, which may also constrain the manner in which jobs execute. However, this constraint is imposed on jobs by scheduling and resource access-control algorithms. It is not a precedence constraint because it is not an intrinsic constraint on the execution order of the jobs.

*3.5   OTHER TYPES OF DEPENDENCIES

Like nonreal-time applications, real-time applications sometimes contain redundant modules, carry out heuristic searches, use multiple versions, execute some job conditionally, and so forth. We add other extensions to the classical precedence graphs in order to model such jobs and dependencies. These extensions include temporal distance, OR jobs, conditional branches, and pipe (or pipeline).

3.5.1   Temporal Dependency

Some jobs may be constrained to complete within a certain amount of time relative to one another. We call the difference in the completion times of two jobs the *temporal distance* [HaLH] between them. Jobs are said to have a *temporal distance constraint* if their temporal distance must be no more than some finite value. Jobs with temporal distance constraints may or may not have deadlines.

As an example, we consider the display of video frames and the accompanying audio when the video is that of a person speaking. To have lip synchronization, the time between the display of each frame and the generation of the corresponding audio segment must be no more than 160 msec [StNa]. Another example is the visual and audio displays of a passive sonar system [MoMW]. The synthesized audio signal and the accompanied visual display must be presented to the operator no more than 100 msec apart. These timing requirements can be stated more naturally in terms of temporal distance constraints than in terms of deadlines of jobs.

In a task graph, temporal distance constraints among jobs are represented by temporal-dependency edges. There is a temporal-dependency edge from a vertex J_i to a vertex J_k if the job J_k must be completed within a certain time after J_i completes. The temporal distance between the jobs is given by the temporal distance parameter of the edge. The value of this parameter is infinite if the jobs have no temporal distance constraint, or equivalently, there is no temporal-dependency edge between the jobs.

3.5.2   AND/OR Precedence Constraints

In the classical model, a job with more than one immediate predecessor must wait until all its immediate predecessors have been completed before its execution can begin. Whenever it is necessary to be specific, we call such jobs *AND jobs* and dependencies among them *AND precedence constraints*. AND jobs are represented by unfilled circles in the task graph in Figure 3–1. An example is the job labeled *J* in this figure. All three of its immediate predecessors must be completed before *J* can begin execution. An *AND* job such as *J* may be the transmission of a message to a user. Its immediate predecessors are the jobs that set up a connection for the message, encrypt the message to safeguard privacy, and check the user's account for the requested quality of the delivery service. These predecessors may execute in any order relative to each other, but they must all be completed before the message transmission job can begin.

In contrast, an *OR job* is one which can begin execution at or after its release time provided one or some of its immediate predecessors has been completed. In Figure 3–1, we represent *OR* jobs by square vertices, as exemplified by the two square vertices at the bottom of the graph. The one labeled *2/3* can begin execution as soon as two out of its three immediate predecessors complete. In a system that uses triple redundancy to increase fault tolerance, a voter can be modeled as a 2/3 job. Its predecessors are three replicated jobs that implement a critical function. The voter executes and in turn allows its successors to begin whenever two out of the three predecessors complete (and produce correct results). Similarly, we can model a two-version computation as the two immediate predecessors of a 1/2 *OR* job. The operating system chooses one of the versions depending on factors such as their resource requirements and quality of their results. Only one of them needs to be completed before the *OR* job can begin execution.

In the task graph, the *in-type* of job (i.e., the vertex representing the job) tells us whether all its immediate predecessors must complete before its execution can begin. By default, the value of this job parameter is *AND*. It can have the value *OR*, if only one of its immediate predecessors must be completed, or *k-out-of-l*, if only *k* out *l* of its immediate predecessor must be completed before its execution can begin.

3.5.3 Conditional Branches

Similarly, in the classical model, all the immediate successors of a job must be executed; an outgoing edge from every vertex expresses an *AND constraint*. This convention makes it inconvenient for us to represent conditional execution of jobs, such as the example in Figure 3–2.

This system can easily be modeled by a task graph that has edges expressing *OR constraints*. Only one of all the immediate successors of a job whose outgoing edges express OR constraints is to be executed. Such a job is called a *branch* job. In a meaningful task graph, there is a *join* job associated with each branch job. In Figure 3–1, these jobs are represented by filled circles. The subgraph that begins from a vertex representing a branch job and ends at the vertex representing the associated join job is called a *conditional block*. Only one conditional branch in each conditional block is to be executed. The conditional block in Figure 3–1 has two conditional branches: Either the upper conditional branch, containing a chain of jobs, or the lower conditional branch, containing only one job, is to be executed.

This natural extension allows us to use a task graph to characterize data-dependent conditional executions exemplified by the program segment in Figure 3–2. As an exercise, you may want to look at Problem 3.2 which asks you to draw a task graph of an application that has conditional branches and for comparison, use as many classical precedence graphs as

For every second do the following:
    Process radar returns.
    Generate track records.
    Perform track association.
    For the target T on each of the established tracks do:
        If the target T is within distance D from self,
            Do the following:
                Analyze the trajectory of T.
                If T is on collision course with self, sound alarm.
            Enddo
                Else
            Compute the current distance of T from self.
            If the current distance is larger than previous distance,
                drop the track of T.
            Endif
        Endif
Endfor

FIGURE 3–2   A program with conditional branches.

necessary to represent all of its possible execution paths. In general, we need to use a classical precedence graph for each branch in each conditional block. For example, the task graph in Figure 3–1 is equivalent to two precedence graphs: One contains only the upper conditional branch, and the other graph contains only the lower conditional branch. We need l^k classical precedence graphs to represent an application system that contains k conditional blocks if each conditional blocks has l branches.

    Similar to the parameter *in-type*, the job parameter *out-type* tells whether all the job's immediate successors are to be executed. The default value of the *out-type* parameter of every job is *AND*, that is, all its immediate successors are to be executed. On the other hand, the *out-type* of a branch job is *OR*, because only one of its immediate successors must be executed.

3.5.4   Pipeline Relationship

A dependency between a pair of producer-consumer jobs that are piped can theoretically be represented by a precedence graph. In this graph, the vertices are the granules of the producer and the consumer. Each granule of the consumer can begin execution when the previous granule of this job and the corresponding granule of the producer job have completed. Problem 3.3 gives an example of how this representation works, but the example also illustrates how inconvenient the representation is. For this reason, we introduce the pipeline relation between jobs.

    In the task graph, we represent a pipeline relationship between jobs by a pipeline edge, as exemplified by the dotted edge between the jobs in the right-bottom corner of the graph in Figure 3–1. There is an edge from J_i to J_k if the output of J_i is piped into J_k and the execution of J_k can proceed as long as there are data for it to process.

3.6   FUNCTIONAL PARAMETERS

While scheduling and resource access-control decisions are made disregarding most functional characteristics of jobs, several functional properties do affect these decisions. The workload model must explicitly describe these relevant properties, and this is done by the values of functional parameters. Among them are preemptivity, criticality, optional interval, and laxity type.

3.6.1   Preemptivity of Jobs

Executions of jobs can often be interleaved. The scheduler may suspend the execution of a less urgent job and give the processor to a more urgent job. Later when the more urgent job completes, the scheduler returns the processor to the less urgent job so the job can resume execution. This interruption of job execution is called *preemption*. A job is *preemptable* if its execution can be suspended at any time to allow the execution of other jobs and, later on, can be resumed from the point of suspension. Computation jobs that execute on CPUs are examples of preemptable jobs. In nonreal-time systems, such jobs are typically scheduled in a round-robin manner; this is possible because they are preemptable.

A job is *nonpreemptable* if it must be executed from start to completion without interruption. This constraint may be imposed because its execution, if suspended and the processor given to other jobs, must be executed again from the beginning. As an example, we consider jobs that model the transmissions of data frames in a token ring (or bus). If transmission of a frame is interrupted before it completes, the partially transmitted frame is discarded by the receiver. The entire frame must be retransmitted from the start. To avoid wasting bandwidth in this way, we make the execution of this job on the ring (or bus) nonpreemptable.

Sometimes, a job may be preemptable everywhere except for a small portion which is constrained to be nonpreemptable. An example is an interrupt handling job. An interrupt handling job usually begins by saving the state of the processor (i.e., storing the processor status register, the stack pointer, the program counter, and so on). This small portion of the job is nonpreemptable because suspending the execution of this portion and giving the CPU to another job may cause serious errors in the data structures shared by the jobs.

During preemption, the system must first save the state of the preempted job at the time of preemption so it can resume the job from that state. Then, the system must prepare the execution environment for the preempting job before starting the job. For example, in the case of CPU jobs, the state of the preempted job includes the contents of its program counter, processor status register, and registers containing temporary results. After saving the contents of these registers in memory and before the preempting job can start, the operating system must load the new processor status register, clear pipelines, and so on. In operating system literature, these actions are collectively called a *context switch*. The amount of time required to accomplish a context switch is called a *context-switch time*. We will use these terms to mean the overhead work done during preemption and the time required to accomplish the work, respectively, for all types of jobs, not just CPU jobs.

Finally, we have focused here on the preemptivity of jobs on processors. The fact that a job is nonpreemptable is treated as a constraint of the job. In Section 3.7, we will see that the nonpreemptivity of a job may be a consequence of a constraint on the usage of some resource. Let us keep this point in mind when we discuss the preemptivity attribute of resources in Section 3.7.

3.6.2   Criticality of Jobs

In any system, jobs are not equally important. The *importance* (or *criticality*) of a job is a positive number that indicates how critical the job is with respect to other jobs; the more critical the job, the larger its importance. In literature, the terms priority and weight are often used to refer to importance; the more important a job, the higher its priority or the larger its weight. We will use the terms priority and weight extensively later to mean attributes that are unrelated to the importance. Throughout this book, we use importance or criticality to measure criticality in order to avoid overloading these terms.

During an overload when it is not possible to schedule all the jobs to meet their deadlines, it may make sense to sacrifice the less critical jobs so that the more critical jobs can meet their deadlines. For this reason, some scheduling and resource access-control algorithms try to optimize weighted performance measures such as weighted average response time (i.e., the average of response time multipled by importance) or weighted average tardiness (i.e., the average of tardiness multiplied by importance) over all jobs. If the system uses one of these algorithms, the information concerning the criticality of jobs must be given to the scheduler. Assigning importance to each job is a natural way to do so.

For example, in a flight control and management system, the job that controls the flight of the aircraft is more critical than the navigation job that determines the current position relative to the chosen course. The navigation job is more critical than the job that adjusts the course and cruise speed in order to minimize fuel consumption. The cabin air flow and temperature control jobs are more critical than the job that runs the in-flight movies, and so on. In the model of this system, the designer may give these jobs different importance values. In this way, the different degrees of criticality of the jobs are explicitly specified.

*3.6.3   Optional Executions

It is often possible to structure an application so that some jobs or portions of jobs are optional. If an *optional job* or an *optional portion* of a job completes late or is not executed at all, the system performance may degrade, but nevertheless function satisfactorily. In contrast, jobs and portions of jobs that are not optional are *mandatory*; they must be executed to completion. Therefore, during a transient overload when it is not possible to complete all the jobs in time, we may choose to discard optional jobs (i.e, leave them unexecuted or partially executed) so that the mandatory jobs can complete in time. In this way, the system can trade the quality of the results it produces and the services it delivers for timeliness of its results and services.

In our model, the optional parameter of each job indicates the portion of the job that is optional. Marking a job or a portion of a job optional is another way for the designer to indicate that the job is not critical. By explicitly identifying the optional jobs and using a scheduling strategy that takes advantage of this information, the designer can control the manner in which the system degrades.

As an example, in a collision avoidance system, we may consider the job that computes the correct evasive action and informs the operator of this action optional. Normally, we want the system to help the operator by choosing the correct action. However, in the presence of a failure and when the system is operating in a degraded mode, it is not possible to complete this computation in time. The collision avoidance system may still function satisfactorily if it skips this computation as long as it generates a warning and displays the course of the object about to collide with it in time.

*3.6.4 Laxity Type and Laxity Function

The laxity type of a job indicates whether its timing constraints are soft or hard. As mentioned earlier, in real-time systems literature, the laxity type of a job is sometimes supplemented by a *usefulness function*. This function gives the usefulness of the result produced by the job as a function of its tardiness.

Figure 3–3 gives several usefulness functions as examples. The ones shown as solid step functions are usually associated with hard real-time jobs. The usefulness of the result becomes zero or negative as soon as the job is tardy. In the latter case, it is better not to execute the job than to execute it and complete it late. In other words, it is "better never than late." As mentioned in Chapter 2, the transmission and execution of a command to release a bomb on a target is an example of jobs with this laxity type.

The dashed and dotted lines in Figure 3–3 show two other usefulness functions. In particular, the dotted ones may be that of a point-of-sales transaction, for example, one that executes to check whether you have enough credit for the current purchase. If the job is late, you and the salesperson become more and more impatient. The usefulness of the result decreases gradually. Eventually, you are likely to give up and walk away. At that point, the usefulness of the result becomes zero. The dashed line shows a function that decreases faster and becomes negative. An example of jobs that have this kind of usefulness function is a stock price update transaction. It may be tolerable if the update completes slightly late and the price x written into the database is somewhat old. However, if the transaction completes so late that the current price differs significantly from x, the result x can be misleading. By that time, the usefulness of this update becomes negative.

We can use these usefulness functions to describe qualitatively the real-time performance objectives of the system. They can guide the choice and implementation of scheduling strategies. However, their utility as the means to specify timing constraints is small, especially if the timing constraints are hard. The only exception are those exemplified by the solid step

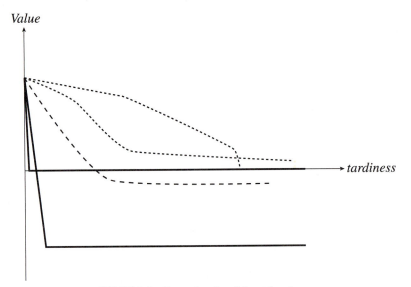

FIGURE 3–3   Examples of usefulness functions.

functions in Figure 3–3, but such constraints can easily be specified without the usefulness functions.

3.7   RESOURCE PARAMETERS OF JOBS AND PARAMETERS OF RESOURCES

Earlier we said that the basic components of the underlying system available to the application system(s) are processors and resources. Every job requires a processor throughout its execution.[3] In addition to a processor, a job may also require some resources. The resource parameters of each job give us the type of processor and the units of each resource type required by the job and the time intervals during its execution when the units are required. These parameters provide the information that is needed to support resource management decisions. In Chapter 8, where we will need these job parameters, we will discuss them in detail.

3.7.1   Preemptivity of Resources

The resource parameters of jobs give us a partial view of the processors and resources from the perspective of the applications that execute on them. We sometimes want to describe the characteristics of processors and resources independent of the application and can do so using parameters of resources. A resource parameter is *preemptivity*. A resource is nonpreemptable if each unit of the resource is constrained to be used serially. In other words, once a unit of a nonpreemptable resource is allocated to a job, other jobs needing the unit must wait until the job completes its use. Otherwise, if jobs can use every unit of a resource in an interleaved fashion, the resource is preemptable. The lock on a data object in a database is an example of nonpreemptable resource. When a job modeling a transaction that reads and writes the data object has acquired the lock, other jobs that also require this lock at the time must wait. The lock is a nonpreemptable resource and, consequently, every transaction job is nonpreemptable in its use of the lock. This does not mean that the job is nonpreemptable on other resources or on the processor. In fact, the transaction may process the data it has already retrieved and, for this purpose, it requires the processor while it holds the lock. The transaction can be preempted on the processor by other transactions that are not waiting for the locks held by it.

In Section 3.6 we used message transmissions on a token ring as an example of where jobs may be constrained to be nonpreemptable. This is a poor way to model the application and the resource. A better alternative is to model the token ring as a nonpreemptable resource and leave message transmission jobs preemptable. The fact that the transmission of a message over a token ring, if interrupted, must be redone from the beginning is a consequence of the way the medium-access protocol works. Hence, nonpreemptivity is a property of the token ring. If we

---

[3]In general, a job may execute in parallel on a number of processors, and the number and types of processors it requires may vary during its execution. Moreover the amount of time required by a job to complete may be a function of the number of processors used to execute the job. (For example, the execution time of a parallelizable computation on a massively parallel machine decreases with the number of processors used to do the computation.) The resource parameters of a job give us the type and number of processors required by a job to execute, as well as how the length of time for which the processors are required depends on the number of processors made available to the job. However, we will rarely be concerned with parallelizable jobs. Except when we state otherwise, we assume that every job executes on one processor.

were to transmit the messages by an ATM switch, we can preempt the transmission of a less urgent message in preference to more urgent messages without having to retransmit the less urgent message in entirety. In other words, message transmission jobs are in fact preemptable.

*3.7.2 Resource Graph

We can describe the configuration of the resources using a *resource graph*. In a resource graph, there is a vertex R_i for every processor or resource R_i in the system. (For the sake of convenience, we now refer to both processors and resources as resources and name each vertex by the name of the resource represented by it.) The attributes of the vertex are the parameters of the resource. In particular, the *resource type* of a resource tells us whether the resource is a processor or a (passive) resource, and its *number* gives us the number of available units.

While edges in task graphs represent different types of dependencies among jobs, edges in a resource graph represent the relationship among resources. Using different types of edges, we can describe different configurations of the underlying system.

There are two types of edges in resource graphs. An edge from a vertex R_i to another vertex R_k can mean that R_k is a component of R_i. (For example, a memory is part of a computer, and so is a monitor.) This edge is an *is-a-part-of edge*. Clearly, the subgraph containing all the is-a-part-of edges is a forest. The root of each tree represents a major component which contains subcomponents represented by vertices in the tree. As an example, the resource graph in a system containing two computers consists of two trees. The root of each tree represents a computer. The children of this vertex include one or more CPUs, main memory, and so on. Each of these subcomponents is represented by a vertex, and there is an edge from the computer vertex to each subcomponent vertex.

Some edges in resource graphs represent connectivity between components. These edges are called *accessibility edges*. In the above example, if there is a connection between two CPUs in the two computers, then each CPU is accessible from the other computer, and there is an accessibility edge from each computer to the CPU on the other computer. Each accessibility edge may have several parameters whose values help to complete the description of the interconnection of the resources. A parameter of an accessibility edge from a processor P_i to another P_k is the cost for sending a unit of data from a job executing on P_i to a job executing on P_k. In Chapter 9, we will describe algorithms that decide on which processors to place jobs and resources in a statically configured system. These algorithms need the information provided by accessibility edges. There we will again discuss this and other parameters that we will need to describe the resources and their interconnections for the purpose of scheduling in multiprocessor and distributed systems.

3.8   SCHEDULING HIERARCHY

Figure 3–4 shows the three elements of our model of real-time systems together. The application system is represented by a task graph, exemplified by the graph on the top of the diagram. This graph gives the processor time and resource requirements of jobs, the timing constraints of each job, and the dependencies of jobs. The resource graph describes the amounts of the resources available to execute the application system, the attributes of the resources, and the rules governing their usage. Between them are the scheduling and resource access-control algorithms used by the operating system.

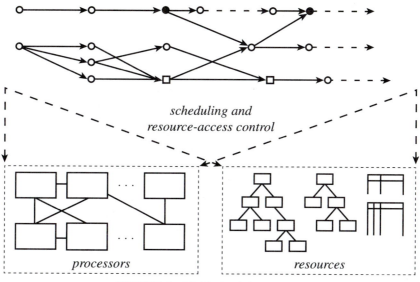

FIGURE 3–4   Model of real-time systems.

3.8.1   Scheduler and Schedules

Jobs are scheduled and allocated resources according to a chosen set of scheduling algorithms and resource access-control protocols. The module which implements these algorithms is called the *scheduler*.

Specifically, the scheduler assigns processors to jobs, or equivalently, assigns jobs to processors. We say that a job is scheduled in a time interval on a processor if the processor is assigned to the job, and hence the job executes on the processor, in the interval. The total amount of (processor) time assigned to a job according to a schedule is the total length of all the time intervals during which the job is scheduled on some processor.

By a *schedule*, we mean an assignment of all the jobs in the system on the available processors produced by the scheduler. Throughout this book, we do not question the correctness of the scheduler; rather, we assume that the scheduler works correctly. By correctness, we mean that the scheduler produces only *valid schedules*; a valid schedule satisfies the following conditions:

1. Every processor is assigned to at most one job at any time.
2. Every job is assigned at most one processor at any time.
3. No job is scheduled before its release time.
4. Depending on the scheduling algorithm(s) used, the total amount of processor time assigned to every job is equal to its maximum or actual execution time.
5. All the precedence and resource usage constraints are satisfied.

Again, an implicit assumption here is that jobs do not run in parallel on more than one processor to speed up their execution.

3.8.2   Feasibility, Optimality, and Performance Measures

A valid schedule is a *feasible schedule* if every job completes by its deadline (or, in general, meets its timing constraints). We say that a set of jobs is *schedulable* according to a scheduling algorithm if when using the algorithm the scheduler always produces a feasible schedule.

The criterion we use most of the time to measure the performance of scheduling algorithms for hard real-time applications is their ability to find feasible schedules of the given application system whenever such schedules exist. Hence, we say that a hard real-time scheduling algorithm is *optimal* if (using) the algorithm (the scheduler) always produces a feasible schedule if the given set of jobs has feasible schedules. (For the sake of simplicity, we will not mention the scheduler; in other words, we will omit the words in the parentheses in the previous sentence. When we say what an algorithm does, we mean what the scheduler does according to the algorithm.) Conversely, if an optimal algorithm fails to find a feasible schedule, we can conclude that the given set of jobs cannot feasibly be scheduled by any algorithm.

In addition to the criterion based on feasibility, other commonly used performance measures include the maximum and average tardiness, lateness, and response time and the miss, loss, and invalid rates. The right choice of performance measure depends on the objective of scheduling. As an example, when a set of jobs is not schedulable by any algorithm, we may settle for a schedule according to which the number of jobs failing to complete in time is the smallest. Hence, an algorithm performs better if it can produce a schedule with a smaller number of late jobs than others. Alternatively, we may not care how many jobs are late, provided that their tardiness is small. In this case, we want to use algorithms that give us small maximum or average tardiness.

The *lateness* of a job is the difference between its completion time and its deadline. Unlike the tardiness of a job which never has negative values, the lateness of a job which completes early is negative, while the lateness of a job which completes late is positive. Sometimes, we want to keep jitters in the completion times small; we can do so by using scheduling algorithms that try to minimize the average absolute lateness of jobs. As an example, suppose that the jobs model the transmission of packets in a packet-switched network. The packets in each message are buffered at the switch at the receiving end, assembled into a message, and then forwarded to the receiving host. The early arrivals must be held in the buffer waiting for the late arrivals. A larger arrival-time jitter means a larger buffer occupancy time and consequently, a larger total demand for buffer space of all messages arriving at the switch. In this example, the average lateness of jobs is a meaningful performance measure, because minimizing it indirectly minimizes the average buffer occupancy time and buffer space requirement.

In the case where all the jobs have the same release time and deadline, the problem of scheduling the jobs to meet their deadline is in essence the same as that of scheduling to minimize the completion time of the job which completes last among all jobs. The response time of this job is the response time of the set of jobs as a whole and is often called the *makespan* of the schedule. This is a performance criterion commonly used to compare scheduling algorithms in classical scheduling literature: an algorithm that produces a schedule with a shorter makespan is better. Clearly, if the makespan is less than or equal to the length of their feasible interval, the jobs can meet their deadline.

By far, the most frequently used performance measure for jobs that have soft deadlines is their average response times. We sometimes compare the performance of scheduling algorithms on a given set of jobs based on the average response times of jobs when scheduled according to them. The smaller the average response time, the better the algorithm, just as for general-purpose, interactive systems. In a system that has a mixture of jobs with hard and soft deadlines, the objective of scheduling is typically to minimize the average response time of jobs with soft deadlines while ensuring that all jobs with hard deadlines complete in time. Since there is no advantage in completing jobs with hard deadlines early, we may delay their execution in order to improve the response time of jobs with soft deadlines. Indeed, you will find scheduling algorithms in Chapters 5 and 7 that use this strategy.

For many soft real-time applications, it is acceptable to complete some jobs late or to discard late jobs. For such an application, suitable performance measures include the *miss rate* and *loss rate*. The former gives the percentage of jobs that are executed but completed too late, and the latter give the percentage of jobs that are discarded, that is, not executed at all. When it is impossible to complete all the jobs on time, a scheduler may choose to discard some jobs. By doing so, the scheduler increases the loss rate but completes more jobs in time. Thus, it reduces the miss rate. Similarly, reducing the loss rate may lead to an increase in miss rate. For this reason when we talk about minimization of the miss rate, we mean that the miss rate is reduced as much as possible subjected to the constraint that the loss rate is below some acceptable threshold. Alternatively, we may want to minimize the lost rate provided the miss rate is below some threshold. A performance measure that captures this trade-off is the *invalid rate*, which is the sum of the miss and loss rates and gives the percentage of all jobs that do not produce a useful result. We want to minimize the invalid rate. If the jobs are transmissions of real-time packets, the miss rate gives the percentage of packets arriving at the receiver too late, the loss rate gives the percentage of packets discarded en route, and the invalid rate gives the percentage of packets that are not useful to the application.

3.8.3 Interaction among Schedulers

Thus far, we have been talking solely of scheduling the application system on the underlying processors and resources. In fact, a system typically has a hierarchy of schedulers. This scheduling hierarchy arises for two reasons. First, some processors and resources used by the application system are not physical entities; they are logical resources. Logical resources must be scheduled on physical resources. The algorithms used for this purpose are typically different from the ones used to schedule the application system. A scheduler that schedules a logical resource may be different from the scheduler that schedules the application system using the resource. Second, a job may model a server that executes on behalf of its client jobs. The time and resources allocated to the server job must in turn be allocated to its client jobs. Again, the algorithm used by the server to schedule its clients may be different from the algorithm used by the operating system to schedule the server with other servers.

In an earlier example, we treated database locks as resources. In fact, these resources are implemented by a database management system whose execution must be scheduled on one or more processors. The scheduler that schedules the database management system may be different from the scheduler that schedules the application system using the locks. The schedulers most likely use different algorithms. Now we have two levels of scheduling. In the higher level, the application system is scheduled on the resources. In the lower level, the jobs that execute in order to implement the resources are scheduled on the processors and resources needed by them.

As an example of servers, we consider an application system containing periodic tasks and aperiodic jobs on one processor. All the aperiodic jobs are placed in a queue when they are released. There is a poller. Together with the periodic tasks, the poller is scheduled to execute periodically. When the poller executes, it checks the aperiodic job queue. If there are aperiodic jobs waiting, it chooses an aperiodic job from the queue and executes the job. Hence, the aperiodic jobs are the clients of the poller. We again have two levels of scheduling. In the lower level the scheduler provided by the operating system schedules the poller and the periodic tasks. In the higher level, the poller schedules its clients.

In every level of the scheduling hierarchy, we can represent the workload by a task graph and the processors and resources required by it by a resource graph. In this way all levels of the scheduling hierarchy can be represented in a uniform way.

3.9   SUMMARY

This chapter describes the general model of real-time systems and introduces the terms that we will use in the subsequent chapters. In the chapters on scheduling and resource management, we will adopt several simpler models that are special cases of this general model.

3.9.1   Characterization of Application Systems

According to this model, the basic components of any real-time application system are jobs. The operating system treats each job as a unit of work and allocates processor and resources to it. For the purpose of scheduling and validation, it suffices to define each job by its temporal, resource, interconnection and functional parameters. Among all the parameters of a job J_i, we work with the following ones most frequently:

- *Release time* (or *arrival time*) r_i: r_i is the instant of time at which the job becomes eligible for execution. The release (arrival) time of the job may be jittery (sporadic), meaning that r_i is in the range $[r_i^-, r_i^+]$ and that only the range of r_i is known but not the actual value of r_i.
- *Absolute deadline* d_i: d_i is the instant of time by which the job must complete.
- *Relative deadline* D_i: D_i is the maximum allowable response time of the job.
- *Laxity type*: The deadline (or timing constraint in general) of the job can be hard or soft.
- *Execution time* e_i: e_i is the amount of time required to complete the execution of J_i when it executes alone and has all the resources it requires. The execution time of J_i may vary, meaning that e_i is in the range $[e_i^-, e_i^+]$ and that this range is known but not the actual value of e_i. Some models assume that J_i always executes for the maximum amount e_i^+ of time; when there is no possible ambiguity, we also use e_i to mean the maximum execution time e_i^+.
- *Preemptivity*: The job may be constrained to be nonpreemptable.
- *Resource requirements*: This parameter gives the processors and resources required by the job in order to execute and the time interval(s) during which each resource is required.

This book assumes that these parameters are known. While others can be deduced from requirements and specification of the system, the execution time and resource parameters are obtained from measurement and analysis. The execution times of most noncomputation jobs

are usually obtained by meaurement. For example, the execution time of a message transmission job is typically obtained by measuring either the transmission time or the length of a
message. On the other hand, analysis is the preferred approach to predicting the maximum execution time of a program because timing analysis techniques guarantee the correctness of the
predicted maximum execution time, while measurement techniques do not. (A prediction is
correct if the actual execution time is never less than the predicted maximum execution time.)
You can find techniques used for this purpose in [AMWH, HeWh, KiMH, LiMW, LBJR].

A set of related jobs is called a task. Jobs in a task may be precedence constrained
to execute in a certain order. Sometimes jobs may be constrained to complete within a certain time from one another (i.e., they are temporal distance constrained). Jobs may have data
dependencies even when they are not precedence constrained.

A periodic task T_i is a sequence of jobs with identical parameters. In addition to the
parameters of its jobs, a periodic task is defined by the following task parameters:

- *Period p_i*: p_i is the minimum length of the intervals between the release times of con-
  secutive jobs (i.e., interrelease interval).
- *Execution time e_i*: e_i of T_i is the maximum execution time of all the jobs in the task.
- *Phase ϕ_i*: ϕ_i is the release time of the first job in T_i.

When the interrelease intervals of a sequence of jobs vary widely and are arbitrarily
small, we model the interrelease intervals as random variables. Similarly, the execution times
of jobs are sometimes modeled as random variables. An aperiodic task or a sporadic task
is a sequence of jobs whose interrelease times are identically distributed according to the
probability distribution $A(x)$ and whose execution times are identically distributed according
to the probability distribution $B(x)$. The deadlines of jobs in an aperiodic task are soft, while
the deadlines of jobs in a sporadic task are hard.

In subsequent chapters, we will use a task graph to represent the application system
when the dependencies among its jobs cannot be described in a few sentences. There is a
vertex in this graph for each job in the system. The edges in this graph represent dependencies
among jobs. An edge from a vertex representing J_i to another vertex representing J_k may
represent a precedence constraint and/or a data dependency between the two jobs. Parameters
of the edge include the type of the edge and the volume of data from J_i to J_k.

3.9.2 Characterization of the Underlying Systems

The resources available to the application system are processors and resources. Jobs and tasks
require them in order to execute. The scheduler decides when each job (or task) has its required
processor and resources.

We usually model CPUs, disks, buses, network links, and so on, that compute, retrieve,
transmit, and so on, as processors. Every job must have a processor in order to execute. Processors that can be used interchangeably are of the same type, while processors that cannot be
used interchangeably are of different types. In addition to its type, a processor is characterized
by the following parameters:

- *Preemptivity*: The execution of jobs on the processor may or may not be preemptable.
- *Context-Switch Time*: This parameter gives the cost in time of each preemption.

We model shared data objects, buffers, sequence numbers, and the like, entities some-times called passive resources, as resources. The amount of time a job requires a resource usually depends on the speed of the processor on which the job executes, not on some pa-rameter of the resource. The resources considered here are reusable, because they are not consumed during use. Each unit of each resource (type) can be used by one job at the time, and the use of every resource (unit) is nonpreemptable. A shared resource that can be used simultaneously by at most x jobs at the same time is modeled as a resource with x units, each of which can be used by at most one job at a time.

3.9.3   Schedulers

A scheduler is a module that allocates processors and resources to jobs and tasks. In most of this book we assume that a scheduler is completely defined by the scheduling and resource management algorithms it implements. The only exception is Chapter 12 on operating sys-tems. There, we will discuss why a real-life scheduler may behave differently from an ideal one and how to minimize and account for the discrepancy.

Except where stated otherwise, we assume that the scheduler works correctly. It pro-duces only valid schedules. According to a valid schedule, no job is scheduled before its release time and the completion of all its predecessors, no job is scheduled on more than one processor at the same time, no processor is scheduled to execute more than one job at the same time, and the total amount of time assigned to every job is equal to the execution time except when the job or a portion of it can be discarded because it is optional. A valid schedule is feasible if, according to the schedule, every job completes by its deadline.

EXERCISES

3.1 Because sporadic jobs may have varying release times and execution times, the periodic task model may be too inaccurate and can lead to unduly underutilization of the processor even when the interrelease times of jobs are bounded from below and their executions are bounded from above. As an example, suppose we have a stream of sporadic jobs whose interrelease times are uniformly distributed from 9 to 11. Their execution times are uniformly distributed from 1 to 3.

(a) What are the parameters of the periodic task if we were to use such a task to model the stream?

(b) Compare the utilization of the periodic task in part (a) with the average utilization of the sporadic job stream.

3.2 Consider the real-time program described by the psuedocode below. Names of jobs are in italic.

```
At 9AM, start: have breakfast and go to office;
At 10AM,
    If there is class,
        teach;
    Else, help students;
    When teach or help is done, eat_lunch;
Until 2PM, sleep;
If there is a seminar,
    If topic is interesting,
        listen;
```

Else, *read*;
Else
　　write in office;
When seminar is over, *attend* social hour;
discuss;
jog;
eat_dinner;
work a little more;
end_the_day;

   (a) Draw a task graph to capture the dependencies among jobs.

   (b) Use as many precedence graphs as needed to represent all the possible paths of the program

3.3 *job_1* | *job_2* denotes a pipe: The result produced by *job_1* is incrementally consumed by *job_2*. (As an example, suppose that *job_2* reads and displays one character at a time as each handwritten character is recognized and placed in a buffer by *job_1*.) Draw a precedence constraint graph to represent this producer-consumer relation between the jobs.

3.4 Draw a task graph to represent the flight control system described by Figure 1-3.

   (a) Assume that producers and consumers do not explicitly synchronize (i.e., each consumer uses the latest result generated by each of its producers but does not wait for the completion of the producer.)

   (b) Repeat part (a), assuming that producers and consumers do synchronize.

CHAPTER 4

Commonly Used Approaches to Real-Time Scheduling

This chapter provides a brief overview of three commonly used approaches to scheduling real-time systems: clock-driven, weighted round-robin and priority-driven. The subsequent five chapters will study in depth the clock-driven and priority-driven approaches, with particular emphasis on the latter. We need to be aware of several important facts about priority-driven scheduling. They are presented here and shown to be true, so they will not be buried in the details later. We will use these facts to motivate and support the arguments presented in later chapters. The weighted round-robin approach is used primarily for scheduling real-time traffic in high-speed switched networks. It will be described in depth in Chapter 11. We discuss here why this approach is not ideal for scheduling jobs on CPUs.

4.1 CLOCK-DRIVEN APPROACH

As the name implies, when scheduling is *clock-driven* (also called *time-driven*), decisions on what jobs execute at what times are made at specific time instants. These instants are chosen a priori before the system begins execution. Typically, in a system that uses clock-driven scheduling, all the parameters of hard real-time jobs are fixed and known. A schedule of the jobs is computed off-line and is stored for use at run time. The scheduler schedules the jobs according to this schedule at each scheduling decision time. In this way, scheduling overhead during run-time can be minimized.

A frequently adopted choice is to make scheduling decisions at regularly spaced time instants. One way to implement a scheduler that makes scheduling decisions periodically is to use a hardware timer. The timer is set to expire periodically without the intervention of the scheduler. When the system is initialized, the scheduler selects and schedules the job(s) that will execute until the next scheduling decision time and then blocks itself waiting for the expiration of the timer. When the timer expires, the scheduler awakes and repeats these actions.

4.2   WEIGHTED ROUND-ROBIN APPROACH

The round-robin approach is commonly used for scheduling time-shared applications. When jobs are scheduled on a round-robin basis, every job joins a First-in-first-out (FIFO) queue when it becomes ready for execution. The job at the head of the queue executes for at most one time slice. (A time slice is the basic granule of time that is allocated to jobs. In a time-shared environment, a time slice is typically in the order of tens of milliseconds.) If the job does not complete by the end of the time slice, it is preempted and placed at the end of the queue to wait for its next turn. When there are n ready jobs in the queue, each job gets one time slice every n time slices, that is, every *round*. Because the length of the time slice is relatively short, the execution of every job begins almost immediately after it becomes ready. In essence, each job gets $1/n$th share of the processor when there are n jobs ready for execution. This is why the round-robin algorithm is also called the processor-sharing algorithm.

The *weighted round-robin algorithm* has been used for scheduling real-time traffic in high-speed switched networks. It builds on the basic round-robin scheme. Rather than giving all the ready jobs equal shares of the processor, different jobs may be given different *weights*. Here, the weight of a job refers to the fraction of processor time allocated to the job. Specifically, a job with weight wt gets wt time slices every round, and the length of a round is equal to the sum of the weights of all the ready jobs. By adjusting the weights of jobs, we can speed up or retard the progress of each job toward its completion.

By giving each job a fraction of the processor, a round-robin scheduler delays the completion of every job. If it is used to schedule precedence constrained jobs, the response time of a chain of jobs can be unduly large. For this reason, the weighted round-robin approach is not suitable for scheduling such jobs. On the other hand, a successor job may be able to incrementally consume what is produced by a predecessor (e.g., as in the case of a UNIX pipe). In this case, weighted round-robin scheduling is a reasonable approach, since a job and its successors can execute concurrently in a pipelined fashion. As an example, we consider the two sets of jobs, $\mathbf{J}_1 = \{J_{1,1}, J_{1,2}\}$ and $\mathbf{J}_2 = \{J_{2,1}, J_{2,2}\}$, shown in Figure 4–1. The release times of all jobs are 0, and their execution times are 1. $J_{1,1}$ and $J_{2,1}$ execute on processor P_1, and $J_{1,2}$ and $J_{2,2}$ execute on processor P_2. Suppose that $J_{1,1}$ is the predecessor of $J_{1,2}$, and $J_{2,1}$ is the predecessor of $J_{2,2}$. Figure 4–1(a) shows that both sets of jobs (i.e., the second jobs $J_{1,2}$ and $J_{2,2}$ in the sets) complete approximately at time 4 if the jobs are scheduled in a weighted round-robin manner. (We get this completion time when the length of the time slice is small compared with 1 and the jobs have the same weight.) In contrast, the schedule in Figure 4–1(b) shows that if the jobs on each processor are executed one after the other, one of the chains can complete at time 2, while the other can complete at time 3. On the other hand, suppose that the result of the first job in each set is piped to the second job in the set. The latter can execute after each one or a few time slices of the former complete. Then it is better to schedule the jobs on the round-robin basis because both sets can complete a few time slices after time 2.

Indeed, the transmission of each message is carried out by switches en route in a pipeline fashion. A switch downstream can begin to transmit an earlier portion of the message as soon as it receives the portion without having to wait for the arrival of the later portion of the message. The weighted round-robin approach does not require a sorted priority queue, only a round-robin queue. This is a distinct advantage for scheduling message transmissions in ultrahigh-speed networks, since priority queues with the required speed are expensive. In

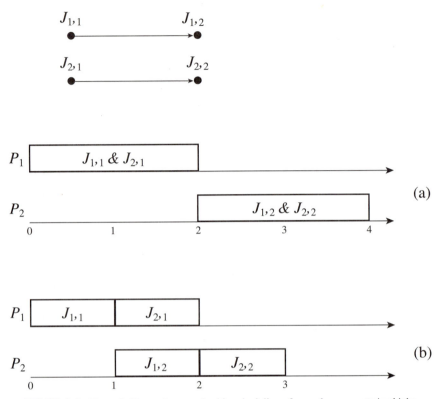

FIGURE 4–1   Example illustrating round-robin scheduling of precedence-constrained jobs.

Chapter 11 we will describe in detail the application of weighted round-robin algorithms to network scheduling.

4.3   PRIORITY-DRIVEN APPROACH

The term *priority-driven* algorithms refers to a large class of scheduling algorithms that never leave any resource idle intentionally. Stated in another way, a resource idles only when no job requiring the resource is ready for execution. Scheduling decisions are made when events such as releases and completions of jobs occur. Hence, priority-driven algorithms are *event-driven*.

Other commonly used names for this approach are *greedy scheduling*, *list scheduling* and *work-conserving scheduling*. A priority-driven algorithm is greedy because it tries to make locally optimal decisions. Leaving a resource idle while some job is ready to use the resource is not locally optimal. So when a processor or resource is available and some job can use it to make progress, such an algorithm never makes the job wait. We will return shortly to illustrate that greed does not always pay; sometimes it is better to have some jobs wait even when they are ready to execute and the resources they require are available.

The term list scheduling is also descriptive because any priority-driven algorithm can be implemented by assigning priorities to jobs. Jobs ready for execution are placed in one or more queues ordered by the priorities of the jobs. At any scheduling decision time, the jobs with the highest priorities are scheduled and executed on the available processors. Hence, a priority-driven scheduling algorithm is defined to a great extent by the list of priorities it assigns to jobs; the priority list and other rules, such as whether preemption is allowed, define the scheduling algorithm completely.

Most scheduling algorithms used in nonreal-time systems are priority-driven. Examples include the FIFO (First-In-First-Out) and LIFO (Last-In-First-Out) algorithms, which assign priorities to jobs according their release times, and the SETF (Shortest-Execution-Time-First) and LETF (Longest-Execution-Time-First) algorithms, which assign priorities on the basis of job execution times. Because we can dynamically change the priorities of jobs, even round-robin scheduling can be thought of as priority-driven: The priority of the executing job is lowered to the minimum among all jobs waiting for execution after the job has executed for a time slice.

Figure 4–2 gives an example. The task graph shown here is a classical precedence graph; all its edges represent precedence constraints. The number next to the name of each job is its execution time. J_5 is released at time 4. All the other jobs are released at time 0. We want to schedule and execute the jobs on two processors P_1 and P_2. They communicate via a shared memory. Hence the costs of communication among jobs are negligible no matter where they are executed. The schedulers of the processors keep one common priority queue of ready jobs. The priority list is given next to the graph: J_i has a higher priority than J_k if $i < k$. All the jobs are preemptable; scheduling decisions are made whenever some job becomes ready for execution or some job completes.

Figure 4–2(a) shows the schedule of the jobs on the two processors generated by the priority-driven algorithm following this priority assignment. At time 0, jobs J_1, J_2, and J_7 are ready for execution. They are the only jobs in the common priority queue at this time. Since J_1 and J_2 have higher priorities than J_7, they are ahead of J_7 in the queue and hence are scheduled. The processors continue to execute the jobs scheduled on them except when the following events occur and new scheduling decisions are made.

- At time 1, J_2 completes and, hence, J_3 becomes ready. J_3 is placed in the priority queue ahead of J_7 and is scheduled on P_2, the processor freed by J_2.
- At time 3, both J_1 and J_3 complete. J_5 is still not released. J_4 and J_7 are scheduled.
- At time 4, J_5 is released. Now there are three ready jobs. J_7 has the lowest priority among them. Consequently, it is preempted. J_4 and J_5 have the processors.
- At time 5, J_4 completes. J_7 resumes on processor P_1.
- At time 6, J_5 completes. Because J_7 is not yet completed, both J_6 and J_8 are not ready for execution. Consequently, processor P_2 becomes idle.
- J_7 finally completes at time 8. J_6 and J_8 can now be scheduled and they are.

Figure 4–2(b) shows a nonpreemptive schedule according to the same priority assignment. Before time 4, this schedule is the same as the preemptive schedule. However, at time 4 when J_5 is released, both processors are busy. It has to wait until J_4 completes (at time 5) before it can begin execution. It turns out that for this system this postponement of the higher priority job benefits the set of jobs as a whole. The entire set completes 1 unit of time earlier according to the nonpreemptive schedule.

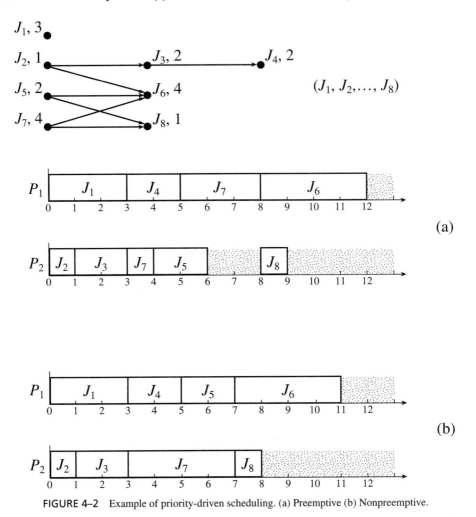

FIGURE 4–2   Example of priority-driven scheduling. (a) Preemptive (b) Nonpreemptive.

In general, however, nonpreemptive scheduling is not better than preemptive scheduling. A fundamental question is, when is preemptive scheduling better than nonpreemptive scheduling and vice versa? It would be good if we had some rule with which we could determine from the given parameters of the jobs whether to schedule them preemptively or nonpreemptively. Unfortunately, there is no known answer to this question in general. In the special case when jobs have the same release time, preemptive scheduling is better when the cost of preemption is ignored. Specifically, in a multiprocessor system, the minimum makespan (i.e., the response time of the job that completes last among all jobs) achievable by an optimal preemptive algorithm is shorter than the makespan achievable by an optimal nonpreemptive algorithm. A natural question here is whether the difference in the minimum makespans achievable by the two classes of algorithms is significant, in particular, whether the theoretical gain in makespan achievable by preemption is enough to compensate for the context switch overhead of preemption. The answer to this question is only known for the two-processor case. Coffman and

Garey [CoGa] recently proved that when there are two processors, the minimum makespan achievable by nonpreemptive algorithms is never more than 4/3 times the minimum makespan achievable by preemptive algorithms when the cost of preemption is negligible. The proof of this seemingly simple results is too lengthy to be included here.

4.4   DYNAMIC VERSUS STATIC SYSTEMS

In the above example, jobs that are ready for execution are placed in a priority queue common to all processors. When a processor is available, the job at the head of the queue executes on the processor. We will refer to such a multiprocessor system as a *dynamic system*, because jobs are *dynamically dispatched* to processors. In the example in Figure 4–2, we allowed each preempted job to resume on any processor and hence, jobs are migratable. We say that a job *migrates* if it starts execution on a processor, is preempted, and later resumes on a different processor.

Another approach to scheduling in multiprocessor and distributed systems is to partition the jobs in the system into subsystems and assign and bind the subsystems statically to the processors. Jobs are moved among processors only when the system must be reconfigured, that is, when the operation mode of the system changes or some processor fails. Such a system is called a *static system*, because the system is *statically configured*. If jobs on different processors are dependent, the schedulers on the processors must synchronize the jobs according to some synchronization and resource access-control protocol. Except for the constraints thus imposed, the jobs on each processor are scheduled by themselves.

As an example, a partition and assignment of the jobs in Figure 4–2 put J_1, J_2, J_3, and J_4 on P_1 and the remaining jobs on P_2. The priority list is segmented into two parts: (J_1, J_2, J_3, J_4) and (J_5, J_6, J_7, J_8). The scheduler of processor P_1 uses the former while the scheduler of processor P_2 uses the latter. It is easy to see that the jobs on P_1 complete by time 8, and the jobs on P_2 complete by time 11. Moreover, J_2 completes by time 4 while J_6 starts at time 6. Therefore, the precedence constraint between them is satisfied.

In this example, the response of the static system is just as good as that of the dynamic system. Intuitively, we expect that we can get better average responses by dynamically dispatching and executing jobs. In later chapters we will return to this discussion. Specifically, we will demonstrate that while dynamic systems may be more responsive on the average, their worst-case real-time performance may be poorer than static systems. More importantly, we do not yet have reliable techniques to validate the timing constraints of dynamic systems while such techniques exist for static systems. For this reason, most hard real-time systems built today are static.

4.5   EFFECTIVE RELEASE TIMES AND DEADLINES

The given release times and deadlines of jobs are sometimes inconsistent with the precedence constraints of the jobs. By this, we mean that the release time of a job may be later than that of its successors, and its deadline may be earlier than that of its predecessors. Therefore, rather than working with the given release times and deadlines, we first derive a set of effective release times and deadlines from these timing constraints, together with the given precedence constraints. The derived timing constraints are consistent with the precedence constraints.

When there is only one processor, we can compute the derived constraints according to the following rules:

Effective Release Time: The effective release time of a job without predecessors is equal to its given release time. The effective release time of a job with predecessors is equal to the maximum value among its given release time and the effective release times of all of its predecessors.

Effective Deadline: The effective deadline of a job without a successor is equal to its given deadline. The effective deadline of a job with successors is equal to the minimum value among its given deadline and the effective deadlines of all of its successors.

The effective release times of all the jobs can be computed in one pass through the precedence graph in $O(n^2)$ time where n is the number of jobs. Similarly, the effective deadlines can be computed in $O(n^2)$ time.

As an example, we look at the set of jobs in Figure 4–3. The numbers in the parentheses next to the name of each job are its given release times and deadlines. Because J_1 and J_2 have no predecessors, their effective release times are the given release times, that is, 2 and 0, respectively. The given release time of J_3 is 1, but the latest effective release time of its predecessors is 2, that of J_1. Hence, the effective release time of J_3 is 2. You can repeat this procedure and find that the effective release times of the rest of the jobs are 4, 2, 4, and 6, respectively. Similarly, J_6 and J_7 have no successors, and their effective deadlines are equal to their given deadlines, 20 and 21, respectively. Since the effective deadlines of the successors of J_4 and J_5 are larger than the given deadlines of J_4 and J_5, the effective deadlines of J_4 and J_5 are equal to their given deadlines. On the other hand, the given deadline of J_3 is equal to 12, which is larger than the minimum value of 8 among the effective deadlines of its successors. Hence, the effective deadline of J_3 is 8. In a similar way, we find that the effective deadlines of J_1 and J_2 are 8 and 7, respectively.

You may have noticed that the calculation of effective release times and deadlines does not take into account the execution times of jobs. More accurately, the effective deadline of a job should be as early as the deadline of each of its successors minus the execution time of the successor. The effective release time of a job is that of its predecessor plus the execution time of the predecessor. The more accurate calculation is unnecessary, however, when there is only one processor. Gary and Johnson [GaJo77] have shown that it is feasible to schedule any

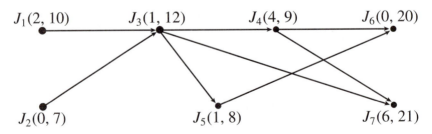

FIGURE 4–3   Example of effective timing constraints.

set of jobs on a processor according to their given release times and deadlines if and only if it is feasible to schedule the set according to their effective release times and deadlines defined above. When there is only one processor and jobs are preemptable, working with the effective release times and deadlines allows us to temporarily ignore the precedence constraints and treat all the jobs as if they are independent. Of course, by doing so, it is possible for an algorithm to produce an invalid schedule that does not meet some precedence constraint. For example, J_1 and J_3 in Figure 4–3 have the same effective release time and deadline. An algorithm which ignores the precedence constraint between them may schedule J_3 in an earlier interval and J_1 in a later interval. If this happens, we can always add a step to swap the two jobs, that is, move J_1 to where J_3 is scheduled and vice versa. This swapping is always possible, and it transforms an invalid schedule into a valid one.

Hereafter, by release times and deadlines, we will always mean effective release times and deadlines. When there is only one processor and jobs are preemptable, we will ignore the precedence constraints.

4.6   OPTIMALITY OF THE EDF AND LST ALGORITHMS

A way to assign priorities to jobs is on the basis of their deadlines. In particular, the earlier the deadline, the higher the priority. The priority-driven scheduling algorithm based on this priority assignment is called the *Earliest-Deadline-First* (*EDF*) algorithm. This algorithm is important because it is optimal when used to schedule jobs on a processor as long as preemption is allowed and jobs do not contend for resources. This fact is stated formally below.

> **THEOREM 4.1.**   When preemption is allowed and jobs do not contend for resources, the EDF algorithm can produce a feasible schedule of a set **J** of jobs with arbitrary release times and deadlines on a processor if and only if **J** has feasible schedules.

Proof.   The proof is based on the following fact: Any feasible schedule of **J** can be systematically transformed into an EDF schedule (i.e., a schedule produced by the EDF algorithm). To see why, suppose that in a schedule, parts of J_i and J_k are scheduled in intervals I_1 and I_2, respectively. Furthermore, the deadline d_i of J_i is later than the deadline d_k of J_k, but I_1 is earlier than I_2 as shown in Figure 4–4.

There are two cases. In the first case, the release time of J_k may be later than the end of I_1. J_k cannot be scheduled in I_1; the two jobs are already scheduled on the EDF basis in these intervals. Hence, we need to consider only the second case where the release time r_k of J_k is before the end of I_1; without loss of generality, we assume that r_k is no later than the beginning of I_1.

To transform the given schedule, we swap J_i and J_k. Specifically, if the interval I_1 is shorter than I_2, as shown in Figure 4–4, we move the portion of J_k that fits in I_1 forward to I_1 and move the entire portion of J_i scheduled in I_1 backward to I_2 and place it after J_k. The result is as shown in Figure 4–4(b). Clearly, this swap is always possible. We can do a similar swap if the interval I_1 is longer than I_2 : We move the entire portion of J_k scheduled in I_2 to I_1 and place it before J_i and move the portion of J_i that fits in I_2 to the interval. The result of this swap is that these two jobs are now scheduled on the

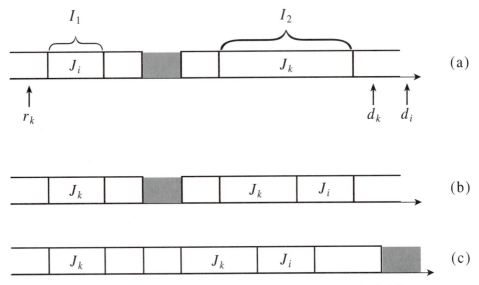

FIGURE 4–4 Transformation of a non-EDF schedule into an EDF schedule.

EDF basis. We repeat this transformation for every pair of jobs that are not scheduled on the EDF basis according to the given non-EDF schedule until no such pair exists.

The schedule obtained after this transformation may still not be an EDF schedule if some interval is left idle while there are jobs ready for execution but are scheduled in a later interval (e.g., as in the schedule in Figure 4–4(b).) We can eliminate such an idle interval by moving one or more of these jobs forward into the idle interval and leave the interval where the jobs were scheduled idle. This is clearly always possible. We repeat this process if necessary until the processor never idles when there are jobs ready for execution as in Figure 4–4(c).

That the preemptive EDF algorithm can always produce a feasible schedule as long as feasible schedules exist follows straightforwardly from the fact that every feasible schedule can be transformed into a preemptive EDF schedule. If the EDF algorithm fails to produce a feasible schedule, then no feasible schedule exists. (If a feasible schedule were to exist, it could be transformed into an EDF schedule, which contradicts the statement that the EDF algorithm fails to produce a feasible schedule.) ☐

When the goal of scheduling is to meet deadlines, there is no advantage to completing any job sooner than necessary. We may want to postpone the execution of hard real-time jobs for some reason (e.g., to enable soft real-time jobs, whose response times are important, to complete earlier). For this reason, we sometimes also use the *latest release time (LRT)* algorithm (or reverse EDF algorithm). This algorithm treats release times as deadlines and deadlines as release times and schedules the jobs backwards, starting from the latest deadline of all jobs, in "priority-driven" manner, to the current time. In particular, the "priorities" are based on the release times of jobs: the later the release time, the higher the "priority." Because it may leave the processor idle when there are jobs ready for execution, the LRT algorithm is not a priority-driven algorithm.

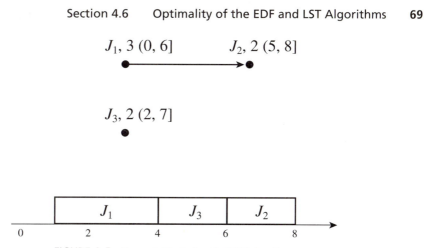

J_1, 3 (0, 6] J_2, 2 (5, 8]

J_3, 2 (2, 7]

FIGURE 4–5   Example illustrating the LRT algorithm.

Figure 4–5 gives an example. In the precedence graph, the number next to the job name is the execution time of the job. Its feasible interval is given by the range of time next to its execution time. The latest deadline among all jobs is 8. Hence time starts at 8 and goes backwards to 0. At time 8, J_2 is "ready" and is scheduled. At time 7, J_3 is also "ready" to be scheduled, but because J_2 has a later release time, it has a higher priority. Consequently, J_2 is scheduled from 7 to 6. When J_2 "completes" at time 6, J_1 is "ready." However, J_3 has a higher priority and is, therefore, scheduled from 6 to 4. Finally J_1 is scheduled from 4 to 1. The result is a feasible schedule.

The following corollary states that the LRT algorithm is also optimal under the same conditions that the EDF algorithm is optimal. Its proof follows straightforwardly from the proof of Theorem 4.1.

> **COROLLARY 4.2.**   When preemption is allowed and jobs do not contend for resources, the LRT algorithm can produce a feasible schedule of a set **J** of jobs with arbitrary release times and deadlines on a processor if and only if feasible schedules of **J** exist.

Another algorithm that is optimal for scheduling preemptive jobs on one processor is the *Least-Slack-Time-First* (*LST*) algorithm (also called the *Minimum-Laxity-First* (*MLF*) algorithm) [LeWh, Mok]. At any time t, the *slack* (or *laxity*) of a job with deadline at d is equal to $d - t$ minus the time required to complete the remaining portion of the job. Take the job J_1 in Figure 4–5 as an example. It is released at time 0, its deadline is 6, and its execution time is 3. Hence, its slack is equal to 3 at time 0. The job starts to execute at time 0. As long as it executes, its slack remains at 3, because at any time t before its completion, its slack is $6 - t - (3 - t)$. Now suppose that it is preempted at time 2 by J_3, which executes from time 2 to 4. During this interval, the slack of J_1 decreases from 3 to 1. (At time 4, the remaining execution time of J_1 is 1, so its slack is $6 - 4 - 1 = 1$.)

The LST algorithm assigns priorities to jobs based on their slacks: the smaller the slack, the higher the priority. The following theorem states that the LST algorithm is also optimal. Its proof is left as an exercise at the end of this chapter.

THEOREM 4.3. When preemption is allowed and jobs do not contend for resources, the LST (MLF) algorithm can produce a feasible schedule of a set **J** of jobs with arbitrary release times and deadlines on a processor if and only if feasible schedules of **J** exist.

While the EDF algorithm does not require any knowledge of the execution times of jobs, the LST algorithm does. This is a serious disadvantage. As discussed earlier, the actual execution times of jobs are often not known until the jobs complete. Obviously, it is impossible for us to calculate the actual amounts of slack under this circumstance. We typically calculate the slack of each job based on its maximum execution time e_i^+ when the range $[e_i^-, e_i^+]$ of execution time e_i of every job is relatively small. Furthermore, we require that the maximum (and sometimes even the actual) execution time of each sporadic or aperiodic job become known upon its arrival since this knowledge is needed for slack computation.

4.7 NONOPTIMALITY OF THE EDF AND THE LST ALGORITHMS

It is natural to ask here whether the EDF and the LST algorithms remain optimal if preemption is not allowed or there is more than one processor. Unfortunately, the answer is no.

The fact that the EDF and the LST algorithms are optimal only when preemption is allowed is illustrated by the example in Figure 4–6. The system shown in this figure has three independent, nonpreemptable jobs J_1, J_2, and J_3. Their release times are 0, 2 and 4, respectively, and are indicated by the arrows above the schedules. Their execution times are

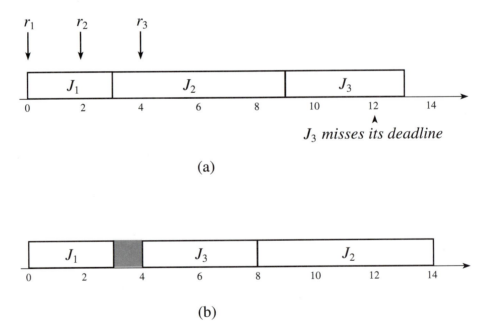

(a)

(b)

FIGURE 4–6 Example illustrating nonoptimality of the nonpreemptive EDF algorithm. (a) An EDF schedule. (b) A non-EDF schedule.

3, 6, and 4; and their deadlines are 10, 14, and 12, respectively. Figure 4–6(a) shows the schedule produced by the EDF algorithm. In particular, when J_1 completes at time 3, J_2 has already been released but not J_3. Hence, J_2 is scheduled. When J_3 is released at time 4, J_2 is executing. Even though J_3 has an earlier deadline and, hence, a higher priority, it must wait until J_2 completes because preemption is not allowed. As a result, J_3 misses its deadline. It is easy to see that the LST algorithm would produce the same infeasible schedule. The fact that these three jobs can meet their deadlines is demonstrated by the feasible schedule in Figure 4–6(b). At time 3 when J_1 completes, the processor is left idle, even though J_2 is ready for execution. Consequently, when J_3 is released at 4, it can be scheduled ahead of J_2, allowing both jobs to meet their deadlines.

We note that the schedule in Figure 4–6(b) cannot be produced by any priority-driven scheduling algorithm. By definition, a priority-driven algorithm never leaves a processor idle when there are jobs ready to use the processor. This example illustrates the fact that not only nonpreemptive EDF and LST algorithms are not optimal, but also no nonpreemptive priority-driven algorithm is optimal when jobs have arbitrary release times, execution times, and deadlines.

The example in Figure 4–7 shows that the EDF algorithm is not optimal for scheduling preemptable jobs on more than one processor. The system in this figure also contains three jobs, J_1, J_2, and J_3. Their execution times are 1, 1, and 5 and their deadlines are 1, 2, and 5, respectively. The release times of all three jobs are 0. The system has two processors. According to the EDF algorithm, J_1 and J_2 are scheduled on the processors at time 0 because they have higher priorities. The result is the schedule in Figure 4–7(a), and J_3 misses its deadline.

On the other hand, an algorithm which assigns a higher priority to J_3 in this case can feasibly schedule the jobs. An example of such algorithms is the LST algorithm. The slacks of the J_1, J_2, and J_3 in Figure 4–7 are 0, 1, and 0, respectively. Hence, this algorithm would

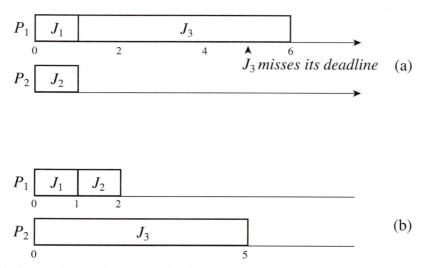

FIGURE 4–7   Example illustrating nonoptimality of the EDF algorithm for multiprocessor scheduling. (a) The EDF schedule. (b) A feasible schedule.

produce the feasible schedule in Figure 4–7(b). Unfortunately, the LST algorithm is also not optimal for scheduling jobs on more than one processor, as demonstrated by the example in Problem 4.4.

4.8 CHALLENGES IN VALIDATING TIMING CONSTRAINTS IN PRIORITY-DRIVEN SYSTEMS

Compared with the clock-driven approach, the priority-driven scheduling approach has many advantages. As examples, you may have noticed that priority-driven schedulers are easy to implement. Many well-known priority-driven algorithms use very simple priority assignments, and for these algorithms, the run-time overhead due to maintaining a priority queue of ready jobs can be made very small. A clock-driven scheduler requires the information on the release times and execution times of the jobs a priori in order to decide when to schedule them. In contrast, a priority-driven scheduler does not require most of this information, making it much better suited for applications with varying time and resource requirements. You will see in later chapters other advantages of the priority-driven approach which are at least as compelling as these two.

Despite its merits, the priority-driven approach has not been widely used in hard real-time systems, especially safety-critical systems, until recently. The major reason is that the timing behavior of a priority-driven system is nondeterministic when job parameters vary. Consequently, it is difficult to validate that the deadlines of all jobs scheduled in a priority-driven manner indeed meet their deadlines when the job parameters vary. In general, this *validation problem* [LiHa] can be stated as follows: Given a set of jobs, the set of resources available to the jobs, and the scheduling (and resource access-control) algorithm to allocate processors and resources to jobs, determine whether all the jobs meet their deadlines.

4.8.1 Anomalous Behavior of Priority-Driven Systems

Figure 4–8 gives an example illustrating why the validation problem is difficult when the scheduling algorithm is priority-driven and job parameters may vary. The simple system contains four independent jobs. The jobs are scheduled on two identical processors in a priority-driven manner. The processors maintain a common priority queue, and the priority order is J_1, J_2, J_3, and J_4 with J_1 having the highest priority. In other words, the system is dynamic. The jobs may be preempted but never migrated, meaning that once a job begins execution on a processor, it is constrained to execute on that processor until completion. (Many systems fit this simple model. For example, the processors may model two redundant data links connecting a source and destination pair, and the jobs are message transmissions over the links. The processors may also model two replicated database servers, and the jobs are queries dynamically dispatched by a communication processor to the database servers.) The release times, deadlines, and execution times of the jobs are listed in the table. The execution times of all the jobs are fixed and known, except for J_2. Its execution time can be any value in the range [2, 6].

Suppose that we want to determine whether the system meets all the deadlines and whether the completion-time jitter of every job (i.e., the difference between the latest and the earliest completion times of the job) is no more than 4. A brute force way to do so is to simulate the system. Suppose that we schedule the jobs according their given priorities, assuming

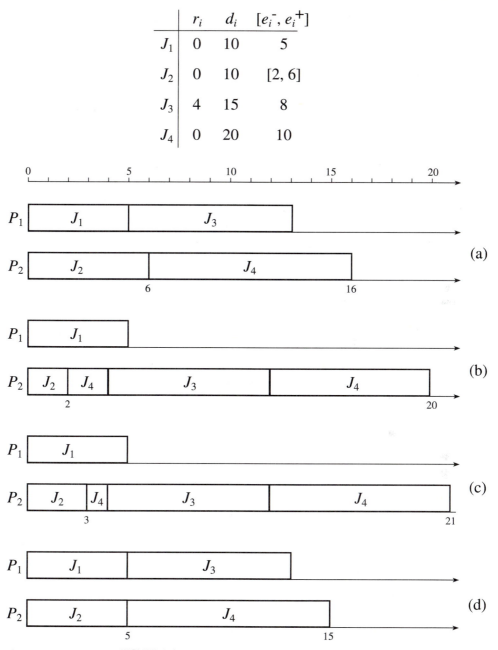

	r_i	d_i	$[e_i^-, e_i^+]$
J_1	0	10	5
J_2	0	10	[2, 6]
J_3	4	15	8
J_4	0	20	10

FIGURE 4–8   Example illustrating scheduling anomalies.

first that the execution time of J_2 has the maximum value 6 and then that it has the minimum value 2. The resultant schedules are shown in Figure 4–8(a) and (b), respectively. Looking at these schedules, we might conclude that all jobs meet their deadlines, and the completion-time jitters are sufficiently small. This would be an incorrect conclusion, as demonstrated by the schedules in Figure 4–8(c) and (d). As far as J_4 is concerned, the worst-case schedule is the one shown in Figure 4–8(c); it occurs when the execution time of J_2 is 3. According to this schedule, the completion time of J_4 is 21; the job misses its deadline. The best-case schedule for J_4 is shown in Figure 4–8(d); it occurs when the execution time of J_2 is 5. From this schedule, we see that J_4 can complete as early as time 15; its completion-time jitter exceeds the upper limit of 4. To find the worst-case and best-case schedules, we must try all the possible values of e_2.

The phenomenon illustrated by this example is known as a *scheduling anomaly*, an unexpected timing behavior of priority-driven systems. Graham [Grah] has shown that the completion time of a set of nonpreemptive jobs with identical release times can be later when more processors are used to execute them and when they have shorter execution times and fewer dependencies. (Problem 4.5 gives the well-known illustrative example.) Indeed, when jobs are nonpreemptable, scheduling anomalies can occur even when there is only one processor. For example, suppose that the execution time e_1 of the job J_1 in Figure 4–6 can be either 3 or 4. The figure shows that J_3 misses its deadline when e_1 is 3. However, J_3 would complete at time 8 and meet its deadline if e_1 were 4. We will see in later chapters that when jobs have arbitrary release times and share resources, scheduling anomalies can occur even when there is only one processor and the jobs are preemptable.

Scheduling anomalies make the problem of validating a priority-driven system difficult whenever job parameters may vary. Unfortunately, variations in execution times and release times are often unavoidable. If the maximum range of execution times of all n jobs in a system is X, the time required to find the latest and earliest completion times of all jobs is $O(X^n)$ if we were to find these extrema by exhaustive simulation or testing. Clearly, such a strategy is impractical for all but the smallest systems of practical interest.

4.8.2   Predictability of Executions

When the timing constraints are specified in terms of deadlines of jobs, the validation problem is the same as that of finding the worst-case (the largest) completion time of every job. This problem is easy whenever the execution behavior of the set **J** is predictable, that is, whenever the system does not have scheduling anomalies. To define predictability more formally, we call the schedule of **J** produced by the given scheduling algorithm when the execution time of every job has its maximum value the *maximal schedule* of **J**. Similarly, the schedule of **J** produced by the given scheduling algorithm when the execution time of every job has its minimum value is the *minimal schedule*. When the execution time of every job has its actual value, the resultant schedule is the *actual schedule* of **J**. So, the schedules in Figure 4–8(a) and (b) are the maximal and minimal schedules, respectively, of the jobs in that system, and all the schedules shown in the figure are possible actual schedules.

Since the range of execution time of every job is known, the maximal and minimal schedules of **J** can easily be constructed when the release-time jitters are negligible. (We assume that release times of all jobs are fixed and known for this discussion. How release-time jitters further complicate the validation problem is beyond the scope of our discussion here.) In contrast, its actual schedule is unknown because the actual values of the execution times are unknown.

The predictability of job execution (behavior) is an intuitive notion: The execution of **J** under the given priority-driven scheduling algorithm is predictable if the actual start time and actual completion time of every job according to the actual schedule are bounded by its start times and completion times according to the maximal and minimal schedules. More formally, we let $s(J_i)$ be the instant of time at which the execution of J_i begins according to the actual schedule of **J**. $s(J_i)$ is the (actual) start time of J_i. Let $s^+(J_i)$ and $s^-(J_i)$ be the start times of J_i according to the maximal schedule and minimal schedule of **J**, respectively. These start times can easily be found by constructing the maximal and minimal schedules and observing when J_i starts according to these schedules. We say that J_i is *start-time predictable* if $s^-(J_i) \leq s(J_i) \leq s^+(J_i)$. As an example, for the job J_4 in Figure 4–8, $s^-(J_4)$ is 2. $s^+(J_4)$ is 6. Its actual start time is in the range [2, 6]. Therefore, J_4 is start-time predictable.

Similarly, let $f(J_i)$ be the actual completion time (also called finishing time) of J_i according to the actual schedule of **J**. Let $f^+(J_i)$ and $f^-(J_i)$ be the completion times of J_i according to the maximal schedule and minimal schedule of **J**, respectively. We say that J_i is *completion-time predictable* if $f^-(J_i) \leq f(J_i) \leq f^+(J_i)$. The execution of J_i is *predictable*, or simply J_i is predictable, if J_i is both start-time and completion-time predictable. The execution behavior of the entire set **J** is predictable if every job in **J** is predictable. Looking at Figure 4–8 again, we see that $f^-(J_4)$ is 20, but $f^+(J_4)$ is 16. It is impossible for the inequality $20 \leq f(J_4) \leq 16$ to hold. Therefore, J_4 is not completion-time predictable, and the system is not predictable.

In general, whether a set of jobs has predictable execution behavior depends not only on the parameters of jobs in the set but also on the algorithm used to schedule the jobs. For example, while the execution of independent, preemptable but nonmigratable jobs is not predictable in general, as exemplified by the jobs in Figure 4–8, it is predictable when the priorities are assigned on the FIFO basis [Ha]. In Chapters 6–9, we will use the following fact, which is true for all priority-driven scheduling algorithms.

THEOREM 4.4.   The execution of every job in a set of independent, preemptable jobs with fixed release times is predictable when scheduled in a priority-driven manner on one processor.

Proof.   That the highest priority job J_1 is predictable is obvious: It always starts at its release time, and its maximum execution time is larger than its actual execution time. Suppose that all the $i - 1$ highest priority jobs $J_1, J_2, \ldots, J_{i-1}$ are predictable. We now show by contradiction that J_i, which has a lower priority than they but a higher priority than all the other jobs in the system, is also predictable.

Suppose that $s^-(J_i) \leq s(J_i) \leq s^+(J_i)$ is not true. In particular, we suppose that $s(J_i) > s^+(J_i)$. Because the scheduler never schedules a job before its release time, $s^+(J_i)$ is no earlier than the release r_i of J_i. Because the scheduling algorithm is priority-driven, every job whose release time is at or earlier than $s^+(J_i)$ and whose priorities are higher than J_i has completed by $s^+(J_i)$ according to the maximal schedule. By induction hypothesis, we know that every such job has completed by $s^+(J_i)$ according to the actual schedule as well. $s(J_i) > s^+(J_i)$ means either that the processor is left idle in the interval $[s^+(J_i), s(J_i)]$ or a job with a priority lower than J_i is scheduled in this interval. This contradicts the fact that the algorithm used to schedule the jobs is priority-driven. Hence, $s(J_i) > s^+(J_i)$ cannot be true.

A similar argument based on the actual and minimal schedules allows us to conclude that $s^-(J_i) > s(J_i)$ cannot be true. In other words, J_i is start-time predictable.

To show that J_i is also completion-time predictable, we note that since $s(J_i) \leq s^+(J_i)$, there is more available time in the interval $[s(J_i), f^+(J_i)]$ than in the interval $[s^+(J_i), f^+(J_i)]$. Moreover, the actual execution time of every job is never larger than the maximum execution time of the job. If J_i remains incomplete at $f^+(J_i)$ according to the actual schedule while it can complete by this time according to the maximal schedule, it must be delayed by one or more jobs with priorities lower than J_i executing in $[s(J_i), f^+(J_i)]$, or the processor must be left idle for some time in this interval. This contradicts the fact that the scheduling algorithm is priority-driven. We can, therefore, conclude that $f(J_i) \leq f^+(J_i)$. A similar argument based on the actual and minimal schedules tells us that $f^-(J_i)$ is never later than $f(J_i)$, or that J_i is also completion-time predictable.   □

Theorem 4.4 tells us that it is relatively easy to validate priority-driven, uniprocessor and static systems when jobs are independent and preemptable. Because the execution behavior of all the jobs is predictable, we can confine our attention to the maximum execution times of all the jobs and ignore the variations in execution times when we want to determine their maximum possible response times. You will see that this is indeed what we will do in most parts of Chapters 6–9. Nonpreemptivity and resource contention invariably introduce unpredictability in execution. Fortunately, it is possible to bound the additional delay suffered by every job due to these factors reasonably accurately. We will describe the methods for doing so as well.

4.8.3   Validation Algorithms and Their Performance

The validation problem has many variants, and that of validating static priority-driven systems is an important variant. Recent advances in real-time scheduling and schedulability analysis have lead to several sufficient conditions and analytical bounds. They are solutions to this variant and the subjects of discussion in Chapters 6–9. These theoretical results form a rigorous basis of good validation algorithms and tools for a wide spectrum of static systems. (A *validation algorithm* allows us to determine whether all jobs in a system indeed meet their timing constraints despite scheduling anomalies.) While there are mature validation algorithms and tools for static systems, good validation algorithms for dynamic, priority-driven systems are not yet available.

Specifically, we say that a validation algorithm is *correct* if it never declares that all timing constraints are met when some constraints may not be. The merits of (correct) validation algorithms are measured in terms of their complexity, robustness, and accuracy. A validation algorithm is good when it achieves a good balance in performance according to these conflicting figures of merit.

For example, some existing validation algorithms run in constant time or $O(n)$ time, where n is the number of tasks in the system. They are well suited for on-line acceptance tests to determine whether the system should admit a new task. More complex ones run in pseudopolynomial time but have better performance in the other dimensions.

Every rigorous validation algorithm is based on a workload model. When applied to a system, the conclusion of the algorithm is correct if all the assumptions of the model are valid for the system. A validation algorithm is said to be *robust* if it remains correct even when some assumptions of its underlying workload model are not valid. The use of a robust validation algorithm significantly reduces the need for an accurate characterization of the applications and the run-time environment and, thus, the efforts in analysis and measurement of the individual applications for the purpose of validating the workload model. We will see in later chapters that existing validation algorithms based on the periodic task model are robust to a great extent. Although the model assumes that jobs in each task are released periodically and execute for an equal amount of time, such a validation algorithm remains correct in the presence of release-time jitters, variations in job execution time, and other deviations from periodic behavior. It is only necessary for us to know the ranges of task parameters (e.g., the minimum interrelease time and maximum execution time of jobs), which are much easier to obtain and validate, either by timing analysis or measurement, than the actual values or probability distributions of the parameters.

Efficiency and robustness can be achieved easily if we are not concerned with the accuracy of the validation test. A validation algorithm is *inaccurate* when it is overly pessimistic and declares tasks unable to meet their timing constraints except when system resources are unduly underutilized. A scheduler using an inaccurate validation algorithm for an acceptance test may reject too many new tasks which are in fact acceptable. Because most validation algorithms are based on conditions that are sufficient but not necessary, they are all inaccurate to some degree, which is the price paid for the sake of robustness. The accuracy of a validation algorithm depends on whether the actual characteristics of the application systems are accurately captured by the underlying workload model. For example, validation algorithms that are based on the periodic task model are sufficiently accurate for applications, such as digital control and constant bit-rate voice and video communications, which are well characterized by the periodic task model but may have poor accuracy when used to validate applications that have widely varying processor-time demands and large release-time jitters.

4.9   OFF-LINE VERSUS ON-LINE SCHEDULING

In Section 4.1, we mentioned that a clock-driven scheduler typically makes use of a precomputed schedule of all hard real-time jobs. This schedule is computed off-line before the system begins to execute, and the computation is based on the knowledge of the release times and processor-time/resource requirements of all the jobs for all times. When the operation mode of the system changes, the new schedule specifying when each job in the new mode executes is also precomputed and stored for use. In this case, we say that scheduling is (done) off-line, and the precomputed schedules are *off-line schedules*.

An obvious disadvantage of off-line scheduling is inflexibility. This approach is possible only when the system is deterministic, meaning that the system provides some fixed set(s) of functions and that the release times and processor-time/resource demands of all its jobs are known and do not vary or vary only slightly. For a deterministic system, however, off-line scheduling has several advantages, the deterministic timing behavior of the resultant system being one of them. Because the computation of the schedules is done off-line, the complexity of the scheduling algorithm(s) used for this purpose is not important. Indeed, as we will see in the next chapter, complex heuristic algorithms are typically used to find good off-line schedules that can make nearly full use of the resources.

We say that scheduling is done *on-line*, or that we use an *on-line scheduling algorithm*, if the scheduler makes each scheduling decision without knowledge about the jobs that will be released in the future; the parameters of each job become known to the on-line scheduler only after the job is released. The priority-driven algorithms described earlier and in subsequent chapters are on-line algorithms. In Chapter 2 we talked about the admission of each new task depending on the outcome of an acceptance test that is based on the parameters of the new task and tasks admitted earlier. Such an acceptance test is on-line.

Clearly, on-line scheduling is the only option in a system whose future workload is unpredictable. An on-line scheduler can accommodate dynamic variations in user demands and resource availability. The price of the flexibility and adaptability is a reduced ability for the scheduler to make the best use of system resources. Without prior knowledge about future jobs, the scheduler cannot make optimal scheduling decisions while a clairvoyant scheduler that knows about all future jobs can.

As a simple example, suppose that at time 0, a nonpreemptive job J_1 with execution time 1 and deadline 2 is released. An on-line scheduler has two options at time 0: It either schedules J_1 to start execution at time 0 or it postpones the execution of J_1 to some later time. Suppose that the on-line scheduler decides to schedule J_1 at time 0. Later at time $x < 1$, a job J_2 with execution time $1 - x$ and deadline 1 is released. J_2 would miss its deadline because it cannot start execution until time 1. In contrast, a clairvoyant scheduler, which knows J_2 at time 0, would schedule J_1 to start execution at time 1 and thus allow both jobs to complete in time. In the second case, the on-line scheduler decides to postpone the execution of J_1 until some later time $x < 1$. Now suppose that at time x, J_3 is released instead of J_2. The execution time of J_3 is 1, and its deadline is 2. It is impossible for the on-line scheduler to schedule both J_1 and J_3 so that they complete in time. Again, a clairvoyant scheduler, knowing the future release of J_3 at time 0, would schedule J_1 to start execution at time 0 so it can complete both J_1 and J_3 on time.

The system is said to be *overloaded* when the jobs offered to the scheduler cannot be feasibly scheduled even by a clairvoyant scheduler. When the system is not overloaded, an optimal on-line scheduling algorithm is one that always produces a feasible schedule of all offered jobs. The example above shows that *no optimal on-line scheduling algorithm exists when some jobs are nonpreemptable*. On the other hand, if all the jobs are preemptable and there is only one processor, optimal on-line algorithms exist, and the EDF and LST algorithms are examples.

During an overload, some jobs must be discarded in order to allow other jobs to complete in time. A reasonable way to measure the performance of a scheduling algorithm during an overload is by the amount of work the scheduler can feasibly schedule according to the algorithm: the larger this amount, the better the algorithm. The competitive factor of an algorithm captures this aspect of performance. To define this performance measure, we say that the *value of a job* is equal to its execution time if the job completes by its deadline according to a given schedule and is equal to zero if the job fails to complete in time according to the schedule. The *value of a schedule* of a sequence of jobs is equal to the sum of the values of all the jobs in the sequence according to the schedule. A scheduling algorithm is optimal if it always produces a schedule of the maximum possible value for every finite set of jobs. An on-line algorithm has a *competitive factor c* if and only if the value of the schedule of any finite sequence of jobs produced by the algorithm is at least c times the value of the schedule of the jobs produced by an optimal clairvoyant algorithm.

In terms of this performance measure, EDF and LST algorithms are optimal under the condition that the jobs are preemptable, there is only one processor, and the processor is not overloaded. Their competitive factors are equal to 1 under this condition. On other hand, when the system is overloaded, their competitive factors are 0. To demonstrate, let us consider two jobs. The first one is released at time 0, and its execution time is 2ε; the deadline is ε for some arbitrarily small positive number ε. At time ε, a job whose relative deadline is equal to its execution time e is released. The value achieved by the EDF or LST algorithm is 0, while the maximum possible value achievable is e.

As it turns out, the EDF and LST algorithms are not the only algorithms with poor performance when the system is overloaded. In general, all on-line scheduling algorithms perform rather poorly. The following theorem due to Baruah, *et al.* [BKMM] gives us the performance limitation of on-line scheduling when the system is overloaded.

THEOREM 4.5.   No on-line scheduling algorithm can achieve a competitive factor greater than 0.25 when the system is overloaded.

Informal Proof of Theorem 4.5.   To gain some insight into why this upper bound of 0.25 is true, we summarize the proof of Theorem 4.5; you can find the complete formal proof in [BKMM]. Suppose that there is an adversary of the on-line scheduler. Over time, the adversary creates two kinds of jobs and offers (i.e., releases) them to the scheduler: major jobs and jobs associated with major jobs. The relative deadline of every job is equal to its execution time. (In other words, the job has no slack; the scheduler should either schedule the job immediately after it is released, or discard it.) We name the major jobs J_i for $i = 0, 1, \ldots, max$ in increasing order of their release times and denote the execution time and release time of each job J_i by e_i and r_i, respectively. (max is some positive integer that we will define shortly.) The adversary creates a sequence of jobs associated with each major job J_i. The execution times of all the associated jobs in the sequence are equal to some small number $\varepsilon > 0$, which is negligible compared with e_i. The first job in the sequence associated with each major job J_i is released at the same time with J_i. If there is more than one associated job in a sequence, each subsequent associated job is released at the deadline of the previous associated job in the sequence. The number of associated jobs in the sequence depends on the action of the on-line scheduler. Specifically, as long as the on-line scheduler chooses to execute J_i, the adversary continues to create jobs associated with J_i until the deadline d_i of J_i. Whenever the scheduler decides to execute a job associated with J_i, the adversary stops releasing any more associated jobs.

Let us now consider a busy interval which begins at r_0 when the adversary releases the first major job J_0 and the first of the sequence of jobs associated with J_0. Depending on the action of the on-line scheduler, the adversary may release major job J_i for $i > 0$ at time r_i; the release time r_i of the ith major job and the first of its associated jobs is equal to $r_{i-1} + e_{i-1} - \varepsilon$. In other words, J_i is released at ε units of time before the deadline of J_{i-1}. It is not possible to schedule both J_{i-1} and J_i to complete in time. At the time r_i, the scheduler must choose either to discard J_{i-1} and start to execute J_i or continue to execute J_{i-1} and therefore discard J_i.

If the scheduler chooses to discard J_{i-1} and begins to execute J_i, the adversary then releases J_{i+1} at r_{i+1}. As long as the scheduler continues to discard the executing major job each time a new major job is released in order to execute the new job, the adversary continues to release the next major job ε units of time before the deadline of the executing job. This process continues until the major job J_{max} is released for some positive integer max, and the busy interval ends at the deadline of this job. In this case, the on-line scheduler discards all the jobs but J_{max}, and the total value achieved by the scheduler in this busy interval is e_{max}. In contrast, the clairvoyant scheduler would schedule the jobs associated with all the major jobs before J_{max} and then the major job J_{max} and achieve the value $\sum_{k=1}^{max} e_k$.

On the other hand, the scheduler may decide to complete J_i and, upon the completion of J_i, execute a job associated with J_{i+1} for $i < max$. In this case, the adversary stops releasing any major job after J_{i+1}. Moreover, it stops releasing jobs associated with J_{i+1} after the first associated job. (Figure 4–9 shows this situation for $i = 2$.) The value achieved in the busy interval by the on-line scheduler is approximately equal to e_i. However, the clairvoyant scheduler would execute all jobs associated with jobs J_0, $J_1, \ldots, J_{i-1}$ and then the job J_i and achieve a value of $\sum_{k=0}^{i} e_i$.

Now suppose that the execution time e_0 of the first major job J_0 is 1, and for $i > 0$, the execution time e_i of the ith major job is given by

$$e_i = ce_{i-1} - \sum_{k=0}^{i-1} e_k$$

If we perform the necessary algebraic manipulation, we will find that competitive factor of the on-line scheduler is either equal to $1/c$, if the scheduler completes J_i followed by an associate job, or is equal to the ratio of e_{max} to the sum $\sum_{k=0}^{max} e_k$, if the scheduler discards all the major jobs except J_{max}. The former is always greater than or equal to the latter for every positive integer max if c is equal to 4 or more. For c equal to 4,

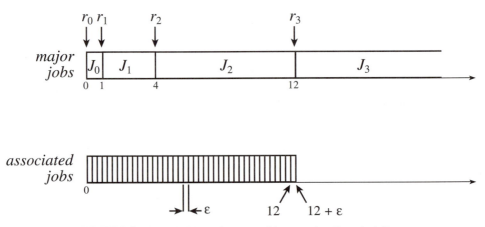

FIGURE 4–9   Example illustrating competitiveness of on-line scheduling.

the competitive factor is 0.25. The execution times of the major jobs are equal to 1, 3, 8, 20, 48, ... Figure 4–9 shows the case where the on-line scheduler executes J_2 to completion. It achieves a value of 8 while a clairvoyant scheduler, knowing that all the jobs shown in the figure will be released at all time, can achieve a value of 32.   □

The system used in the proof of Theorem 4.5 is extremely overloaded. It is not surprising that the performance of on-line scheduling algorithms is poor when the system is so overloaded. Intuitively, we expect that some on-line algorithms should perform well when the system is only slightly overloaded. To state this more precisely, we let $x(t, t')$ $(t' > t)$ denote the *load ratio* of the interval $[t, t']$: It is the ratio of the total execution time of all jobs whose feasible intervals are contained in the interval $[t, t']$ to the length $t' - t$ of the interval. A system is said to have a *loading factor* X if the load ratio of the system is equal to or less than X for all intervals. Our intuition says that if the loading factor of a system is $1 + \varepsilon$ for some very small positive number ε, there should be on-line algorithms whose competitiveness factors are close to 1. Unfortunately, our intuition fails us. Baruah, *et al.* showed that the competitiveness factor of an on-line scheduling algorithm is at most equal to 0.385 for any system whose loading factor is just slightly over 1.

The results on competitiveness of on-line algorithms tell us that when scheduling is done on-line, it is important to keep the system from being overloaded using some overload management or load shedding algorithms. Most overload management algorithms take into account the criticality factors of jobs, not just their timing parameters, when choosing jobs to be discarded. We will describe a few of them in later chapters.

4.10   SUMMARY

This chapter gave a brief overview of the clock-driven, weighted round-robin and priority-driven approaches to scheduling. They are the subjects of in-depth discussion of the next few chapters. This chapter also discussed several important facts about the priority-driven approach. We need to keep them in mind at all times.

An algorithm for scheduling hard real-time jobs is optimal if it can produce a feasible schedule as long as feasible schedules of the given jobs exist, that is, when the system is not overloaded. This is the criterion of merit we use most of the time in this book. The EDF (Earliest-Deadline-First) algorithm is optimal for scheduling preemptable jobs on one processor. LST (Least-Slack-Time) algorithm is also optimal for preemptable jobs on one processor, but it requires information on the execution times of all jobs while the EDF algorithm does not. Neither algorithm is optimal when jobs are nonpreemptable or when there is more than one processor.

Another important concept is predictability of the timing behavior of jobs. The execution behavior of a system is predictable if the system exhibits no anomalies. We can conclude that the jobs in a predictable system can always meet their deadlines if the jobs meet their deadlines according to the maximal schedule of the system, that is, when every job in the system executes for as long as its maximum execution time. We have shown that when the jobs are independent and preemptable and are scheduled on one processor, their execution behavior is predictable. This fact allows us to ignore the variations in job execution times during validation and work with their maximum execution times. Indeed, this is what we will do in most parts of subsequent chapters.

In general, systems that use priority-driven scheduling have scheduling anomalies. In subsequent chapters we will discuss efficient validation algorithms that allow us to verify the timely completions of jobs despite scheduling anomalies. Such an algorithm is correct if it never concludes that some job completes in time when the job may fail to do so. The merits of correct validation algorithms are measured by their efficiency, robustness, and accuracy. These measures tell us how much time a validation algorithm takes to reach its conclusion on the schedulability of each job or the entire system, whether its conclusion remains correct when some assumptions of its underlying model are no longer valid, and whether the algorithm is overly pessimistic.

Finally, the EDF and LST algorithms are not optimal when the system is overloaded so some jobs must be discarded in order to allow other jobs to complete in time. In fact, these algorithms perform poorly for overloaded systems: Their competitive factors are equal to zero. Some kind of overload management algorithm should be used with these algorithms.

4.11   EXERCISES

4.1 The feasible interval of each job in the precedence graph in Figure 4P–1 is given next to its name. The execution time of all jobs are equal to 1.

    (a) Find the effective release times and deadlines of the jobs in the precedence graph in Figure 4P–1.

    (b) Find an EDF schedule of the jobs

    (c) A job is said to be at level i if the length of the longest path from the job to jobs that have no successors is i. So, jobs J_3, J_6, and J_9 are at level 0, jobs J_2, J_5, and J_8 are at level 1, and so on. Suppose that the priorities of the jobs are assigned based on their levels: the higher the level, the higher the priority. Find a priority-driven schedule of the jobs in Figure 4P–1 according to this priority assignment.

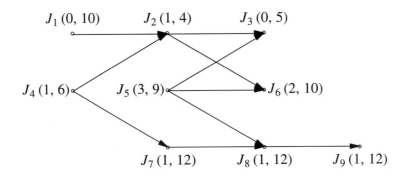

4.2 (a) The execution times of the jobs in the precedence graph in Figure 4P–2 are all equal to 1, and their release times are identical. Give a nonpreemptive optimal schedule that minimizes the completion time of all jobs on three processors. Describe briefly the algorithm you used to find the schedule.

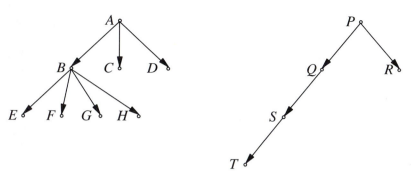

    (b) If the execution times of jobs are arbitrary rational numbers, can your algorithm be modified so that it will produce optimal preemptive schedules of such jobs? Explain your answer.

4.3 Prove Theorem 4.3 on the optimality of the LST algorithm for scheduling preemptive jobs on one processor.

4.4 Consider a system that has five periodic tasks, A, B, C, D, and E, and three processors P_1, P_2, P_3. The periods of A, B, and C are 2 and their execution times are equal to 1. The periods of D and E are 8 and their execution times are 6. The phase of every task is 0, that is, the first job of the task is released at time 0. The relative deadline of every task is equal to its period.

    (a) Show that if the tasks are scheduled dynamically on three processors according to the LST algorithm, some jobs in the system cannot meet their deadlines.

    (b) Find a feasible schedule of the five tasks on three processors.

    (c) Parts (a) and (b) allow us to conclude that the LST algorithm is not optimal for scheduling on more than one processor. However, when all the jobs have the same release time or when they have the same deadline, the LST algorithm is optimal. Prove this statement.

4.5 [Grah] A system contains nine nonpreemptable jobs named J_i, for $i = 1, 2, \ldots, 9$. Their execution times are 3, 2, 2, 2, 4, 4, 4, 4, and 9, respectively, their release times are equal to 0, and their deadlines are 12. J_1 is the immediate predecessor of J_9, and J_4 is the immediate predecessor of J_5, J_6, J_7, and J_8. There is no other precedence constraints. For all the jobs, J_i has a higher priority than J_k if $i < k$.

    (a) Draw the precedence graph of the jobs.

    (b) Can the jobs meet their deadlines if they are scheduled on three processors? Explain your answer.

    (c) Can the jobs meet their deadlines if we make them preemptable and schedule them preemptively. Explain your answer.

    (d) Can the jobs meet their deadlines if they are scheduled nonpreemptively on four processors? Explain your answer.

    (e) Suppose that due to an improvement of the three processors, the execution time of every job is reduced by 1. Can the jobs meet their deadlines? Explain your answer.

4.6 Consider a system that has two processors and uses an on-line preemptive scheduler to schedule jobs on the processors. At time 0, three independent jobs, J_1, J_2, and J_3, with execution time 1, 1, and 2, respectively, are released. Their deadlines are 2, 2, and 4, respectively. The scheduler either schedules a portion of J_3 before time 1, or it does not schedule J_3 before time 1. We now consider these two cases.

    (a) In case (1), the scheduler schedules a portion of J_3 before time 1. Now suppose that two more independent jobs, J_4 and J_5, are released at time 2. Their execution times are both equal to 1, and their deadlines are equal to 2. Show that in this case, the scheduler can no longer feasibly schedule all the jobs, while a clairvoyant scheduler, which foresees the releases of J_4 and J_5, would not schedule any part of J_3 before time 1 and therefore could feasibly schedule all the jobs.

(b) In case (2), the on-line scheduler does not schedule any portion of J_3 before time 1. Show by constructing an example that there exist future jobs which the on-line scheduler will not be able to schedule feasibly, while the jobs could feasibly be scheduled if the on-line scheduler had scheduled J_3 before time 1.

4.7 Consider the set of jobs in Figure 4-3. Suppose that the jobs have identical execution time.

(a) What maximum execution time can the jobs have and still can be feasibly scheduled on one processor? Explain your answer.

(b) Suppose that the release times of J_1 and J_2 are jittery. The release time of J_1 can be as early as 0 and as late as 3, and the release time of J_2 can be as late as 1. How can you take into account this variation when you want to determine whether the jobs can all meet their deadlines?

C H A P T E R 5

Clock-Driven Scheduling

The previous chapter gave a skeletal description of clock-driven scheduling. This chapter fleshes out this description and discusses the advantages and disadvantages of this approach.

5.1 NOTATIONS AND ASSUMPTIONS

As it will become evident shortly, the clock-driven approach to scheduling is applicable only when the system is by and large deterministic, except for a few aperiodic and sporadic jobs to be accommodated in the deterministic framework. For this reason, we assume a restricted periodic task model throughout this chapter. The following are the restrictive assumptions that we will remove in subsequent chapters:

1. There are n periodic tasks in the system. As long as the system stays in an operation mode, n is fixed.
2. The parameters of all periodic tasks are known a priori. In particular, variations in the interrelease times of jobs in any periodic task are negligibly small. In other words, for all practical purposes, each job in T_i is released p_i units of time after the previous job in T_i.
3. Each job $J_{i,k}$ is ready for execution at its release time $r_{i,k}$.

We refer to a periodic task T_i with phase ϕ_i, period p_i, execution time e_i, and relative deadline D_i by the 4-tuple (ϕ_i, p_i, e_i, D_i). For example, $(1, 10, 3, 6)$ is a periodic task whose phase is 1, period is 10, execution time is 3, and relative deadline is 6. Therefore the first job in this task is released and ready at time 1 and must be completed by time 7; the second job is ready at 11 and must be completed by 17, and so on. Each of these jobs executes for at most 3 units of time. The utilization of this task is 0.3. By default, the phase of each task is 0, and its relative deadline is equal to its period. We will omit the elements of the tuple that have their default values. As examples, both $(10, 3, 6)$ and $(10, 3)$ have zero phase. Their relative deadlines are 6 and 10, respectively.

Also, there are aperiodic jobs released at unexpected time instants. For now we assume that there are no sporadic jobs. We will discuss how to schedule sporadic jobs in Section 5.6. Most of this chapter focuses on scheduling tasks on one processor. The discussion on how to generalize the clock-driven uniprocessor scheduling strategy to schedule jobs in multiprocessor systems is postponed to Section 5.7.

5.2 STATIC, TIMER-DRIVEN SCHEDULER

For the sake of concreteness, we assume that the operating system maintains a queue for aperiodic jobs. When an aperiodic job is released, it is placed in the queue without the attention of the scheduler. We are not concerned with how the aperiodic jobs are ordered in this queue but simply assume that they are ordered in a manner suitable for the applications in the system. Whenever the processor is available for aperiodic jobs, the job at the head of this queue executes.

Whenever the parameters of jobs with hard deadlines are known before the system begins to execute, a straightforward way to ensure that they meet their deadlines is to construct a *static schedule* of the jobs off-line. This schedule specifies exactly when each job executes. According to the schedule, the amount of processor time allocated to every job is equal to its maximum execution time, and every job completes by its deadline. During run time, the scheduler dispatches the jobs according to this schedule. Hence, as long as no job ever *overruns* (i.e., some rare or erroneous condition causes it to execute longer than its maximum execution time), all deadlines are surely met. Because the schedule is computed off-line, we can afford to use complex, sophisticated algorithms. Among all the feasible schedules (i.e., schedules where all jobs meet their deadlines), we may want to choose one that is good according to some criteria (e.g., the processor idles nearly periodically to accommodate aperiodic jobs).

As an example, we consider a system that contains four independent periodic tasks. They are $T_1 = (4, 1)$, $T_2 = (5, 1.8)$, $T_3 = (20, 1)$, and $T_4 = (20, 2)$. Their utilizations are 0.25, 0.36, 0.05, and 0.1, respectively, and the total utilization is 0.76. It suffices to construct a static schedule for the first hyperperiod of the tasks. Since the least common multiple of all periods is 20, the length of each hyperperiod is 20. The entire schedule consists of replicated segments of length 20. Figure 5–1 shows such a schedule segment on one processor. We see that T_1 starts execution at time 0, 4, 9.8, 13.8, and so on; T_2 starts execution at 2, 8, 12, 18, and so on. All tasks meet their deadlines.

Some intervals, such as (3.8, 4), (5, 6), and (10.8, 12), are not used by the periodic tasks. These intervals can be used to execute aperiodic jobs. For this purpose, it may be advantageous to have the unused intervals scattered more or less periodically in the schedule. If no aperiodic jobs are ready for execution during these intervals, we can use the time to execute background nonreal-time jobs whose response times are uncritical to the performance of the system or some built-in self-test job that checks the status and monitors the health of the system.

A straightforward way to implement the scheduler is to store the precomputed schedule as a table. Each entry $(t_k, T(t_k))$ in this table gives a *decision time* t_k, which is an instant when a scheduling decision is made, and $T(t_k)$, which is either the name of the task whose job should start at t_k or I. The latter indicates an idle interval during which no periodic task is scheduled. During initialization (say at time 0), the operating system creates all the tasks that are to be executed. (In other words, it allocates a sufficient amount of memory for the code

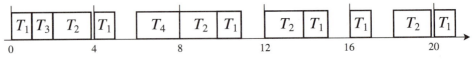

FIGURE 5–1 An arbitrary static schedule.

and data of every task and brings the code executed by the task into memory.) The scheduler makes use of a timer. Immediately after all the tasks have been created and initialized and then at every scheduling decision time, the scheduler sets the timer so the timer will expire and request an interrupt at the next decision time. Upon receiving a timer interrupt at t_k, the scheduler sets the timer to expire at t_{k+1} and prepares the task $T(t_k)$ for execution. It then suspends itself, letting the task have the processor and execute. When the timer expires again, the scheduler repeats this operation.

The pseudocode in Figure 5–2 describes the operation of such a scheduler. H is the length of the hyperperiod of the system. N is the number of entries in the schedule of each hyperperiod. The description assumes the existence of a timer. The timer, once set to expire at a certain time, will generate an interrupt at that time. This interrupt wakes up the scheduler, which is given the processor with a negligible amount of delay.

In the example in Figure 5–1, the stored table contains 17 entries. They are $(0, T_1)$, $(1, T_3)$, $(2, T_2)$, $(3.8, I)$, $(4, T_1)$, . . . $(19.8, I)$. Hence, the timer is set to expire at 0, 1, 2, 3.8, and so on. At these times, the scheduler schedules the execution of tasks T_1, T_3, T_2, and an aperiodic or background job, respectively. The table is used again during the next hyperperiod, and new decision times 20, 21, 22, 23.8, and so on, can be obtained from the times in the first hyperperiod as described in Figure 5–2.

We call a periodic static schedule a *cyclic schedule*. Again, this approach to scheduling hard real-time jobs is called the *clock-driven* or *time-driven* approach because each scheduling decision is made at a specific time, independent of events, such as job releases and completions, in the system. It is easy to see why a clock-driven system never exhibits the anomalous timing behavior of priority-driven systems.

Input: Stored schedule $(t_k, T(t_k))$ for $k = 0, 1, \ldots N - 1$.
Task SCHEDULER:
    set the next decision point i and table entry k to 0;
    set the timer to expire at t_k.
    do forever:
      accept timer interrupt;
      if an aperiodic job is executing, preempt the job;
      current task $T = T(t_k)$;
      increment i by 1;
      compute the next table entry $k = i \, mod(N)$;
      set the timer to expire at $\lfloor i/N \rfloor H + t_k$;
      if the current task T is I,
        let the job at the head of the aperiodic job queue execute;
      else, let the task T execute;
      sleep;
end SCHEDULER

FIGURE 5–2   A clock-driven scheduler.

5.3   GENERAL STRUCTURE OF CYCLIC SCHEDULES

Rather than using ad hoc cyclic schedules, such as the one in Figure 5–1, we may want to use a schedule that has a certain structure. By making sure that the structure has the desired characteristics, we can ensure that the cyclic schedule and the scheduler have these characteristics.

5.3.1   Frames and Major Cycles

Figure 5–3 shows a good structure of cyclic schedules [BaSh]. A restriction imposed by this structure is that scheduling decisions are made periodically, rather than at arbitrary times. The scheduling decision times partition the time line into intervals called *frames*. Every frame has length f; f is the *frame size*. Because scheduling decisions are made only at the beginning of every frame, there is no preemption within each frame. The phase of each periodic task is a nonnegative integer multiple of the frame size. In other words, the first job of every task is released at the beginning of some frame.

In addition to choosing which job to execute, we want the scheduler to carry out monitoring and enforcement actions at the beginning of each frame. In particular, we want the scheduler to check whether every job scheduled in the frame has indeed been released and is ready for execution. We also want the scheduler to check whether there is any overrun and take the necessary error handling action whenever it finds any erroneous condition. These design objectives make some choices of frame size more desirable than the others.

5.3.2   Frame Size Constraints

Ideally, we want the frames to be sufficiently long so that every job can start and complete its execution within a frame. In this way, no job will be preempted. We can meet this objective if we make the frame size f larger than the execution time e_i of every task T_i. In other words,

$$f \geq \max_{1 \leq i \leq n} (e_i) \qquad (5.1)$$

To keep the length of the cyclic schedule as short as possible, the frame size f should be chosen so that it divides H, the length of the hyperperiod of the system. This condition is met when f divides the period p_i of at least one task T_i, that is,

$$\lfloor p_i/f \rfloor - p_i/f = 0 \qquad (5.2)$$

for at least one i. When this condition is met, there is an integer number of frames in each hyperperiod. We let F denote this number and call a hyperperiod that begins at the beginning of the $(kF + 1)$st frame, for any $k = 0, 1, \ldots$, a *major cycle*.

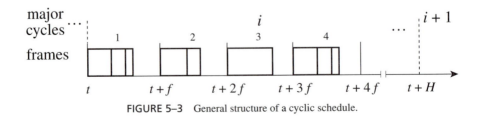

FIGURE 5–3   General structure of a cyclic schedule.

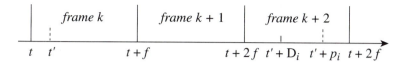

FIGURE 5–4   A constraint on the value of frame size.

On the other hand, to make it possible for the scheduler to determine whether every job completes by its deadline, we want the frame size to be sufficiently small so that between the release time and deadline of every job, there is at least one frame. Figure 5–4 illustrates the suitable range of f for a task $T_i = (p_i, e_i, D_i)$. When f is in this range, there is at least one frame between the release time and deadline of every job in the task. In this figure, t denotes the beginning of a frame (called the kth frame) in which a job in T_i is released, and t' denotes the release time of this job. We need to consider two cases: $t' > t$ and $t' = t$. If t' is later than t, as shown in this figure, we want the $(k+1)$st frame to be in the interval between the release time t' and the deadline $t' + D_i$ of this job. For this to be true, we must have $t + 2f$ equal to or earlier than $t' + D_i$, that is, $2f - (t' - t) \leq D_i$. Because the difference $t' - t$ is at least equal to the greatest common divisor $gcd(p_i, f)$ of p_i and f, this condition is met if the following inequality holds:

$$2f - gcd(p_i, f) \leq D_i \tag{5.3}$$

We want the inequality of Eq. (5.3) to hold for all $i = 1, 2, \ldots, n$. In the special case when t' is equal to t, it suffices to choose a frame size that is equal to or smaller than D_i. The condition $f \leq D_i$ is satisfied for all values of f that satisfy Eq. (5.3) and, hence, does not need to be considered separately. We refer to Eqs. (5.1), (5.2) and (5.3) as the *frame-size constraints*.

For the four tasks in Figure 5–1, we see that Eq (5.1) constrains the frame size to be no less than 2. Their hyperperiod length is 20; hence, 2, 4, 5, 10 and 20 are possible frame sizes according to Eq. (5.2). However, only 2 satisfies Eq. (5.3). Therefore, we must choose this frame size and can use the cyclic schedule shown in Figure 5–5.

As another example, we consider the tasks (15, 1, 14), (20, 2, 26), and (22, 3). Because of Eq. (5.1), we must have $f \geq 3$; because of Eq. (5.2), we must have $f = 3, 4, 5, 10, 11, 15, 20,$ and 22; and because of Eq. (5.3), we must have $f = 3, 4$ or 5. Therefore the possible choices of the frame size are 3, 4, and 5.

5.3.3   Job Slices

Sometimes, the given parameters of some task systems cannot meet all three frame size constraints simultaneously. An example is the system $\mathbf{T} = \{(4, 1), (5, 2, 7), (20, 5)\}$. For Eq. (5.1) to be true, we must have $f \geq 5$, but to satisfy Eq. (5.3) we must have $f \leq 4$. In this situation,

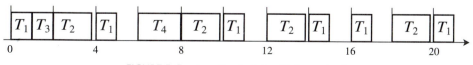

FIGURE 5–5   A cyclic schedule with frame size 2.

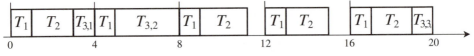

FIGURE 5–6   A preemptive cyclic schedule of $T_1 = (4, 1)$, $T_2 = (5, 2, 7)$ and $T_3 = (20, 5)$.

we are forced to partition each job in a task that has a large execution time into slices (i.e., subjobs) with smaller execution times. (When the job is a message transmission, we divide the message into several segments. When the job is a computation, we partition the program into procedures, each of which is to be executed nonpreemptively.) In this way, we can reduce the lower bound of f imposed by Eq. (5.1).

For $\mathbf{T} = \{(4, 1), (5, 2, 7), (20, 5)\}$, we can divide each job in $(20, 5)$ into a chain of three slices with execution times 1, 3, and 1. In other words, the task $(20, 5)$ now consists of three subtasks $(20, 1)$, $(20, 3)$ and $(20, 1)$. The resultant system has five tasks for which we can choose the frame size 4. Figure 5–6 shows a cyclic schedule for these tasks. The three original tasks are called T_1, T_2 and T_3, respectively, and the three subtasks of T_3 are called $T_{3,1}$, $T_{3,2}$, and $T_{3,3}$.

You may question why we choose to decompose $(20, 5)$ into three subtasks. To satisfy Eq. (5.1), it suffices for us to partition each job in the task into two slices, one with execution time 3 and the other with execution time 2. However, a look at the schedule in Figure 5–6 shows the necessity of three slices. It would not be possible to fit the two tasks $(20, 3)$ and $(20, 2)$ together with T_1 and T_2 in five frames of size 4. T_1, with a period of 4, must be scheduled in each frame. T_2, with a period of 5, must be scheduled in four out of the five frames. (The fact that the relative deadline of T_2 is 7 does not help.) This leaves one frame with 3 units of time for T_3. The other frames have only 1 unit of time left for T_3. We can schedule two subtasks each with 1 unit of execution time in these frames, but there is no time in any frame for a subtask with execution time 2.

From this example, we see that in the process of constructing a cyclic schedule, we have to make three kinds of design decisions: choosing a frame size, partitioning jobs into slices, and placing slices in the frames. In general, these decisions cannot be made independently. The more slices a job is partitioned into, the higher the context switch and communication overhead. Therefore, we want to partition each job into as few slices as necessary to meet the frame-size constraints. Unfortunately, this goal is not always attainable. There may not be any feasible schedule for the choices of frame size and job slices because it is impossible to pack the large job slices into the frames by their deadlines. In contrast, feasible schedules may exist if we choose smaller job slices. For this reason, we sometimes are forced to partition some jobs into more slices than needed to meet the frame size constraints. We will present in Section 5.8 an algorithm for the construction of good cyclic schedules and will discuss this issue again.

5.4   CYCLIC EXECUTIVES

The clock-driven scheduler described in Figure 5–1 must be modified to accommodate the restriction that scheduling decisions are made only at frame boundaries. The cyclic executive approach is a way. In real-time systems literature, the term "cyclic executive" refers to a scheduler that deterministically interleaves and sequentializes the execution of periodic-tasks on a CPU according to a given cyclic schedule. Each job slice is a procedure. The cyclic executive executes a single do loop. Starting from the beginning of each frame, it executes in turn the slices scheduled in the frame. The flight controller in Figure 1–3 is an example.

Here, we use the term *cyclic executive* in a more general sense to mean a table-driven cyclic scheduler for all types of jobs in a multithreaded system. Similar to the scheduler in Figure 1–3, it makes scheduling decisions only at the beginning of each frame and deterministically interleaves the execution of periodic tasks. However, it allows aperiodic and sporadic jobs to use the time not used by periodic tasks. The pseudocode in Figure 5–7 describes such a cyclic executive on a CPU. The stored table that gives the precomputed cyclic schedule has F entries, where F is the number of frames per major cycle. Each entry (say the kth) lists the names of the job slices that are scheduled to execute in frame k. In Figure 5–7, the entry is denoted by $L(k)$ and is called a *scheduling block*, or simply a block. The current block refers to the list of periodic job slices that are scheduled in the current frame.

In essence, the cyclic executive takes over the processor and executes at each of the clock interrupts, which occur at the beginning of frames. When it executes, the cyclic executive copies the table entry for the current frame into the current block. It then wakes up a job, called periodic task server,[1] and lets the server execute the job slices in the current block. Upon

---

Input: Stored schedule: $L(k)$ for $k = 0, 1, \ldots, F - 1$;
   Aperiodic job queue
Task CYCLIC_EXECUTIVE:
   the current time $t = 0$;
   the current frame $k = 0$;
   do forever
      accept clock interrupt at time tf;
      currentBlock = $L(k)$;
      $t = t + 1$;
      $k = t \bmod F$;
      if the last job is not completed, take appropriate action;
      if any of the slices in currentBlock is not released, take appropriate action;
      wake up the periodic task server to execute the slices in currentBlock;
      sleep until the periodic task server completes;
      while the aperiodic job queue is nonempty,
         wake up the job at the head of the aperiodic job queue;
         sleep until the aperiodic job completes;
         remove the aperiodic job from the queue;
      endwhile;
      sleep until the next clock interrupt;
   enddo;
end CYCLIC_EXECUTIVE

FIGURE 5–7   A table-driven cyclic executive.

---

[1] In a system where periodic tasks never overrun, the periodic task server is not needed; the cyclic executive simply executes the job slices.

the completion of the periodic task server, the cyclic executive wakes up the aperiodic jobs in the aperiodic job queue in turn and allows them to use the remaining time in the frame. The assumption here is that whenever the server or a job completes, the cyclic executive wakes up and executes. Alternatively, the system may have an aperiodic task server, which when awaked executes aperiodic jobs in the aperiodic job queue.

In addition to scheduling, the cyclic executive also checks for overruns at the beginning of each frame. If the last job executed in the previous frame is not complete at that time, the cyclic executive preempts the execution of the job if the last job is an aperiodic job. The job remains in the aperiodic job queue and will be resumed whenever there is time again for aperiodic jobs. If the cyclic executive finds the periodic task server still executing at the time of a clock interrupt, a *frame overrun* occurs; some slice(s) scheduled in the previous frame has executed longer than the time allocated to it by the precomputed cyclic schedule. The cyclic executive takes an appropriate action to recover from this frame overrun. (We will discuss ways to handle frame overruns in Section 5.7.)

After checking for overruns, the cyclic executive makes sure that all the job slices scheduled in the current block are ready for execution and then wakes up the periodic task server to execute them. If there is still time after all the slices in the current block are completed and the aperiodic job queue is nonempty, it lets the job at the head of the aperiodic job queue execute.

To conclude this section, let us examine two important assumptions that we have made here; these assumptions must be valid in order for the cyclic executive to work as intended. The first assumption is the existence of a timer. The timer generates interrupts periodically without intervention. The second assumption is that each timer interrupt is handled by the cyclic executive within a bounded amount of delay. Specifically, either this delay is negligibly small, or at least we know how large it can be and therefore can take this delay into account when we compute the cyclic schedule. As we will see in Chapter 12, both assumptions are valid in most modern operating systems.

5.5 IMPROVING THE AVERAGE RESPONSE TIME OF APERIODIC JOBS

Thus far we have paid no attention to the performance of the scheduler as far as the aperiodic jobs are concerned. They are scheduled in the background after all the job slices with hard deadlines scheduled in each frame are completed. However, the strategy of delaying the execution, and hence the completion, of aperiodic jobs in preference of periodic tasks is not a good one. There is no advantage to completing a job with a hard deadline early. On the other hand, an aperiodic job is released and executed by the system in response to an event. The sooner an aperiodic job completes, the more responsive the system is. For this reason, minimizing the response time of each aperiodic job or the average response time of all the aperiodic jobs is typically one of the design goals of real-time schedulers.

5.5.1 Slack Stealing

A natural way to improve the response times of aperiodic jobs is by executing the aperiodic jobs ahead of the periodic jobs whenever possible. This approach, called *slack stealing*, was originally proposed for priority-driven systems [RaLe]. For the slack-stealing scheme described below to work, every periodic job slice must be scheduled in a frame that ends no later than its deadline. Let the total amount of time allocated to all the slices scheduled in the frame k be x_k. The *slack* (time) available in the frame is equal to $f - x_k$ at the beginning of the frame. If the aperiodic job queue is nonempty at this time, the cyclic executive can let aperiodic jobs execute for this amount of time without causing any job to miss its deadline.

When an aperiodic job executes ahead of slices of periodic tasks, it consumes the slack in the frame. After y units of slack time are used by aperiodic jobs, the available slack is reduced to $f - x_k - y$. The cyclic executive can let aperiodic jobs execute in frame k as long as there is slack, that is, the available slack $f - x_k - y$ in the frame is larger than 0.

When the cyclic executive finds the aperiodic job queue empty, it lets the periodic task server execute the next slice in the current block. The amount of slack remains the same during this execution. As long as there is slack, the cyclic executive returns to examine the aperiodic job queue after each slice completes.

Figure 5–8 gives an illustrative example. Figure 5–8(a) shows the first major cycle in the cyclic schedule of the periodic tasks. Figure 5–8(b) shows three aperiodic jobs A_1, A_2, and A_3. Their release times are immediately before 4, 9.5. and 10.5, and their execution times are 1.5, 0.5 and 2, respectively. Figure 5–8(c) shows when the aperiodic jobs execute if we use the cyclic executive shown in Figure 5–7, which schedules aperiodic jobs after the slices of periodic tasks in each frame are completed. The execution of A_1 starts at time 7. It does not complete at time 8 when the frame ends and is, therefore, preempted. It is resumed at time 10 after both slices in the next frame complete. Consequently, its response time is 6.5. A_2 executes after A_1 completes and has a response time equal to 1.5. Similarly, A_3 follows A_2 and is preempted once and completes at the end of the following frame. The response time of A_3 is 5.5. The average response time of these three jobs is 4.5.

Figure 5–8(d) shows what happens if the cyclic executive does slack stealing. At time 4, the cyclic executive finds A_1 in the aperiodic job queue, and there is 1 unit of slack. Hence it lets A_1 execute. At time 5, there is no more slack. It preempts A_1 and lets the periodic task

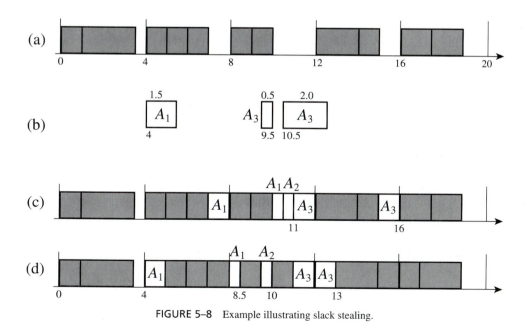

FIGURE 5–8   Example illustrating slack stealing.

server execute the job slices scheduled in the frame. At the beginning of the next frame, the available slack is 2. It resumes A_1, which completes at time 8.5. At the time, the first slice in the current block is executed, since the aperiodic job queue is empty. Upon completion of the slice at time 9.5, the cyclic executive checks the aperiodic job queue again, finds A_2 ready, and lets A_2 execute. When the job completes at time 10, the cyclic executive finds the aperiodic job queue empty and lets the periodic task server execute the next job slice in the current block. At time 11, it finds A_3 and lets the job execute during the last unit of time in the frame, as well as in the beginning of the next frame. The job completes by time 13. According to this schedule, the response times of the jobs are 4.5, 0.5, and 2.5, with an average of 2.5.

Let us now examine how to implement slack stealing. The initial amount of slack in each frame can be precomputed along with the cyclic schedule and stored in the table defining the schedule. It is necessary for the cyclic executive to keep track of the amount of available slack and update this amount as it consumes the slack. This can be done using an interval timer. At the beginning of each frame, the cyclic executive sets the timer to the value of the initial slack in the frame. The timer counts down whenever an aperiodic job executes ahead of any slice in the current block. When the timer expires, indicating that there is no more slack, the cyclic executive preempts the executing aperiodic job and lets the execution of the next job slice in the current block begin. Unfortunately as you will see in Section 12.2.2, most operating systems do not offer interval timers of submillisecond granularity and accuracy. So, this scheme is practical only when the temporal parameters of periodic tasks are in orders of hundreds of milliseconds or seconds.

5.5.2 Average Response Time

While we are not required to ensure the completion of aperiodic jobs by some specific times, we are often required to guarantee that their average response time is no greater than some value. To give this guarantee, we need to be able estimate the average response time of these jobs.

In general, an accurate estimate of the average response time can be found only by simulation and/or measurement. This process is time consuming and can be done only after a large portion of the system is designed and built. On the other hand, we can apply known results in queueing theory to get a rough estimate of the average response time as soon as we know some statistical behavior of the aperiodic jobs. For example, a requirement of the system may be that it must respond satisfactorily as long as the average rate of arrival (i.e., releases) of aperiodic jobs is within a given limit. We can estimate the average response time of the system for this average arrival rate. We also need to know the mean and mean square values of the execution times of aperiodic jobs. These values can be estimated by analysis, simulation, and/or measurement of the jobs' execution by themselves.

To express average response time in terms of these parameters, let us consider a system in which there are n_a aperiodic tasks. (The term aperiodic task was introduced earlier in Chapter 3; each aperiodic task consists of a stream of aperiodic jobs that execute in response to a type of event.) The jobs in each aperiodic task have the same interarrival-time and execution-time distributions and the same response-time requirement. Suppose that the average rate of arrival of aperiodic jobs in the ith aperiodic task is λ_i jobs per unit of time. The sum λ of λ_i over all $i = 1, 2, \ldots a$ is the total number of aperiodic job arrivals per unit of time. The mean and the mean square values of the execution times of jobs in the ith aperiodic task are $E[\beta_i]$

and $E[\beta_i^2]$, respectively. (Here $E[x]$ denotes the mean value of the random variable x. $E[x]$ is also called the expected value of x, hence the choice of the letter E.) Let u_i denote the average utilization of the ith task; it is the average fraction of processor time required by all the jobs in the task. u_i is equal to $\lambda_i E[\beta_i]$. We call the sum U_A of u_i over all aperiodic tasks the *total average utilization of aperiodic tasks*; it is the average fraction of processor time required by all the aperiodic tasks in the system.

Let U be the total utilization of all the periodic tasks. $1 - U$ is the fraction of time that is available for the execution of aperiodic jobs. We call it the *aperiodic (processor) bandwidth*. If the total average utilization of the aperiodic jobs is larger than or equal to the aperiodic bandwidth of the system (i.e., $U_A \geq 1 - U$), the length of the aperiodic job queue and the average response time will grow without bound. Hence we consider here only the case where $U_A < 1 - U$.

When the jobs in all aperiodic tasks are scheduled on the FIFO basis, we can estimate the average response time W (also known as waiting time) of any aperiodic job by the following expression [Klie]:

$$W = \sum_{i=1}^{na} \frac{\lambda_i E[\beta_i]}{\lambda(1 - U)} + \frac{W_0}{(1 - U)^2[1 - U_A/(1 - U)]} \tag{5.4a}$$

where W_0 is given by

$$W_0 = \sum_{i=1}^{na} \frac{\lambda_i E[\beta_i^2]}{2} \tag{5.4b}$$

The first term in Eq. (5.4a) gives the average amount of time required by an aperiodic job to complete execution if it does not wait for any aperiodic job. The second term gives us the average queueing time, which is the average amount of time a job waits in the queue.

Figure 5–9 shows the behavior of the average queueing time, normalized with respect to the average execution time $\sum_{i=1}^{na} \lambda_i E[\beta_i]/\lambda$ of all the aperiodic jobs, as a function of the total average utilization U_A of aperiodic jobs for different values of aperiodic bandwidth $(1 - U)$. The average queueing time is inversely proportional to the square of the aperiodic bandwidth. It remains small for a large range of U_A but increases rapidly and approaches infinity when U_A approaches $(1 - U)$.

We can improve the average response time of some aperiodic tasks at the expense of some others by prioritizing the aperiodic tasks. Without loss of generality, suppose that we index the aperiodic tasks so that the smaller the index, the higher the priority. Instead of one FIFO queue, we put the jobs in each aperiodic task in a separate FIFO queue. The jobs in the queue for the ith aperiodic task are executed only when the queues of all the higher priority aperiodic tasks are empty. We let U_H denote the sum $\sum_{k=1}^{i-1} u_k$; it is the average total utilization of all aperiodic tasks with priority higher than the ith aperiodic task. The average response time W_i of a job in the ith aperiodic task is given by

$$W_i = \frac{E[\beta_i]}{(1 - U)} + \frac{W_0}{(1 - U)^2[1 - U_H/(1 - U)][1 - (U_H + u_i)/(1 - U)]} \tag{5.5}$$

approximately, where W_0 is given by Eq. (5.4b).

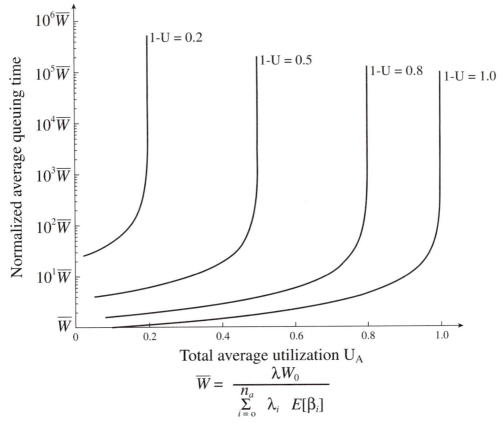

$$\overline{W} = \frac{\lambda W_0}{\sum\limits_{i=0}^{n_a} \lambda_i \; E[\beta_i]}$$

FIGURE 5–9   Average queueing time versus total average utilization.

5.6   SCHEDULING SPORADIC JOBS

Like jobs in periodic tasks, sporadic jobs have hard deadlines. On the other hand, their minimum release times and maximum execution times are unknown a priori. Consequently, it is impossible to guarantee a priori that all sporadic jobs can complete in time.

5.6.1   Acceptance Test

A common way to deal with this situation is to have the scheduler perform an acceptance test when each sporadic job is released. During an *acceptance test*, the scheduler checks whether the newly released sporadic job can be feasibly scheduled with all the jobs in the system at the time. Here, by *a job in the system*, we mean either a periodic job, for which time has already been allocated in the precomputed cyclic schedule, or a sporadic job which has been scheduled but not yet completed. If according to the existing schedule, there is a sufficient amount of time in the frames before its deadline to complete the newly released sporadic job without causing any job in the system to complete too late, the scheduler accepts and schedules the job. Otherwise, the scheduler rejects the new sporadic job. By rejecting a sporadic job that cannot be scheduled to complete in time immediately after the job is released, the scheduler gives the application system as much time as there is to take any necessary recovery action.

To illustrate that this approach is a reasonable one, we consider a quality control system. A sporadic job that activates a robotic arm is released when a defective part is detected. The arm, when activated, removes the part from the conveyor belt. This job must complete before the part moves beyond the reach of the arm. When the job cannot be scheduled to complete in time, it is better for the system to have this information as soon as possible. The system can slow down the belt, stop the belt, or alert an operator to manually remove the part. Otherwise, if the sporadic job were scheduled but completed too late, its lateness would not be detected until its deadline. By the time the system attempts a recovery action, the defective part may already have been packed for shipment, too late for simple recovery actions to be effective.

We assume that the maximum execution time of each sporadic job becomes known upon its release. It is impossible for the scheduler to determine which sporadic jobs to admit and which to reject unless this information is available. Therefore, the scheduler must maintain information on the maximum execution times of all types of sporadic jobs that the system may execute in response to the events it is required to handle. We also assume that all sporadic jobs are preemptable. Therefore, each sporadic job can execute in more than one frame if no frame has a sufficient amount of time to accommodate the entire job.

Conceptually, it is quite simple to do an acceptance test. To explain, let us suppose that at the beginning of frame t, an acceptance test is done on a sporadic job $S(d, e)$, with deadline d and (maximum) execution time e. (When it is not necessary to mention the deadline and execution time of the job, we will simply refer to it as S without these parameters.) Suppose that the deadline d of S is in frame $l+1$ (i.e., frame l ends before d but frame $l+1$ ends after d) and $l \geq t$. Clearly, the job must be scheduled in the lth or earlier frames. The job can complete in time only if the *current (total) amount of slack time* $\sigma_c(t, l)$ in frames $t, t+1, \ldots l$ is equal to or greater than its execution time e. Therefore, the scheduler should reject S if $e > \sigma_c(t, l)$. As we will see shortly, the scheduler may let a new sporadic job execute ahead of some previously accepted sporadic jobs. Therefore, the scheduler also checks whether accepting the new job may cause some sporadic jobs in the system to complete late. The scheduler accepts the new job $S(d, e)$ only if $e \leq \sigma_c(t, l)$ and no sporadic jobs in system are adversely affected.

In general, more than one sporadic job may be waiting to be tested at the same time. A good way to order them is on the Earliest-Deadline-First (EDF) basis. In other words, newly released sporadic jobs are placed in a waiting queue ordered in nondecreasing order of their deadlines: the earlier the deadline, the earlier in the queue. The scheduler always tests the job at the head of the queue and removes the job from the waiting queue after scheduling it or rejecting it.

5.6.2   EDF Scheduling of the Accepted Jobs

By virtue of its optimality, the EDF algorithm is a good way to schedule accepted sporadic jobs. For this purpose, the scheduler maintains a queue of accepted sporadic jobs in nondecreasing order of their deadlines and inserts each newly accepted sporadic job into this queue in this order. Whenever all the slices of periodic tasks scheduled in each frame are completed, the cyclic executive lets the jobs in the sporadic job queue execute in the order they appear

---

Input: Stored schedule: $L(k)$ for $k = 0, 1, \ldots F - 1$;
    Aperiodic job queue, sporadic-job waiting queue, and accepted-sporadic-job EDF queue;
Task CYCLIC_EXECUTIVE:
  the current time $t = 0$;
  the current frame $k = 0$;
  do forever
    accept clock interrupt at time tf;
    currentBlock $= L(k)$;
    $t = t + 1$;
    $k = t \bmod F$;
    if the last job is not completed, take appropriate action;
    if any of the slices in the currentBlock is not released, take appropriate action;
    while the sporadic-job waiting queue is not empty,
      remove the job at the head of the sporadic job waiting queue;
      do an acceptance test on the job;
      if the job is acceptable,
        insert the job into the accepted-sporadic-job queue in the EDF order;
      else, delete the job and inform the application;
    endwhile;
    wake up the periodic task server to execute the slices in currentBlock;
    sleep until the periodic task server completes;
    while the accepted sporadic job queue is nonempty,
      wake up the job at the head of the sporadic job queue;
      sleep until the sporadic job completes;
      remove the sporadic job from the queue;
    endwhile;
    while the aperiodic job queue is nonempty,
      wake up the job at the head of the aperiodic job queue;
      sleep until the aperiodic job completes;
      remove the aperiodic job from the queue;
    endwhile;
    sleep until the next clock interrupt;
  enddo;
end CYCLIC_EXECUTIVE

FIGURE 5–10   A cyclic executive with sporadic and aperiodic job scheduling capability.

in the queue. Figure 5–10 gives a pseudocode description of the modified cyclic executive that integrates the scheduling of sporadic jobs with that of aperiodic and periodic jobs. The cyclic executive assumes that each newly released sporadic job is placed in a waiting queue without the intervention of the scheduler. The scheduler allows aperiodic jobs to execute only when the accepted sporadic job queue is empty. Again, whenever a server or job completes, the cyclic executive wakes up to execute. Like the version in Figure 5–7, this version does not steal slack but can easily be modified to do so.

    Figure 5–11 gives an example. The frame size used here is 4. The shaded boxes show where periodic tasks are scheduled.

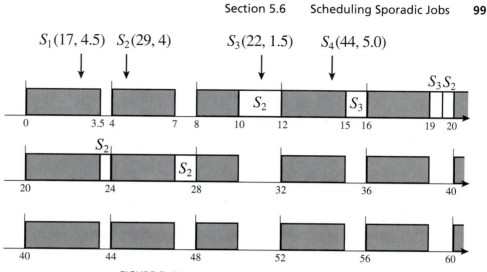

FIGURE 5–11   Example of scheduling sporadic jobs.

- Suppose that at time 3, a sporadic job $S_1(17, 4.5)$ with execution time 4.5 and deadline 17 is released. The acceptance test on this job is done at time 4, that is, the beginning of frame 2. S_1 must be scheduled in frames 2, 3, and 4. In these frames, the total amount of slack time is only 4, which is smaller than the execution time of S_1. Consequently, the scheduler rejects the job.

- At time 5, $S_2(29, 4)$ is released. Frames 3 through 7 end before its deadline. During the acceptance test at 8, the scheduler finds that the total amount of slack in these frames is 5.5. Hence, it accepts S_2. The first part of S_2 with execution time 2 executes in the current frame.

- At time 11, $S_3(22, 1.5)$ is released. At time 12, the scheduler finds 2 units of slack time in frames 4 and 5, where S_3 can be scheduled. Moreover, there still is enough slack to complete S_2 even though S_3 executes ahead of S_2. Consequently, the scheduler accepts S_3. This job executes in frame 4.

- Suppose that at time 14, $S_4(44, 5)$ is released. At time 16 when the acceptance test is done, the scheduler finds only 4.5 units of time available in frames before the deadline of S_4, after it has accounted for the slack time that has already been committed to the remaining portions of S_2 and S_3. Therefore, it rejects S_4. When the remaining portion of S_3 completes in the current frame, S_2 executes until the beginning of the next frame.

- The last portion of S_2 executes in frames 6 and 7.

5.6.3   Implementation of the Acceptance Test

We now describe how to implement the acceptance test when accepted sporadic jobs are scheduled on the EDF basis. Specifically, we focus on an acceptance test at the beginning of frame t to decide whether a sporadic job $S(d, e)$ should be accepted or rejected. The acceptance test consists of the following two steps:

1. The scheduler first determines whether the current total amount of slack in the frames before the deadline of job S is at least equal to the execution time e of S. If the answer is no, it rejects S. If the answer is yes, the second step is carried out.

2. In the second step, the scheduler determines whether any sporadic job in the system will complete late if it accepts S. If the acceptance of S will not cause any sporadic job in the system to complete too late, it accepts S; otherwise, it rejects S.

Again, a sporadic job in the system is one that was accepted earlier but is not yet complete at the time. We note that there is no need to check whether any periodic job might miss its deadline because sporadic jobs in the system never affect the execution of any periodic job slice scheduled in any frame.

To do an acceptance test, the scheduler needs the current total amount of slack time $\sigma_c(i, k)$ in frames i through k for every pair of frames i and k. We can save computation time during run time by precomputing the *initial (total) amounts of slack* $\sigma(i, k)$, for $i, k = 1, 2, \ldots F$ and storing them in a slack table along with the precomputed cyclic schedule at the cost of $O(F^2)$ in storage space. From the initial amounts of slack in the frames in the first major cycle, initial amounts of slack in any later frames can be computed as follows. For any $0 < j < j'$ and any i and k equal to $1, 2, \ldots F$, the initial amount of slack time in frames from frame i in major cycle j through frame k in major cycle j' is given by

$$\sigma(i + (j - 1)F, k + (j' - 1)F) = \sigma(i, F) + \sigma(1, k) + (j - j' - 1)\sigma(1, F)$$

As an example, we look at Figure 5–11 again. For this system, F is 5. Only $\sigma(i, k)$ for $i, k = 1, 2, \ldots, 5$ are stored. To compute the initial amount of slack time $\sigma(3, 14)$ in frames 3 through 14, we note that frame 3 is in the first major cycle (i.e., $j = 1$), and frame 14 is in the third major cycle (i.e., $j' = 3$). The term i in the above formula is equal to 3, and $\sigma(i, F) = \sigma(3, 5) = 4$. Similarly, $k = 4$, and $\sigma(1, 4)$ is 4.5. Since $\sigma(1, F)$ is 5.5, we have $\sigma(3, 14)$ equal to $4 + 4.5 + (3 - 1 - 1) \times 5.5 = 14$.

Suppose that at the beginning of current frame t, there are n_s sporadic jobs in the system. We call these jobs $S_1, S_2, \ldots, S_{n_s}$. Let d_k and e_k denote the deadline and execution time of S_k, respectively, and ξ_k denote the execution time of the portion of S_k that has been completed at the beginning of the current frame. Suppose that the deadline d of the job $S(d, e)$ being tested is in frame $l + 1$. The current total amount of slack time $\sigma_c(t, l)$ in frames t through l can be computed from the initial amount of slack time in these frames according to

$$\sigma_c(t, l) = \sigma(t, l) - \sum_{d_k \leq d}(e_k - \xi_k) \tag{5.6a}$$

The sum in this expression is over all sporadic jobs in the system that have deadlines equal to or less than d. Because the slack time available in these frames must be used to execute the remaining parts of these jobs first, only the amount leftover by them is available to $S(d, e)$.

If S is accepted, the amount of slack σ before its deadline is equal to

$$\sigma = \sigma_c(t, l) - e \tag{5.6b}$$

We say that the job has σ units of slack. Clearly, we can accept S only if its slack σ is no less than zero. If S is accepted, its slack is stored for later use.

Since the accepted jobs are scheduled on the EDF basis, the acceptance of S may cause an existing sporadic job S_k whose deadline is after d to complete too late. Specifically, if S is accepted, the slack σ_k of S_k is reduced by the execution time e of S. If the reduced amount remains to be no less than zero, S_k will not miss its deadline. The scheduler must consider every sporadic job that is still in the system and has a deadline after d. It accepts S only if the reduced slack of every such job is no less than zero.

In summary, the data maintained by the scheduler for the sake of acceptance tests consist of the following:

1. The precomputed slack table whose entry $\sigma(i, k)$ gives the initial total amount of slack time in frames i through k, for every pair of $i, k = 1, 2, \ldots, F$;
2. The execution time ξ_k of the completed portion of every sporadic job S_k in the system at the beginning of the current frame t; and
3. The current slack σ_k of every sporadic job S_k in the system.

Whenever a sporadic job S_k is executed in a frame, the scheduler updates ξ_k at end of the frame. The slack time of a sporadic job S is given by Eq. (5.6b) when the job is accepted. Later whenever a new sporadic job with an earlier deadline is accepted, the slack of S is decremented by the execution time of the new sporadic job. The complexity of this update operation, as well as the computation needed to accept or reject each sporadic job, is $O(N_s)$ where N_s is the maximum number of sporadic jobs in the system.

We conclude this section with the old example in Figure 5–11 and run through the acceptance tests of the sporadic jobs, following the procedure described above.

1. At time 4 when the scheduler checks whether $S_1(17, 4.5)$ can be accepted, it finds that the slack $\sigma(2, 4)$ in frames before the deadline of S_1 is only 4. Hence, it rejects the job.
2. At time 8, when the scheduler tests $S_2(29, 4)$, the current slack $\sigma_c(3, 7)$ in frames 3 through 7 is equal to $\sigma(3, 5) + \sigma(1, 2) = 4 + 1.5 = 5.5$. This amount is larger than the execution time of S_2. Since there is no other sporadic job in the system, the fact that S_2 passes this step suffices, and the scheduler accepts S_2. The slack σ_2 of S_2 is 1.5.
3. At time 12 when the scheduler tests $S_3(22, 1.5)$, the slack σ_2 of S_2 is still 1.5. There is no sporadic job with deadline before 20, the end of the frame before 22. Hence, the sum on the right-hand side of Eq. (5.6a) is 0, and the current slack $\sigma_c(4, 5)$ before 22 is equal to $\sigma(4, 5) = 2$. Since $2 > 1.5$, S_3 passes the first step of its acceptance test. The acceptance of S_3 would reduce σ_2 to 0. Therefore, S_3 is acceptable. When S_3 is accepted, its slack σ_3 is 0.5, and σ_2 is 0.
4. At time 16, when the acceptance test on $S_4(44, 5.0)$ is performed, ξ_2 is 2 and ξ_3 is 1.0. The current slack time $\sigma_c(5, 11)$ in the frames before 44 is $7 - 2 - 0.5 = 4.5$ according to Eq. (5.6a). Since this slack is insufficient to complete S_4 by time 44, the scheduler rejects S_4.

We call the scheme described above the *cyclic EDF* algorithm.

5.6.4 Optimality of Cyclic EDF Algorithm

We have claimed that the cyclic EDF algorithm is good. Now is the time to ask just how good it is. To answer this question, we first compare it only with the class of algorithms that perform acceptance tests at the beginnings of frames. The cyclic EDF algorithm is optimal in the following sense: As long as the given string of sporadic jobs is schedulable (i.e., all the jobs can be accepted and scheduled to complete by their deadlines) by any algorithm in this class, the EDF algorithm can always find a feasible schedule of the jobs. This statement follows directly from Theorem 4.1 on the optimality of the EDF algorithm.

However, the cyclic EDF algorithm is not optimal when compared with algorithms that perform acceptance tests at arbitrary times. If we choose to use an interrupt-driven scheduler which does an acceptance test upon the release of each sporadic job, we should be able to do better. The example in Figure 5–11 illustrates this fact. Suppose that the scheduler were to interrupt the execution of the job slices in frame 1 and do an acceptance test at time 3 when $S_1(17, 4.5)$ is released. It would find an additional 0.5 units of slack in frame 1, making it possible to accept S_1. Because it waits until time 4 to do the acceptance test, the 0.5 unit of slack time in frame 1 is wasted. Consequently, it cannot accept S_1.

However, the advantage of the interrupt-driven alternative is outweighed by a serious shortcoming: It increases the danger for periodic-job slices to complete late. Because the release times of sporadic jobs are unpredictable, the execution of periodic job slices may be delayed by an unpredictable number of the context switches and acceptance tests in the middle of each frame. Because of this shortcoming, it is better to stay within the cyclic scheduling framework and make scheduling decisions, including acceptance tests, only at the beginning of the frames.

The cyclic EDF algorithm for scheduling sporadic jobs is an on-line algorithm. You recall from our discussion in Section 4.9 that we measure the merit of an on-line algorithm by the value (i.e., the total execution time of all the accepted jobs) of the schedule produced by it: the higher the value, the better the algorithm. At any scheduling decision time, without prior knowledge on when the future jobs will be released and what their parameters will be, it is not always possible for the scheduler to make an optimal decision. Therefore, it is not surprising that the cyclic EDF algorithm is not optimal in this sense when some job in the given string of sporadic jobs must be rejected. In the example in Figure 5–11, because the scheduler has already accepted and scheduled S_3 at time 12, it must reject S_4. The value of the schedule of these four sporadic jobs is only 5.5, instead of the maximum possible value of 9 obtained by rejecting S_3 and accepting S_4. If we were to modify the scheduling algorithm so that the scheduler rejects S_3, the value of the resultant schedule is again less than the maximum possible if S_4 is not released later or if its execution time is less than 1.5.

5.7   PRACTICAL CONSIDERATIONS AND GENERALIZATIONS

Thus far, we have ignored many practical problems, such as how to handle frame overruns, how to do mode changes, and how to schedule tasks on multiprocessor systems. We discuss them now.

5.7.1   Handling Frame Overruns

A frame overrun can occur for many reasons. For example, when the execution time of a job is input data dependent, it can become unexpectedly large for some rare combination of input values which is not taken into account in the precomputed schedule. A transient hardware fault in the system may cause some job to execute longer than expected. A software flaw that was undetected during debugging and testing can also cause this problem. There are many ways to handle a frame overrun. Which one is the most appropriate depends on the application and the reason for the overrun.

A way to handle overruns is to simply abort the overrun job at the beginning of the next frame and log the premature termination of the job. Such a fault can then be handled by some recovery mechanism later when necessary. This way seems attractive for applications where late results are no longer useful. An example is the control-law computation of a robust digital controller. When the computation completes late or terminates prematurely, the result it produces is erroneous. On the other hand, as long as such errors occur infrequently, the erroneous trajectory of the controlled system remains sufficiently close to its correct trajectory. In this case, we might as well terminate the computation if it does not complete in time.

However, premature termination of overrun jobs may put the system in some inconsistent state, and the actions required to recover from the state and maintain system integrity may be costly. For this reason, in most real-life systems, a job that overruns its allocated time and is found executing at the end of the frame is preempted immediately, if it is not in a critical section at the time, or as soon as it exits the critical section, if it is. The unfinished portion executes as an aperiodic job during the slack time in the subsequent frame(s) or in the background whenever there is spare time.

Another way to handle an overrun is to continue to execute the offending job. The start of the next frame and the execution of jobs scheduled in the next frame are then delayed. Letting a late job postpone the execution and completion of jobs scheduled after it can in turn cause these jobs to be late. This way is appropriate only if the late result produced by the job is nevertheless useful, and an occasional late completion of a periodic job is acceptable.

5.7.2 Mode Changes

As stated earlier, the number n of periodic tasks in the system and their parameters remain constant as long as the system stays in the same (operation) mode. During a *mode change*, the system is reconfigured. Some periodic tasks are deleted from the system because they will not execute in the new mode. Periodic tasks that execute in the new mode but not in the old mode are created and added to the system. The periodic tasks that execute in both modes continue to execute in a timely fashion. When the mode change completes, the new set of periodic tasks are scheduled and executed.

We assume that the parameters of periodic tasks to be executed in the new mode are also known. The schedule of the tasks executed in the new mode is also precomputed. However, the new schedule table may not be in memory during the old mode. This table must be brought into memory. Similarly, the code of the new tasks must be brought into memory and memory space for data accessed by them must be allocated before their execution begins. The work to configure the system is a mode-change job; the job is released in response to a mode-change command. We need to consider two cases: The mode-change job has either a soft or hard deadline. In both cases, we assume that periodic tasks are independent and hence can be added and deleted independently. We will return in Section 8.11 to discuss how a mode changer should work when this assumption is not true.

Aperiodic Mode Change.   A reasonable way to schedule a mode-change job that has a soft deadline is to treat it just like an ordinary aperiodic job, except that it may be given the highest priority and executed ahead of other aperiodic jobs. Once the job begins to execute, however, it may modify the old schedule in order to speed up the mode change. A periodic task that will not execute in the new mode can be deleted and its memory space and processor time freed as soon as the current job in the task completes. This scheme can be implemented by letting the scheduler or the mode-change job mark each periodic task that is to be deleted. During mode change, the scheduler continues to use the old schedule table. Before the periodic task server begins to execute a periodic job, however, it checks whether the corresponding task is marked and returns immediately if the task is marked. In this way, the schedule of the periodic tasks that execute in both modes remain unchanged during mode change, but the time allocated to the deleted task can be used to execute the mode-change job. Once the new schedule table and code of the new tasks are in memory, the scheduler can switch to use the new table.

A question that remains to be answered is how aperiodic and sporadic jobs in the system should be dealt with during mode changes. It may no longer be safe to execute some of these jobs; they should be deleted as well. Since the deadlines of the remaining aperiodic jobs are soft, their execution can be delayed until after the mode change. On the other hand, the sporadic jobs should not be affected by the mode change, since their on-time completion has been guaranteed. One way to ensure their on-time completion is to defer the switchover from the old schedule table to the new schedule table until all the sporadic jobs in the system complete. Clearly this option can lengthen the response time of the mode change. Another option is have the mode-change job check whether the sporadic jobs in the system can complete in time according to the new schedule. The schedule switchover is deferred only when some sporadic job cannot complete in time according to the new schedule. In the case when the delay thus introduced is unacceptably long, the scheduler may be forced to switchover to the new schedule, let some sporadic jobs complete late, and leave the affected applications to handle the timing faults.

As a summary of our discussion, Figure 5–12 describes a mode changer. It assumes that in addition to the precomputed schedule of each mode, the lists of new tasks to be created and old tasks to be deleted are available for every possible pair of old and new modes. The scheduler is a cyclic executive which executes accepted sporadic jobs on the EDF basis and the mode changer at the highest priority among all aperiodic jobs. When informed of a mode change, the cyclic executive stops to perform acceptance tests. In addition, it checks for periodic tasks to be deleted and executes the mode changer during the times allocated to the deleted periodic tasks. Finally, when the new schedule and all the new tasks are in memory, it switches over to use the new schedule table at the beginning of the next major cycle and resumes doing acceptance tests.

Sporadic Mode Change.   A sporadic mode change has to be completed by a hard deadline. There are two possible approaches to scheduling this job. We can treat it like an ordinary sporadic job and schedule it as described in Section 5.6. This approach can be used only if the application can handle the rejection of the job. Specifically, if the mode-change job is not schedulable and is therefore rejected, the application can either postpone the mode change or take some alternate action. In this case, we can use mode changer described in Figure 5–12.

---

task MODE_CHANGER (oldMode, newMode):
    fetch the deleteList of periodic tasks to be deleted;
    mark each periodic task in the deleteList;
    inform the cyclic executive that a mode change has commenced;
    fetch the newTaskList of periodic tasks to be executed in newMode;
    allocate memory space for each task in newTaskList and create each of these task;
    fetch the newSchedule;
    perform acceptance test on each sporadic job in the system according to the newSchedule,
    if every sporadic job in system can complete on time according to the newSchedule,
      inform the cyclic executive to use the newSchedule;
      else,
        compute the latestCompletionTime of all sporadic jobs in system;
        inform the cyclic executive to use the newSchedule at
          max (latestCompletionTime, thresholdTime);
End Mode_Changer

FIGURE 5–12   A mode changer.

As an example, when a computer-controlled bulldozer moves to the pile of hazardous waste, the mode change to slow down its forward movement and carry out the digging action should complete in time; otherwise the bulldozer will crash into the pile. If this mode change cannot be made in time, an acceptable alternative action is for the bulldozer to stop completely. The time required by the controller to generate the command for the stop action is usually much shorter, and the sporadic job to stop the bulldozer is more likely to be acceptable.

On the other hand, the action to stop the bulldozer cannot be postponed. The scheduler must admit and schedule the job to activate the brakes in time. In general, the mode changer in Figure 5–12 cannot be used when a sporadic mode change cannot be rejected. The only alternative is to schedule each sporadic mode-change job that cannot be rejected periodically, with a period no greater than half the maximum allowed response time. The flight control system in Figure 1–3 is an example. The mode selection task is polled at 30 Hz. In this example, a mode change does not involve deletion and creation of tasks, only changes in the input data. The time required by the mode selection task is very small and is allocated to the task periodically. In general, the (maximum) execution time of a sporadic mode-change job may be large. Setting aside a significant amount of processor bandwidth for it leads to a reduction in the processing capacity available for periodic tasks. However, this is not a problem as long as the other periodic tasks are schedulable. The cyclic executive described in earlier sections reclaims the time allocated to but not used by the mode-change task and uses the time to execute aperiodic jobs.

5.7.3   General Workloads and Multiprocessor Scheduling

It is probably obvious to you that the clock-driven approach is equally applicable to other types of workload, not just those executed on a CPU. For example, a bus arbitrator can use a scheduler similar to the one in Figure 5–7 to interleave the data transmissions from different I/O devices on a system bus.

The clock-driven approach is applicable to workloads that are not characterizable by the periodic task model. As long as the parameters of the jobs are known a priori, a static schedule can be computed off-line. Precedence constraints and other types of dependencies and contentions for resources among jobs constrain when the jobs may be scheduled relative to each other. The algorithms used to search for a feasible schedule can take these constraints into account. Once a feasible schedule is found and stored as a table, the static scheduler described in Figure 5–2 can use the table in the same manner as schedule tables of periodic tasks.

It is conceptually straightforward to schedule tasks on several processors whenever the workload parameters are known a priori and there is a global clock. We can construct a global schedule which specifies on what processor each job executes and when the job executes. As long as the clock drifts on the processors are sufficiently small, we can use the uniprocessor schedulers described in earlier sections on each processor to enforce the execution of the jobs according to the global schedule.

Sometimes, a precomputed multiprocessor schedule can be found straightforwardly from a precomputed uniprocessor schedule. As an example, Figure 5–13(a) shows a system containing several CPUs connected by a system bus. Each task consists of a chain of jobs, which executes on one of the CPUs and sends or receives data from one of the I/O devices via the system bus. In a system with such an architecture, the system bus is sometimes the bottleneck. By the bus being the bottleneck, we mean that if there is a feasible schedule of all the data transfer activities on the bus, it is always possible to feasibly schedule the jobs that send and receive the data on the respective CPUs. To illustrate, Figure 5–13(b) shows a cyclic schedule of the data-transfer activities on the bus and the schedules of CPUs and I/O device interfaces that produce and consume the data. The shaded boxes on the time lines of CPUS1 and CPUS2 show when the CPUs execute in order to produce and consume the data that occupy the bus in time intervals shown by shaded boxes on the time line of the bus. Similarly, the CPUD is the producer of the data transferred to an I/O device during intervals shown as dotted boxed on the bus time line. We can see that the schedules of the CPUs and I/O devices can be derived directly from the schedule of the bus. Computing the schedule for the entire system is simplified to computing the schedule of the system bus. This example is based on the Boeing 777 Airplane Information Management System (AIMS) [DrHo]. The system uses a table-driven system bus protocol. The protocol controls the timing of all data transfers. The intervals when the bus interface unit of each CPU must execute (and hence when each CPU must execute) are determined by the schedule of the system bus in a manner illustrated by this example.

In general, searching for a feasible multiprocessor schedule is considerably more complex than searching for a uniprocessor schedule. However, since the search is done off-line, we can use exhaustive and complex heuristic algorithms for this purpose. The next section presents a polynomial time hueristic algorithm for this purpose.

*5.8   ALGORITHM FOR CONSTRUCTING STATIC SCHEDULES

The general problem of choosing a minor frame length for a given set of periodic tasks, segmenting the tasks if necessary, and scheduling the tasks so that they meet all their deadlines is NP-hard. Here, we first consider the special case where the periodic tasks contain no nonpreemptable section. After presenting a polynomial time solution for this case, we then discuss how to take into account practical factors such as nonpreemptivity.

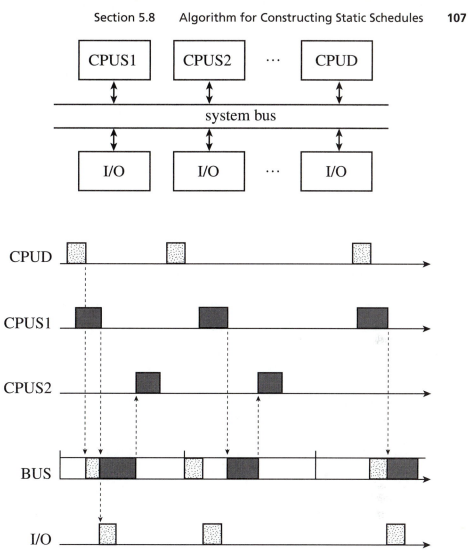

FIGURE 5–13   A simple clock-driven multiprocessor schedule.

5.8.1 Scheduling Independent Preemptable Tasks

We will prove later in Section 6.3 that a system of independent, preemptable periodic tasks whose relative deadlines are equal to or greater than their respective periods is schedulable if and only if the total utilization of the tasks is no greater than 1. Because some tasks may have relative deadlines shorter than their periods and the cyclic schedule is constrained to have the structure described earlier, a feasible schedule may not exist even when this condition is met. The iterative algorithm described below enables us to find a feasible cyclic schedule if one exists. The algorithm is called the *iterative network-flow algorithm*, or the *INF algorithm* for short. Its key assumptions are that tasks can be preempted at any time and are independent. (We note that the latter assumption imposes no restriction. Because we work with jobs' effective release times and deadlines, which were defined in Section 4.5, we can temporarily ignore all the precedence constraints.)

Before applying the INF algorithm on the given system of periodic tasks, we find all the possible frame sizes of the system: These frame sizes met the constraints of Eqs. (5.2) and (5.3) but not necessarily satisfy Eq. (5.1). [For example, the possible frame sizes of tasks $T_1 = (4, 1)$, $T_2 = (5, 2, 7)$, and $T_3 = (20, 5)$ are 2 and 4. They satisfy Eqs. (5.2) and (5.3), but not Eq. (5.1).] The INF algorithm iteratively tries to find a feasible cyclic schedule of the system for a possible frame size at a time, starting from the largest possible frame size in order of decreasing frame size. A feasible schedule thus found tells us how to decompose some tasks into subtasks if their decomposition is necessary. If the algorithm fails to find a feasible schedule after all the possible frame sizes have been tried, the given tasks do not have a feasible cyclic schedule that satisfies the frame size constraints even when tasks can be decomposed into subtasks.

Network-Flow Graph.   The algorithm used during each iteration is based on the well-known network-flow formulation [Blas] of the preemptive scheduling problem. In the description of this formulation, it is more convenient to ignore the tasks to which the jobs belong and name the jobs to be scheduled in a major cycle of F frames $J_1, J_2, \ldots, J_N$. The constraints on when the jobs can be scheduled are represented by the *network-flow graph* of the system. This graph contains the following vertices and edges; the capacity of an edge is a nonnegative number associated with the edge.

1. There is a *job vertex* J_i representing each job J_i, for $i = 1, 2, \ldots, N$.
2. There is a *frame vertex* named j representing each frame j in the major cycle, for $j = 1, 2, \ldots, F$.
3. There are two special vertices named *source* and *sink*.
4. There is a directed edge (J_i, j) from a job vertex J_i to a frame vertex j if the job J_i can be scheduled in the frame j, and the *capacity* of the edge is the frame size f.
5. There is a directed edge from the *source* vertex to every job vertex J_i, and the capacity of this edge is the execution time e_i of the job.
6. There is a directed edge from every frame vertex to the *sink*, and the capacity of this edge is f.

A *flow of an edge* is a nonnegative number that satisfies the following constraints: (1) It is no greater than the capacity of the edge and (2) with the exception of the *source* and *sink*, the sum of the flows of all the edges into every vertex is equal to the sum of the flows of all the edges out of the vertex.

Figure 5–14 shows part of a network-flow graph. For simplicity, only job vertices J_i and J_k are shown. The label "(capacity), flow" of the each edge gives its capacity and flow. This graph indicates that job J_i can be scheduled in frames x and y and the job J_k can be scheduled in frames y and z.

A *flow of a network-flow graph*, or simply a flow, is the sum of the flows of all the edges from the *source*; it should equal to the sum of the flows of all the edges into the *sink*. There are many algorithms for finding the maximum flows of network-flow graphs. The time complexity of straightforward ones is $O((N + F)^3)$. One of the fastest is by Goldberg [Gold].

Jobs   Frames

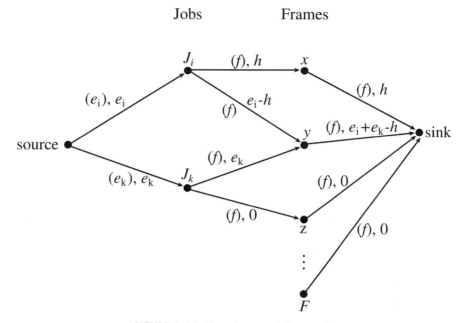

FIGURE 5–14   Part of a network-flow graph.

Its worst-case run time complexity is pseudopolynomial in the length of the major cycle F, but on average, it can find a maximum flow in a much shorter time.

Maximum Flow and Feasible Preemptive Schedule.   Clearly, the maximum flow of a network-flow graph defined above is at most equal to the sum of the execution times of all the jobs to be scheduled in a major cycle. The set of flows of edges from job vertices to frame vertices that gives this maximum flow represents a feasible preemptive schedule of the jobs in the frames. Specifically, *the flow of an edge* (J_i, j) *from a job vertex* J_i *to a frame vertex* j *gives the amount of time in frame* j *allocated to job* J_i. (For example, the flows in Figure 5–14 indicate that the job J_i is allocated h units of time in frame x and $e_i - h$ units of time in frame y and that it shares the frame y with J_k.) The total amount of time allocated to a job J_i is represented by the total flow out of all the edges from the job vertex J_i. Since this amount is equal to the flow into J_i, this amount is e_i. Since the flow of the only edge out of every frame vertex is at most f, the total amount of time in every frame allocated to all jobs is at most f.

As an example, we again look at the tasks $T_1 = (4, 1)$, $T_2 = (5, 2, 7)$, and $T_3 = (20, 5)$. The possible frame sizes are 4 and 2. The network-flow graph used in the first iteration is shown in Figure 5–15. The frame size is 4. We want every job slice to be scheduled in a frame which begins no sooner than its release time and ends no later than its deadline. This is reason for the edges from the job vertices to the frame vertices. The maximum flow of this graph is 18, which is the total execution time of all jobs in a hyperperiod. Hence the flows of edges from the job vertices to the frame vertices represent a schedule of the tasks, in particular, the schedule shown in Figure 5–6.

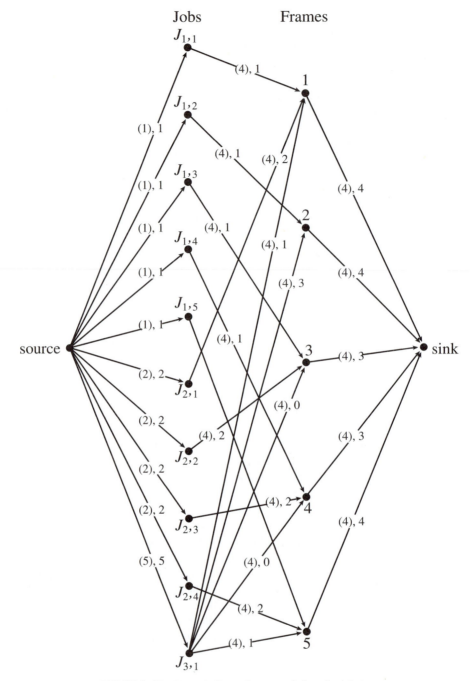

FIGURE 5–15 Example illustrating network-flow formulation.

It is possible that the maximum flow of a network-flow graph is less than the sum of the execution times of all N jobs. This fact indicates that the given tasks have no feasible schedule with the frame size used to generate the graph. For example, the possible frame sizes of tasks $T_1 = (4, 3)$ and $T_2 = (6, 1.5)$ are also 4 and 2. During the first iteration when we try to find a schedule using frame size 4, we find that the maximum flow is only 11, while the total execution time of all jobs in each hyperperiod is 12. (This is because both jobs in T_2 cannot be scheduled in the second frame.) Hence, there is no feasible schedule with frame size 4. We must carry out the second iteration using frame size 2, making it necessary to segment every job into two slices.

Generalization to Arbitrary Release Times and Deadlines. By the way, the network-flow formulation of the preemptive scheduling problem can easily be generalized to find schedules of independent jobs that have arbitrary known release times and deadlines. In this case, the release times and deadlines of all N jobs to be scheduled partition the time from the earliest release time to the latest deadline into at most $2N - 1$ intervals. Rather than frame vertices, the network-flow graph for this problem has a vertex representing each of these intervals. The capacity of each edge into or out of an interval vertex is equal to the length of the interval represented by the vertex. Again, a set of flows that gives the maximum flow equal to the total execution times of all the jobs represents a preemptive schedule of the job.

5.8.2 Postprocessing

The feasible schedule found by the INF algorithm may not meet some of the constraints that are imposed on the cyclic schedule. Examples are precedence order of jobs and restrictions on preemptions. Precedence constraints among jobs can easily be taken into account as follows. You recall that we work with the effective release time and deadline of each job. The network-flow graph for each possible frame size is generated based on the assumption that the jobs are independent. Hence, the jobs may be scheduled in some wrong order according to a feasible schedule found by the INF algorithm. We can always transform the schedule into one that meets the precedence constraints of the jobs by swapping the time allocations of jobs that are scheduled in the wrong order. In Section 4.5 we discussed why this swapping can always be done.

We can try to transform a feasible preemptive schedule produced by the INF algorithm into one that satisfies constraints on the number of preemptions and times of preemptions. Unfortunately, there is no efficient optimal algorithm to do this transformation. This is not surprising since the problem of finding a feasible nonpreemptive schedule of jobs with different release times and deadlines is NP-hard, even on one processor.

5.9 PROS AND CONS OF CLOCK-DRIVEN SCHEDULING

The clock-driven approach to scheduling has many advantages. The most important one is its conceptual simplicity. We can take into account complex dependencies, communication delays, and resource contentions among jobs in the choice and construction of the static schedule, making sure there will be no deadlock and unpredictable delays. A static schedule can be represented by a table of start times and completion times that is interpreted by the scheduler at run time. By changing the table, jobs can be scheduled according to different static schedules in different operation modes. There is no need for concurrency control. Precedence constraints and other types of dependency can be taken care of by the choice of the schedule. Hence, there is no need for any synchronization mechanism. Some applications have tight completion-time jitter requirements. Again, such requirements can be taken into account in the choice of the cyclic schedule.

When the workload is mostly periodic and the schedule is cyclic, timing constraints can be checked and enforced at each frame boundary. Context switching and communication overhead can be kept low by choosing as large a frame size as possible so as many jobs as possible can execute from start to finish without interruption. This is a good scheduling strategy for applications where variations in time and resource requirements are small. Many traditional real-time applications (e.g., the patient care system and the flight control system mentioned in Sections 1.1 and 1.2) are examples.

There are many ways to simplify clock-driven scheduling further from what we have described. Here, we have allowed the periods of periodic tasks to be arbitrary. Moreover, we have allowed the releases of the sporadic and aperiodic jobs to be *event-triggered* [Kope]. The system invokes aperiodic and sporadic computations, communications, I/O operations, and so on, in response to external events which can occur at any time. In practice, systems based on the clock-driven scheduling paradigm are typically *time-triggered*. In a time-triggered system, interrupts in response to external events are queued and polled periodically. The periods are chosen to be integer multiples of the frame size. This design choice simplifies the construction of the static schedules and eliminates the waste in slack time. The system and its static schedule(s) can be simplified further if the periods of periodic tasks are chosen to be harmonic, as exemplified by the flight controller in Figure 1–3.

Time-triggered systems based on the clock-driven scheduling approach are relatively easy to validate, test, and certify. Because the times when jobs execute are deterministic, a system scheduled in this manner will not exhibit the kind of anomalies described in Section 4.8. For this reason, it is possible to determine whether the system indeed meets all of its timing requirements by exhaustive simulation and testing.

However, the clock-driven approach also has many disadvantages. The most obvious one is that a system based on this approach is brittle: It is relatively difficult to modify and maintain. For example, an enhancement that leads to changes in execution times of some tasks or the addition of new tasks often requires that a new schedule be constructed. Consequently, the approach is suited only for systems (e.g., small embedded controllers) which are rarely modified once built.

Other disadvantages include the ones listed below.

1. The release times of all jobs must be fixed. In contrast, priority-driven algorithms do not require fixed release times. We will see in Chapter 6 that we can guarantee the timely completion of every job in a priority-driven system as long as the interrelease times of all jobs in each periodic task are never less than the period of the task. This relaxation of the release-time jitter requirement often eliminates the need for global clock synchronization and permits more design choices.

2. In a clock-driven system, all combinations of periodic tasks that might execute at the same time must be known a priori so a schedule for the combination can be precomputed. This restriction is clearly not acceptable for applications which must be recon-

figurable on-line and the mix of periodic tasks cannot be predicted in advance. As we will see in the next chapter, a priority-driven system does not have this restriction. We can vary the number and parameters of periodic tasks in the system provided we subject each new periodic task to an on-line acceptance test.

3. The pure clock-driven approach is not suitable for many systems that contain both hard and soft real-time applications. You may have noticed that the methods for scheduling aperiodic and sporadic tasks in the midst of periodic tasks described in earlier sections in fact schedule the aperiodic and sporadic tasks in a priority-driven manner.

5.10 SUMMARY

This chapter described clock-driven schedulers that schedule periodic tasks according to some cyclic schedule. To use this type of scheduler, the number of periodic tasks and the parameters of the tasks in the system at all times must be known a priori. Each cyclic schedule used by the scheduler is computed off-line based on this information and stored as a table for use by the scheduler at run time.

It is desirable for cyclic schedules to satisfy the frame size constraints (5.1), (5.2), and (5.3). According to such a schedule, scheduling decisions are made at the beginning of each frame. The execution of every job starts in a frame which begins after the release time of the job. Similarly, every job is scheduled to complete in a frame which ends before the deadline of the job. Hence, at the beginning of each frame, the scheduler can verify that all jobs whose deadlines are earlier than that time have indeed completed and that all jobs which are scheduled in the current frame have indeed been released. The scheduler takes appropriate recovery action if any of these conditions are not satisfied.

Aperiodic jobs can be scheduled in the background after the periodic jobs scheduled in each frame have completed. Alternatively, we can improve the average response time of aperiodic jobs by scheduling them in the slack in each frame, that is, ahead of the periodic job slices for as long as there is slack in the frame.

Similarly, sporadic jobs are also scheduled during the slack times not used by periodic job slices in the frames. A sporadic job S is accepted only when (1) the total slack time not used by periodic job slices and existing sporadic jobs in frames before its deadline is no less than the execution time of the sporadic job S and (2) the slack of every existing sporadic job which has a later deadline than S is no less than execution time of S. Once a sporadic job is accepted, it is scheduled among all sporadic jobs in the EDF order during the time intervals not used by periodic jobs slices.

EXERCISES

5.1 Each of the following systems of periodic tasks is scheduled and executed according to a cyclic schedule. For each system, choose an appropriate frame size. Preemptions are allowed, but the number of preemptions should be kept small.

    (a) (6, 1), (10, 2), and (18, 2).

    (b) (8, 1), (15, 3), (20, 4), and (22, 6).

    (c) (4, 0.5), (5, 1.0), (10, 2), and (24, 9).

      (d) $(5, 0.1)$, $(7, 1.0)$, $(12, 6)$, and $(45, 9)$.

      (e) $(9, 5.1, 1, 5.1)$, $(8, 1)$, $(13, 3)$, and $(0.5, 22, 7, 22)$.

      (f) $(7, 5, 1, 5)$, $(9, 1)$, $(12, 3)$, and $(0.5, 23, 7, 21)$.

      (g) $(10, 1, 12)$, $(15, 1.5, 11)$, $(21, 12, 15)$, and $(32, 4, 24)$.

5.2 A system uses the cyclic EDF algorithm to schedule sporadic jobs. The cyclic schedule of periodic tasks in the system uses a frame size of 5, and a major cycle contains 6 frames. Suppose that the initial amounts of slack time in the frames are 1, 0.5, 0.5, 0.5, 1, and 1.

      (a) Suppose that a sporadic job $S_1(23, 1)$ arrives in frame 1, sporadic jobs $S_2(16, 0.8)$ and $S_3(20, 0.5)$ arrive in frame 2. In which frame are the accepted sporadic jobs scheduled?

      (b) Suppose that an aperiodic job with execution time 3 arrives at time 1. When will it be completed, if the system does not do slack stealing?

5.3 Draw a network-flow graph that we can use to find a preemptive cyclic schedule of the periodic tasks $T_1 = (3, 1, 7)$, $T_2 = (4, 1)$, and $T_3 = (6, 2.4, 8)$.

5.4 A system contains the following periodic tasks: $T_1 = (5, 1)$, $T_2 = (7, 1, 9)$, $T_3 = (10, 3)$, and $T_4 = (35, 7)$.

      (a) If the frame size constraint (5-1) is ignored, what are the possible frame sizes?

      (b) Use the largest frame size you have found in part (a), draw the network-flow graph of the system.

      (c) Find a cyclic schedule by solving the network-flow problem in part (b) or show that the system cannot be feasibly scheduled according to a cyclic schedule of the frame size used in part (b).

C H A P T E R   6

Priority-Driven Scheduling of Periodic Tasks

This chapter describes well-known priority-driven algorithms for scheduling periodic tasks on a processor and examines the merits and limitations of these algorithms. It is the first of three chapters devoted to priority-driven scheduling on one processor of applications characterizable by the periodic task model. The simplifying assumptions made in this chapter are that

1. the tasks are independent and
2. there are no aperiodic and sporadic tasks.

In the next chapter we will describe ways to integrate the scheduling of aperiodic and sporadic tasks with periodic tasks. In Chapter 8, we will introduce other resources and discuss the effects of resource contention. We will also describe resource access-control protocols designed to keep bounded the delay in job completion caused by resource contentions.

In most of this chapter, we will confine our attention to the case where every job is ready for execution as soon as it is released, can be preempted at any time, and never suspends itself. Scheduling decisions are made immediately upon job releases and completions. Moreover, the context switch overhead is negligibly small compared with execution times of the tasks, and the number of priority levels is unlimited. At the end of the chapter, we will remove these restrictions and discuss the effects of these and other practical factors.

Since there will be no ambiguity in this chapter, we often refer to periodic tasks simply as tasks. We now remove the restrictive assumption on fixed interrelease times which we made in Chapter 5. Hereafter we again use the term *period* to mean *the minimum interrelease time* of jobs in a task, as the term was defined in Chapter 3.

Most of our discussion is in terms of a fixed number of periodic tasks. The assumption here is that some protocol is used to regulate changes in the number or parameters of periodic tasks. In particular, when an application creates a new task, the application first requests the scheduler to add the new task by providing the scheduler with relevant parameters of the task, including its period, execution time, and relative deadline. Based on these parameters, the scheduler does an acceptance test on the new periodic task. In this test, the scheduler uses one of the methods described in this chapter to determine whether the new task can be feasibly scheduled with all the other existing tasks in the system. It accepts and adds the new task to the system only if the new task and all other existing tasks can be feasibly scheduled. Otherwise, the scheduler rejects the new task. (We assume that the application system deals with the rejections of new task requests and recovers in an application-dependent way.) When tasks are independent, the scheduler can delete any task and add an acceptable task at any time without causing any missed deadline. Later in Chapter 8 and 9, we will consider periodic tasks that share resources and have precedence constraints. Such tasks cannot be added and deleted at any time. We will describe a mode change protocol that tries to complete task additions and deletions as soon as possible.

6.1 STATIC ASSUMPTION

Again, these three chapters focus on uniprocessor systems. You may question why we examine the problems of uniprocessor scheduling and synchronization in so much detail when most real-time systems today and in the future contain more than one processor. To answer this question, we recall that a multiprocessor priority-driven system is either dynamic or static. In a static system, all the tasks are partitioned into subsystems. Each subsystem is assigned to a processor, and tasks on each processor are scheduled by themselves. In contrast, in a dynamic system, jobs ready for execution are placed in one common priority queue and dispatched to processors for execution as the processors become available.

The dynamic approach should allow the processors to be more fully utilized on average as the workload fluctuates. Indeed, it may perform well most of the time. However, in the worst case, the performance of priority-driven algorithms can be unacceptably poor. A simple example [DhLi] demonstrates this fact. The application system contains $m + 1$ independent periodic tasks. The first m tasks T_i, for $i = 1, 2, \ldots m$, are identical. Their periods are equal to 1, and their execution times are equal to 2ε, where ε is a small number. The period of the last task T_{m+1} is $1 + \varepsilon$, and its execution time is 1. The tasks are in phase. Their relative deadlines are equal to their periods. Suppose that the priorities of jobs in these tasks are assigned on an EDF basis. The first job $J_{m+1,1}$ in T_{m+1} has the lowest priority because it has the latest deadline. Figure 6–1 shows an EDF schedule of these jobs if the jobs are dispatched and scheduled dynamically on m processors. We see that $J_{m+1,1}$ does not complete until $1 + 2\varepsilon$ and, hence, misses its deadline. The total utilization U of these $m + 1$ periodic tasks is $2m\varepsilon + 1/(1 + \varepsilon)$. In the limit as ε approaches zero, U approaches 1, and yet the system remains unschedulable. We would get the same infeasible schedule if we assigned the same priority to all the jobs in each task according to the period of the task: the shorter the period, the higher the priority. On the other hand, this system can be feasibly scheduled statically. As long as the total utilization of the first m tasks, $2m\varepsilon$, is equal to or less than 1, this system can be feasibly scheduled on two processors if we put T_{m+1} on one processor and the other tasks on the other processor and schedule the task(s) on each processor according to either of these priority-driven algorithms.

It is arguable that the poor behavior of dynamic systems occurs only for some pathological system configurations, and some other algorithms may perform well even for the pathological cases. In most cases, the performance of dynamic systems is superior to static systems. The more troublesome problem with dynamic systems is the fact that we often do not know how to determine their worst-case and best-case performance. The theories and algorithms

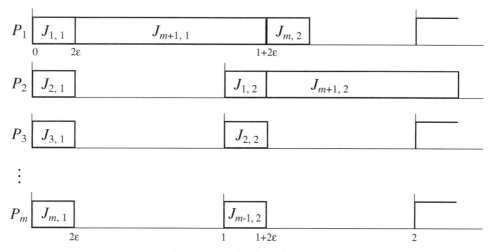

FIGURE 6–1   A dynamic EDF schedule on m processors.

presented in this and subsequent chapters make it possible for us to validate efficiently, robustly, and accurately the timing constraints of static real-time systems characterizable by the periodic task model. There are very few similar theories and algorithms for dynamic systems to date, as we discussed in Section 4.8. Until they become available, the only way to validate a dynamic system is by simulating and testing the system. This is prohibitively time consuming if done exhaustively, or unreliable if the coverage of the test is incomplete.

For these reasons, most hard real-time systems built and in use to date and in the near future are static. In the special case when tasks in a static system are independent, we can consider the tasks on each processor independently of the tasks on the other processors. The problem of scheduling in multiprocessor and distributed systems is reduced to that of uniprocessor scheduling. In general, tasks may have data and control dependencies and may share resources on different processors. As you will see in Chapter 9, uniprocessor algorithms and protocols can easily be extended to synchronize tasks and control their accesses to global resources in multiprocessor and distributed environments.

6.2   FIXED-PRIORITY VERSUS DYNAMIC-PRIORITY ALGORITHMS

As stated in Section 4.9, a priority-driven scheduler (i.e., a scheduler which schedules jobs according to some priority-driven algorithm) is an on-line scheduler. It does not precompute a schedule of the tasks. Rather, it assigns priorities to jobs after they are released and places the jobs in a ready job queue in priority order. When preemption is allowed at any time, a scheduling decision is made whenever a job is released or completed. At each scheduling decision time, the scheduler updates the ready job queue and then schedules and executes the job at the head of the queue.

Priority-driven algorithms differ from each other in how priorities are assigned to jobs. We classify algorithms for scheduling periodic tasks into two types: fixed priority and dynamic priority. A *fixed-priority* algorithm assigns the same priority to all the jobs in each task. In other words, the priority of each periodic task is fixed relative to other tasks. In contrast, a *dynamic-priority* algorithm assigns different priorities to the individual jobs in each task. Hence the priority of the task with respect to that of the other tasks changes as jobs are released and completed. This is why this type of algorithm is said to be "dynamic."

As you will see later, most real-time scheduling algorithms of practical interest assign fixed priorities to individual jobs. The priority of each job is assigned upon its release when it is inserted into the ready job queue. Once assigned, the priority of the job relative to other jobs in the ready job queue does not change. In other words, at the level of individual jobs, the priorities are fixed, even though the priorities at the task level are variable. Indeed, we have three categories of algorithms: fixed-priority algorithms, task-level dynamic-priority (and job-level fixed-priority) algorithms, and job-level (and task-level) dynamic algorithms. Except where stated otherwise, by dynamic-priority algorithms, we mean task-level dynamic-priority (and job-level fixed-priority) algorithms.

6.2.1 Rate-Monotonic and Deadline-Monotonic Algorithms

A well-known fixed-priority algorithm is the *rate-monotonic* algorithm [LiLa]. This algorithm assigns priorities to tasks based on their periods: the shorter the period, the higher the priority. The *rate* (of job releases) of a task is the inverse of its period. Hence, the higher its rate, the higher its priority. We will refer to this algorithm as the RM algorithm for short and a schedule produced by the algorithm as an RM schedule.

Figure 6–2 gives two examples. Figure 6–2(a) shows the RM schedule of the system whose cyclic schedule is in Figure 5-8. This system contains three tasks: $T_1 = (4, 1)$, $T_2 = (5, 2)$, and $T_3 = (20, 5)$. The priority of T_1 is the highest because its rate is the highest (or equivalently, its period is the shortest). Each job in this task is placed at the head of the priority

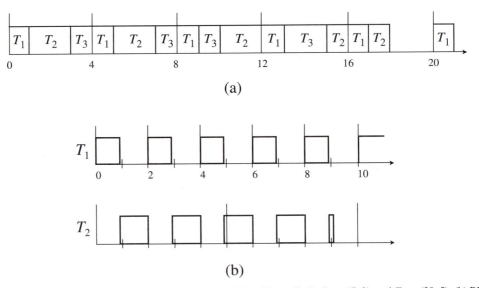

(a)

(b)

FIGURE 6–2 Examples of RM schedules. (a) RM schedule of $T_1 = (4, 1)$, $T_2 = (5, 2)$, and $T_3 = (20, 5)$. (b) RM schedule of $T_1 = (2, 0.9)$ and $T_2 = (5, 2.3)$.

queue and is executed as soon as the job is released. T_2 has the next highest priority. Its jobs execute in the background of T_1. For this reason, the execution of the first job in T_2 is delayed until the first job in T_1 completes, and the fourth job in T_2 is preempted at time 16 when the fifth job in T_1 is released. Similarly, T_3 executes in the background of T_1 and T_2; the jobs in T_3 execute only when there is no job in the higher-priority tasks ready for execution. Since there is always at least one job ready for execution until time 18, the processor never idles until that time.

The schedule in Figure 6–2(b) is for the tasks $T_1 = (2, 0.9)$ and $T_2 = (5, 2.3)$. The tasks are in phase. Here, we represent the schedule in a different form. Instead of using one time line, sometimes called a Gantt chart, to represent a schedule on a processor as we have done thus far, we use a time line for each task. Each time line is labeled at the left by the name of a task; the time line shows the intervals during which the task executes. According to the RM algorithm, task T_1 has a higher-priority than task T_2. Consequently, every job in T_1 is scheduled and executed as soon as it is released. The jobs in T_2 are executed in the background of T_1.

Another well-known fixed-priority algorithm is the *deadline-monotonic algorithm*, called the DM algorithm hereafter. This algorithm assigns priorities to tasks according their relative deadlines: the shorter the relative deadline, the higher the priority. Figure 6–3 gives an example. The system consists of three tasks. They are $T_1 = (50, 50, 25, 100)$, $T_2 = (0, 62.5, 10, 20)$, and $T_3 = (0, 125, 25, 50)$. Their utilizations are 0.5, 0.16, and 0.2, respectively. The total utilization is 0.86. According to the DM algorithm, T_2 has the highest priority because its relative deadline 20 is the shortest among the tasks. T_1, with a relative deadline of 100, has the lowest priority. The resultant DM schedule is shown in Figure 6–3(a). According to this schedule, all the tasks can meet their deadlines.

Clearly, when the relative deadline of every task is proportional to its period, the RM and DM algorithms are identical. When the relative deadlines are arbitrary, the DM algorithm performs better in the sense that it can sometimes produce a feasible schedule when the RM algorithm fails, while the RM algorithm always fails when the DM algorithm fails. The example above illustrates this fact. Figure 6–3(b) shows the RM schedule of the three tasks which Figure 6–3(a) has shown to be feasible when scheduled deadline-monotonically. According to the RM algorithm, T_1 has the highest priority, and T_3 has the lowest priority. We see that because the priorities of the tasks with short relative deadlines are too low, these tasks cannot meet all their deadlines.

6.2.2 Well-Known Dynamic Algorithms

The EDF algorithm assigns priorities to individual jobs in the tasks according to their absolute deadlines; it is a dynamic-priority algorithm. Figure 6–4 shows the EDF schedule of the two tasks T_1 and T_2 whose RM schedule is depicted in Figure 6–2(b).

- At time 0, the first jobs $J_{1,1}$ and $J_{2,1}$ of both tasks are ready. The (absolute) deadline of $J_{1,1}$ is 2 while the deadline of $J_{2,1}$ is 5. Consequently, $J_{1,1}$ has a higher priority and executes. When $J_{1,1}$ completes, $J_{2,1}$ begins to execute.
- At time 2, $J_{1,2}$ is released, and its deadline is 4, earlier than the deadline of $J_{2,1}$. Hence, $J_{1,2}$ is placed ahead of $J_{2,1}$ in the ready job queue. $J_{1,2}$ preempts $J_{2,1}$ and executes.
- At time 2.9, $J_{1,2}$ completes. The processor then executes $J_{2,1}$.

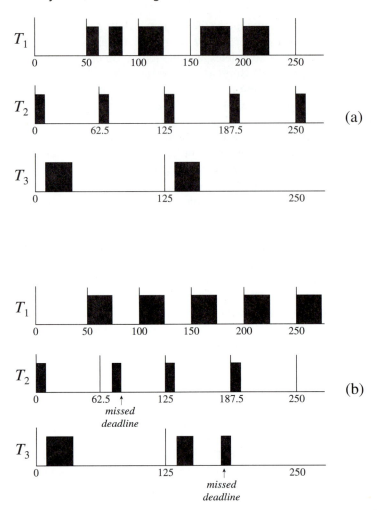

FIGURE 6–3   Fixed-priority schedules of $T_1 = (50, 50, 25, 100)$, $T_2 = (0, 62.5, 10, 20)$ and $T_3 = (0, 125, 25, 50)$.

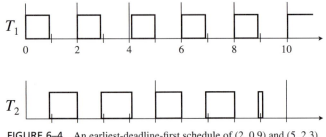

FIGURE 6–4   An earliest-deadline-first schedule of $(2, 0.9)$ and $(5, 2.3)$.

- At time 4, $J_{1,3}$ is released; its deadline is 6, which is later than the deadline of $J_{2,1}$. Hence, the processor continues to execute $J_{2,1}$.

- At time 4.1, $J_{2,1}$ completes, the processor starts to execute $J_{1,3}$, and so on.

We note that the priority of T_1 is higher than the priority of T_2 from time 0 until time 4.0. T_2 starts to have a higher priority at time 4. When the job $J_{2,2}$ is released, T_2 again has a lower priority. Hence, the EDF algorithm is a task-level dynamic-priority algorithm. On the other hand, once a job is placed in the ready job queue according to the priority assigned to it, its order with respect to other jobs in the queue remains fixed. In other words, the EDF algorithm is a job-level fixed-priority algorithm. Later on in Chapter 8, we will make use of this property.

Another well-known dynamic-priority algorithm is the *Least-Slack-Time-First* (LST) algorithm. You recall that at time t, the slack of a job whose remaining execution time (i.e., the execution of its remaining portion) is x and whose deadline is d is equal to $d - t - x$. The scheduler checks the slacks of all the ready jobs each time a new job is released and orders the new job and the existing jobs on the basis of their slacks: the smaller the slack, the higher the priority.

Coincidentally, the schedule of T_1 and T_2 in the above example produced by the LST algorithm happens to be identical to the EDF schedule in Figure 6–4. In general, however, the LST schedule of a system may differ in a fundamental way from the EDF schedule. To illustrate, we consider a more complicated system that consists of three tasks: $T_1 = (2, 0.8)$, $T_2 = (5, 1.5)$, and $T_3 = (5.1, 1.5)$. When the first jobs $J_{1,1}$, $J_{2,1}$ and $J_{3,1}$ are released at time 0, their slacks are 1.2, 3.5, and 3.6, respectively. $J_{1,1}$ has the highest priority, and $J_{3,1}$ has the lowest. At time 0.8, $J_{1,1}$ completes, and $J_{2,1}$ executes. When $J_{1,2}$ is released at time 2, its slack is 1.2, while the slacks of $J_{2,1}$ and $J_{3,1}$ become 2.7 and 1.6, respectively. Hence, $J_{1,2}$ has the highest priority, but now $J_{3,1}$ has a higher-priority than $J_{2,1}$! From this example, we see that the LST algorithm is a job-level dynamic-priority algorithm, while the EDF algorithm is a job-level fixed-priority algorithm. As we will see in Chapter 8, this change in the relative priorities of jobs makes resource access control much more costly.

Because scheduling decisions are made only at the times when jobs are released or completed, this version of the LST algorithm does not follow the LST rule of priority assignment at all times. If we wish to be specific, we should call this version of the LST algorithm the *nonstrict LST* algorithm. If the scheduler were to follow the LST rule strictly, it would have to monitor the slacks of all ready jobs and compare them with the slack of the executing job. It would reassign priorities to jobs whenever their slacks change relative to each other. As an example, according to the schedule in Figure 6–4, the scheduler would find that at time 2.7, the slack of $J_{2,1}$ becomes $(5 - 2.7 - 1.2) = 1.1$, the same as that of $J_{1,2}$. It would schedule the two ready jobs in a round-robin manner until $J_{1,2}$ completes. The run-time overhead of the strict LST algorithm includes the time required to monitor and compare the slacks of all ready jobs as time progresses. Moreover, by letting jobs with equal slacks execute in a round-robin manner, these jobs suffer extra context switches. For this reason, the strictly LST algorithm is an unattractive alternative, and we will not consider it further.

According to our classification, FIFO and Last-in-First-Out (LIFO) algorithms are also dynamic-priority algorithms. As an example, suppose that we have three tasks: $T_1 = (0, 3, 1, 3)$, $T_2 = (0.5, 4, 1, 1)$, and $T_3 = (0.75, 7.5, 2, 7.5)$. Suppose that the jobs in them are scheduled on the FIFO basis. Clearly, $J_{1,1}$ has a higher priority than $J_{2,1}$, which in turn has a higher priority than $J_{3,1}$. In other words, T_1 has the highest priority, and T_3 has the lowest priority initially. Later, $J_{1,4}$, $J_{2,3}$, and $J_{3,2}$ are released at the times 9, 8.5, and 8.25, respectively, and T_3 has the highest priority while T_1 has the lowest priority.

6.2.3   Relative Merits

Algorithms that do not take into account the urgencies of jobs in priority assignment usually perform poorly. Dynamic-priority algorithms such as FIFO and LIFO are examples. (If the two tasks in Figure 6–4 were scheduled on the FIFO basis, most of the jobs in T_1 would miss their deadlines.) An example of fixed-priority algorithms of this nature is one which assigns priorities to tasks on the basis of their functional criticality: the more critical the task, the higher the priority. (Suppose that T_1 in this example is a video display task while T_2 is a task which monitors and controls a patient's blood pressure. The latter is clearly more functionally critical. If it were given the higher-priority, T_1 would miss most of its deadlines. This sacrifice of T_1 for T_2 is unnecessary since both tasks can be feasibly scheduled.) Hereafter, we confine our attention to algorithms that assign priorities to jobs based on one or more temporal parameters of jobs and have either optimal or reasonably good performance. The RM, DM, EDF, and the LST algorithm are such algorithms.

A criterion we will use to measure the performance of algorithms used to schedule periodic tasks is the schedulable utilization. The *schedulable utilization* of a scheduling algorithm is defined as follows: *A scheduling algorithm can feasibly schedule any set of periodic tasks on a processor if the total utilization of the tasks is equal to or less than the schedulable utilization of the algorithm.*

Clearly, the higher the schedulable utilization of an algorithm, the better the algorithm. Since no algorithm can feasibly schedule a set of tasks with a total utilization greater than 1, an algorithm whose schedulable utilization is equal to 1 is an optimal algorithm. In the subsequent sections, we will show that the EDF algorithm is optimal in this sense as expected, but the RM and DM algorithms are not.

While by the criterion of schedulable utilization, optimal dynamic-priority algorithms outperform fixed-priority algorithms, an advantage of fixed-priority algorithms is predictability. The timing behavior of a system scheduled according to a fixed-priority algorithm is more predictable than that of a system scheduled according to a dynamic-priority algorithm. When tasks have fixed priorities, overruns of jobs in a task can never affect higher-priority tasks. It is possible to predict which tasks will miss their deadlines during an overload.

In contrast, when the tasks are scheduled according to a dynamic algorithm, it is difficult to predict which tasks will miss their deadlines during overloads. This fact is illustrated by the examples in Figure 6–5. The tasks shown in Figure 6–5(a) have a total utilization of 1.1. According to their EDF schedule shown here, the job $J_{1,5}$ in $T_1 = (2, 1)$ is not scheduled until 10 and misses its deadline at 10. Deadlines of all jobs in T_2 are met in the schedule segment. The tasks in Figure 6–5(b) also have a total utilization of 1.1. According to the EDF schedule in Figure 6–5(b), $J_{1,5}$ in $T_1 = (2, 0.8)$, as well as every job in T_2, cannot complete on time. There is no easy test, short of an exhaustive one, that allows us to determine which tasks will miss their deadlines and which tasks will not.

The EDF algorithm has another serious disadvantage. We note that a late job which has already missed its deadline has a higher-priority than a job whose deadline is still in the future.

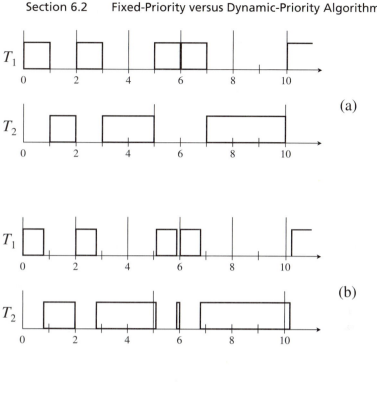

(a)

(b)

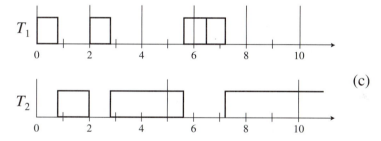

(c)

FIGURE 6–5 Unpredictability and instability of the EDF algorithm. (a) An EDF schedule of $T_1 = (2, 1)$ and $T_2 = (5, 3)$ with $U = 1.1$. (b) An EDF schedule of $T_1 = (2, 0.8)$ and $T_2 = (5, 3.5)$ with $U = 1.1$. (c) An EDF schedule of $T_1 = (2, 0.8)$ and $T_2 = (5, 4.0)$ with $U = 1.2$.

Consequently, if the execution of a late job is allowed to continue, it may cause some other jobs to be late. As an example, we examine the schedule shown in Figure 6–5(c). When $J_{2,1}$ becomes late at 5, it continues to execute because its priority is higher than the priority of $J_{1,3}$. As a consequence, $J_{1,3}$ is late also. In fact, after $J_{1,4}$, every job in both tasks will be late. This unstable behavior of the EDF algorithm, that one job being late causes many other jobs to be late, makes the algorithm unsuitable for systems where overload conditions are unavoidable.

   A good overrun management strategy is crucial to prevent this kind of instability. An overrun management strategy is to schedule each late job at a lower priority than the jobs that are not late. An alternative is to complete the late job, but schedule some functional noncritical jobs at the lowest priority until the system recovers from the overload condition. There are many other alternatives. Invariably, the scheduler either lowers the priorities of some or all the late jobs (or portions of jobs), or discards some jobs if they cannot complete by their deadlines and logs this action. Clearly, what alternatives are suitable depends on the application.

6.3   MAXIMUM SCHEDULABLE UTILIZATION

Again, we say that a system is *schedulable* by an algorithm if the algorithm always produces a feasible schedule of the system. A system is schedulable (and *feasible*) if it is schedulable by some algorithm, that is, feasible schedules of the system exist. We now ask how large the total utilization of a system can be in order for the system to be surely schedulable.

6.3.1   Schedulable Utilizations of the EDF Algorithm

We first focus on the case where the relative deadline of every task is equal to its period. (This choice of the relative deadline arises naturally from throughput considerations. The job in each period completes before the next period starts so there is no backlog of jobs.) The following theorem tells us that any such system can be feasibly scheduled if its total utilization is equal to or less than one, no matter how many tasks there are and what values the periods and execution times of the tasks are. In the proof of this and later theorems, we will use the following terms. At any time t, the *current period* of a task is the period that begins before t and ends at or after t. We call the job that is released in the beginning of this period the *current job*.

> **THEOREM 6.1.**   A system T of independent, preemptable tasks with relative deadlines equal to their respective periods can be feasibly scheduled on one processor if and only if its total utilization is equal to or less than 1.

> ***Proof.***   That the system is not feasible if its total utilization is larger than 1 is obvious so we focus on the *if* part of the proof. As stated in Theorem 4.1, the EDF algorithm is optimal in the sense that it can surely produce a feasible schedule of any feasible system. Hence, it suffices for us to prove that the EDF algorithm can surely produce a feasible schedule of any system with a total utilization equal to 1. We prove this statement by showing that if according to an EDF schedule, the system fails to meet some deadlines, then its total utilization is larger than 1. To do so, let us suppose that the system begins to execute at time 0 and at time t, the job $J_{i,c}$ of task T_i misses its deadline.
>
> For the moment, we assume that prior to t the processor never idles. We will remove this assumption at the end of the proof. There are two cases to consider: (1) The current period of every task begins at or after $r_{i,c}$, the release time of the job that misses its deadline, and (2) the current periods of some tasks begin before $r_{i,c}$. The two cases are illustrated in Figure 6–6. In this figure, we see that the current jobs of all tasks T_k, for all $k \neq i$, have equal or lower priorities than $J_{i,c}$ because their deadlines are at or after t.
>
> **Case (1):** This case is illustrated by the time lines in Figure 6–6(a); each tick on the time line of a task shows the release time of some job in the task. The fact that

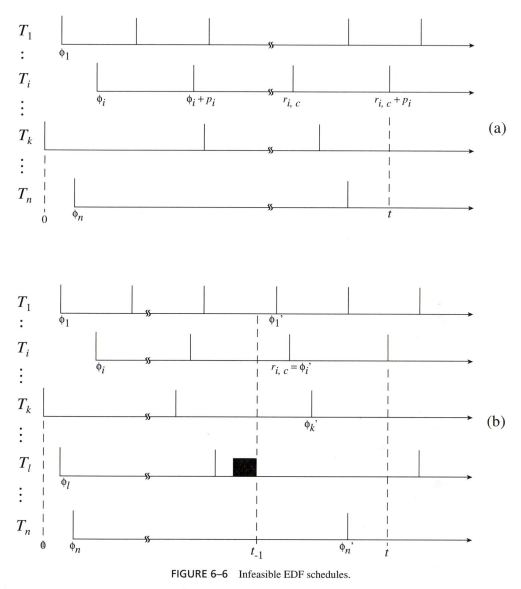

FIGURE 6–6   Infeasible EDF schedules.

$J_{i,c}$ misses its deadline at t tells us that any current job whose deadline is after t is not given any processor time to execute before t and that the total processor time required to complete $J_{i,c}$ and all the jobs with deadlines at or before t exceeds the total available time t. In other words,

$$t < \frac{(t - \phi_i)e_i}{p_i} + \sum_{k \neq i} \left\lfloor \frac{t - \phi_k}{p_k} \right\rfloor e_k \qquad (6.1)$$

(You recall that ϕ_k, p_k and e_k are the phase, period, and execution time of task T_k, respectively.) $\lfloor x \rfloor$ $(x \geq 0)$ denotes the largest integer less than or equal to x. The first term on the right-hand side of the inequality is the time required to complete all the jobs in T_i with deadlines before t and the job $J_{i,c}$. Each term in the sum gives the total amount of time before t required to complete jobs that are in a task T_k other than T_i and have deadlines at or before t. Since $\phi_k \geq 0$ and $e_k/p_k = u_k$ for all k, and $\lfloor x \rfloor \leq x$ for any $x \geq 0$,

$$\frac{(t - \phi_i)e_i}{p_i} + \sum_{k \neq i} \left\lfloor \frac{t - \phi_k}{p_k} \right\rfloor e_k \leq t\frac{e_i}{p_i} + t\sum_{k \neq i}\frac{e_k}{p_k} = t\sum_{k=1}^{n} u_k = tU$$

Combining this inequality with the one in Eq. (6.1), we have $U > 1$.

Case (2): The time lines in of Figure 6–6(b) illustrate case (2). Let $\mathbf{T}'$ denote the subset of $\mathbf{T}$ containing all the tasks whose current jobs were released before $r_{i,c}$ and have deadlines after t. It is possible that some processor time before $r_{i,c}$ was given to the current jobs of some tasks in $\mathbf{T}'$. In the figure, T_l is such a task.

Let t_{-1} be the end of the latest time interval I (shown as a black box in Figure 6–6(b)) that is used to execute some current job in $\mathbf{T}'$. We now look at the segment of the schedule starting from t_{-1}. In this segment, none of the current jobs with deadlines after t are given any processor time. Let ϕ_k' denote the release time of the first job of task T_k in $\mathbf{T} - \mathbf{T}'$ in this segment. Because $J_{i,c}$ misses its deadline at t, we must have

$$t - t_{-1} < \frac{(t - t_{-1} - \phi_i')e_i}{p_i} + \sum_{T_k \in \mathbf{T} - \mathbf{T}'} \left\lfloor \frac{t - t_{-1} - \phi_k'}{p_k} \right\rfloor e_k$$

(Tasks in $\mathbf{T}'$ are not included the sum; by definition of t_{-1}, these tasks are not given any processor time after t_{-1}.) This inequality is the same as the one in Eq. (6.1) except that t is replaced by $t - t_{-1}$ and ϕ_k is replaced by ϕ_k'. We can used the same argument used above to prove that $\sum_{T_k \in \mathbf{T} - \mathbf{T}'} u_k > 1$, which in turn implies that $U > 1$.

Now we consider the case where the processor idles for some time before t. Let t_{-2} be the latest instant at which the processor idles. In other words, from t_{-2} to the time t when $J_{i,c}$ misses its deadline, the processor never idles. For the same reason that Eq. (6.1) is true, the total time required to complete all the jobs that are released at and after t_{-2} and must be completed by t exceeds the total available time $t - t_{-2}$. In other words, $U > 1$. $\qquad \square$

The following facts follow straightforwardly from this theorem.

1. *A system of independent, preemptable periodic tasks with relative deadlines longer than their periods can be feasibly scheduled on a processor as long as the total utilization is equal to or less than 1.*

2. *The schedulable utilization $U_{EDF}(n)$ of the EDF algorithm for n independent, preemptable periodic tasks with relative deadlines equal to or larger than their periods is equal to 1.*

The EDF algorithm is not the only algorithm with this schedulable utilization. In particular, *the schedulable utilization of the LST algorithm is also 1*. This follows straightforwardly from Theorem 4.3 which states that the LST algorithm is also optimal for scheduling independent, preemptable jobs on one processor.

When the relative deadlines of some tasks are less than their respective periods, the system may no longer be feasible, even when its total utilization is less than 1. As an example, the task with period 5 and execution time 2.3 in Figure 6–4 would not be schedulable if its relative deadline were 3 instead of 5.

We call the ratio of the execution time e_k of a task T_k to the minimum of its relative deadline D_k and period p_k the *density* of the task. In other words, the density of T_k is $e_k/\min(D_k, p_k)$. The sum of the densities of all tasks in a system is the *density* of the system and is denoted by Δ. When $D_i < p_i$ for some task T_i, $\Delta > U$. If the density of a system is larger than 1, the system may not be feasible. For example, this sum is larger than 1 for $(2, 0.9)$ and $(5, 2.3, 3)$, and the tasks are not schedulable by any algorithm. On the other hand, any system is feasible if its density is equal to or less than 1. We state this fact in the following theorem which generalizes Theorem 6.1; its proof is similar to the proof of Theorem 6.1 and is left to you as an exercise.

THEOREM 6.2.   A system **T** of independent, preemptable tasks can be feasibly scheduled on one processor if its density is equal to or less than 1.

The condition given by this theorem is not necessary for a system to be feasible. A system may nevertheless be feasible when its density is greater than 1. The system consisting of $(2, 0.6, 1)$ and $(5, 2.3)$ is an example. Its density is larger than 1, but it is schedulable according to the EDF algorithm.

6.3.2 Schedulability Test for the EDF Algorithm

Hereafter, we call a test for the purpose of validating that the given application system can indeed meet all its hard deadlines when scheduled according to the chosen scheduling algorithm a *schedulability test*. If a schedulability test is efficient, it can be used as an on-line acceptance test.

Checking whether a set of periodic tasks meet all their deadlines is a special case of the validation problem that can be stated as follows: We are given

1. the period p_i, execution time e_i, and relative deadline D_i of every task T_i in a system $\mathbf{T} = \{T_1, T_2, \ldots T_n\}$ of independent periodic tasks, and
2. a priority-driven algorithm used to schedule the tasks in **T** preemptively on one processor.

We are asked to determine whether all the deadlines of every task T_i, for every $1 \leq i \leq n$, are always met. We note that in the above statement, the phases of tasks are not given. If we were also given the phases and if the values of all the given parameters would never vary, this problem could be solved by simulation. We simply construct a segment of the schedule of these tasks according to the given scheduling algorithm. A segment of length $2H + \max_i p_i +$

$\max_i D_i$ suffices [BaHR]. T_i meets all its deadlines if we observe no missed deadline in this schedule segment. However, this method does not work whenever the parameters of the tasks do vary; some of the reasons were discussed in Section 4.8.

When the scheduling algorithm is the EDF algorithm, Theorems 6.1 and 6.2 give us the theoretical basis of a very simple schedulability test. To determine whether the given system of n independent periodic tasks surely meets all the deadlines when scheduled according to the preemptive EDF algorithm on one processor, we check whether the inequality

$$\sum_{k=1}^{n} \frac{e_k}{\min(D_k, p_k)} \leq 1 \tag{6.2}$$

is satisfied. We call this inequality the *schedulability condition* of the EDF algorithm. If it is satisfied, the system is schedulable according to the EDF algorithm. When Eq. (6.2) is not satisfied, the conclusion we may draw from this fact depends on the relative deadlines of the tasks. If $D_k \geq p_k$ for all k from 1 to n, then Eq. (6.2) reduces to $U \leq 1$, which is both a necessary and sufficient condition for a system to be feasible. On the other hand, if $D_k < p_k$ for some k, Eq. (6.2) is only a sufficient condition; therefore we can only say that the system may not be schedulable when the condition is not satisfied.

This schedulability test is not only simple but also robust. Theorem 4.4 states that the execution of independent jobs on one processor according to a preemptive schedule is predictable. This theorem allows us to conclude that the system remains schedulable if some jobs execute for less time than their respective (maximum) execution times. The proof of Theorems 6.1 (and similarly the proof of Theorem 6.2) never makes use of the actual values of the periods; it only makes use of the total demand for processor time by the jobs of each task T_k in any interval of length t. If the actual interrelease times are sometimes longer than p_k, the total demand will in fact be smaller. Hence if according to Eq. (6.2) the system is schedulable on the EDF basis, it remains schedulable when the interrelease times of jobs in some tasks are sometimes longer than the respective periods of tasks. We will return to state this fact more formally in Section 7.4 when we discuss sporadic tasks.

We can also use Eq. (6.2) as a rule to guide the choices of the periods and execution times of the tasks while we design the system. As a simple example, we consider a digital robot controller. Its control-law computation takes no more than 8 milliseconds on the chosen processor to complete. The desired sampling rate is 100 Hz, that is, the control-law task executes once every 10 milliseconds. Clearly the task is feasible if the control-law task is the only task on the processor and its relative deadline is equal to the period. Suppose that we also need to use the processor for a Built-In Self-Test (BIST) task. The maximum execution time of this task is 50 milliseconds. We want to do this test as frequently as possible without causing the control-law task to miss any deadline, but never less frequently than once a second. Equation (6.2) tells us that if we schedule the two tasks according to the EDF algorithm, we can execute the BIST task as frequently as once every 250 milliseconds. Now suppose that we need to add a telemetry task. Specifically, to send or receive each message, the telemetry task must execute 15 milliseconds. Although the interarrival times of messages are very large, we want the relative deadline of message processing jobs to be as small as feasible. Equation (6.2) tells us that if we are willing to reduce the frequency of the BIST task to once a second, we can make the relative deadline of the telemetry task as short as 100 milliseconds. If this guaranteed maximum response time of the telemetry task is not acceptable and we must redesign the three tasks, Eq. (6.2) can guide us in the process of trading off among the task parameters in order to keep the entire system feasible.

6.4 OPTIMALITY OF THE RM AND DM ALGORITHMS

Hereafter in our discussion on fixed-priority scheduling, we index the tasks in decreasing order of their priorities except where stated otherwise. In other words, the task T_i has a higher priority than the task T_k if $i < k$. By indexing the tasks in this manner, our discussion implicitly takes into consideration the scheduling algorithm. Sometimes, we refer to the priority of a task T_i as priority π_i. π_i's are positive integers $1, 2, \ldots, n$, 1 being the highest priority and n being the lowest priority. We denote the subset of tasks with equal or higher priority than T_i by $\mathbf{T}_i$ and its total utilization by $U_i = \sum_{k=1}^{i} u_k$. You may have noticed that we implicitly assume here that the tasks have distinct priorities. At the end of the chapter we will return to remove this assumption, as well as to discuss the effects of a limited number of priority levels when it is not possible to give tasks distinct priorities.

Because they assign fixed priorities to tasks, fixed-priority algorithms cannot be optimal: Such an algorithm may fail to schedule some systems for which there are feasible schedules. To demonstrate this fact, we consider a system which consists of two tasks: $T_1 = (2, 1)$ and $T_2 = (5, 2.5)$. Since their total utilization is equal to 1, we know from Theorem 6.1 that the tasks are feasible. $J_{1,1}$ and $J_{1,2}$ can complete in time only if they have a higher priority than $J_{2,1}$. In other words, in the time interval $(0, 4]$, T_1 must have a higher-priority than T_2. However, at time 4 when $J_{1,3}$ is released, $J_{2,1}$ can complete in time only if T_2 (i.e., $J_{2,1}$) has a higher priority than T_1 (i.e., $J_{1,3}$). This change in the relative priorities of the tasks is not allowed by any fixed priority algorithm.

While the RM algorithm is not optimal for tasks with arbitrary periods, it is optimal in the special case when the periodic tasks in the system are simply periodic and the deadlines of the tasks are no less than their respective periods. A system of periodic tasks is *simply periodic* if for every pair of tasks T_i and T_k in the system and $p_i < p_k$, p_k is an integer multiple of p_i. An example of a simply periodic task system is the flight control system in Figure 1-3. In that system, the shortest period is 1/180 seconds. The other two periods are two times and six times 1/180 seconds. The following theorem states that the RM algorithm is optimal for scheduling such a system.

THEOREM 6.3.   A system of simply periodic, independent, preemptable tasks whose relative deadlines are equal to or larger than their periods is schedulable on one processor according to the RM algorithm if and only if its total utilization is equal to or less than 1.

To see why this theorem is true, we suppose for now that the tasks are in phase (i.e., the tasks have identical phases) and the processor never idles before the task T_i misses a deadline for the first time at t. (In the next section we will justify why it suffices for us to consider the case where the tasks are in phase and the processor never idles before t.) t is an integer multiple of p_i. Because the tasks are simply periodic, t is also an integer multiple of the period p_k of every higher-priority task T_k, for $k = 1, 2, \ldots, i - 1$. Hence the total time required to complete all the jobs with deadlines before and at t is equal to $\sum_{k=1}^{i}(e_k t/p_k)$, which is equal to t times the total utilization $U_i = \sum_{k=1}^{i} u_k$ of the i highest priority tasks. That T_i misses a deadline at t means that this demand for time exceeds t. In other words, $U_i > 1$.

Despite the fact that fixed-priority scheduling is not optimal in general, we may nevertheless choose to use this approach because it leads to a more predictable and stable system. For this reason, we want to know among all the fixed-priority algorithms, which one(s) is the best. The answer is that the DM algorithm is the optimal fixed-priority algorithm. Theorem 6.4 states this fact more precisely. We will return shortly to clarify the sense in which this theorem supports the claim that the DM algorithm is optimal even though the theorem is stated for tasks with identical phase, that is, in phase.

> **THEOREM 6.4.**   A system **T** of independent, preemptable periodic tasks that are in phase and have relative deadlines equal to or less than their respective periods can be feasibly scheduled on one processor according to the DM algorithm whenever it can be feasibly scheduled according to any fixed-priority algorithm.

This theorem is true because we can always transform a feasible fixed-priority schedule that is not a DM schedule into one that is. Specifically, suppose that a system has a feasible fixed-priority schedule that is not a DM schedule. We scan the tasks, starting from task T_1 with the shortest relative deadline in order of increasing relative deadlines. When we find two tasks T_i and $T_i + 1$ which are such that D_i is less than D_{i+1} but T_i has a lower priority than T_{i+1} according to this schedule, we switch the priorities of these two tasks and modify the schedule of the two tasks accordingly. After the switch, the priorities of the two tasks are assigned on the DM basis relative to one another. By repeating this process, we can transform the given schedule into a DM schedule. The step of showing that when the tasks are in phase, it is always possible to switch the priorities of tasks T_i and T_{i+1} and hence the time intervals in which jobs in these tasks are scheduled without leading to any missed deadline is left to you as an exercise.

In some systems, the relative deadline of every task T_i is equal to δp_i for some constant $0 < \delta$. For such systems, the DM and RM algorithms are the same. As a corollary to the above theorem, *the RM algorithm is optimal among all fixed-priority algorithms whenever the relative deadlines of the tasks are proportional to their periods*.

6.5 A SCHEDULABILITY TEST FOR FIXED-PRIORITY TASKS WITH SHORT RESPONSE TIMES

We now describe a pseudopolynomial time schedulability test developed by Lehoczky, *et al.* [LeSD] and Audsley, *et al.* [ABTR] for tasks scheduled according to a fixed-priority algorithm. In this section we confine our attention to the case where the response times of the jobs are smaller than or equal to their respective periods. In other words, every job completes before the next job in the same task is released. We will consider the general case where the response times may be larger than the periods in the next section. Since no system with total utilization greater than 1 is schedulable, we assume hereafter that the total utilization U is equal to or less than 1.

6.5.1 Critical Instants

The schedulability test uses as inputs the given sets $\{p_i\}$ and $\{e_i\}$ of periods and execution times of the tasks in **T** and checks one task T_i at a time to determine whether the response times of all its jobs are equal to or less than its relative deadline D_i. Because we cannot count on any relationship among the release times to hold, we must first identify the worst-case combination of release times of any job $J_{i,c}$ in T_i and all the jobs that have higher priorities than $J_{i,c}$. This combination is the worst because the response time of a job $J_{i,c}$ released under this condition is the largest possible for all combinations of release times. For this purpose, the notion of critical instant was first introduced in [LiLa] and subsequently refined by others (e.g., [Bake] pointed out the need to consider case (2) below.) A *critical instant* of a task T_i is a time instant which is such that

1. the job in T_i released at the instant has the maximum response time of all jobs in T_i, if the response time of every job in T_i is equal to or less than the relative deadline D_i of T_i, and

2. the response time of the job released at the instant is greater than D_i if the response time of some jobs in T_i exceeds D_i.

We call the response time of a job in T_i released at a critical instant the *maximum (possible) response time* of the task and denote it by W_i. The following theorem gives us the condition under which a critical instant of each task T_i occurs.

> **THEOREM 6.5.**   In a fixed-priority system where every job completes before the next job in the same task is released, a critical instant of any task T_i occurs when one of its job $J_{i,c}$ is released at the same time with a job in every higher-priority task, that is, $r_{i,c} = r_{k,l_k}$ for some l_k for every $k = 1, 2, \ldots, i - 1$.

> ***Proof.***   We first show that the response time of the first job $J_{i,1}$ is the largest when the tasks in the subset $\mathbf{T}_i$ of i highest priority tasks are in phase, that is, when the condition stated in the theorem is met. To do so, we take as the time origin the minimum of all the phases of tasks in $\mathbf{T}_i$. It suffices for us to consider the case where the processor remains busy executing jobs with higher priorities than $J_{i,1}$ before $J_{i,1}$ is released at ϕ_i.[1]
>
> Let $W_{i,1}$ denote the response time of $J_{i,1}$. From the release time ϕ_k of the first job in T_k to the instant $\phi_i + W_{i,1}$ when the first job $J_{i,1}$ in T_i completes, at most $\lceil (W_{i,1} + \phi_i - \phi_k)/p_k \rceil$ jobs in T_k become ready for execution. Each of these jobs demands e_k units of processor time. Hence the total amount of processor time demanded by $J_{i,1}$ and all the jobs that must be completed before $J_{i,1}$ is given by
>
> $$e_i + \sum_{k=1}^{i-1} \left\lceil \frac{W_{i,1} + \phi_i - \phi_k}{p_k} \right\rceil e_k$$

---

[1] If during some intervals before ϕ_i the processor idles or executes lower priority jobs, we can ignore the segment of the schedule before the end of the latest of such intervals, take this time instant as the time origin, and call the first job in every higher-priority task released after this instant the first job of the task.

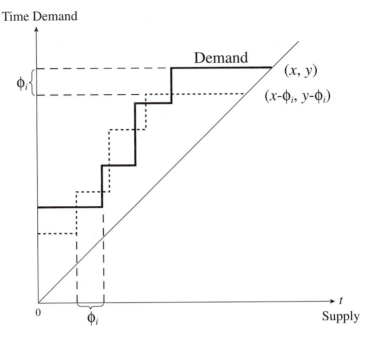

Time Demand

FIGURE 6–7 Dependency of response time on phases.

At time $W_{i,1} + \phi_i$ when $J_{i,1}$ completes, the supply of processor time becomes sufficient to meet this total demand for the processor time for first time since time 0. In other words, $W_{i,1}$ is equal to the smallest of all solutions of

$$W_{i,1} = e_i + \sum_{k=1}^{i-1} \left\lceil \frac{W_{i,1} + \phi_i - \phi_k}{p_k} \right\rceil e_k - \phi_i \qquad (6.3)$$

if this equation has solutions in the range $(0, p_i]$. If the equation does not have a solution in this range, then $J_{i,1}$ cannot complete in time and misses its deadline.

To see how $W_{i,1}$ depends on the phase ϕ_k of each higher-priority task, we note that the expression in the right-hand side of this equation is a staircase function of $W_{i,1}$. It lies above the 45° straight line $y(W_{i,1}) = W_{i,1}$ until it intersects the straight line; the value of $W_{i,1}$ at this intersection is the solution of Eq. (6.3). From Eq. (6.3), it is clear that the staircase function has the largest value, and hence its intersection with the 45° straight line has the largest value, when ϕ_k is 0 for every $k = 1, 2, \ldots, i - 1$. In other words, the job $J_{i,1}$ has the largest response time when all the higher-priority tasks are in phase.

We now let ϕ_k be 0 for all $k < i$. The time instant when the processor first completes all the ready jobs in higher-priority tasks released since time 0 is independent when $J_{i,1}$ is released, and this is the first instant when $J_{i,1}$ can begin execution. Therefore, the sooner $J_{i,1}$ is released, the longer it must wait to start execution and the larger its response time. This observation leads us to conclude that the response time $W_{i,1}$ of $J_{i,1}$ has the largest possible value when ϕ_i is also equal to zero.[2]

To show that an arbitrary job $J_{i,c}$ in T_i has the maximum possible response time whenever it is released at the same time with a job in every higher-priority task, we let the release time of this job be ϕ'_i and the release time of the job in T_k that is current at time ϕ'_i be ϕ'_k. Because every job completes in the period in which it is released, there is no need for us to consider the jobs in each task T_k that are released before ϕ'_k. Hence we can take the minimum among the release times ϕ'_k, for $k = 1, 2, \ldots, i$, of the current jobs as the time origin and consider the segment of the schedule starting from this new origin independently from the earlier segment. The above argument can be repeated and allows us to reach the conclusion that the response time of $J_{i,c}$ has the maximum value when the release times of all the current jobs in $\mathbf{T}_i$ are the same.

It follows from the above arguments that the maximum possible response time W_i of all jobs in T_i is, therefore, equal to the smallest value of t that satisfies the equation

$$t = e_i + \sum_{k=1}^{i-1} \left\lceil \frac{t}{p_k} \right\rceil e_k \tag{6.4}$$

It is easy to see that if Eq. (6.3) does not have a solution equal to or less than D_i, neither does this equation. □

Figure 6–8 gives an illustrative example. Figure 6–8(a) shows an RM schedule of the three jobs, (2, 0.6), (2.5, 0.2), and (3, 1.2) when they are in phase. Time 0 is a critical instant of both lower-priority tasks. The response times of the jobs in (2.5, 0.2) are 0.8, 0.3, 0.2, 0.2, 0.8, and so on. These times never exceed the response time of the first job. Similarly, the response times of the jobs in (3, 1.2) are 2, 1.8, 2, 2, and so on, which never exceed 2, the response time of the first job in (3, 1.2). Figure 6–8(b) shows an RM schedule when the phase of the task with period 2.5 is one, while the phases of the other tasks are 0. We see that 6 is a critical instant of the two lower-priority tasks. The jobs of these tasks released at this instant have the maximum possible response times of 0.8 and 2, respectively.

We are now ready to clarify a point that was left fuzzy at the end of the last section. Although Theorem 6.4 is stated in terms of tasks that are in phase, we claimed that the DM algorithm is an optimal fixed-priority algorithm. Theorem 6.5 gives us justification. Whenever release-time jitters are not negligible, the information on release times cannot be used to determine whether any algorithm can feasibly schedule the given system of tasks. Under this

---

[2]Rather than relying on this intuitive argument, we can arrive at this conclusion by examining how the solution in Eq. (6.3) depends on ϕ_i when ϕ_k equal 0 for every $k = 1, 2, \ldots, i - 1$. The solid graph in Figure 6–7 shows the general behavior of the staircase function when ϕ_i is also equal to 0. Each rise occurs when $W_{i,1}$ is an integer multiple of some p_k. When ϕ_i is nonzero, the staircase function behaves as indicated by the dotted line. Each rise in the dotted line occurs when $W_{i,1} + \phi_i$ is an integer multiple of some period p_k. Hence, corresponding to each rise in the solid staircase function at some value z of $W_{i,1}$, there is a rise in the dotted function at $z - \phi_i$. The step sizes at the corresponding rises of both staircase functions are the same. However, every plateau in the dotted function is ϕ_i units lower than the corresponding plateau in the solid function. In short, we can obtain the dotted staircase function by shifting the solid staircase function to the right by ϕ_i units and down for ϕ_i units. From this, we can see that if the solid staircase function intersects the 45° straight line for the first time at some point (x, y), as shown in Figure 6–7, the dotted staircase function intersects the straight line at $(x - \phi_i, y - \phi_i)$. Therefore, the response time of $J_{i,1}$ for an arbitrary ϕ_i is equal to its response time for zero phase minus ϕ_i.

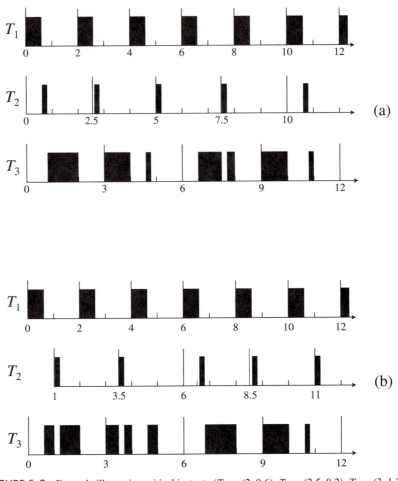

FIGURE 6–8   Example illustrating critical instants ($T_1 = (2, 0.6)$, $T_2 = (2.5, 0.2)$, $T_3 = (3, 1.2)$).

circumstance, we have no choice but to judge a fixed-priority algorithm according to its performance for tasks that are in phase because all fixed-priority algorithms have their worst-case performance for this combination of phases.

6.5.2   Time-Demand Analysis

The schedulability test [LeSD, ABTR] described below makes use of the fact stated in Theorem 6.5. To determine whether a task can meet all its deadlines, we first compute the total demand for processor time by a job released at a critical instant of the task and by all the higher-priority tasks as a function of time from the critical instant. We then check whether this demand can be met before the deadline of the job. For this reason, we name this test a *time-demand analysis*.

To carry out the time-demand analysis on **T**, we consider one task at a time, starting from the task T_1 with the highest priority in order of decreasing priority. To determine whether a task T_i is schedulable after finding that all the tasks with higher priorities are schedulable, we focus on a job in T_i, supposing that the release time t_0 of the job is a critical instant of T_i. At time $t_0 + t$ for $t \geq 0$, the total (processor) time demand $w_i(t)$ of this job and all the higher-priority jobs released in $[t_0, t]$ is given by

$$w_i(t) = e_i + \sum_{k=1}^{i-1} \left\lceil \frac{t}{p_k} \right\rceil e_k, \qquad \text{for } 0 < t \leq p_i \tag{6.5}$$

This job of T_i can meet its deadline $t_0 + D_i$ if at some time $t_0 + t$ at or before its deadline, the supply of processor time, which is equal to t, becomes equal to or greater than the demand $w_i(t)$ for processor time. In other words, $w_i(t) \leq t$ for some $t \leq D_i$, where D_i is equal to or less than p_i. Because this job has the maximum possible response time of all jobs in T_i, we can conclude that all jobs in T_i can complete by their deadlines if this job can meet its deadline.

If $w_i(t) > t$ for all $0 < t \leq D_i$, this job cannot complete by its deadline; T_i, and hence the given system of tasks, cannot be feasibly scheduled by the given fixed-priority algorithm. More specifically, as long as the variations in the interrelease times of tasks are not negligibly small, we have to make this conclusion because a critical instant of T_i can occur. However, if the given tasks have known phases and periods and the jitters in release times are negligibly small, it is possible to determine whether any job of T_i is ever released at the same time as a job of every higher priority task. If this condition can never occur, a critical instant of T_i can never occur; no job in T_i can ever have the maximum possible response time. T_i may nevertheless be schedulable even though the time-demand analysis test indicates that it is not.

Because of Theorem 6.5, we can say that $w_i(t)$ given by the Eq. (6.5) is the maximum time demanded by any job in T_i, plus all the jobs that must be completed before this job, at any time $t < p_i$ since its release. We call $w_i(t)$ the *time-demand function* of the task T_i.

As an example, we consider a system containing four tasks: $T_1 = (\phi_1, 3, 1)$, $T_2 = (\phi_2, 5, 1.5)$, $T_3 = (\phi_3, 7, 1.25)$, and $T_4 = (\phi_4, 9, 0.5)$, where the phases of the tasks are arbitrary. Their total utilization is 0.87. The given scheduling algorithm is the RM algorithm. In Figure 6–9, the solid lines show the time-demand functions of these four tasks. The dotted lines show the total contributions of higher-priority tasks to the time-demand function of each lower-priority task. For example, the job in T_2 being considered is released at t equal to 0. In the time interval $(0, 5)$, it contributes 1.5 units of time to its time-demand function $w_2(t)$. T_1 contributes a total of 1 unit from time 0 to 3 and 2 units from time 3 to 6, and so on. Because at time $t = 2.5$ the total demand $w_2(t)$ of 2.5 units is met, the maximum possible response time of jobs in T_2 is 2.5. Since the relative deadline of T_2 is 5, the task is schedulable. From Figure 6–9, we can see that every task in this system is schedulable. In particular, the dot at the intersection of $w_i(t)$ and the straight line $y(t) = t$ marks the time instant from a critical instant of T_i at which the job in T_i released at the critical instant completes. From this graph, we can tell that the maximum possible response times of the tasks are 1, 2.5, 4.75, and 9, respectively.

Suppose that in addition to these four tasks, there is a fifth task with period 10 and execution time 1. It is easy to see that the time-demand function of this task lies entirely above the supply function t from 0 to 10. For this reason, we can conclude that this task cannot be feasibly scheduled by the given scheduling algorithm.

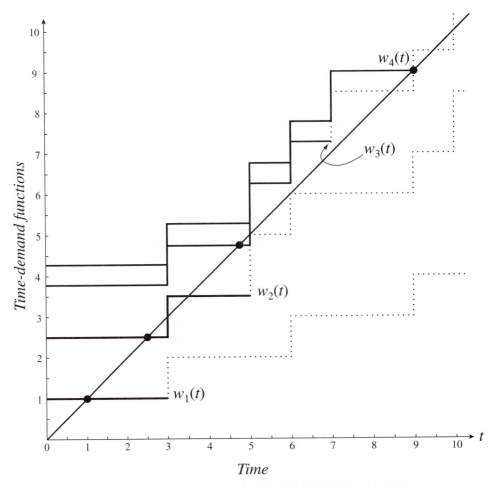

FIGURE 6–9   Time-demand analysis (3,1), (5, 1.5), (7, 1.25), and (9, 0.5).

This example illustrates the fact that the time-demand function of any task T_i is a staircase function. The rises in the function occur at time instants which are integer multiples of periods of higher-priority tasks. Immediately before each rise in each function $w_i(t)$, the shortage $w_i(t) - t$ between the processor-time demand and the supply is the smallest for all t in the interval from the previous rise. (In this example, in the range of t from 0 to 3, $w_2(t) - t$ is the smallest at t equal to 3; in the range from 3 to 5, this difference is the smallest at t equal to 5.) Hence, if we are not interested in the value of its maximum possible response time, only whether a task is schedulable, it suffices for us to check whether the time-demand function of the task is equal to or less than the supply at these instants.

In summary, to determine whether T_i can be feasibly scheduled by the given scheduling algorithm using the *time-demand analysis method* proposed by Lehoczky, *et al.* [LeSD], we

1. compute the time-demand function $w_i(t)$ according to Eq. (6.5), and

2. check whether the inequality

$$w_i(t) \leq t \qquad\qquad (6.6a)$$

is satisfied for values of t that are equal to

$$t = jp_k; \qquad k = 1, 2, \ldots i; j = 1, 2, \ldots, \lfloor \min(p_i, D_i)/p_k \rfloor \qquad (6.6b)$$

If this inequality is satisfied at any of these instants, T_i is schedulable.

Let $q_{n,1}$ denote the *period ratio* of the system, that is, the ratio of the largest period p_n to the smallest period p_1. The time complexity of the time-demand analysis for each task is $O(nq_{n,1})$.

For task T_3 in this example, we need to check whether its time-demand function $w_3(t)$ is equal to or less than t at t equal to 3, 5, 6, and 7. In doing so, we find that the inequality is not satisfied at 3 but is satisfied at 5. Hence, we can conclude that the maximum response time of T_3 is between 3 and 5 and the task is schedulable. As a more complicated example, suppose that we are given a set of tasks with periods 2, 3, 5, and 11 and we want to determine whether the task with period 11 is schedulable. We check whether Eq. (6.6a) is satisfied at 2, 4, 6, 8, and 10, which are integer multiples of 2 less than 11; 3, 6, and 9, which are integer multiples of 3 less than 11; 5 and 10, which are integer multiples of 5 less than 11, and finally 11.

We now use the example in Figure 6–9 to explain intuitively why the time-demand analysis method is robust: The conclusion that a task T_i is schedulable remains correct when the execution times of jobs may be less than their maximum execution times and interrelease times of jobs may be larger than their respective periods. We replotted the time-demand functions for the two highest priority tasks in Figure 6–10(a). Suppose that the execution times of jobs in T_1 are in the range $[0.9, 1]$ and those of jobs in T_2 are in the range $[1.25, 1.5]$. $w_2(t)$, calculated according to Eq. (6.5), is the maximum time-demand function of T_2. Its actual time-demand function can be anywhere in the shaded area. Clearly, the intersection of the actual time-demand function with the time supply line t is a point at most equal to 2.5. Similarly, the dotted lines in Figure 6–10(b) show the time-demand function $w_3(t)$ of T_3, which is calculated according to Eq. (6.5), as well as the contribution of T_1 and T_2 to the function. The dashed lines show the contribution of T_1 and T_2 to the actual time-demand function of T_3 when the actual interrelease times of the jobs in T_1 and T_2 are larger than their periods. We see again that the actual time-demand function of T_3, depicted by the solid line, lies below the time-demand function depicted by the dotted line. T_3 remains schedulable despite these variations in release times.

6.5.3 Alternatives to Time-Demand Analysis

For the simple case considered here, Theorem 6.5 lets us identify the worst-case condition for the schedulability of a fixed-priority system. Instead of carrying out a time-demand analysis, we can also determine whether a system of independent preemptable tasks is schedulable by simply simulating this condition and observing whether the system is then schedulable. In other words, a way to test the schedulability of such a system is to construct a schedule of it according to the given scheduling algorithm. In this construction, we assume that the tasks are in phase and the actual execution times and interrelease times of jobs in each task T_i are equal to e_i and p_i, respectively. As long as Theorem 6.5 holds, it suffices for us to construct only the initial segment of length equal to the largest period of the tasks. If there is no missed deadline in this segment, then all tasks are feasibly scheduled by the given algorithm. Figure 6–11 shows the worst-case initial segment of the RM schedule of the system in Figure 6–9.

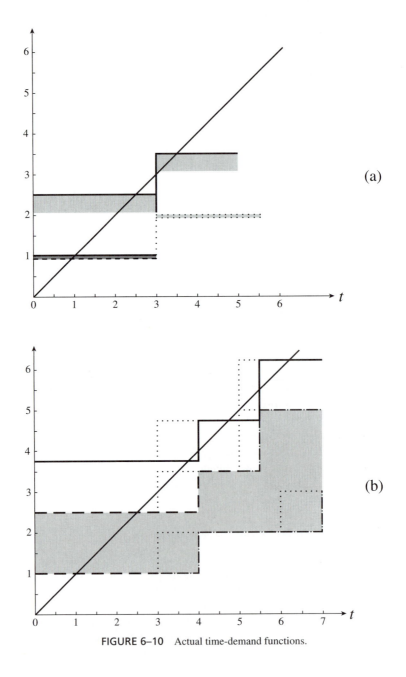

FIGURE 6–10   Actual time-demand functions.

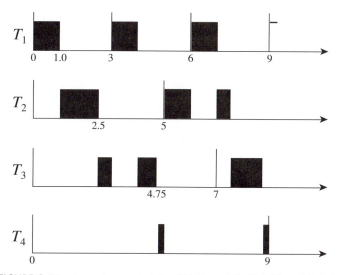

FIGURE 6–11   A worst-case schedule of (3, 1), (5, 1.5), (7, 1.25), and (9, 0.5).

This schedule allows us to draw the same conclusion about the maximum response times of the four tasks. We refer to this alternative as the *worst-case simulation method*. It is easy to see that the time complexity of this method is also $O(nq_{n,1})$, where $q_{n,1}$ is the ratio p_n/p_1.

For now, it appears that the more conceptually complex time-demand analysis method has no advantage over the simulation method. Later in the chapter, it will become evident that we can easily extend the time-demand analysis method to deal with other factors, such as nonpreemptivity and self-suspension, that affect the schedulability of a system, but we cannot easily extend the simulation method. When these factors must be taken into account, either we no longer know the worst-case condition for each task or the worst-case conditions for different tasks are different. In either case, the need to construct a large number of worst-case conditions greatly increases the complexity of the simulation method and makes it impractical for large systems.

If we want to know the maximum possible response time W_i of each task T_i, we must solve Eq. (6.4). This can be done in an iterative manner [ABTR], starting from an initial guess $t^{(1)}$ of W_i. (Since the response time of a job is at least equal to its execution time, we can always use e_i as the initial value.) During the lth iteration for $l \geq 1$, we compute the value $t^{(l+1)}$ on the right-hand side of Eq. (6.4) according to

$$t^{(l+1)} = e_i + \sum_{k=1}^{i-1} \left\lceil \frac{t^{(l)}}{p_k} \right\rceil e_k \tag{6.7}$$

We terminate the iteration either when $t^{(l+1)}$ is equal to $t^{(l)}$ and $t^{(l)} \leq p_i$ for some l or when $t^{(l+1)}$ becomes larger than p_i, whichever occurs sooner. In the former case, W_i is equal to $t^{(l)}$, and T_i is schedulable. In the latter case, we fail to find W_i, and T_i is not schedulable.

For example, we consider the task $T_3 = (7, 1.25)$ in Figure 6–9. Substituting the parameters of this task and the higher-priority tasks (3, 1) and (5, 1.5) into Eq. (6.4), we have

$$t = 1.25 + 1 \left\lceil \frac{t}{3} \right\rceil + 1.5 \left\lceil \frac{t}{5} \right\rceil$$

As an initial guess $t^{(1)}$ of W_3, we use its execution time 1.25. Evaluating the right-hand side of this equation, we find $t^{(2)}$ equal to 3.75. Substituting this value into the right-hand side again, we find $t^{(3)}$ equal to 4.75. $t^{(4)}$ calculated from $t^{(3)} = 4.75$ is equal to 4.75. Hence, W_3 is 4.75.

6.6   SCHEDULABILITY TEST FOR FIXED-PRIORITY TASKS WITH ARBITRARY RESPONSE TIMES

This section describes a general time-demand analysis method developed by Lehoczky [Leho] to determine the schedulability of tasks whose relative deadlines are larger than their respective periods. Since the response time of a task may be larger than its period, it may have more than one job ready for execution at any time. Ready jobs in the same task are usually scheduled on the FIFO basis. We assume here that this policy is used.

6.6.1   Busy Intervals

We will use the term level-π_i busy interval. A *level-π_i busy interval* $(t_0, t]$ begins at an instant t_0 when (1) all jobs in $\mathbf{T}_i$ released before the instant have completed and (2) a job in $\mathbf{T}_i$ is released. The interval ends at the first instant t after t_0 when all the jobs in $\mathbf{T}_i$ released since t_0 are complete. In other words, in the interval $(t_0, t]$, the processor is busy all the time executing jobs with priorities π_i or higher, all the jobs executed in the busy interval are released in the interval, and at the end of the interval there is no backlog of jobs to be executed afterwards. Hence, when computing the response times of jobs in $\mathbf{T}_i$, we can consider every level-π_i busy interval independently from other level-π_i busy intervals.

With a slight abuse of the term, we say that a level-π_i busy interval is *in phase* if the first jobs of all tasks that have priorities equal to or higher than priority π_i and are executed in this interval have the same release time. Otherwise, we say that the tasks have arbitrary phases in the interval.

As an example, Figure 6–12 shows the schedule of three tasks $T_1 = (2, 1)$, $T_2 = (3, 1.25)$, and $T_3 = (5, 0.25)$ in the first hyperperiod. The filled rectangles depict where jobs in T_1 are scheduled. The first busy intervals of all levels are in phase. The priorities of the tasks are $\pi_1 = 1$, $\pi_2 = 2$, and $\pi_3 = 3$, with 1 being the highest priority and 3 being the lowest priority. As expected, every level-1 busy interval always ends 1 unit time after it begins. For this system, all the level-2 busy intervals are in phase. They begin at times 0, 6, and so on which are the least common multiples of the periods of tasks T_1 and T_2. The lengths of these intervals are all equal to 5.5. Before time 5.5, there is at least one job of priority 1 or 2 ready for execution, but immediately after 5.5, there are none. Hence at 5.5, the first job in T_3 is scheduled. When this job completes at 5.75, the second job in T_3 is scheduled. At time 6, all the jobs released before time 6 are completed; hence, the first level-3 busy interval ends at this time. The second level-3 busy interval begins at time 6. This level-3 busy interval is not in phase since the release times of the first higher-priority jobs in this interval are 6, but the first job of T_3 in this interval is not released until time 10. The length of this level-3 busy

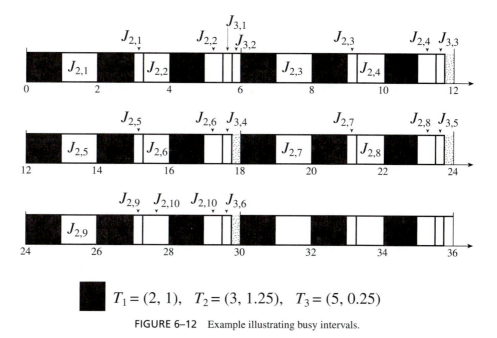

$$T_1 = (2, 1), \quad T_2 = (3, 1.25), \quad T_3 = (5, 0.25)$$

FIGURE 6–12   Example illustrating busy intervals.

interval is only 5.75. Similarly, all the subsequent level-3 busy intervals in the hyperperiod have arbitrary phases.

6.6.2 General Schedulability Test

The general schedulability test described below relies on the fact that when determining the schedulability of a task T_i in a system in which the response times of jobs can be larger than their respective periods, it still suffices to confine our attention to the special case where the tasks are in phase. However, the first job $J_{i,1}$ may no longer have the largest response time among all jobs in T_i. (This fact was illustrated by Lehoczky, *et al.* [LSST] by the example of two tasks: $T_1 = (70, 26)$ and $T_2 = (100, 62)$. Seven jobs of T_2 execute in the first level-2 busy interval. Their response times are 114, 102, 116, 104, 118, 106, and 94, respectively. The response times of both the third and fifth jobs in T_2 are larger than the response time of the first job.) Consequently, we must examine all the jobs of T_i that are executed in the first level-π_i busy interval. (Obviously, this busy interval is in phase when the tasks are in phase.) If the response times of all these jobs are no greater than the relative deadline of T_i, T_i is schedulable; otherwise, T_i may not be schedulable.

Specifically, the following general schedulability test developed by Lehoczky [Leho] for tasks with arbitrary relative deadlines works in this manner.

General Time-Demand Analysis Method

Test one task at a time starting from the highest priority task T_1 in order of decreasing priority. For the purpose of determining whether a task T_i is schedulable, assume that all the tasks are in phase and the first level-π_i busy interval begins at time 0.

While testing whether all the jobs in T_i can meet their deadlines (i.e., whether T_i is schedulable), consider the subset $\mathbf{T}_i$ of tasks with priorities π_i or higher.

(i) If the first job of every task in $\mathbf{T}_i$ completes by the end of the first period of the task, check whether the first job $J_{i,1}$ in T_i meets its deadline. T_i is schedulable if $J_{i,1}$ completes in time. Otherwise, T_i is not schedulable.

(ii) If the first job of some task in $\mathbf{T}_i$ does not complete by the end of the first period of the task, do the following:

(a) Compute the length of the in phase level-π_i busy interval by solving the equation $t = \sum_{k=1}^{i}\lceil\frac{t}{p_k}\rceil e_k$ iteratively, starting from $t^{(1)} = \sum_{k=1}^{i} e_k$ until $t^{(l+1)} = t^{(l)}$ for some $l \geq 1$. The solution $t^{(l)}$ is the length of the level-π_i busy interval.

(b) Compute the maximum response times of all $\lceil t^{(l)}/p_i \rceil$ jobs of T_i in the in-phase level-π_i busy interval in the manner described below and determine whether they complete in time.

T_i is schedulable if all these jobs complete in time; otherwise T_i is not schedulable.

It is easy to compute the response time of the first job $J_{i,1}$ of T_i in the first in-phase level-π_i busy interval. The time-demand function $w_{i,1}(t)$ is still given by the expression in the right-hand side of Eq. (6.5). An important difference is that the expression remains valid for all $t > 0$ before the end of the level-π_i busy interval. For the sake of convenience, we copy the expression here.

$$w_{i,1}(t) = e_i + \sum_{k=1}^{i-1}\left\lceil\frac{t}{p_k}\right\rceil e_k, \qquad \text{for } 0 < t \leq w_{i,1}(t) \tag{6.8}$$

The maximum possible response time $W_{i,1}$ of $J_{i,1}$ is equal to the smallest value of t that satisfies the equation $t = w_{i,1}(t)$. To obtain $W_{i,1}$, we solve the equation iteratively and terminate the iteration only when we find $t^{(l+1)}$ equal to $t^{(l)}$. Because U_i is no greater than 1, this equation always has a finite solution, and the solution can be found after a finite number of iterations.

Let $W_{i,j}$ denote the maximum possible response time of the jth job in a level-π_i busy interval. The following lemma tells us how to compute $W_{i,j}$.

LEMMA 6.6. The maximum response time $W_{i,j}$ of the jth job of T_i in an in-phase level-π_i busy period is equal to the smallest value of t that satisfies the equation

$$t = w_{i,j}(t + (j-1)p_i) - (j-1)p_i \tag{6.9a}$$

where $w_{i,j}()$ is given by

$$w_{i,j}(t) = je_i + \sum_{k=1}^{i-1}\left\lceil\frac{t}{p_k}\right\rceil e_k, \qquad \text{for } (j-1)p_i < t \leq w_{i,j}(t) \tag{6.9b}$$

As an example, Figure 6–13(a) shows the time-demand functions $w_{1,1}(t)$, $w_{2,1}(t)$ and $w_{3,1}(t)$ of the first jobs $J_{1,1}$, $J_{2,1}$ and $J_{3,1}$ in the system in Figure 6–12. Since $w_{2,1}(t)$ lies entirely above the supply t line from 0 to 3, $J_{2,1}$ does not complete at 3. Solving for the response time $W_{2,1}$ of this job, we find that $W_{2,1}$ equals 3.25. Similarly, the first intersection of $w_{3,1}(t)$ with the supply line t is at 5.75; this is the response time of $J_{3,1}$.

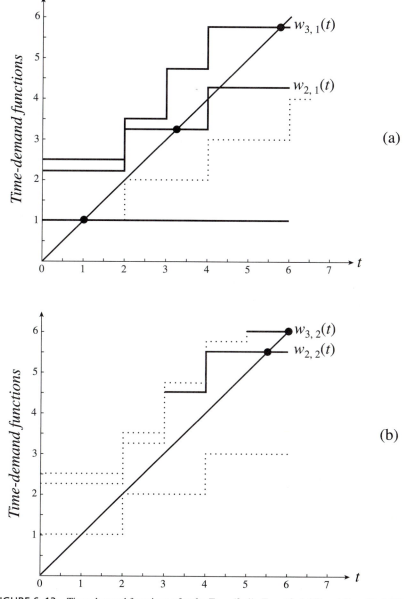

FIGURE 6–13   Time-demand functions of tasks $T_1 = (2, 1)$, $T_2 = (3, 1.25)$ and $T_3 = (5, 0.25)$.

Figure 6–13(b) shows the time-demand functions $w_{2,2}(t)$ and $w_{3,2}(t)$ of the second jobs of T_2 and T_3 in the first busy intervals, respectively. We see that these functions are equal to t when t is equal to 5.5 and 6, respectively. Therefore, $J_{2,2}$ completes at $t = 5.5$, and $J_{3,2}$ completes at $t = 6$. Subtracting their release times, we find that $W_{2,2}$ is 2.5 and $W_{3,2}$ is 1.

Computationally, it is more efficient to find $W_{i,j}$ by solving Eq. (6.9) iteratively in a manner similar to Eq. (6.7). For example, to find $W_{2,2}$, we substitute the parameters of the tasks into Eq. (6.9) to obtain

$$t = 2 \times 1.25 + \lceil (t + 3)/2 \rceil - 3$$

To solve this equation iteratively, we begin with the initial guess $t^{(1)}$ of 1.25, the execution time of $J_{2,2}$. Substituting t on the right-hand side of the equation by this value, we obtain $t^{(2)} = 2.5$. When we substitute t on the right-hand side by 2.5, we obtain $t^{(3)} = 2.5$. This allows us to terminate the iteration and conclude that $W_{2,2}$ is 2.5. Similarly, $W_{3,2} = 1$ is the minimum solution of the equation

$$t = 2 \times 0.25 + \lceil (t + 5)/2 \rceil + 1.25 \lceil (t + 5)/3 \rceil - 5$$

Again, an alternative is the worst-case simulation approach. To determine whether T_i is schedulable, we generate the schedule of the tasks in $\mathbf{T}_i$ according to the given fixed-priority algorithm, assuming that the tasks are in phase. (The schedule in Figure 6–12 is an example.) If we do not observe any missed deadlines within the first level-π_i busy interval, we can conclude that all the tasks in $\mathbf{T}_i$ are schedulable. Otherwise, we cannot guarantee that all tasks in $\mathbf{T}_i$ always meet their deadlines.

Finally, to determine whether the jth job in an in-phase level-π_i busy interval completes in time, we can check whether the inequality $w_{i,j}(t) \le t$ is ever satisfied for some instant t in the range from $(j - 1)p_i$ to $(j - 1)p_i + D_i$. As with Eq. (6.6), we only need to check for the satisfiability of this inequality at time instants which are integer multiples of p_k, for $k = 1, 2, \dots, i$, in this range of time.

*6.6.3 Correctness of the General Schedulability Test

The general schedulability test described above makes a key assumption: The maximum response time of some job $J_{i,j}$ in an in-phase level-π_i busy interval is equal to the maximum possible response time of all jobs in T_i. Therefore, to determine whether T_i is schedulable, we only need to check whether the maximum response times of all jobs in this busy interval are no greater than the relative deadline of T_i. This subsection presents several lemmas as proof that this assumption is valid.

We begin by considering an arbitrary job $J_{i,c}$ of T_i. When computing the maximum possible response time of this job, we must consider the possibility that some jobs released before the release time t_0 of $J_{i,c}$ may remain incomplete at the time. Since some of these jobs are executed before $J_{i,c}$, their processor time demands must be included in the time-demand function of $J_{i,c}$. As it turns out, because of Lemma 6.7, we need not be concerned with the jobs released before t_0 if $J_{i,c}$ is released at the same time as a job in every higher-priority task.

LEMMA 6.7. Let t_0 be a time instant at which a job of every task in $\mathbf{T}_i$ is released. All the jobs in $\mathbf{T}_i$ released before t_0 have been completed at t_0.

Intuitively, we can see why this lemma is true by focusing on the latest level-π_i busy interval before t_0. Suppose that this interval begins at t_{-1}. We can use an argument similar to the one used in the proof of Theorem 6.1 to show that the amount of processor time demanded by all the jobs of priorities π_i or higher that are released in the interval (t_{-1}, t_0) cannot exceed $t_0 - t_{-1}$ since the total utilization U_i of $\mathbf{T}_i$ is no greater than 1. Consequently, at t_0 there is no backlog of jobs in $\mathbf{T}_i$, that is, every job in $\mathbf{T}_i$ released before t_0 is completed at t_0.

Lemma 6.7 tells us that any instant which is the release time of a job from every task in $\mathbf{T}_i$ is the beginning of an in-phase level-π_i busy interval. As a consequence, Lemma 6.8 is true.

LEMMA 6.8. When a system of independent, preemptive periodic tasks is scheduled on a processor according to a fixed-priority algorithm, the time-demand function $w_{i,1}(t)$ of a job in T_i released at the same time as a job in every higher-priority task is given by Eq. (6.8).

To see how the response time of an arbitrary job in a busy interval depends on the phases of the tasks for the interval, we again look at the first busy interval, and this time, we assume that each task T_k has an arbitrary phase ϕ_k. The response time of the jth job $J_{i,j}$ in the first level-π_i busy period is the smallest value of t that satisfies the equation

$$ t = je_i + \sum_{k=1}^{i-1} \left\lceil \frac{t + \phi_i - \phi_k}{p_k} \right\rceil e_k - \phi_i - (j-1)p_i $$

Again, we take as the time origin the smallest of all the phases. The argument used in the proof of Theorem 6.5 can be used again to show that the response time of this job is the largest when all the tasks $\mathbf{T}_i$ have zero phase. This fact remains true for any arbitrary level-π_i busy interval, not just the first one. We restate this fact below.

LEMMA 6.9. The response time $W_{i,j}$ of the jth job of T_i executed in an in-phase level-π_i busy interval is no less than the response time of the jth job of T_i executed in any level-π_i busy interval.

Finally, the correctness of the general schedulability test depends on the following lemma

LEMMA 6.10. The number of jobs in T_i that are executed in an in-phase level-π_i busy interval is never less than the number of jobs in this task that are executed in a level-π_i busy interval of arbitrary phase.

Figure 6–12 illustrates this fact. Each of the later level-3 busy intervals is not in-phase. Only one job of T_3 executes in such an interval. In contrast, two jobs of T_3 execute in the first interval that is in phase. To see why this lemma is true in general, we note that during the time when each job of T_i is waiting to complete, new jobs with priorities π_i and higher are released and become ready. The rates at which the new jobs are released are independent of the response time of the waiting job. The longer this job of T_i waits, the more new jobs become ready. Hence, this lemma follows directly from Lemma 6.9.

In summary, Lemmas 6.7—6.10 tell us that the busy interval we examine according to the general time-demand analysis method contains the most number of jobs in T_i that can possibly execute in any level-π_i busy interval. Moreover, the response time of each job in the examined busy interval is larger than the response time of the corresponding job executed in any level-π_i busy interval. This is why if we find that none of the examined jobs completes late, we know that no job in T_i will.

6.7 SUFFICIENT SCHEDULABILITY CONDITIONS FOR THE RM AND DM ALGORITHMS

When we know the periods and execution times of all the tasks in an application system, we can use the schedulability test described in the last section to determine whether the system is schedulable according to the given fixed-priority algorithm. However, before we have completed the design of the application system, some of these parameters may not be known. In fact, the design process invariably involves the trading of these parameters against each other. We may want to vary the periods and execution times of some tasks within some range of values for which the system remains feasible in order to improve some aspects of the system. For this purpose, it is desirable to have a schedulability condition similar to the ones given by Theorems 6.1 and 6.2 for the EDF and the LST algorithms. These schedulability conditions give us a flexible design guideline for the choices of the periods and execution times of tasks. The schedulable utilizations presented in this section give us similar schedulability conditions for systems scheduled according to the RM or DM algorithms. An acceptance test based on such a schedulable utilization can decide whether to accept or reject a new periodic task in constant time. In contrast, the more accurate time-demand analysis test takes $O(nq_{n,1})$ time; moreover, the accurate test is less robust because its result is sensitive to the values of periods and execution times.

6.7.1 Schedulable Utilization of the RM Algorithm for Tasks with $D_i = p_i$

Specifically, the following theorem from [LiLa] gives us a schedulable utilization of the RM algorithm. We again focus on the case when the relative deadline of every task is equal to its period. For such systems, the RM and DM algorithms are identical.

> **THEOREM 6.11.** A system of n independent, preemptable periodic tasks with relative deadlines equal to their respective periods can be feasibly scheduled on a processor according to the RM algorithm if its total utilization U is less than or equal to
>
> $$U_{RM}(n) = n(2^{1/n} - 1) \tag{6.10}$$

$U_{RM}(n)$ is the schedulable utilization of the RM algorithm when $D_i = p_i$ for all $1 \leq k \leq n$. Figure 6–14 shows its value as a function of the number n of tasks in the set. When n is equal to 2, $U_{RM}(n)$ is equal to 0.828. It approaches $\ln 2$ (0.693), shown by the dashed line, for large n.

Specifically, $U(n) \leq U_{RM}(n)$ is a sufficient schedulability condition for any system of n independent, preemptable tasks that have relative deadlines equal to their respective periods to be schedulable rate-monotonically. (We use the notation $U(n)$ in place of U in our subsequent discussion whenever we want to bring the number of tasks n to our attention.) As long as

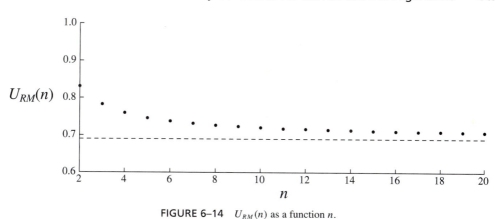

FIGURE 6–14 $U_{RM}(n)$ as a function n.

the total utilization of such a system satisfies this condition, it will never miss any deadline. In particular, we can reach this conclusion without considering the individual values of the phases, periods, and execution times.

As an example, we consider the system **T** of 5 tasks: $(1.0, 0.25)$, $(1.25, 0.1)$, $(1.5, 0.3)$, $(1.75, 0.07)$, and $(2.0, 0.1)$. Their utilizations are 0.25, 0.08, 0.2, 0.04, and 0.05. The total utilization is 0.62, which is less than 0.743, the value of $U_{RM}(5)$. Consequently, we can conclude that we can feasibly schedule **T** rate-monotonically. Suppose that the system is later enhanced. As a result, the tasks are modified, and the resultant tasks are $(0.3, 1.3, 0.1)$, $(1.0, 1.5, 0.3)$, $(1.75, 0.1)$, $(2.0, 0.1)$, and $(7.0, 2.45)$. Since their total utilization is 0.737, which is still less than 0.743, we know for sure that the system remains schedulable. There is no need for us to do the more complex time-demand analysis to verify this fact. On the other hand, suppose that to make the above five-task system more modular, we divide the task with period 7.0 into three smaller tasks with periods 5, 6, and 7, while keeping the total utilization of the system at 0.737. We can no longer use this condition to assure ourselves that the system is schedulable because $U_{RM}(7)$ is 0.724 and the total utilization of the system exceeds this bound.

Since $U(n) \leq U_{RM}(n)$ is not a necessary condition, a system of tasks may nevertheless be schedulable even when its total utilization exceeds the schedulable bound. For example, the total utilization of the system with the four tasks $(3, 1)$, $(5, 1.5)$, $(7, 1.25)$, and $(9, 0.5)$ is 0.85, which is larger than $U_{RM}(4) = 0.757$. Earlier in Figure 6–9, we have shown by the time-demand analysis method that this system is schedulable according to the RM algorithm.

*6.7.2 Proof of Theorem 6.11

While the schedulable utilization of the EDF algorithm given by Theorem 6.1 is intuitively obvious, the schedulable utilization $U_{RM}(n)$ given by Theorem 6.11 is not. We now present an informal proof of this theorem in order to gain some insight into why it is so.

The proof first shows that the theorem is true for the special case where the longest period p_n is less than or equal to two times the shortest period p_1. After the truth of the theorem is established for this special case, we then show that the theorem remains true when this restriction is removed. As before, we assume that the priorities of all tasks are distinct. Here, this means that $p_1 < p_2 < \cdots < p_n$.

Proof for the Case of $p_n \leq 2p_1$.   The proof for the case where $p_n \leq 2p_1$ consists of the four steps that are described below. Their goal is to find the most difficult-to-schedule system of n tasks among all possible combinations of n tasks that are difficult-to-schedule rate-monotonically. We say that a system is *difficult to schedule* if it is schedulable according to the RM algorithm, but it fully utilizes the processor for some interval of time so that any increase in the execution time or decrease in the period of some task will make the system unschedulable. The system sought here is the *most difficult* in the sense that its total utilization is the smallest among all difficult-to-schedule n-task systems. The total utilization of this system is the schedulable utilization of the RM algorithm, and any system with a total utilization smaller than this value is surely schedulable. Each of the following steps leads us closer to this system and the value of its total utilization.

Step 1:   In the first step, we identify the phases of the tasks in the most difficult-to-schedule system. For this we rely on Theorem 6.5. You recall that according to that theorem, a job has its maximum possible response time if it is released at the same time as a job in every higher-priority task. The most difficult-to-schedule system must have one or more in-phase busy intervals. Therefore, in the search for this system, we only need to look for it among in-phase systems.

Step 2:   In the second step, we choose a relationship among the periods and execution times and hypothesize that the parameters of the most difficult-to-schedule system of n tasks are thus related. In the next step, we will verify that this hypothesis is true. Again from Theorem 6.5, we know that in making this choice, we can confine our attention to the first period of every task. To ensure that the system is schedulable, we only need to make sure that the first job of every task completes by the end of the first period of the task. Moreover, the parameters are such that the tasks keep the processor busy once some task begins execution, say at time 0, until at least p_n, the end of the first period of the lowest priority task T_n.

The combination of n periods and execution times given by the pattern in Figure 6–15 meets these criteria. By construction, any system of n tasks whose execution times are related to their periods in this way is schedulable. It is easy to see that any increase in execution time of any task makes this system unschedulable. Hence systems whose parameters satisfy this relationship are difficult to schedule. Expressing analytically the dependencies of execution times on the periods of tasks that are given by Figure 6–15, we have

$$e_k = p_{k+1} - p_k \qquad \text{for } k = 1, 2, \ldots, n-1 \qquad (6.11a)$$

Since each of the other tasks execute twice from 0 to p_n the execution time of the lowest priority task T_n is

$$e_n = p_n - 2\sum_{k=1}^{n-1} e_k \qquad (6.11b)$$

Step 3:   We now show that the total utilization of any difficult-to-schedule n-task system whose execution times are not related to their periods according to Eq. (6.11) is larger than or equal to the total utilization of any system whose periods and execution times are thus

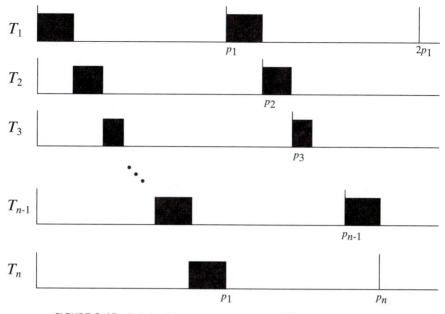

FIGURE 6–15   Relationship among parameters of difficult-to-schedule tasks.

related. Since we are looking for the difficult-to-schedule system with the least total utilization, we need not consider any system whose parameters are not thus related.

To do so, we construct new systems, whose parameters do not satisfy Eq. (6.11), from an original system whose parameters satisfy Eq. (6.11). There are two ways to do this. One way is by increasing the execution time of a higher-priority task from the value given by Eq. (6.11) by a small amount $\varepsilon > 0$. Without loss of generality, let this task be T_1. In other words, in the new system, the execution time e'_1 of T_1 is equal to

$$e'_1 = p_2 - p_1 + \varepsilon = e_1 + \varepsilon$$

For the new system to be schedulable, some other task must have a smaller execution time. From Figure 6–15, we see that the first job in every task can complete in time if we let the execution time of any other task be ε units less than the value given by Eq. (6.11a). Suppose that we choose T_k, for some $k \neq 1$, to be this task and make its new execution time equal to

$$e'_k = e_k - \varepsilon$$

The execution times of the tasks other than T_1 and T_k are still given by Eq. (6.11). The new system still keeps the processor busy in the interval $(0, p_n]$. The difference between the total utilization U' of the new system and the total utilization U of the original system is

$$U' - U = \frac{e'_1}{p_1} + \frac{e'_k}{p_k} - \frac{e_1}{p_1} - \frac{e_k}{p_k} = \frac{\varepsilon}{p_1} - \frac{\varepsilon}{p_k}$$

Since $p_1 < p_k$, this difference is positive, and the total utilization of the new system is larger. (You may want to convince yourself that we would reach the same conclusion if in the construction of the new system, we make the execution time of some task other than T_1 larger by ε units and make the execution times of one or more tasks with priorities lower than this task smaller by a total of ε units.)

Another way to construct a new difficult-to-schedule system from the original one is to let the execution time of a higher-priority task be ε units smaller than the value given by Eq. (6.11). Again, suppose that we choose T_1 to be this task, that is, its new execution time is

$$e_1'' = p_2 - p_1 - \varepsilon$$

From Figure 6–15, we see that if we do not increase the execution time of some other task, the processor will be idle for a total of 2ε units of time in $(0, p_n]$. To keep the processor busy throughout this interval and the system schedulable, we can increase the execution time of any of the other tasks by 2ε units, that is,

$$e_k'' = e_k + 2\varepsilon$$

for some $k \neq 1$. It is easy to see that with this increase accompanying the decrease in the execution time of T_1, the first job of every task in the new system can still complete by its deadline and the processor never idles from 0 to p_n. Comparing the total utilization U'' of this new system with that of the original system, we find that

$$U'' - U = \frac{2\varepsilon}{p_k} - \frac{\varepsilon}{p_1}$$

Since $p_k \leq 2p_1$ for all $k \neq 1$, this difference is never negative. (Again, we could also divide the 2ε units of time arbitrarily among the $n - 1$ lower-priority tasks and get a new system with a total utilization larger than or equal to U.)

Step 4:   As a result of step 3, we know that the parameters of the most difficult-to-schedule system of tasks must be related according to Eq. (6.11). To express the total utilization of a system whose parameters are given by Eq. (6.11) in terms of periods of the tasks in it, we substitute Eq. (6.11) into the sum $\sum_{k=1}^{n} e_k/p_k$ and thus obtain

$$U(n) = q_{2,1} + q_{3,2} + \cdots + q_{n,(n-1)} + \frac{2}{q_{2,1} q_{3,2} \cdots q_{n,(n-1)}} - n \qquad (6.12)$$

where $q_{k,i}$, for $k > i$, is the ratio of the larger period p_k to the smaller period p_i, that is, $q_{k,i} = p_k/p_i$. In particular, the total utilization of any n-task system whose parameters are related according to Eq. (6.11) is a function of the $n - 1$ *adjacent period ratios* $q_{k+1,k}$ for $k = 1, 2, \ldots, n - 1$.

This equation shows that $U(n)$ is a symmetrical convex function of the adjacent period ratios. It has a unique minimum, and this minimum is the schedulable utilization $U_{RM}(n)$ of the RM algorithm. To find the minimum, we take the partial derivative of $U(n)$ with respect to each adjacent period ratio $q_{k+1,k}$ and set the derivative to 0. This gives us the following $n - 1$ equation:

$$1 - \frac{2}{q_{2,1} q_{3,2} \cdots q_{(k+1),k}^2, \cdots q_{n,(n-1)}} = 0$$

for all $k = 1, 2, \ldots, n - 1$.

Solving these equations for $q_{k+1,k}$, we find that $U(n)$ is at its minimum when all the $n - 1$ adjacent period ratios $q_{k+1,k}$ are equal to $2^{1/n}$. Their product $q_{2,1} q_{3,2} \cdots q_{n,(n-1)}$ is the ratio $q_{n,1}$ of the largest period p_n to the smallest period p_1. This ratio, being equal to $2^{(n-1)/n}$, satisfies the constraint that $p_n \leq 2p_1$. Substituting $q_{k+1,k} = 2^{1/n}$ into the right-hand side of Eq. (6.12), we get the expression of $U_{RM}(n)$ given by Theorem 6.11.

For more insight, let us look at the special case where n is equal to 3. The total utilization of any difficult-to-schedule system whose parameters are related according to Eq. (6.11) is given by

$$U(3) = q_{2,1} + q_{3,2} + + \frac{2}{q_{3,2} q_{2,1}} - 3$$

$U(3)$ is a convex function of $q_{2,1}$ and $q_{3,1}$. Its minimum value occurs at the point $q_{2,1} = q_{3,2} \geq 2^{1/3}$, which is equal to 1.26. In other words, the periods of the tasks in the most difficult-to-schedule three-task system are such that $p_3 = 1.26p_2 = 1.59p_1$.

Generalization to Arbitrary Period Ratios.   The ratio $q_{n,1} = p_n/p_1$ is the *period ratio* of the system. To complete the proof of Theorem 6.11, we must show that any n-task system whose total utilization is no greater than $U_{RM}(n)$ is schedulable rate-monotonically, not just systems whose period ratios are less than or equal to 2. We do so by showing that the following two facts are true.

1. Corresponding to every difficult-to-schedule n-task system whose period ratio is larger than 2 there is a difficult-to-schedule n-task system whose period ratio is less than or equal to 2.
2. The total utilization of the system with period ratio larger than 2 is larger than the total utilization of the corresponding system whose period ratio is less than or equal to 2.

Therefore, the restriction of period ratio being equal to or less than 2, which we imposed earlier in steps 1–4, leads to no loss of generality.

We show that fact 1 is true by construction. The construction starts with any difficult-to-schedule n-task system $\{T_i = (p_i, e_i)\}$ whose period ratio is larger than 2 and step-by-step transforms it into a system with a period ratio less than or equal to 2. Specifically, in each step, we find a task T_k whose period is such that $lp_k < p_n \leq (l+1)p_k$ where l is an integer equal to or larger than 2; the transformation completes when no such task can be found. In this step, we modify only this task and the task T_n with the largest period p_n. T_k is transformed into a new task whose period is equal to lp_k and whose execution time is equal to e_k. The period of the task with period p_n is unchanged, but its execution time is increased by $(l-1)e_k$. Figure 6–16 shows the original tasks and the transformed tasks. Clearly, the ratio of p_n and the period of the task transformed from T_k is less than or equal to 2, and the system thus obtained is also a difficult-to-schedule system. By repeating this step until $p_n \leq 2p_k$ for all $k \neq n$, we systematically transform the given system into one in which the ratio of p_n and the period of every other task is less than or equal to 2.

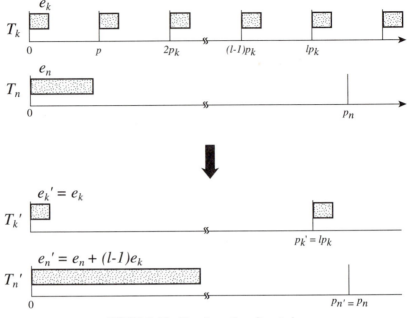

FIGURE 6–16   Transformation of two tasks.

To show fact 2 is true, we compute the difference between the total utilization of the system before the transformation of each task and the total utilization of the system after the transformation. This difference is

$$\frac{e_k}{p_k} - \frac{e_k}{lp_k} - \frac{(l-1)e_k}{p_n} = \left(\frac{1}{lp_k} - \frac{1}{p_n}\right)(l-1)e_k$$

which is larger than 0 because $lp_k < p_n$. This allows us to conclude that the system with a period ratio less than 2 obtained when the transformation completes has a smaller total utilization than the given system.

*6.7.3   Schedulable Utilization of RM Algorithm as Functions of Task Parameters

When some of the task parameters are known, this information allows us to improve the schedulable utilization of the RM algorithm. We now give several schedulable utilizations that are larger than $U_{RM}(n)$ for independent, preemptive periodic tasks whose relative deadlines are equal to their respective periods. These schedulable utilizations are expressed in terms of known parameters of the tasks, for example, the utilizations of individual tasks, the number n_h of disjoint subsets each containing simply periodic tasks, and some functions of the periods of the tasks. The general schedulable utilization $U_{RM}(n)$ of the RM algorithm is the minimum value of these specific schedulable utilizations. Because they are larger than $U_{RM}(n)$, when applicable, these schedulable utilizations are more accurate criteria of schedulability. They are particularly suited for on-line acceptance tests. When checking whether a new periodic task can be scheduled with existing tasks, many of the task parameters are already known, and computing one of these schedulable utilizations takes a constant amount of time, much less than the time required to do a time-demand analysis.

Schedulable Utilization $U_{RM}(u_1, u_2, \ldots u_n)$ as a Function of Task Utilizations. Rather than replacing the individual periods in Eq. (6.11a) by adjacent period ratios as we did earlier, we rewrite the equation as follows:

$$p_{k+1} = p_k(1 + u_k) \qquad \text{for } k = 1, 2, \ldots, n - 1$$

Moreover, from Eq. (6.11b) and the fact that $p_n \leq 2p_1$, we can conclude that

$$p_n(1 + u_n) \leq 2p_1$$

Combining these two expressions, we have the following corollary.

> **COROLLARY 6.12.** n independent, preemptable periodic tasks with relative deadlines equal to their respective periods are schedulable rate-monotonically if their utilizations $u_1, u_2, \ldots, u_n$ satisfy the inequality
>
> $$(1 + u_1)(1 + u_2) \cdots (1 + u_n) \leq 2 \tag{6.13}$$

We denote the total utilization of the tasks whose utilizations satisfy the constraint Eq. (6.13) by $U_{RM}(u_1, u_2, \ldots, u_n)$.

As an example, we consider a system of two tasks T_1 and T_2. The schedulable utilization $U_{RM}(u_1, u_2)$ of the system is equal to 0.957, 0.899, 0.861, and 0.828, respectively, when the ratio u_1/U of the utilization of T_1 to the total utilization of both tasks is equal to 0.05, 0.1, 0.25, and 0.5. The minimum of $U(u_1, u_2)$ is at the point $u_1 = 0.5U$ (i.e., when $u_1 = u_2$) and is 0.828, the Liu and Layland bound for n equal to 2.

For arbitrary n, the inequality Eq. (6.13) becomes $(1 + U(n)/n)^n \leq 2$ when the utilizations of all the tasks are equal. For this combination of utilizations, the inequality Eq. (6.13) becomes the same as the Liu and Layland bound $U(n) \leq n(2^{1/n} - 1)$.

Schedulable Utilization of Subsets of Simply Periodic Tasks. We now consider a system of periodic tasks that are not simply periodic but can be partitioned into n_h subsets of simply periodic tasks. For example, we can partition the system **T** of tasks with periods 4, 7, 8, 14, 16, 28, 32, 56, and 64 into two subsets $\mathbf{Z}_1$ and $\mathbf{Z}_2$. $\mathbf{Z}_1$ contains the tasks with period 4, 8, 16, 32, and 64; and $\mathbf{Z}_2$ contains tasks with periods 7, 14, 28, and 56. Let $U(\mathbf{Z}_1)$ and $U(\mathbf{Z}_2)$ denote the total utilization of the tasks in $\mathbf{Z}_1$ and $\mathbf{Z}_2$, respectively. Kuo, *et al.* [KuMo91] have shown that if $U(\mathbf{Z}_1) + U(\mathbf{Z}_2) \leq 0.828$ [i.e., $U_{RM}(2)$], all these tasks are schedulable rate-monotonically. In contrast, if we were to treat the tasks separately, we would have to use the bound $U_{RM}(9)$, which is only 0.712.

The following theorem by Kuo, *et al.* [KuMo91] states this fact in general.

> **THEOREM 6.13.** If a system **T** of independent, preemptable periodic tasks, whose relative deadlines are equal to their respective periods, can be partitioned into n_h disjoint

subsets, $\mathbf{Z}_1, \mathbf{Z}_2, \ldots, \mathbf{Z}_{n_h}$, each of which contains simply periodic tasks, then the system is schedulable rate-monotonically if the total utilizations $U(\mathbf{Z}_i)$, for $i = 1, 2, \ldots, n_h$, of the tasks in the subsets satisfy the inequality

$$(1 + U(\mathbf{Z}_1))(1 + U(\mathbf{Z}_2)) \cdots (1 + U(\mathbf{Z}_{n_h})) \leq 2.$$

It follows that such a system $\mathbf{T}$ is schedulable rate-monotonically if its total utilization is equal to or less than $U_{RM}(n_h)$.

To see intuitively why this theorem is true, we replace each subset $\mathbf{Z}_i$ by a single periodic task T_i'. The period p_i' of this task is equal to the shortest period all the tasks in $\mathbf{Z}_i$, and its execution time is equal to $p_i'U(\mathbf{Z}_i)$. Clearly, the set of n_h new tasks T_i''s are schedulable rate-monotonically if either one of the conditions in Theorem 6.13 is satisfied. The fact that T_i' is schedulable means that within each interval of length p_i', T_i' has $p_i'U(\mathbf{Z}_i)$ units of processor time. Because the tasks in $\mathbf{Z}_i$ are simply periodic, the total amount of time demanded by all the tasks during any period p ($\geq p_i'$) of any task in $\mathbf{Z}_i$ is equal to $pU(\mathbf{Z}_i) = kp_i'U(\mathbf{Z}_i)$ for some integer k. Since this demand is met by any schedule in which all jobs in T_i' complete in time, every job in any task in $\mathbf{Z}_i$ can always complete in time. (This argument is not a proof because it neglects the fact that tasks with longer periods are scheduled at lower priorities. A complete proof of this theorem can be found in [KuMo91].)

The schedulable utilization given by Theorem 6.13 is particularly useful for any system that contains a small number n of large application modules. If we can make the tasks in each module simply periodic, we do not need to be concerned with the number of tasks in each module. Provided that the total utilization of all the modules is no greater than $U_{RM}(n)$, we are assured of the schedulability of all the tasks in the system. For example, in a system containing a large number of multirate controllers, n is the rate groups (i.e., the number of controllers). We need not be concerned with how many control-law computations per controller the system must perform when the rates in each group are related in a harmonic way.

Dependency of Schedulable Utilization on Periods of Tasks.   The schedulable utilization of the RM algorithm depends on the periods of tasks in two ways. First, it increases with the minimum adjacent period ratio and, hence, the period ratio of the system, and second, it increases as the tasks become closer to being simply periodic.

Dependency on Period Ratio.   The fact that the schedulable utilization of the RM algorithm increases with the period ratio of the system has been demonstrated statistically in a study by Lehoczky, *et al.* [LeSD] who simulated systems in which task periods are uniformly distributed over a wide range. We expect the schedulable utilization of the RM algorithm to increase with the minimum adjacent period ratio for the following reason. During any period of a task T_i, it is possible for a higher priority task T_k ($k < i$) to consume an extra e_k units of processor time beyond $u_k p_i$. This is why the schedulable utilization $U_{RM}(i)$ is less than 1. However, when the ratio p_i/p_k becomes larger, the extra amount e_k becomes a smaller fraction of $u_k p_i$. In the limit as the adjacent period ratios approach infinity, the amount of time in each period of T_i used by higher-priority tasks approaches $U_{i-1}p_i$, the amount of time available to T_i approaches $1 - U_{i-1}$, and the schedulable utilization of the i tasks approaches 1.

We can also observe from the proof of Theorem 6.11 that the period ratio of the most difficult-to-schedule n-task system is $2^{(n-1)/n}$, which is equal to 1.414 when n is equal to 2 and is approximately equal to 2 when n is large. Moreover in this system, the ratios of all $n-1$ adjacent periods are equal to $2^{1/n}$. The total utilization of a difficult-to-schedule system increases as the minimum adjacent period ratio increases. Hence, the performance of the RM algorithm in terms of its schedulable utilization is the worst when the minimum adjacent period ratio of the system is $2^{1/n}$ and improves as the ratio increases.

Dependency on Values of Periods.   Theorem 6.3 tells us that any number of simply periodic, independent, preemptable tasks can be feasibly scheduled rate-monotonically as long as their total utilization is no more than 1. We, therefore, expect that the closer the tasks are to being simply periodic, the larger the total schedulable utilization of the RM algorithm is. The schedulable utilization found by Burchard, *et al.* [BLOS] quantifies this statement.

Specifically, Burchard, *et al.* [BLOS] expresses the schedulable utilization in terms a parameter ζ which measures how far the tasks of a system deviate from being simply periodic. ζ is defined as follows:

$$\zeta = \max_{1 \le i \le n} X_i - \min_{1 \le i \le n} X_i \qquad (6.14a)$$

where

$$X_i = log_2 p_i - \lfloor \log_2 p_i \rfloor \qquad (6.14b)$$

THEOREM 6.14.   The schedulable utilization $U_{RM}(\zeta, n)$ of the RM algorithm as a function of ζ and n is given by

$$U_{RM}(n, \zeta) = (n-1)(2^{\zeta/(n-1)} - 1) + 2^{1-\zeta} - 1 \qquad \text{for } \zeta < 1 - 1/n \quad (6.14c)$$
$$n(2^{1/n} - 1) \qquad \text{for } \zeta \ge 1 - 1/n$$

Theorem 6.11 follows straightforwardly from this theorem.

Before we examine the behavior of $U_{RM}(n, \zeta)$ as ζ varies, we first examine how ζ depends on the periods of the tasks. To do so, we write p_i as 2^{x_i} for some $x_i > 0$. If x_i is an integer, the value X_i defined above is 0. X_i increases as x_i increases and deviates more from the integer value and becomes 0 again when it assumes the next larger integer value. For example, X_i is 0 if $p_i = 2^3 = 8$. It has the values 0.322, 0.585, and 0.807 when p_i is equal to 10, 12, and 14, respectively. Similarly, X_i is 0 when p_i is equal to $2^4 = 16$ (or $2^2 = 4$) and is equal to these values when p_i is equal to 20, 24, and 28 (or 5, 6, and 7), respectively. Hence, for a system of n tasks, ζ is equal to 0 when the period p_i of every task T_i is equal to $y2^{x_i}$ for some $y > 0$ independent of i and some positive integer x_i. (In other words, the period of every task is divisible by some power of 2.) In the extreme when ζ approaches one, there must be a task whose period is slightly larger than some power of 2 and some other task whose period is slightly smaller than some power of 2 (i.e., the periods are relatively prime).

Figure 6–17 plots $U_{RM}(n, \zeta)$ as a function of ζ and n. In the region where $\zeta < 1 - 1/n$, $U_{RM}(n, \zeta)$ is larger than the general schedulable utilization $U_{RM}(n)$ given by Eq. (6.10). In particular, as ζ approaches zero, $U_{RM}(n, \zeta)$ approaches one for all n as expected.

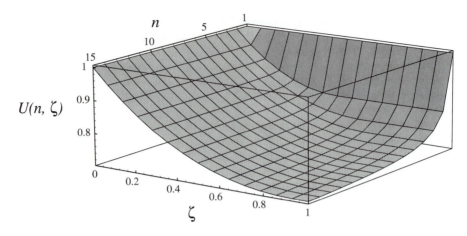

FIGURE 6–17 $U_{RM}(n, \zeta)$ as a function of n and ζ.

Yet Another Schedulability Test Making Use of Task Periods.   For a given system **T** of tasks, let **T′** be a set of tasks which has the following property. There is a task T_i' in **T′** if and only if there is task T_i in **T**. Moreover, the execution time of T_i' is equal to the execution time of T_i, and the period of T_i' is shorter than the period of T_i. **T′** is called an *accelerated set* of **T**.

We now try to make use of the fact demonstrated by the example in Figure 6–9 at the end of Section 6.5.2. It follows from the observation made there that any system **T** is schedulable according to a fixed-priority algorithm if it has an accelerated set **T′** that is schedulable according to the algorithm. In particular, we have the following theorem regarding the RM algorithm.

> **THEOREM 6.15.**   A system **T** of independent, preemptive periodic tasks whose relative deadlines are equal to their respective periods is schedulable according the RM algorithm if it has an accelerated set **T′** which is simply periodic and has a total utilization equal to or less than 1.

The theorem follows from the above observation and Theorem 6.3. Han [Han] gives an $O(n^2 \log n)$ algorithm and an $O(n^3)$ algorithm that apply Theorem 6.15 to determine the schedulability of rate-monotonically scheduled systems. The more complex algorithm is more accurate. Both are more accurate than the test based on the schedulable utilizations [Eqs. (6.10) and (6.14)]. Section 10.2.3 will describe an algorithm that can be used for this purpose as well.

6.7.4   Schedulable Utilization of Fixed Priority Tasks with Arbitrary Relative Deadlines

Obviously, a system of n tasks with a total utilization $U_{RM}(n)$ may not be schedulable rate-monotonically when the relative deadlines of some tasks are shorter than their periods. On the other hand, if the relative deadlines of the tasks are larger than the respective task periods, we expect the schedulable utilization of the RM algorithm to be larger than $U_{RM}(n)$. We now consider the case where the relative deadline D_i of every task is equal to δ times its period

p_i for some $0 < \delta$. The following theorem proven by Lehoczky et al. [Leho, LeSh, LSST] gives us a schedulable utilization $U_{RM}(n, \delta)$ as a function of δ and the number n of tasks. The schedulable utilization $U_{RM}(n)$ given by Theorem 6.11 is equal to this upper bound in the special case where $\delta = 1$.

> **THEOREM 6.16.**   A system of n independent, preemptable periodic tasks with relative deadlines $D_i = \delta p_i$ for all $1 \le i \le n$ is schedulable rate-monotonically if its total utilization is equal to or less than
>
> $$U_{RM}(n, \delta) = \delta(n-1)\left[\left(\frac{\delta+1}{\delta}\right)^{1/n-1} - 1\right], \qquad \text{for } \delta = 2, 3, \dots \quad (6.15)$$
>
> $$n((2\delta)^{1/n} - 1) + 1 - \delta, \qquad\qquad 0.5 \le \delta \le 1$$
>
> $$\delta, \qquad\qquad\qquad\qquad\qquad 0 \le \delta \le 0.5$$

Figure 6–18 lists the values of $U_{RM}(n, \delta)$ for several values of n and δ. For any n, this schedulable utilization is larger than $U_{RM}(n)$ when δ is an integer larger than 1. In the limit when n is equal to infinity, this upper bound on the total utilization approaches $\delta \ln((\delta+1)/\delta)$, for $\delta = 1, 2, \dots$. It approaches 1 as δ approaches infinity, as expected; since $U(n)$ is no greater than one, every job eventually completes.

Figure 6–18 also plots $U_{RM}(n, \delta)$ as a function of n and δ in the range $0 \le \delta \le 1$. We see that in this range of δ, $U_{RM}(n, \delta)$ decreases from $U_{RM}(n)$ given by Eq. (6.10) as δ decreases.

As an example, let us consider the system consisting of tasks $(3, 0.6)$, $(4, 1.0)$ and $(5, 1)$. The total utilization of the tasks is 0.65. Since $U_{RM}(3)$ is equal to 0.779, the tasks are schedulable. Now, suppose that as a way to control completion-time jitters, we require that every job completes in half the period; in other words, δ is equal to 0.5. Because $U_{RM}(3, 0.5)$ is 0.5, the schedulable utilization does not ensure us that the tasks are schedulable. In fact, the task $(5, 1)$ is not schedulable. However, if δ is equal to 0.69, $U_{RM}(3, \delta)$ is equal to 0.65 and hence, it guarantees that the tasks are schedulable.

*6.7.5   Schedulable Utilization of the RM Algorithm for Multiframe Tasks

We know that the periodic task model is sometimes inaccurate, and the prediction on schedulability based on the model can be unduly pessimistic. An example is a task that models the transmission of an MPEG compressed video over a network link. Jobs in this task, modeling the transmissions of individual video frames, are released periodically. Because the size of I-frames can be very large compared with that of B- and P-frames, the execution times of the jobs can vary widely. When modeled as a periodic task, the execution time of the task is equal to the transmission time of an I-frame. Hence, if we were to determine whether a system of such tasks is schedulable based on the schedulability tests described above, we would surely underutilize the processor. The *multiframe task model* developed by Mok and Chen [MoCh] is a more accurate model and leads to more accurate schedulability tests.

The example used by Mok and Chen to motivate the multiframe task model is a system of two tasks: T_1 and T_2. T_2 is a task with period 5 and execution time 1. The period of T_1 is 3. The maximum execution time of $J_{1,k}$ is equal to 3, if k is odd and is equal to 1 if k is

n	$\delta = 4.0$	$\delta = 3.0$	$\delta = 2.0$	$\delta = 1.0$	$\delta = 0.9$	$\delta = 0.8$	$\delta = 0.7$	$\delta = 0.6$	$\delta = 0.5$
2	0.944	0.928	0.898	0.828	0.783	0.729	0.666	0.590	0.500
3	0.926	0.906	0.868	0.779	0.749	0.708	0.656	0.588	0.500
4	0.917	0.894	0.853	0.756	0.733	0.698	0.651	0.586	0.500
5	0.912	0.888	0.844	0.743	0.723	0.692	0.648	0.585	0.500
6	0.909	0.884	0.838	0.734	0.717	0.688	0.646	0.585	0.500
7	0.906	0.881	0.834	0.728	0.713	0.686	0.644	0.584	0.500
8	0.905	0.878	0.831	0.724	0.709	0.684	0.643	0.584	0.500
9	0.903	0.876	0.829	0.720	0.707	0.682	0.642	0.584	0.500
∞	0.892	0.863	0.810	0.693	0.687	0.670	0.636	0.582	0.500

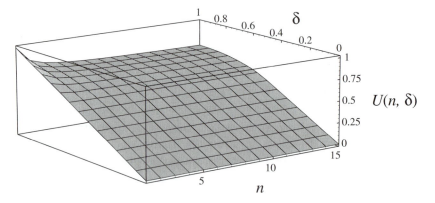

FIGURE 6–18 $U_{RM}(n, \delta)$ as a function of n for $0 \le \delta \le 1$. (a) Values of $U_{RM}(n, \delta)$. (b) Behavior of $U_{RM}(n, \delta)$ in the range of $\delta < 1$.

even. The relative deadlines of the tasks are equal to their respective periods. We can treat T_1 as the periodic task $(3, 3)$, but if we were to do so, we would conclude that the system is not schedulable. This conclusion would be too pessimistic because the system is in fact schedulable. Indeed, as we will see shortly, by modeling T_1 more accurately as a multiframe task, we can reach the correct conclusion.

Specifically, in the multiframe task model, each (multiframe) task T_i is characterized by a 4-tuple $(p_i, \xi_i, e_i^P, e_i^n)$. In the 4-tuple, p_i is the period of the task and has the same meaning as the period of a periodic task. Jobs in T_i have either one of two possible maximum execution times: e_i^P and e_i^n, where $e_i^P \ge e_i^n$. The former is its *peak execution time*, and the latter is its *normal execution time*. Each period which begins at the release time of a job with the peak execution time is called a *peak frame*, and the other periods are called *normal frames*. Each peak frame is followed by $\xi_i - 1$ normal frames, which in turn are followed by a peak frame and so on. The utilization u_i of the multiframe task $T_i = (p_i, \xi_i, e_i{}^p, e_i{}^n)$ is equal to $(e_i{}^p + (\xi_i - 1)e_i{}^n)/\xi_i p_i$ when ξ_i is larger than 1. A periodic task (p_i, e_i) is the special multiframe task $(p_i, 1, e_i, e_i)$.

According to the multiframe task model, the task T_1 in the example above is $(3, 2, 3, 1)$; its period is 3, peak execution time is 3, normal execution time is 1, and each peak frame is followed by one normal frame. It utilization is equal to $(3 + 1)/6 = 0.667$. The task $(33, 6, 1.0, 0.3)$ can model an MPEG video transmission task. The period of the task is 33 milliseconds. The execution time of the job in each peak frame, which models the transmission of an I-frame in the video stream, is never more than one millisecond. It is followed by five normal frames. The execution times of jobs released in normal frames are never more than 0.3. These jobs model the transmissions of B- and P-frames in the video. They are followed by the transmission of an I-frame, that is, a peak frame, which is in turn followed by five normal frames, and so on.

We observe that the response time of a job $J_{i,k}$ in T_i has the maximum possible value if the kth period, which begins when $J_{i,k}$ is released, is a peak frame and this peak frame begins at the same time as a peak frame in every high-priority task. In other words, a critical instant of a multiframe task T_i occurs under this condition. (The proof of this claim is left to you as an exercise.) Consequently, when the relative deadlines D_i's are such that $D_k \leq p_k$ for all $1 \leq k \leq n$, a task T_i is schedulable if the job in the task released at a critical instant completes in time.

Given a system of n multiframe tasks, the *load variation*, denoted by Ξ, of the system is $\min_{1 \leq i \leq n}(e_i{}^p/e_i{}^n)$. We expect that the schedulable utilization of the RM algorithm is an increasing function of the load variation. Mok and Chen [MoCh] found that it depends on Ξ as stated below.

THEOREM 6.17.   A system of n independent, preemptable multiframe tasks, whose relative deadlines are equal to the respective periods, is schedulable according to the RM algorithm if their total utilization is no greater than

$$U_{RM}(n, \Xi) = \Xi n \left(\left(\frac{\Xi + 1}{\Xi} \right)^{1/n} - 1 \right) \tag{6.16}$$

Figure 6–19 shows this schedulable utilization as function of Ξ and n. Indeed, as Ξ increases, this upper bound increases. However, we would still declare the tasks $T_1 = (3, 2, 3, 1)$ and $T_2 = (5, 1, 1, 1)$ mentioned earlier unschedulable if we were to use this schedulable utilization as the criterion of schedulability. The load variation of this system is 1. $U_{RM}(n, \Xi = 1)$ is 0.828, but the total utilization of this system is 0.867.

6.8   PRACTICAL FACTORS

Thus far, we have assumed that every job is preemptable at any time; once a job is released, it never suspends itself and hence is ready for execution until it completes; scheduling and context-switch overhead is negligible; the scheduler is event-driven and acts immediately upon event occurrences; every task (or job) has a distinct priority; and every job in a fixed-

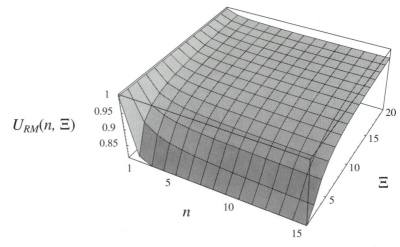

$U_{RM}(n, \Xi)$

FIGURE 6–19   Schedulable utilization of the RM algorithm for n multiframe tasks.

priority system is scheduled at a constant priority. These assumptions are often not valid. We now discuss how these factors affect the schedulability of fixed-priority and dynamic-priority systems. In this discussion, we will need two new terms: blocking and priority inversion. A (ready) job J_i is *blocked* when it is prevented from executing by a lower-priority job: The lower-priority job executes while J_i waits. We say that a *priority inversion* occurs whenever a lower-priority job executes while some ready higher-priority job waits.

6.8.1 Nonpreemptability

There are many reasons for a job, or a portion of it, to be nonpreemptable. When a job is using a resource (e.g., a critical section) that must be used in a mutual exclusive manner, making the job nonpreemptable while it has the resource is one way to ensure mutual exclusion. Some system calls (or parts of the calls) are nonpreemptable for the same reason; consequently, a job that makes such a call is nonpreemptable during the execution of the call. Sometimes, preemption may be too costly. An example is disk scheduling. If reads and writes of files on a disk were preemptable, it would take an additional seek to resume the read or write of a file each time such an operation were preempted. Since seek and latency times are large on average, a significant amount of bandwidth might be lost if preemption were allowed. Consequently, disk scheduling is typically nonpreemptive.

Blocking Time Due to Nonpreemptivity.   A higher-priority job that becomes ready when a nonpreemptable lower-priority job is executing is blocked until the nonpreemptable portion of the lower-priority job completes. The delay due to blocking may cause the higher-priority job to miss its deadline. Consequently, when we want to determine whether a task can meet all its deadlines, we must consider not only all the tasks that have higher priorities than it, but also the nonpreemptable portions of lower-priority tasks.

As an example, we consider a system of three fixed-priority tasks: $T_1 = (\varepsilon, 4, 1)$, $T_2 = (\varepsilon, 5, 1.5)$, and $T_3 = (9, 2)$, where $\varepsilon > 0$ is very small compared with the other timing parameters of the tasks. The total utilization is 0.77. The time-demand functions of the three tasks are shown in Figure 6–20(a). If all the tasks are preemptable, they are schedulable according to both the schedulable utilization $U_{RM}(3) = 0.78$ and the time-demand analysis.

Now, suppose that T_3 is nonpreemptable. When the jobs $J_{1,1}$ and $J_{2,1}$ become ready at ε, the first job $J_{3,1}$ of T_3 is executing. Because $J_{3,1}$ cannot be preempted, the higher-priority jobs are blocked until time 2 when $J_{3,1}$ completes; there is a priority inversion during $(\varepsilon, 2)$. $J_{2,1}$ is forced to wait for the lower-priority job $J_{3,1}$ in addition to the higher-priority task T_1. As a consequence, it misses its deadline at time 5. Because both the schedulable utilization $U_{RM}(n)$ given by Eq. (6.10) and the time-demand functions given by Eq. (6.5) do not take into account the delay suffered by T_2 due to priority inversion, they would mislead us into believing that T_2 can meet all its deadlines.

From this example, we can see that one way to take into account the effect of priority inversion is to add its duration into the time-demand functions of T_1 and T_2. The result is shown in Figure 6–20(b). The time-demand function $w_2(t)$ that includes the 2 units of time consumed by $J_{3,1}$ lies entirely above the time supply function t. It leads us to a correct conclusion that T_2 is not schedulable. Similarly, we can account for these 2 units of time in the computation of the total utilization of T_1 and T_2. Because a job in T_2 may be forced to wait for 2 additional units of time, the total fraction of time required by T_2 and the higher-priority job T_1 can be as high as $1/4 + (1.5 + 2)/5$. This sum is 0.95, higher than $U_{RM}(2)$.

In general, let $b_i(np)$ denote the longest time for which any job in the task T_i can be blocked each time it is blocked due to nonpreemptive lower-priority tasks. We call $b_i(np)$ its *blocking time per blocking due to nonpreemptivity*. A job $J_{i,j}$ of T_i is blocked if when it is released, a nonpreemptive lower-priority job is executing at the time. In the worst case, this lower-priority job is the one that has the longest nonpreemptable portion among all lower-priority jobs. In other words, for the sake of determining whether the system is schedulable, we do not need to keep track of the execution times of all the nonpreemptable portions, only the longest nonpreemptable portion of each job. We use θ_i ($\theta_i \leq e_i$) to denote the maximum execution time of the longest nonpreemptable portion of jobs in the task T_i. In a fixed-priority system, $b_i(np)$ is given by

$$b_i(np) = \max_{i+1 \leq k \leq n} \theta_k \tag{6.17}$$

If the task T_i never suspends itself, once the job $J_{i,j}$ or a ready higher-priority job begins to execute, no lower-priority job can ever get the processor until $J_{i,j}$ completes. So, when T_i never self-suspends, $b_i(np)$ is the total blocking time of T_i due to nonpreemptivity.

Effect of Blocking on Schedulability.   As will become evident later, a job may be blocked for many reasons. $b_i(np)$ is only one of the factors that contribute to the blocking time of T_i. The term *blocking time*, denoted by b_i, refers to the maximum total duration for which each job in task T_i may be delayed by both lower-priority tasks and deferred execution of higher-priority tasks. (We will return shortly to explain the latter.)

To see how to take into account blocking times of fixed-priority tasks, let us suppose that we have found the total blocking time b_i of every task T_i. If a job $J_{i,j}$ is to meet its deadline, the total time demanded by itself and all the higher-priority jobs that must be completed before it, plus the time that may be taken by a nonpreemptable lower-priority job and other blocking factors, must be met by the supply of time before its deadline. Therefore, the time-demand

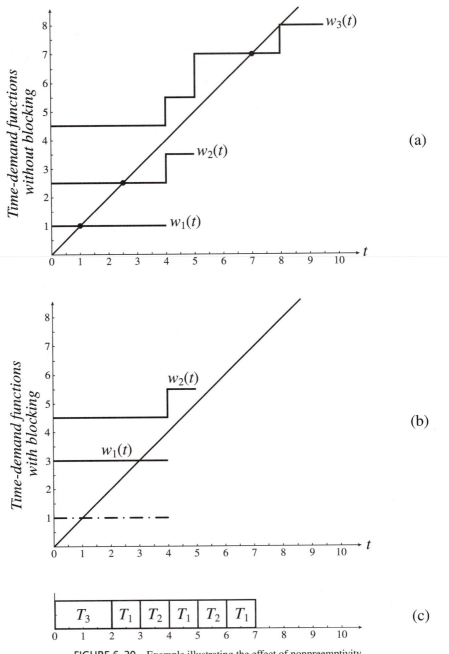

FIGURE 6–20 Example illustrating the effect of nonpreemptivity.

function $w_i(t)$ of the task T_i, including its blocking time b_i, is given by

$$w_i(t) = e_i + b_i + \sum_{k=1}^{i-1} \left\lceil \frac{t}{p_k} \right\rceil e_k, \qquad \text{for } 0 < t \le \min(D_i, p_i) \qquad (6.18)$$

When we use this expression of the time-demand function, instead of the one given by Eq. (6.5), in the time-demand analysis of a system where $D_i \le p_i$ for all i, we correctly take into account the effect of blocking. Similarly, we add b_i in the expressions of $w_{i,j}(t)$ in Eq. (6.9b) when the response times and relative deadlines of some tasks are larger than p_i, that is,

$$w_{i,j}(t) = je_i + b_i + \sum_{k=1}^{i-1} \left\lceil \frac{t}{p_k} \right\rceil e_k, \qquad \text{for } (j-1)p_i < t \le w_{i,j}(t) \qquad (6.19)$$

Clearly, if we want to use the schedulable utilizations such as those in Section 6.7 to determine the schedulability of tasks that are sometimes blocked, we must also take into account the effect of blocking. Because the jobs in different tasks may be blocked for different amounts of time and blocking affects different tasks to different degrees, we need to do the test one task at a time. In the worst case, every job in a task, say T_i, can be blocked; the amount of time per period required by the job is $e_i + b_i$. b_i/p_i is the fraction of time that is not accounted for by the utilization u_i of the task. Hence, *in a fixed-priority system, the task T_i, for $1 \le i < n$, is schedulable if*

$$\frac{e_1}{p_1} + \frac{e_2}{p_2} + \cdots + \frac{e_i + b_i}{p_i} = U_i + \frac{b_i}{p_i} \le U_X(i) \qquad (6.20)$$

where U_i is the total utilization of the i highest priority tasks and $U_X(i)$ denotes the appropriate schedulable utilization of the fixed-priority algorithm X used to schedule the tasks.

To compute the blocking time $b_i(np)$ of a task T_i in a deadline-driven system (i.e., when tasks are scheduled on a EDF basis), we make use of the following theorem [Bake91].

THEOREM 6.18. In a system where jobs are scheduled on the EDF basis, a job J_k with relative deadline D_k can block a job J_i with relative deadline D_i only if D_k is larger than D_i.

Proof. The following observations allow us to conclude that the theorem is true.

1. In order for J_k to block J_i, J_k must have a lower priority than J_i. Since priorities are assigned on the EDF basis, this implies that the deadline d_k of J_k must be later than the deadline d_i of J_i. In other words, $d_k > d_i$.
2. In addition, when the higher-priority job J_i is released, the lower-priority job J_k must be executing if J_k is to block J_i. This means that J_k must be released earlier than J_i, or $r_k < r_i$.

Both inequalities can be true only when $D_k > D_i$. □

Suppose that we index all periodic tasks according to their relative deadlines; the smaller the relative deadline, the smaller the index. Then, it follows from this theorem that in a deadline-driven system, the blocking time of each periodic task T_i due to nonpreemptivity is also given by Eq. (6.17). *A task T_i with a total blocking time b_i is schedulable with other independent periodic tasks on a processor according to the EDF algorithm if*

$$\sum_{k=1}^{n} \frac{e_k}{\min(D_k,\,p_k)} + \frac{b_i}{\min(D_i,\,p_i)} \leq 1 \qquad (6.21)$$

The system is schedulable if the condition is met for every $i = 1, 2, \ldots, n$.

6.8.2 Self-Suspension

While executing, a job may invoke some external operation, for example, an I/O operation or a remote procedure, that is executed on another processor. *Self-blocking* or *self-suspension* occurs when the job is suspended and waits until such an operation completes before its execution can continue. While it waits, the operating system removes it from the ready queue and places it in a blocked queue. We assume that the maximum amount of time each external operation takes to complete and, hence, the maximum duration of each self-suspension, is known. (This time can be an upper bound on the maximum response time of the external operation obtained by doing a time-demand analysis of all the tasks on the processor where the operation executes.)

In a special case, every job in a task T_i self-suspends for x units of time immediately after it is released (e.g., due to input data transmission). The job is ready for execution x time units after it is released. Hence, the time from the instant when the job is ready to its deadline is only $D_i - x$, not D_i. To determine whether the task T_i is schedulable, we use the shortened deadline $D_i - x$ in the schedulability test; there is no need to modify any of the methods otherwise.

A job may self-suspend after its execution has begun, and the amounts of time for which jobs in a task self-suspend may differ. As a consequence, the task no longer behaves as a periodic task. In particular, it may demand more time in some interval than a periodic task. For example, we consider two tasks $T_1 = (4, 2.5)$ and $T_2 = (3, 7, 2.0)$. The tasks are schedulable rate-monotonically if jobs in both tasks never self-suspend. The schedule in Figure 6–21 shows what happens when the first job $J_{1,1}$ in T_1 self-suspends for 1.5 units of time shortly after it begins execution. Because the execution of $J_{1,1}$ is deferred, T_1 now

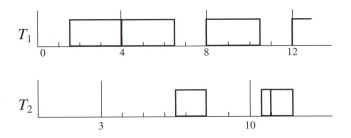

FIGURE 6–21 Example illustrating the effect of self-suspension: $T_1 = (4, 2.5)$, $T_2 = (3, 7, 2.0)$.

demands 5.5 units of time in the interval (3, 10]. (In contrast, if the execution of $J_{1,1}$ were not deferred, T_1 would demand only 4.5 units of time.) As a consequence, $J_{2,1}$ misses its deadline.

From this example, we see that one way to account for the extra delay suffered by a task T_i in a fixed-priority system due to its own self-suspension and the suspension of higher-priority tasks is to treat this delay as a factor of the blocking time of T_i. We denote this factor by $b_i(ss)$. At the risk of abusing the term blocking, we call $b_i(ss)$ the *blocking time of T_i due to self-suspension.*

To determine $b_i(ss)$, we suppose that the *maximum self-suspension time* of any job in each higher-priority task T_k ($k < i$) is x, that is, no job in T_k ever self-suspends for more than x units of time. The difference between the total amounts of time demanded by T_k in the feasible interval of any job in T_i when T_k never self-suspends and when T_k does self-suspend is never more than x units and is never more than e_k. Therefore, we can bound the blocking time $b_i(ss)$ of T_i due to self-suspension in a fixed-priority system by

$$b_i(ss) = \text{maximum self-suspension time of } T_i \qquad (6.22)$$

$$+ \sum_{k=1}^{i-1} \min(e_k, \text{maximum self-suspension time of } T_k)$$

In the example in Figure 6–21, the maximum self-suspension time of T_1 is 1.5, which is smaller than its execution time of 2.5. Hence $b_2(ss)$ is equal to 1.5.

We must include $b_i(ss)$ in the total blocking time b_i of each task T_i, of course. In a system where some tasks are nonpreemptable, the effect of self-suspension is more severe than this factor indicates, however. The reason is that every time a job suspends itself, it loses the processor. It may be blocked again by a nonpreemptive lower-priority job when it resumes after the suspension. Therefore, if each job in a task T_i can self-suspend for a maximum number K_i times after it starts execution, its total blocking time b_i is given by

$$b_i = b_i(ss) + (K_i + 1)b_i(np) \qquad (6.23)$$

6.8.3   Context Switches

We now confine our attention to job-level fixed-priority assignment, that is, each job is given a fixed priority throughout its execution. In such a system, each job preempts at most one job if there is no self-suspension. Hence, each job suffers at most one context switch when it starts execution and another context switch when it completes. We can account for the context-switch overhead in a schedulability test by including the time spent for the two context switches at the start and completion of each job as part of the execution time of the job. If the job is preempted and later resumed, the time spent for the two context switches is accounted for in the same way: Include the context-switch time in the execution time of the preempting job.

We let CS denote the *context-switch time* of the system, that is, the maximum amount of time the system spends per context switch. CS includes the time required to maintain the context of the jobs involved in the context switch, as well as the time spent by the scheduler to service the event interrupt that triggers the context switch and to carry out the scheduling action at the context switch. If no job ever self-suspends, we increase the execution time of every task T_i to $e_i + 2CS$, for $i = 1, 2, \ldots, n$ when the context-switch overhead is not negligible. If some job self-suspends, the job incurs two more context switches each time it self-suspends. Therefore, if each job in any task T_i can self-suspend a maximum of K_i times after its execution starts, we add $2(K_i + 1)CS$ to the execution time e_i.

In a job-level dynamic-priority system, for example, in a system scheduled according to the LST algorithm described in Section 6.2.2, we can bound the effect of context-switch overhead if we can find an upper bound to the number of times a job may preempt another job. In addition to complications in resource access control, which we will discuss in Chapter 8, and higher scheduling overhead, the difficulty in accounting for the effect of context switching accurately in such systems is another disadvantage of job-level dynamic-priority algorithms.

6.8.4 Limited-Priority Levels

A real-life system can support only a limited number Ω_s of priority levels. (For example, the IEEE 802.5 token ring provides only 8 priority levels, and real-time operating systems provide no more than 256 priority levels.) As a consequence, tasks (or jobs) may have nondistinct priorities.

Time Demand Functions of Fixed-Priority Tasks with Nondistinct Priorities. When tasks in a fixed-priority system have nondistinct priorities, a job $J_{i,j}$ of T_i may be delayed by a job of an equal priority task T_k. This is due to the fact that jobs of equal priorities are scheduled either on a FIFO basis or on a round-robin basis. The delay suffered by $J_{i,j}$ due to equal priority tasks is the largest when a job from each of these tasks is released immediately before $J_{i,j}$. Let $\mathbf{T}_E(i)$ denote the subset of tasks, other than T_i, that have the same priority as T_i. This delay is at most equal to the sum of the execution times of all the tasks in $\mathbf{T}_E(i)$.

Therefore, when the priorities of tasks are not distinct, the time-demand function $w_i(t)$ of any task T_i in a system where $D_k \le p_k$ for all k is

$$w_i(t) = e_i + b_i + \sum_{T_k \in \mathbf{T}_E(i)} e_k + \sum_{T_k \in \mathbf{T}_H(i)} \left\lceil \frac{t}{p_k} \right\rceil e_k, \qquad \text{for } 0 < t \le \min(D_i, p_i) \quad (6.24a)$$

where $\mathbf{T}_H(i)$ denotes the subset of tasks that have higher priorities than T_i. Similarly, in a system where the response times of some tasks are larger than their respective periods, we compute the time-demand function of the jth-job of T_i in a level-i busy interval according to

$$w_{i,j}(t) = je_i + b_i + \sum_{T_k \in \mathbf{T}_E(i)} \left(\left\lceil \frac{(j-1)p_i}{p_k} \right\rceil + 1 \right) e_k + \sum_{T_k \in \mathbf{T}_H(i)} \left\lceil \frac{t}{p_k} \right\rceil e_k \qquad (6.24b)$$

for $(j-1)p_i < t \le w_{i,j}(t)$.

Schedulability Loss of Fixed-Priority Systems.   Whenever the number Ω_n of priorities assigned to tasks (called assigned priorities) by a fixed-priority scheduling algorithm is larger than the number Ω_s of priority levels supported by the system, the Ω_n assigned priorities must be mapped onto Ω_s system priorities. The performance of the scheduling algorithm critically depends on this mapping.

In the description of this mapping, we continue to use positive integers $1, 2, \dots, \Omega_n$ to denote the assigned priorities, 1 being the highest priority and Ω_n the lowest. We denote the system priorities by $\pi_1, \pi_2, \ldots, \pi_{\Omega_s}$, where π_k ($1 \leq k \leq \Omega_s$) is a positive integer in the range $[1, \Omega_n]$ and π_j is less than π_k if $j < k$. The set $\{\pi_1, \pi_2, \ldots, \pi_{\Omega_s}\}$ is a priority grid. We map the assigned priorities onto this grid so that all the assigned priorities equal to or higher than π_1 are mapped to π_1 and all assigned priorities in the range $(\pi_{k-1}, \pi_k]$ are mapped to the system priority π_k for $1 < k \leq \Omega_s$.

A natural mapping is the uniform mapping. According to this method, the priority grid is uniformly distributed in the range of the assigned priorities. Specifically, let Q denote the integer $\lfloor \Omega_n / \Omega_s \rfloor$. $\pi_k = kQ$ for $k = 1, 2, \ldots, \Omega_s - 1$ and π_{Ω_s} is equal to Ω_n. Hence, the highest Q assigned priorities $1, 2, \ldots, Q$ are mapped to $\pi_1 = Q$, the next Q highest assigned priorities are mapped to $\pi_2 = 2Q$, and so on. As an example, suppose that a system has 10 tasks whose assigned priorities are equal to $1, 2, \ldots, 10$. Suppose that the system can support only three priority levels. According to uniform mapping, the system priorities are $\pi_1 = 3$, $\pi_2 = 6$, and $\pi_3 = 10$. The assigned priorities 1, 2, and 3 are mapped to the same system priority $\pi_1 = 3$, the assigned priorities 4, 5, and 6 are mapped to system priority $\pi_2 = 6$, and the assigned priorities 7, 8, 9, and 10 are mapped to the lowest system priority $\pi_3 = 10$. The scheduler then schedules the tasks according to their system priorities. Because jobs in tasks with the same system priority are scheduled on a FIFO basis, with linear mapping, the schedulable utilization can be very small.

A better method is the *constant ratio mapping* [LeSh]. This method keeps the ratios of $(\pi_{i-1} + 1)/\pi_i$, for $i = 2, 3, \ldots, \Omega_s$ as equal as possible. Consequently, there are more system priority levels at the higher-priority end of the assigned priority range than at the lower-priority end. In the example above, we can let $\pi_1 = 1$, $\pi_2 = 4$, and $\pi_3 = 10$. $(\pi_1 + 1)/\pi_2$ is 1/2, and $(\pi_2 + 1)/\pi_3$ is also 1/2. With this grid, the assigned priority 1 is mapped to system priority 1; the assigned priorities 2, 3, and 4 are mapped to system priority 4 and the five lowest assigned priorities are mapped to system priority 10.

Let g denote the minimum of the grid ratios, that is, $g = \min_{2 \leq i \leq \Omega_s}(\pi_{i-1} + 1)/\pi_i$. Lehoczky and Sha [LeSh] showed that when constant ratio mapping is used, the schedulable utilization of the RM algorithm for large n and $D_i = p_i$ for all i is equal to $ln(2g) + 1 - g$, if $g > 1/2$ and is equal to g, if $g \leq 1/2$. The ratio of this schedulable utilization to $\ln 2$ is the *relative schedulability*; it measures the deterioration in schedulability due to an insufficient number of system priorities. For a system containing 100,000 tasks (i.e., $\Omega_n = 100,000$), the relative schedulability is equal to 0.9986 when Ω_s is equal to 256. Hence, 256 system priority levels are sufficient even for the most complex rate-monotonically scheduled systems.

Schedulability Loss of Deadline-Driven Systems.   As we will see in Chapter 12, one way to implement EDF algorithm is to put ready jobs with the same relative deadline in a FIFO queue. These jobs are naturally ordered among themselves according to their deadlines. Hence, the job with earliest deadline among the jobs at heads of all the nonempty FIFO queues is the one with the earliest deadline among all ready jobs. In general, the number Ω_s of FIFO queues maintained by the scheduler may be fewer than the number Ω_n of distinct relative deadlines of all tasks in the system. Some scheme, such as the constant ratio mapping scheme described above, is needed to map relative deadlines of jobs to the relative deadline grid supported by the system. A question then is, what is the loss in schedulable utilization when the system supports Ω_s relative deadlines?

To answer this question, we suppose that according to some mapping rule, the scheduler maps all relative deadlines in the range $[D_{i,\min}, D_{i,\max}]$ to $D_{i,\min}$. In other words, the minimum and maximum relative deadlines of all jobs in the ith FIFO queue are $D_{i,\min}$ and $D_{i,\max}$, respectively, and the absolute deadline of every job in the queue is equal to its release time plus $D_{i,\min}$. The grid ratio g is the minimum of the ratios $D_{i,\min}/D_{i,\max}$ among all Ω_s distinct relative deadline grid points. A sufficient schedulability condition for the on-time completion of all jobs is that the total density of all periodic tasks be no greater than g. (This condition follows directly from Theorem 7.4 discussed in Section 7.4.1.)

6.8.5   Tick Scheduling

An important assumption underlying all the schedulability tests described above is that the scheduler is event-driven: Upon the occurrence of every scheduling event, the scheduler executes immediately. Hence, every job is inserted into the ready job queue immediately after it becomes ready. This assumption is sometimes not valid. A way to implement the scheduler is to make it time-driven. By this we mean that the execution of the scheduler is triggered by a timer which is set to expire periodically. Scheduling decisions are made at these time instants, called *clock interrupts*. This method is called *tick scheduling* or time-based scheduling. We now focus on the case when the scheduler executes only at clock interrupts.

Tick scheduling introduces two additional factors that must be accounted for in schedulability analysis. First, the fact that a job is ready may not be noticed and acted upon by the scheduler until the next clock interrupt. The delayed action of the scheduler may delay the completion of the job. Second, a ready job that is yet to be noticed by the scheduler must be held somewhere other than the ready job queue. Let us call this place the pending (job) queue; it holds the jobs that have been released or unblocked since the last clock interrupt. When the scheduler executes, it moves the jobs in the pending queue to the ready job queue and places them there in order of their priorities. Once in the ready queue, the jobs execute in priority order without intervention by the scheduler. The time the scheduler takes to move the jobs introduces additional scheduling overhead.

Let p_0 denote the *tick size*, that is, the length of time between consecutive clock interrupts. We can model the scheduler as a periodic task T_0 whose period is p_0. This task has the highest priority among all tasks in the system. Its execution time e_0 is the amount of time the scheduler takes to service the clock interrupt. This time is spent even when there is no job in the pending job queue. Let CS_0 denote the maximum amount of time that the scheduler takes to move a job from the pending queue to the ready job queue. This overhead occurs each time a job is placed into the ready queue.

As an example, we consider a fixed-priority system consisting of three tasks $T_1 = (0.1, 4, 1)$, $T_2 = (0.1, 5, 1.8)$ and $T_3 = (20, 5)$. The first section of T_3 is nonpreemptable, and the execution time of this section is 1.1. The relative deadlines of the tasks are equal to their respective periods. According to the time-demand analysis method described in Section 6.5, the maximum response times of the tasks are equal to 2.1, 3.9, and 14.4, respectively. They are correct upper bounds if the scheduler executes whenever a job is released, completes, or leaves a nonpreemptable section.

Now suppose that the scheduler executes only at clock interrupts 0, 1, 2, ... (i.e., p_0 is 1). It takes 0.05 unit of time to service a clock interrupt (i.e., e_0 is 0.05) and 0.06 unit of time to move a job from the pending queue to the ready queue (i.e., CS_0 is 0.06). (On a modern processor, these times are a few microseconds.) We now have the schedule in Figure 6–22.

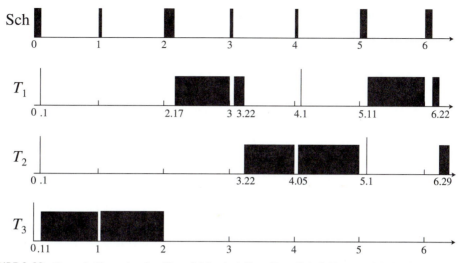

FIGURE 6–22 Example illustrating the effect of tick scheduling: ($T_1 = (0.1, 4, 1), T_2 = (0.1, 5, 1.8), T_3 = (20, 5)$; $p_0 = 1, e_0 = 0.05$, and $CS_0 = 0.06$).

1. At time 0.05 after the scheduler finishes serving the clock interrupt at time 0, it finds only $J_{3,1}$ in the pending queue and moves the job to ready queue. This job begins to execute at time 0.11 and immediately enters its nonpreemptable section.

2. At time 1, both $J_{1,1}$ and $J_{2,1}$ have been released, but they are not ready for execution because $J_{3,1}$ is still in its nonpreemptable section. The scheduler does nothing. $J_{3,1}$ executes, exits its nonpreemptable section, and continues to execute.

3. At time 2, the scheduler finds $J_{1,1}$ and $J_{2,1}$ unblocked and moves them to the ready queue. The total time spent by the scheduler is 0.17. Hence, $J_{1,1}$ begins to execute at time 2.17.

4. At time 3, the scheduler finds no job in the pending queue. $J_{1,1}$ continues to execute after the scheduler completes servicing the clock interrupt. Upon the completion of $J_{1,1}$, the next job $J_{2,1}$ in the ready queue executes.

5. At time 4, the scheduler again finds no job in the pending queue. $J_{2,1}$ continues to execute.

6. At time 5, $J_{2,1}$ is still not complete. The scheduler finds $J_{1,2}$ in the pending queue. (The job was released at time 4.1.) It moves $J_{1,2}$ to the ready queue and places it ahead of $J_{2,1}$. Consequently, when the scheduler completes at time 5.11, $J_{1,2}$ begins to execute.

7. At time 6, the scheduler finds $J_{2,2}$ in the pending queue, moves the job to the ready queue, and places the job after $J_{1,2}$ and $J_{2,1}$. At time 6.11, $J_{1,2}$ executes. The job completes at 6.22. $J_{2,1}$ resumes and subsequently completes at time 6.29. Then, $J_{2,1}$ begins to execute and so on.

The response time of the first job in T_2 is 6.19, larger than its relative deadline 5. Because the time-demand analysis method in Sections 6.5 and 6.6 ignores the effect of tick scheduling, it fails to predict the missed deadline at time 5.1.

Fixed-Priority Systems.   We can take into account the additional time demand introduced by tick scheduling in a fixed-priority system by using the following modified task parameters in the computation of the time-demand function of task T_i:

1. include the task $T_0 = (p_0, e_0)$ in the set of higher-priority tasks;
2. add $(K_k + 1)CS_0$ to the execution time e_k of every higher-priority task T_k (i.e., for $k = 1, 2, \ldots, i$), where K_k is the number times T_k may self-suspend;
3. for every lower-priority task $T_k, k = i + 1, \ldots, n$, add a task (p_k, CS_0) in the set of higher-priority tasks; and
4. make the blocking time $b_i(np)$ due to nonpreemptability of T_i equal to

$$\left(\left\lceil \max_{i+1 \leq k \leq n} \theta_k / p_0 \right\rceil + 1 \right) p_0,$$

where θ_k is the maximum execution time of nonpreemptable sections of the lower-priority task T_k.

Rule 1 is obvious. It takes into account the clock interrupt service overhead of the scheduler. Each time a job in T_i or a task with a higher or equal priority than T_i becomes ready, the scheduler spends CS_0 units of time to move the job to the ready queue. This time is taken care of by rule 2. Similarly, because of rule 3, the time the scheduler takes to move lower-priority jobs from the pending queue to the ready queue is added to the time-demand function of T_i. Because lower-priority jobs never execute in a level-π_i busy interval, we need not be concerned with whether they self-suspend.

To see the rationale behind rule 4, we note that a job in T_i may suffer up to p_0 units of delay waiting in the pending queue each time when it becomes ready, and we can treat this delay as a factor of its blocking time. This is why the blocking term $b_i(np)$ is equal to p_0 even when lower-priority tasks do not have nonpreemptable sections (i.e., θ_k is 0 for all $k > i$.) If some lower-priority tasks have nonpreemptable sections, a job may wait in the pending queue longer than the maximum execution time of the nonpreemptable sections. In the worst case, a job may be released shortly after the $(x - 1)$th clock interrupt for some x, a lower priority job enters a nonpreemptable section shortly before the xth clock interrupt, and exits the section shortly after the yth clock interrupt $(y \geq x)$. The job waits in the pending queue for approximately p_0 units before the xth clock interrupt, $(y - x)p_0$ units between clock interrupts x and y, and p_0 units after the yth clock interrupt. This is the reason for the expression of the blocking time.

To apply the above rules to the example in Figure 6–22, we compute the time-demand function of T_2 as if it were in the system of the following five tasks: $T_0 = (1, 0.05)$, $T_{0'} = (20, 0.06)$, $T_1 = (4, 1.06)$, $T_2 = (5, 1.86)$, $T_3 = (20, 5)$. T_0 and $T_{0'}$ have higher priorities than the other tasks. $b_2(np)$ is equal to $(\lceil 1.1/1.0 \rceil + 1) \times 1.0 = 3.0$. Substituting the parameters of these tasks into the expression in Eq. (6.18), we have

$$w_2(t) = 1.86 + 3.0 + 0.05 \left\lceil \frac{t}{1.0} \right\rceil + 0.06 \left\lceil \frac{t}{20.0} \right\rceil + 1.06 \left\lceil \frac{t}{4.0} \right\rceil$$

Solving $t = w_2(t)$ iteratively, we find that the maximum possible response time of T_2 is 7.44. This bound would lead us to the correct conclusion that T_2 is not schedulable. Using the same method, we find that the maximum response times of T_1 and T_3 are 4.43 and 18.75, respectively. So, only T_3 is surely schedulable.

You can see that the conclusion on the schedulability of T_1 is pessimistic. For this example, the major source of inaccuracy is the seemingly loose bound on the blocking time $b_1(np)$. However, this bound cannot be tightened in general. The blocking time of T_1 and T_2 would be approximately 3 if $J_{3,1}$ were to enter its nonpreemptable section shortly before time 1.0 and exit the section after 2. The value of p_0 in this example was chosen to highlight the effect of tick scheduling. Usually, the period between clock interrupts is in the order of milliseconds, small compared with the periods of tasks. By choosing a smaller p_0, we can reduce the extra blocking time introduced by tick scheduling at the expense of a higher overhead for servicing clock interrupts.

Tindell and Clark [TiCl] pointed out that the time required by the scheduler to move each of the subsequent jobs from the pending queue to the ready queue is smaller than the time it requires to move the first job in the pending queue. We can, therefore, improve the accuracy of the time-demand function by keeping track of the number of moves within the time interval $(t_0, t + t_0]$ and counting the cost of moving jobs more accurately. In our example, the scheduler moves two job at clock interrupt 2, and the time taken to do the moves would be only 0.09 (not 0.12 as shown in Figure 6–22) if the scheduler takes only 0.03 unit of time to move the second job. The improvement in the accuracy of the time-demand function can be significant only when the number of tasks are large (and hence the number of jobs in the pending queue at each clock interrupt can be large).

Dynamic-Priority Systems.   We can take into account of the effect of tick scheduling in a dynamic-priority system in a similar way. Specifically, when checking the schedulability of a task T_i, we modify the task parameters as follows.

1. Add the task $T_0 = (p_0, e_0)$.
2. Add $(K_k + 1) C S_0$ to the execution time e_k of every task T_k for $k = 1, 2, \ldots, n$.
3. Make the blocking time $b_i(np)$ due to nonpreemptability of T_i equal to

$$(\lceil \max_{i+1 \leq k \leq n} \theta_k / p_0 \rceil + 1) p_0,$$

where θ_k is the maximum execution time of nonpreemptable sections of a task T_k whose relative deadline is larger than the relative deadline of T_i.

6.8.6 Varying Priority in Fixed-Priority Systems

Thus far, we have confined our attention to fixed-priority systems in which every job has a constant priority. In general, each job in a task T_i may have more than one segment and the segments may have different priorities. There are many reasons for doing so. When tasks contend for resources, we sometimes raise the priority of a job segment during which the job holds some nonpreemptable resource in order to speed up the release of the resource. (In Chapter 8 we will discuss this matter in depth.) Sometimes, raising the priority of a job segment is a way to make the job, and hence the task containing it, schedulable. As an example, the system of two tasks $T_1 = (2, 1)$ and $T_2 = (5, 2.5)$ is not schedulable on a fixed-priority basis. However, if each job in T_2 is divided into two segments whose execution times are 2.0 and 0.5, respectively, and if the first segment has a lower priority than T_1 but the second segment has a higher priority than T_1, then both tasks would be schedulable. (This "fixed-priority assignment" in fact emulates the EDF assignment.)

This subsection describes an extension of the time-demand analysis method developed by Harbour, *et al.* [HaKL, KRPO] to determine the schedulability of fixed-priority systems containing tasks that have subtasks of different priorities. The method described here assumes that jobs do not suspend themselves, every job can be preempted at any time, and context-switch overhead is negligible. Moreover, jobs in each task are scheduled on a FIFO basis. Therefore, before a job completes, the subsequent jobs in the same task do not compete for processor time with jobs in other tasks.

Subtasks, Canonical Form, and Interference Block.   We let $n(i)$ denote the number of segments in each job of a periodic task T_i. These segments have different priorities. In a fixed-priority system, the corresponding segments of all the jobs in the same task have the same priority. It is convenient to think of each such task T_i as composed of $n(i)$ subtasks $T_{i,1}, T_{i,2}, \ldots, T_{i,n(i)}$. A job in $T_{i,k}$ is the kth segment of a job in T_i.

The jth job in each subtask of T_i is released at the beginning of the jth period of T_i. The job in $T_{i,1}$ is ready as soon as it is released. The subtask $T_{i,k-1}$ is the immediate predecessor of $T_{i,k}$, and $T_{i,k}$ is the immediate successor of $T_{i,k-1}$. By this we mean that the jth job in $T_{i,k}$ is ready when the jth job in $T_{i,k-1}$ completes, for all $1 < k \leq n(i)$. The maximum execution times of the subtasks are $e_{i,1}, e_{i,2}, \ldots, e_{i,n(i)}$, respectively. The sum of these execution times is e_i.

The relative deadlines of the subtasks of T_i are $D_{i,1}, D_{i,2}, \ldots, D_{i,n(i)}$, respectively. Clearly, for the relative deadlines of the subtasks to be consistent with the precedence constraints among their jobs, we must have $D_{i,1} \leq D_{i,2} \leq \cdots \leq D_{i,n(i)}$, and $D_{i,n(i)}$ is equal to D_i. In practice, the relative deadline of every subtask $T_{i,k}$ of T_i is usually equal to D_i, that is, it does not matter when the individual job segments complete, provided that each job as a whole completes in time. We focus here on this special case.

The subtasks of each task T_i have fixed priorities $\pi_{i,1}, \pi_{i,2}, \ldots, \pi_{i,n_i}$, respectively, and $\pi_{i,k-1} \neq \pi_{i,k}$ for all $1 < k \leq n(i)$. Since we are concerned here with how to determine whether a system of independent periodic tasks with varying priorities is schedulable, not how priorities should be assigned to them, we assume that priorities of all subtasks of all tasks are given.

A task is in *canonical form* if every later subtask has a higher priority than its immediate predecessor subtask. A task that is not in canonical form can be transformed into canonical form in the following manner. Starting with the last subtask, we examine the subtasks of the task in turn in reverse precedence order. We lower the priority of each immediate predecessor to the priority of the immediate successor if the given priority of the immediate predecessor is higher; otherwise, we leave the priority of the immediate predecessor unchanged. We repeat this process until the priority of the first subtask is thus determined. If in this process the priorities of adjacent subtasks become the same, we combine these subtasks into one subtask and decrement the number of subtasks accordingly.

As an example, suppose that the task T_i has four subtasks. It is not in canonical form if the priorities of the subtasks are 4, 1, 3, and 2, respectively. To transform it into canonical form for the sake of time-demand analysis, we leave the priorities of fourth and third subtasks unchanged since the fourth subtask has a higher priority. We lower the priority of second subtask to 3, the priority of the third subtask. Since the first subtask has a lower priority than 3, we leave its priority unchanged. After this step, the second and third subtasks have the same priority. So, we concatenate them into one new subtask $T_{i,2}$. The execution time of this new subtask is the sum of the execution times of the original second and third subtasks. The first and third subtask of the transformed task are the original first and fourth subtasks, respectively.

An *interference block* of a subtask $T_{i,k}$ is a chain of one or more contiguous subtasks $T_{l,x}, T_{l,x+1}, \ldots, T_{l,y}$ in another task T_l, for some $l \neq i$ and $y \geq x$, that have the following properties. (1) All of these subtasks have equal or higher priorities than the priority $\pi_{i,k}$ of $T_{i,k}$; (2) either $T_{l,x}$ has no predecessor or the priorities of its immediate predecessor are lower than $\pi_{i,k}$; and (3) either $T_{l,y}$ has no successor or the priority of its immediate successor is lower than $\pi_{i,k}$.

Extended General Time-Demand Analysis.   We are now ready to describe the extended general time-demand analysis method [HaKL]. As in Section 6.6, we compute the maximum possible response time of one task at a time. We call the task for which we are doing the computation the *target task*. In our discussion here, the target task is T_i.

Transforming the Target Task.   Rather than working with the given target task, we first transform it into canonical form if the task is not already in the form. The maximum response time of the transformed target task is no less than the maximum response time of the given task. (The proof of this statement can be found in [HaKL].) Therefore, the extended time-demand analysis method will never lead us to conclude that the target task is schedulable when it is not. Hereafter, by subtasks $T_{i,1}, T_{i,2}, \ldots, T_{i,n(i)}$, we mean the subtasks of the transformed target task. Therefore, $T_{i,1}$ has the lowest priority, and the later subtasks have increasingly higher priorities.

Identifying the Interference Blocks.   After making sure that the task is in canonical form, the next step is to compute the maximum length of a level-$\pi_{i,1}$ busy interval and the maximum number of jobs in T_i released in the busy interval. In this computation, we focus on the first subtask $T_{i,1}$ of the target task and examine every task T_l other than T_i (i.e., $l \neq i$) to identify the interference blocks of $T_{i,1}$. Let h_l denote the number of interference blocks in T_l and $E_{l,x}$ denote the sum of the execution times of all the subtasks in the xth interference block in T_l. (For simplicity, we omit in these notations any reference to the target subtask $T_{i,1}$. It is important to keep in mind that the values of h_l and $E_{l,x}$ are different for different target subtasks.) Rather than keeping track of individual subtasks in T_l when trying to account for the processor time demand of T_l, we keep track of the processor time demands of interference blocks in T_l.

Computing the Length of Level-$\pi_{i,1}$ Busy Interval.   With respect to $T_{i,1}$, we partition the other tasks in the system into the following disjoint subsets according to the priorities of their subtasks:

L(1): A task is in this subset if it contains no interference block of the target subtask $T_{i,1}$.

H(1): A task is in this subset if all its subtasks form a single interference block of $T_{i,1}$.

H/L(1): A task is in this subset if it contains at least one interference block of $T_{i,1}$, and either its first subtask or its last subtask or both are not in an interference block.

HLH(1): A task is in this subset if its first and last subtasks are in two different interference blocks.

Let t_0 denote the beginning of a level-$\pi_{i,1}$ busy interval. Since no job of tasks in $\mathbf{L}(1)$ can execute after t_0, we can ignore this subset of tasks. Clearly, every task T_l in $\mathbf{H}(1)$ may repeatedly preempt the subtask $T_{i,1}$ and may demand $\lceil t/p_l \rceil e_l$ units of processor time in the interval $(t_0, t_0 + t]$ for any $t \geq 0$.

In contrast, at most one interference block of each task T_l in the subset $\mathbf{H/L}(1)$ can execute in the interval $(t_0, t_0 + t]$. The reason is that when the interference block completes, the subtasks following the interference block have lower priorities than $T_{i,1}$ (and subsequent subtasks of T_i) and cannot start execution until the current job in T_i completes. Specifically, the amount of processor time demanded by a task T_l in the subset $\mathbf{H/L}(1)$ is the largest if the first subtask in the interference block with the largest total maximum execution time among all the interference blocks in T_l becomes ready for execution at t_0. Similarly, if the xth ($1 \leq x \leq h_l - 1$) interference block in T_l in the subset $\mathbf{HLH}(1)$ is ready at time t_0, the amount of processor time demanded by the task in $(t_0, t_0 + t]$ is no more than $\max_{1 \leq x \leq h_l - 1} E_{l,x}$. If the last interference block is ready at time t_0, however, the amount of processor time demanded by T_l can be as large as $E_{l,h_l} + E_{l,1}$. It follows that the maximum amount of processor time demanded by all the tasks in the subsets $\mathbf{H/L}$ and $\mathbf{HLH}(1)$ is equal to

$$a(1) = \sum_{T_l \in \mathbf{H/L}(1)} \max_{1 \leq x \leq h_l} E_{l,x} + \sum_{T_l \in \mathbf{HLH}(1)} \max \left(\max_{2 \leq x \leq h_l - 1} E_{l,x}, E_{l,1} + E_{l,h_l} \right) \qquad (6.25a)$$

Let B_i denote the maximum length of a level-$\pi_{i,1}$ busy interval. B_i is the minimum solution of the equation

$$t = b_i + a(1) + \lceil t/p_i \rceil e_i + \sum_{T_l \in \mathbf{H}(1)} \left\lceil \frac{t}{p_l} \right\rceil e_l \qquad (6.25b)$$

where b_i is the blocking time of T_i. We can solve this equation iterative starting from the initial value $b_i + e_i + a(1)$. Let N_i denote the number of jobs in each busy interval.

$$N_i = \lceil B_i/p_i \rceil \qquad (6.25c)$$

Maximum Response Time of $T_{i,1}$.   The time-demand function $w_{i,1;j}(t)$ of the jth job of $T_{i,1}$ in a level-$\pi_{i,1}$ busy interval is given by

$$w_{i,1;j}(t) = b_i + e_{i,1} + (j - 1)e_i + a(1) + \sum_{T_l \in \mathbf{H}(1)} \left\lceil \frac{t}{p_l} \right\rceil e_l \qquad (6.26a)$$

We use $f_{i,k;j}$ to denote the latest completion time of the jth job in the subtask $T_{i,k}$, for $k = 1, 2, \ldots, n(i)$, in a level-$\pi_{i,1}$ busy interval. $f_{i,1;j}$ is the minimum solution of the equation

$$t = w_{i,1;j}(t) \qquad (6.26b)$$

We can find the solution by solving the above equation iteratively starting from the initial guess $b_i + e_{i,1} + (j - 1)e_i + a(1)$.

Maximum Response Times of Later Subtasks.   After finding the time-demand function $w_{i,k-1;j}(t)$ and the latest completion time $f_{i,k-1;j}$ of the jth job in the subtask $T_{i,k-1}$ for each $k > 1$, we then find the time-demand function $w_{i,k;j}(t)$ and the latest completion time $f_{i,k;j}$ of the jth job of $T_{i,k}$. (Now, $T_{i,k}$ is the target subtask.) During the computation of $w_{i,k-1,j}(t)$, we have identified the subset $\mathbf{H}(k-1)$ of tasks that contain no subtasks with priorities lower than $T_{i,k-1}$. Because $T_{i,k}$ has a higher priority than $T_{i,k-1}$, some tasks in $\mathbf{H}(k-1)$ may contain subtasks with lower priorities than the current target subtask $T_{i,k}$. These tasks cannot repeatedly preempt $T_{i,k}$. We therefore further partition the subset $\mathbf{H}(k-1)$ into the following disjoint subsets according to the priorities of their subtasks when compared with the priority $\pi_{i,k}$ of $T_{i,k}$.

$\mathbf{H}(k)$: A task is in this subset if all its subtasks form a single interference block of $T_{i,k}$.

$\mathbf{H/L}(k)$: A task is in this subset if it contains at least one interference block of $T_{i,k}$, and either its first subtask or its last subtask or both are not in an interference block.

$\mathbf{HLH}(k)$: A task is in this subset if its first and last subtasks are in two different interference blocks of the subtask $T_{i,k}$.

$\mathbf{L}(k)$: A task is in this subset if all its subtasks have priorities lower than $\pi_{i,k}$.

Again, each task in $\mathbf{H}(k)$ can repeatedly preempt the job $J_{i,k;j}$ in the target subtask $T_{i,k}$. For the same reason that leads us to Eq. (6.25a), the total processor time demanded by all the tasks in the subsets $\mathbf{H/L}(k)$ and $\mathbf{HLH}(k)$ after the completion time $f_{i,k-1;j}$ of the intermediate predecessor job $J_{i,k-1;j}$ is given by

$$a(k) = \sum_{T_l \in \mathbf{H/L}(k)} \max_{1 \leq x \leq h_l} E_{l,x} + \sum_{T_l \in \mathbf{HLH}(k)} \max \left(\max_{2 \leq x \leq h_l - 1} E_{l,x}, E_{l,1} + E_{l,h_l} \right) \tag{6.27a}$$

where h_l and $E_{l,x}$ are parameters of interference blocks of $T_{i,k}$. The time-demand function $w_{i,k;j}(t)$ of the the jth job in the target subtask $T_{i,j}$ is given by

$$w_{i,k;j}(t) = b_i + (j-1)e_i + \sum_{x=1}^{k} \left[e_{i,x} + a(x) + \sum_{T_l \in \mathbf{H}(x-1) - \mathbf{H}(x)} \left\lceil \frac{f_{i,x-1;j}}{p_l} \right\rceil e_l \right] + \sum_{T_l \in \mathbf{H}(k)} \left\lceil \frac{t}{p_l} \right\rceil e_l \tag{6.27b}$$

where the completion time $f_{i,0;j}$ of jth job of an nonexisting subtask $T_{i,0}$ is 0 and $\mathbf{H}(0)$ is $\mathbf{T}$. The latest completion time $f_{i,k;j}$ of the jth job of $T_{i,k}$ in a level-$\pi_{i,1}$ busy interval is equal to the minimum solution of the equation

$$t = w_{i,k;j}(t) \tag{6.27c}$$

Maximum Response Time W_i.   The maximum response time W_i of the target task is given by

$$W_i = \max_{1 \leq j \leq N_i} (f_{i,n(i);j} - (j-1)p_i) \tag{6.28}$$

The Procedure.   In summary, to determine the schedulability of a fixed-priority system of periodic tasks that contain subtasks of different priorities we carry out the following steps to compute the maximum response time W_i of a task T_i at a time.

1. Transform the target task T_i into canonical form. After the transformation, its subtasks $T_{i,k}$ for $k = 1, 2, \ldots, n(i)$ have increasing priorities $\pi_{i,1}, \pi_{i,2}, \ldots, \pi_{i,n(i)}$.

2. Compute the length B_i of the longest level-$\pi_{i,1}$ busy interval and maximum number N_i jobs of T_i in the busy interval according to Eq. (6.25).

3. For $j = 1, 2, \ldots, N_i$, compute the latest completion time of $f_{i,n(i);j}$ of the jth job in T_i. This is done by computing the latest completion time $f_{i,k;j}$ of the jth job in each subtask $T_{i,k}$ of T_i, for $k = 1, 2, \ldots, n(i)$, starting from the first subtask in precedence order until the last subtask. The time-demand functions used for this computation are given by Eqs. (6.26) and (6.27).

4. Compute an upper bound W_i of the maximum response time of T_i according to Eq. (6.28).

An Example.   As an example, we compute below the maximum response time W_2 of the task T_2 in the fixed-priority system whose parameters are listed in Table 6-1. The blocking time of all the tasks is 0. T_2 has two subtasks, $T_{2,1}$ and $T_{2,2}$. The task is already in canonical form, so we proceed to compute the maximum length B_2 of a level-5 busy interval.

Comparing with $\pi_{2,1} = 5$, we divide the other three tasks into subsets. Both **L**(1) and **H/L**(1) are empty. **H**(1) = $\{T_1, T_4\}$, and **HLH** = $\{T_3\}$. T_3 has three interference blocks of $T_{2,1}$ and their execution times are 0.6, 0.7, and 0.5. From Eq. (6.25a), $a(1) = 0.6 + 0.5 = 1.1$.

Substituting this value and the parameters of the tasks into Eq. (6.25b), we have

$$ t = 1.1 + 2.5 \left\lceil \frac{t}{7} \right\rceil + 2.5 \left\lceil \frac{t}{10} \right\rceil + 3.0 \left\lceil \frac{t}{15} \right\rceil $$

The minimum solution of this equation is 19.6. Hence $B_2 = 19.6$, and $N_2 = 2$.

To find the maximum completion time $f_{2,1;1}$ of the first job in $T_{2,1}$ in a level-5 busy interval, we have from Eq. (6.26a)

$$ w_{2,1}; 1(t) = 0.9 + 1.1 + 2.5 \left\lceil \frac{t}{7} \right\rceil + 3.0 \left\lceil \frac{t}{15} \right\rceil $$

$f_{2,1;1} = 10$ because $w_{2,1;1}(t)$ becomes equal to t at $t = 10$.

TABLE 6–1   Tasks with Subtasks of Different Priorities

Subtask	p_i	D_i	$e_{i,k}$	$\pi_{i,k}$
$T_{1,1}$	7	7	2.5	1
$T_{2,1}$	10	15	0.9	5
$T_{2,2}$	10	15	1.6	2
$T_{3,1}$	12	20	0.6	2
$T_{3,2}$	12	20	0.1	6
$T_{3,3}$	12	20	0.7	2
$T_{3,4}$	12	20	0.1	6
$T_{3,5}$	12	20	0.5	3
$T_{4,1}$	15	15	1.0	2
$T_{4,2}$	15	15	0.5	1
$T_{4,3}$	15	15	1.5	4

Now we examine the subset $\mathbf{H}(1)$ and partition it into subsets in the way as described above. $\mathbf{H}(2) = \{T_1\}$, and $\mathbf{H/L}(2) = \{T_4\}$. Moreover the execution time of the interference block of $T_{2,2}$ in T_4 is equal to the sum the execution times of $T_{4,1}$ and $T_{4,2}$; hence, $a(2)$ is equal to 1.5. From Eq. (6.27), we have

$$w_{2,2;1}(t) = 2.5 + 1.1 + 1.5 + 3\left\lceil\frac{10}{15}\right\rceil + 2.5\left\lceil\frac{t}{7}\right\rceil$$

Solving the equation $t = w_{2,2;1}(t)$ iteratively, we have $f_{2,2;1} = 13.1$. In other words, the first job of T_2 in a level-5 busy interval completes by 13.1.

Similarly, the maximum completion time $f_{2,1;2}$ of the second job in $T_{2,1}$ is given by the minimum solution of the equation

$$t = 2.5 + 0.9 + 1.1 + 2.5\left\lceil\frac{t}{7}\right\rceil + 3.0\left\lceil\frac{t}{15}\right\rceil$$

$f_{2,1;2}$ is equal to 18. Finally, the solution of

$$t = w_{2,2;2}(t) = 2.5 + 2.5 + 1.1 + 1.5 + 3\left\lceil\frac{18}{15}\right\rceil + 2.5\left\lceil\frac{t}{7}\right\rceil$$

is $f_{2,2;2} = 23.6$. The maximum response time W_2 of the task T_2 is $\max(13.1 - 0, 23.6 - 10.0) = 13.6$. Since the relative deadline of the task is 15, this task is schedulable.

You may have noticed that the upper bound $f_{2,2;2} = 23.6$ is a loose one. Since the first level-5 busy interval ends at time 19.6, $f_{2,2;2}$ is surely no greater than 19.6. A careful examination of the above expression of $w_{2,2;2}(t)$ tells us that the source of inaccuracy is the inclusion of $a(2) = 1.5$, which is the execution time of the interference block $\{T_{4,1}, T_{4,2}\}$ in $\mathbf{H/L}(2)$. In this case, this time is already included in the term $3\lceil 18/15\rceil$ and is therefore counted twice. In general, when a task has a long chain of subtasks, the maximum completion time of a job in a later subtask computed from the time-demand function in Eq. (6.27b) can be rather loose for this reason. Unfortunately, we cannot tighten this bound in general. The term $a(x)$ must be included to ensure the correctness of the bound. In our example, if the completion time of predecessor job $J_{2,1;2}$ were 15, not 18, we would have to include the term $a(2)$.

6.8.7   Schedulability Test of Hierarchically Scheduled Periodic Tasks

Earlier in Chapter 3, we mentioned that the scheduling scheme may be hierarchical. The application system consists of a number of disjoint subsets of periodic tasks. Each subset is a major component, called a subsystem here. (As an example, a flight management system contains flight control, avionics, and navigation modules as subsystems.) The scheduler may use one approach to schedule individual subsystems on the processor and use another approach to divide the time given to each subsystem among the tasks in the subsystem.

Two common hierarchical scheduling schemes are the priority-driven/round-robin scheme and fixed-time partitioning scheme. In a *priority-driven/round-robin* system, the scheduler schedules the subsystems in a priority-driven manner. The tasks in each subsystem are scheduled in a round-robin manner in the intervals assigned to the subsystem. According to the *fixed-time partitioning* scheme, the schedulers schedules the subsystems according to a cyclic schedule. The tasks in each subsystem are scheduled according to the scheduling algorithm chosen for the subsystem. We do not need any new method to determine the schedulability of a priority-driven/round-robin system. For the sake of schedulability analysis, all the tasks in each subsystem have the same priority, and their schedulability can be determined using the method described in Section 6.8.4.

This section focuses on fixed-time partitioning systems and considers only the simplest case: The subsystems are scheduled in a weighted round-robin manner. In particular, the cyclic scheduler at the low level partitions the time into intervals of a fixed length RL. Each interval is a *round*. The round length RL must be smaller than the minimum period and the minimum relative deadline of all tasks in the system. We consider a subsystem that has n independent, preemptable periodic tasks and is given a slot of length τ in each round by the cyclic scheduler.

As a specific example, suppose that the subsystem contains three periodic tasks: $T_1 = (\phi_1, 8, 0.5)$, $T_2 = (\phi_2, 10, 1.2)$, and $T_2 = (\phi_3, 14, 0.8)$. Their phases are unknown. The total utilization of the subsystem is 0.24. The subsystem is given a slot of length 1 every round of length 3, and the tasks in it are scheduled rate-monotonically in its slots. Figure 6–23 shows a segment of the worst-case schedule. (We take as the time origin a critical instant of the tasks; in the worst case, this critical instant occurs immediately after the end of a slot assigned to the subsystem.) According to this schedule, the maximum response times of the tasks are 2.5, 5.7, and 9.0, respectively.

Schedulability of Fixed-Priority Tasks. In general, the time-demand function of any task T_i in a subsystem whose tasks are scheduled on a fixed-priority basis is still given by Eq. (6.24). However, the amount $supply(t)$ of time available to the subsystem in the time interval $(t_0, t_0 + t)$ following a critical instant t_0 of T_i is no longer t. Rather,

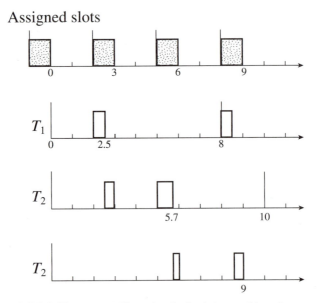

FIGURE 6–23 Example illustrating the fixed-time partition scheme.

$$supply(t) \leq \left\lfloor \frac{t}{RL} \right\rfloor \tau + \max \left(0, \tau - RL + t - \left\lfloor \frac{t}{RL} \right\rfloor RL \right) \qquad (6.29)$$

The first term in this expression gives the amount of time allocated to the subsystem in rounds that lie entirely in the interval $(t_0, t_0 + t)$. The second term gives the amount of time that is allocated to the subsystem and is in the last of all the rounds which start before $t_0 + t$. The equality holds when the critical instant t_0 is immediately after the end of a slot that is allocated to the subsystem. We can use the general schedulability analysis method described in Section 6.6 to determine whether T_i is schedulable, provided that we use this expression of time supply.

To find the maximum possible response time of task T_3 in Figure 6–23, we solve for the minimum value of t satisfying the equation

$$0.8 + 0.5 \left\lceil \frac{t}{8} \right\rceil + 1.2 \left\lceil \frac{t}{10} \right\rceil \leq \left\lfloor \frac{t}{3} \right\rfloor + \max \left(0, 1 - 3 + t - 3 \left\lfloor \frac{t}{3} \right\rfloor \right)$$

Again, we can solve this equation iteratively. The initial guess $t^{(1)}$ ($= 2.5$) is the sum of execution times of the three tasks. Substituting this value of t, we find the left-hand side is equal to 2.5, but the right-hand side is only 0.5. For the second iteration, we try $t^{(2)} = 9.0$, which is $\lceil t^{(1)}/(\tau/RL) \rceil$ and find that for this value of t, the two sides of the above expressions have the same value. Hence, the maximum possible response time of the T_3 is 9.0.

Schedulability of Deadline-Driven Tasks. A subsystem of n periodic tasks with relative deadlines no less than their respective periods is schedulable on the EDF basis when its total utilization is no greater than

$$U(RL, \tau) = \frac{\tau}{RL} - \frac{RL - \tau}{\min_{1 \leq i \leq n} p_i}$$

The proof of this statement is to you as an exercise.

6.9 SUMMARY

This chapter focused on the performance of priority-driven algorithms for scheduling independent, preemptive periodic tasks. Such algorithms are divided into two classes: fixed priority and dynamic priority. Examples of fixed-priority algorithms are the Rate-Monotonic (RM) and Deadline-Monotonic (DM) algorithms, which assign priorities to tasks on the basis of their periods and relative deadlines, respectively; the shorter the period or relative deadline, the higher the priority. Examples of dynamic-priority algorithms are the EDF (Earliest-Deadline-First) and LST (Least-Slack-Time) algorithms. The former assigns priorities to individual jobs on the basis of their absolute deadlines, while the latter does so on the basis of their slacks. We further divide dynamic priority algorithms into two subclasses: job-level fixed-priority and job-level dynamic-priority algorithms. The EDF algorithm is an example of the former because the priority of each job once assigned remains fixed relative to priorities of existing jobs. The LST algorithm is an example of the latter.

6.9.1 Sufficient Schedulability Conditions

A criterion commonly used to measure the performance of an algorithm for scheduling periodic tasks is the schedulable utilization of the algorithm. As long as the total utilization of a system of periodic tasks is less than or equal to the schedulable utilization of an algorithm, the system is schedulable according to the algorithm. Therefore, the higher the schedulable utilization of an algorithm, the better the algorithm.

Schedulable Utilization or Density of Optimal Dynamic-Priority Algorithms. The schedulable utilization of the EDF and LST algorithms is one when the periodic tasks scheduled on one processor are independent and preemptable and have relative deadlines equal to or larger than their respective periods. When the relative deadline D_k of some task T_k is shorter than its period p_i, a system of independent, preemptive periodic tasks is schedulable according to the EDF algorithm if

$$\sum_{k=1}^{n} \frac{e_k}{\min(D_k, p_k)} \leq 1$$

where e_k is the execution time of task T_k and n is the number of periodic tasks in the system.

Schedulable Utilizations of Optimal Fixed-Priority Algorithms.   No fixed-priority algorithm is optimal, because there exist schedulable systems for which no fixed-priority algorithm can find feasible schedules. Among fixed-priority algorithms, the DM algorithm is optimal. It is identical to the RM algorithm when $D_k = \delta p_k$, for $k = 1, 2, \ldots, n$ and some constant δ. For such a system, the schedulable utilization of these algorithms is

$$U_{RM}(n, \delta) = \delta(n-1)\left[\left(\frac{\delta+1}{\delta}\right)^{1/n-1} - 1\right], \qquad \text{for } \delta = 2, 3, \ldots$$

$$n\left((2\delta)^{1/n} - 1\right) + 1 - \delta, \qquad\qquad 0.5 \leq \delta \leq 1$$

$$\delta, \qquad\qquad 0 \leq \delta \leq 0.5$$

A sufficient schedulability condition for a system of n independent, preemptive periodic tasks to be scheduled rate-monotonically is that its total utilization $U(n)$ be equal to or less than $U_{RM}(n, \delta)$.

There are several less robust but more accurate schedulable utilizations of the RM algorithm. All of them rely on making use of some values of individual task parameters. Specifically, the following schedulable utilizations were presented earlier:

- $U_{RM}(u_1, u_2, \ldots u_n)$ given by Eq. (6.13) for systems with known task utilizations,
- the improved schedulable utilization given by Theorem 6.13 for tasks that can be partitioned into disjoint subsets of simply periodic tasks,
- the schedulable utilization given by Eq. (6.14) for tasks with known periods,
- the sufficient condition given by Theorem 6.15 for tasks with known periods and execution times based on the existence of a simply periodic, accelerated set with total utilization equal to or less than one, and
- the schedulable utilization given by Eq. (6.16) for multiframe tasks.

6.9.2 Necessary and Sufficient Schedulability Test for Fixed-Priority Systems

The general time-demand analysis method presented in Section 6.6.2 is a pseudopolynomial time schedulability test for fixed-priority systems that is both necessary and sufficient. This test examines the execution times and periods of all tasks and hence can be used only when you know the values of these parameters. The method works as follows:

1. To determine whether a system of independent, preemptable periodic tasks is schedulable, we test one task at a time starting from the highest priority task T_1 in order of decreasing priority.

2. While checking whether T_i is schedulable, we consider the subset $\mathbf{T}_i$ of tasks with priorities π_i or higher, assume that the tasks in this subset are in phase, and examine the jobs in the first level-π_i busy interval.

   a. If the first job of every task in $\mathbf{T}_i$ completes by the end of the first period of the task, we check whether the first job of T_i meets its deadline. T_i is schedulable if the job completes in time. Otherwise, T_i may not be schedulable.

   b. If the first job of some task in $\mathbf{T}_i$ does not complete by the end of the first period of the task, we examine every job of T_i that is executed in the busy interval. T_i is schedulable if every examined job completes in time.

The length B_i of an in phase level-π_i busy interval is equal to the minimum value of t that satisfies the equation $t = \sum_{k=1}^{i} \lceil t/p_k \rceil e_k$. There are no more than $\lceil B_i/p_i \rceil$ jobs of T_i in this busy interval. The maximum possible response time $W_{i,j}$ of the jth job of T_i in an in-phase level-π_i busy interval is equal to the minimum value of t that satisfies Eq. (6.9).

6.9.3 Effect of Practical Factors

Section 6.8 described ways to take into account the effect of practical factors such as nonpreemptability, self-suspension, and so on. These ways are summarized below.

Nondistinct Priorities.   When tasks do not have distinct priorities, the time-demand function $w_{i,j}(t)$ of the jth job of T_i in an in-phase level-π_i busy interval is given by Eq. (6.24), that is,

$$w_{i,j}(t) = je_i + b_i + \sum_{T_k \in \mathbf{T}_E(i)} \left(\left\lceil \frac{(j-1)p_i}{p_k} \right\rceil + 1 \right) e_k$$

$$+ \sum_{T_k \in \mathbf{T}_H(i)} \left\lceil \frac{t}{p_k} \right\rceil e_k, \quad \text{for } (j-1)p_i < t \leq w_{i,j}(t)$$

where $\mathbf{T}_E(i)$ is the subset of tasks other than T_i that have the same priority as T_i and $\mathbf{T}_H(i)$ is the subset of tasks that have higher priorities than T_i.

Blocking Time.   The term b_i in the above equation gives the total amount time that a job in T_i may be blocked. If the job may self-suspend K_i times after it starts execution, the total blocking time b_i it may suffer is equal to

$$b_i = b_i(ss) + (K_i + 1)b_i(np)$$

$b_i(ss)$ is the blocking time due to deferred execution of T_i and higher-priority tasks. Each higher-priority task T_k ($1 \leq k \leq i$) contributes $\min(e_k$, maximum self-suspension time of T_k) units of time to this term. $b_i(np)$ is the blocking time which a job in T_i may suffer due to nonpreemptable lower-priority tasks. It is equal to $\max_{i+1 \leq k \leq n} \theta_k$, where θ_k is the execution time of the longest nonpreemptable section in T_k.

We must also include the blocking time b_i of task T_i in the computation of the total utilization of the tasks in $\mathbf{T}_i$ when we want to check whether T_i is schedulable using the schedulable utilization of the algorithm. For example, a sufficient condition for a task T_i in a rate-monotonically scheduled system to be schedulable is

$$\frac{e_1}{p_1} + \frac{e_2}{p_2} + \cdots + \frac{e_i + b_i}{p_i} = U_i + \frac{b_i}{p_i} \leq U_{RM}(i)$$

where U_i is the total utilization of the i highest priority tasks and $U_{RM}(i)$ is schedulable utilization of the RM algorithm.

Context Switch.   In any job-level fixed-priority system, we can take into account the context-switch overhead by adding $2(K_i + 1)CS$ to the execution time of each task T_i, where CS is the maximum amount of time to do a context switch.

Tick Scheduling.   When the scheduler makes scheduling decisions only at clock interrupts that are p_0 units of time apart, a newly released or unblocked job must wait in the pending queue until the next clock interrupt. We need to consider the following two factors: the delay suffered by each job waiting to be noticed by the scheduler and the time taken by the scheduler to move each job from the pending queue to the ready queue. To determine the schedulability of system, we modify the given task parameters following the rules given in Section 6.8.5 and do the schedulability test using the modified task parameters.

Varying Priority.   In some fixed-priority system, each job in a task T_i may have more than one segment, the segments may have different priorities, and the corresponding segments of all the jobs in the same task have the same priority. A general time-demand analysis procedure for such tasks is given in Section 6.8.6.

Hierarchical Scheduling.   Section 6.8.7 described how to determine the schedulability of each subsystem when the subsystem is allocated a slot of τ time units in each round of length RL and periodic tasks in the subsystem are scheduled on a priority-driven basis during the time slots allocated to the subsystem.

EXERCISES

6.1 The static Least-Slack-Time (LST) algorithm [LeWh] is also called the Minimum Laxity (ML) algorithm. This algorithm assigns priorities on the basis of laxity of tasks, where the laxity of each task is equal to its relative deadline less its execution time.

(a) Show that the dynamic system in Figure 6–1 is schedulable according to this algorithm. For this system, T_m has the highest priority, and the other n tasks have a lower priority.

(b) Is it true that ML algorithm can always make good use of all the processors in a dynamic system, that is, the total utilization of all the periodic tasks that can be feasibly dispatched and scheduled in an m processor system according to this algorithm is proportional to m? Give an informal proof or a counterexample.

6.2 Prove that Theorem 6.2 is true.

6.3 Complete the proof of Theorem 6.4, by showing that it is always possible to swap T_i and T_{i+1} in a feasible, fixed-priority schedule so that after the swapping, T_i and T_{i+1} are scheduled deadline-monotonically. By swapping T_i and T_{i+1}, we mean move the task T_i to some of the intervals where T_{i+1} is scheduled and vice versa without affecting other tasks.

6.4 A system **T** contains four periodic tasks, $(8, 1)$, $(15, 3)$, $(20, 4)$, and $(22, 6)$. Its total utilization is 0.87. Construct the initial segment in the time interval $(0, 50)$ of a rate-monotonic schedule of the system.

6.5 Which of the following systems of periodic tasks are schedulable by the rate-monotonic algorithm? By the earliest-deadline-first algorithm? Explain your answer.
(a) $\mathbf{T} = \{(8, 3), (9, 3), (15, 3)\}$
(b) $\mathbf{T} = \{(8, 4), (12, 4), (20, 4)\}$
(c) $\mathbf{T} = \{(8, 4), (10, 2), (12, 3)\}$

6.6 Give two different explanations of why the periodic tasks $(2, 1)$, $(4, 1)$, and $(8, 2)$ are schedulable by the rate-monotonic algorithm.

6.7 This problem is concerned with the performance and behavior of rate-monotonic and earliest-deadline-first algorithms.
(a) Construct the initial segments in the time interval $(0, 750)$ of a rate-monotonic schedule and an earliest-deadline-first schedule of the periodic tasks $(100, 20)$, $(150, 50)$, and $(250, 100)$, whose total utilization is 0.93.
(b) Construct the initial segments in the time interval $(0, 750)$ of a rate-monotonic schedule and an earliest-deadline-first schedule of the periodic tasks $(100, 20)$, $(150, 50)$, and $(250, 120)$, whose total utilization is 1.1.

6.8 (a) Use the time-demand analysis method to show that the rate-monotonic algorithm will produce a feasible schedule of the tasks $(6, 1)$, $(8, 2)$, and $(15, 6)$.
(b) Change the period of one of the tasks in part (a) to yield a set of tasks with the maximal total utilization which is feasible when scheduled using the rate-monotonic algorithm. (Consider only integer values for the period.)
(c) Change the execution time of one of the tasks in part (a) to yield a set of tasks with the maximal total utilization which is feasible when scheduled using the rate-monotonic algorithm. (Consider only integer values for the execution time.)

6.9 The periodic tasks $(3, 1)$, $(4, 2)$, and $(6, 1)$ are scheduled according to the rate-monotonic algorithm.
(a) Draw the time-demand functions of the tasks.
(b) Are the tasks schedulable? Why or why not?
(c) Can this graph be used to determine whether the tasks are schedulable according to an arbitrary priority-driven algorithm? Explain your answer.

6.10 Which of the following fixed-priority tasks(s) is not schedulable? Explain your answer.

$$T_1 = (5, 1), \ T_2 = (3, 1), \ T_3 = (7, 2.5), \ \text{and} \ T_4 = (16, 1)$$

6.11 Find the maximum possible response time of task T_4 in the following fixed-priority system by solving the equation $w_4(t) = t$ iteratively.

$$T_1 = (5, 1), \ T_2 = (3, 1), \ T_3 = (8, 1.6), \ \text{and} \ T_4 = (18, 3.5)$$

6.12 **(a)** Show that the periodic tasks $(10, 2)$, $(15, 5)$, and $(25, 9)$ are schedulable by the rate-monotonic algorithm.

   (b) Show that the periodic tasks $(10, 2)$, $(12, 5)$, and $(15, 4)$ are not schedulable by the rate-monotonic algorithm.

   (c) Construct the initial segments in the time interval $(0, 75)$ of a rate-monotonic schedule and a earliest-deadline-first schedule of the periodic tasks $(10, 2)$, $(15, 5)$, and $(25, 12)$.

6.13 Find the length of an in-phase level-3 busy interval of the following fixed-priority tasks:

$$T_1 = (5, 1), \quad T_2 = (3, 1), \quad T_3 = (8, 1.6), \text{ and } T_4 = (18, 3.5)$$

6.14 A system **T** contains four periodic tasks: $(9, 5.1, 1, 5.1)$, $(8, 1)$, $(13, 3)$, and $(0.5, 22, 7, 22)$. The total utilization of **T** is 0.87. Is this system scheduled according to the rate-monotonic algorithm? Explain how you arrive at your conclusion.

6.15 A system consists of three periodic tasks: $(3, 1)$, $(5, 2)$, and $(8, 3)$.

   (a) What is the total utilization?

   (b) Construct an earliest-deadline-first schedule of this system in the interval $(0, 32)$. Label any missed deadlines.

   (c) Construct a rate-monotonic schedule for this system in the interval $(0, 32)$. Label any missed deadlines.

   (d) Suppose we want to reduce the execution time of the task with period 3 in order to make the task system schedulable according to the earliest-deadline-first algorithm. What is the minimum amount of reduction necessary for the system to be schedulable by the earliest-deadline-first algorithm?

6.16 **(a)** The total utilization of the periodic tasks $\{(7, 10, 1, 10), (12, 2,), (25, 9)\}$ is 0.63. Is it schedulable by the rate-monotonic algorithm? Explain how you arrive at your conclusion.

   (b) The total utilization of the periodic tasks $\{(7, 10, 1, 10), (12, 6), (25, 9)\}$ is 0.96. Is it schedulable by the rate-monotonic algorithm? Explain how you arrive at your conclusion.

   (c) Suppose that we increase the execution time of the task with period 10 by 1 [i.e., the parameters of the task become $(7, 10, 2, 10)$ after the change] and reduce the relative deadline of the task with period 25 by 5 [i.e., the task become $(25, 9, 20)$]. We want to reduce the execution time of the task with period 12 in order to make the task system schedulable rate-monotonically. What is the minimum amount of reduction necessary? Write a brief description of the method you used to find this amount.

6.17 A system contains five periodic tasks T_i, for $i = 1, 2, \ldots, 5$. Their utilizations are $u_1 = 0.8$ $u_2 = u_3 = u_4 = u_5 = 0.01$. Are these tasks schedulable rate-monotonically? Be sure to explain your answer.

6.18 The following systems of periodic tasks are scheduled rate-monotonically on one processor. Determine whether each system is schedulable using a method that is fast and/or uses the least amount of information on the tasks.

   (a) $T_1 = (2, 0.5, 4)$, $T_2 = (3, 1.0, 10)$, $T_1 = (5, 1.0, 10)$, and $T_1 = (7, 0.45, 15)$.

   (b) $T_1 = (2, 0.1)$, $T_2 = (3, 0.15)$, $T_3 = (4, 0.20)$, $T_4 = (5, 0.25)$, $T_5 = (7, 1.4)$, $T_6 = (9, 0.45)$, $T_7 = (8, 0.4)$, $T_8 = (10, 0.5)$, $T_9 = (16, 0.8)$, $T_{10} = (20, 1.0)$, $T_{11} = (32, 1.6)$, $T_{12} = (40, 2.0)$

   (c) $T_1 = (10, 4.0)$, $T_2 = (12, 4.0)$, $T_3 = (20, 1.0)$, and $T_4 = (25, 0.5)$

6.19 Many operating systems schedule tasks with the same priority on a round-robin basis. We must modify the time-demand method used to determine whether a system of periodic tasks is schedulable by the rate-monotonic (or deadline-monotonic) algorithm to handle this case.

   (a) Suppose that the temporal parameters of the tasks are large compared with the length of the time slices. How should the method be modified?

   (b) What if the parameters have values that are comparable with the length of the time slices?

6.20 A digital control loop can be implemented as a periodic task as follows:

```
Do forever
    Waitfor(new sample);
    GetSample(value);
    Calculate control output;
    Do D_A conversion;
    Update state;
EndDo
```

where a digital sample is generated periodically by the A_D converter. A problem with this implementation is that the length of the time interval between when a sample is taken and when D_A conversion is done may vary widely. Ideally, we want the length of this interval to be fixed. One way to accomplish this objective is to split the task into two logically as follows:

```
Do forever
    Waitfor(sample);              First half of the task starts at t approx.
    GetSample(value, t);
    Calculate control output;
    Waitfor(t + x)                Second half of the task starts.
    Do D_A conversion;
    Update state;
EndDo
```

where t is when a sample is read and x is chosen so that by $t + x$ the computation step is surely completed.

Suppose that the following three periodic tasks are implemented in this manner.

$$T_1: p_1 = 100 \quad e_{1,1} = 10 \quad e_{1,2} = 15$$
$$T_2: p_2 = 75 \quad e_{2,1} = 6 \quad e_{2,2} = 9$$
$$T_3: p_3 = 130 \quad e_{3,1} = 9 \quad e_{3,1} = 10$$

For $i = 1, 2, 3$, $e_{i,1}$ and $e_{i,2}$ are the maximum execution times of the first half $T_{i,1}$ and second half $T_{i,2}$ of task T_i, respectively. x_i is the length of the delay between the release of a job in $T_{i,1}$ and the release of the corresponding job in $T_{i,2}$ (i.e., when D_A conversion starts). Suppose that the tasks have fixed priorities: T_1 has the highest priority and T_3 has the lowest priority. What are the minimum values of x_i, for $i = 1, 2, 3$?

6.21 (a) Use the time-demand analysis method to show that the set of periodic tasks $\{(5, 1), (8, 2), (14, 4)\}$ is schedulable according to the rate-monotonic algorithm.

    (b) Suppose that we want the make the first x units of each request in the task $(8, 2)$ nonpreemptable. What is the maximum value of x so the system remains schedulable according to the rate-monotonic algorithm?

6.22 Suppose that it is possible to shorten the nonpreemptable portion of T_3 in the system whose time-demand functions are shown in Figure 6–20. Using the time-demand functions in this figure, determine how short the nonpreemptable portion of T_3 must be so that all tasks are schedulable.

6.23 A system contains tasks $T_1 = (10, 3)$, $T_2 = (16, 4)$, $T_3 = (40, 10)$, and $T_1 = (50, 5)$. The total blocking due to all factors of the tasks are $b_1 = 5$, $b_2 = 1$, $b_3 = 4$, and $b_4 = 10$, respectively. These tasks are scheduled on the EDF basis. Which tasks (or task) are (or is) schedulable? Explain your answer.

6.24 A system contains three periodic tasks: $T_1 = (2, 0.5)$, $b_1 = 0.75$; $T_2 = (3, 1)$; and $T_3 = (5, 1)$. The tasks are scheduled by the rate-monotonic algorithms. Suppose that the lengths of interarrival intervals of interrupts are never less than 50 time units, and each interrupt requires 2 time unit or less to complete.

   (a) Suppose that each interrupt is executed nonpreemptively at the lowest priority until it completes. Show that the periodic task system is not schedulable.

   (b) Suppose that we allow the execution of each interrupt to be preempted a limited number of times. Choose the length of time for which the interrupt service task is allowed to execute nonpreemptively and the length of the time interval between consecutive times this task executes so that the interrupt service task is preempted a minimum number of times and all periodic tasks meet their deadlines.

6.25 Section 6.8.1 states that to account for the effect of blocking, it suffices to add the blocking time b_i of the task T_i to the expression in the right-hand side of Eq. (6.9b) to obtain the time-demand function $w_{i,j}(t)$ of the jth job of T_i in an in phase level-π_i busy period. Explain why it is not necessary to add more than one b_i, that is, why not jb_i.

6.26 Consider a fixed-priority system of three periodic tasks, $T_1 = (4, 1)$, $T_2 = (7, 2.1)$, and $T_3 = (10, 2)$. T_1 has the highest priority and T_3 the lowest.

   (a) Are the tasks schedulable? Why?

   (b) Suppose that the context switch time is 0.2. To compensate for this additional demand for processor time, we increase the relative deadline of T_3 so it is schedulable. What is the minimum increase?

   (c) We again assume that the context switch overhead is negligible. However, T_1 may suspend itself for 3 units of time, and T_3 is nonpreemptable. Identify the task (or tasks) that is (or are) no longer schedulable.

6.27 The *instantaneous utilization* of a periodic task at any time t is equal to the ratio of the execution time of the current job to the length of the current period. Consider a system of n independent, preemptable periodic tasks. The relative deadline of every job is the equal to the length of the period in which it is released. The periods and execution times of jobs in some tasks vary widely. However, the instantaneous utilization of each task T_k never exceeds $\hat{u}_k$.

   (a) Show that the system is schedulable according to the EDF algorithm if total instantaneous utilization $\sum_{k=1}^{n} \hat{u}_k$ is equal to or less than 1.

   (b) In contrast, none of the fixed-priority algorithms can feasibly schedule such a system. Give a simple example to prove this statement.

6.28 Prove the schedulable utilization in Theorem 6.16 for tasks whose relative deadlines are shorter than the respective periods.

6.29 Consider a system of multiframe tasks defined in Section 6.7.5. The tasks are scheduled on a fixed-priority basis.

   (a) Suppose that every job completes by the time the next job in the same task is released. Show that the response time of a job $J_{i,k}$ in T_i has the maximum possible value if the period k, which begins when $J_{i,k}$ is released, is a peak frame and this peak frame begins at the same time as a peak frame in every high-priority task. In other words, a critical instant of a multiframe task T_i occurs under this condition.

   (b) Suppose that the relative deadline of every task is equal to its period. Show that the RM algorithm is an optimal algorithm among all fixed-priority algorithms.

   (c) Modify Eq. (6.5) to express the time-demand function of the task T_i, that is, the amount of processor time demanded by the job $J_{i,k}$ since its release time t_0 plus the total time demanded by all jobs that have higher priorities than $J_{i,k}$ and must be completed before $J_{i,k}$.

   (d) Extend the time-demand analysis method described in Section 6.5 so it can be applied to test for the schedulability of multiframe tasks whose relative deadlines are equal to their respective periods. Briefly describe your extension and apply it on multiframe tasks $T_1 = (3, 4, 3, 1)$, $T_2 = (5, 3, 1, 0.5)$, and $T_3 = (11, 1)$. Are the tasks schedulable if their relative deadlines are 3, 5, and 11, respectively? What are the maximum possible response times of these tasks?

(e) Can the general time-demand analysis method described in Section 6.6 be similarly extended? If yes, briefly explain how. If no, briefly explain your reason.

6.30 A system uses the rate-monotonic algorithm to schedule three computation tasks $T_1 = (2.5, 0.5)$, $T_2 = (90, 15)$, and $T_3 = (150, 24)$. In addition, the system processes messages from two sources. The tasks that process the messages can be modeled as two periodic I/O tasks $I_1 = (20, 2)$, and $I_2 = (360, 3)$. (In other words, the minimum interarrival times of messages from the sources are 20 and 360, and the maximum amounts of time required to process each message from the sources are 2 and 3, respectively.) Whenever a message arrives, the processor handles interrupt immediately for 0.9 unit of time to identify the message source. Interrupt handling is executed nonpreemptively. When interrupt handling completes, one of the I/O tasks is called to process the message. Are the tasks schedulable? Explain your answer.

6.31 Interrupts typically arrive sporadically. When an interrupt arrives, interrupt handling is serviced (i.e., executed on the processor) immediately and in a nonpreemptable fashion. The effect of interrupt handling on the schedulability of periodic tasks can be accounted for in the same manner as blocking time. To illustrate this, consider a system of four tasks: $T_1 = (2.5, 0.5)$, $T_2 = (4, 1)$, $T_3 = (10, 1)$, and $T_4 = (30, 6)$. Suppose that there are two streams of interrupts. The interrelease time of interrupts in one stream is never less than 9, and that of the other stream is never less than 25. Suppose that it takes at most 0.2 unit of time to service each interrupt. Like the periodic tasks, interrupt handling tasks (i.e., the stream of interrupt handling jobs) are given fixed priorities. They have higher priorities than the periodic tasks, and the one with a higher rate (i.e., shorter minimum interrelease time) has a higher priority.

(a) What is the maximum amount of time each job in each periodic task may be delayed from completion by interrupts?

(b) Let the maximum delay suffered by each job of T_i in part (a) be b_i, for $i = 1, 2, 3$, and 4. Compute the time-demand functions of the tasks and use the time-demand analysis method to determine whether every periodic task T_i can meet all its deadlines if D_i is equal to p_i.

(c) In one or two sentences, explain why the answer you obtained in (b) about the schedulability of the periodic tasks is correct and the method you use works not only for this system but also for all independent preemptive periodic tasks.

6.32 Consider the following five fixed-priority tasks:

$$T_1 = (10, 2.0), \quad T_2 = (14, 2), \quad T_3 = (15, 3), \quad T_4 = (50, 1) \text{ and } T_5 = (24, 3).$$

(a) Suppose that each context switch takes 0.1 unit of time. Write the time-demand function $w_3(t)$ of T_3.

(b) Modify your time-demand function in part (a) to take into account of the fact that T_3 can self-suspend for 1 unit of time and T_5 contains a nonpreemptable section with execution time 0.5.

(c) Suppose that the scheduler makes a scheduling decision every 1 unit of time, that is, the tick size is 1.0. Each time, it takes 0.1 unit of time regardless of whether there are jobs waiting to be scheduled and 0.2 additional unit of time to schedule each waiting job. Modify your time demand function in part (b). Is T_3 schedulable?

6.33 Describe how to determine by simulation the schedulability of each task in a system of independent periodic tasks which may be nonpreemptable and may suspend itself.

6.34 Consider a system of independent, preemptable periodic tasks whose relative deadlines are equal to or larger than their respective periods. The tasks are scheduled rate-monotonically.

(a) Suppose that the utilizations u_{j_i} of k ($j < n$) tasks T_{j_i} for $i = 1, 2, \ldots, k$ are known and $(1 + u_{j_1})(1 + u_{j_2}) \cdots (1 + u_{j_k})$ is less than 2. Show that the other $n - k$ tasks are schedulable provided their total utilization is equal to or less than

$$(n - k)\left[\left(\frac{2}{(1 + u_{j_1})(1 + u_{j_2}) \cdots (1 + u_{j_k})}\right)^{1/(n-k)} - 1\right]$$

(b) Given that the utilizations of two tasks in a system of seven tasks are 0.01 and 0.02. How large can the total utilization of the other five tasks be for the system to be guaranteed schedulable rate-monotonically according to the criterion in part (a).

6.35 It is known that the periods of a system of independent, preemptable periodic tasks are 2, 3, 4, 5, 7, 8, 9, 11, 14, 16, 22, 25, 27, 28, 32, 33, 64, 81, 125, and 500. Moreover, the total utilization of the system is equal to 0.725. Is the system schedulable rate-monotonically, if the relative deadline of every task is equal to its period? Explain your answer.

6.36 Section 6.5.3. states that one way to determine whether a fixed-priority system of independent, preemptable tasks which are never blocked is by simulation. The simulation assumes that all tasks are in phase. If no task misses its first deadline in a schedule of the tasks according to their priorities, the system is schedulable. Alternatively, one can compute the maximum response time of each task by the iterative method described there.

(a) Explain briefly why the simulation approach no longer works when tasks may be blocked by nonpreemptive lower-priority tasks and self-suspension of higher-priority tasks. Is there a straightforward fix of the simulation method so we can take into account of these types of blocking reliably? Explain your answer.

(b) We can solve the equation $w_i(t) = t$ iteratively to find an upper bound of the response time of the task T_i. Explain briefly why, if we use the expression of $w_i(t)$ given by Eq. (6.18), the upper bound thus obtained is not tight unless b_i is 0.

6.37 Let $U_{RM}(n; \gamma)$ denote the schedulable utilization of the RM algorithm when it is used to schedule tasks whose adjacent period ratios are all larger than some integer $\gamma \geq 1$. $U_{RM}(n)$ is the schedulable utilization of n tasks when no restriction is placed on their adjacent period ratios, that is, $\gamma = 1$. Show the following corollary of Theorem 6.11 is true: Two independent, preemptable periodic tasks whose relative deadlines are equal to their respective periods is schedulable if its total utilization is no greater than

$$U_{RM}(2; \gamma) = 2[\gamma(\gamma + 1)]^{1/2} - 2\gamma$$

Moreover, this bound is tight. (*Hint*: Consider the tasks T_1 and T_2 whose execution times are related to their periods according to $e_1 = p_2 - \gamma p_1$ and $e_2 = p_2 - (\gamma + 1)e_1$.)

6.38 Compute the maximum response times the tasks T_3 and T_4 in the system whose parameters are listed Table 6-1.

6.39 Consider a system consisting of three fixed priority tasks: $T_1 = (100, 30)$, $T_2 = (150, 40)$, and $T_3 = (190, 35)$.

(a) Compute the maximum response time of T_3 ignoring all the practical factors discussed in Section 6.8.

(b) Suppose that scheduler executes periodically. The tick size p_0 is 10, e_0 is 0.03, and it takes 0.05 unit of time to move a job from pending queue to the ready queue. Moreover, each context switch takes 0.04 unit of time. What is the maximum response time of T_3?

6.40 Intuitively, it seems that in a fixed-time partitioning system, a subsystem of n independent, preemptable periodic tasks should be schedulable rate-monotonically if its total utilization is no greater than $U_{RM}(n)(\tau/RL)$, when the subsystem is allocated a slot of length τ in every round of length RL.

(a) Show that this statement is wrong. (The example in Figure 6–23 gives a good starting point.)

(b) Find a schedulable utilization of such a subsystem as a function of n, τ, and RL.

6.41 Consider a fixed-priority system of three tasks: $T_1 = (10, 3)$, $T_2 = (25, 7)$, and $T_3 = (70, 15)$. They are scheduled by a rate-monotonic scheduler which operates periodically. Specifically,

(a) The period p_0 of clock interrupts is 1.0 and the scheduler tasks 0.05 unit of time to complete when there are no ready jobs to be moved to the ready queue.

(b) The scheduler takes 0.02 unit of time to move a job from the waiting queue to the ready queue.

(c) Each context switch takes 0.1 unit of time.

(d) T_1 may self-suspend once during its execution.

Find the set of transformed tasks we should use to determine the schedulability of the periodic tasks.

6.42 In Section 6.8.7, we found the maximum possible response time of a task in the fixed-time partitioning subsystem shown in Figure 6–23 by solving for the minimum solution of the equation $w_i(t) = supply(t)$ where $w_i(t)$ and $supply(t)$ are given by Eqs. (6.24) and (2.29), respectively. The section gave an ad hoc way to seek the solution of this equation. Develop an algorithm that will surely find the minimum solution.

6.43 Suppose that the tasks in Figure 6–21 are scheduled according to the EDF algorithm; what is the blocking time of each task due to self-suspension? From the insight gained from this example, derive a formula for blocking time due to self-suspension in a deadline-driven system.

CHAPTER 7

Scheduling Aperiodic and Sporadic Jobs in Priority-Driven Systems

This chapter describes algorithms for scheduling aperiodic and sporadic jobs among periodic tasks in a priority-driven system. After discussing the assumptions made here on both types of jobs, we first focus on algorithms for scheduling aperiodic jobs. We then describe algorithms for scheduling sporadic jobs, while ignoring aperiodic jobs. We conclude the chapter by describing ways to integrate the scheduling of both aperiodic and sporadic jobs with periodic tasks.

7.1 ASSUMPTIONS AND APPROACHES

As in Chapters 5 and 6, we assume that there is only one processor and the periodic tasks in the system are independent. Aperiodic and sporadic jobs are also independent of each other and of the periodic tasks. We assume that every job can be preempted at any time. The effects of nonpreemptability and other practical factors can be taken into accounted in the manner described in Section 6.8.

We do not make any assumptions on the interrelease-times and execution times of aperiodic jobs. Indeed, most algorithms used to schedule aperiodic jobs do not even require the knowledge of their execution times after they are released. In contrast, throughout our discussion, we assume that the parameters of each sporadic job become known after it is released. Sporadic jobs may arrive at any instant, even immediately after each other. Moreover, their execution times may vary widely, and their deadlines are arbitrary. As we discussed in Chapter 5, in general, it is impossible for some sporadic jobs to meet their deadlines no matter what algorithm we use to schedule them. The only alternatives are (1) to reject the sporadic jobs that cannot complete in time or (2) to accept all sporadic jobs and allow some of them to complete late. Which alternative is appropriate depends on the application. This chapter focuses primarily on the first alternative. Only Section 7.8 discusses the second alternative.

7.1.1 Objectives, Correctness, and Optimality

Throughout this chapter, we assume that we are given the parameters $\{p_i\}$ and $\{e_i\}$ of all the periodic tasks and a priority-driven algorithm used to schedule them. Moreover, when the periodic tasks are scheduled according to the given algorithm and there are no aperiodic and sporadic jobs, the periodic tasks meet all their deadlines.

For the sake of concreteness, we assume that the operating system maintains the priority queues shown in Figure 7–1. The ready periodic jobs are placed in the periodic task queue, ordered by their priorities that are assigned according to the given periodic task scheduling algorithm. Similarly, each accepted sporadic job is assigned a priority and is placed in a priority queue, which may or may not be the same as the periodic task queue. Each newly arrived aperiodic job is placed in the aperiodic job queue. Moreover, aperiodic jobs are inserted in the aperiodic job queue and newly arrived sporadic jobs are inserted into a waiting queue to await acceptance without the intervention of the scheduler.

The algorithms described in this chapter determine when aperiodic or sporadic jobs are executed. We call them *aperiodic job and sporadic job scheduling algorithms*; they are solutions to the following problems:

1. Based on the execution time and deadline of each newly arrived sporadic job, the scheduler decides whether to accept or reject the job. If it accepts the job, it schedules the job so that the job completes in time without causing periodic tasks and previously accepted sporadic jobs to miss their deadlines. The problems are how to do the acceptance test and how to schedule the accepted sporadic jobs.

2. The scheduler tries to complete each aperiodic job as soon as possible. The problem is how to do so without causing periodic tasks and accepted sporadic jobs to miss their deadlines.

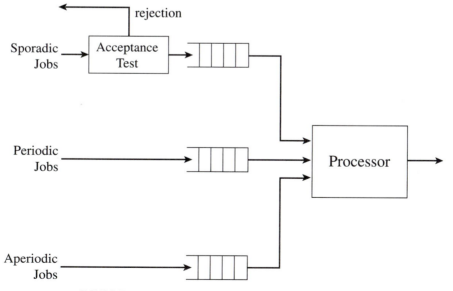

FIGURE 7–1   Priority queues maintained by the operating system.

Hereafter, by algorithm, we mean specifically an aperiodic job or sporadic job scheduling algorithm, except when it is stated otherwise. Such an algorithm is *correct* if it produces only correct schedules of the system. By a *correct schedule*, we mean one according to which periodic and accepted sporadic jobs never miss their deadlines. We consider only correct algorithms. In our subsequent discussion, we will omit the reminder that the actions of the scheduler according to the algorithm being described must never cause any periodic or sporadic job in the system to be late.

Finally, we assume that the queueing discipline used to order aperiodic jobs among themselves is given. An aperiodic job scheduling algorithm is optimal if it minimizes either the response time of the aperiodic job at the head of the aperiodic job queue or the average response time of all the aperiodic jobs for the given queueing discipline. An algorithm for (accepting and) scheduling sporadic jobs is optimal if it accepts each sporadic job newly offered to the system and schedules the job to complete in time if and only if the new job can be correctly scheduled to complete in time by some means. You recall from our discussion in Chapters 4 and 5 that such an algorithm is an optimal on-line algorithm only when all the sporadic jobs offered to the system are schedulable and is not optimal in general when some sporadic jobs must be rejected.

7.1.2 Alternative Approaches

All the algorithms described in this chapter attempt to provide improved performance over the three commonly used approaches. These approaches are background, polled, and interrupt-driven executions. For the sake of simplicity and clarity, we ignore sporadic jobs for now.

Background and Interrupt-Driven Execution versus Slack Stealing. According to the *background* approach, aperiodic jobs are scheduled and executed only at times when there is no periodic or sporadic job ready for execution. Clearly this method always produces correct schedules and is simple to implement. However, the execution of aperiodic jobs may be delayed and their response times prolonged unnecessarily.

As an example, we consider the system of two periodic tasks $T_1 = (3, 1)$ and $T_1 = (10, 4)$ shown in Figure 7–2. The tasks are scheduled rate monotonically. Suppose that an aperiodic job A with execution time equal to 0.8 is released (i.e., arrives) at time 0.1. If this job is executed in the background, its execution begins after $J_{1,3}$ completes (i.e., at time 7) as shown in Figure 7–2(a). Consequently, its response time is 7.7.

An obvious way to make the response times of aperiodic jobs as short as possible is to make their execution interrupt-driven. Whenever an aperiodic job arrives, the execution of periodic tasks are interrupted, and the aperiodic job is executed. In this example, A would execute starting from 0.1 and have the shortest possible response time. The problem with this scheme is equally obvious: If aperiodic jobs always execute as soon as possible, periodic tasks may miss some deadlines. In our example, if the execution time of A were equal to 2.1, both $J_{1,1}$ and $J_{2,1}$ would miss their deadlines.

The obvious solution is to postpone the execution of periodic tasks only when it is safe to do so. From Figure 7–2(a), we see that the execution of $J_{1,1}$ and $J_{2,1}$ can be postponed by 2 units of time because they both have this much slack. (Again, at any time t, the *slack* of a job with deadline d and remaining execution time e is equal to $d - t - e$.) By postponing the execution of $J_{1,1}$ and $J_{2,1}$, the scheduler allows aperiodic job A to execute immediately after

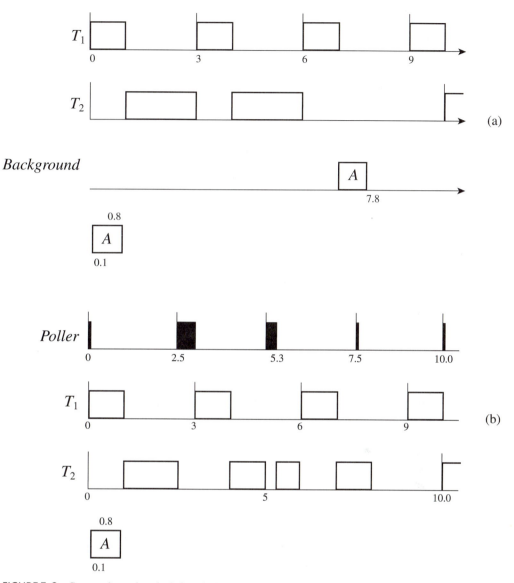

FIGURE 7–2 Commonly used methods for scheduling aperiodic jobs: $T_1 = (3, 1), T_2 = (10, 4)$, poller $= (2.5, 0.5)$. (a) Background execution. (b) Polling.

its arrival. The response time of A is equal to 0.8, which is as short as possible. The periodic job $J_{1,1}$ completes at time 1.8, and $J_{2,1}$ completes at 7.8. Both of them meet their deadlines. On the other hand, if the execution time of A is 2.1, only the first two units of the job can complete as soon as possible. After A has executed for 2 units of time, periodic tasks have no more slack and must execute. The last 0.1 unit of A must wait until time 9.0 when both periodic tasks have slack again. (We will return in Section 7.6 to explain this example further.)

Algorithms that make use of the available slack times of periodic and sporadic jobs to complete aperiodic jobs early are called *slack-stealing algorithms*, which were first proposed by Chetto, *et al.* [ChCh] and Lehoczky, *et al.* [LeRa]. In systems where slack-stealing can be done with an acceptable amount of overhead, it allows us to realize the advantage of interrupt-driven execution without its disadvantage. We saw in Chapter 5 that slack-stealing is algorithmically simple in clock-driven systems (although it complicates the implementation of clock-driven scheduling considerably). As you will see in Sections 7.5 and 7.6 slack stealing is significantly more complex in priority-driven systems.

Polled Executions versus Bandwidth-Preserving Servers. Polling is another commonly used way to execute aperiodic jobs. In our terminology, a *poller* or *polling server* (p_s, e_s) is a periodic task: p_s is its polling period, and e_s is its execution time. The poller is ready for execution periodically at integer multiples of p_s and is scheduled together with the periodic tasks in the system according to the given priority-driven algorithm. When it executes, it examines the aperiodic job queue. If the queue is nonempty, the poller executes the job at the head of the queue. The poller suspends its execution or is suspended by the scheduler either when it has executed for e_s units of time in the period or when the aperiodic job queue becomes empty, whichever occurs sooner. It is ready for execution again at the beginning of the next polling period. On the other hand, if at the beginning of a polling period the poller finds the aperiodic job queue empty, it suspends immediately. It will not be ready for execution and able to examine the queue again until the next polling period.

We now use the poller as an example to introduce a few terms and jargon which are commonly used in real-time systems literature. We will use them to describe variations of the poller in subsequent sections. We call a task that behaves more or less like a periodic task and is created for the purpose of executing aperiodic jobs a *periodic server*. A periodic server (p_s, e_s) is defined partially by its period p_s and execution time e_s. (Roughly speaking, the server never executes for more than e_s units of time in any time interval of length p_s. However, this statement is not true for some kinds of servers.) The parameter e_s is called the *execution budget* (or simply *budget*) of the server. The ratio $u_s = e_s/p_s$ is the *size* of the server. A poller (p_s, e_s) is a kind of periodic server. At the beginning of each period, the budget of the poller is set to e_s. We say that its budget is *replenished* (by e_s units) and call a time instant when the server budget is replenished a *replenishment time*.

We say that the periodic server is *backlogged* whenever the aperiodic job queue is nonempty and, hence, there is at least an aperiodic job to be executed by the server. The server is *idle* when the queue is empty. The server is *eligible* (i.e., ready) *for execution only when it is backlogged and has budget* (i.e., its budget is nonzero). When the server is eligible, the scheduler schedules it with the ready periodic tasks according to the algorithm used for scheduling periodic tasks as if the server is the periodic task (p_s, e_s). When the server is scheduled and executes aperiodic jobs, it *consumes* its budget at the rate of one per unit time. We say that the server budget becomes *exhausted* when the budget becomes zero. Different kinds of periodic servers differ in how the server budget changes when the server still has budget but the server is idle. As an example, the budget of a poller becomes exhausted instantaneously whenever the poller finds the aperiodic job queue empty, that is, itself idle.

Figure 7–2(b) shows a poller in the midst of the two fixed-priority periodic tasks $T_1 = (3, 1)$ and $T_2 = (10, 4)$. The poller has period 2.5 and execution budget 0.5. It is treated by the scheduler as the periodic task $(2.5, 0.5)$ and is given the highest priority among periodic tasks. At the beginning of the first polling period, the poller's budget is replenished, but when it executes, it finds the aperiodic job queue empty. Its execution budget is consumed instantaneously, and its execution suspended immediately. The aperiodic job A arrives a short time later and must wait in the queue until the beginning of the second polling period when the poller's budget is replenished. The poller finds A at head of the queue at time 2.5 and executes the job until its execution budget is exhausted at time 3.0. Job A remains in the aperiodic job queue and is again executed when the execution budget of the poller is replenished at 5.0. The job completes at time 5.3, with a response time of 5.2. Since the aperiodic job queue is empty at 5.3, the budget of the poller is exhausted and the poller suspends.

This example illustrates the shortcoming of the polling approach. An aperiodic job that arrives after the aperiodic job queue is examined and found empty must wait for the poller to return to examine the queue again a polling period later. If we can *preserve* the execution budget of the poller when it finds an empty queue and allow it to execute later in the period if any aperiodic job arrives, we may be able to shorten the response times of some aperiodic jobs. In this example, if the poller were able to examine the queue again at time 0.1, then job A would complete in the second polling period, making its response time significantly shorter.

Algorithms that improve the polling approach in this manner are called *bandwidth-preserving server* algorithms. Bandwidth-preserving servers are periodic servers. Each type of server is defined by a set of *consumption* and *replenishment* rules. The former give the conditions under which its execution budget is preserved and consumed. The latter specify when and by how much the budget is replenished. We will return in Chapters 11 and 12 to discuss the implementation of such servers in networks and operating systems. For now, we assume that they work as follows:

- A backlogged bandwidth-preserving server is ready for execution when it has budget. The scheduler keeps track of the consumption of the server budget and suspends the server when the server budget is exhausted or the server becomes idle. The scheduler moves the server back to the ready queue once it replenishes the server budget if the server is still backlogged at the time.
- The server suspends itself whenever it finds the aperiodic job queue empty, that is, when it becomes idle. When the server becomes backlogged again upon of arrival of an aperiodic job, the scheduler puts the server back to the ready queue if the server has budget at the time.

The next three sections describe three types of bandwidth-preserving servers. They are (1) deferrable servers [LeSS, StLS, GhBa], (2) sporadic servers [SpSL, GhBa], and (3) constant utilization/total bandwidth servers [DeLS, SpBu] and weighted fair-queueing servers [DeKS].

7.2 DEFERRABLE SERVERS

A *deferrable server* is the simplest of bandwidth-preserving servers. Like a poller, the execution budget of a deferrable server with period p_s and execution budget e_s is replenished periodically with period p_s. Unlike a poller, however, when a deferrable server finds no aperiodic job ready for execution, it preserves its budget.

7.2.1 Operations of Deferrable Servers

Specifically, the consumption and replenishment rules that define a deferrable server (p_s, e_s) are as follows.

Consumption Rule

> The execution budget of the server is consumed at the rate of one per unit time whenever the server executes.

Replenishment Rule

> The execution budget of the server is set to e_s at time instants kp_k, for $k = 0, 1, 2, \ldots$.

We note that the server is not allowed to cumulate its budget from period to period. Stated in another way, any budget held by the server immediately before each replenishment time is lost.

As an example, let us look again at the system in Figure 7–2. Suppose that the task $(2.5, 0.5)$ is a deferrable server. When it finds the aperiodic job queue empty at time 0, it suspends itself, with its execution budget preserved. When aperiodic job A arrives at 0.1, the deferrable server resumes and executes A. At time 0.6, its budget completely consumed, the server is suspended. It executes again at time 2.5 when its budget is replenished. When A completes at time 2.8, the aperiodic job queue becomes empty. The server is suspended, but it still has 0.2 unit of execution budget. If another aperiodic job arrives later, say at time 4.0, the server resumes at that time.

Figure 7–3 gives another example. Figure 7–3(a) shows that the deferrable server $T_{DS} = (3, 1)$ has the highest priority. The periodic tasks $T_1 = (2.0, 3.5, 1.5)$ and $T_2 = (6.5, 0.5)$ and the server are scheduled rate-monotonically. Suppose that an aperiodic job A with execution time 1.7 arrives at time 2.8.

1. At time 0, the server is given 1 unit of budget. The budget stays at 1 until time 2.8. When A arrives, the deferrable server executes the job. Its budget decreases as it executes.

2. Immediately before the replenishment time 3.0, its budget is equal to 0.8. This 0.8 unit is lost at time 3.0, but the server acquires a new unit of budget. Hence, the server continues to execute.

3. At time 4.0, its budget is exhausted. The server is suspended, and the aperiodic job A waits.

4. At time 6.0, its budget replenished, the server resumes to execute A.

5. At time 6.5, job A completes. The server still has 0.5 unit of budget. Since no aperiodic job waits in the queue, the server suspends itself holding this budget.

Figure 7–3(b) shows the same periodic tasks and the deferrable server scheduled according to the EDF algorithm. At any time, the deadline of the server is equal to the next replenishment time.

1. At time 2.8, the deadline of the deferrable server is 3.0. Consequently, the deferrable server executes at the highest-priority beginning at this time.

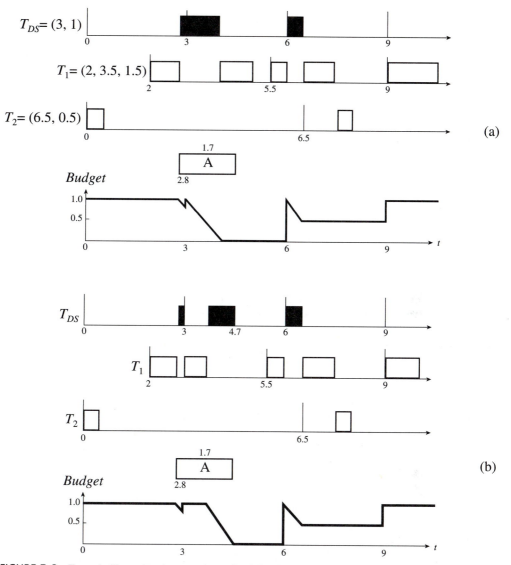

FIGURE 7–3 Example illustrating the operations of a deferrable server: ($T_{DS} = (3, 1)$, $T_1 = (2, 3.5, 1.5)$, and $T_2 = (6.5, 0.5)$. (a) Rate-monotonic schedule. (b) EDF schedule.

2. At time 3.0, when the budget of the deferrable server is replenished, its deadline for consuming this new unit of budget is 6. Since the deadline of $J_{1,1}$ is sooner, this job has a higher priority. The deferrable server is preempted.

3. At time 3.7, $J_{1,1}$ completes. The deferrable server executes until time 4.7 when its budget is exhausted.

4. At time 6 when the server's budget is replenished, its deadline is 9, which is the same as the deadline of the job $J_{1,2}$. Hence, $J_{1,2}$ would have the same priority as the server. The figure shows that the tie is broken in favor of the server.

Again, the scheduler treats a deferrable server as a periodic task. As you can see from the rules of the deferrable server algorithm, the algorithm is simple. The scheduling overhead of a deferrable server is no higher than that of a poller.

The responsiveness of the system can be further improved if we combine the use of a deferrable server with background execution. In other words, we also use a *background server*. This server is scheduled whenever the budget of the deferrable server has been exhausted and none of the periodic tasks is ready for execution. When the background server is scheduled, it also executes the aperiodic job at the head of the aperiodic job queue. With such a server, job A in Figure 7–3(a) would be executed from time 4.7 and completed by time 5.2, rather than 6.5, as shown in the figure.

7.2.2 Schedulability of Fixed-Priority Systems Containing Deferrable Server(s)

You may question the need of a background server in the above example. The schedule in Figure 7–3 may lead us to wonder whether we can get the same improved response by making the execution budget of the server bigger, for example, let it be 1.5 instead of 1.0. As it turns out, if we were to make the server budget bigger, the task (3.5, 1.5) would not be schedulable. This fact is shown by Figure 7–4. Suppose that an aperiodic job with execution time 3.0 or more arrives to an empty aperiodic job queue at time t_0, 1 unit of time before the replenishment time of the server (3, 1). At t_0, the server has 1 unit of budget. The server begins to execute from time t_0. Its budget is replenished at $t_0 + 1$, and it continues to execute as shown. Suppose that a job of each of the periodic tasks is released at time t_0. For this combination of release

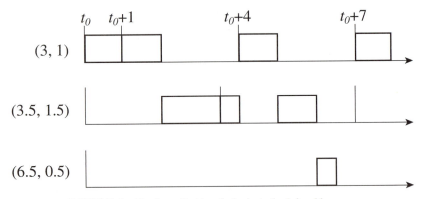

FIGURE 7–4 The factor limiting the budget of a deferrable server.

times, the task with period 3.5 would not complete in time if the budget of the server were bigger than 1.0. Since we cannot be sure that this combination of release times can never occur, the budget of the server must be chosen based the assumption that this combination can occur. This consideration limits the size of the server.

This example illustrates the condition under which a critical instant of a periodic task occurs in a system containing a deferrable server when all tasks have fixed priorities and the deferrable server has the highest priority. Lemma 7.1 [LeSS, StLS] stated below follows straightforwardly from Theorem 6.5.

LEMMA 7.1. In a fixed-priority system in which the relative deadline of every independent, preemptable periodic task is no greater than its period and there is a deferrable server (p_s, e_s) with the highest priority among all tasks, a critical instant of every periodic task T_i occurs at time t_0 when all the following are true.

1. One of its jobs $J_{i,c}$ is released at t_0.
2. A job in every higher-priority task is released at the same time.
3. The budget of the server is e_s at t_0, one or more aperiodic jobs are released at t_0, and they keep the server backlogged hereafter.
4. The next replenishment time of the server is $t_0 + e_s$.

Figure 7–5 shows the segment of a fixed-priority schedule after a critical instant t_0. Task T_{DS} is the deferrable server (p_s, e_s). As always, the other tasks are indexed in decreasing order of their priorities. As far as the job $J_{i,c}$ that is released at t_0 is concerned, the demand for processor time by each of the higher-priority tasks in its feasible interval $(r_{i,c}, r_{i,c} + D_i]$ is the largest when (1) and (2) are true. When (3) and (4) are true, the amount of processor time consumed by the deferrable server in the feasible interval of $J_{i,c}$ is equal to $e_s + \lceil (D_i - e_s)/p_s \rceil e_s$, and this amount the largest possible.

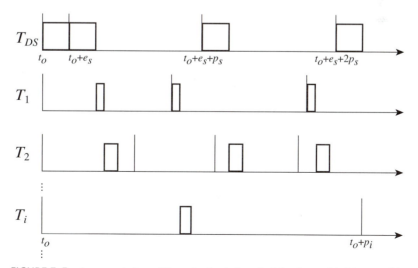

FIGURE 7–5   A segment of an arbitrary fixed-priority schedule after a critical instant of T_i.

Time-Demand Analysis Method.   We can use the time-demand method to determine whether all the periodic tasks remain schedulable in the presence of a deferrable server (p_s, e_s). For a job $J_{i,c}$ in T_i that is released at a critical instant t_0, we add the maximum amount $e_s + \lceil (t - e_s)/p_s \rceil e_s$ of processor time demanded by the server at time t units after t_0 into the right-hand side of Eq. (6.18). Hence, the time-demand function of the task T_i is given by

$$w_i(t) = e_i + b_i + e_s + \left\lceil \frac{t - e_s}{p_s} \right\rceil e_s + \sum_{k=1}^{i-1} \left\lceil \frac{t}{p_k} \right\rceil e_k \qquad \text{for } 0 < t \leq p_i \qquad (7.1)$$

when the deferrable server (p_s, e_s) has the highest priority.

To determine whether the response time of T_i ever exceeds its relative deadline D_i in the case of $D_k \leq p_k$ for all $k = 1, 2, \ldots, i$, we check whether $w_i(t) \leq t$ is satisfied at any of the values of t that are less than or equal to D_i. Again, we only need to check at values of t that are integer multiples of p_k for $k = 1, 2, \ldots, i - 1$ and at D_i. In addition, since $w_i(t)$ also increases at the replenishment times of the server at or before the deadline of $J_{i,c}$ (i.e., at e_s, $e_s + p_s, e_s + 2p_s, \ldots e_s + \lfloor (D_i - e_s)/p_s \rfloor p_s$), we also need to check whether $w_i(t) \leq t$ at these values of t. The response time of T_i is always equal to or less than D_i if the time supply t ever becomes equal to or larger than the time demand $w_i(t)$ at any of these values of t.

It is also easy to modify the time-demand analysis method for periodic tasks whose response times are longer than the respective periods to account for the effect of a deferrable server. When the server has the highest priority, we add the time demand of the server (which is equal to $e_s + \lceil (t - e_s)/p_s \rceil e_s$) to the expression of $w_{i,j}(t)$ given by Eq. (6.19).

Figure 7–6 shows the time-demand functions of T_1 and T_2 in the system shown in Figure 7–3. To determine whether T_2 is schedulable, we must check whether $w_i(t) \leq t$ at 1 and

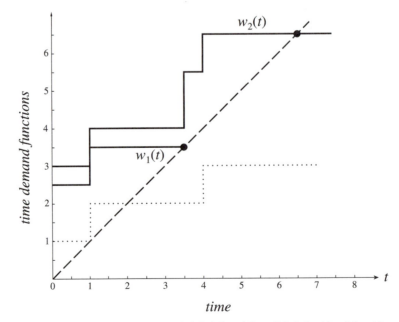

FIGURE 7–6   The time demand functions of $T_1 = (2, 3.5, 1.5)$ and $T_2 = (6.5, 0.5)$ with a deferrable server $(3, 1.0)$.

4, which are the replenishment times of the server before the deadline 6.5 of the first job in T_2, in addition to 3.5, which is the period of T_1, and 6.5. As expected, both tasks are schedulable according to this test.

Because of Lemma 7.1, we can also determine the schedulability of the fixed-priority periodic tasks by examining a segment of the schedule immediately after a critical instant of the periodic tasks. (The schedule in Figure 7–4 is an example.) Similarly, using the expression of $w_i(t)$ given by Eq. (7.1), we can find the maximum response time of each periodic task when scheduled together with a deferrable server by solving the equation $w_i(t) = t$ iteratively.

Schedulable Utilization.   There is no known schedulable utilization that assures the schedulability of a fixed-priority system in which a deferrable server is scheduled at an arbitrary priority. The only exception is the special case when the period p_s of the deferrable server is shorter than the periods of all periodic tasks and the system is scheduled rate-monotonically. In particular, the following theorem gives the schedulable utilization of a special class of systems [LeSS, StLS].

> **THEOREM 7.2.**   Consider a system of n independent, preemptable periodic tasks whose periods satisfy the inequalities $p_s < p_1 < p_2 < \cdots < p_n < 2p_s$ and $p_n > p_s + e_s$ and whose relative deadlines are equal to their respective periods. This system is schedulable rate-monotonically with a deferrable server (p_s, e_s) if their total utilization is less than or equal to
>
> $$U_{RM/DS}(n) = (n-1)\left[\left(\frac{u_s+2}{u_s+1}\right)^{1/(n-1)} - 1\right]$$
>
> where u_s is the utilization e_s/p_s of the server.

The proof is similar to that of Theorem 6.5 and is left to you as an exercise (Problem 7.7).

When the server's period is arbitrary, we can use the schedulable utilization $U_{RM}(n)$ given by Eq. (6.10) to determine whether each periodic task T_i is schedulable if the periodic tasks and the server are scheduled rate-monotonically and the relative deadlines of the periodic tasks are equal to their respective periods. To see how, we focus on the feasible interval $(r_{i,c}, r_{i,c} + D_i]$ of a job $J_{i,c}$ in any periodic task T_i that has a lower priority than the server. As far as this job is concerned, the server behaves just like a periodic task (p_s, e_s), except that the server may execute for an additional e_s units of time in the feasible interval of the job. We can treat these e_s units of time as additional "blocking time" of the task T_i: T_i is surely schedulable if

$$U_i + u_s + \frac{e_s + b_i}{p_i} \le U_{RM}(i+1)$$

where U_i is the total utilization of the i highest-priority tasks in the system.

As an example, consider a deferrable server with period 4 and execution budget 0.8. It is scheduled rate-monotonically with three preemptable periodic tasks $T_1 = (3, 0.6)$, $T_2 = (5.0, 0.5)$, and $T_3 = (7, 1.4)$. T_1 has a higher priority than the server and is not affected by the server. To determine whether T_2 is schedulable, we compute $U_2 + u_s + e_s/p_2$. The value of this expression is 0.66. Since it is less than $U_{RM}(3) = 0.757$, we know that T_2 is schedulable. To check whether T_3 is schedulable in the same manner, we find that $U + u_s + e_s/p_3 = 0.814$

exceeds the schedulable utilization of the RM algorithm for four tasks. This sufficient but not necessary test says that the task T_3 may not be schedulable. However, if we use the right-hand side of Eq. (7.1) as the time-demand function of T_3 and do a time-demand analysis, we will find that T_3 is in fact schedulable.

Deferrable Server with Arbitrary Fixed Priority. You recall that any budget of a deferrable server that remains unconsumed at the end of each server period is lost. For this reason, when the server is not scheduled at the highest priority, the maximum amount of processor time it can consume (and hence is demanded) depends not only on the release times of all the periodic jobs relative to replenishment times of the server, but also on the execution times of all the tasks. For some combinations of task and server parameters, the time demand of the server in a time interval of length t may never be as large as $e_s + \lceil (t - e_s)/p_s \rceil e_s$, the terms we included in the right-hand side of Eq. (7.1). However, these terms do give us an upper bound to the amount of time demanded by the server and allows us to account for the effect of the server on the schedulability of lower-priority tasks correctly if not accurately.

From this observation, we can conclude that in a system where the deferrable server is scheduled at an arbitrary priority, the time-demand function of a task T_i with a lower-priority than the server is bounded from above by the expression of $w_i(t)$ in Eq. (7.1). Using this upper bound, we make the time-demand analysis method a sufficient schedulability test for any fixed-priority system containing one deferrable server.

A system may contain several aperiodic tasks. We may want to use different servers to execute different aperiodic tasks. By adjusting the parameters and priorities of the servers, the response times of jobs in an aperiodic task may be improved at the expense of the response times of jobs in other aperiodic tasks. It is easy to see that when there is more than one deferrable server, we can take the effect of each server into account by including its processor-time demand in the computation of the time-demand function of each lower-priority periodic task in the same manner. Specifically, the time-demand function $w_i(t)$ of a periodic task T_i with a lower priority than m deferrable servers, each of which has period $p_{s,k}$ and execution budget $e_{s,k}$, is given by

$$w_i(t) \le e_i + b_i + \sum_{k=1}^{m} \left(1 + \left\lceil \frac{t - e_{s,k}}{p_{s,k}} \right\rceil \right) e_{s,k} + \sum_{k=1}^{i-1} \left\lceil \frac{t}{p_k} \right\rceil e_k \qquad \text{for } 0 < t \le p_i \qquad (7.2)$$

7.2.3 Schedulability of Deadline-Driven Systems in the Presence of Deferrable Server

We now derive the schedulable utilization of a system of n independent periodic tasks that is scheduled according to the EDF algorithm together with a deferrable server of period p_s and execution budget e_s. Let t be the deadline of a job $J_{i,c}$ in some periodic task T_i and t_{-1} ($< t$) be the latest time instant at which the processor is either idle or is executing a job whose deadline is after t. We observe that if $J_{i,c}$ does not complete by t, the total amount $w_{DS}(t - t_{-1})$ of processor time consumed by the deferrable server in the interval $(t_{-1}, t]$ is at most equal to

$$e_s + \left\lfloor \frac{t - t_{-1} - e_s}{p_s} \right\rfloor e_s \qquad (7.3)$$

Figure 7–7 shows the condition under which the server consumes this amount of time.

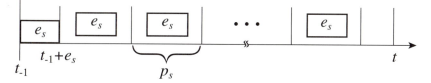

FIGURE 7–7   the condition under which the deferrable server consumes the most time.

1. At time t_{-1}, its budget is equal to e_s and the deadline for consuming the budget is (and hence the budget is to be replenished at) $t_{-1} + e_s$.
2. One or more aperiodic jobs arrive at t_{-1}, and the aperiodic job queue is never empty hereafter, at least until t.
3. The server's deadline $t_{-1} + e_s$ is earlier than the deadlines of all the periodic jobs that are ready for execution in the interval $(t_{-1}, t_{-1} + e_s]$.

Under this condition, the server executes continuously in $(t_{-1}, t_{-1} + e_s]$. If the current period (i.e., the period which begins before t and ends at or after t) of the server also ends at t, the argument of the floor function in Eq. (7.3) is an integer; the floor function is equal to this integer. Otherwise, if the current period of the server ends after t, the server has a lower-priority than $J_{i,c}$ and is not given any time during this period. In either case, the total amount of the time consumed by the server after $t_{-1} + e_s$ is given by the second term in Eq. (7.3).

Since $\lfloor x \rfloor \leq x$ for all $x \geq 0$ and $u_s = e_s/p_s$, $w_{DS}(t - t_{-1})$ must satisfy the following inequality if the job $J_{i,c}$ does not complete by its deadline at t:

$$w_{DS}(t - t_{-1}) \leq e_s + \frac{t - t_{-1} - e_s}{p_s} e_s = u_s(t - t_{-1} + p_s - e_s) \qquad (7.4)$$

This observation leads to Theorem 7.3 [GhBa]. This theorem allows us to determine whether any periodic task T_i is schedulable when the periodic tasks are scheduled together with a deferrable server according to the EDF algorithm.

THEOREM 7.3.   A periodic task T_i in a system of n independent, preemptive periodic tasks is schedulable with a deferrable server with period p_s, execution budget e_s, and utilization u_s, according to the EDF algorithm if

$$\sum_{k=1}^{n} \frac{e_k}{\min(D_k, p_k)} + u_s \left(1 + \frac{p_s - e_s}{D_i} \right) \leq 1 \qquad (7.5)$$

Proof.   We suppose that a job misses its deadline at t and consider the interval $(t_{-1}, t]$. The interval begins at the latest time instant t_{-1} at which time the processor is either idle or is executing a job whose deadline is after t. The total amount of processor time used by each periodic task T_k in the time interval is bounded from above by $e_k(t - t_{-1})/p_k$. The fact that a job misses its deadline at t tells us that the total amount of time in this time interval used by all the periodic jobs with deadlines at or before t and the deferrable server exceeds the length of this interval. In other words,

$$t - t_{-1} \leq \sum_{k=1}^{n} \frac{e_k}{p_k}(t - t_{-1}) + u_s(t - t_{-1} + p_s - e_s)$$

Dividing both sides of this inequality by $t - t_{-1}$, we get Eq. (7.5) for the case of $D_k \geq p_k$.

□

As an example, let us consider again the system of three periodic tasks $T_1 = (3, 0.6)$, $T_2 = (5.0, 0.5)$, and $T_3 = (7, 1.4)$, which we studied earlier. The total utilization of the tasks is 0.5. If they are scheduled with a deferrable server whose period is 4 and execution time is 0.8, the values of the expression on the left-hand side of Eq. (7.5) for the three tasks are 0.913, 0.828 and 0.792, respectively. Hence, all three tasks are schedulable.

From Eq. (7.5), we see that just as in a fixed-priority system, a deferrable server in a deadline-driven system behaves like a periodic task (p_s, e_s) except that it may execute an extra amount of time in the feasible interval of any job. We treat this extra amount as the blocking time suffered by the job. In a fixed-priority system, the blocking time can be as large as e_s. In contrast, Theorem 7.3 says that the blocking caused by a deferrable server in a deadline-driven system is only $(p_s - e_s)u_s$. (The latter is always less than the former. In our earlier example, e_s is 0.8, while $(p_s - e_s)u_s$ is only 0.64.)

We can take into account the effect of any number of deferrable servers in this way. (This corollary is stated as an exercise at the end of the chapter.) To illustrate, suppose that in addition to the server $(4, 0.8)$ in the previous example, we have another deferrable server $(2, 0.1)$ with utilization 0.05. The blocking time contributed by this server is 0.095. Adding the contribution of the second server to the left-hand side of (7.5) (i.e., adding $0.05 + 0.095/3.0$ to 0.913), we get 0.995 for T_1. Hence we can conclude that T_1 remains to be schedulable. Similarly, T_2 and T_3 are schedulable.

7.3 SPORADIC SERVERS

We have just seen that a deferrable server may delay lower-priority tasks for more time than a period task with the same period and execution time. This section describes a class of bandwidth-preserving servers, called *sporadic servers* [SpSL, GhBa], that are designed to improve over a deferrable server in this respect. The consumption and replenishment rules of sporadic server algorithms ensure that each sporadic server with period p_s and budget e_s never demands more processor time than the periodic task (p_s, e_s) in any time interval. Consequently, we can treat the sporadic server exactly like the periodic task (p_s, e_s) when we check for the schedulability of the system. A system of periodic tasks containing a sporadic server may be schedulable while the same system containing a deferrable server with the same parameters is not.

For example, we mentioned earlier that it is not possible to make the execution time of the deferrable server in Figure 7–3 larger than 1.0 when the system is scheduled rate-monotonically. In contrast, if we replace the deferrable server by a sporadic server, we can increase the server execution time to 1.25, while keeping its period at 3.0, or decrease its period to 2.5, while keeping its execution time at 1.0. You may want to convince yourself that a sporadic server with these sets of parameters will be able to complete the aperiodic job at 6.25 and 6.0, respectively, instead of 6.5 accomplished by the deferrable server in Figure 7–3.

With slight abuse of the notation, we will sometimes refer to a sporadic server with period p_s and budget e_s as the periodic task $T_s = (p_s, e_s)$ and say that a server job is released when the server becomes eligible. Different kinds of sporadic servers differ in their consumption and replenishment rules. More complicated rules allow a server to preserve its budget for a longer time, replenish the budget more aggressively, and, in a deadline-driven system, execute at a higher priority. By using different rules, you can trade off the responsiveness of the server for the overhead in its implementation.

7.3.1   Sporadic Server in Fixed-Priority Systems

We first confine our attention to fixed-priority systems. For the moment, we assume that there is only one sporadic server in a fixed-priority system $\mathbf{T}$ of n independent, preemptable periodic tasks. The server has an arbitrary priority π_s. (If the server has the same priority as some periodic task, the tie is always broken in favor of the server.) We use $\mathbf{T}_H$ to denote the subset of periodic tasks that have higher priorities than the server. We say that the system $\mathbf{T}$ of periodic tasks (or the higher-priority subsystem $\mathbf{T}_H$) idles when no job in $\mathbf{T}$ (or $\mathbf{T}_H$) is ready for execution; $\mathbf{T}$ (or $\mathbf{T}_H$) is busy otherwise. By definition, the higher-priority subsystem remains busy in any busy interval of $\mathbf{T}_H$. Finally, a *server busy interval* is a time interval which begins when an aperiodic job arrives at an empty aperiodic job queue and ends when the queue becomes empty again.

Since our focus here is on the consumption and replenishment rules of the server, we assume that we have chosen the parameters p_s and e_s and have validated that the periodic task (p_s, e_s) and the system $\mathbf{T}$ are schedulable according to the fixed-priority algorithm used by the system. When doing the schedulability test, we assume that the relative deadline for consuming the server budget is finite but arbitrary. In particular, we allow this deadline to be larger than p_s. During an interval when the aperiodic job queue is never empty, the server behaves like the periodic task (p_s, e_s) in which some jobs may take longer than one period to complete.

We state below the consumption and replenishment rules that define a simple sporadic server. In the statement, we use the following notations. (Their names may not make sense for now. We will return shortly to explain why they are called by these names and to discuss the rationales behind the consumption and replenishment rules.)

- t_r denotes the latest (actual) replenishment time.
- t_f denotes the first instant after t_r at which the server begins to execute.
- t_e denotes the latest *effective replenishment time*.
- At any time t, *BEGIN* is the beginning instant of the earliest busy interval among the latest contiguous sequence of busy intervals of the higher-priority subsystem $\mathbf{T}_H$ that started before t. (Two busy intervals are contiguous if the later one begins immediately after the earlier one ends.)
- *END* is the end of the latest busy interval in the above defined sequence if this interval ends before t and equal to infinity if the interval ends after t.

The scheduler sets t_r to the current time each time it replenishes the server's execution budget. When the server first begins to execute after a replenishment, the scheduler determines the latest effective replenishment time t_e based on the history of the system and sets the next replenishment time to $t_e + p_s$. (In other words, the next replenishment time is p_s units away from t_e, as if the budget was last replenished at t_e and hence the name effective replenishment time.)

Simple Sporadic Server.   In its simpliest form, a sporadic server is governed by the following consumption and replenishment rules. We call such a server a *simple sporadic server*. A way to implement the server is to have the scheduler monitor the busy intervals of $\mathbf{T}_H$ and maintain information on *BEGIN* and *END*.

- *Consumption Rules of Simple Fixed-Priority Sporadic Server*: At any time t after t_r, the server's execution budget is consumed at the rate of 1 per unit time until the budget is exhausted when either one of the following two conditions is true. When these conditions are not true, the server holds its budget.

  C1 The server is executing.

  C2 The server has executed since t_r and *END* $< t$.

- *Replenishment Rules of Simple Fixed-Priority Sporadic Server*:

  R1 Initially when the system begins execution and each time when the budget is replenished, the execution budget $= e_s$, and $t_r =$ the current time.

  R2 At time t_f, if *END* $= t_f$, $t_e = \max(t_r, BEGIN)$. If *END* $< t_f$, $t_e = t_f$. The next replenishment time is set at $t_e + p_s$.

  R3 The next replenishment occurs at the next replenishment time, except under the following conditions. Under these conditions, replenishment is done at times stated below.

    (a) If the next replenishment time $t_e + p_s$ is earlier than t_f, the budget is replenished as soon as it is exhausted.

    (b) If the system $\mathbf{T}$ becomes idle before the next replenishment time $t_e + p_s$ and becomes busy again at t_b, the budget is replenished at $\min(t_e + p_s, t_b)$.

Rules C1 and R1 are self-explanatory. Equivalently, rule C2 says that the server consumes its budget at any time t if it has executed since t_r but at t, it is suspended and the higher-priority subsystem $\mathbf{T}_H$ is idle. Rule R2 says that the next replenishment time is p_s units after t_r (i.e., the effective replenishment time t_e is t_r) only if the higher-priority subsystem $\mathbf{T}_H$ has been busy throughout the interval (t_r, t_f). Otherwise, t_e is later; it is the latest instant at which an equal or lower-priority task executes (or the system is idle) in (t_r, t_f).

Figure 7–8 gives an illustrative example. Initially the budget of the server $(5, 1.5)$ is 1.5. It is scheduled rate-monotonically with three periodic tasks: $T_1 = (3, 0.5)$, $T_2 = (4, 1.0)$, and $T_3 = (19, 4.5)$. They are schedulable even when the aperiodic job queue is busy all the time.

1. From time 0 to 3, the aperiodic job queue is empty and the server is suspended. Since it has not executed, its budget stays at 1.5. At time 3, the aperiodic job A_1 with execution time 1.0 arrives; the server becomes ready. Since the higher-priority task $(3, 0.5)$ has a job ready for execution, the server and the aperiodic job wait.

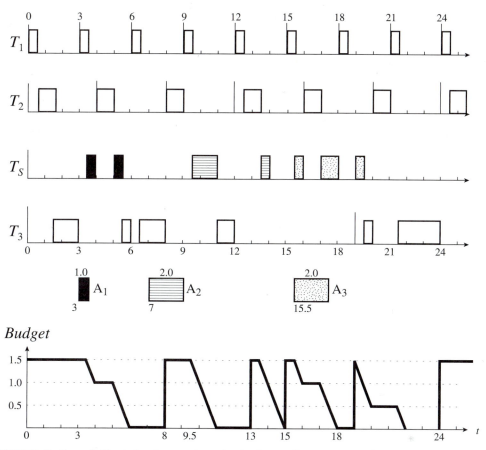

FIGURE 7–8 Example illustrating the operations of a simple sporadic server: $T_1 = (3, 0.5)$, $T_2 = (4, 1.0)$, $T_3 = (19, 4.5)$, $T_s = (5, 1.5)$.

2. The server does not begin to execute until time 3.5. At the time, t_r is 0, *BEGIN* is equal to 3, and *END* is equal to 3.5. According to rule R2, the effective replenishment time t_e is equal to $\max(0, 3.0) = 3$, and the next replenishment time is set at 8.

3. The server executes until time 4; while it executes, its budget decreases with time.

4. At time 4, the server is preempted by T_2. While it is preempted, it holds on to its budget.

5. After the server resumes execution at 5, its budget is consumed until exhaustion because first it executes (C1) and then, when it is suspended again, T_1 and T_2 are idle (or equivalently, *END*, which is 5.0, is less than the current time) (C2).

6. When the aperiodic job A_2 arrives at time 7, the budget of the server is exhausted; the job waits in the queue.

7. At time 8, its budget replenished (R3), the server is ready for execution again.

8. At time 9.5, the server begins to execute for the first time since 8. t_e is equal to the latest replenishment time 8. Hence the next replenishment time is 13. The server executes

until its budget is exhausted at 11; it is suspended and waits for the next replenishment time. In the meantime, A_2 waits in the queue.

9. Its budget replenished at time 13, the server is again scheduled and begins to execute at time 13.5. This time, the next replenishment time is set at 18. However at 13.5, the periodic task system **T** becomes idle. Rather than 18, the budget is replenished at 15, when a new busy interval of **T** begins, according to rule R3b.

10. The behavior of the later segment also obeys the above stated rules. In particular, rule R3b allows the server budget to be replenished at 19.

This example does not give us an opportunity to illustrate rule R3a. To illustrate this rule, we consider the situation shown in Figure 7–9. Before t_r some lower-priority task T_l executed, but after t_r only higher-priority tasks (i.e., tasks in $\mathbf{T}_H$) execute until t_f. At t_f the server is finally scheduled. The next replenishment time $t_e + p_s$ computed based on rule R2 is earlier than t_f. The figure shows that as soon as the budget is exhausted, it is replenished, allowing the server to continue until it is preempted.

*Informal Proof of Correctness of the Simple Sporadic Server. We now explain why a server following the above stated rules emulates the periodic task $T_s = (p_s, e_s)$; therefore, when checking for the schedulability of the periodic tasks, we can simply treat the server as the periodic task T_s. (The actual interrelease-times of jobs in T_s are sometimes larger than p_s, and their execution times are sometimes smaller than e_s. We saw in Chapter 6 that the schedulability of lower-priority tasks are not adversely affected by these variations.) In this

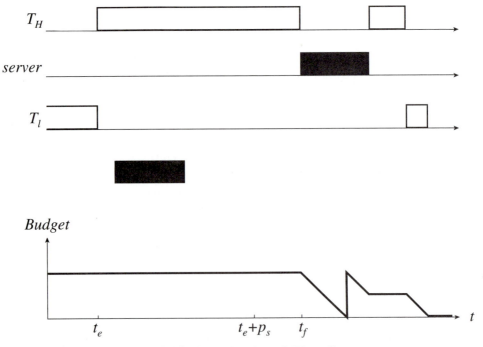

FIGURE 7–9 A situation where rule R3a applies.

sense, the rules and, hence, the sporadic server are correct. The only exception is when rule R3b is applied; we will show that despite this exception, the server is correct.

For the moment, let us confine our attention to an interval when the periodic task system **T** has not been idle and hence the rule R3b has never been applied. It is convenient to view each replenishment time as the nominal "release time" of a server job. The actual release-time of the server job is at t_e, which may be later than its nominal release time. The term current job refers to the "server job" which was "released" at the latest replenishment time t_r or the latest effective replenishment time t_e.

The consumption rule C1 ensures that each server job never executes for more time than its execution budget e_s. C2 applies when the server becomes idle while it still has budget. This rule says that unlike a deferrable server, the budget of an idle simple sporadic server continues to decrease with time as if server were executing. Because of these two rules, each server job never executes at times when the corresponding job of the periodic task T_s does not.

C2 also means that the server holds on to its budget at any time t after its budget is replenished at t_r when (a) some higher-priority job is executing or (b) the server has not executed since t_r. When condition (a) occurs, the server waits for higher-priority tasks; its budget does not decrease because the server is not scheduled independent of whether the server is ready or suspended. To see that condition (b) will not cause the server to demand for more processor time than the periodic task T_s, we note that t_r is the nominal release time of the current server job. Its actual release-time can be as late as t_f when it first starts to execute since t_r. This emulates the situation when the current job of the periodic task T_s is released late.

To show the correctness of the replenishment rules R2 and R3a, we note that the next replenishment time is always set at the p_s time units after the effective release-time t_e of the current server job and the next release-time is never earlier than the next replenishment time. Hence according to these two rules, consecutive replenishments occurs at least p_s units apart.

Specifically, rule R2 is designed to make the effective replenishment time as soon as possible (so that the next replenishment time can be as soon as possible) without making the server behave differently from a periodic task. At time t_f when the server executes for the first time after t_r, the effective replenishment time t_e is set at t_r if higher-priority tasks have executed throughout the interval (t_r, t_f); this emulates a job in T_s released at t_r but has to wait for higher-priority tasks to become idle before it can execute. On the other hand, if lower-priority tasks executed in this interval, t_e is set to the latest time instant when a lower-priority task executes. This emulates a job in T_s that is released at t_e and waits for higher-priority tasks to become idle and then begins execution.

Rule R3a applies when the current server job has to wait for more than p_s units of time before its execution can begin. This rule allows the budget to be replenished as soon as it is exhausted. When this rule applies, the server emulates the situation when a job in T_s takes more than one server period to complete. In fact, it starts to execute after the subsequent job of T_s is released. This rule works correctly if at the time when the server parameters were chosen and schedulability of the periodic tasks were determined, the fact that the response time of the server can be larger than the server period was taken into consideration.

When rule R3b applies, the server may behave differently from the periodic task T_s. This rule is applicable only when a busy interval of the periodic task system **T** ends. As a result of this rule, the server budget is replenished when the next busy interval of **T** begins. In other words, a server job is "released" at the same time as the job in **T** which begins the new busy interval. This condition was taken into account in the schedulability test that found **T** to be schedulable together with the periodic task T_s, and the behavior of the system in the new busy interval is independent of that in the previous busy interval. Hence, the early replenishment of the server budget will not adversely affect the schedulability of lower-priority tasks.

7.3.2 Enhancements of Fixed-Priority Sporadic Server

We now discuss several enhancements as an exercise in server design. If we are willing to make sporadic servers somewhat more complex and pay for slightly higher scheduling overhead, there are many ways to replenish the execution budget more aggressively and preserve it longer. One point to keep in mind in this discussion is the relationship between the replenishment and consumption rules. If we change one rule, we may need to change some other rule(s) in order for the entire set of rules to remain correct.

Sporadic/Background Server.   The example in Figure 7–8 tells us that rule R3b of the simple fixed-priority sporadic server is overly conservative. At time 18.5, the periodic system becomes idle. The aperiodic job A_3 remains incomplete, but the server budget is exhausted. According to this rule, the budget is not replenished until the job $J_{3,2}$ is released at 19. While A_3 waits, the processor idles. It is clear that the schedulability of the periodic system will not be adversely affected if we replenish the server budget at 18.5 and let the server execute until 19 with its budget undiminished. In this way, the server claims all the background time that is not used by the periodic task system. For this example, A_3 would complete by time 19 if the server were allowed to claim the background time.

We call a sporadic server that claims the background time a *sporadic/background server*; in essence, it is a combination of a sporadic server and a background server and is defined by the following rules.

- *Consumption rules of simple sporadic/background servers* are the same as the rules of simple sporadic servers except when the period task system is idle. As long as the periodic task system is idle, the execution budget of the server stays at e_s.
- *Replenishment rules of simple sporadic/background servers* are same as those of the simple sporadic server except R3b. The budget of a sporadic/background server is replenished at the beginning of each idle interval of the periodic task system. t_r is set at the end of the idle interval.

When there is only one server in the system, there is no reason not to make it a sporadic/ background server. When there is more than one sporadic/background server, the highest priority server gets the background time whenever it can execute at the time. This may or may not be desirable. For this reason, we may want to keep some servers simple and give the background time to some other servers, or even make all sporadic servers simple servers and use a separate background server to execute in the background of the periodic task system and the servers.

As an example, suppose that a system has two aperiodic tasks. The jobs in one task are released whenever the operator issues a command, and their execution times are small. We use a sporadic server to execute these jobs. In order to make the system responsive to the operator, we choose to make the server period 100 milliseconds and execution budget sufficiently large to complete a job (at least most of time). Each job of the other aperiodic task is released to process a message. The messages arrive infrequently, say one a minute on the average. The execution times of jobs in this task vary widely because the messages have widely differing lengths. To execute these jobs, we use a sporadic server with a much longer period. Suppose that the system is scheduled rate-monotonically. We may want to give all the background time to the message-processing server. This can be done by making the command-processing server a simple sporadic server and the message-processing server a sporadic/background server.

Cumulative Replenishment. A reason for the simplicity of simple sporadic servers is that all the budget a server has at any time was replenished at the same time. In particular, a simple server is not allowed to cumulate its execution budget from replenishment to replenishment. This simplifies the consumption and replenishment rules. A way to give the server more budget is to let the server keep any budget that remains unconsumed. In other words, rather than setting the budget to e_s, we increment its budget by e_s units at each replenishment time. Hence the budget of a server may exceed e_s. As a result of this change in replenishment rule R1, the server emulates a periodic task in which some jobs do not complete before the subsequent jobs in the task are released. Of course, as stated in the beginning of this section, we must take into account the fact that the response times of some server jobs may be longer than the server period when we check for the schedulability of the periodic tasks and choose the server parameters p_s and e_s accordingly.

Figure 7–10 gives an example. The server with period 15 and execution budget 6 cannot consume its budget at time 15 when its budget is replenished. This example illustrates that it is safe to increment its budget by 6 units. By doing so, the server emulates the periodic task $(15, 6)$ whose first job cannot complete within one period. As a consequence of this enhancement, the server completes the aperiodic job A_2 by time 27. In contrast, a simple sporadic server cannot complete the job until time 36.

Let us now examine an enhanced sporadic server which increments its budget by e_s units at each replenishment and see what its consumption rules should be. Clearly, the budget still should be consumed at the rate of 1 per time unit whenever the server is executing; rule C1 of simple sporadic servers always applies. However, we need to modify rule C2 of simple sporadic servers to make it work for an enhanced sporadic server. In particular, it is necessary to treat the e_s-unit chunk of new budget replenished at the latest replenishment time differently from the chunk of old budget left unconsumed at the time. Whenever the server has both new budget and old budget, it always consumes the old budget first; this emulates the behavior that jobs in a periodic task are executed in the FIFO order whenever more than one job of the task is ready for execution at the same time.

At any time t after the latest replenishment time t_r, it is still safe to consume the new budget according to C1 and C2. However, we cannot use rule C2 to govern the consumption of the old budget. To see why, we note that because of the way t_r was determined, the server must have executed in the interval between the replenishment time of the old budget and t_r. Hence after t_r, the old budget should be consumed at the rate of 1 per unit time when the server is suspended and the higher-priority subsystem $\mathbf{T}_H$ is idle independent of whether the server has executed since t_r. To illustrate this point, we look at the example in Figure 7–10 again and suppose that job A_2 is released at time 17 instead. From time 15 to 17 while the lower-priority task $(59, 5)$ is executing, the server holds on to its new budget replenished at time 15 according to rule C2. However, the 1-unit chunk of old budget should be consumed by

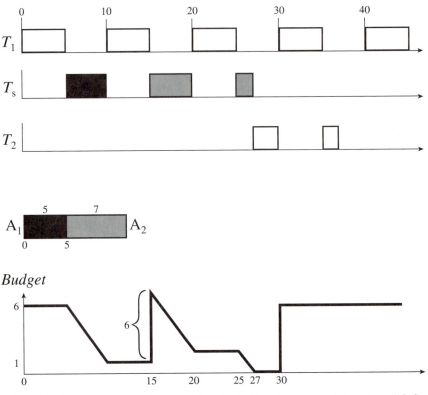

FIGURE 7–10   A more aggressive replenishment rule. $T_1 = (10, 5)$, $T_2 = (59, 5)$, $T_s = (15, 6)$.

time 16, leaving the server with only its new budget at 16. You may want to convince yourself that if the server were to consume the old budget according to rule C2 (i.e., holding on the budget as long as its has not executed since t_r), it would in essence defer the use of the old budget, and this deference might affect the schedulability of some lower-priority task.

It is easy to see that we can further improve the replenishment rule R3a as follows: Replenish the budget at time $t_r + p_s$ whenever the higher-priority subsystem $\mathbf{T}_H$ has been busy throughout the interval $(t_r, t_r + p_s]$. This additional change in replenishment rules in turn makes it necessary to treat the budget that is not consumed in this interval with care. As an exercise in server design, you may want to write up consumption and replenishment rules of enhanced sporadic servers. You can find the statement of this exercise in Problem 7.11.

SpSL Sporadic Servers.   If you look up the reference [SpSL] and read the description of the sporadic servers, you will find that their rules allow a server to consume and replenish its budget in chunks rather than as a whole as we have done thus far. Specifically, a Sprunt, Sha, and Lehoczky (SpSL) sporadic server preserves unconsumed chunks of budget whenever possible and replenishes the consumed chunks as soon as possible. By doing so, a SpSL server with period p_s and execution budget e_s emulates several periodic tasks with the same period and total execution time equal to e_s.

To explain, we return to the example in Figure 7–8. The figure shows that at time 5.5 when the simple sporadic server is suspended, the server has already consumed a 1-unit chunk of budget. Its remaining 0.5-unit chunk of budget is consumed as the lower-priority task T_3 executes. If an aperiodic job A_4 with 0.5 unit of execution time were to arrive at 6.5, the server would have to wait until time 9.5 to execute the job. In contrast, a SpSL server holds on to the remaining chunk of 0.5 unit of budget as T_3 executes. Figure 7–11 illustrates the operations of a SpSL server.

1. Suppose that at time 6.5, A_4 indeed arrives. The SpSL server can execute the job immediately, and in the process, consumes its remaining chunk of budget.
2. At time 8, rather than the entire budget of 1.5 units, the SpSL server replenishes only the chunk of 1.0 unit which was consumed from time 3.5 to 5.5. This 1.0 unit is treated as one chunk because the execution of the server was interrupted only by a higher-priority task during the time interval when this chunk was consumed.

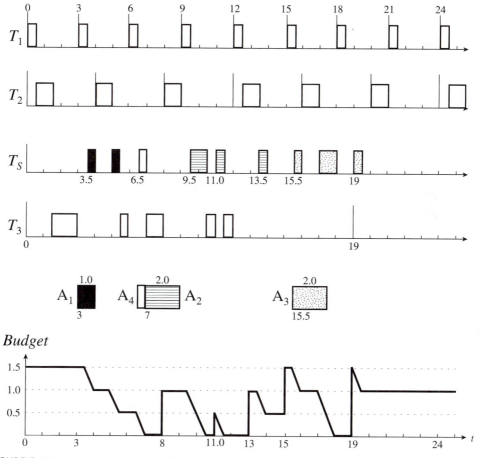

FIGURE 7–11   Example illustrating SpSL sporadic servers: $T_1 = (3, 0.5)$, $T_2 = (4, 1.0)$, $T_3 = (19, 4.5)$, $T_s = (5, 1.5)$.

3. At time 11.0, 5 units of time from the effective replenishment time of the second chunk, the 0.5 unit of budget is replenished. [The effective replenishment time of the second chunk is 6.0 because at time t_f (= 6.5), the first execution time of this chunk, *BEGIN* is 6.0, the time instant when T_1 begins to execute.]

4. Similarly, at time 13, only the first chunk is replenished.

5. Later at 13.5, when the higher-priority tasks are no longer busy, the server executes and completes A_2. At this time, it still has 0.5 units of budget, and this chunk is preserved. By now, the server has three different chunks of budget: the chunk that was replenished at time 11.0 and consumed at 11.5, the chunk that was replenished at 13 and consumed by 14.0, and the leftover chunk at 14.0.

6. As it is, the system becomes idle at 14.0. All the chunks can be replenished at time 15 following rule R3b of the simple sporadic server, and the server has only one 1.5-unit chunk of budget again.

This example illustrates the advantage of SpSL servers over simple sporadic servers. During time intervals when the aperiodic job queue is continuously nonempty or empty for a larger number of server periods, these two types of servers behave in the same manner. However, when the queue frequently alternates from being nonempty to empty and vice versa, a SpSL server oftentimes can respond sooner to new arrivals of aperiodic jobs than a simple sporadic server.

Conceptually, a SpSL server emulates several periodic tasks, one per chunk. As time progresses and its budget breaks off into more and more chunks, the original periodic task (p_s, e_s) breaks up into more and more periodic tasks whose total execution time is e_s. The additional cost of SpSL servers over simple servers arises due to the need of keeping track of the consumption and replenishment of different chunks of budget. In particular, it is necessary to keep track when each chunk was replenished so as to ensure that individual chunks are not replenished too soon. This requires more complicated replenishment rules than those given in [SpSL]. (Problem 7.12 gives the statement of the consumption and replenishment rules in [SpSL] and an example to illustrate the problem which can arise because these rules do not deal with different chunks separately when they should. As a consequence, the server is not correct because it may cause some lower-priority periodic tasks to miss their deadlines.)

The consumption and replenishment rules below define an enhanced fixed-priority sporadic server that holds onto its execution budget except when it is actually executing. We also call this server the SpSL server. It differs from the original version in that it works correctly and it does not claim the background time when the periodic task system becomes idle.

Rules of SpSL Server

- Breaking of Execution Budget into Chunks

    B1 Initially, the budget $= e_s$ and $t_r = 0$. There is only one chunk of budget.

    B2 Whenever the server is suspended, the last chunk of budget being consumed just before suspension, if not exhausted, is broken up into two chunks: The first chunk is the portion that was consumed during the last server busy interval, and the second chunk is the remaining portion. The first chunk inherits the next replenishment time of the original chunk. The second chunk inherits the last replenishment time of the original chunk.

- Consumption Rules

    C1 The server consumes the chunks of budget in order of their last replenishment times.

    C2 The server consumes its budget only when it executes.

- Replenishment Rules: The next replenishment time of each chunk of budget is set according to rules R2 and R3 of the simple sporadic server. The chunks are consolidated into one whenever they are replenished at the same time.

The overhead of the SpSL server over the simple version consists of the time and space required to maintain the last and the next replenishment times of individual chunks of the server budget. In the worst case, this can be as high as $O(N)$, where N is the number of jobs in a hyperperiod of the periodic tasks.

However, as we will see in Section 12.2.2, it is relatively simple for the operating system to monitor the budget consumption of a SpSL server, because its budget is consumed only when it executes. In contrast, the budget of a simple sporadic server may also be consumed during the execution of lower-priority tasks. Consequently, it is more complex to monitor the budget consumption of a simple sporadic server accurately.

***Priority Exchanges.**   In addition to allowing the budget to be divided up into chunks as a SpSL server does, there is another way to preserve the server budget. To see how, we begin by reexamining rule C2 of the simple sporadic server. (For simplicity, we consider only the option where there is only one chunk of budget.) According to this rule, once the server has executed since a replenishment, it consumes its budget except during the time interval(s) when it is preempted. In particular, its budget decreases when the server is idle and some lower-priority task executes. We can stop the consumption under this condition by allowing the server to trade time with the executing lower-priority task.

The schedule segments in Figure 7–12 illustrate what we mean. T_l is a lower-priority task. The schedule in part (a) illustrates the situation when the aperiodic job queue remains nonempty after the server begins to execute at time t_f. The server continues to execute until its budget is exhausted at time $t_f + e_s$. The lower-priority task T_l must wait until this time to execute and completes later at time t_l. The schedule in part (b) illustrates the situation that the server busy interval ends and the server becomes idle and, therefore, suspended at time $t_f + \varepsilon$ before its budget is exhausted. A job in the lower priority task T_l begins to execute at this time. Because T_l is able to use the $e_s - \varepsilon$ units of time which would be given to the server if it were not suspended, T_l can complete sooner. This means that $e_s - \varepsilon$ units of time before t_l is no longer needed by the lower-priority task; they can be given to the server as budget. In order to ensure that the other lower-priority tasks are not affected by this exchange, the chunk of budget the server gets from the lower-priority task should be scheduled at the priority of the task, not at the priority of the server. Figure 7–12(b) shows that an aperiodic job arrives later at time t_0, and it can be executed by the server if the server has the traded budget, while a simple sporadic server has no budget at this time.

In general, we may have the situation where (1) the server becomes idle and is therefore suspended while it still has budget and (2) some lower priority tasks $T_l, T_{l+1}, \ldots, T_{l+k}$ execute in the time interval where the server would be scheduled if it were not suspended. We say that

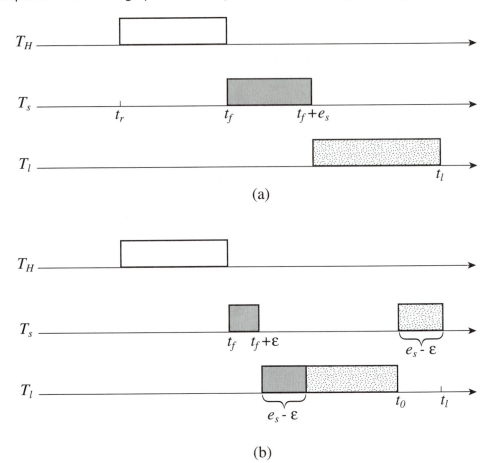

FIGURE 7–12   Priority exchange between the server and a lower-priority task.

these lower-priority tasks execute at the server's priority in this interval. Let x_j denote the amount of time the lower-priority task T_{l+j} executes in this interval. The server is allowed to keep x_j units of budget. When the server later uses this budget, it will be scheduled at the priority of the task T_{l+j}.

Trading time and priorities among the server and the lower-priority tasks in this manner is exactly what a *priority-exchange server* [LeSS, SpSL] does. Intuitively, we can see that priority exchange is particularly advantageous when the aperiodic job queue becomes empty frequently. However, without special hardware to support priority exchange, the run time overhead of a priority-exchange server is significantly higher than that of a simple sporadic server or an SpSL server. The high overhead of priority exchange makes this type of servers impractical.

7.3.3   Simple Sporadic Servers in Deadline-Driven Systems

When the periodic tasks are scheduled on the EDF basis, the priorities of the tasks vary as their jobs are released and completed. Consequently, the membership of the subset of tasks with higher priorities than the server varies with time. Some of the rules of simple sporadic servers stated earlier for fixed-priority systems must be modified for this reason. The rationales behind the modified rules remain the same: a simple sporadic server of period p_s and budget e_s following the rules behave like a periodic task (p_s, e_s).

The consumption and replenishment rules of simple sporadic servers in a system where all tasks are scheduled according to the EDF algorithm are stated below. We again use t_r to denote the latest replenishment time. However the notation t_e, the effective latest replenishment time, has a different meaning from that of a fixed-priority sporadic server. Specifically, rule R2 below governs how the value of t_e is determined. The server is ready for execution only when it is backlogged (i.e., the aperiodic job queue is nonempty) and its deadline d (and hence its priority) is set. The server is suspended whenever its deadline is undefined or when the server is idle (i.e., the aperiodic job queue becomes empty).

- *Consumption Rules of Simple Deadline-Driven Sporadic Server*: The server's execution budget is consumed at the rate of one per unit time until the budget is exhausted when either one of the following two conditions is true. When these conditions are not true, the server holds its budget.

    C1 The server is executing.

    C2 The server deadline d is defined, the server is idle, and there is no job with a deadline before d ready for execution.

- *Replenishment Rules of Simple Deadline-Driven Sporadic Server*:

    R1 Initially and at each replenishment time, t_r is the current time, and the budget $=$ e_s. Initially, t_e and the server deadline d are undefined.

    R2 Whenever t_e is defined, $d = t_e + p_s$, and the next replenishment time is $t_e + p_s$. Otherwise, when t_e is undefined, d remains undefined. t_e is determined (defined) as follows:

    (a) At time t when an aperiodic job arrives at an empty aperiodic job queue, the value of t_e is determined based on the history of the system before t as follows:

    i. If only jobs with deadlines earlier than $t_r + p_s$ have executed throughout the interval (t_r, t), $t_e = t_r$.

    ii. If some job with deadline after $t_r + p_s$ has executed in the interval (t_r, t), $t_e = t$.

    (b) At replenishment time t_r,

    i. if the server is backlogged, $t_e = t_r$, and

    ii. if the server is idle, t_e and d become undefined.

    R3 The next replenishment occurs at the next replenishment time, except under the following conditions. Under these conditions, the next replenishment is done at times stated below.

(a) If the next replenishment time $t_e + p_s$ is earlier than the time t when the server first becomes backlogged since t_r, the budget is replenished as soon as it is exhausted.

(b) The budget is replenished at the end of each idle interval of the periodic task system **T**.

As you can see, the differences in rules of simple sporadic servers in deadline-driven and fixed-priority systems are small. It just so happens that if we schedule the periodic tasks in Figure 7–8 according to the EDF algorithm and make the sporadic server follow the rules of deadline-driven simple sporadic servers, the schedule segment we get is essentially the same as the one shown in the figure. The possible differences may arise if when the server has the same priority as the periodic tasks, we alway break the tie in favor of the server.

Like SpSL servers, a deadline-driven sporadic server proposed by Ghazalie and Baker [GhBa], which we call a GhBa server, also consumes and replenishes its budget in chunks. The consumption and replenishment rules of GhBa servers are given in Problem 7.13. Unlike the rules of SpSL servers given in [SpSL], these rules do ensure that each chunk is never replenished sooner than one server period since its last replenishment. Consequently, lower-priority jobs never miss their deadlines because the server takes too much time. The rules of GhBa servers are somewhat more complex than the rules of simple deadline-driven sporadic servers. Both kinds of servers are considerably more complex than the constant utilization, total bandwidth, and weighted fair-queueing servers described in the next section.

7.4 CONSTANT UTILIZATION, TOTAL BANDWIDTH, AND WEIGHTED FAIR-QUEUEING SERVERS

We now describe three bandwidth preserving server algorithms that offer a simple way to schedule aperiodic jobs in deadline-driven systems. They are constant utilization [DeLS], total bandwidth [SpBu], and weighted fair-queueing [DeKS] algorithms. These algorithms belong to a class of algorithms that more or less emulate the Generalized Processor Sharing (GPS) algorithm. GPS, sometimes called fluid-flow processor sharing, is an idealized weighted round-robin algorithm; it gives each backlogged server in each round an infinitesmally small time slice of length proportional to the server size.[1]

Clearly, infinitesmally fine-grain time slicing cannot be implemented in practice. The algorithms which we are about to describe behave like the GPS algorithm to different degrees. In particular, each server maintained and scheduled according to any of these algorithms offers timing isolation to the task(s) executed by it; by this statement, we mean that the worst-case response times of jobs in the task are independent the processor-time demands of tasks executed by other servers. While such a server works in a way that is similar to sporadic servers, its correctness relies on a different principle. Before we describe the rules governing the operations of such a server, we digress briefly to describe a schedulability condition of sporadic jobs scheduled on the EDF basis. The correctness of these algorithms follows from the condition.

---

[1]The GPS algorithm is sometimes called a bit-by-bit or instruction-by-instruction round-robin algorithm because the lengths of time slices are equal to the time to transmit a few bits in a packet or to execute a few instructions or processor cycles in a program. It is a generalization of the processor sharing model first used by Klienrock [Klie].

7.4.1 Schedulability of Sporadic Jobs in Deadline-Driven Systems

In Chapter 6, we showed that a system of independent, preemptable periodic tasks whose relative deadlines are equal to or larger than their respective periods is schedulable according to the EDF algorithm if the total utilization of the tasks is equal to or less than 1. We also argued that if the execution times of some jobs in some task are smaller than the execution time of the task and the interrelease times between some jobs are larger than its period, the system is schedulable if it is schedulable according to this criterion. We now carry this point further to a more general sufficient schedulability condition for independent, preemptable sporadic jobs. This schedulability condition is in terms of densities of sporadic jobs. The *density* of a sporadic job J_i that has release time r_i, maximum execution time e_i and deadline d_i is the ratio $e_i/(d_i - r_i)$. A sporadic job is said to be *active* in its feasible interval $(r_i, d_i]$; it is not active outside of this interval.

> **THEOREM 7.4.** A system of independent, preemptable sporadic jobs is schedulable according to the EDF algorithm if the total density of all active jobs in the system is no greater than 1 at all times.

> **Proof.** We prove the theorem by contradiction. Suppose that a job misses its deadline at time t, and there is no missed deadline before t. Let t_{-1} be the latest time instant before t at which either the system idles or some job with a deadline after t executes. Suppose that k jobs execute in the time interval $(t_{-1}, t]$. We call these jobs $J_1, J_2, \ldots, J_k$ and order them in increasing order of their deadlines. (Ties in deadlines are broken arbitrarily.) J_k is the job that misses its deadline at t. Because the processor remains busy in $(t_{-1}, t]$ executing jobs of equal or higher priorities than J_k and J_k misses its deadline at time t, we must have $\sum_{i=1}^{k} e_i > t - t_{-1}$.
>
> We let the number of job releases and completions during the time interval (t_{-1}, t) be l, and t_i be the time instant when the ith such event occurs. In terms of this notation, $t_{-1} = t_1$ and, for the sake of convenience, we also use t_{l+1} to denote t. These time instants partition the interval $(t_{-1}, t]$ into l disjoint subintervals, $(t_1, t_2], (t_3, t_3], \ldots, (t_l, t_{l+1}]$. The active jobs in the system and their total density remain unchanged in each of these subintervals. Let $\mathbf{X}_i$ denote the subset containing all the jobs that are active during the subinterval $(t_i, t_{i+1}]$ for $1 \leq i \leq l$ and Δ_i denote the total density of the jobs in $\mathbf{X}_i$.
>
> The total time demanded by all the jobs that execute in the time interval $(t_{-1}, t]$ is $\sum_{i=1}^{k} e_i$. We can rewrite the sum as

$$\sum_{i=1}^{k} \frac{e_i}{d_i - r_i}(d_i - r_i) = \sum_{j=1}^{l}(t_{j+1} - t_j) \sum_{J_k \in \mathbf{X}_j} \frac{e_k}{d_k - r_k} = \sum_{j=1}^{l} \Delta_j (t_{j+1} - t_j)$$

> Since $\Delta_j \leq 1$ for all $j = 1, 2, \ldots, l - 1$, we have

$$\sum_{i=1}^{k} e_i \leq \sum_{j=1}^{l}(t_{j+1} - t_j) = t_{l+1} - t_1 = t - t_{-1}$$

> This leads to a contradiction.   □

The condition stated in Theorem 7.4 is not necessary: Sporadic jobs may be schedulable on the EDF basis when this condition is not satisfied. As an example, we consider three sporadic jobs each of which has a relative deadline of 2 and execution time of 1. They are released at time instants 0, 0.5, and 1.0. The total density of jobs is 1.5 in (1, 2], yet they are schedulable on the EDF basis.

You recall that a sporadic task S_i is a stream of sporadic jobs. Let $S_{i,j}$ denote the jth job in the task S_i (i.e., the release time of $S_{i,j}$ is later than the release times of $S_{i,1}, S_{i,2}, \ldots, S_{i,j-1}$). Let $e_{i,j}$ denote the execution time of $S_{i,j}$, and $p_{i,j}$ denote the length of time between the release times of $S_{i,j}$ and $S_{i,j+1}$. At the risk of abusing the term, we call $p_{i,j}$ the *period* of the sporadic job $S_{i,j}$ and the ratio $e_{i,j}/p_{i,j}$ the *instantaneous utilization* of the job. The *instantaneous utilization* $\tilde{u}_i$ of a sporadic task is the maximum of the instantaneous utilizations of all the jobs in this task (i.e., $\tilde{u}_i = \max_j(e_{i,j}/p_{i,j})$). As with execution times and periods of periodic tasks, we assume that the instantaneous utilization of a sporadic task is a known parameter of the task.

In a system of n sporadic tasks whose total instantaneous utilization is equal to or less than one, the total density of all active jobs is equal to or less than 1 at all times. Consequently, the following sufficient schedulability condition of sporadic tasks scheduled according to the EDF algorithm follows straightforwardly from Theorem 7.4.

> **COROLLARY 7.5.** A system of n independent, preemptable sporadic tasks, which is such that the relative deadline of every job is equal to its period, is schedulable on a processor according to the EDF algorithm if the total instantaneous utilization (i.e., $\sum_{i=1}^{n} \tilde{u}_i$), is equal to or less than 1.

Because the utilization $u_i = \max_j(e_{i,j})/\min_j(p_{i,j})$ of any task S_i is always larger than its instantaneous utilization $\tilde{u}_i = \max_j(e_{i,j}/p_{i,j})$, we have the following corollary.

> **COROLLARY 7.6.** A system of independent, preemptable periodic and sporadic tasks, which is such that the relative deadline of every job is equal to its period, is schedulable on a processor according to the EDF algorithm if the sum of the total utilization of the periodic tasks and the total instantaneous utilization of the sporadic tasks is equal to or less than 1.

This corollary gives us theoretical basis of the constant utilization server algorithm described below.

7.4.2 Constant Utilization Server Algorithm

We now return our attention to the problem of scheduling aperiodic jobs amid periodic tasks in a deadline-driven system. For the purpose of executing aperiodic jobs, there is a basic *constant utilization server*. The server is defined by its *size*, which is its instantaneous utilization $\tilde{u}_s$; this fraction of processor time is reserved for the execution of aperiodic jobs. As with deferrable servers, the deadline d of a constant utilization server is always defined. It also has an execution budget which is replenished according to the replenishment rules described below. The server is eligible and ready for execution only when its budget is nonzero. When the server is ready, it is scheduled with the periodic tasks on the EDF basis. While a sporadic server emulates a periodic task, a constant utilization server emulates a sporadic task with a constant instantaneous utilization, and hence its name.

Consumption and Replenishment Rules.   The consumption rule of a constant utilization server, as well as that of a total bandwidth or weighted fair-queueing server, is quite simple. *A server consumes its budget only when it executes.* You will see shortly that such a server never has any budget when there is no aperiodic job ready for execution. Hence the problem of dealing with chunks of budget never arises.

The budget of a basic constant utilization server is replenished and its deadline set according to the following rules. In the description of the rules, $\tilde{u}_s$ is the size of the server, e_s is its budget, and d is its deadline. t denotes the current time, and e denotes the execution time of the job at the head the aperiodic job queue. The job at the head of the queue is removed when it completes. The rules assume that the execution time e of each aperiodic job becomes known when the job arrives. We will return later to discuss how to remove this restriction.

Replenishment Rules of a Constant Utilization Server of Size $\tilde{u}_s$

R1 Initially, $e_s = 0$, and $d = 0$.

R2 When an aperiodic job with execution time e arrives at time t to an empty aperiodic job queue,

    (a) if $t < d$, do nothing;

    (b) if $t \geq d$, $d = t + e/\tilde{u}_s$, and $e_s = e$.

R3 At the deadline d of the server,

    (a) if the server is backlogged, set the server deadline to $d + e/\tilde{u}_s$ and $e_s = e$;

    (b) if the server is idle, do nothing.

In short, a constant utilization server is always given enough budget to complete the job at the head of its queue each time its budget is replenished. Its deadline is set so that its instantaneous utilization is equal to $\tilde{u}_s$.

Figure 7–13 illustrates how a constant utilization server works. This system of periodic tasks and aperiodic jobs is essentially the same as the system in Figure 7–8. (For this system, the simple fixed-priority and deadline-driven sporadic servers happen to behave the same.) The only difference between them is that in Figure 7–13, aperiodic job A_2 arrives at time 6.9 instead of 7.0. The size of the constant utilization server is 0.25, slightly smaller than the size of the sporadic server in Figure 7–8.

1. Before time 3.0, the budget of the server is 0. Its deadline is 0. The server does not affect other tasks because it is suspended.

2. At time 3, A_1 arrives. The budget of the server is set to 1.0, the execution time of A_1, and its deadline is $3 + 1.0/0.25 = 7$ according to R2b. The server is ready for execution. It completes A_1 at time 4.5.

3. When A_2 arrives at time 6.9, the deadline of the server is later than the current time. According to R2a, nothing is done except putting A_2 in the aperiodic job queue.

4. At the next deadline of the server at 7, the aperiodic job queue is checked and A_2 is found waiting. The budget of the server is replenished to 2.0, the execution time of A_2, and its deadline is $7 + 2.0/0.25 = 15$. The server is scheduled and executes at time 7, is preempted by T_2 at time 8, resumes execution at 9.5 and completes A_2 at time 10.5.

5. At time 15, the aperiodic job queue is found empty. Nothing is done.

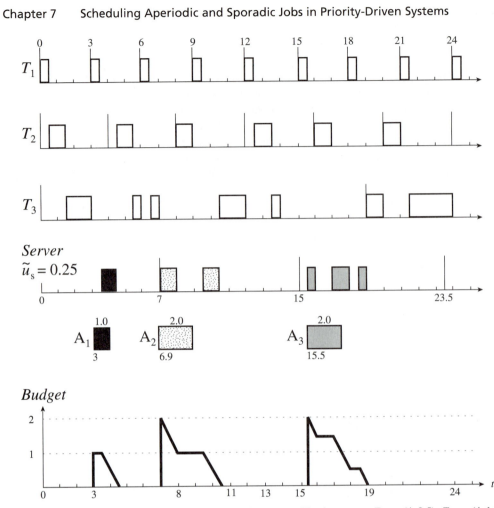

FIGURE 7–13 Example illustrating the operations of constant utilization server: $T_1 = (4, 0.5)$, $T_2 = (4, 1.0)$, $T_3 = (19, 4.5)$.

6. At time 15.5, A_3 arrives. At the time, the deadline of the server is 15. Hence according to rule R2b, its deadline is set at 23.5, and the server budget is set to 2.0. This allows the server to execute A_3 to completion at time 19.

We see that the constant utilization server completes each of the aperiodic jobs earlier than a simple sporadic server.

From Theorem 7.4 and its corollaries, we see that for a given system of periodic tasks with total density Δ, we can divide the leftover processor bandwidth among an arbitrary number of constant utilization servers. [You recall that the density of a periodic task (p_i, e_i, D_i) is $e_i / \min(D_i, p_i)$.] We are sure that no deadlines will be missed as long as the total size (i.e., the total instantaneous utilization) of all the servers is equal to or less than $1 - \Delta$.

Scheduling Aperiodic Jobs with Unknown Execution Times. In the description of the constant utilization server algorithm, we assume that the execution times of aperiodic jobs become known upon their arrival. This restrictive assumption can be removed by modifying the replenishment rules of constant utilization (or total bandwidth) servers. One way is to give the server a fixed size budget e_s and fixed period $e_s/\tilde{u}_s$ just like sporadic and deferrable servers. Since the execution time of each aperiodic job can be determined after it is completed with little overhead, we can adjust the server deadline based on this knowledge upon the completion of the job. Specifically, when an aperiodic job with execution time e shorter than e_s completes, we reduce the current deadline of the server by $(e_s - e)/\tilde{u}_s$ units before replenishing the next e_s units of budget and setting the deadline accordingly. This action clearly can improve the performance of the server and does not make the instantaneous utilization of the server larger than $\tilde{u}_s$.

An aperiodic job with execution time larger than e_s is executed in more than one server period. We can treat the last chunk of such a job in the manner described above if the execution time of this chunk is less than e_s.

7.4.3   Total Bandwidth Server Algorithm

To motivate the total bandwidth server algorithm [SpBu], let us return to the example in Figure 7–13. Suppose that A_3 were to arrive at time 14 instead. Since 14 is before the current server deadline 15, the scheduler must wait until time 15 to replenish the budget of the constant utilization server. A_3 waits in the interval from 14 to 15, while the processor idles! Clearly, one way to improve the responsiveness of the server is to replenish its budget at time 14. This is exactly what the total bandwidth server algorithm does.

Specifically, the total bandwidth server algorithm improves the responsiveness of a constant utilization server by allowing the server to claim the background time not used by periodic tasks. This is done by having the scheduler replenish the server budget as soon as the budget is exhausted if the server is backlogged at the time or as soon as the server becomes backlogged. We now show that a constant utilization server works correctly if its budget is replenished in this aggressive manner. In particular, we can change the replenishment rules as follows and get a *total bandwidth server*. You can see that the rules of a total bandwidth server are even simpler than the rules of a constant utilization server.

Replenishment Rules of a Total Bandwidth Server of size $\tilde{u}_s$

R1 Initially, $e_s = 0$ and $d = 0$.

R2 When an aperiodic job with execution time e arrives at time t to an empty aperiodic job queue, set d to $\max(d, t) + e/\tilde{u}_s$ and $e_s = e$.

R3 When the server completes the current aperiodic job, the job is removed from its queue.

  (a) If the server is backlogged, the server deadline is set to $d + e/\tilde{u}_s$, and $e_s = e$.

  (b) If the server is idle, do nothing.

Comparing a total bandwidth server with a constant utilization server, we see that for a given set of aperiodic jobs and server size, both kinds of servers have the same sequence of deadlines, but the budget of a total bandwidth server may be replenished earlier than that of a constant utilization server. As long as a total bandwidth server is backlogged, it is always ready for execution. In the above example, this means that the server's budget is replenished at 6.9 and, if A_3 were to arrive at 14, at 14, and the deadline of the server is 15 and 23.5, respectively, A_3 would be completed at time 17.5 if it were executed by a total bandwidth server but would be completed at 19 by a constant bandwidth server.

Clearly, a total bandwidth server does not behave like a sporadic task with a constant instantaneous utilization. To see why it works correctly, let us examine how the server affects periodic jobs and other servers when its budget is set to e at a time t before the current server deadline d and its deadline is postponed to the new deadline $d' = d + e/\tilde{u}_s$. In particular, we compare the amount of processor time demanded by the server with the amount of time demanded by a constant utilization server of the same size $\tilde{u}_s$ before the deadline $d_{i,k}$ of a periodic job $J_{i,k}$ whose deadline is later than the server's new deadline d'. (We do not need to consider periodic jobs with deadlines earlier than d' because they have higher priorities than the server.) If the job $J_{i,k}$ is ready at t, then the amounts of time consumed by both servers are the same in the interval from t to $d_{i,k}$. If $J_{i,k}$ is not yet released at t, then the time demanded by the total bandwidth server in the interval $(r_{i,k}, d']$ is less than the time demanded by the constant utilization server because the total bandwidth server may have executed before $r_{i,k}$ and has less budget in this interval. In any case, the total bandwidth server will not cause a job such as $J_{i,k}$ to miss its deadline if the constant utilization server will not. By a similar argument, we can show that a total bandwidth server will not cause another server to become unschedulable if a constant utilization server of the same size will not.

We state the correctness of constant utilization and total bandwidth server algorithms in the following corollaries so we can refer to them later. In the statement of the corollaries, we use the expression "a server meets its deadline" (or "a server is schedulable," as we said in the last paragraph). By this, we mean that the budget of the server is always consumed by the deadline set at the time when the budget was replenished. If we think of the server as a sporadic task and each replenishment of the budget of e units as the release of a sporadic job that has this execution time and the corresponding deadline, then every job in this sporadic task completes in time.

COROLLARY 7.7.   When a system of independent, preemptable periodic tasks is scheduled with one or more total bandwidth and constant utilization servers on the EDF basis, every periodic task and every server meets its deadlines if the sum of the total density of periodic tasks and the total size of all servers is no greater than 1.

When some periodic tasks and sporadic jobs have nonpreemptable portions, the effect of nonpreemptability is a reduction in the schedulable utilization. Alternatively, the schedulable utilization can be maintained at the expense of a bounded amount of tardiness. These facts are stated in the following corollaries. In the statement of these corollaries, $b_{max}(np)$ denotes the maximum execution time of nonpreemptable portions of all periodic tasks and jobs executed by servers. D_{min} denotes the minimum of the relative deadlines of all periodic tasks and the effective execution times of jobs executed by all servers in the system. By the effective execution time of a job executed by a server, we mean the ratio of the job execution time and the server size. These corollaries give the theoretical foundation of delay bounds of nonpreemptive versions of these algorithms. (The nonpreemptive version of the total bandwidth server algorithm is called the *virtual clock algorithm* [Zhan]. It is one of the well-known algorithms for scheduling packets in switched networks.)

COROLLARY 7.8.   When a system of periodic tasks is scheduled with one or more total bandwidth and constant utilization servers on the EDF basis, every periodic task and every server meets its deadlines if the sum of the total density of the periodic tasks and the total size of all servers is no greater than $1 - b_{max}(np)/D_{min}$.

COROLLARY 7.9.   If the sum of the total density of all the periodic tasks and the total size of total bandwidth and constant utilization servers that are scheduled on the EDF basis is no greater than 1, the tardiness of every periodic task or server is no greater than $b_{max}(np)$.

7.4.4   Fairness and Starvation

Thus far, we have ignored fairness [DeKS, PaGa93] of our algorithms.[2] By a scheduling algorithm being fair within a time interval, we mean that the fraction time of processor time in the interval attained by each server that is backlogged throughout the interval is proportional to the server size. For many applications (e.g., data transmission in switched networks), fairness is important.

It is well known in communication literature that the virtual clock algorithm (i.e., non-preemptive total bandwidth server algorithm) is unfair. To illustrate that this is also true for the total bandwidth server algorithm, let us consider a system consisting solely of two total bandwidth servers, TB_1 and TB_2, each of size 0.5. Each server executes an aperiodic task; jobs in the task are queued in the server's own queue. It is easy to see that if both servers are never idle, during any time interval of length large compared to the execution times of their jobs, the total amount of time each server executes is approximately equal to half the length of the interval. In other words, each server executes for its allocated fraction of time approximately.

Now suppose that in the interval $(0, t)$, for some $t > 0$, server TB_1 remains backlogged, but server TB_2 remains idle. By time t, TB_1 have executed for t units of time and its deadline is at least equal to $2t$. If at time t, a stream of jobs, each with execution time small compared with t, arrives and keeps TB_2 backlogged after t. In the interval $(t, 2t)$, the deadline of TB_2 is earlier than the deadline of TB_1. Hence, TB_2 continues to execute, and TB_1 is starved during this interval. While processor time is allocated fairly during $(0, 2t)$, the allocation is unfair during $(t, 2t)$. Since t is arbitrary, the duration of unfairness is arbitrary. As a consequence, the response time of jobs executed by TB_1 can arbitrarily be large after t. This is not acceptable for many applications. (An example is an aperiodic task that is executed in response to keyboard entries of a video game. The player will not happy if the system becomes sluggish for a considerable length of time, no matter how responsive it was in the past.)

In the remainder of this section, we first formally define fairness and then present two solutions. We will discuss this issue further in Chapter 11 which is on real-time communication. That chapter will present other solutions found in communication literature.

Definition of Fairness.   Since fairness is not an important issue for periodic tasks, we confine our attention here to systems containing only aperiodic and sporadic jobs. Specifically, we consider a system consisting solely of n (> 1) servers. Each server executes an aperiodic or sporadic task. For $i = 1, 2, \ldots, n$, the size of the ith server is $\tilde{u}_i$. $\sum_{i=1}^{n} \tilde{u}_i$ is no greater than 1, and hence every server is schedulable. $\tilde{w}_i(t_1, t_2)$, for $0 < t_1 < t_2$, denotes the total

---

[2]At the risk of a bad pun, it is fair to say that when the total utilization of periodic tasks is significant and there is only one server, fairness is not an issue. Moreover, bandwidth-preserving algorithms described in earlier sections do not have any serious problem in starvation and fairness.

attained processor time of the ith server in the time interval (t_1, t_2), that is, the server executes for $\tilde{w}_i(t_1, t_2)$ units of time during this interval.

The ratio $\tilde{w}_i(t_1, t_2)/\tilde{u}_i$ is called the *normalized service* attained by the ith server [StVa98a]. A scheduler (or the scheduling algorithm used by the scheduler) is *fair* in the interval (t_1, t_2) if the normalized services attained by all servers that are backlogged during the interval differ by no more than the *fairness threshold* $FR \geq 0$.

In the ideal case, FR is equal to zero, and

$$\frac{\tilde{w}_i(t_1, t_2)}{\tilde{w}_j(t_1, t_2)} = \frac{\tilde{u}_i}{\tilde{u}_j}$$

for any $t_2 > t_1$ and ith and jth servers that are backlogged throughout the time interval (t_1, t_2). Equivalently,

$$\tilde{w}_i(t_1, t_2) = \tilde{u}_i(t_2 - t_1)$$

It should not be a surprise that only an algorithm that infinitesmally fine-grain time slices among ready servers can achieve ideal fairness. Hence, ideal fairness is not realizable in practice. For a given scheduling algorithm, the difference in the values of the two sides of the above expression depends on the length $t_2 - t_2$ of the time interval over which fairness is measured. In general, FR is a design parameter. By allowing processor time allocation to be somewhat unfair (i.e., for some acceptable $FR > 0$) over some time interval length, we admit simple and practical schemes to keep scheduling fair.

Elimination of Starvation.   Let us examine again the previous example of two total bandwidth servers. The starvation problem is due to the way in which the total bandwidth server algorithm makes background time available to TB_1; in general, the deadline of a back-logged total bandwidth server is allowed to be arbitrarily far in the future when there is spare processor time. The simple scheme presented below, as well as the weighted fair-queueing algorithm presented in the next subsection, eliminates starvation and improve fairness by keeping the deadlines of backlogged servers sufficiently close to the current time.

A simple solution is to use only constant utilization servers. Since the budget of such a server is never replenished before the current server deadline, the current deadline of a backlogged constant utilization server CU_i of size $\tilde{u}_i$ is never more than $e_{i,\max}/\tilde{u}_i$ units of time from the current time. ($e_{i,\max}$ is the maximum execution time of all the jobs executed by the server.) Hence the length of starvation suffered by any server is bounded by $\max_i(e_{i,\max}/\tilde{u}_i)$. To allow these servers to use background time, we add rule R4 to the constant utilization server budget replenishment rules given in Section 7.4.2.

Replenishment Rules of a Starvation-Free Constant Utilization/Background Server

R1–R3 Within any busy interval of the system, replenish the budget of each backlogged server following rules of a constant utilization server.

R4 Whenever a busy interval of the system ends, replenish the budgets of all backlogged servers.

To illustrate, we look at the example in Figure 7–14. The system contains four aperiodic tasks A_1, A_2, A_3, and A_4, each a stream of jobs with identical execution times. Specifically,

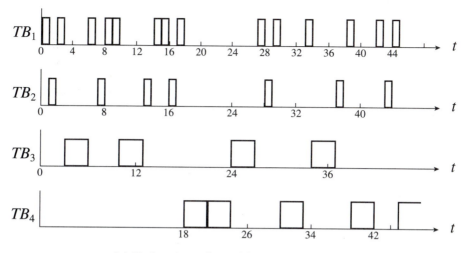

(a) Behavior of total bandwidth servers.

FIGURE 7–14 Example illustrating starvation and fairness: $\tilde{u}_1 = \frac{1}{4}$, $\tilde{u}_2 = \frac{1}{8}$, $\tilde{u}_3 = \frac{1}{4}$, $\tilde{u}_4 = \frac{3}{8}$. $A_1 \equiv$ jobs with execution times $= 1$ arriving from $t = 0$; $A_2 \equiv$ jobs with execution times $= 1$ arriving from $t = 0$; $A_3 \equiv$ jobs with executiong times $= 3$ arriving from $t = 0$; $A_4 \equiv$ jobs with executiong times $= 3$ arriving from $t = 18$.

the execution times of jobs in these tasks are 1, 1, 3, and 3, respectively. Each aperiodic task is executed by a server. The sizes of the servers for the tasks are 1/4, 1/8, 1/4, and 3/8, respectively. Starting from time 0, the jobs in A_1, A_2, and A_3 arrive and keep their respective servers backlogged continuously. The first job in A_4 arrives at time 18, and afterwards, the server for A_4 also remains backlogged.

Figure 7–14(a) shows their schedules when the servers are total bandwidth servers. Server TB_i executes A_i, for $i = 1, 2, 3, 4$. The numbers under each time line labeled by a server name give the deadlines of the server as time progresses. (You recall that the budget of a backlogged server is replenished and its deadline set each time it completes a job.) In particular, when the first job in A_4 arrives at time 18, the deadlines of servers TB_1, TB_2, and TB_3 are 36, 40, and 36, respectively. Since the deadline of TB_4 is first set to 26 and, upon the completion of the first job in A_4, to 34, TB_4 executes until 24, starving the other servers in $(18, 24)$. Before time 18, the amounts of time allocated to the servers according to their sizes are 4.5, 2.25, and 4.5 respectively, but because TB_4 is idle and the time left unused by it is shared by backlogged servers, the servers have executed for 8, 4, and 6 units of time, respectively. In contrast, their fair shares of processor time should be 7.2, 3.6, and 7.2, respectively. (The fair fractional share of a backlogged server in a time interval is equal to its size divided by the sum of sizes of all servers backlogged during the interval. So the fair shares of the three servers are 2/5, 1/5, and 2/5 of 18.) This example supports our intuition: The closer the consecutive deadlines (i.e., the larger the server size and the smaller the execution times of jobs), the larger share of background time a server attains at the expense of other backlogged servers.

Now suppose that each aperiodic task A_i is executed by a starvation-free constant utilization/background server CU_i, for $i = 1, 2, 3, 4$. We have the schedule shown in Figure 7–14(b). At time 6, the budgets of all three backlogged servers are exhausted, and the system

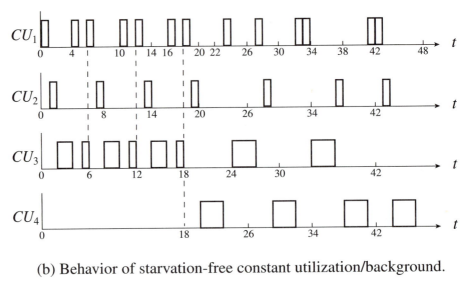

(b) Behavior of starvation-free constant utilization/background.

FIGURE 7-14 (continued)

becomes idle. According to rule R4, all three servers gets their new budgets and deadlines. Similarly, their budgets are replenished at time 12. Starting from time 18, all four servers are backlogged, and hence the schedule shown here. It is evident that none of the servers suffers starvation. After time 18, the normalized services of all servers are identical in time intervals of length 24 or more. Before 18, the background time left unused by the idle server is not distributed to backlogged servers in proportion to their sizes, however. In this example, the servers have executed for 6, 3, and 9 units of time before 18. This illustrates that although the enhanced constant utilization server algorithm eliminates starvation, it does not ensure fairness. Moreover, it is difficult to determine how the background processor time will be distributed among backlogged server in general.

7.4.5 Preemptive Weighted Fair-Queueing Algorithm

The well-known Weighted Fair-Queueing (WFQ) algorithm [DeKS] is also called the PGPS (packet-by-packet GPS algorithm). It is a nonpreemptive algorithm for scheduling packet transmissions in switched networks. Here, we consider the preemptive version of the weighted fair-queueing algorithm for CPU scheduling and leave the nonpreemptive, original version, to Chapter 11. Hereafter, by the WFQ algorithm, we mean the preemptive version.

The WFQ algorithm is designed to ensure fairness [DeKS] among multiple servers. As you will see shortly, the algorithm closely resembles the total bandwidth server algorithm. Both are greedy, that is, work conserving. Both provide the same schedulability guarantee, and hence, the same worst-case response time. At a quick glance, the replenishment rules of a WFQ server appear to be the same as those of a total bandwidth server, except for how the deadline is computed at each replenishment time. This difference, however, leads to a significant difference in their behavior: The total bandwidth server algorithm is unfair, but the WFQ algorithm gives bounded fairness.

Emulation of GPS Algorithm.   Again, a WFQ server consumes its budget only when it executes. Its budget is replenished when it first becomes backlogged after being idle. As long as it is backlogged, its budget is replenished each time it completes a job. At each replenishment time, the server budget is set to the execution time of the job at the head of its queue.

In short, the replenishment rules of the WFQ algorithm are such that a WFQ server emulates a GPS server of the same size; the deadline of the WFQ server is the time at which a GPS server would complete the job at the head of the server queue. To illustrate, we look at the example in Figure 7–14 again. Figure 7–14(c) shows the schedule of the four tasks A_i, for $i = 1, 2, 3, 4$, when they are scheduled according to the GPS algorithm. Specifically, the figure shows that they are executed by GPS servers GPS_1, GPS_2, GPS_3, and GPS_4, respectively, and the sizes of these servers are $1/4, 1/8, 1/4$, and $3/8$, respectively. The scheduler schedules backlogged servers on a weighted round-robin basis, with an infinitesmally small round length and the time per round given to each server is proportional to the server size.

The numbers below each time line in Figure 7–14(c) give the completion times of jobs executed by the respective server.

- Before time 18, server GPS_4 being idle, the backlogged servers share the processor proportionally. In other words, the servers attain $2/5, 1/5$, and $2/5$ of available time, and each of their jobs completes in 2.5, 5, and 7.5 units of time, respectively.

- By time 18, the eighth, fourth, and third jobs of A_1, A_2 and A_3 are at the heads of the queues of the backlogged servers, and their remaining execution times are 0.8, 0.4, and 1.8 respectively.

- Starting from 18, all four servers being backlogged, each server now attains $1/4, 1/8, 1/4$, and $3/8$ of available time, respectively. This is why the first three servers take an additional 3.2, 3.2, and 7.2 units of time to complete the jobs at the heads of their respective queues. (These jobs are completed at 21.2, 21.2, and 25.2, respectively.) Afterwards, each server GPS_i completes each job in A_i in 4, 8, 12, and 8, units of time, for $i = 1, 2, 3, 4$, respectively.

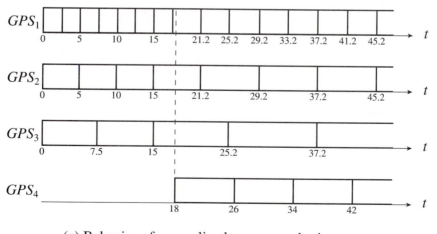

(c) Behavior of generalized processor sharing servers.

FIGURE 7–14   (continued)

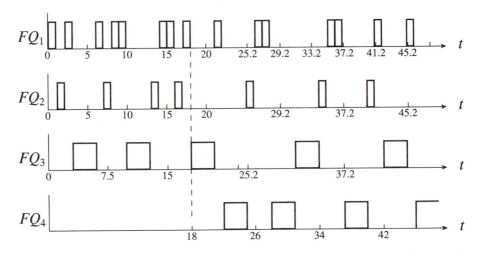

(d) Behavior of weighted fair-queuing servers with deadlines given in real time.

FIGURE 7–14   (continued)

Figure 7–14(d) gives the corresponding WFQ schedule. The budget of each WFQ server (called FQ_i in the figure) is replenished in the same manner as the corresponding total bandwidth server, except for the way the server deadline is computed. Specifically, we note the following.

- Before time 18, the backlogged WFQ servers behave just like total bandwidth servers, except each of the backlogged servers gets 2/5, 1/5, and 2/5 of processor time, respectively. Hence whenever a WFQ server FQ_i completes a job, the scheduler gives the server 1, 1, or 3 units of budget and sets its deadline at its current deadline plus 2.5 (i.e., $1 \times 5/2$), 5 (i.e., $1 \times 5/1$), or 7.5 (i.e., $3 \times 5/2$) for $i = 1, 2, 3$, respectively.
- Immediately before time 18, the three backlogged servers have completed 8, 4, and 2 jobs and their deadlines are at 22.5, 25, and 22.5, respectively.
- At time 18 when FQ_4 also becomes backlogged, the scheduler recomputes the deadlines of FQ_1, FQ_2 and FQ_3 and make them equal to the completion times of the ninth job, fifth job and third job of corresponding tasks according to the GPS schedule. Their completion times are 25.2, 29.2, and 25.2, respectively. These are the new deadlines of servers FQ_1, FQ_2, and FQ_3. Also, at this time, the scheduler gives FQ_4 3 units of budget and sets its deadline at 26. The scheduler then queues the servers according to their new deadlines.
- After time 18, the WFQ servers behave just like total bandwidth servers again.

Virtual Time versus Real-Time.   We note that if the scheduler were to replenish server budget in the manner illustrated by the above example, it would have to recompute the deadlines of all backlogged servers whenever some server changes from idle to backlogged and vice versa. While this recomputation may be acceptable for CPU scheduling, it is not for scheduling packet transmissions. A "budget replenishment" in a packet switch corresponds to the scheduler giving a ready packet a time stamp (i.e., a deadline) and inserting the packet in the outgoing queue sorted in order of packet time stamps. To compute a new deadline and time stamp again of an already queued packet would be unacceptable, from the standpoint of both scheduling overhead and switch complexity. Fortunately, this recomputation of server deadlines is not necessary if instead of giving servers deadlines measured in real time, as we have done in this example, the scheduler gives servers virtual-time deadlines, called finish numbers. The *finish number* of a server gives the number of the round in which the server budget would be exhausted if the backlogged servers were scheduled according to the GPS algorithm.

Figure 7–14(e) shows how finish numbers are related to time for our example. Before time 18, the total size of backlogged servers is only 5/8. If the tasks were executed according to the GPS algorithm, the length of each round would be only 5/8 of what the round length would be when the total size of backlogged servers is 1. In other words, the finish number of the system increases at the rate of 8/5 per unit time. So, at time 2.5, the system just finishes round 4 ($= 2.5 \times 8/5$); at time 5, the system just finishes round 8, and at time 18, the system is in round 28.8 ($= 18 \times 8/5$). After 18, the total size of backlogged servers is 1. Consequently, the finish number of the system increases at the rate of 1 per unit time.

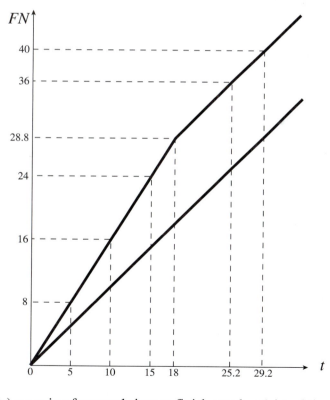

(e) mapping from real-time to finish number (virtual time).

FIGURE 7–14   (continued)

From this argument, we can see that an alternative is for the scheduler to give each server a finish number each time it replenishes the server budget. It then schedules eligible servers according to their finish numbers; the smaller the finish number, the higher the priority. If the scheduler were to use this alternative in our example, the finish numbers of the servers FQ_i, for $i = 1, 2, 3$, would be the numbers under the time lines of TB_i, respectively, in Figure 7–14(a). At time 18, the system is in round 28.8, and it takes 8 rounds to complete each job in A_4. Hence, at time 18, the scheduler sets the finish number of FQ_4 to 36.8. At this time, the finish numbers of FQ_1, FQ_2 and FQ_3 are 36, 40, 36, respectively. If we were construct a schedule according to these finish numbers, we would get the schedule in Figure 7–14(d).

Rules of Preemptive Weighted Fair-Queueing Algorithm.   We are now ready to state the rules that define the WFQ algorithm. The scheduling and budget consumption rules of a WFQ server are esentially the same as those of a total bandwidth server.

> *Scheduling Rule*: A WFQ server is ready for execution when it has budget and a finish time. The scheduler assigns priorities to ready WFQ servers based their finish numbers: the smaller the finish number, the higher the priority.
>
> *Consumption Rule*: A WFQ server consumes its budget only when it executes.

In addition to these rules, the weighted fair-queueing algorithm is defined by rules governing the update of the total size of backlogged servers and the finish number of the system and the replenishment of server budget. In the statement of these rules, we use the following notations:

- t denotes the current time, except now we measure this time from the start of the current system busy interval. (In other words, t is the length of time interval from the beginning of the current system busy interval to the current time.)
- f_n_i denotes the finish number of the server FQ_i, e_i its budget, and $\tilde{u}_i$ its size. e denotes the execution time of the job at the head of the server queue.
- U_b denotes the total size of all backlogged servers at t, and F_N denotes the finish number of system at time t. t_{-1} denotes the previous time when F_N and U_b were updated.

Finally, the system contains n servers whose total size is no greater than one.

Initialization Rules

> **I1** For as long as all servers (and hence the system) are idle, $F\_N = 0$, $U_b = 0$, and $t_{-1} = 0$. The budget and finish numbers of every server are 0.
>
> **I2** When the first job with execution time e arrives at the queue of some server FQ_k and starts a busy interval of the system,
>> **(a)** $t_{-1} = t$, and increment U_b by $\tilde{u}_k$, and
>> **(b)** set the budget e_k of FQ_k to e and its finish number f_n_k to $e/\tilde{u}_k$.

Rules for Updating F_N and Replenishing Budget of FQ_i during a System Busy Interval

> **R1** When a job arrives at the queue of FQ_i, if FQ_i was idle immediately prior to this arrival,
>> **(a)** increment system finish number F_N by $(t - t_{-1})/U_b$,

(b) $t_{-1} = t$, and increment U_b by $\tilde{u}_i$, and

(c) set budget e_i of FQ_i to e and its finish number f_n_i to $F\_N + e/\tilde{u}_i$ and place the server in the ready server queue in order of nonincreasing finish numbers.

R2 Whenever FQ_i completes a job, remove the job from the queue of FQ_i,

(a) if the server remains backlogged, set server budget e_i to e and increment its finish number by $e/\tilde{u}_i$.

(b) if the server becomes idle, update U_b and F_N as follows:

i. Increment the system finish number F_N by $(t - t_{-1})/U_b$,

ii. $t_{-1} = t$ and decrement U_b by $\tilde{u}_i$.

In summary, the scheduler updates the finish number F_N of the system and the total size U_b of all backlogged servers each time an idle server becomes backlogged or a backlogged server becomes idle. So, suppose that in our example in Figure 7–14(d), server FQ_1 were to become idle at time 37 and later at time 55 become backlogged again.

- At time 37, t_{-1} is 18, the value of F_N computed at 18 is 28.8, and the U_b in the time interval (18, 37] is 1. Following rule R2b, F_N is incremented by $37 - 18 = 19$ and hence becomes 47.8. U_b becomes 3/4 starting from 37, and $t_{-1} = 37$.
- At time 55 when FQ_1 becomes backlogged again, the new values of F_N, U_b and t_{-1} computed according to rule R1 are $47.8 + (55-37)/0.75 = 71.8$, 1, and 55, respectively.

Once the system finish number is found when an idle server becomes backlogged, the finish numbers of the server are computed in the same way as the deadlines of a backlogged total bandwidth server.

We conclude by observing that the response time bound achieved by a WFQ server is the same as that achieved by a total bandwidth server. The completion time of every job in a stream of jobs executed by such a server of size $\tilde{u}$ is never later than the completion time of the job when the job stream is executed by a virtual processor of speed $\tilde{u}$ times the speed of the physical processor. Corollary 7.7 substantiates this claim. In particular, this real-time performance of the server is guaranteed regardless of the characteristics of aperiodic tasks executed by other servers, as long as the total size of all servers is no greater than 1 and the execution of every job is preemptable.

*7.5 SLACK STEALING IN DEADLINE-DRIVEN SYSTEMS

We now describe how to do slack-stealing in priority-driven systems. As you will see shortly that slack-stealing algorithms for deadline-driven systems are conceptually simpler than slack-stealing algorithms for fixed-priority systems. For this reason, we first focus on systems where periodic tasks are scheduled according to the EDF algorithm.

In this section, it is convenient for us to think that aperiodic jobs are executed by a *slack stealer*. The slack stealer is ready for execution whenever the aperiodic job queue is nonempty and is suspended when the queue is empty. The scheduler monitors the periodic tasks in order to keep track of the amount of available slack. It gives the slack stealer the highest priority whenever there is slack and the lowest priority whenever there is no slack. When the slack stealer executes, it executes the aperiodic job at the head of the aperiodic job queue. This kind of slack-stealing algorithm is said to be *greedy*: The available slack is always used if there is an aperiodic job ready to be executed.

As an example, we consider again the system of two periodic tasks, $T_1 = (2.0, 3.5, 1.5)$ and $T_2 = (6.5, 0.5)$, which we studied earlier in Figure 7–3. Suppose that in addition to the aperiodic job that has execution time 1.7 and is released at 2.8, another aperiodic job with execution time 2.5 is released at time 5.5. We call these jobs A_1 and A_2, respectively. Figure 7–15 shows the operation of a slack stealer.

1. Initially, the slack stealer is suspended because the aperiodic job queue is empty. When A_1 arrives at 2.8, the slack stealer resumes. Because the execution of the last 0.7 units of $J_{1,1}$ can be postponed until time 4.8 (i.e., $5.5 - 0.7$) and T_2 has no ready job at the time, the system has 2 units of slack. The slack stealer is given the highest priority. It preempts $J_{1,1}$ and starts to execute A_1. As it executes, the slack of the system is consumed at the rate of 1 per unit time.

2. At time 4.5, A_1 completes. The slack stealer is suspended. The job $J_{1,1}$ resumes and executes to completion on time.

3. At time 5.5, A_2 arrives, and the slack stealer becomes ready again. At this time, the execution of the second job $J_{1,2}$ of T_1 can be postponed until time 7.5, and the second job $J_{2,2}$ of T_2 can be postponed until 12.5. Hence, the system as a whole has 2.0 units of slack. The slack stealer has the highest priority starting from this time. It executes A_2.

4. At time 7.5, all the slack consumed, the slack stealer is given the lowest priority. $J_{1,2}$ preempts the slack stealer and starts to execute.

5. At time 9, $J_{1,2}$ completes, and the system again has slack. The slack stealer now has the highest priority. It continues to execute A_2.

6. When A_2 completes, the slack stealer is suspended again. For as long as there is no job in the aperiodic job queue, the periodic tasks execute on the EDF basis.

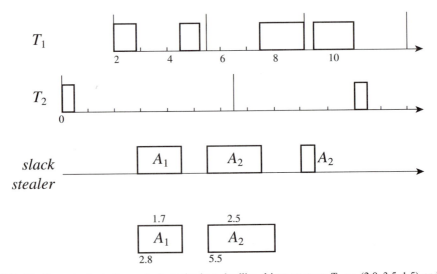

FIGURE 7–15   Example ilustrating a slack stealer in a deadline-driven system: $T_1 = (2.0, 3.5, 1.5)$ and $T_2 = (6.5, 0.5)$.

This example shows that in principle slack stealing in a priority-driven system is almost as straightforward as in a clock-driven system. The key step in slack stealing is the computation to determine whether the system has any slack. While this is a simple step in a clock-driven system, it is considerably more complex in a priority-driven system. The remainder of this section and most of the following section are devoted to algorithms for computing the amount of available slack. We call these algorithms *slack computation algorithms*.

A slack computation algorithm is *correct* if it never says that the system has slack when the system does not, since doing so may cause a periodic job to complete too late. An *optimal slack computation algorithm* gives the exact amount of slack the system has at the time of the computation; hence, it is correct. A correct slack computation algorithm that is not optimal gives a lower bound to the available slack.

There are two approaches to slack computation: *static* and *dynamic*. The method used to compute slack in a clock-driven system exemplifies the static approach. According to this approach, the initial slacks of all periodic jobs are computed off-line based on the given parameters of the periodic tasks. The scheduler only needs to update the slack information during run time to keep the information current, rather than having to generate the information from scratch. Consequently, the run-time overhead of the static approach is lower. A serious limitation of this approach is that the jitters in the release times of the periodic jobs must be negligibly small. We will show later that the slack computed based on the precomputed information may become incorrect when the actual release-times of periodic jobs differ from the release times used to generate the information.

According to the *dynamic* approach, the scheduler computes the amount of available slack during run time. When the interrelease times of periodic jobs vary widely, dynamic-slack computation is the only choice. The obvious disadvantage of the dynamic-slack computation is its high run-time overhead. However, it has many advantages. For example, the scheduler can integrate dynamic-slack computation with the reclaiming of processor time not used by periodic tasks and the handling of task overruns. This can be done by keeping track of the cumulative unused processor time and overrun time and taking these factors into account in slack computation.

7.5.1   Static-Slack Computation

To give us some insight into the complexity of slack computation, let us look at the system containing two periodic tasks: $T_1 = (4, 2)$ and $T_2 = (6, 2.75)$. There is an aperiodic job with execution time 1.0 waiting to be executed at time 0. The previous example gives us the impression that we may be able to determine the available slack at time 0 by examining only the slacks of the two current jobs $J_{1,1}$ and $J_{2,1}$. Since we can postpone the execution of $J_{1,1}$ until time 2, this job has 2 units of slack. Similarly, since only 4.75 units of time before the deadline of $J_{2,1}$ are required to complete $J_{2,1}$ and $J_{1,1}$, $J_{2,1}$ has 1.25 units of slack. If we were to conclude from these numbers that the system has 1.25 units of slack and execute the aperiodic job to completion, we would cause the later job $J_{1,3}$ to miss its deadline. The reason is that $J_{1,3}$ has only 0.5 unit of slack. Consequently, the system as a whole has only 0.5 unit of slack. In general, to find the correct amount of slack, we must find the minimum among the slacks of all N jobs in the current hyperperiod. If this computation is done in a brute force manner, its time complexity is $O(N)$ (i.e., the computation is pseudopolynomial in time). Indeed, this is the complexity of some slack computation algorithms (e.g., [ChCh]).

We now describe an optimal static-slack computation algorithm proposed by Tia [Tia]. The complexity of this algorithm is $O(n)$. The number n of periodic tasks is usually significantly smaller than N. To achieve its low run-time overhead, the algorithm makes use of a precomputed slack table that is $O(N^2)$ in size. *The key assumption of the algorithm is that the jobs in each periodic task are indeed released periodically.*

To describe this algorithm, it is more convenient for us to ignore the periodic task to which each job belongs. The individual periodic jobs in a hyperperiod are called J_i for $i = 1, 2, \ldots, N$. The deadline of J_i is d_i. In particular, we index the periodic jobs modulo N in nonincreasing priority order. Hence, the deadline d_i of the job J_i is equal to or earlier than the deadline d_k of J_k if $i < k$. The ith jobs in all the hyperperiods are named J_i.

We use t_c to denote the time of a slack computation and $\sigma_i(t_c)$ to denote the *slack* of the periodic job J_i computed at time t_c. $\sigma_i(t_c)$ is equal to the difference between the total available time in $(t_c, d_i]$ and the total amount of time required to complete J_i and all the jobs that are ready in this interval and have the same or earlier deadlines than J_i. [As far as this job is concerned, $\sigma_i(t_c)$ units of time can be used to execute aperiodic jobs at time t_c without causing it to miss its deadline.] The *slack of the system* $\sigma(t_c)$ at time t_c is the minimum of the slacks of all the jobs with deadlines after t_c. In the following, we first describe the precomputed slack table and then the way to compute the slack of the system during run time based on the information provided by this table and the history of the system.

Precomputed Slack Table.   We take as the time origin the instant when the system begins to execute. For now, we assume that in the absence of aperiodic jobs, the beginning of every hyperperiod coincides with the beginning of a busy interval of the periodic tasks. (We will return to discuss when this condition may not be true and what additional slack information other than the information described here is required.) Before the system begins to execute, we compute the initial slack of the N periodic jobs $J_1, J_2, \ldots, J_N$ in each hyperperiod of the periodic tasks. Specifically, the initial slack $\sigma_i(0)$ of the job J_i is given by

$$\sigma_i(0) = d_i - \sum_{d_k \leq d_i} e_k \tag{7.6}$$

Let $\omega(j; k)$ denote the minimum of all $\sigma_i(0)$ for $i = j, j + 1, \ldots, k - 1, k$. $\omega(j; k)$ is the *minimum slack* of the periodic jobs whose deadlines are in the range $[d_j, d_k]$. Expressed in terms of this notation, the initial slack of the system is $\omega(1; N)$. The initial slack $\sigma_i(0)$ of the job J_i is $\omega(i; i)$. Rather than storing the $\sigma_i(0)$'s, the precomputed slack table stores the N^2 initial minimum slacks $\omega(j; k)$ for $1 \leq j, k \leq N$.

Figure 7–16 gives an example. The system contains three periodic tasks $T_1 = (2, 0.5)$, $T_2 = (0.5, 3, 1)$, and $T_3 = (1, 6, 1.2)$. The relative deadline of every task is equal to its period. An aperiodic job with execution time 1.0 arrives at time 5.5. The figure shows the schedule of the system during the first two hyperperiods, as well as the slack table which gives the initial minimum slacks $\omega(j; k)$ for $j, k = 1, 2, \ldots, 6$.

Dependency of the Current Slack on Past History.   Once the system starts to execute, the slack of each individual job changes with time. In particular, the precomputed initial slack of each job J_i does not take into account the events that the processor idles, lower-priority jobs execute, and the slack stealer executes. When any of these events occurs before

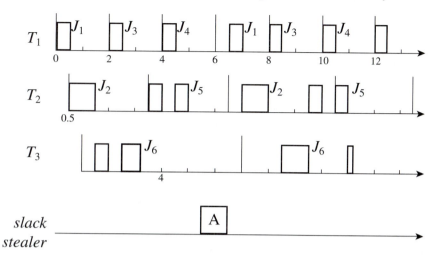

FIGURE 7–16   Slack table of $T_1 = (2, 0.5)$, $T_2 = (0.5, 3, 1.0)$, and $T_3 = (1, 6, 1.2)$.

d_i and takes away some available time from J_i, the slack of the job becomes smaller than the precomputed value.

For example, J_6 in Figure 7–16 executes for 0.5 unit of time before time 2. The precomputed initial slack of J_3 does not take into account this 0.5 unit of time. At time 2, the slack of J_3 is not equal to the precomputed value 2; rather it is equal to 1.5. At time 6.5, the slack stealer has executed since the beginning of the second hyperperiod for 0.5 unit of time. For this reason, the slacks of all the jobs in the hyperperiod is reduced by 0.5 unit from their respective precomputed values.

In general, to facilitate slack computation, the scheduler maintains the following information on the history of the system:

1. the *total idle time* I, which is the total length of time the processor idles since the beginning of the current hyperperiod.
2. the *total stolen time* ST, which is the time consumed by the slack stealer since the beginning of the current hyperperiod, and
3. the execution time ξ_k of the completed portion of each periodic job J_k in the current hyperperiod.

At time t_c of a slack computation, the slack of a job J_i that is in the current hyperperiod and has a deadline after t_c is equal to

$$\sigma_i(t_c) = \sigma_i(0) - I - ST - \sum_{d_i < d_k} \xi_k \qquad (7.7)$$

Since the initial slacks of jobs in each subsequent hyperperiod are computed assuming that time starts at the beginning the hyperperiod, the slacks of those jobs are not affected by the events in the current hyperperiod. We need to consider only the jobs in the current hyperperiod when we compute the current slack of the system, provided that we recompute the slack of the system at the beginning of each hyperperiod.

In the previous example, at time 2, ξ_6 is 0.5, I and ST are 0. Hence, the slacks of J_3, J_4 and J_5 are reduced by 0.5 unit from their initial values 2.0, 3.5, and 3, respectively. At time 3.5, ξ_6 is 1.2, I is 0.3, and ST is equal to 0. The slacks of J_4 and J_5 are reduced to 2.0 and 1.5, respectively. If we want to compute the slack of the system at this time, we need to find only the minimum slack of the jobs J_4, J_5, and J_6. When the second hyperperiod begins, the values of I, ST and ξ_i's are all 0, and the slack of the system is given by $\omega(1; 6)$, which is 1.5. At time 6.5, ST becomes 0.5; the slack of every job in the second hyperperiod is reduced by 0.5 unit, and the slack of the system is reduced to 1.0.

Computing the Current Slack of the System.   Again, if we were to compute the slack of the system by updating the slacks of all the jobs according to Eq. (7.7) and searching for the minimum among them, it would take $O(N)$ time to do so. Fortunately, we can speed up the slack computation by first partitioning all the jobs into n disjoint subsets. It suffices for us to compute and examine the slack of a job in each set. By doing so, we can compute the slack of the system in $O(n)$ time.

To see why this speedup is possible, we remind ourselves that at t_c, only one job per periodic task is current, and only current jobs could have executed before t_c. To distinguish current jobs from the other jobs in the hyperperiod, we call the current job of T_i J_{c_i}, for $i = 1, 2, \ldots, n$. The deadline of J_{c_i} is d_{c_i}. The current jobs are sorted by the scheduler in nondecreasing order of their deadlines in the priority queue of ready periodic jobs. Without loss of generality, suppose that $d_{c_1} < d_{c_2} < \cdots < d_{c_n}$. We now partition all the periodic jobs that are in the hyperperiod and have deadlines after t_c into n subsets Z_i for $i = 1, 2, \ldots, n$ as follows. A job is in the subset Z_i if its deadline is in the range $[d_{c_i}, d_{c_{i+1}})$ for $i = 1, 2, \ldots,$ $n - 1$. Hence, Z_i is $\{J_{c_i}, J_{c_i+1}, \ldots, J_{c_{i+1}-1}\}$. The subset Z_n contains all the jobs in the current hyperperiod whose deadlines are equal to or larger than d_{c_n}. This partition is illustrated by Figure 7–17. The tick marks show the deadlines of the current jobs and of the jobs in each of the subsets. The job that has the latest deadline among all the jobs in Z_i is $J_{c_{i+1}-1}$. This partition can be done in $O(n)$ time since the jobs are presorted and we know the index of every job.

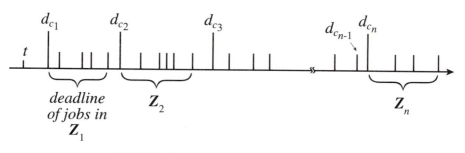

FIGURE 7–17   Partitioning of all jobs into n subsets.

The values of ξ_k's are nonzero only for current jobs. From this observation and Eq. (7.7), we can conclude that *in the computation of the current slacks of all the jobs in each of the subset $\mathbf{Z}_i$, the amounts subtracted from their respective initial slacks are the same.* In particular, for every job in $\mathbf{Z}_i$, the sum in the right-hand side of Eq. (7.7) includes the execution times of the completed portions of current jobs $J_{c_{i+1}}, J_{c_{i+2}}, \ldots, J_{c_n}$ because their deadlines are larger than its own. (This sum does not include the execution times of the completed portions of $J_{c_1}, J_{c_2}, \ldots, J_{c_i}$, because the execution time of these current jobs have already been taken into account in the computation of the initial slacks.)

To illustrate, let us suppose that we want to compute the slack of the system in Figure 7–16 at time 1.75. Both total idle time I and stolen time ST are zero. The current jobs at the time are J_1, J_2, and J_6, and the execution times of their completed portions are 0.5, 1.0, and 0.25, respectively. The deadlines of these three jobs partition the six jobs in this hyperperiod into three subsets: $\mathbf{Z}_1 = \{J_1\}$, $\mathbf{Z}_2 = \{J_2, J_3, J_4, J_5\}$, and $\mathbf{Z}_3 = \{J_6\}$. We need not be concerned with J_1 and J_2 since they are already completed at time 1.75. The slacks of the other jobs in $\mathbf{Z}_2$ are equal to their respective initial slacks minus 0.25, the execution time of the completed portion of the current job J_6, because d_6 is later than their own deadlines. On the other hand, the slack of the J_6, the only job in $\mathbf{Z}_3$, is equal to its initial slack because there is no current job whose deadline is later than d_6.

Since the slack of every job in each subset $\mathbf{Z}_i$ is equal to its initial slack minus the same amount as all the jobs in the subset, the job that has the smallest initial slack also has the smallest current slack. In other words, the minimum slack of all the jobs in $\mathbf{Z}_i$ is

$$\omega_i(t_c) = \omega(c_i; c_{i+1} - 1) - I - ST - \sum_{k=i+1}^{n} \xi_{c_k} \tag{7.8a}$$

for $i = 1, 2, \ldots, n - 1$, and

$$\omega_n(t_c) = \omega(c_n; N) - I - ST \tag{7.8b}$$

The slack $\sigma(t_c)$ of the system is given by

$$\sigma(t_c) = \min_{1 \le i \le n} \omega_i(t_c) \tag{7.8c}$$

The scheduler can keep the values of I, ST and ξ_{c_i}'s up to date by using $n + 2$ registers, one for each of these variables, together with a counter. These variables are set to 0 at the beginning of each hyperperiod. The counter is loaded with the current value of total idle time

Precomputed Slack Table: $\omega(i; k)$ gives the minimum slack of all periodic jobs with deadlines in the range $[d_i, d_k]$ for $i, k = 1, 2, \ldots, N$.

Slack Computation at time t

1. Obtain from the ready periodic job queue the sorted list of current jobs J_{c_i} for $i = 1, 2, \ldots, n$.
2. Partition the periodic jobs that are in the current hyperperiod and have deadlines after t into n subsets such that the subset $\mathbf{Z}_i$ contains all the jobs with deadlines equal to or larger than d_{c_i} but less than $d_{c_{i+1}}$.
3. Compute the slack $\sigma(t)$ of the system according to Eq. (7.8).

Operations of the Scheduler

- Initialization:
    - Create a slack stealer and suspend it.
    - Set I, ST, and ξ_i for $i = 1, 2, \ldots, N$ to 0 at the beginning of each hyperperiod.
- Schedule periodic jobs in the EDF order as follows: Whenever a job is released or complete or when the slack is exhausted do the following:
    - Update I, ST, or ξ_i for $i = 1, 2, \ldots, N$.
    - If the aperiodic job queue is nonempty,
        * Do slack computation to find $\sigma(t)$.
        * If $\sigma(t) > 0$, then schedule the slack stealer.
          Else, schedule the highest priority periodic job.
      Else, schedule the highest priority periodic job.

FIGURE 7–18 Operations of an EDF scheduler to accommodate a slack stealer.

whenever the processor becomes idle and is incremented as long as the processor idles. The content of the counter replaces the old value of I when the processor starts to execute again. Similarly, the counter keeps tracks of the amount of time spent executing the slack stealer or a periodic job each time it executes. The value of ST is updated at each time instant when the aperiodic job queue becomes empty (and the slack stealer becomes suspended) or when the slack stealer is preempted. The execution time ξ_{c_i} of the completed portion of each current job J_{c_i} is updated whenever the job completes or is preempted, as well as when the slack of the system needs to be computed.

The pseudocode description in Figure 7–18 summarizes the operation of a scheduler in a deadline-driven system where aperiodic jobs are executed by a slack stealer. The description does not include the actions to place ready jobs in the appropriate queues in priority order. We can see from this description that even when slack computation can be done in $O(n)$ time, the scheduling overhead is considerably higher than that of bandwidth-preserving servers described in earlier sections.

7.5.2 Practical Considerations

We now consider two complicating factors of differing significance. The first can be taken care of easily. The second one points to the limitation of static-slack computation and the need for dynamic-slack computation.

Effect of Phases.   When the phases of periodic tasks are arbitrary, the end of the first hyperperiod may not be the end of a busy interval. In this case, even in the absence of aperiodic jobs, the schedule of the second hyperperiod may not be the same as that of the first hyperperiod. As an example, we consider a system of two tasks, $T_1 = (2, 1)$ and $T_2 = (1, 3, 1.5)$. The length of a hyperperiod is 6 and the number N of jobs in each hyperperiod is five. If we were to compute the slack of the system based on the precomputed slacks of the first five jobs, we would conclude that the system has 0.5 unit of slack in each hyperperiod. This information is not correct, however; the total utilization of the system is 1 and, hence, the system has no slack after time 4. The 0.5 unit of slack is available initially because the periodic tasks have different phases.

In general, when the periodic tasks are not in phase, we need to determine whether the end of the first hyperperiod (i.e., at time H since the execution of the periodic task system begins) is also the end of a busy interval of the periodic tasks in the absence of aperiodic jobs. If it is, as exemplified by the system in Figure 7–16, the schedule of the periodic task system in the absence of aperiodic jobs and release-time jitters is cyclic with period H from the start. It suffices for us to precompute the slacks of the first N jobs and use them to compute the slack of the system for all times. On the other hand, if the end of the first hyperperiod is in the midst of a busy interval, the schedule of the periodic tasks has an initial transient segment which ends when the first busy interval ends and then is cyclic with period H. Therefore, we need to precompute the slacks of periodic jobs that execute in the first busy interval and then the slacks of the N jobs in the hyperperiod that begins when the second busy interval begins. The slack of the system should be computed based on the latter N entries once the second busy interval begins. In the previous example, the first busy intervals ends at 3.5. Jobs J_1 and J_3 of T_1 and J_2 of T_2 execute in the first busy interval. After time 4.0, we compute the system slack based on the precomputed slacks of jobs $J_4, \ldots, J_8$.

Effect of Release-Time Jitters.   Release-time jitters are often unavoidable and the periodic task model and priority-driven scheduling algorithms allow for the jitters. A critical question is, therefore, whether the results of a static-slack computation based on the assumption that the jobs in each task are released periodically remain correct when the interrelease times of jobs in each task may be larger than the period of the task. An examination of the example in Figure 7–16 can give us some insight into this question.

Suppose that the release times of J_3 and J_4 are delayed to 2.1 and 4.3, respectively, while the other jobs in this hyperperiod are released at their nominal release times. The initial slacks of the jobs J_1, J_3, and J_4 given by the precomputed slack table are 1.5, 2.0, and 3.5. Since the actual deadline of the J_1 remains to be 2.0, its initial slack is still 1.5. However, the actual deadlines of J_3 and J_4 are 4.1 and 6.3, respectively. Therefore, their actual initial slacks are 2.1 and 3.8, respectively. Similarly, if the release time of J_5 is delayed by a small amount, say by 0.1 unit, the actual initial slack of this job is 0.1 unit more than is given by the precomputed slack table. The precomputed initial slacks of other jobs remain accurate despite these late releases. In this case, the precomputed initial slacks give us lower bounds to the actual initial slacks.

In general, as long as the jitters in the release times are so small that priorities of all the jobs are not changed as a consequence (i.e., the order of the jobs sorted by their deadlines remains the same), Eq. (7.8) continues to be correct. However, when the release-time jitters are large compared to the separations between deadlines, the actual order and the priorities of the jobs may differ from their precomputed values. Take J_4 in Figure 7–16 for instance. If this job is released at time 5.5 instead, its deadline becomes later than that of J_6. The computation given by Eq. (7.8) uses the presorted list $(J_1, J_2, \ldots, J_6)$ to partition the jobs into subsets $\mathbf{Z}_i$. This partition is no longer correct, and the result of the slack computation may no longer be correct.

7.5.3 Dynamic-Slack Computation

In the presence of release-time jitters, the slack of a system may have to be computed dynamically during run time. We focus here on an algorithm that computes a lower bound on the slack of the system at time t_c when the scheduler needs the bound, without relying on any precomputed slack information. So, the adjectives "current" and "next" are relative with respect to the slack computation time t_c.

You recall that schedule segments during different busy intervals of the periodic tasks are independent of each other. Therefore, when computing the slack $\sigma(t_c)$, it is safe to consider only the periodic jobs that execute in the current busy interval, provided that any available slack in subsequent busy intervals is not included in $\sigma(t_c)$. This is the basis of the algorithm described below.

Information Maintained by the Scheduler. We let ξ_{c_i} denote the execution time of the completed portion of the current job J_{c_i} of the periodic task T_i. To support dynamic slack computation, the scheduler keeps up to date the value of ξ_{c_i} for each periodic task T_i.

Let $\tilde{\phi}_i$ denote the earliest possible release time of the next job in T_i. The scheduler can keep the value of $\tilde{\phi}_i$ up-to-date by adding p_i to the actual release time of the current job in T_i when the job is released.

Estimated Busy Interval Length. The slack computation is done in two steps. In the first step, the scheduler computes an upper bound on the length X of time to the end of the current busy interval of the periodic tasks. The length X is the longest when the jobs in each task T_i are released periodically with period p_i. Under this condition, the maximum processor-time demand $w(x)$ of all periodic jobs during the interval $(t_c, t_c + x)$ is given by

$$w(x) = \sum_{i=1}^{n}(e_i - \xi_i) + \sum_{i=1}^{n}\left\lceil \frac{(t_c + x - \tilde{\phi}_i)u_{-1}(t_c + x - \tilde{\phi}_i)}{p_i} \right\rceil e_i$$

where $u_{-1}(t)$ denotes a unit step function which is equal to zero for $t < 0$ and is equal to one when $t \geq 0$. The first sum on the right-hand side of this equation gives the total remaining execution time of all the current periodic jobs at time t_c. The second sum gives the total maximum execution time of all the jobs that are released in $(t_c, t_c + x)$. The length X is equal to the minimum of the solutions of $w(x) = x$ and can be found by solving this equation iteratively in the manner described in Section 6.5.

The current busy interval ends at time $END = t_c + X$. Let $BEGIN$ be the earliest possible instant at which the next busy interval can begin. Since $\lfloor(END - \tilde{\phi}_i)/p_i\rfloor$ jobs of T_i are released after $\tilde{\phi}_i$ and before END for all i, the earliest possible time $BEGIN$ at which next busy interval can begin is given by

$$BEGIN = \min_{1 \leq i \leq n}\left(\tilde{\phi}_i + \left\lceil \frac{(END - \tilde{\phi}_i)u_{-1}(END - \tilde{\phi}_i)}{p_i} \right\rceil p_i\right)$$

Slack Computation.   We can save some time in slack computation by considering only jobs in the current busy interval. Let $\mathbf{J}_c$ denote the subset of all the periodic jobs that execute in the interval (t_c, END). In the second step, the scheduler considers only the jobs in $\mathbf{J}_c$, computes a lower bound on the slack of each of these jobs, and takes as the slack of the system the minimum of the lower bounds.

Specifically, a lower bound on the slack of any job J_i in the set $\mathbf{J}_c$ is the difference between $\min(d_i, BEGIN)$ and the total execution time of all the jobs that are in $\mathbf{J}_c$ and have deadlines equal to or before d_i. (This difference is a lower bound because if d_i is after $BEGIN$, we may be able to postpone the execution of J_i to sometime after $BEGIN$, making the slack of the job larger than the difference.) By using this lower bound, the scheduler eliminates the need to examine jobs that are released in the next busy interval. Again, the slack of the system is equal to the minimum of such lower bounds on slacks of all the jobs in $\mathbf{J}_c$. This computation can be done in $O(N_b)$ time where N_b is the maximum number of jobs in a busy interval. In the special case where the relative deadline of every periodic task is equal to its period, $BEGIN - END$ is a lower bound to the slack of the system.

As an example, we consider a system of three periodic tasks, $T_1 = (4, 1)$, $T_2 = (5, 2)$, and $T_3 = (11, 2.1)$. The length of their hyperperiod is 220 and N is 119. Suppose that the scheduler computes the slack of the system at time $t = 2.0$. At that time, ξ_{c_1} is 1.0, ξ_{c_2} is 1.0, and ξ_{c_3} is 0. The execution time of the remaining portion of the current jobs are 0, 1.0, and 2.1. The earliest release times of the next jobs in the three periodic tasks are 4, 5, and 11, respectively. According to the above expression of the processor-time demand $w(x)$, we have

$$w(x) = 0 + 1.0 + 2.1 + \left\lceil \frac{x-2}{4} \right\rceil + 2 \left\lceil \frac{x-3}{5} \right\rceil$$

for $3 \leq x < 9$. The solution X of $w(x) = x$ is 7.1. Hence END is equal to $2 + 7.1 = 9.1$. $BEGIN$ is equal to

$$\min\left(4 + 4 \left\lceil \frac{9.1-4}{4} \right\rceil, 5 + 5 \left\lceil \frac{9.1-5}{5} \right\rceil, 11\right) = \min(12, 10, 11) = 10$$

Since the relative deadline of every periodic task is equal to its period, the slack of the system at time 2.0 is $10 - 9.1 = 0.9$. On the other hand, suppose that the actual release-time of first job in T_2 is 1. $BEGIN$ becomes 11, because $\tilde{\phi}_2$ is 6, and the slack is 1.9.

The lower bound of the system slack thus computed can be extremely pessimistic. For example, suppose that the execution time of T_3 in the above system were 2.0 instead. The scheduler would find that the current busy interval ends at 8 and the next busy interval begins at time 8. It would then conclude that the system has no slack. In fact, the system has 1 unit of slack at time 2, and the scheduler would find this slack if it were to consider not only the current busy interval but also the next busy interval, which ends at 9. Often, we can obtain more accurate information on the available slack by examining more periodic jobs. In the limit, if we are willing to compute the slacks of all N jobs in a hyperperiod and incur an overhead of $O(N)$, we can obtain the tightest lower bound on the amount of slack.

*7.6 SLACK STEALING IN FIXED-PRIORITY SYSTEMS

In principle, slack stealing in a fixed-priority system works in the same way as slack stealing in a deadline-driven system. However, both the computation and the usage of the slack are more complicated in fixed-priority systems.

7.6.1 Optimality Criterion and Design Consideration

To illustrate the issues, Tia [Tia] provided the example in Figure 7–19. The system contains three periodic tasks: $T_1 = (3, 1)$, $T_2 = (4, 1)$, and $T_3 = (6, 1)$. They are scheduled rate-monotonically. If the system were deadline-driven, it would have 2 units of slack in the interval $(0, 3]$, but this system has only 1 unit. The reason is that once $J_{1,2}$ becomes ready, $J_{2,1}$ must wait for it to complete. As a consequence, $J_{2,1}$ must complete by time 3, although its deadline is 4. In essence, 3 is the effective deadline of $J_{2,1}$, and its slack is determined by the effective deadline.

Figure 7–19(a) shows the schedule for the case when the 1 unit of slack is not used before time 3. At time 3, $J_{3,1}$ has already completed. $J_{1,2}$ and $J_{2,2}$ can start as late as time 5 and 7, respectively, and still complete in time. Therefore, the system has two units of slack at time 3. Figure 7–19(b) shows the schedule for the other case: The 1 unit of slack is used before time 3. $J_{3,1}$ is not yet complete at time 3. Consequently, $J_{1,2}$ and $J_{2,2}$ must execute immediately after they are released, even though their deadlines are 6 and 8; otherwise, $J_{3,1}$ cannot complete in time. Under this condition, the system has no more slack until time 6.

Now suppose that aperiodic jobs A_1 and A_2 arrive at times 2 and 3, respectively, and their execution times are equal to 1. If the slack stealer executes A_1 immediately upon arrival, the job can be completed at 3 and have the minimum response time of 1. Since the system has no more slack until time 6, A_2 cannot be completed until time 7 (i.e., its response time is 4). On the other hand, if the scheduler waits until time 3 and then schedules the slack stealer, the aperiodic jobs are completed at times 4 and 5, respectively. A_2 now has the minimum response time of 2. This reduction is achieved at the expense of A_1, whose response time is no longer the minimum possible.

As a variation, suppose that A_1 is the only aperiodic job. We have just seen that when its execution time is 1, its response time is minimum if the job is executed immediately upon its arrival. However, if the execution time of the job were larger than 1 but no greater than 2, the scheduler would do better by waiting until time 3 to start its execution; the response time of the job would be 3 or less but would be more than 4 if the job were executed starting from time 2. If the execution time of A_1 were between 2 and 3, the scheduler would again do better by letting the job be executed immediately upon its arrival; the job would be completed by time 8.

This example points out the following important facts. These facts provide the rationales for the slack-stealing algorithm described below.

1. *No slack-stealing algorithm can minimize the response time of every aperiodic job in a fixed-priority system even when prior knowledge on the arrival times and execution times of aperiodic jobs is available.* (Using a similar argument, Tia [Tia] also showed that *no on-line slack-stealing algorithm can minimize the average response time of all the aperiodic jobs*; however a clairvoyant algorithm can.)

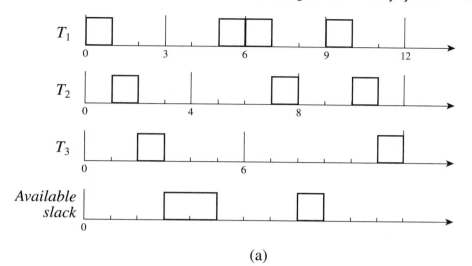

(a)

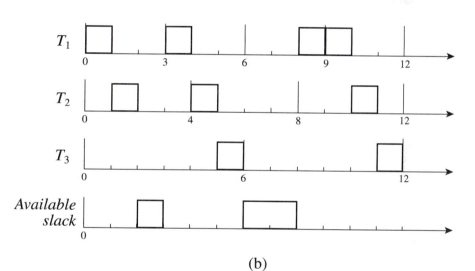

(b)

FIGURE 7–19   Example illustrating slack stealing in fixed-priority systems containing $T_1 = (3, 1)$, $T_2 = (4, 1)$, $T_3 = (6, 1)$.

2. The amount of slack a fixed-priority system has in a time interval may depend on when the slack is used. To minimize the response time of an aperiodic job, the decision on when to schedule the job must take into account the execution time of the job.

Because of (1), we use here a weaker optimality criterion: A slack-stealing algorithm for fixed-priority systems is *optimal in the weak sense* if it is correct and it minimizes the response time of the job at the head of the aperiodic job queue. Because of (2), an optimal slack-stealing algorithm for fixed-priority systems does not use available slack greedily. The remainder of this section describes a slack-stealing algorithm. The algorithm is defined by a static-slack computation algorithm used to compute available slack and a scheduling algorithm for deciding when the available slack is used. It is optimal in the weak sense. To achieve optimality in the weak sense, it requires and uses the knowledge of the execution times of aperiodic jobs after their arrivals.

7.6.2 Static Slack Computation in Fixed-Priority Systems

The previous example pointed out that the slack of each periodic job should be computed based on its effective deadline, not its deadline. The effective deadline of every job in the highest priority periodic task is equal to its deadline. For $i > 1$, the *effective deadline* $d_{i,j}^e$ of a job $J_{i,j}$ is equal to the deadline $d_{i,j}$ of the job if higher-priority periodic tasks have no ready jobs immediately before $d_{i,j}$. Otherwise, if $d_{i,j}$ is amid or at the end of a level-π_{i-1} busy interval, $d_{i,j}^e$ is equal to the beginning of this busy interval. (As always, we index fixed-priority tasks in nondecreasing priority order. So, a level-π_{i-1} busy interval is a busy interval of the subset $\mathbf{T}_{i-1}$ of periodic tasks with priorities equal to or higher than T_i. $\mathbf{T}_{i-1}$ does not include T_i.)

Just as in deadline-driven systems, a static-slack computation at any time t_c within a hyperperiod begins with the precomputed initial slack $\sigma_{i,j}(0)$ of every periodic job $J_{i,j}$ in the hyperperiod. The initial slack of $J_{i,j}$ is given by

$$\sigma_{i,j}(0) = \max\left(0, d_{i,j}^e - \sum_{k=1}^{i} e_k \left\lceil \frac{d_{i,j}^e}{p_k} \right\rceil \right) \tag{7.9}$$

The effective deadlines of all N periodic jobs in a hyperperiod can be determined by constructing a schedule of the periodic tasks for the hyperperiod when $\sigma_{i,j}(0)$'s are computed. The N effective deadlines and initial amounts of slack are stored for use at run time. The effective deadlines and initial slacks of jobs in subsequent hyperperiods can easily be computed from the respective stored values of jobs in the first hyperperiod.

Slack Functions. Table 7–1 lists the notations used in the subsequent description of the slack-stealing algorithm. The scheduler does a slack computation when it needs to decide the priority of the slack stealer. Let t be a future time instant (i.e., $t > t_c$) and $J_{i,j}$ be the first job in T_i whose effective deadline is after t. In other words, $d_{i,j-1}^e \leq t < d_{i,j}^e$.

$$\sigma_i(t_c, t) = \begin{cases} \sigma_{i,j}(0) - I - ST - \Xi_i & \text{if } J_{i,j} \text{ is not completed at } t \\ \sigma_{i,j+1}(0) - I - ST - \Xi_i & \text{if } J_{i,j} \text{ is completed at } t \end{cases} \tag{7.10a}$$

gives the amount of time before $x_i(t)$ that is not needed by jobs in $\mathbf{H}_i(t_c, x_i(t))$ for them to complete before $x_i(t)$. We call $\sigma_i(t_c, t)$ the *slack function* of T_i. The *minimum slack function* of the periodic tasks

$$\sigma^*(t_c, t) = \min_{1 \leq i \leq n} \sigma_i(t_c, t) \tag{7.10b}$$

gives the minimum amount of available slack from t_c to $x_i(t)$.

To support the computation of $\sigma_i(t_c, t)$, the scheduler keeps up-to-date the total idle time I and stolen time ST. (We have already described in the previous section how the scheduler

---

TABLE 7–1   Notations Used in the Description of the Slack-Stealing Algorithm

t_c:	the time at which a slack computation is carried out
t_0:	the beginning of the current hyperperiod, the beginning of the first hyperperiod being 0
$d_{i,j}^e$:	the effective deadline of the job $J_{i,j}$
$\sigma_{i,j}(0)$:	precomputed initial slack of the jth job $J_{i,j}$ of T_i in the current hyperperiod
I:	the total idle time, i.e., the cumulative amount of time since t_0 during which the processor idles
ST:	the total stolen time, i.e., the cumulative amount of time since t_0 during which aperiodic jobs execute.
ξ_i, for $i = 1, 2, \ldots, n$:	the cumulative amount of processor time since t_0 used to execute T_i
Ξ_i, for $i = 1, 2, \ldots, n$:	the cumulative amount of time since t_0 used to execute periodic tasks with priorities lower than T_i
$x_i(t)$, for a time instant t in the range $[d_{i,j-1}^e, d_{i,j}^e)$:	$x_i(t)$ is equal to the effective deadline $d_{i,j}^e$ of $J_{i,j}$ if the job is not complete by time t, and is equal to $d_{i,j+1}^e$ if $J_{i,j}$ is complete by t.
$\mathbf{T}_{i-1}$:	the subset of tasks, other than T_i, with priorities equal to or higher than T_i.
$\mathbf{H}_i(t_c, t)$, $t > t_c$:	the subset of periodic jobs that are in T_i or $\mathbf{T}_{i-1}$ and are active at some time during the interval $(t_c, t]$—A job is active in the interval between its release time and its effective deadline.
$\sigma_{i,j}(t_c, t)$:	the slack function of T_i
$\sigma^*(t_c, t)$:	the slack function of the system
$y_1 < y_2 < \ldots, < y_k$:	locations of steps of $\sigma^*(t_c, t)$, i.e., the values of t at which $\sigma^*(t_c, t)$ increases
$\sigma^*(y_k)$:	the amount of slack from t_c to y_k
z_i:	the next step of $\sigma_i(t_c, t)$ after t_c and the latest known step of $\sigma^*(t_c, t)$
A:	the aperiodic job at the head of the aperiodic job queue
e_A:	the remaining execution time of A

can do this.) In addition, for each periodic task T_i in the system, the scheduler updates the cumulative amount ξ_i of time during which the processor executes T_i each time when a job in the task completes or is preempted. Because $\Xi_i = \Xi_{i-1} + \xi_{i-1}$, the scheduler can obtain the values of Ξ_i's needed in Eq. (7.10a) by a single pass through the ξ_i's. This takes $O(n)$ time.

To illustrate, we return to the previous example. The effective deadline of every job except $J_{2,1}$ is equal to its deadline. Because $d_{2,1}$ is at the end of a busy interval of T_1 that begins at 3, $d_{2,1}^e$ is 3. At time 0, I, ST, and Ξ_i are equal to 0. Figure 7–20(a) shows the slack functions $\sigma_i(0, t)$ computed at time 0 for $i = 1$, 2, and 3 and t in the first hyperperiod (0, 12). The minimum slack function $\sigma^*(0, t)$ shows that the periodic tasks have 1 unit of slack before 6 and 2 more units after 6. Figure 7–20(b) shows the slack functions computed at time 3 for the case where the slack is not used before 3. At the time, $J_{2,1}$ is complete. According to Eq. (7.10a), the slack function $\sigma_2(3, t)$ for $t \leq 8$ is equal to the initial slack (= 3) of $J_{2,2}$ minus Ξ_3 (= 1) and hence is 2. Similarly, $J_{3,1}$ is completed. For $t > 3$, the slack function $\sigma_3(3, t)$ is equal to initial slack $\sigma_{3,2}(0) = 3$ of $J_{3,2}$. The amount of slack available before 6 increases by 1 at time 3. This is what we observed earlier from Figure 7–19.

Computation Procedure.   From Eq. (7.10) and Figure 7–20, we see that in general, the slack function $\sigma_i(t_c, t)$ of each task T_i is a staircase function and it has a step (increase) at

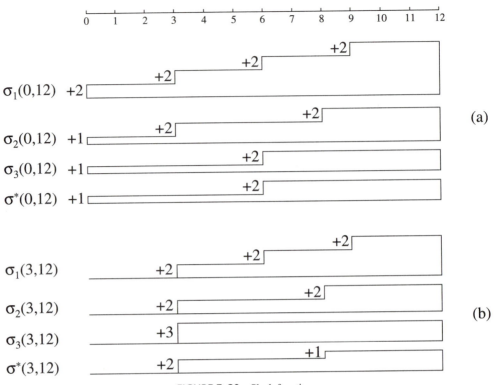

FIGURE 7–20 Slack functions.

the effective deadline of each job in T_i. Consequently, the minimum slack function $\sigma^*(t_c, t)$ is also a staircase function. Let $y_1 < y_2 < \cdots < y_k \ldots$ be the values of t at which $\sigma^*(t_c, t)$ increases. Each y_k is the effective deadline of some periodic job. With a slight abuse of the term, we call these time instants the steps of $\sigma^*(t_c, t)$. A computation of $\sigma^*(t_c, t)$ amounts to finding the steps of the function and the increase in slack at each step.

According to the algorithm proposed by Tia [Tia], each slack computation finds the next step of the minimum slack function and the value of the function until the step. The initial step y_0 occurs immediately after the beginning of the current hyperperiod, and the slack of each task T_i at the initial step is equal to $\sigma_{i,1}(0)$. Let y_{k-1} $(k > 0)$ denote the step of the minimum slack function found during the initial or the previous slack computation. z_i denotes the next step of $\sigma_i(t_c, t)$, that is, the earliest step of this function after $\max(t_c, y_{k-1})$. z_{min} denotes the step among z_i for $1 \le i \le n$ that has the least slack. In other words, $\sigma_{min}(t_c, z_{min}^-) \le \sigma_i(t_c, z_i^-)$ for all i. (v^- is an instant immediately before v.) If there is a tie, z_{min} is the latest among the z_i's that have the minimum slack. The next step y_k is equal to z_{min}. The minimum slack function $\sigma^*(t_c, t)$ is equal to $\sigma_{min}(t_c, z_{min}^-)$ and is the slack of the system until y_k. The job in T_{min} whose effective deadline is z_{min} is called the *constraining job*.

As an example, suppose that the scheduler does a slack computation at time 1. The next step z_i of $\sigma_i(1, t)$ is equal to 3, 3, and 6 for $i = 1, 2,$ and 3, respectively. Immediately before their corresponding next steps, the slack functions of the tasks are equal to 2, 2, and 1, respectively. Hence, the next step y_1 of the minimum slack function is $z_3 = 6$. $\sigma^*(t_c, y_1)$ is 1. The constraining job is $J_{3,1}$.

If the scheduler keeps effective deadlines of each task T_i in a list sorted in increasing order, it can find the next step z_i in $O(1)$ time from this list and the step found during the previous slack computation. It takes $O(n)$ time to update all the Ξ_i's; hence the complexity of each slack computation is $O(n)$.

7.6.3   Scheduling Aperiodic Jobs

In addition to maintaining I, ST and ξ_i for $i = 1, 2, \ldots, n$ as stated above, the scheduler also updates the remaining execution time e_A of the aperiodic job A at the head of the aperiodic job queue if the job is preempted before it is completed. The scheduler controls when any available slack is used by varying the priority of the slack stealer relative to the fixed priorities of the periodic tasks. We have the following two observations about the constraining job J found at the time t_c of the kth slack computation.

1. There can be no more than $\sigma^*(t_c, y_k)$ units of slack before y_k unless the constraining job J is completed before y_k.

2. Scheduling the constraining job J so that it completes as soon as possible will not lead to a decrease in the amount of slack before y_k.

If J completes at some time t before y_k, we may be able to delay the execution of some periodic jobs in $\mathbf{H}_i(t_c, y_k)$ until after y_k and thus create more slack before y_k.

Scheduler Operations.   These observations are the rationales behind the slack-stealing algorithm defined by the following rules.

R0   Maintain history information, that is, I, SI, and ξ_i, for $i = 1, 2, \ldots, n$, and update e_A before A starts execution and when it is preempted.

R1   Slack Computation: Carry out a slack computation each time when

- an aperiodic job arrives if the aperiodic job queue is empty prior to the arrival,
- an aperiodic job completes and the aperiodic job queue remains nonempty, and
- a constraining job completes.

The next step and minimum slack found by the slack computation are y, y being the effective deadline of a job in T_{min}, the available slack until y is $\sigma^*(t_c, y) = \sigma_{min}(t_c, y)$.

R2   Assigning Priority to Slack Stealer: Each time following a slack computation, assign the slack stealer the highest priority if $\sigma^*(t_c, y) \geq e_A$. Otherwise, the priority of the slack stealer is between that of T_{min} and T_{min+1}.

R2   Periodic jobs and slack stealers execute according to their priorities.

We again use the example in Figure 7–19 to illustrate. Suppose that shortly after time 0, an aperiodic job A with execution time equal to 1.5 arrives. The slack functions of all tasks being as shown in Figure 7–20(a), the next step y is 6, the effective deadline of constraining job $J_{3,1}$. Since the $\sigma^*(0, 6)$ (= 1) is less than the remaining execution time e_A (= 1.5), the slack stealer is given a lower priority than $J_{3,1}$. Upon the completion of $J_{3,1}$ at 3, the slack is computed again. This time the slack of the system is equal to 2. Therefore, the slack stealer is given the highest priority. It starts to execute at 3 and completes A at 4.5.

On the other hand, suppose that the execution time of A is 2.5. At time 3, the slack stealer is given a priority lower than the constraining job $J_{2,2}$ but higher than $J_{3,2}$. This allows $J_{2,2}$ to complete at 5. When the slack is completed again at 5, the system has 3 units of slack. Consequently, the slack stealer is given the highest priority and it completes A at time 7.5.

Performance.   Tia [Tia] showed that the slack-stealing algorithm described above is optimal in the weak sense, that is, it minimizes the response time of the job at the head of the aperiodic job queue. From his simulation study, Tia found that this algorithm performs only slightly better when compared with slack-stealing algorithms [LeRa, DaTB] that use the available slack greedily. The greedy algorithms have the advantage that they do not require knowledge of execution times of aperiodic jobs.

The slack-stealing approach gives smaller response times when compared with the sporadic server scheme even when the sporadic server is allowed to use background time. This is especially true when the total utilization of periodic tasks is higher than 75 percent. When the total utilization of periodic tasks is this large, one is forced to give a sporadic server a small size. As a consequence, the performance of a sporadic server becomes closer to that of a background server. In contrast, by letting the slack stealer executes aperiodic jobs while the periodic tasks have slack, one can reduce their response times significantly. Therefore, when the release-time jitters of periodic tasks are negligible and when the $O(n)$ slack computation overhead is tolerable, slack stealing should be the preferred approach.

7.7   SCHEDULING OF SPORADIC JOBS

This and the next sections focus on algorithms for scheduling sporadic jobs. We ignore aperiodic jobs. After seeing how we can schedule sporadic jobs with hard deadlines in the midst of periodic tasks, we will discuss the real-time performance that existing algorithms can provide to sporadic jobs with soft deadlines.

Here we take the approach discussed in Chapter 5: The scheduler performs an acceptance test on each sporadic job upon its arrival. We now describe how to do acceptance tests in priority-driven systems. As in Chapter 5, we assume that acceptance tests are performed on sporadic jobs in the EDF order. Once accepted, sporadic jobs are ordered among themselves in the EDF order. In a deadline-driven system, they are scheduled with periodic jobs on the EDF basis. In a fixed-priority system, they are executed by a bandwidth preserving server. In both cases, no new scheduling algorithm is needed.

In our subsequent discussion, we refer to each individual sporadic job as S_i. When we want to call attention to the fact that the job is released at time t and has maximum execution time e and (absolute) deadline d, we call the job $S_i(t, d, e)$. We say that an acceptance test is optimal if it accepts a sporadic job if and only if the sporadic job can be feasibly scheduled without causing periodic jobs or sporadic jobs in the system to miss their deadlines.

7.7.1 A Simple Acceptance Test in Deadline-Driven Systems

Theorem 7.4 says that in a deadline-driven system where the total density of all the periodic tasks is Δ, all the accepted sporadic jobs can meet their deadlines as long as the total density of all the active sporadic jobs is no greater than $1 - \Delta$ at all times. This fact gives us a theoretical basis of a very simple acceptance test in a system where both the periodic and sporadic jobs are scheduled on the EDF basis.

Acceptance Test Procedure.   The acceptance test on the first sporadic job $S(t, d, e)$ is simple indeed. The scheduler accepts S if its density $e/(d - t)$ is no greater than $1 - \Delta$. If the scheduler accepts the job, the (absolute) deadline d of S divides the time after t into two disjoint time intervals: the interval I_1 at and before d and the interval I_2 after d. The job S is active in the former but not in the latter. Consequently, the total densities $\Delta_{s,1}$ and $\Delta_{s,2}$ of the active sporadic jobs in these two intervals are equal to $e/(d - t)$ and 0, respectively.

We now consider the general case. At time t when the scheduler does an acceptance test on $S(t, d, e)$, there are n_s active sporadic jobs in the system. For the purpose of scheduling them and supporting the acceptance test, the scheduler maintains a nondecreasing list of (absolute) deadlines of these sporadic jobs. These deadlines partition the time interval from t to the infinity into $n_s + 1$ disjoint intervals: $I_1, I_2, \ldots, I_{n_s+1}$. I_1 begins at t and ends at the first (i.e., the earliest) deadline in the list. For $1 \leq k \leq n_s$, each subsequent interval I_{k+1} begins when the previous interval I_k ends and ends at the next deadline in the list or, in the case of I_{n_s+1}, at infinity. (Some of these intervals have zero length when the sporadic jobs have nondistinct deadlines.) The scheduler also keeps up-to-date the total density $\Delta_{s,k}$ of the sporadic jobs that are active during each of these intervals.

Let I_l be the time interval containing the deadline d of the new sporadic job $S(t, d, e)$. Based on Theorem 7.4, the scheduler accepts the job S if

$$\frac{e}{d - t} + \Delta_{s,k} \leq 1 - \Delta \tag{7.11}$$

for all $k = 1, 2, \ldots l$.

If these conditions are satisfied and S is accepted, the scheduler divides the interval I_l into two intervals: The first half of I_l ends at d, and the second half of I_l begins immediately after d. We now call the second half I_{l+1} and rename the subsequent intervals $I_{l+2}, \ldots, I_{n_s+2}$. (Here, we rename the intervals for the sake of clarity. In the actual implementation of the acceptance test, this step is not necessary provided some appropriate data structure is used to allow efficient insertion and deletion of the intervals and update of the total densities associated with individual intervals.) The scheduler increments the total density $\Delta_{s,k}$ of all active sporadic jobs in each of the intervals $I_1, I_2, \ldots, I_l$ by the density $e/(d - t)$ of the new job. Thus, the scheduler becomes ready again to carry out another acceptance test. The complexity of this acceptance test is $O(N_s)$ where N_s is the maximum number of sporadic jobs that can possibly be in the system at the same time.

As an example, we consider a deadline-driven system in Figure 7–21. The system has two periodic tasks $T_1 = (4, 1)$ and $T_2 = (6, 1.5)$. The relative deadline of each task is equal to the period of the task. Their total density is 0.5, leaving a total density of 0.5 for sporadic jobs.

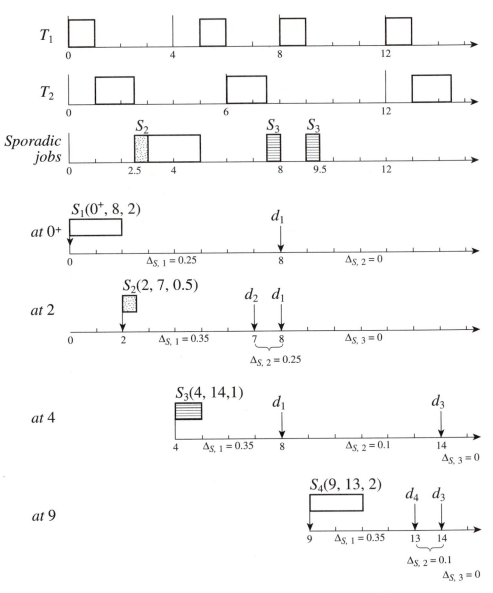

FIGURE 7–21 An acceptance test on $T_1 = (4, 1)$, and $T_2 = (6, 1.5)$.

1. Suppose that the first sporadic job $S_1(0^+, 8, 2)$ is released shortly after time 0. Since the density of S_1 is only 0.25, the scheduler accepts it. The deadline 8 of S_1 divides the future time into two intervals: $I_1 = (0^+, 8]$ and $I_2 = (8, \infty)$. The scheduler updates the total densities of active sporadic jobs in these intervals: $\Delta_{s,1} = 0.25$ and $\Delta_{s,2} = 0$. The scheduler then inserts S_1 into the queue of ready periodic and sporadic jobs in the EDF order.

2. At time 2, the second sporadic job $S_2(2, 7, 0.5)$ with density 0.1 is released. Its deadline 7 is in I_1. Since the condition $0.1 + 0.25 \le 0.5$ defined by Eq. (7.11) is satisfied, the

scheduler accepts and schedules S_2. We now call the interval I_2 I_3. The interval I_1 is divided into $I_1 = (2, 7]$ and $I_2 = (7, 8]$. The scheduler increments the total density $\Delta_{s,1}$ by the density of S_2. Now, $\Delta_{s,1} = 0.35$, $\Delta_{s,2} = 0.25$, and $\Delta_{s,3} = 0$.

3. At time 4, $S_3(4, 14, 1)$ is released. S_2 has already completed. The only sporadic job in the system is S_1. $\Delta_{s,1} = 0.25$ (for interval I_1 before 8) and $\Delta_{s,2} = 0$ (for interval I_2 after 8). The deadline of S_3 is in the interval I_2. The conditions the scheduler checks are whether $0.25 + 0.1$ and 0.1 are equal to or less than 0.5. Since both are satisfied, the scheduler accepts S_3. The intervals maintained by the scheduler are now $I_1 = (4, 8]$, $I_2 = (8, 14]$, and $I_3 = (14, \infty]$. Moreover, $\Delta_{s,i}$ are $0.35, 0.1$, and 0 for $i = 1, 2$, and 3, respectively.

4. At time 9, $S_4(9, 13, 2)$ is released. Now, the only active sporadic job in the system is S_3. I_1 is $(9, 14]$ and I_2 is $(14, \infty)$. Since for I_1, the total density of existing active sporadic jobs is 0.1 and the density of S_4 is 0.5, their sum exceeds 0.5. Consequently, the scheduler rejects S_4.

Enhancements and Generalization.   Two points are worthy of observing. First, the acceptance test is not optimal, meaning that a sporadic job may be rejected while it is schedulable. The reason is that the schedulability condition given by Theorem 7.4 is sufficient but not necessary. In the example above, the system becomes idle at time 9.5 and does not become busy again until time 12. So, S_4 is acceptable. In fact, as we will see shortly, it would be acceptable even if its execution time were 4.0, making its density 1.0!

An enhancement is to have the scheduler also compute the slack of the system. In this example, suppose that the scheduler were to compute the slack of the system dynamically at time 9. It would find that the current busy interval of the periodic tasks and accepted sporadic jobs ends at time 9.5 and the next busy interval does not begin until time 12. This leaves the system with 2.5 units of slack before time 13, the deadline of S_4. Hence, S_4 is acceptable. The shortcoming of an acceptance test that makes use of dynamic-slack computation is its high run-time overhead. The next subsection describes an optimal acceptance test algorithm that makes use of static-slack computation. According to that test, S_4 would be acceptable as long as its execution time is no more than 4. However, that acceptance test can be used only when periodic tasks have little or no release-time jitters.

The second point worth noting is that the acceptance test described above assumes that every sporadic job is ready for execution upon its arrival. In general, its feasible interval may begin some time after its acceptance test time. (As an example, suppose that that S_3 in the above example were offered to the scheduler for acceptance testing at time 3, but it is ready for execution at time 4.) We can modify the simple acceptance test in a straightforward fashion to accommodate arbitrary ready times of sporadic jobs. The ready times and deadlines of sporadic jobs in the system partition the future time into disjoint time intervals. The scheduler maintains information on these intervals and the total densities of active sporadic jobs in them in a similar manner, but now it may have to maintain as many as $2N_s + 1$ intervals, where N_s is the maximum number of sporadic jobs in the system.

*7.7.2 An Acceptance Test Based on Slack Computation in Deadline-Driven Systems

We now describe an algorithm that uses static-slack computation and is for systems where periodic and accepted sporadic jobs are scheduled on the EDF basis [Tia]. The time complexity of the acceptance test based on this algorithm is $O(n + N_s)$. Other existing algorithms for an acceptance test based on static-slack computation in deadline-driven systems include those described in [ChCh] and [SiCE]. These algorithms have pseudopolynomial complexity $O(N + N_s)$. Alternatives are to compute the available slack dynamically (e.g., in [McEl]) or to subject periodic jobs to an acceptance test as well as sporadic jobs (e.g., in [ScZh]). Both alternatives have their own shortcomings. Except when an extreme high run-time overhead can be tolerated, we are forced to use dynamically computed lower bounds on the available slack. These bounds tend to be loose. As a consequence, the acceptance test is no longer optimal and may not have significant advantage over the simple acceptance test described earlier. Subjecting periodic jobs to an acceptable test is not only time consuming, especially since the acceptance test in [ScZh] is pseudopolynomial time in complexity, but may also result in the rejection of some periodic jobs, which is incorrect according to the correctness criterion used here.

Major Steps.   As in Section 7.5, we call the ith periodic job in each hyperperiod J_i for $i = 1, 2, \ldots, N$. The N jobs are indexed so that the deadline d_i of J_i is equal to or less than the deadline d_k of J_k if $i < k$. Suppose that at the time t when an acceptance test is done on a new sporadic job S, there are also n_s sporadic jobs in the system. We call the sporadic jobs $S_1, S_2, \ldots, S_{n_s}$. Let $e_{s,k}$ and $d_{s,k}$ denote the maximum execution time and absolute deadline of S_k, respectively. We again assume that every sporadic job is ready for execution as soon as it is released. We continue to use $\sigma_k(t)$ to denote the slack of the periodic job J_k at time t in the absence of any sporadic jobs. The notation for the slack of the sporadic job S_k at t is $\sigma_{s,k}(t)$.

Specifically, when a sporadic job $S_i(t, d, e)$ is released at time t, the scheduler carries out the following steps to accept and schedule S_i or to reject S_i.

1. The scheduler computes the slack $\sigma_{s,i}(t)$ of the tested job S_i. If $\sigma_{s,i}(t)$ is less than 0, it rejects S_i. Otherwise, it carries out the next step.

2. The scheduler accepts S_i and carries out step 3 if the current slack of every job whose deadline is at or after d is at least equal to the execution time e of S_i; otherwise, it rejects S_i.

3. When the scheduler accepts $S_i(t, e, d)$, it inserts the job into the EDF priority queue of all ready jobs, allocates a register for the storage of the execution time $\xi_{s,i}$ of the completed portion of S_i, stores the initial slack $\sigma_{s,i}(t)$ of S_i, and decrements the slack of every existing sporadic job whose deadline is at or after d by e.

To support slack computation, the scheduler updates the total amount TE of time in the current hyperperiod that is used to execute completed sporadic jobs whenever a sporadic job completes. It also maintains the total amount I of time the system has been been idle since the beginning of the current hyperperiod, as well as the execution time ξ_k (or $\xi_{s,k}$) of the completed portion of each current periodic (or existing sporadic) job in the system.

As you can see, the acceptance test described here is the same as the test for clock-driven systems (it was described in Section 5.6) in principle. The difference between the two tests is the more complex slack computation in deadline-driven systems. The static computation algorithm described in Section 7.5 can easily be extended for this purpose. In the description of this extension, we first assume that the deadline of every sporadic job released in a hyperperiod is in the same hyperperiod period. After describing how slack computation is done when this simplifying assumption is true, we then show how a simple modification allows us to remove this restrictive assumption.

Finally, in this description, by a sum over sporadic jobs, we mean sporadic jobs that are still in the system; the completed sporadic jobs are not included. For a given sporadic job $S_i(t, d, e)$ being tested, we let J_l denote the periodic job whose deadline d_l is the latest among all the periodic jobs whose deadlines are at or before d, if there are such jobs. This job is called the *leverage job* of S_i. If the deadline d of S_i is earlier than the deadline of the first periodic job in the hyperperiod, its leverage job is a nonexisting periodic job; for the sake of convenience, we let the slack and deadline of this nonexisting periodic job be 0. Since the set of candidates of J_l contains only one job per periodic task, the job J_l can be found in $O(n)$ time.

Acceptance Test for the First Sporadic Job.   To compute the slack of the first sporadic job $S_1(t, d, e)$ tested in the current hyperperiod, the scheduler first finds its leverage job J_l. In addition to the slack of J_l, which can be used to execute S_1, the interval $(d_l, d]$ is also available. Hence the slack of S_1 is given by

$$\sigma_{s,1}(t) = \sigma_l(t) + (d - d_l) - e \qquad (7.12a)$$

(An implicit assumption here is that ties in deadlines, and hence priorities, are broken in favor of sporadic jobs.) The slack of the job J_l in the absence of any sporadic job is given by Eq. (7.7) if there are aperiodic jobs in the system and a slack stealer to execute them. Otherwise, if there is no slack stealer, as we have assumed here,

$$\sigma_l(t) = \omega(l; l) - I - \sum_{d_k > d} \xi_k \qquad (7.12b)$$

When the deadline of the first periodic job in the hyperperiod is later than d, $\sigma_l(t)$ and d_l are zero by definition, and $\sigma_{s,1}(t)$ is simply equal to $d - e$.

In the first step of the acceptance test, the scheduler computes $\sigma_{s,1}(t)$ in this way. It rejects the new sporadic job S_1 if $\sigma_{s,1}(t)$ is less than 0. Otherwise, it proceeds to check whether the acceptance of the S_1 may cause periodic jobs with deadlines after d to miss their deadlines. For this purpose, it computes the minimum of the current slacks $\sigma_k(t)$ of all the periodic jobs J_k for $k = l + 1, l + 2, \ldots, N$ whose deadlines are after d. The minimum slack of these jobs can be found using the static-slack computation method described in Section 7.5. This computation and the subsequent actions of the scheduler during the acceptance test also take $O(n)$ time.

Acceptance Test for the Subsequent Sporadic Jobs.   In general, when the acceptance of the sporadic job $S_i(t, d, e)$ is tested, there may be n_s sporadic jobs in the system waiting to complete. Similar to Eq. (7.12), the slack of S_i at time t can be expressed in terms of the slack $\sigma_l(t)$ of its leverage job J_l as follows.

$$\sigma_{s,i}(t) = \sigma_l(t) + (d - d_l) - e - TE - \sum_{d_{s,k} \leq d} e_{s,k} - \sum_{d_{s,k} > d} \xi_{s,k} \qquad (7.13)$$

To see why this equation is correct, we note that among the possible $\sigma_l(t) + (d - d_l)$ units of time available to S_i, TE units were used to complete sporadic jobs that have executed and completed in the current hyperperiod. The first sum on the right-hand side of the equation gives the total amount of time in the current hyperperiod committed to the yet-to-be-completed sporadic jobs whose deadlines are at or before d. The second sum gives the total amount of time in the current hyperperiod that was used to execute the completed portion of the sporadic jobs whose deadlines are after d.

After computing the slack $\sigma_{s,i}(t)$ available to S_i in this manner, the scheduler proceeds to the second step of the acceptance test if $\sigma_{s,i}(t) \geq 0$. This time, the second step has two substeps. First, the scheduler checks whether the acceptance of S_i would cause any yet-to-be-completed sporadic job S_k whose deadline is after d to be late. This can be done by comparing the current slack $\sigma_{s,k}(t)$ of S_k with the execution time e of the new job S_i. S_i is acceptable only when the slack of every affected sporadic job in the system is no less than e.

If the new job $S_i(t, d, e)$ passes the first substep, the scheduler then checks whether the minimum of current slacks of periodic jobs whose deadlines are at or after d is at least as large as e. The method for computing this minimum is similar to the one based on Eq. (7.8). Specifically, the periodic jobs are now partitioned into at most $n+n_s$ disjoint subsets according to the deadlines of the current periodic jobs and the yet-to-be completed sporadic jobs in the manner described in Section 7.5.1. Let $\mathbf{Z}_j$ denote one of these subsets and J_x and J_y denote the periodic jobs that have the earliest deadline d_x and latest deadline d_y, respectively, among the jobs in this subset. The minimum slack of all periodic jobs in $\mathbf{Z}_j$ is given by

$$\omega_j(t) = \omega(x; y) - I - TE - \sum_{d_{s,k} \leq d_x} e_{s,k} - \left(\sum_{d_{s,k} > d_y} \xi_{s,k} + \sum_{d_k > d_y} \xi_k \right) \tag{7.14}$$

Again, we have the expression on the right-hand side because the precomputed value $\omega(x; y)$ of the minimum slack $\omega_j(t)$ of the periodic jobs in $\mathbf{Z}_j$ does not take into account the following factors: (1) the total idle time I since the beginning of the current hyperperiod, (2) the total time TE in the current hyperperiod used for the execution of completed sporadic jobs; (3) the total time already committed to yet-to-be-completed sporadic jobs whose deadlines are before or at the deadline of the first job J_x in $\mathbf{Z}_j$; and (4) the total time already used to execute the completed portion of yet-to-be-completed jobs whose deadlines are after the deadline d_y of the last job J_y in $\mathbf{Z}_j$. Therefore, these factors are subtracted from the precomputed minimum initial slack $\omega(x, y)$.

Clearly, the minimum slack of all periodic jobs whose deadlines are after d is

$$\min_{1 \leq j \leq n+n_s} \omega_j(t).$$

The scheduler accepts the new job $S_i(t, d, e)$ only if this minimum slack is no less than e. The slack computation takes $O(n + n_s)$ time.

Acceptance Tests for Sporadic Jobs with Arbitrary Deadlines. Finally, let us consider a sporadic job $S_i(t, d, e)$ that arrives in the current hyperperiod and its deadline d is in some later hyperperiod. Without loss of generality, suppose that the current hyperperiod starts at time 0 and the deadline d is in zth hyperperiod. In other words, $0 < t \leq (z - 1)H < d \leq zH$. For this sporadic job, the leverage job J_l is the last job among all the periodic jobs that are in the zth hyperperiod and have deadlines at or before d, if there are such jobs, or a nonexisting job whose slack is 0 and deadline is $(z - 1)H$, if there is no such periodic job.

In this case, the time available to the new job S_i consists of three terms: the slack a_1 in the current hyperperiod, the slack a_2 in the second through $(z - 1)$th hyperperiods and the slack a_3 in the zth hyperperiod. a_1 is given by

$$a_1 = \sigma_N(0) - I - TE - \sum_{d_{s,k} \leq d_N} e_{s,k} - \sum_{d_{s,k} > d_N} \xi_{s,k} \tag{7.15a}$$

The total amount a_2 of time during the second through the $(z - 1)$th hyperperiods that is available to S_i is equal the total initial slack in $z - 2$ hyperperiods minus the amount of time already committed to sporadic jobs in system that have deadlines in these hyperperiods. In other words,

$$a_2 = (z - 2)\sigma_N(0) - \sum_{d_N < d_{s,k} \leq (z-1)d_N} e_{s,k} \tag{7.15b}$$

The time in the zth hyperperiod available to S_i is equal to

$$a_3 = \sigma_l(0) + (d - d_l) - \sum_{(z-1)H < d_{s,k} \leq d_l} e_{s,k} \tag{7.15c}$$

In the first step, the scheduler computes the available slack of the new job $S_i(t, d, e)$ according to

$$\sigma_{s,i}(t) = a_1 + a_2 + a_3 - e \tag{7.15d}$$

The scheduler proceeds to do step 2 of the acceptance test if $\sigma_{s,i}(t)$ is no less than 0. In the second step, the scheduler only needs to check whether the periodic jobs that are in the zth hyperperiod and have deadlines at or after d may be adversely affected by the acceptance of S_i. This can be done in the manner described earlier.

We are now ready to look at the example in Figure 7–21 which we used earlier to illustrate the simple acceptance test based on Theorem 7.4. The periodic tasks in the system are $T_1 = (4, 1)$ and $T_2 = (6, 1.5)$. The length H of each hyperperiod is 12, and N is equal to 5. The initial slack $\sigma_i(0)$ of the five periodic jobs are 3.0, 3.5, 4.5, 7.0, and 6.0, respectively, for i equal to 1, 2, 3, 4, and 5.

1. At time 0^+, $S_1(0^+, 8, 2)$ is tested. For this sporadic job, the leverage job is J_2 (i.e., $J_{2,1}$ with deadline 6). In the first step, the scheduler finds $\sigma_{s,1}(0^+)$, which is equal to $\sigma_2(0) + (8 - 6) - 2 = 3.5$ according to Eq. (7.12a). In the second step, it finds the minimum slack of periodic jobs J_3, J_4, and J_5. This minimum is equal to 2.5 if S_1 is accepted. Hence, the scheduler accepts S_1, inserts it into the EDF queue of ready periodic and sporadic jobs, stores $\sigma_{s,1}(0^+) = 3.5$ for later use. It also creates a register to store the current value of $\xi_{s,1}$ of S_1.

2. At time 2, $S_2(2, 7, 0.5)$ is tested. Its leverage job J_l is also J_2. Up until time 2, the system has never been idle and no sporadic job has completed. Hence, I and TE are both 0. $\xi_{s,1}$ is also equal to 0. No periodic job with deadline after 7 has executed. According to Eq. (7.13), $\sigma_{s,2}(2)$ is equal to $3.5 + 1 - 0.5 = 4.0$. Since it is larger than 0.5, the scheduler proceeds to step 2 of the acceptance test. Since none of the jobs with deadlines after 7 will be adversely affected, the scheduler accepts S_2. In addition to do all the bookkeeping work on S_2, the scheduler updates the slack of S_1: $\sigma_{s,1}(2) = 3.5 - 0.5 = 3.0$.

3. By time 4.0 when $S_3(4, 14, 1)$ is released and tested, S_2 has completed. TE is therefore equal to 0.5. I is still zero. The deadline of S_3 is in the second hyperperiod. The scheduler first computes a_1 according to Eq. (7.15a): $a_1 = 6 - 0.5 - 2 = 3.5$. a_2 is equal to zero. Since no existing sporadic job has a deadline in the second hyperperiod, according to Eq. (7.15c), a_3 is equal to 2 (the difference between d and the beginning of the second hyperperiod). Hence $\sigma_{s,3}(4) = 3.5 + 2 - 1 = 4.5$.

   In the second step, the scheduler needs to check only whether the jobs with deadlines in the second hyperperiod would be late if S_3 is accepted. Since all of their slacks are larger than the execution time of S_3, S_3 is acceptable and is accepted.

4. When $S_4(9, 13, 2)$ is tested at time 9, $I = 0$, and $TE = 2.5$. There is only one sporadic job S_3 in the system, and $\xi_{s,3}(9) = 0.5$. The scheduler finds a_1 equal to $6 - 0 - 2.5 - 0.5 = 3.0$. a_3 is equal to 1.0. Hence the slack $\sigma_{s,4}(9) = 3 + 1 - 2 = 2$.

   Since the slack $\sigma_{s,3}(9)$ is 4.5, S_3 will not be late if S_4 is accepted. Moreover, none of the periodic jobs in the second hyperperiod will be late; S_4 is acceptable and is accepted in the second step.

We observe that if the execution time of S_4 were 4.0, this test would accept the job, and the action would be correct.

7.7.3 A Simple Acceptance Test in Fixed-Priority Systems

One way to schedule sporadic jobs in a fixed-priority system is to use a sporadic server to execute them. Because the server (p_s, e_s) has e_s units of processor time every p_s units of time, the scheduler can compute the least amount of time available to every sporadic job in the system. This leads to a simple acceptance test.

As always, we assume that accepted sporadic jobs are ordered among themselves on an EDF basis. When the first sporadic job $S_1(t, d_{s,1}, e_{s,1})$ arrives, the server has at least $\lfloor (d_{s,1} - t)/p_s \rfloor e_s$ units of processor time before the deadline of the job. Therefore, the scheduler accepts S_1 if the slack of the job

$$\sigma_{s,1}(t) = \lfloor (d_{s,1} - t)/p_s \rfloor e_s - e_{s,1}$$

is larger than or equal to 0.

To decide whether a new job $S_i(t, d_{s,i}, e_{s,i})$ is acceptable when there are n_s sporadic jobs in the system, the scheduler computes the slack $\sigma_{s,i}$ of S_i according to

$$\sigma_{s,i}(t) = \lfloor (d_{s,i} - t)/p_s \rfloor e_s - e_{s,i} - \sum_{d_{s,k} < d_{s,i}} (e_{s,k} - \xi_{s,k})$$

where $\xi_{s,k}$ is the execution time of the completed portion of the existing sporadic job S_k. The new job S_i cannot be accepted if its slack is less than 0.

If $\sigma_{s,i}(t)$ is no less than 0, the scheduler then checks whether any existing sporadic job S_k whose deadline is after $d_{s,i}$ may be adversely affected by the acceptance of S_i. This can easily be done by checking whether the slack $\sigma_{s,k}(t)$ of S_k at the time is equal to or larger than $e_{s,i}$. The scheduler accepts S_i if $\sigma_{s,k}(t) - e_{s,i} \geq 0$ for every existing sporadic job S_k with deadline equal to or later than $d_{s,i}$. If the scheduler accepts S_i, it stores $\sigma_{s,i}(t)$ for later use and decrements the slack of every sporadic job with a deadline equal to or later than $d_{s,i}$ by the execution time $e_{s,i}$ of the new job.

7.7.4 Integrated Scheduling of Periodic, Sporadic, and Aperiodic Tasks

In principle, we can schedule sporadic and aperiodic tasks together with periodic tasks according to either the bandwidth-preserving server approach or the slack-stealing approach, or both. However, it is considerably more complex to do slack stealing in a system that contains both sporadic tasks with hard deadlines and aperiodic tasks. If we steal slack from sporadic and periodic jobs in order to speed up the completion of aperiodic jobs, some sporadic jobs may not be acceptable later while they may be acceptable if no slack is used. The presence of sporadic jobs further increases the complexity of slack computation. In contrast, both the implementation and validation of the system are straightforward when we use bandwidth-preserving servers to execute aperiodic or sporadic jobs.

7.8 REAL-TIME PERFORMANCE FOR JOBS WITH SOFT TIMING CONSTRAINTS

For many applications, occasional missed deadlines are acceptable; their sporadic jobs have soft deadlines. This section discusses the performance of the algorithms described in previous sections when used to schedule this type of jobs. In the remainder of this section, except where it is stated otherwise, by a sporadic job, we mean one whose deadline is soft.

7.8.1 Traffic Models

You recall that each sporadic task is a stream of sporadic jobs that have the same interrelease-time and execution-time distributions and the same real-time performance requirements. The real-time performance experienced by each sporadic task is typically measured in terms of such criteria as the maximum tardiness and miss rate of jobs in it. (These terms were defined in Section 3.8.) In a system that provides each sporadic task with some kind of performance guarantee, the system subjects each new sporadic task to an acceptance test. Once a sporadic task is admitted into the system, the scheduler accepts and schedules every job in it.

Specifically, when requesting admission into the system, each sporadic task presents to the scheduler its *traffic parameters*. (These parameters are collectively called the flow specification of the task in communications literature.) These parameters define the constraints on the interarrival times and execution times of jobs in the task. The performance guarantee provided by the system to each task is *conditional*, meaning that the system delivers the guaranteed performance conditioned on the fact that the task meets the constraints defined by its traffic parameters. The flip side is that if the task misbehaves (i.e., its actual parameters deviate from its traffic parameters), the performance experienced by it may deteriorate.

Different traffic models use different traffic parameters to specify the behavior of a sporadic task. In addition the periodic task and sporadic task models, there are also the Ferrari and Verma (FeVe) model [FeVe], the (λ, β) model [Cruz], and the leaky bucket model [Turn, ClSZ]. These models are commonly used to characterize real-time traffic in communication networks.

FeVe and (λ, β) Models.   According to the FeVe model, each sporadic task is characterized by a 4-tuple $(e, p, \overline{p}, I)$: e is the maximum execution time of all jobs in the task; p is the minimum interarrival time of the jobs; $\overline{p}$ is their average interarrival time, and this average is taken over a time interval of length I. Each job may model the transmission of a message (or packet) and each sporadic task the transmission of a message stream. It is also a good model of other types of sporadic tasks (e.g., computations) when the execution times of jobs in each task are roughly the same but their interarrival times may vary widely.

The (λ, β) model, characterizes each sporadic task by a rate parameter λ and a burst parameter β. The total execution time of all jobs that are released in any time interval of length x is no more than $\beta + \lambda x$.

Leaky Bucket Model.   To define the *leaky bucket model*, we first introduce the notion of a (Λ, E) leaky bucket filter. Such a filter is specified by its (input) rate Λ and size E: The filter can hold at most E tokens at any time and it is being filled with tokens at a constant rate of Λ tokens per unit time. A token is lost if it arrives at the filter when the filter already contains E tokens.

We can think of a sporadic task that meets the (Λ, E) leaky bucket constraint as if its jobs were generated by the filter in the following manner. The filter may release a job with execution time e when it has at least e tokens. Upon the release of this job, e tokens are removed from the filter. No job can be released when the filter has no token. Therefore, no job in a sporadic task that satisfies the (Λ, E) leaky bucket constraint has execution time larger than E. Indeed, the total execution time of all jobs that are released within any time interval of length E/Λ is surely less than $2E$. A periodic task with period equal to or larger than E/Λ and execution time equal to or less than E satisfies the (Λ, E) leaky bucket constraint. A sporadic task $S = (1, p, \overline{p}, I)$ that fits the FeVe model satisfies this constraint if $\overline{p} = 1/\Lambda$ and $E = (1 - p/\overline{p})I/\overline{p}$.

Figure 7–22 shows an example. The arrows above the time line indicate the release times of jobs of a sporadic task in a time interval of length 70. The execution times of the jobs are given by the numbers above the boxes symbolizing the jobs, and their relative deadlines are all equal to 15.

- Of course, we can model the task as a periodic task $(5, 2, 15)$ since the minimum inter-release time is 5 and the maximum execution time of all instances is 2. However, this

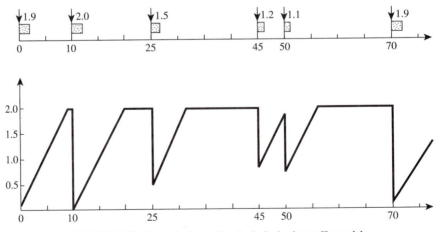

FIGURE 7–22   Example illustrating the leaky bucket traffic model.

is not an accurate characterization; the utilization of this periodic task is 0.4, which is many times larger than its average utilization of 0.11.

- Following the sporadic task model, we can characterize the task by the sequence of instantaneous utilizations of its jobs: 0.19, 0.133, 0.075, 0.24, 0.055, and so on. The maximum instantaneous utilization of the stream is 0.24.

- This task satisfies the (0.2, 2.0)-leaky bucket constraint. The diagram at the bottom of the figure shows the number of token remaining in a (0.2, 2.0)-leaky bucket filter as a function of time. The bucket is full at time 0. In fact, the task satisfies this constraint provided the size of the leaky bucket is no less than 2.0 and its rate is no less than 0.19.

7.8.2   Performance of Bandwidth-Preserving Server Algorithms

Because no job of any accepted sporadic task is rejected by the scheduler, it is possible for a sporadic task to overload the processor. For this reason, the scheduler must provide firewall protection not only to tasks and jobs that have hard deadlines, but also to each existing sporadic task so the performance guarantee of the task will not be violated when other sporadic tasks misbehave. The bandwidth-preserving server algorithms described in earlier sections are designed to provide such protection and, therefore, are ideally suited for scheduling sporadic tasks with soft deadlines.

We focus here on systems which use a bandwidth-preserving server to execute each sporadic task. During an acceptance test, the scheduler can use an appropriate schedulability test to determine the maximum schedulable size of the server chosen to execute the new task. Hence, whether a new sporadic task is acceptable is reduced to the question of whether its required performance can be achieved when its server has the maximum schedulable size. This question can be answered by analyzing the new sporadic task alone without regard to other tasks.

We now ask what is the maximum response time of jobs in a sporadic task that is executed by a constant utilization, total bandwidth, or WFQ server in a deadline-driven system. Clearly, the size $\tilde{u}$ of the server must at least be equal to the average utilization u (i.e., the ratio of the average execution time to the average interarrival time) of the sporadic task S. Queueing theory tells us that even when $\tilde{u} = u$, the average response time of the jobs in S is unbounded if their execution times and interarrival times are not otherwise constrained.

$(e, p, \overline{p}, I)$-Constrained Sporadic Tasks.   Suppose that the sporadic task fits the FeVe model: $S = (e, p, \overline{p}, I)$, and $u = e/p$. Specifically, we suppose that the number of jobs in S released in any interval of length I is never more than $I/\overline{p}$. (In the remainder of this section, by jobs, we mean jobs in S and will omit this reminder most of the time.) Corollary 7.7 tells us that if the server size $\tilde{u}$ is equal to u and the server is schedulable, the response time of every job is never more than $\overline{p}$ if their interarrival times are at least $\overline{p}$. Because their interarrival times can be smaller than $\overline{p}$, their response times can be larger than $\overline{p}$. The question we want to answer here is how large their response times can be when the jobs are executed in FIFO order. Corollary 7.7 tells us as long as the total server size is no greater than 1, we can answer this question without regard to jobs executed by other servers.

To find the maximum possible response time W of all jobs in S, we look at a busy interval of the server that begins at the arrival time t_0 of the first of a bursty sequence of X jobs. By their arrivals being bursty, we mean that the interarrival times of these X jobs are all

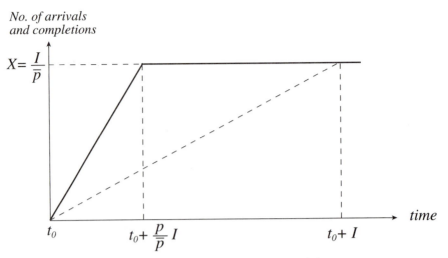

FIGURE 7–23 Number of arrivals and completions.

equal to the minimum possible value p. Because S meets the $(e, p, \overline{p}, I)$ constraint, $X \leq I/\overline{p}$. The solid line in Figure 7–23 shows the number of arrivals of jobs in S as a function of time from t_0, and the dotted line in the figure shows the number of completions of these jobs. The vertical difference between the two lines at any time gives the number of jobs waiting to be executed at the time. It is evident that the response time of the Xth job in the busy interval is larger than the response times of all other jobs executed in the busy interval.

To find the response time of the Xth job (and hence the maximum response time of the sporadic task S), we note that immediately before the release time of the Xth job in S, there are no more than $(X - 1) - \lfloor (X - 1)p/\overline{p} \rfloor$ jobs waiting to be completed. Since it may take the server $\overline{p}$ units of time to complete each job, maximum response time of the Xth job is bounded from above by

$$
W = \begin{cases} \left(X - \dfrac{(X - 1)p}{\overline{p}} \right) \overline{p} + \overline{p} = p + \overline{p} + I\left(1 - \dfrac{p}{\overline{p}} \right) & \text{if } p < \overline{p} \\ \overline{p} & \text{if } p = \overline{p} \end{cases} \qquad (7.16)
$$

The upper bound W for the case of $p < \overline{p}$ is loose because we obtain the expression above by replacing the floor function $\lfloor x \rfloor$ by its lower bound $x - 1$. However, it differs from the tight bound by no more than p because the maximum response time can be as large as $\overline{p} + I(1 - p/\overline{p})$, which is obtained by replacing $\lfloor x \rfloor$ by x.

$(1/\overline{p}, I/\overline{p})$-Leaky Bucket Constrained Tasks. An important special case is when the sporadic task S models the transmission of a packet stream over a network. In this case, the maximum execution time of all jobs is the time required to transmit a maximum size packet. For simplicity, we let this time be 1. Suppose that the task $S = (1, p, \overline{p}, I)$ also satisfies the $(1/\overline{p}, I/\overline{p})$ *leaky bucket constraint*.

In this case, the largest response time occurs when the leaky bucket is full at the beginning t_0 of a busy interval of the server. Starting from t_0, one job with execution time 1 is removed from the bucket every p units of time, while it is being filled at the rate of one job every $\overline{p}$ units of time. At the time the Xth job is ready for transmission, the bucket is empty. In other words,

$$X = \frac{I}{p} + \left\lfloor \frac{(X-1)p}{\overline{p}} \right\rfloor \leq \frac{I + (X-1)p}{\overline{p}}$$

which gives us

$$X \leq \frac{I - p}{\overline{p} - p}$$

The above observations allow us to conclude that the maximum response time of all jobs in S is bounded from above by

$$W = \left(X + 1 - \frac{(X-1)p}{\overline{p}} \right) \overline{p} = I + \overline{p} \qquad (7.17)$$

Again the above upper bound is not tight, but the tight bound is no less than I.

We observe that the maximum response time W of a leaky bucket constrained sporadic task is independent of the minimum interarrival time p of jobs. In particular, the maximum response time is bounded by the above expression if the leaky bucket is emptied at time t_0, that is, $I/\overline{p}$ jobs arrive at t_0. W depends only on the length I of time required to fill the leaky bucket. A smaller I means a smaller W, but also a more regular arrival time pattern.

The derivation of the bound in Eq. (7.16) relies only on the fact that the server can complete each job within $\overline{p}$ units of time after the job reaches the head of the queue of the sporadic task. A deferrable or sporadic server $(\overline{p}, e)$ in a fixed-priority system can also give this performance guarantee if the server is schedulable (i.e., its budget is alway consumed by the end of every period as long as the server is backlogged). Therefore, $I + \overline{p}$ is also an upper bound on the response times of all jobs in a sporadic task S that meets the $(1/\overline{p}, I/\overline{p})$ leaky bucket constraint and is executed by a schedulable deferrable or sporadic server server $(\overline{p}, e)$ in a fixed-priority system.

7.9   A TWO-LEVEL SCHEME FOR INTEGRATED SCHEDULING

This section describes a two-level scheduling scheme [DeLS] that provides timing isolation to individual applications executed on one processor. Each application contains an arbitrary number and types of tasks. By design, the two-level scheme allows different applications to use different scheduling algorithms (e.g., some may be scheduled in a clock-driven manner while the others in a priority-driven manner). Hence, each application can be scheduled in a way best for the application. More importantly, the schedulability and real-time performance of each application can be determined independently of other applications executed on the same processor. By emulating an infinitesmally fine-grain time slicing scheme, the two-level scheme creates a slower virtual processor for each applications in the system.

7.9.1 Overview and Terminology

According to the two-level scheme, each application is executed by a server. The scheduler at the lower level is called the *OS scheduler*. It replenishes the budget and sets the deadline of each server in the manners described below and schedules the ready servers on the EDF basis. At the higher level, each server has a *server scheduler*; this scheduler schedules the jobs in the application executed by the server according to the algorithm chosen for the application.

Required Capability. In the description below, we use $\mathbf{T}_i$ for $i = 1, 2, \ldots, n$ to denote n real-time applications on a processor; each of these applications is executed by a server. To determine the schedulability and performance of each application $\mathbf{T}_i$, we examine the tasks in it as if the application executes alone on a slower processor whose speed is a fraction s of the speed of the physical processor. In other words, we multiple the execution time of every job in the application by a factor $1/s > 1$ and use the product in place of the execution time in the schedulability test on the application. The minimum fraction of speed at which the application is schedulable is called its *required capacity* s_i. The required capacity of every application must be less than 1.

For example, the required capacity of an application that contains two periodic tasks $(2, 0.5)$ and $(5, 1)$ is 0.5 if it is scheduled rate-monotonically. The reason is that we can multiple the execution time of each task by 2 and the resultant tasks $(2, 1.0)$ and $(5, 2)$ are schedulable, but if the multiplication factor were bigger, the resultant tasks would not be schedulable. If these tasks are scheduled on the EDF basis, its required capacity is 0.45.

The system may also have one or more nonreal-time applications. All nonreal-time applications are executed by a total bandwidth or WFQ server of size $0 < \tilde{u}_0 < 1$. The jobs in these applications are scheduled by the server scheduler in a time-shared manner; so the budget of the server is replenished periodically. In essence, the two-level scheduler creates for all the nonreal-time applications a virtual time-shared processor of speed $\tilde{u}_0$.

Predictable versus Nonpredictable Applications. As we will see shortly, in order to correctly maintain the server of an application that is scheduled according to a preemptive priority-driven algorithm, the OS scheduler needs an estimate of the occurrence time of every event of the application that may trigger a context switch within the application. Such events include the releases and completions of jobs and their requests and releases of resources. At any time t, the *next event* of application $\mathbf{T}_i$ is the one that would have the earliest occurrence time after t among all events of $\mathbf{T}_i$ if the application were to execute alone on a slow processor with speed s_i equal to its required capacity. We call an application that is scheduled according to a preemptive, priority-driven algorithm and contains aperiodic and sporadic tasks and/or periodic tasks with release-time jitters an *unpredictable application*. The reason for this name is that the OS scheduler needs an estimate of its next event (occurrence) time at each replenishment time of its server, but its server scheduler cannot compute an accurate estimate.

All other types of applications are *predictable*. An application that contains only periodic tasks with fixed release times and known resource request times is predictable because its server scheduler can compute accurately the occurrence times of its future events. (In fact, for such an application, the event occurrence times can be computed a priori before the application requests to execute in the real-time mode and stored for use at run time.) All time-driven applications are predictable because scheduling decisions are triggered by clock interrupts which occur at known time instants. As we will see shortly, the OS scheduler does not need to know the event occurrence times of a nonpreemptively scheduled application. We say that nonpreemptively scheduled applications are predictable.

7.9.2 Scheduling Predictable Applications

An important property of all types of predictable applications is that such an application is schedulable according to the two-level scheme if the size of its server is equal to its required capability and its server is schedulable. In contrast, a nonpredictable application requires a server of a size larger than than its required capability, as we will explain below.

Nonpreemptively Scheduled Applications.   Specifically, according to the two-level scheme, each nonpreemptively scheduled application T_i is executed by a constant utilization server whose size $\tilde{u}_i$ is equal to the required capacity s_i of the application. The server scheduler orders jobs in T_i according to the algorithm used by T_i. Let B denote the maximum execution time of nonpreemptable sections[3] of all jobs in all applications in the system and $D_{\min}$ denote the minimum of relative deadlines of all jobs in these applications. Corollary 7.8 says that all servers are schedulable if the total size of all servers is no greater than $1 - B/D_{\min}$.

To show that every job in a nonpreemptively scheduled real-time application T_i completes in time when scheduled according to the two-level scheme, we consider a time instant at which the OS scheduler replenishes the server budget and sets the server deadline to execute a job in T_i. This time instant is the same as the scheduling decision time at which the job would be scheduled if T_i were executed alone on a slow processor whose speed is s_i times the speed of the physical processor. The job would complete on the slow processor at the deadline of the server. Since the server is schedulable, it surely will execute for as long as the execution time of the job (hence complete the job) by the server deadline according to the two-level scheme.[4]

Applications Scheduled according to a Cyclic Schedule.   Each application T_i that is scheduled according to a cyclic schedule is also executed by a constant utilization server of size equal to s_i. The OS replenishes the budget of the server at the beginning of each frame. At each replenishment, the budget is set to $s_i f$, where f is the length of the frames, and the server deadline is the beginning of the next frame. The server scheduler schedules the application according to its precomputed cyclic schedule.

Preemptively Scheduled Predictable Applications.   As with other predictable applications, the size $\tilde{u}_i$ of the server for a predictable application T_i that is scheduled in a preemptive, priority-driven manner is equal to its required capacity. However, the OS scheduler cannot maintain the server according to the constant utilization/total bandwidth server

---

[3]By definition, jobs in a nonpreemptively scheduled application never preempt each other. However, because the server of the application may be preempted by other servers, these jobs may be preempted by jobs in other applications. In contrast, the server is never preempted, and hence the job it is executing is never preempted, when the job is nonpreemptable.

[4]This discussion assumes that actual execution time of every job is equal to its maximum execution time. The consumption rule of the server must be modified when the actual execution time can be smaller. The modification is simple: The remaining budget provided to the server to execute a job is consumed immediately when the job completes. In other words, the server does not reclaim the time allocated to the job. Rather, this time is made available to nonreal-time applications.

algorithms. Rather, it replenishes the server budget in the slightly different manner described below.

To motivate the modified replenishment rule, we consider two jobs, J_1 and J_2. The execution time of each is 0.25. Their feasible intervals are (0.5, 1.5] and (0, 2], respectively. The jobs are scheduled preemptively in a priority-driven manner: J_1 has the higher priority and J_2 the lower. These jobs would be schedulable if they were to execute by themselves on a slow processor of speed 0.25. Now, suppose that they are executed by a server of size 0.25 according to the two-level scheme on a processor of speed one. Moreover, suppose that the server is maintained according to the constant utilization server or total bandwidth server algorithm: At time 0, the server is given 0.25 unit of budget, and its deadline is set at 1. The server may execute for 0.25 unit of time and complete J_2 by time 0.5 when J_1 is released. When the server budget is replenished again, the deadline for consuming the budget is 2. J_1 may complete as late as time 2 and, hence, may miss its deadline.

Deng, *et al.* [DeSL] showed that if the server for a preemptive, priority-driven application were maintained according to the constant utilization/total bandwidth server algorithms, we could guarantee the schedulability of the application only if the size of its server is 1, even when the required capacity of the application is much smaller than 1. This means that it cannot share the processor with any other application! A look at the above example tells us why. From time 0 to 0.5, the server is given (and is allowed to consume) 0.125 unit of budget more than what is required to complete the portion of J_2 that could be completed before time 0.5 if J_2 were executed on the slower processor. This 0.125 unit of budget should be saved to execute the higher-priority job J_1 after 0.5. By giving the server a budget equal to the execution time or the remaining execution time of the job at the head of the server's ready queue, the OS scheduler may introduce a form of priority inversion: A lower-priority job is able to make more progress according to the two-level schedule at the expense of some higher-priority job. We say that this priority inversion is due to the overreplenishment of the server budget.

A way to prevent this kind of priority inversion works as follows. At each replenishment time of the server for a preemptively scheduled application $\mathbf{T}_i$, let t be the current server deadline or the current time, whichever is later. Let t' be the next release-time of $\mathbf{T}_i$, that is, t' is the earliest release time after t of all jobs in $\mathbf{T}_i$ (in general, the occurrence time of the earliest possible context switch). t' is computed by the server scheduler; this is possible when the release times of all jobs in $\mathbf{T}_i$ are known. Knowing that a preemption within $\mathbf{T}_i$ may occur at t', the OS scheduler sets the server budget to $\min(e_r, (t' - t)\tilde{u}_i)$, where e_r is the execution time of the remaining portion of the job at the head of the server queue, and sets the deadline of the server at $\min(t + e_r/\tilde{u}_i, t')$. Therefore, if $\mathbf{T}_i$ were to execute alone on a slower processor of speed $\tilde{u}_i$, it would not have any context switch between any replenishment time and the corresponding server deadline. This condition, together with conditions that the server size is equal to the required capacity and the total size of all servers is no greater than $1 - B/D_{\min}$, gives a sufficient condition for $\mathbf{T}_i$ to be schedulable when executed according to the two-level scheme.

7.9.3 Scheduling Nonpredictable Applications

In general, the actual release-times of some jobs in a nonpredictable application $\mathbf{T}_i$ may be unknown. It is impossible for its server scheduler to determine the next release-time t' of $\mathbf{T}_i$ precisely. Therefore, some priority inversion due to overreplenishment of the server budget is unavoidable. Fortunately, the bad effect on the schedulability of $\mathbf{T}_i$ can be compensated by making the size $\tilde{u}_i$ of the server larger than the required capacity s_i of the application.

Budget Replenishment.   Let t'_e denote an estimate of the next release time t' of $\mathbf{T}_i$. The server scheduler computes this estimate at each replenishment time t of the server as follows. If the earliest possible release time of every job in $\mathbf{T}_i$ is known, the server scheduler uses as t'_e the minimum of the future earliest release times plus an error factor $\varepsilon > 0$. When the earliest release times of some jobs in $\mathbf{T}_i$ are unknown, t'_e is equal to the $t + \varepsilon$, where t is the current time. After obtaining the value t'_e from the server scheduler, the OS scheduler sets the server budget to $\min(e_r, (t'_e - t)\tilde{u}_i)$ and the server deadline at $\min(t + e_r/\tilde{u}_i, t'_e)$.

ε is a design parameter. It is called the *quantum size* of the two-level scheduler. In the absence of any knowledge on the release-times of jobs in an application, the OS scheduler replenishes the budget of its server every ε units of time. Hence, the smaller the quantum size, the more frequent the server replenishments, and the higher the server maintenance overhead. However, the size of the server required to execute the application grows with the quantum size, as it will become evident below.

Required Server Size.   It is easy to see that if $\mathbf{T}_i$ were to execute alone on a slower processor, it would not have any context switch from the current replenishment time to ε time units before the new server deadline. The extra budget that the OS scheduler may inadvertently give to the server is no greater than $\varepsilon\tilde{u}_i$. Hence, the length of priority inversion due to the overreplenishment of the server budget is at most $\varepsilon\tilde{u}_i$. We can treat this time as the blocking time of any higher-priority job that may be released between the current replenishment time and server deadline.

Let $D_{i,\min}$ be the minimum relative deadline of all jobs in $\mathbf{T}_i$. Section 6.8 tells us that if the size of the server for $\mathbf{T}_i$ satisfies the inequality $s_i + \varepsilon\tilde{u}_i/D_{i,\min} \leq \tilde{u}_i$, any higher-priority job that may suffer this amount of blocking can still complete in time. Rewriting this inequality and keeping the equality sign, we get

$$\tilde{u}_i = s_i \frac{D_{i,\min}}{D_{i,\min} - \varepsilon}$$

In conclusion, a nonpredictable application $\mathbf{T}_i$ with required capacity s_i and minimum relative deadline $D_{i,\min}$ is schedulable according to the two-level scheme if the size of its server is given by the expression above and the total size of all servers in the system is no greater than $1 - B/D_{\min}$.

7.10   SUMMARY

This chapter describes algorithms for scheduling aperiodic and sporadic jobs in a system of periodic tasks. Algorithms for scheduling aperiodic jobs try to complete these jobs as soon as possible without causing any periodic or sporadic job to miss its deadline. A correct algorithm for scheduling sporadic jobs accepts and schedules each sporadic job newly offered to the system only if the new job, as well as all the periodic tasks and previously accepted sporadic jobs, can be scheduled to complete in time.

7.10.1 Algorithms for Scheduling Aperiodic Jobs

There are two types of aperiodic job scheduling algorithms. They are bandwidth-preserving algorithms and slack-stealing algorithms.

Bandwidth-Preserving Algorithms.   According to a bandwidth-preserving algorithm, aperiodic jobs are executed by one or more servers; each bandwidth-preserving server emulates one or more periodic tasks or a sporadic task. Bandwidth-preserving algorithms can tolerate release-time jitters of periodic tasks. Many of them are simple to implement.

Deferrable Server.   The budget of a deferrable server (p_s, e_s) is set to e_s at time instants kp_s, for $k = 0, 1, 2, \ldots$. The server consumes its budget only when it executes. Such a server emulates a periodic task whose execution may be suspended and deferred. Section 7.2.2 discussed how to take into account the presence of deferrable servers on the schedulability of fixed-priority periodic tasks. The inequality Eq. (7.5) gives an upper bound to the size of a deferrable server in a deadline-driven system.

Sporadic Server.   A simple sporadic server (p_s, e_s) described in Section 7.3.1 or 7.3.3 emulates a periodic task of period p_s and execution time e_s. SpSL and GhBa servers described in Sections 7.3.2 and 7.3.3 are enhanced sporadic servers. Such a server emulates several periodic tasks when its budget is broken up into chunks to be replenished at different times. We can account for the effect of a sporadic server on schedulability of periodic tasks by treating the server as a periodic task or several periodic tasks with period p_s and total execution time e_s.

Constant Utilization and Total Bandwidth Servers.   A constant utilization server emulates a sporadic task that has a constant instantaneous utilization. It can be used only in deadline-driven systems. A total bandwidth server is an enhanced constant utilization server that is allowed to claim the background time not used by periodic tasks. The total size of all the constant utilization and total bandwidth servers in a system of independent, preemptable periodic tasks whose total density is Δ must be no greater than $1 - \Delta$. When this condition is satisfied, the worst-case response times of jobs executed by such a server depend only on the size of the server and can be determined independent of the workload executed by other servers in the system.

Weighted Fair-Queueing Server.   For many applications, it is important that the scheduling algorithm be fair. The total bandwidth server algorithm is not fair; a server can be starved for an arbitrary amount of time. The weighted fair-queueing algorithm does not have this problem and can achieve the same worst-case response time as the total bandwidth server algorithm. The nonpreemptive version of this algorithm is also called packet-by-packet generalized processor sharing algorithm and is for scheduling transmissions of packets in switched networks.

Slack-Stealing Algorithms.   In a system that does slack stealing, the scheduler schedules aperiodic jobs whenever the periodic tasks and sporadic jobs in the system have slack, that is, their execution can be safely postponed without causing them to miss their deadlines. Sections 7.5 and 7.6 described slack-stealing algorithms for use in deadline-driven and fixed-priority systems, respectively.

The scheduling overhead of slack-stealing is primarily the time spent to do slack computations: the work that the scheduler must do to determine how much slack the system has at each scheduling decision time. This overhead is $O(N)$, where N is the number of periodic jobs in a busy interval or hyperperiod, when the scheduler does slack computations dynamically without making use of precomputed slack information. In a system of n periodic tasks, the overhead can be reduced to $O(n)$ if the scheduler uses static computation, that is, it computes the current slack from the precomputed initial slack. The limitation of static slack-stealing algorithms is that they can be used only when the release-time jitters of periodic tasks are negligible. When they can be used, however, the slack-stealing algorithms typically offer better performance than bandwidth-preserving algorithms, especially when the total utilization of periodic tasks is large (e.g., 75% or larger).

7.10.2 Algorithms for Scheduling Sporadic Jobs

Section 7.7 described how to schedule sporadic jobs that have hard deadlines among periodic tasks. The key assumptions are that (1) the scheduler subjects each new sporadic job to an acceptance test and (2) the accepted sporadic jobs are ordered among themselves in the EDF order.

      Acceptance Tests for Deadline-Driven Systems.   The simplest acceptance test algorithm is based on Theorem 7.4, and it is applicable only when periodic tasks are scheduled on a EDF basis. It works as follows. In a system where the total density of periodic tasks is Δ, the scheduler accepts a new sporadic task $S(t, d, e)$ at the time t of its arrival if the total density of all the existing sporadic jobs whose deadlines are at or before the deadline d of the new job is less than or equal to $1 - \Delta - e/(d - t)$.

      The simple acceptance test is not accurate. Its accuracy can be improved if the scheduler also computes and makes use of the slack of the system at each acceptance test. The dynamic-slack computation algorithm described in Section 7.5 can be used for this purpose. When the periodic tasks have fixed release times, the acceptance test described in Section 7.7.2 can be used. This test uses static-slack computation. Its time complexity is $O(n + N_s)$, where n and N_s are the number of periodic tasks and sporadic jobs, respectively, in the system.

      Acceptance Tests for Fixed-Priority Systems.   A simple and effective way to schedule sporadic jobs is to use a bandwidth-preserving server (p_s, e_s). The fact that the server is guaranteed to have e_s units of processor time every p_s units of time makes it possible for the scheduler to compute the latest completion times of the new sporadic job and existing sporadic jobs. The simple acceptance test described in Section 7.7.3 is based on this fact.

7.10.3 Scheduling Sporadic Jobs with Soft Deadlines

Section 7.8 described three well-known model of sporadic tasks that have soft deadlines. They are the FeVe model [FeVe], the (λ, β) model [Cruz], and the leaky bucket model [Turn, ClSZ].

      The scheduler performs an acceptance test on each such sporadic task based on the traffic parameters of the task. If the scheduler accepts a task, it provides the task with a bandwidth-preserving server of sufficiently large size to execute jobs in the task and hereafter accepts every job in the task. Eq. (7.17) gives the worst-case response time of jobs in a task that meets the leaky bucket constraint in terms of parameters of the leaky bucket.

7.10.4 Integrated Scheduling of Periodic, Sporadic, and Aperiodic Tasks

Finally, Section 7.9 describes a two-level priority-driven scheme for integrated scheduling of all types of tasks on a single processor. This scheme emulates infinitesimally fine-grain time slicing under a set of conditions that can be easily met. Under these conditions, the schedulability of each application consisting a subset of all the tasks in the system can be analyzed independently of the other applications in the system.

EXERCISES

7.1 A system contains three periodic tasks. They are $(2.5, 1)$, $(4, 0.5)$, $(5, 0.75)$, and their total utilization is 0.475.

  (a) The system also contains a periodic server $(2, 0.5)$. The server is scheduled with the periodic tasks rate-monotonically.

      i. Suppose that the periodic server is a basic sporadic server. What are the response times of the following two aperiodic jobs: One arrives at 3 and has execution time 0.75, and one arrives at 7.5 and has execution time 0.6.

      ii. Suppose that the period server is a deferrable server. What are the response times of the above two aperiodic jobs.

  (b) Note that the utilization of the periodic server in part (a) is 0.25. We can give the server different periods while keeping its utilization fixed at 0.25. Repeat (i) and (ii) in part (a) if the period of the periodic server is 1.

  (c) Can we improve the response times by increasing the period of the periodic server?

  (d) Suppose that as a designer you were given (1) the characteristics of the periodic tasks, that is, (p_1, e_1), (p_2, e_2), ..., (p_n, e_n), (2) the minimum interval p_a between arrivals of aperiodic jobs, and (3) the maximum execution time required to complete any aperiodic job. Suppose that you are asked to choose the execution budget and period of a deferrable server. Suggest a set of good design rules.

7.2 A system contains three periodic tasks. They are $(3, 1)$, $(4, 0.5)$, $(5, 0.5)$.

  (a) The task system also contains a sporadic server whose period is 2. The sporadic server is scheduled with the periodic tasks rate-monotonically. Find the maximum utilization of the server if all deadlines of periodic tasks are surely met.

      i. Suppose that the server in part (a) is a pure polling server. What are the response times of the following two aperiodic jobs: One arrives at 2.3 and has execution time 0.8, and one arrives at 12.7 and has execution time 0.6?

      ii. Suppose that the server in part (a) is a basic sporadic server. What are the response times of the above two aperiodic jobs?

  (b) We can give the server different periods while keeping its utilization fixed. Repeat (ii) in part (a) if the period of the sporadic server whose utilization is given by your answer to (a) is 1 or 4.

7.3 Consider a system containing the following periodic tasks: $T_1 = (10, 2)$, $T_2 = (14, 3)$, and $T_3 = (21, 4)$. A periodic server of period 8 is used to schedule aperiodic jobs.

  (a) Suppose that the server and the tasks are scheduled rate-monotonically.

      i. If the periodic server is a deferrable server, how large can its maximum execution budget be?

      ii. If the periodic server is a sporadic server, how large can its maximum execution budget be?

iii. Suppose that the sporadic server in (ii) is a simple sporadic server. If the aperiodic job queue is rarely empty, which server you should use and why?

iv. Suppose that aperiodic jobs arrive more or less regularly every 7 units of time apart and their execution times are around half of the execution budget of the server. Which server is better and why?

v. Suppose that the sporadic server is a SpSL server. Which server is better and why for aperiodic jobs in (iv)?

(b) Suppose that the server and the tasks are scheduled on the EDF basis.

i. Repeat (i) and (ii) in part (a).

ii. Suppose that the server is a total bandwidth server. How large can the size of the server be? Will it perform at least as well as the deferrable server under the conditions in (ii) and (iv) in part (a)?

7.4 Consider a system that contains two periodic tasks $T_1 = (7, 2)$ and $T_2 = (10, 3)$. There is a bandwidth-preserving server whose period is 6. Suppose that the periodic tasks and the server are scheduled rate-monotonically.

(a) Suppose that the server is a deferrable server.

i. What is the maximum server size?

ii. Consider two aperiodic jobs A_1 and A_2. The execution times of the jobs are equal to 1.0 and 2.0, respectively. Their arrival times are 2 and 5. What are their response times?

(b) Suppose that the server is a simple sporadic or SpSL sporadic server.

i. What is the maximum server size?

ii. Find the response times of jobs A_1 and A_2 in (ii) in part (a) if the server is a SpSL server.

7.5 Suppose that the periodic tasks in the previous problem are scheduled along with a server on the earliest-deadline-first basis.

(a) What is the maximum server size if the server is a deferrable server? Is this size a function of the period of the server? If not, why not? If yes, what is the best choice of server size?

(b) What is the maximum server size if the server is a total bandwidth server?

(c) Find the response times of A_1 and A_2 in Problem 7.4 for servers in parts (a) and (b).

7.6 A system contains three periodic tasks: $(2.5, 0.5)$, $(3, 1)$, and $(5, 0.5)$.

(a) The system also contains a sporadic server whose period is 4. The server is scheduled with the periodic tasks rate-monotonically. Find the maximum execution budget of the server so the periodic tasks remain schedulable.

(b) We want improve the responsiveness of the system by increasing the size of the server obtained in part (a). In particular, we want to reduce its period while keeping its execution budget fixed. Find the minimum server period.

(c) Suppose that the server is a sporadic/background server whose parameters are $(3.5, 0.75)$. There are two aperiodic jobs. One arrives at 1.9, and the other arrives at 4.8. Each of these jobs requires 1 unit of processor time to complete. Construct a schedule for this system in the time interval $[0, 15]$. What are the response times of the jobs?

(d) Suppose that the aperiodic jobs in part (c) are executed by a slack stealer.

i. Compute the initial slack time in the interval $[0, 10]$.

ii. What is the amount of slack time when the first aperiodic job arrives at 1.9?

iii. Find the response time of the aperiodic jobs.

7.7 You are ask to prove Theorem 7.2 using an argument similar to the one used in the proof of Theorem 6.11.

(a) We begin by guessing that the execution times and periods of the periodic tasks and the server in the most difficult-to-schedule system are related according to the following equations:

$$e_s = (p_1 - p_s)/2$$

$$e_k = p_{k+1} - p_k \qquad \text{for } k = 1, 2, \ldots, n-1$$

$$e_n = p_n - 3e_s - 2\sum_{k=1}^{n-1} e_k$$

Draw a segment of the schedule starting from a critical instant t_0 of all the periodic tasks to the time $t_0 + p_n$. Verify that the periodic tasks and the deferrable server with these parameters are schedulable and that they keep the processor busy in this time interval. We call a system whose parameters are thus related a difficult-to-schedule system.

(b) The total utilization of a system is equal to the total utilization of the periodic tasks plus the utilization of the deferrable server. Show that the total utilization of any system whose parameters are not related according to the equations in part (a) is larger than the total utilization of any difficult-to-schedule system.

(c) Express the total utilization of a difficult-to-schedule system in terms of the adjacent period ratios $q_{1,s}, q_{2,1}, \ldots, q_{n,n-1}$.

(d) Show that the minimum value of the total utilization in part (c) is $U_{RMS/DS}(n)$ plus u_s given by Theorem 7.2.

7.8 In Theorem 7.2, one of the conditions on the periods of the tasks is that $p_s + e_s \leq p_n < 2p_s$. When $p_s + e_s > p_n$, $U_{RM/DS}(n)$ given by the theorem is no longer the schedulable utilization of the periodic tasks. This problem intends to show you that the schedulable utilization of the periodic tasks may be very poor when $p_s + e_s > p_n$.

(a) Consider a system containing a periodic task with period 2 and execution time $\varepsilon > 0$ that is scheduled rate-monotonically together with a deferrable server whose period is 1.9 and execution budget is 1.0. Show that the periodic task is not schedulable for all values of $\varepsilon > 0$.

(b) Consider a system containing n independent periodic tasks and a deferrable server (p_s, e_s) that are scheduled rate-monotonically. The periods of the tasks and the parameters of the server are such that $p_s + e_s > p_n$.

    i. Show that when u_s is less than 0.5, the system is schedulable if the total utilization of the periodic tasks is equal to or less than $1 - 2u_s$. (*Hint:* It will be helpful if you first show that the statement is true for n equal to 1 and then reduce the problem for arbitrary n to the case of n equal to 1.)

    ii. Show that when u_s is larger than 0.5, no periodic task with period larger than p_s is schedulable.

7.9 Show that a periodic task $T_i = (p_k, e_k)$ in a system of n independent, preemptable periodic tasks is schedulable according to the EDF algorithm, together with m deferrable servers, each of which has period $p_{s,k}$, execution budget $e_{s,k}$ and utilization $u_{s,k}$, if

$$\sum_{k=1}^{n} \frac{e_k}{\min(D_k, p_k)} + \sum_{k=1}^{m} u_{s,k}\left(1 + \frac{p_{s,k} - e_{s,k}}{D_i}\right) \leq 1$$

7.10 In a fixed-priority system of two periodic tasks $T_1 = (3, 1)$ and $T_3 = (9, 3)$, there is a sporadic server $(p_s, e_s) = (8, 2)$. Suppose that two aperiodic jobs A_1 and A_2 arrive at time 0.5 and 5, respectively. Their execution times are both equal to 1.

(a) What is the response time of A_2 if the server is a simple sporadic server?

(b) What is the response time of A_2 if the server is a SpSL server?

7.11 Section 7.3 described informally an enhanced sporadic server algorithm. The primary difference between an enhanced sporadic server and a simple sporadic server with the same period p_s and execution budget e_s is that the former is allowed to keep its unconsumed budget at each replenishment time, while the latter is not. Stated more precisely, at each replenishment time, the budget of an enhanced sporadic server is incremented by e_s, and if the higher-priority subsystem $\mathbf{T}_H$ is busy throughout the interval $(t_r, t_r + p_s]$ since the latest replenishment time, the budget is replenished at $t_r + p_s$.

  (a) Write the replenishment rules of such a server.

  (b) Write the consumption rules of enhanced sporadic servers so that such a server emulates a periodic task (p_s, e_s) in which the response times of some jobs are longer than p_s.

7.12 The consumption and replenishment rules of SpSL sporadic servers stated in [SpSL] are as follows. Let p_s and e_s denote the server period and execution budget, respectively.

  - Consumption rule: The budget is consumed at the rate of 1 per unit time only when the server is executed.
  - Replenishment rules

    R1 The budget is initially set at e_s.

    R2 The next replenishment time is set at $t + p_s$ when at time t the server or a task in the higher-priority subsystem $\mathbf{T}_H$ becomes ready for execution after the processor has been executing tasks with priorities lower than the server. The amount of budget replenished at this replenishment time is determined when the processor starts to execute a lower-priority task after having executed the server or a task in $\mathbf{T}_H$: The amount to be replenished is equal to the time consumed by the SpSL server since the last time the replenishment time was set.

    R3 The execution budget is set at e_s when the processor becomes idle.

  (Note that because of rule R3, the SpSL server is a sporadic/background server.)

  (a) Show that the system containing two periodic tasks $(3, 1)$ and $(8, 3)$ is schedulable rate-monotonically together with a SpSL server that has period 4 and execution budget 1.0 if the server behaves just like the periodic task $(4, 1)$.

  (b) Apply the rules stated above to this system. There are two aperiodic jobs. A_1 with execution time 0.5 arrives at time 0, and A_2 with execution time 4 arrives at time 4. List the time instants in the interval $(0, 10)$ at which the next replenishment time is set and the instants when the amount to be replenished is determined, together with the corresponding amounts to be replenished.

  (c) If your answer in part (b) is correct, you should find that the lower-priority task $(8, 3)$ fails to meet its deadline at 8. In other words, the server does not behave like a periodic task. Discuss briefly the reason why it fails to behave correctly.

  (d) How should the rules stated above be modified to ensure the correctness of the server?

7.13 GhBa servers [GhBa] are sporadic servers that are designed to work in a deadline-driven system where all the tasks are scheduled on the EDF basis. As stated in Section 7.3, a GhBa server differs from a simple deadline-driven sporadic server in that its execution budget is consumed and replenished in chunks. When the budget of the server is replenished for the first time, the server has one chunk of budget of size e_s. As time goes on, chunks of budget are created and deleted as described below. The server is eligible for execution when the server is backlogged and has at least one chunk of budget. The server consumes its budget only when it executes. It uses and consumes chunks of budget replenished at different times in order of their replenishment. Whenever the server has exhausted a chunk of budget, the chunk is deleted. It is scheduled for replenishment at the current deadline d of the server. When the server becomes idle after it has consumed x units of a chunk of budget, a new chunk of size x is scheduled for replenishment at the current deadline d. The size of the chunk being consumed is reduced by x.

  The server has a deadline which is sometimes undefined. When the deadline is defined, it is scheduled with the periodic tasks on the EDF basis based on its deadline. The deadline of the server is determined according to the following rule.

  (1) Initially the server deadline is undefined, and budget $= e_s$.

(2) If the deadline is undefined, it is set to $t + p_s$ when any of the following events occurs at t:

    i. The server becomes eligible for execution.

    ii. A task with deadline earlier than $t + p_s$ starts to execute.

(3) If the deadline d_s of the server is defined, it is updated as described below whenever any of the following events occurs at t:

    i. A task with deadline d after the server deadline but at or before $t + p_s$ starts to execute, set the server deadline to d.

    ii. A task with deadline d after $t + p_s$ begins to execute, the deadline of the server becomes undefined.

    iii. The server begins to use a new chunk of budget whose replenishment time is after $d_s - p_s$, set the deadline of the server to the replenishment time of just consumed chunk plus p_s.

Repeat parts (b) in Problem 7.12, using the GhBa server instead.

7.14 A *priority-exchange server* [LeSS, SpSL] with period p_s and budget e_s is a periodic server whose budget is set to e_s at time instants that are integer multiples of p_s. Its budget is consumed at the rate of 1 per unit time whenever it is executing. If when the server is suspended some lower priority tasks $T_{l,1}, T_{l,2}, \ldots, T_{l,k}$ execute in the time interval where the server would be scheduled if it were not suspended, we say that these lower-priority tasks execute at the server's priority in this interval. Let x_j denote the amount of time the task $T_{l,j}$ executes at the server's priority in a period of the server. The server is allowed to preserve x_j units of its budget in the period. However, these x_j units the server gets by trading time with the lower-priority task $T_{l,j}$ has the priority of $T_{l,j}$; when the server later wants to use this budget, it will be scheduled at the priority of the task $T_{l,j}$. Suppose that there is no special hardware to support priority exchange. Describe in pseudocode an implementation of a priority exchange server. Give an estimate of the scheduling overhead and compare it with that of a simple sporadic server.

7.15 **(a)** Are deferrable server and simple sporadic server algorithms fair in fixed-priority systems? If yes, give an informal proof; if no, give an example to illustrate.

    (b) Repeat part (a) for the deferrable server algorithm and the simple sporadic server algorithm in deadline-driven systems.

7.16 A system contains three weighted fair-queueing servers FQ_1, FQ_2, and FQ_3. Their sizes are $\tilde{u}_1 = 0.5$, $\tilde{u}_2 = 0.2$, and $\tilde{u}_3 = 0.3$, respectively. Suppose that before time 0, all servers were idle.

- Starting from time 0, all servers become backlogged.
- At time 5, FQ_3 becomes idle.
- At time 10, FQ_1 also becomes idle.
- At time 20, FQ_3 becomes backlogged again.
- At time 25, FQ_2 becomes idle.
- At time 35, FQ_1 becomes backlogged again.

What is the finish number of the system at time 35?

7.17 Stiliadis, *et al.* [StVa96] put total bandwidth and WFQ servers in a class of bandwidth-preserver server algorithms which they call *latency-rate server* algorithms. The definition of a latency-rate server makes use of the notion of a server busy interval. A busy interval of a server of size $\tilde{u}$ starts at time x if, immediately prior to x, the queue of the server is empty and, at x, a job joins the queue. The busy interval ends at the first time instant x' after x when the total execution time of all jobs that join the server queue at and after x becomes equal to $\tilde{u}(x' - x)$. A server is a latency-rate server if, and only if, at every time instant t in a server busy interval $(x, x']$, the total attained time $\tilde{w}(x, t)$ of the server (i.e., the total amount of time the server executes in this interval) is such that

$$\tilde{w}(x, t) \geq \max(0, \tilde{u}(t - x - \delta))$$

where δ is the minimum of all nonnegative, finite numbers that satisfy this inequality. δ is the latency of the server because it is the additional delay a job may suffer over the time required to complete the job when the job and all the jobs executed by the server before it were executed by a processor whose speed is $\tilde{u}$ of the physical processor and there were no other servers in the system.

Which one(s) of the bandwidth-preserving servers described in this chapter is(are) not latency-rate servers? For each server that is not latency-rate, briefly explain why. For each server that is a latency-rate server, compute its latency.

7.18 Consider a system of three periodic tasks $T_1 = (3, 1)$, $T_2 = (4, 1)$, and $T_3 = (6, 1.5)$. The periodic tasks are scheduled according to the EDF algorithm.

    (a) Compute the initial slacks and the slack table of the jobs in the first hyperperiod of the tasks. Assume that when jobs have the same deadline, the tie in priority is broken on the basis of their periods. The job of the task with a shorter period has a higher priority.

    (b) An aperiodic job with execution time 1.0 arrives at time 3.5, and we want to find the slack of the system at the time. What are the elements of the three subsets $\mathbf{Z}_i$ for $i = 1, 2, 3$?

    (c) Find the minimum slack of the jobs in each of the subsets and the slack of the system.

7.19 Davis, *et al.* [DaWe] suggested a dual-priority scheme for scheduling aperiodic jobs in the midst of periodic tasks. According to the dual-priority scheme, the system keeps three bands of priority, each containing one or more priority levels. The highest band contains real-time priorities; they are for hard real-time tasks. Real-time priorities are assigned to hard real-time tasks according to some fixed priority scheme. The middle priority band is for aperiodic jobs. The lowest priority band is also for hard real-time tasks. Specifically, when a job $J_{i,k}$ in a periodic task $T_i = (p_i, e_i, D_i)$ is released, it has a priority in the lowest priority band until its priority promotion time. At its priority promotion time, its priority is raised to its real-time priority. Let W_i denote the maximum response time of all jobs in T_i when they execute at the real-time priority of the task. The priority promotion time of each job is $Y_i = D_i - W_i$ from its release time. Since W_i can be computed off-line or at admission control time, the relative promotion time Y_i for jobs in each task T_i needs to be computed only once. By delaying as much as possible the scheduling of every hard real-time job at its real-time priority, the scheduler automatically creates slacks for aperiodic jobs.

    (a) Give an initiutive argument to support the claim that this scheme will not cause any periodic job to miss its deadline if the system of periodic tasks is schedulable.

    (b) A system contains three periodic tasks: They are (2.5, 0.5), (3, 1), and (5, 0.5). Compute the priority promotion times for jobs in each of the tasks if the tasks are scheduled rate-monotonically.

    (c) Suppose that there are two aperiodic jobs. One arrives at 1.9, and the other arrives at 4.8. Their execution times are 2. Compute the response times of these jobs in a dual-priority system in which there is only one priority level in the middle priority band and one priority level in the lowest priority band. How much improvement is gained over simply scheduling the aperiodic jobs in the background of rate-monotonically scheduled periodic tasks?

    (d) Can the dual-priority scheme be modified and used in a system where periodic tasks are scheduled according to the EDF algorithm? If no, briefly explain why; if yes, briefly describe the necessary modification.

7.20 A system of three periodic tasks $T_1 = (3, 1)$, $T_2 = (5, 1.5)$, and $T_3 = (8, 2)$ is scheduled on the EDF basis. The precomputed amounts of slack of the six jobs in a hyperperiod are 2, 2.5, 2.5,

2.5, 2.5, and 2, respectively. Suppose that the first aperiodic job arrives at time 3.5. What are the slacks of the jobs J_i for $i = 3, 4, 5, 6$, and 7. (The jobs are indexed in nondecreasing order of their deadlines.)

7.21 The static slack computation algorithm based on Eq. (7.8) assumes that periodic jobs have distinct priorities. In other words, jobs that have the same deadlines are assigned distinct priorities. Does the algorithm remain correct if these jobs are given the same priority and ties are broken in a nondeterministic manner? If yes, explain why. If no, describe how the algorithm must be modified.

7.22 Section 7.8.2 mentioned that a sporadic task $S = (1, p, \overline{p}, I)$ according the FeVe model satisfies the (Λ, E) leaky bucket if $\overline{p} > 1/\Lambda$ and $I(1 - p/\overline{p})/\overline{p}$. Show that this statement is true.

7.23 Suppose that the intervals between arrivals of sporadic jobs are known to be in the range (a, b). The execution time of each sporadic job is at most $e\ (\leq a)$ units.

    (a) Suppose relative deadlines of sporadic jobs are equal to a. You are asked to design a bandwidth-preserving server that will be scheduled rate-monotonically with other periodic tasks. Sporadic jobs waiting to be completed are executed on the first-in-first-out basis in the time intervals where the periodic server is scheduled. Choose the period and utilization of this server so that all sporadic jobs will be completed by their deadlines and the utilization of the periodic server is as small as possible.

    (b) Repeat part (a) for the cases where the relative deadlines of sporadic jobs are equal to d: $d < a$ and $d > a$.

7.24 Suppose that the intervals between arrivals of sporadic jobs with hard deadlines are known to be uniformly distributed in the range $[1, 2]$.

    (a) The execution times of the sporadic jobs are at most equal to 1 unit and are ready upon arrival.

        (i) Suppose that relative deadlines of sporadic jobs are equal to 1. You are asked to design a sporadic/background server that will be scheduled rate-monotonically with periodic tasks. Sporadic jobs waiting to be completed are executed on the FIFO basis in the time intervals where the server is scheduled. (Note that since all sporadic jobs have the same relative deadline, FIFO ordering is the same as EDF ordering.) Choose the period and utilization of this server so that as long as the sporadic server is schedulable, all sporadic jobs will be completed by their deadlines. Make the utilization of the server as small as possible.

        (ii) What should the server parameters be if the relative deadlines of the sporadic jobs are 0.75?

    (b) Suppose that the execution time of a sporadic job is equal to $0.1K$ where K is a random variable that assumes only integer values. The probability for K being k is $0.1(0.9)^k$ for $k = 1, 2, \ldots$. If the relative deadlines of the sporadic jobs are equal to 1, what is the probability that a sporadic job will miss its deadline if your server in (i) of part (a) is used?

C H A P T E R   8

Resources and Resource Access Control

In Section 3.1, we briefly mentioned the fact that in addition to a processor, each job may require some other resource in order to execute, but thus far we have ignored this requirement in order to focus on the problems in processor scheduling. We are now ready to take into account the resource requirements.

This chapter first extends our workload model to include resources and introduces additional notations needed in later sections. It then discusses how resource contention affects the execution behavior and schedulability of jobs, how various resource access-control protocols work to reduce the undesirable effect of resource contention, and how well these protocols succeed in achieving this goal. We focus on priority-driven systems. Clock-driven systems do not have these problems as we can avoid resource contention among jobs by scheduling them according to a cyclic schedule that keeps jobs' resource accesses serialized.

8.1 ASSUMPTIONS ON RESOURCES AND THEIR USAGE

We continue to focus on the case where the system contains only one processor. In addition, the system also contains ρ types of serially reusable resources named $R_1, R_2, \ldots, R_\rho$. There are ν_i indistinguishable units of resource (of type) R_i, for $1 \leq i \leq \rho$. Serially reusable resources are typically granted (i.e., allocated) to jobs on a nonpreemptive basis and used in a *mutually exclusive* manner. In other words, when a unit of a resource R_i is granted to a job, this unit is no longer available to other jobs until the job frees the unit. Again, examples of such resources are mutexes, reader/writer locks, connection sockets, printers, and remote servers. A binary semaphore is a resource (type) that has only 1 unit while a counting semaphore has many units. A system containing five printers has 5 units of the printer resource. There is only 1 unit of an exclusive write-lock.

A resource that has an infinite number of units has no effect on the timing behavior of any job since every job can have the resource at any time; there is no need to include the resource in our model. Therefore, we lose no generality by assuming that every resource R_i has a finite number of units.

Some resources can be used by more than one job at the same time. We model such a resource as a resource type that has many units, each used in a mutually exclusive manner. For example, a file that can be read by at most ν users at the same time is modeled as a resource that has ν exclusive units. By modeling shared resources in this manner, we do not need to treat them differently.

8.1.1 Enforcement of Mutual Exclusion and Critical Sections

For the most part of this chapter, we assume that a lock-based concurrency control mechanism is used to enforce mutually exclusive accesses of jobs to resources. (We make this assumption for the sake of clarity. As you will see later, commonly used resource access control protocols can be implemented without locks.) When a job wants to use η_i units of resource R_i, it executes a *lock* to request them. We denote this lock request by $L(R_i, \eta_i)$. The job continues its execution when it is granted the requested resource. When the job no longer needs the resource, it releases the resource by executing an *unlock*, denoted by $U(R_i, \eta_i)$. When a resource R_i has only 1 unit, we use the simpler notations $L(R_i)$ and $U(R_i)$ for lock and unlock, respectively. When there are only a few resources and each has only 1 unit, we simply call them by capital letters, such as X, Y, and Z, or by names, such as *Black*, *Shaded*, and so on.

Following the usual convention, we call a segment of a job that begins at a lock and ends at a matching unlock a *critical section*. Furthermore, resources are released in the last-in-first-out order. Hence overlapping critical sections are properly nested.

As an example, Figure 8–1 shows three jobs, J_1, J_2, and J_3, and the time instants when locks and unlocks are executed if each job executes alone starting from time 0. Resources R_1, R_2, and R_3 have only 1 unit each, while resources R_4 and R_5 have many units. Job J_3 has three overlapping critical sections that are properly nested. A critical section that is not included in other critical sections is an *outermost critical section*; the critical section delimited by $L(R_1)$ and $U(R_1)$ in J_3 is an example. Other examples are the critical sections delimited by $L(R_2)$ and $U(R_2)$ in J_2, the second pair of $L(R_3)$ and $U(R_3)$ in J_2 and $L(R_3)$ and $U(R_3)$ in J_1.

When the execution times of the critical sections and the way they are nested are relevant in our discussion, we denote each critical section by a square bracket $[R, \eta; e]$. The entries in the bracket give the name R and the number of units η of the resource used by the job when in the critical section and the (maximum) execution time e of the critical section. In the case where R has only 1 unit, we omit the value of η and use the simpler notation $[R; e]$ instead. In the example in Figure 8–1, the critical section in J_3 that begins at $L(R_5, 4)$ is $[R_5, 4; 3]$ because in this critical section, the job uses 4 units of R_5 and the execution time of this critical section is 3. Concatenations and nestings of the brackets allow us to describe different com-

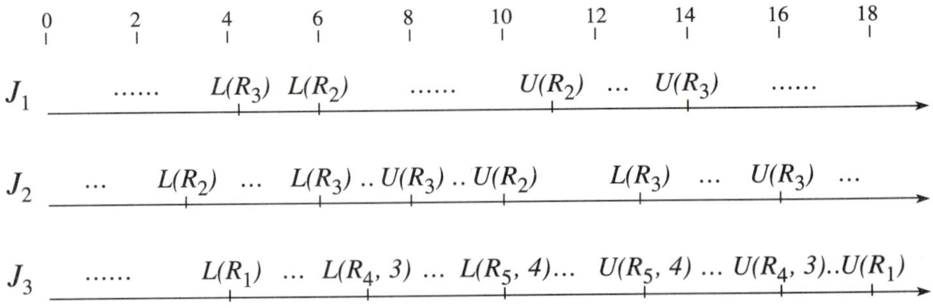

FIGURE 8–1   Examples of critical sections

binations of critical sections. Specifically, we denote nested critical sections by nested square brackets. For example, the nested critical section in J_3 is $[R_1; 14 [R_4, 3; 9 [R_5, 4; 3]]]$. This notation indicates that the critical section beginning from $L(R_1)$ includes the one beginning from $L(R_4, 3)$, which in turn includes the one beginning from $L(R_5, 4)$. Similarly, critical sections in J_2 are $[R_2; 7 [R_3; 2]][R_3; 3]$, indicating that there are two nonlapping critical sections in this job.

8.1.2   Resource Conflicts and Blocking

Two jobs *conflict* with one another, or have a *resource conflict*, if some of the resources they require are of the same type. The jobs *contend* for a resource when one job requests a resource that the other job already has. We use these terms interchangeably as the distinction between them is often not important. The scheduler always denies a request if there are not enough free units of the resource to satisfy the request. Sometimes, as we will see later, a scheduler may deny a request even when the requested resource units are free in order to prevent some undesirable execution behavior.

When the scheduler does not grant η_i units of resource R_i to the job requesting them, the lock request $L(R_i, \eta_i)$ of the job fails (or is denied). When its lock request fails, the job is *blocked* and loses the processor. A blocked job is removed from the ready job queue. It stays blocked until the scheduler grants it η_i units of R_i for which the job is waiting. At that time, the job becomes *unblocked*, is moved backed to the ready job queue, and executes when it is scheduled.

The example in Figure 8–2 illustrates the effect of resource contentions. In this example, there are three jobs, J_1, J_2, and J_3, whose feasible intervals are (6, 14], (2, 17] and (0, 18], respectively. The release time and deadline of each job are marked by the vertical bar on each of the time lines. The jobs are scheduled on the processor on the earliest-deadline-first basis. Hence, J_1 has the highest priority and J_3 the lowest. All three jobs require the resource R, which has only 1 unit. In particular, the critical sections in these jobs are $[R; 2]$, $[R; 4]$, and $[R; 4]$, respectively. Below is a description of this schedule segment. The black boxes in Figure 8–2 show when the jobs are in their critical sections.

1. At time 0, only J_3 is ready. It executes.
2. At time 1, J_3 is granted the resource R when it executes $L(R)$.

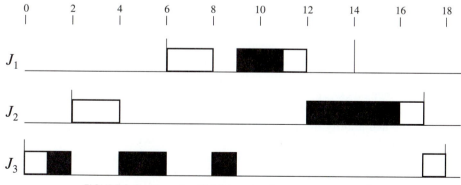

FIGURE 8–2   Example of job interaction due to resource contention.

3. J_2 is released at time 2, preempts J_3, and begins to execute.

4. At time 4, J_2 tries to lock R. Because R is in use by J_3, this lock request fails. J_2 becomes blocked, and J_3 regains the processor and begins to execute.

5. At time 6, J_1 becomes ready, preempts J_3 and begins to execute.

6. J_1 executes until time 8 when it executes a $L(R)$ to request R. J_3 still has the resource. Consequently, J_1 becomes blocked. Only J_3 is ready for execution, and it again has the processor and executes.

7. The critical section of J_3 completes at time 9. The resource R becomes free when J_3 executes $U(R)$. Both J_1 and J_2 are waiting for it. The priority of the former is higher. Therefore, the resource and the processor are allocated to J_1, allowing it to resume execution.

8. J_1 releases the resource R at time 11. J_2 is unblocked. Since J_1 has the highest priority, it continues to execute.

9. J_1 completes at time 12. Since J_2 is no longer blocked and has a higher priority than J_3, it has the processor, holds the resource, and begins to execute. When it completes at time 17, J_3 resumes and executes until completion at 18.

This example illustrates how resource contention can delay the completion of higher-priority jobs. It is easy to see that if J_1 and J_2 do not require the resource, they can complete by times 11 and 14, respectively.

8.2   EFFECTS OF RESOURCE CONTENTION AND RESOURCE ACCESS CONTROL

A *resource access-control protocol*, or simply an *access-control protocol*, is a set of rules that govern (1) when and under what conditions each request for resource is granted and (2) how jobs requiring resources are scheduled. Before moving on to describe several well-known resource access-control protocols and their performance, let us examine in more detail the undesirable effects of resource contention. By looking more closely at what can happen when jobs contend for resources, we should see more clearly the specific design objectives of such a protocol.

8.2.1   Priority Inversion, Timing Anomalies, and Deadlock

In Section 6.8, we saw that priority inversion can occur when the execution of some jobs or portions of jobs is nonpreemptable. Resource contentions among jobs can also cause priority inversion. Because resources are allocated to jobs on a nonpreemptive basis, a higher-priority job can be blocked by a lower-priority job if the jobs conflict, even when the execution of both jobs is preemptable. In the example in Figure 8–2, the lowest priority job J_3 first blocks J_2 and then blocks J_1 while it holds the resource R. As a result, priority inversion occurs in intervals (4, 6] and (8, 9].

When priority inversion occurs, timing anomalies invariably follow. Figure 8–3 gives an example. The three jobs are the same as those shown in Figure 8–2, except that the critical section in J_3 is [R; 2.5]. In other words, the execution time of the critical section in J_3 is shortened by 1.5. If we were not warned earlier in Section 4.8 about timing anomalies, our intuition might tell us that as a consequence of this reduction in J_3's execution time, all jobs

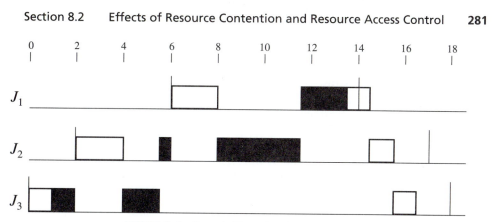

FIGURE 8–3   Example illustrating timing anomaly.

should complete sooner. Indeed, this reduction does allow jobs J_2 and J_3 to complete sooner. Unfortunately, rather than meeting its deadline at 14, J_1 misses its deadline because it does not complete until 14.5.

More seriously, without good resource access control, the duration of a priority inversion can be unbounded. The example in Figure 8–4 illustrates this fact. Here, jobs J_1 and J_3 have the highest priority and lowest priority, respectively. At time 0, J_3 becomes ready and executes. It acquires the resource R shortly afterwards and continues to execute. After R is allocated to J_3, J_1 becomes ready. It preempts J_3 and executes until it requests resource R at time 3. Because the resource is in use, J_1 becomes blocked, and a priority inversion begins. While J_3 is holding the resource and executes, a job J_2 with a priority higher than J_3 but lower than J_1 is released. Moreover, J_2 does not require the resource R. This job preempts J_3 and executes to completion. Thus, J_2 lengthens the duration of this priority inversion. In this situation, the priority inversion is said to be uncontrolled [ShRL90]. There can be an arbitrary number of jobs with priorities lower than J_1 and higher than J_3 released in the meantime. They can further lengthen the duration of the priority inversion. Indeed, when priority inversion is uncontrolled, a job can be blocked for an infinitely long time.

Nonpreemptivity of resource allocation can also lead to deadlocks. The classic example is one where there are two jobs that both require resources X and Y. The jobs are in deadlock

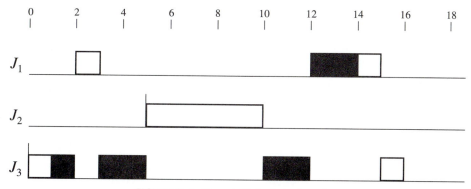

FIGURE 8–4   Uncontrolled priority inversion.

when one of them holds X and requests for Y, while the other holds Y and requests for X. The conditions that allow this circular wait of jobs for each other (i.e., a deadlock) to occur are well-known [Crow, SiGa].

From these examples, we see that no resource access-control protocol can eliminate the priority inversion and anomalous behavior caused by resource contention. A more realistic goal of such a protocol is that it keeps the delays thus incurred as short as possible. For this reason, a criterion we use to measure the performance of a resource access-control protocol is the blocking time of each job. A good resource access-control protocol should control priority inversion and prevent deadlock and, thus, keep the blocking time of every job bounded from the above.

8.2.2 Additional Terms, Notations, and Assumptions

In most parts of this chapter, we ignore all the other factors that can cause a job to be blocked, so, *no job ever suspends itself and every job is preemptable on the processor*. We will discuss the effect of self-suspension and nonpreemptivity at the end of the chapter.

We sometimes use J_h and J_l to denote a higher-priority job and a lower-priority job, respectively. The priorities of these jobs are denoted by π_h and π_l, respectively. In general, the priority of a job J_i is π_i. As in earlier chapters, we represent priorities by integers; the smaller the integer, the higher the priority.

A higher-priority job J_h is said to be *directly blocked* by a lower-priority job J_l when J_l holds some resource which J_h requests and is not allocated. In the example in Figure 8–2, J_3 directly blocks J_2 at time 5.

We describe the dynamic-blocking relationship among jobs using a wait-for graph. In the *wait-for graph* of a system, every job that requires some resource is represented by a vertex labeled by the name of the job. There is also a vertex for every resource in the system, labeled by the name and the number of units of the resource. At any time, the wait-for graph contains an (ownership) edge with label x from a resource vertex to a job vertex if x units of the resource are allocated to the job at the time. There is a (wait-for) edge with label y from a job vertex to a resource vertex if the job requested y units of the resource earlier and the request was denied. In other words, the job is waiting for the resource. (Clearly, y plus the sum of all the labels of edges from the resource vertex is larger than the number of units of the resource.) Therefore, a path in a wait-for graph from a higher-priority job to a lower-priority job represents the fact that the former is directly blocked by the latter. A cyclic path in a wait-for graph indicates a deadlock.

The simple graph in Figure 8–5 is an example. It represents the state of the system in Figure 8–2 at time 5: The resource R is allocated to J_3 and J_2 is waiting for the resource. The path from J_2 to J_3 indicates that J_2 is directly blocked by J_3. Later, J_1 will also be directly

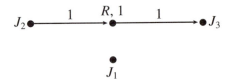

FIGURE 8–5   A wait-for-graph of the system in Figure 8–2 at time 5.

blocked by J_3 when it requests and is denied the resource, and the wait-for graph of the system will have an additional edge from J_1 to R. Since there is only one resource, deadlock can never occur.

In a system of periodic tasks, we say that a periodic task T_i has a critical section $[R, x; y]$, or that the task requires x units of resource R for y units of time, if every job in the task requires at most x units of R for at most y units of time. We sometimes denote the periodic task by the tuple $(\phi_i, p_i, e_i, D_i, [R, x; y])$. In general, when jobs in the task require more than one resource and hence have more than one critical section, we put all the critical sections in the tuple. Hence if J_2 in Figure 8–1 is a job in a periodic task of period 100, execution time 20, zero phase, and relative deadline 100, and if no job in the task has any longer critical section, we call the task $(100, 20; [R_2; 7[R_3; 2]][R_3; 3])$. When the parameters of the critical sections are not relevant, we also denote the task T_i by a tuple $(\phi_i, p_i, e_i, D_i; c_i)$; the last element c_i is the maximum execution time of the longest critical section of the jobs in the periodic task. (The execution times of all the critical sections are included in the execution time e_i of the task.) In this simpler way, the task $(100, 20; [R_2; 7[R_3; 2]][R_3; 3])$ is also called $(100, 20; 7)$.

We will specify resource requirements of a system by a bipartite graph in which there is a vertex for every job (or periodic task) and every resource. Each vertex is named by the name of the job (or task) or resource it represents. The integer next to each resource vertex R_i gives the number v_i of units of the resource. The fact that a job J (or task T) *requires* a resource R_i is represented by an edge from the job (or task) vertex J (or T) to the resource vertex R_i. We may label each edge by one or more 2-tuples or numbers, each for a critical section of the job (or task) which uses the resource. The first element of each 2-tuple gives the number of units used in the critical section. We usually omit this element when there is only 1 unit of the resource. The second element, which is always given, specifies the duration of the critical section. Figure 8–6 gives two examples. The simple graph in Figure 8–6(a) gives

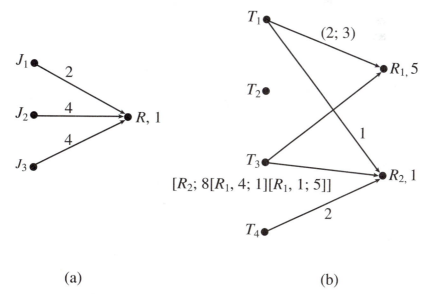

(a)   (b)

FIGURE 8–6   Graphs that specify resource requirements.

the resource requirements of the jobs in the system in Figure 8–2. The labels of the edges are the durations of the critical sections of the respective jobs. The graph in Figure 8-6(b) uses a combination of ways to specify resource requirements. The system has four periodic tasks. The edges from T_1 tells us that (each job in) this task requires 2 units of R_1 for at most 3 units of time and it requires the resource R_2 for at most 1 unit of time. Similarly, T_4 requires R_2 for 2 units of time. Rather than specifying the resource requirement of T_3 by complicated labels of edges connecting vertex T_3 to resource vertices, we simply provide the information on critical sections of T_3 next to the vertex T_3. There is no edge from T_2, meaning that this task does not require any resource.

Finally, to avoid verboseness whenever there is no ambiguity, by a critical section, we mean an outermost critical section. By a critical section of a periodic task, we mean a critical section of each job in the periodic task.

8.3 NONPREEMPTIVE CRITICAL SECTIONS

The simplest way to control access of resources is to schedule all critical sections on the processor nonpreemptively [Mok]. (In other words, when a job requests a resource, it is always allocated the resource. When a job holds any resource, it executes at a priority higher than the priorities of all jobs.) This protocol is called the *Nonpreemptive Critical Section* (*NPCS*) *protocol*. Because no job is ever preempted when it holds any resource, deadlock can never occur.

Take the jobs in Figure 8–4 for example. Figure 8–7(a) shows the schedule of these jobs when their critical sections are scheduled nonpreemptively on the processor. According to this schedule, J_1 is forced to wait for J_3 when J_3 holds the resource. However, as soon as J_3 releases the resource, J_1 becomes unblocked and executes to completion. Because J_1 is not delayed by J_2, it completes at time 10, rather than 15 according to the schedule in Figure 8–4.

In general, uncontrolled priority inversion illustrated by Figure 8–4 can never occur. The reason is that a job J_h can be blocked only if it is released when some lower-priority job is in a critical section. If it is blocked, once the blocking critical section completes, all resources are free. No lower-priority job can get the processor and acquire any resource until J_h completes. Hence, J_h can be blocked only once, and its blocking time due to resource conflict is at most equal to the maximum execution time of the critical sections of all lower-priority jobs.

Specifically, the blocking time $b_i(rc)$ due to resource conflict of a periodic task T_i in a fixed-priority system of n periodic tasks is equal to

$$b_i(rc) = \max_{i+1 \leq k \leq n} (c_k) \qquad (8.1)$$

when the tasks are indexed in order of nonincreasing priority. In a system where periodic tasks are scheduled on the EDF basis, a job in task T_i with relative deadline D_i can be blocked only by jobs in tasks with relative deadlines longer than D_i. This was stated in Theorem 6.18. Therefore, the blocking time $b_i(rc)$ of T_i is again given by Eq. (8.1) if we index the periodic tasks according to their relative deadlines so that $i < j$ if $D_i < D_j$.

As an example, suppose that the tasks in the system in Figure 8–6(b) are scheduled on a fixed-priority basis. The blocking time $b_1(rc)$ of the highest priority task T_1 is 8, the execution time of the (outermost) critical section of T_3. Similarly, $b_2(rc)$ is 8, while $b_3(rc)$ is 2, the execution time of the critical section of T_4. No task blocks T_4 since it has the lowest

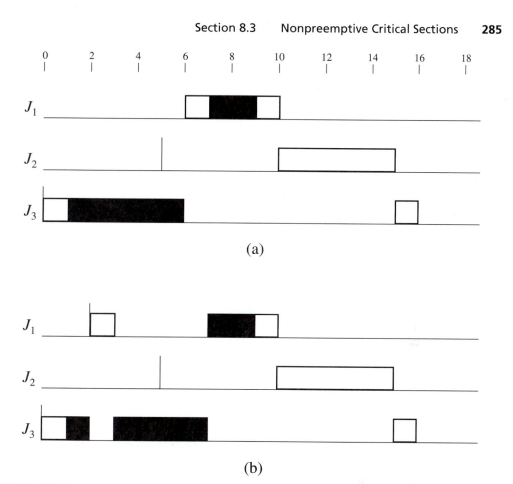

FIGURE 8–7   Example to illustrate two simple protocols. (a) Controlling priority inversion by disallowing preemption of critical section. (b) Controlling priority inversion by using priority inheritance.

priority. Suppose that the relative deadlines of the tasks are $D_1 < D_2 < D_3 < D_4$ and the tasks are scheduled on an EDF basis. Then the blocking times $b_i(rc)$ for $i = 1, 2, 3$, and 4 are also 8, 8, 2, and 0, respectively.

The most important advantage of the NPCS protocol is its simplicity, especially when the numbers of resource units are arbitrary. The protocol does not need any prior knowledge about resource requirements of jobs. It is simple to implement and can be used in both fixed-priority and dynamic-priority systems. It is clearly a good protocol when all the critical sections are short and when most of the jobs conflict with each other.

An obvious shortcoming of this protocol is that every job can be blocked by every lower-priority job that requires some resource even when there is no resource conflict between them. When the resource requirements of all jobs are known, an improvement is to let a job holding any resource execute at the highest priority of all jobs requiring the resource. This is indeed how the *ceiling-priority protocol* supported by the Real-Time Systems Annex of Ada95 [Cohe96] works. We will discuss the ceiling-priority protocol and its worst-case performance in detail in Section 8.6, after examining two other well-known protocols that aim at improving upon the NPCS protocol.

8.4 BASIC PRIORITY-INHERITANCE PROTOCOL

The priority-inheritance protocol proposed by Sha, *et al.* [ShRL90] is also a simple protocol. It works with any preemptive, priority-driven scheduling algorithm. Like the NPCS protocol, it does not require prior knowledge on resource requirements of jobs. The priority-inheritance protocol does not prevent deadlock. When there is no deadlock (i.e., when some other method is used to prevent deadlock), the protocol ensures that no job is ever blocked for an indefinitely long time because uncontrolled priority inversion cannot occur.

In this and the next three sections, we confine our attention to the special case where there is only 1 unit of each resource. (This is the reason for calling the version described here the basic version.) By doing so, we relieve ourselves temporarily of the details that arise due to multiple resource units, so we can focus on the essence of the protocols and the behavior of the system under their control. We will return in Section 8.9 to remove this restrictive assumption.

8.4.1 Definition of Basic Priority-Inheritance Protocol

In the definition of this protocol, as well as other protocols described later, we call the priority that is assigned to a job according to the scheduling algorithm its *assigned priority*. As you will see shortly, at any time t, each ready job J_l is scheduled and executes at its *current priority* $\pi_l(t)$, which may differ from its assigned priority and may vary with time. In particular, the current priority $\pi_l(t)$ of a job J_l may be raised to the higher priority $\pi_h(t)$ of another job J_h. When this happens, we say that the lower-priority job J_l *inherits* the priority of the higher priority job J_h and that J_l executes at its *inherited priority* $\pi_h(t)$. Hereafter, when there is no need to be specific or there is no possible confusion, we will simply say priority when we mean either current or assigned priority.

In its simplest form, the *priority-inheritance protocol* is defined by the following rules. These rules govern the ways current priorities of jobs are set and jobs are scheduled when some of them contend for resources. Again, this version assumes that every resource has only 1 unit.

Rules of the Basic Priority-Inheritance Protocol

1. *Scheduling Rule*: Ready jobs are scheduled on the processor preemptively in a priority-driven manner according to their current priorities. At its release time t, the current priority $\pi(t)$ of every job J is equal to its assigned priority. The job remains at this priority except under the condition stated in rule 3.

2. *Allocation Rule*: When a job J requests a resource R at time t,

   (a) if R is free, R is allocated to J until J releases the resource, and

   (b) if R is not free, the request is denied and J is blocked.

3. *Priority-Inheritance Rule*: When the requesting job J becomes blocked, the job J_l which blocks J inherits the current priority $\pi(t)$ of J. The job J_l executes at its inherited priority $\pi(t)$ until it releases R; at that time, the priority of J_l returns to its priority $\pi_l(t')$ at the time t' when it acquires the resource R.

According to this protocol, a job J is denied a resource only when the resource requested by it is held by another job. (You will see shortly that this is not true for some other protocols.) At time t when it requests the resource, J has the highest priority among all ready jobs. The current priority $\pi_l(t)$ of the job J_l directly blocking J is never higher than the priority $\pi(t)$ of J. Rule 3 relies on this fact.

The simple example in Figure 8–7(b) illustrates how priority inheritance affects the way jobs are scheduled and executed. The three jobs in this figure are the same as the ones in Figure 8–7(a). When J_1 requests resource R and becomes blocked by J_3 at time 3, job J_3 inherits the priority π_1 of J_1. When job J_2 becomes ready at 5, it cannot preempt J_3 because its priority π_2 is lower than the inherited priority π_1 of J_3. As a consequence, J_3 completes its critical section as soon as possible. In this way, the protocol ensures that the duration of priority inversion is never longer than the duration of an outermost critical section each time a job is blocked.

Figure 8–8 gives a more complex example. In this example, there are five jobs and two resources *Black* and *Shaded*. The parameters of the jobs and their critical sections are listed in part (a). As usual, jobs are indexed in decreasing order of their priorities: The priority π_i of J_i is i, and the smaller the integer, the higher the priority. In the schedule in part (b) of this figure, black boxes show the critical sections when the jobs are holding *Black*. Shaded boxes show the critical sections when the jobs are holding *Shaded*.

1. At time 0, job J_5 becomes ready and executes at its assigned priority 5. At time 1, it is granted the resource *Black*.

2. At time 2, J_4 is released. It preempts J_5 and starts to execute.

3. At time 3, J_4 requests *Shaded*. *Shaded*, being free, is granted to the job. The job continues to execute.

4. At time 4, J_3 is released and preempts J_4. At time 5, J_2 is released and preempts J_3.

5. At time 6, J_2 executes $L(Black)$ to request *Black*; $L(Black)$ fails because *Black* is in use by J_5. J_2 is now directly blocked by J_5. According to rule 3, J_5 inherits the priority 2 of J_2. Because J_5's priority is now the highest among all ready jobs, J_5 starts to execute.

6. J_1 is released at time 7. Having the highest priority 1, it preempts J_5 and starts to execute.

7. At time 8, J_1 executes $L(Shaded)$, which fails, and becomes blocked. Since J_4 has *Shaded* at the time, it directly blocks J_1 and, consequently, inherits J_1's priority 1. J_4 now has the highest priority among the ready jobs J_3, J_4, and J_5. Therefore, it starts to execute.

8. At time 9, J_4 requests the resource *Black* and becomes directly blocked by J_5. At this time the current priority of J_4 is 1, the priority it has inherited from J_1 since time 8. Therefore, J_5 inherits priority 1 and begins to execute.

9. At time 11, J_5 releases the resource *Black*. Its priority returns to 5, which was its priority when it acquired *Black*. The job with the highest priority among all unblocked jobs is J_4. Consequently, J_4 enters its inner critical section and proceeds to complete this and the outer critical section.

10. At time 13, J_4 releases *Shaded*. The job no longer holds any resource; its priority returns to 4, its assigned priority. J_1 becomes unblocked, acquires *Shaded*, and begins to execute.

Job	r_i	e_i	π_i	Critical Sections
J_1	7	3	1	[*Shaded*; 1]
J_2	5	3	2	[*Black*; 1]
J_3	4	2	3	
J_4	2	6	4	[*Shaded*; 4 [*Black*; 1.5]]
J_5	0	6	5	[*Black*; 4]

(a)

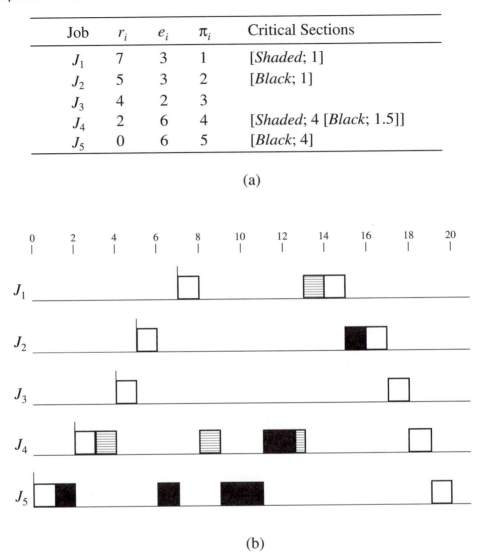

(b)

FIGURE 8–8 Example illustrating transitive inheritance of priority inheritance. (a) Parameters of jobs. (b) Schedule under priority inheritance.

11. At time 15, J_1 completes. J_2 is granted the resource *Black* and is now the job with the highest priority. Consequently, it begins to execute.

12. At time 17, J_2 completes. Afterwards, jobs J_3, J_4, and J_5 execute in turn to completion.

8.4.2 Properties of the Priority-Inheritance Protocol

This example illustrates that when resource accesses are controlled by the priority-inheritance protocol, there are two types of blocking: direct blocking and *priority-inheritance blocking* (or simply *inheritance blocking*). J_2 is directly blocked by J_5 in (6, 11] and by J_4 in (11, 12.5], and J_1 is directly blocked by J_4 in (8, 13]. In addition, J_3 is blocked by J_5 in (6, 7] because the latter inherits a higher priority in this interval. Later at time 8, when J_4 inherits priority 1 from J_1, J_3 becomes blocked by J_4 as a consequence. Similarly, the job J_2 in Figure 8–7(b) suffers inheritance blocking by J_3 in (5, 7]. This type of blocking suffered by jobs that are not involved in resource contention is the cost for controlling the durations of priority inversion suffered by jobs that are involved in resource contention.

The example in Figure 8–8 also illustrates the fact that jobs can *transitively block* each other. At time 9, J_5 blocks J_4, and J_4 blocks J_1. So, *priority inheritance is transitive*. In the time interval (9, 11), J_5 inherits J_4's priority, which J_4 inherited from J_1. As a consequence, J_5 indirectly inherits the J_1's priority.

The priority-inheritance protocol does not prevent deadlock. To see why, let us suppose that J_5 in this example were to request the resource *Shaded* sometime after *Shaded* has been granted to J_4 (e.g., at time 6.5). These two jobs would be deadlocked.

In addition, *the priority-inheritance protocol does not reduce the blocking times suffered by jobs as small as possible*. It is true that in the absence of a deadlock, a job can be blocked directly by any lower-priority job for at most once for the duration of one outermost critical section. However, in the worst case, a job that requires v resources and conflicts with k lower-priority jobs can be blocked for $\min(v, k)$ times, each for the duration of an outermost critical section. Figure 8–9 shows the worst-case scenario when v is equal to k. Here the job J_1 has the highest priority; it is blocked k times.

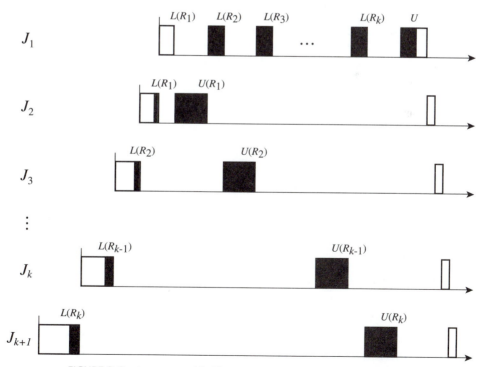

FIGURE 8–9   A worst-case blocking scenario for priority-inheritance protocol.

8.5 BASIC PRIORITY-CEILING PROTOCOL

The *priority-ceiling protocol* [ShRL88, ShRL90] extends the priority-inheritance protocol to prevent deadlocks and to further reduce the blocking time. This protocol makes two key assumptions:

1. The assigned priorities of all jobs are fixed.
2. The resources required by all jobs are known a priori before the execution of any job begins.

To define the protocol, we need two additional terms. The protocol makes use of a parameter, called priority ceiling, of every resource. The *priority ceiling* of any resource R_i is the highest priority of all the jobs that require R_i and is denoted by $\Pi(R_i)$. For example, the priority ceiling $\Pi(Black)$ of the resource *Black* in the example in Figure 8–8 is 2 because J_2 is the highest priority job among the jobs requiring it. Similarly, $\Pi(Shaded)$ is 1. Because of assumption 2, the priority ceilings of all resources are known a priori. We note that if the resource access control protocol includes the priority-inheritance rule, then a job can inherit a priority as high as x during its execution if it requires a resource with priority ceiling x.

At any time t, the *current priority ceiling* (or simply the *ceiling*) $\hat{\Pi}(t)$ of the system is equal to the highest priority ceiling of the resources that are in use at the time, if some resources are in use. If all the resources are free at the time, the current ceiling $\hat{\Pi}(t)$ is equal to Ω, a nonexisting priority level that is lower than the lowest priority of all jobs. As an example, we again look at the system in Figure 8–8. In the interval [0, 1) when both resources in the system are free, the current ceiling of the system is equal to Ω, lower than 5, the priority of the lowest priority job J_5. In (1, 3], *Black* is held by J_5; hence, the current ceiling of the system is 2. In (3, 13] when *Shaded* is also in use, the current ceiling of the system is 1, and so it is in (13, 14].

8.5.1 Definition of the Basic Priority-Ceiling Protocol

We now define the priority-ceiling protocol for the case when there is only 1 unit of every resource.

Rules of Basic Priority-Ceiling Protocol

1. *Scheduling Rule*:
   (a) At its release time t, the current priority $\pi(t)$ of every job J is equal to its assigned priority. The job remains at this priority except under the condition stated in rule 3.
   (b) Every ready job J is scheduled preemptively and in a priority-driven manner at its current priority $\pi(t)$.
2. *Allocation Rule*: Whenever a job J requests a resource R at time t, one of the following two conditions occurs:
   (a) R is held by another job. J's request fails and J becomes blocked.
   (b) R is free.
      (i) If J's priority $\pi(t)$ is higher than the current priority ceiling $\hat{\Pi}(t)$, R is allocated to J.

(ii) If J's priority $\pi(t)$ is not higher than the ceiling $\hat{\Pi}(t)$ of the system, R is allocated to J only if J is the job holding the resource(s) whose priority ceiling is equal to $\hat{\Pi}(t)$; otherwise, J's request is denied, and J becomes blocked.

3. *Priority-Inheritance Rule*: When J becomes blocked, the job J_l which blocks J inherits the current priority $\pi(t)$ of J. J_l executes at its inherited priority until the time when it releases every resource whose priority ceiling is equal to or higher than $\pi(t)$; at that time, the priority of J_l returns to its priority $\pi_l(t')$ at the time t' when it was granted the resource(s).

We note that (ii) in rule 2 assumes that only one job holds all the resources with priority ceiling equal to $\hat{\Pi}(t)$. Similarly, rule 3 assumes that only one job is responsible for J's request being denied, because it holds either the requested resource or a resource with priority ceiling $\hat{\Pi}(t)$. We will return shortly to show that these assumptions are true.

Figure 8–10 shows the schedule of the system of jobs whose parameters are listed in Figure 8–8(a) when their accesses to resources are controlled by the priority-ceiling proto-

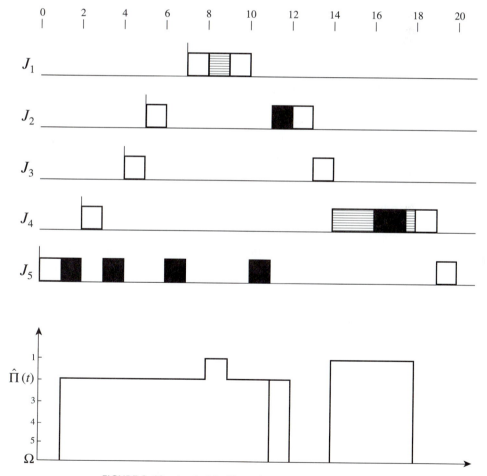

FIGURE 8–10   A schedule illustrating priority-ceiling protocol.

col. As stated earlier, the priority ceilings of the resources *Black* and *Shaded* are 2 and 1, respectively.

1. In the interval (0, 3], this schedule is the same as the schedule shown in Figure 8–8, which is produced under the basic priority-inheritance protocol. In particular, the ceiling of the system at time 1 is Ω. When J_5 requests *Black*, it is allocated the resource according to (i) in part (b) of rule 2. After *Black* is allocated, the ceiling of the system is raised to 2, the priority ceiling of *Black*.

2. At time 3, J_4 requests *Shaded*. *Shaded* is free; however, because the ceiling $\hat{\Pi}(3)$ (= 2) of the system is higher than the priority of J_4, J_4's request is denied according to (ii) in part (b) of rule 2. J_4 is blocked, and J_5 inherits J_4's priority and executes at priority 4.

3. At time 4, J_3 preempts J_5, and at time 5, J_2 preempts J_3. At time 6, J_2 requests *Black* and becomes directly blocked by J_5. Consequently, J_5 inherits the priority 2; it executes until J_1 becomes ready and preempts it. During all this time, the ceiling of the system remains at 2.

4. When J_1 requests *Shaded* at time 8, its priority is higher than the ceiling of the system. Hence, its request is granted according to (i) in part (b) of rule 2, allowing it to enter its critical section and complete by the time 10. At time 10, J_3 and J_5 are ready. The latter has a higher priority (i.e., 2); it resumes.

5. At 11, when J_5 releases *Black*, its priority returns to 5, and the ceiling of the system drops to Ω. J_2 becomes unblocked, is allocated *Black* [according to (i) in part (b) of rule 2], and starts to execute.

6. At time 14, after J_2 and J_3 complete, J_4 has the processor and is granted the resource *Shaded* because its priority is higher than Ω, the ceiling of the system at the time. It starts to execute. The ceiling of the system is raised to 1, the priority ceiling of *Shaded*.

7. At time 16, J_4 requests *Black*, which is free. The priority of J_4 is lower than $\hat{\Pi}(16)$, but J_4 is the job holding the resource (i.e., *Shaded*) whose priority ceiling is equal to $\hat{\Pi}(16)$. Hence, according to (ii) of part (b) of rule 2, J_4 is granted *Black*. It continues to execute. The rest of the schedule is self-explanatory.

Comparing the schedules in Figures 8–8 and 8–10, we see that when priority-ceiling protocol is used, J_4 is blocked at time 3 according to (ii) of part (b) of rule 2. A consequence is that the higher priority jobs J_1, J_2, and J_3 all complete earlier at the expense of the lower priority job J_4. This is the desired effect of the protocol.

8.5.2 Differences between the Priority-Inheritance and Priority-Ceiling Protocols

A fundamental difference between the priority-inheritance and priority-ceiling protocols is that the former is greedy while the latter is not. You recall that the allocation rule (i.e., rule 2) of the priority-inheritance protocol lets the requesting job have a resource whenever the resource is free. In contrast, according to the allocation rule of the priority-ceiling protocol, a job may be denied its requested resource even when the resource is free at the time. (This is what happens to J_4 at time 3 in the above example.) We will return shortly to discuss the consequence of this action.

The priority-inheritance rules of these two protocols are essentially the same. In principle, both rules say that whenever a lower priority job J_l blocks the job J whose request is just denied, the priority of J_l is raised to J's priority $\pi(t)$. The difference arises because of

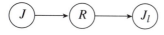

(a) Direct blocking

(b) Priority-inheritance blocking

$\Pi(X)$ is equal to or higher than $\pi(t)$

(c) Avoidance blocking

FIGURE 8–11   Ways for a job to block another job. (a) Direct blocking. (b) Priority-inheritance blocking. (c) Avoidance blocking.

the nongreedy nature of the priority-ceiling protocol. It is possible for J to be blocked by a lower-priority job which does not hold the requested resource according to the priority-ceiling protocol, while this is impossible according to the priority-inheritance protocol.

The wait-for graphs in Figure 8–11 illustrate the three ways in which a job J can be blocked by a lower-priority job when resource accesses are controlled by the priority-ceiling protocol. Of course, J can be directly blocked by a lower-priority job J_l, as shown by the wait-for graph [Figure 8–11(a)]. As a consequence of the priority-inheritance rule, a job J can also be blocked by a lower-priority job J_l which has inherited the priority of a higher-priority job J_h. The wait-for graph in Figure 8–11(b) shows this situation. (For simplicity, we show only the inheritance due to direct blocking.) As stated in Section 8.4, this is priority-inheritance blocking.

The allocation rule may cause a job J to suffer priority-ceiling blocking, which is represented by the graph in Figure 8–11(c). The requesting job J is blocked by a lower-priority job J_l when J requests a resource R that is free at the time. The reason is that J_l holds another resource X whose priority ceiling is equal to or higher than J's priority $\pi(t)$. Rule 3 says that a lower-priority job directly blocking or priority-ceiling blocking the requesting job J inherits J's priority $\pi(t)$.

Priority-ceiling blocking is sometimes referred to as *avoidance blocking*. The reason for this term is that the blocking caused by the priority-ceiling rule is the cost for avoidance of deadlocks among jobs. Hereafter, we will use the terms avoidance blocking and priority-ceiling blocking interchangeably.

8.5.3   Deadlock Avoidance by Priority-Ceiling Protocol

You recall from your study on principles of operating systems that one way to avoid deadlock is to use the ordered-resource technique [Have]. The set of priority ceilings of resources impose a linear order on all the resources. It may not surprise you that deadlock can never occur under the priority-ceiling protocol.

In order to gain a deeper insight into how the protocol works to prevent deadlock, we pause to look at a more complicated example. In the example in Figure 8–12, there are three jobs: J_1, J_2, and J_3 with priorities 1, 2, and 3, respectively. Their release times are 3.5, 1, and 0 and their critical sections are [*Dotted*; 1.5], [*Black*; 2 [*Shaded*; 0.7]], and [*Shaded*; 4.2 [*Black*; 2.3]], respectively. In this schedule, the intervals during which the jobs are in their critical sections are shown as the dotted box (the critical section associated with resource *Dotted*),

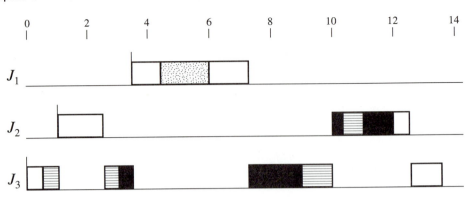

$$\Pi(Dotted) = \pi_1, \Pi(Black) = \Pi(Shaded) = \pi_2$$

FIGURE 8–12 Example illustrating how priority-ceiling protocol prevents deadlock.

shaded boxes (critical sections associated with resource *Shaded*), and black boxes (critical sections associated with resource *Black*).

1. When J_3 requests *Shaded* at time 0.5, no resource is allocated at the time. J_3's request is granted. When job J_2 becomes ready at time 1, it preempts J_3.

2. At time 2.5, J_2 requests *Black*. Because *Shaded* is already allocated to J_3 and has priority ceiling 2, the current ceiling of the system is 2. J_2's priority is 2. According to (ii) of part (b) of rule 2, J_2 is denied *Black*, even though the resource is free. Since J_2 is blocked, J_3 inherits the priority 2 (rule 3), resumes, and starts to execute.

3. When J_3 requests *Black* at time 3, it is holding the resource whose priority ceiling is the current ceiling of the system. According to (ii) of part (b) of rule 2, J_3 is granted the resource *Black*, and it continues to execute.

4. J_3 is preempted again at time 3.5 when J_1 becomes ready. When J_1 requests *Dotted* at time 4.5, the resource is free and the priority of J_1 is higher than the ceiling of the system. (i) of part (b) of rule 2 applies, and *Dotted* is allocated to J_1, allowing the job to enter into its critical section and proceed to complete at 7.3. The description of the segment after this time is left to you.

We now use this example to explain intuitively why priority-ceiling protocol prevents deadlock. To see the rationale behind (ii) of part (b) of rule 2, which leads to the denial of J_2's request for *Black*, we note that at the time *Black* is free but *Shaded* is already allocated to J_3. The fact that the priority ceiling of *Shaded* is 2 indicates that some job with priority 2 requires this resource and this job may very well be J_2, as is indeed the case in this example. If J_2 were allowed to have *Black*, it might later request *Shaded* and would be blocked by J_3. J_3 would execute and might later request *Black*. Denying J_2's access to *Black* is one way to prevent this deadlock. On the other hand, suppose that the priority ceiling of *Shaded* were lower than the priority of J_2. This fact would indicate that J_2 does not require *Shaded*. Moreover, no job with priority equal to or higher than J_2 requires this resource. Consequently, it would not be possible for the job holding *Shaded* to later inherit a higher priority than J_2, preempt J_2, and request *Black*. This is the rationale of (i) of part (b) of rule 2. Indeed, this is the reason that J_1 was granted *Dotted*.

Let us now state in general terms what was said above. At any time t, the priority $\pi(t)$ of a job J being higher than the current ceiling $\hat{\Pi}(t)$ of the system means that (1) job J will not require any of the resources in use at t and (2) jobs with priorities equal to or higher than J will not require any of these resource. In other words, the priority ceiling $\hat{\Pi}(t)$ of the system tells us the subset of all jobs to which we can safely grant free resources at time t; this subset contains all the jobs that have higher priorities than $\hat{\Pi}(t)$. Because of (1), J will not request any resource that is in use at the time. Because of (2), no job holding any resource at the time can inherit a higher priority than J, later preempt J, and request resources allocated to J after t. For these reasons, (i) of part (b) of rule 2 will not lead to any deadlock.

(ii) in part (b) of rule 2 states an exception to the rule that J's request for any resource is denied if its priority is not higher than the ceiling of the system. The exception applies when J is the job holding the resource(s) whose priority ceiling(s) is equal to $\hat{\Pi}(t)$; under this condition, J is granted the resource it requests at t. (This exception is necessary in order to ensure that a job can make progress as it acquires resources. Otherwise, the job would block itself!) J's priority $\pi(t)$ must be equal to $\hat{\Pi}(t)$ when it is granted its requested resource under this condition. Moreover, because of (i) and (ii) in part (b) of rule 2, no other job is holding resources with priority ceiling equal to $\hat{\Pi}(t)$. Consequently, (ii) in part (b) of rule 2 cannot lead to any deadlock.

The following theorem summarizes this discussion. A formal proof of the theorem can be found in [ShRL90].

THEOREM 8.1.   When resource accesses of a system of preemptive, priority-driven jobs on one processor are controlled by the priority-ceiling protocol, deadlock can never occur.

8.5.4 Duration of Blocking

We saw earlier that under the priority-ceiling protocol, a job may be directly blocked, avoidance blocked, and inheritance blocked by lower-priority jobs. A question is whether as a cost of its ability to prevent deadlock, this protocol can cause a job to be blocked for a longer duration than the priority-inheritance protocol. In the worst case, the answer is no. You recall that a job may be blocked for a multiple number of times under the basic priority-inheritance protocol when it conflicts with more than one job over more than one resource. In contrast, under the priority-ceiling protocol, every job is blocked at most once for the duration of a critical section, no matter how many jobs conflict with it. This is stated formally below [ShRL90].

THEOREM 8.2.   When resource accesses of preemptive, priority-driven jobs on one processor are controlled by the priority-ceiling protocol, a job can be blocked for at most the duration of one critical section.

Informal Proof of Theorem 8.2.   Rather than proving the theorem formally, we use an intuitive argument to convince you that the theorem is true. There are two parts to this argument: (1) When a job becomes blocked, it is blocked by only one job, and (2) a job which blocks another job cannot be blocked in turn by some other job. State (2) in another way, *there can be no transitive blocking under the priority-ceiling protocol.*

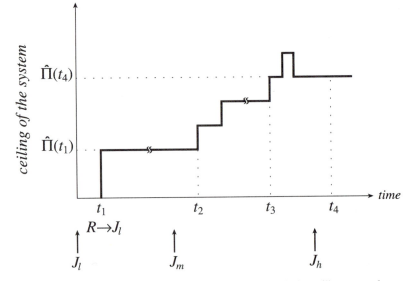

FIGURE 8–13   Scenario illustrating a property of basic priority-ceiling protocol.

We use the scenario in Figure 8–13 to to convince you that (1) is true. There are three jobs, J_l, J_m and J_h. Their release times are indicated by the arrows below the graph, which plots the ceiling of the system as a function of time. The priority π_l of J_l is lower than the priority π_m of J_m, which is in turn lower than the priority π_h of J_h. Suppose that at time t_1, J_l requests and is granted a resource R. As a consequence, the ceiling of the system rises to $\hat{\Pi}(t_1)$, which is the priority ceiling of R. Later, J_m preempts J_l and acquires some resources (say at and after t_2) while it executes. Clearly this is possible only if its priority π_m is higher than $\hat{\Pi}(t_1)$. Suppose that at time t_4, J_h becomes blocked. We note that it is not possible for J_h to be directly blocked by J_l. Otherwise, the ceiling of the system would be at least as high as π_h when J_m requests resources, and J_m would not be able to acquire any resource. If all the resources allocated since t_2 are held by J_m at time t_4, we have shown that J_m is the only job blocking J_h. On the other hand, suppose that at some time t_3 before t_4, a resource R' is allocated to some other job J_k. Then, J_m cannot be blocking J_h for the same reason that J_l cannot be blocking J_h.

This inductive argument allows us to conclude that J_h is either directly blocked or priority-ceiling blocked by only one job, and this job holds the resource that has the highest priority ceiling among all the resources in use when J_h becomes blocked. For simplicity, we have assumed in this scenario that all three jobs have their assigned priorities. It is easy to see that above argument remains valid even when the jobs have inherited priorities, as long as the priority of J_h is the highest and the priority of J_l is the lowest.

To show that (2) is true, let us suppose that the three jobs J_l, J_m and J_h are blocked transitively. Because the jobs are scheduled according to their priorities, it must be that J_l is preempted after having acquired some resource(s) and later at t, J_m is granted some other resource(s). This can happen only if J_m and all the jobs with higher priorities do not require any of the resources held by J_l at t. Until J_m completes, J_l cannot execute and acquire some other resources. Consequently, J_l cannot inherit a priority equal to or higher than $\pi_m(t)$ until J_m

completes. If transitive blocking were to occur, J_m would inherit $\pi_h(t)$, and J_l would inherit a priority higher than $\pi_m(t)$ indirectly. This leads to a contradiction. Hence, the supposition that the three jobs are transitively blocked must be false.

Computation of Blocking Time.   Theorem 8.2 makes it easy for us to compute an upper bound to the amount of time a job may be blocked due to resource conflicts. We call this upper bound the *blocking time (due to resource conflicts)* of the job.

To illustrate how to do this computation, let us consider the system of jobs whose resource requirements are given by Figure 8–14. As always, the jobs are indexed in order of decreasing priorities. We see that J_1 can be directed blocked by J_4 for 1 unit of time. The blocking time $b_1(rc)$ of J_1 is clearly one. Although J_2 and J_3 do not require the resource *Black*, they can be priority-inheritance blocked by J_4 since J_4 can inherit priority π_1. Hence, the blocking times $b_2(rc)$ and $b_3(rc)$ are also one.

Figure 8–15(a) shows a slightly more complicated example. Even for this small system, it is error prone if we compute the blocking times of all jobs by inspection, as we did earlier. The tables in Figure 8–15(b) give us a systematic way. There is a row for each job that can be blocked. (In these tables, there is a row for every job except J_6.) The tables list only the nonzero entries; all the other entries are zero. Since jobs are not blocked by higher-priority jobs, the entries at and below "*" in each column are zero.

The leftmost part is the direct-blocking table. It lists for each job the duration for which it can be directly blocked by each of the lower-priority jobs. The entries in this table come directly from the resource requirement graph of the system. Indeed, for the purpose of calculating the blocking times of the jobs, this table gives a complete specification of the resource requirements of the jobs.

The middle part of Figure 8–15(b) is the priority-inheritance blocking table. It lists the maximum duration for which each job can be priority-inheritance blocked by each of the lower-priority jobs. For example, J_6 can inherit priority π_1 of J_1 for 2 units of time when it directly blocks J_1. Hence, it can block all the other jobs for 2 units for time. In the table, we show 2 units of inheritance blocking time of J_2 and J_3 by J_6. However, because J_6 can also inherit π_3 for 4 units of time, it can block J_4 and J_5 for 4 units of time. This is the reason that the entries in the fourth and fifth rows of column 6 are 4. In general, a systematic way to get the entries in each column of this table from the entries in the corresponding column of the direct-blocking table is as follows. *The entry at column k and row i of the inheritance blocking table is the maximum of all the entries in column k and rows $1, 2, \ldots, i - 1$ of the direct-blocking table.*

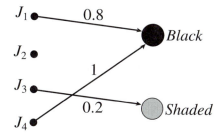

FIGURE 8–14   Example on duration of blocking.

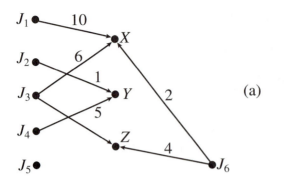

(a)

	Directly blocked by					Priority-inher blocked by					Priority-ceiling blocked by				
	J_2	J_3	J_4	J_5	J_6	J_2	J_3	J_4	J_5	J_6	J_2	J_3	J_4	J_5	J_6
J_1		6			2										
J_2	*		5			*	6			2	*	6			2
J_3		*		4			*	5		2		*	5		2
J_4			*					*		4			*		4
J_5				*					*	4				*	

(b)

FIGURE 8–15   Example illustrating the computation of blocking times.

The rightmost table in Figure 8–15(b) is the avoidance (priority-ceiling) blocking table. It lists the maximum duration for which each job can be avoidance blocked by each lower-priority job. Again, let us focus on column 6. When J_6 holds resource X (whose priority ceiling is the highest in the system), it avoidance blocks all the jobs which require any resource. Similarly, when it holds Z, it avoidance blocks J_4. Therefore, except for the entry in row 5, all entries in column 6 of the avoidance blocking table are the same as the corresponding entries in column 6 of the inheritance blocking table. J_5 does not require any resource and is never directly or avoidance blocked. In general, *when the priorities of all the jobs are distinct, the entries in the avoidance blocking table are equal to corresponding entries in the priority-inheritance blocking table, except for jobs which do not require any resources.* Jobs which do not require any resource are never avoidance blocked, just as they are never directly blocked.

The blocking time $b_i(rc)$ of each job J_i is equal to the maximum value of all the entries in the ith row of the three tables. From Figure 8–15(b), we have $b_i(rc)$ is equal to 6, 6, 5, 4, 4, and 0 for $i = 1, 2, \ldots, 6$, respectively

For this example, every entry in the avoidance blocking table is either equal to or smaller than the corresponding entries in the direct blocking or inheritance blocking tables. Since we are taking the maximum value of the entries of each row, there is no need for us to compute the avoidance blocking table. Indeed, we do not need this table whenever the priorities of all the jobs are distinct. When the priorities of jobs are not distinct, a job may be avoidance blocked by a job of equal priority. The avoidance blocking table gives this information. For example, suppose that in addition to the jobs in Figure 8–15(a), there is a job J_1' whose priority is also π_1, and this job requires a resource V for 9 units of time. Then the blocking time of J_1' is 10, the amount of time J_1 holds the resource X and priority-ceiling blocks J_1'. Similarly, the blocking time of J_1 is 9, the duration for which it is priority-ceiling blocked by J_1'. In this case, we need the avoidance blocking table to give us these blocking times.

In Problem 8.14, you are asked to provide a pseudocode description of an algorithm that computes the blocking time $b_i(rc)$ of all the jobs from the resource requirement graph of the system. For the sake of efficiency, you may want to first identify for each job J_i the subset of all the jobs that may block the job. This subset is called the *blocking set* of J_i. (In our simple example, J_5 is not included in the blocking set of any other job, since it cannot block any job. The blocking set of J_i includes all the lower-priority jobs other than J_5.)

8.5.5   Fixed-Priority Scheduling and Priority-Ceiling Protocol

The priority-ceiling protocol is an excellent algorithm for controlling the accesses to resources of periodic tasks when the tasks are scheduled on a fixed-priority basis. It is reasonable to assume that the resources required by every job of every task and the maximum execution times of their critical sections are known a priori, just like the other task parameters. All the jobs in each periodic task have the same priority. Hence, the priority ceiling of each resource is the highest priority of all the tasks that require the resource. This makes it possible for us to analyze and determine the potential of resource contentions among tasks statically. The effect of resource contentions on the schedulability of the tasks can be taken care of by including the blocking time $b_i(rc)$ in the schedulability test of the system.

For example, suppose that the jobs in Figure 8–14 belong to four periodic tasks. The tasks are $T_1 = (\varepsilon, 2, 0.8; [Black; 0.8])$, $T_2 = (\varepsilon, 2.2, 0.4)$, $T_3 = (\varepsilon, 5, 0.2; [Shaded; 0.2])$, and $T_4 = (10, 1.0; [Black; 1.0])$, where ε is a small positive number. For all i, J_i in Figure 8–14 is a job in T_i. Figure 8–16 shows the initial segment of the schedule of the tasks according to the rate-monotonic algorithm and priority-ceiling protocol. We see that T_2 misses it is deadline at time $2.2 + \varepsilon$. A schedulability test can predict this miss. The time-demand function of T_2 is equal to 2.2 (i.e., $0.8 + 0.4 + 1.0$) in $(0, 2.0 + \varepsilon]$ when the blocking time $b_2(rc) = 1.0$ of T_2 is included and becomes 3.0 at $2.0 + \varepsilon$ (i.e., the beginning of the second period of T_1). Obviously, the time supply by T_2's first deadline at $2.2 + \varepsilon$ cannot meet this demand. Similarly, if the jobs J_i, for $i = 1, 2, \ldots, 6$, in Figure 8–15 are jobs in periodic tasks T_i, respectively, we can take the effect of resource conflicts into account in our determination of whether the tasks are schedulable by including the blocking time $b_i(rc)$ computed above in the schedulability test.

To summarize this section, we recall that two factors contribute to the time-demand function of each task in addition to the execution times of its jobs and execution times of equal and higher-priority jobs. They are blocking time and context-switching time. When the system is scheduled on a fixed-priority basis and uses the priority-ceiling protocol, we can compute the blocking time $b_i(rc)$ of each task T_i due to its resource conflicts with other tasks in the way described above. After we have thus obtained $b_i(rc)$, we include this blocking factor with the other types of blocking times (e.g., due to nonpreemptivity of lower-priority

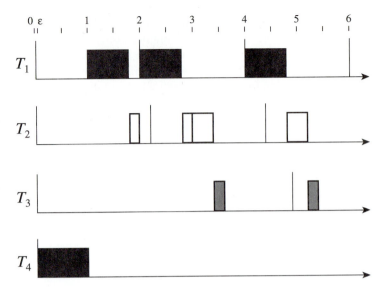

FIGURE 8–16   Example on fixed-priority scheduling and priority-ceiling protocol. ($T_1 = (\varepsilon, 2, 0.8; [Black; 0.8])$, $T_2 = (\varepsilon, 2.2, 0.4)$, $T_3 = (\varepsilon, 5, 0.2; [Shaded; 0.2])$, $T_4 = (10, 1; [Black; 1.0])$).

jobs and self-suspension) which the task may suffer to obtain the total blocking time b_i of the task.

In Section 6.8, we showed that each job in a system of fixed-priority tasks suffers at most two context switches when the tasks are independent. When the tasks contend for resources under the control of the basic priority-ceiling protocol, each job can be blocked at most once. In particular, a job that requires some resources may be blocked and lose the processor when it requests some resource and, as a consequence, suffers two additional context switches. In contrast, a job which does not require any resource suffers only two context switches: one when it starts and one when it ends. (You recall that the context-switch time when a job is preempted is attributed to the preempting job.) Hence, to account for the context switch overhead in schedulability test, we add

1. *two CS to the execution time of each task that does not require any resource and*
2. *four CS to the execution time of each task that requires one or more resource,*

where CS is the maximum time to complete a context switch.[1]

8.6   STACK-BASED, PRIORITY-CEILING (CEILING-PRIORITY) PROTOCOL

In this section, we give two different definitions of a protocol that is simpler than the priority-ceiling protocol but has the same worst-case performance as the priority-ceiling protocol. The different definitions arise from two different motivations: to provide stack-sharing capability

---

[1]It is important to remember the assumption that no job ever suspends itself. We will discuss the effect of self-suspension in Section 8.11.

and to simplify the priority-ceiling protocol. They led to the two different names of the same protocol.

8.6.1 Motivation and Definition of Stack-Sharing Priority-Ceiling Protocol

A resource in the system is the run-time stack. Thus far, we have assumed that each job has its own run-time stack. Sometimes, especially in systems where the number of jobs is large, it may be necessary for the jobs to share a common run-time stack, in order to reduce overall memory demand. (According to Baker [Bake91], if there are 10 jobs at each of 10 priority levels, the storage saving is 90 percent.) Space in the (shared) stack is allocated to jobs contiguously in the last-in-first-out manner. When a job J executes, its stack space is on the top of the stack. The space is freed when the job completes. When J is preempted, the preempting job has the stack space above J's. J can resume execution only after all the jobs holding stack space above its space complete, free their stack spaces, and leave J's stack space on the top of the stack again.

Clearly, if all the jobs share a common stack, schedules such as the one in Figure 8–10 should not be allowed. You can see that if the jobs were to execute according this schedule, J_5 would resume after J_4 is blocked. Since J_4 is not complete, it still holds the space on the top of the stack at this time. The stack space of J_5 would be noncontiguous after this time, which is not allowed, or J_5 would not be allowed to resume, which would result in a deadlock between J_5 and J_4 (i.e., J_5 holds *Black* and avoidance blocks J_4 and J_4 holds the "top of the stack" and blocks J_5).

From this example, we see that to ensure deadlock-free sharing of the run-time stack among jobs, we must ensure that no job is ever blocked because it is denied some resource once its execution begins. This observation leads to the following modified version of the priority-ceiling protocol, called the *stack-based, priority-ceiling protocol*. It is essentially the same as the stack-based protocol designed by Baker [Bake91], which we will describe in the next section. Like Baker's protocol, *this protocol allows jobs to share the run-time stack if they never self-suspend*.

In the statement of the rules of the stack-based, priority-ceiling protocol, we again use the term (current) ceiling $\hat{\Pi}(t)$ of the system, which is the highest-priority ceiling of all the resources that are in use at time t. Ω is a nonexisting priority level that is lower than the lowest priority of all jobs. The current ceiling is Ω when all resources are free.

Rules Defining Basic Stack-Based, Priority-Ceiling Protocol

    0. *Update of the Current Ceiling*: Whenever all the resources are free, the ceiling of the system is Ω. The ceiling $\hat{\Pi}(t)$ is updated each time a resource is allocated or freed.

    1. *Scheduling Rule*: After a job is released, it is blocked from starting execution until its assigned priority is higher than the current ceiling $\hat{\Pi}(t)$ of the system. At all times, jobs that are not blocked are scheduled on the processor in a priority-driven, preemptive manner according to their assigned priorities.

    2. *Allocation Rule*: Whenever a job requests a resource, it is allocated the resource.

We note that according to the scheduling rule, when a job begins to execute, all the resources it will ever need during its execution are free. (Otherwise, if one of the resources it will need is not free, the ceiling of the system is equal to or higher than its priority.) This is why the allocation rule is as simple as stated above. More importantly, *no job is ever blocked once its execution begins*. Likewise, when a job J is preempted, all the resources the preempting job will require are free, ensuring that the preempting job can always complete so J can resume. Consequently, *deadlock can never occur*.

The schedule in Figure 8–17 shows how the system of jobs in Figure 8–10 would be scheduled if the stack-based, priority-ceiling protocol were used instead of the basic priority-ceiling protocol. To better illustrate the stack-based protocol, we let J_2 be released at 4.8 and the execution time of the critical section of J_2 be 1.2. At time 2 when J_4 is released, it is blocked from starting because its priority is not higher than the ceiling of the system, which is equal to 2 at the time. This allows J_5 to continue execution. For the same reason, J_3 does not start execution when it is released. When J_2 is released at time 4.8, it cannot start execution because the ceiling of the system is 2. At time 5, the resource held by J_5 becomes free and the ceiling of the system is at Ω. Consequently, J_2 starts to execute since it has the highest priority among all the jobs ready at the time. As expected, when it requests the resource *Black* at time 6, the resource is free. It acquires the resource and continues to execute. At time 7 when J_1 is released, its priority is higher than the ceiling of the system, which is 2 at the time. (Again, this fact indicates that the resource *Shaded*, which it will require later, is free.) J_1, therefore, preempts J_2 and holds the space on the top of the stack until it completes at time 10. J_2 then resumes and completes at 11. Afterwards, J_3, J_4, and J_5 complete in the order of their priorities.

From this example, we see that the scheduling rule of the stack-based priority-ceiling protocol achieves the same objective as the more complicated priority-inheritance rule of the basic priority-ceiling protocol. (As a consequence of this rule, J_5 is not preempted by J_4 and J_3 while it holds *Black*.) When we compare the schedule in Figure 8–17 with the schedule in Figure 8–10, which is produced by the basic priority-ceiling protocol, we see that the higher-

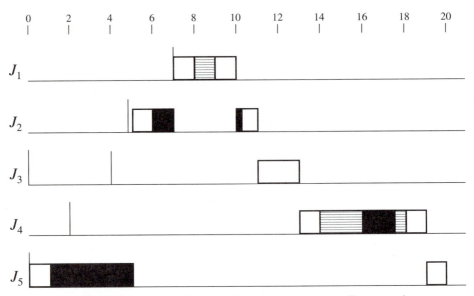

FIGURE 8–17   Schedule illustrating the stack-based, priority-ceiling protocol.

priority jobs J_1, J_2 and J_3 either complete earlier than or at the same time as when they are scheduled according to the basic priority-ceiling protocol.

8.6.2   Definition of Ceiling-Priority Protocol

As we will see shortly, the worst-case performance of the stack-based and the basic priority-ceiling protocols are the same. The former is considerably simpler and has a lower context switching overhead. This is a good reason for using the stack-based version if jobs never self-suspend even when the jobs have their own stacks. Indeed, the stack-based version is the protocol supported by the Real-Time Systems Annex of Ada95 [Cohe96]. In Section 8.3, we mentioned that it is called the *ceiling-priority protocol*. The following rules defines it more formally.

Rules Defining the Ceiling-Priority Protocol

  1. *Scheduling Rule*:
   (a) Every job executes at its assigned priority when it does not hold any resource. Jobs of the same priority are scheduled on the FIFO basis.
   (b) The priority of each job holding any resource is equal to the highest of the priority ceilings of all resources held by the job.
  2. *Allocation Rule*: Whenever a job requests a resource, it is allocated the resource.

We note that when jobs never self-suspend, the stack-based priority-ceiling and ceiling-priority protocols are the same. By saying these protocols are the same we mean that they will produce the same schedule for all jobs. (If you are not convinced, you may want to apply this set of rules on the example given by Figure 8–8(a). The schedule you will produce should be same as one in Figure 8–17.) *The two sets of rules give two implementations of the same protocol.*

Sometimes, jobs of equal priority are scheduled on the round-robin basis. We must modify the definition of the ceiling-priority protocol to make it work for these jobs. This modification is left as an exercise to you in Problem 8.5.

8.6.3   Blocking Time and Context-Switching Overhead

Because of the following theorem [Bake91], we can use the same method to find the blocking time $b_i(rc)$ of every job J_i for both versions of the priority-ceiling protocol.

THEOREM 8.3.   The longest blocking time suffered by every job is the same for the stack-based and basic priority-ceiling protocols.

To see why this theorem is true, we observe first that a higher-priority job J_h can be blocked only by the currently executing job J_l under the stack-based priority-ceiling protocol. The reason is that if a job J_l can start to execute at t, its priority is higher than the ceiling of the system at t. This means that none of the resources in use at t are required by J_l or any higher-priority job. Furthermore, similar arguments allow us to conclude that under the stack-based protocol, no job is ever blocked due to resource conflict more than once.

Now let us suppose that under the stack-based priority-ceiling protocol, a job J_h is blocked by the currently executing job J_l. This can happen only if J_h is released after J_l has acquired a resource X whose priority ceiling is equal to or higher than the priority π_h of J_h and at the time when J_h is released, J_l still holds X. The occurrence of this sequence of events is not dependent on the protocol used; the sequence can also occur under the basic priority-ceiling protocol. Moreover, under this circumstance, J_h is also blocked by J_l under the basic priority-ceiling protocol. In the worst case, J_h is blocked for as long as the job J_l holds such a resource. Theorem 8.3 follows from the fact that we can repeat this argument for every lower-priority job which can block J_h.

While the (worst-case) blocking time of individual jobs and periodic tasks are the same for both versions of the priority-ceiling protocol, the context-switch overhead is smaller under the stack-based version. Because no job is ever blocked once its execution starts, no job ever suffers more than two context switches. In particular, to take into account the context-switching overhead in the schedulability analysis of a system of periodic tasks scheduled according to a fixed-priority algorithm and stack-based priority-ceiling protocol, we add $2CS$ to the execution time of every task.

8.7   USE OF PRIORITY-CEILING PROTOCOL IN DYNAMIC-PRIORITY SYSTEMS

While both versions of the priority-ceiling protocol are relatively simple to implement and perform well when periodic tasks are scheduled on a fixed-priority basis, it is another matter in a dynamic-priority system. In a dynamic-priority system, the priorities of the periodic tasks change with time while the resources required by each task remain constant. As a consequence, the priority ceilings of the resources may change with time.

As an example, let us look at the EDF schedule of two tasks $T_1 = (2, 0.9)$ and $T_2 = (5, 2.3)$ in Figure 6–4. In its first two periods (i.e., from time 0 to 4), T_1 has priority 1 while T_2 has priority 2, but from time 4 to 5, T_2 has priority 1 and T_1 has priority 2. Suppose that the task T_1 requires a resource X while T_2 does not. The priority ceiling of X is 1 from time 0 to 4 and becomes 2 from time 4 to 5, and so on.

For some dynamic systems, we can still use the priority-ceiling protocol to control resource accesses provided we update the priority ceiling of each resource and the ceiling of the system each time task priorities change. This is the approach taken by the dynamic-priority-ceiling protocol proposed by Chen and Lin [ChLi]. As it will become evident shortly, except for this update, the priority-ceiling protocol can be applied without modification in job-level fixed-priority systems. In such a system, the priorities of jobs, once assigned, remain fixed with respect to each other. In particular, the order in which jobs in the ready job queue are sorted among themselves does not alter each time a newly released job is inserted in the queue. This assumption is true for systems scheduled on the EDF and LIFO basis, for example.

8.7.1   Implementation of Priority-Ceiling Protocol in Dynamic-Priority Systems

One way to implement the basic priority-ceiling protocol in a job-level fixed-priority system is to update the priority ceilings of all resources whenever a new job is released. Specifically, when a new job is released, its priority relative to all the jobs in the ready queue is assigned according to the given dynamic-priority algorithm. Then, the priority ceilings of all the resources are updated based on the new priorities of the tasks, and the ceiling of the system is updated based on the new priority ceilings of the resources. The new priority ceilings are used until they are updated again upon the next job release. Chen and Lin [ChLi] showed that the protocol remains effective (i.e., it prevents deadlock and transitive blocking and no job is ever blocked for longer than the length of one critical section) in a job-level fixed-priority system.

The example in Figure 8–18 illustrates the use of this protocol in an EDF system. The system shown here has three tasks: $T_1 = (0.5, 2.0, 0.2; [Black; 0.2])$, $T_2 = (3.0, 1.5; [Shaded; 0.7])$, and $T_1 = (5.0, 1.2; [Black; 1.0 [Shaded; 0.4])$. The priority ceilings of the two resources *Black* and *Shaded* are updated at times 0, 0.5, 2.5, 3, 4.5, 5, 6, and so on. We use consecutive positive integers to denote the priorities of all the ready jobs, the highest priority being 1.[2] In the following description, we focus primarily on how priority ceilings of resources and ceiling of the systems are updated and leave to you many details on how the priority-ceiling protocol works to produce the schedule segment shown in this figure. To emphasize that the priority ceiling of a resource R_i may change with time, we denote it by $\Pi_t(R_i)$.

1. At time 0, there are only two ready jobs, $J_{2,1}$ and $J_{3,1}$. $J_{2,1}$ (and hence T_2) has priority 1 while T_3 has priority 2, the priority of $J_{3,1}$. The priority ceilings of *Black* and *Shaded* are 2 and 1, respectively. Since $J_{2,1}$ has a higher priority, it begins to execute. Because no resource is in use, the ceiling of the system is Ω. At time 0.3, $J_{2,1}$ acquires *Shaded*, and the ceiling of the system rises from Ω to 1, the priority ceiling of *Shaded*.

2. At time 0.5, $J_{1,1}$ is released, and it has a higher priority than $J_{2,1}$ and $J_{3,1}$. Now the priorities of T_1, T_2, and T_3 become 1, 2, and 3, respectively. The priority ceiling Π_t (*Black*) of *Black* is 1, the priority of $J_{1,1}$ and T_1. The priority ceiling Π_t (*Shaded*) of *Shaded* becomes 2 because the priority of $J_{2,1}$ and T_2 is now 2. The ceiling of the system based on these updated values is 2. For this reason, $J_{1,1}$ is granted the resource *Black*. The ceiling of the system is 1 until $J_{1,1}$ releases *Black* and completes at time 0.7. Afterwards, $J_{2,1}$ continues to execute, and the ceiling of the system is again 2. When $J_{2,1}$ completes at time 1.7, $J_{3,1}$ commences to execute and later acquires the resources as shown.

3. At time 2.5, $J_{1,2}$ is released. It has priority 1, while $J_{3,1}$ has priority 2. This update of task priorities leads to no change in priority ceilings of the resources. Since the ceiling of the system is at 1, $J_{1,2}$ becomes blocked at 2.5. At time 2.9, $J_{3,1}$ releases *Black*, and $J_{1,2}$ commences execution.

4. At time 3.0, only T_1 and T_2 have jobs ready for execution. Their priorities are 1 and 2, respectively. The priority ceilings of the resources remain unchanged until time 4.5.

5. At time 4.5, the new job $J_{1,3}$ of T_1 has a later deadline than $J_{2,2}$. (Again, T_3 has no ready job.) Hence, the priority of T_1 is 2 while the priority of T_2 becomes 1. This change in task priorities causes the priority ceilings of *Black* and *Shaded* to change to 2 and 1, respectively.

6. At time 5 when $J_{3,2}$ is released, it is the only job ready for execution at the time and hence has the highest priority. The priority ceilings of both resources are 1. These values remain until time 6.

---

[2]Each time a job is completed, it is removed from the ready job queue. Therefore, when priorities and priority-ceiling values are recomputed, some task may not have any job in the ready job queue. We can either ignore such a task or let it have the lowest (nonexisting) priority Ω until the next update instant. In this example, we choose the former for the sake of simplicity.

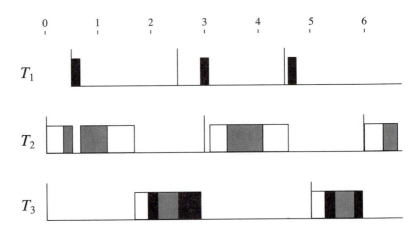

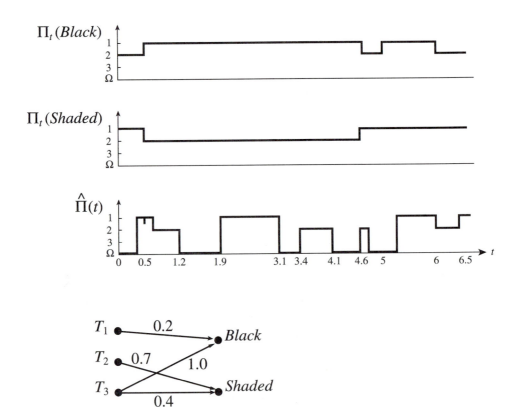

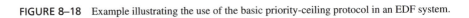

FIGURE 8–18   Example illustrating the use of the basic priority-ceiling protocol in an EDF system.

7. At time 6, both $J_{2,3}$ and $J_{3,2}$ are ready, and the former has an earlier deadline. We now have the same condition as at time 0.

In a system with ρ resources, each of which is required by $\bar{n}$ periodic tasks on average, the time required to update the priority ceilings of all resources is $O(\rho)$ each time a new job is released. This is a significant amount of overhead. For systems where the release-time jitters are negligible, we can save this run-time overhead by precomputing and storing the priority ceilings of all the resources for every time interval between consecutive releases of all N jobs in the entire hyperperiod. Each time a new job is released, we use the precomputed priority ceilings of the interval beginning from the release time of the job. The storage overhead for this purpose is $O(N\rho)$.

It is easy to see that the stack-based priority-ceiling protocol can also be used without modification for job-level fixed-priority assignments. Each time a new job is released, the question is whether its priority is sufficiently high for it to join the ready job queue.

8.7.2 Duration of Blocking

Although in principle every job is blocked at most once for the duration of one outermost critical section, the worst-case blocking time $b_i(rc)$ due to resource conflict of each task is in general larger in a dynamic-priority system than in a fixed-priority system. In particular, when it is possible for the jobs in every task to have a higher priority and preempt jobs in every other task, the worst-case blocking time $b_i(rc)$ of a task T_i is the execution time of the longest critical sections of all tasks other than T_i. For example, suppose that the jobs in Figure 8–15 are in six periodic tasks which are scheduled on the LIFO basis. The worst-case blocking times of all tasks except T_1 (i.e., the task containing J_1) are equal to 10, and the worst-case blocking time of T_1 is 6.

On the other hand, in a deadline-driven system, jobs with relative deadline D_i are never preempted by jobs with relative deadlines equal to or larger than D_i. Hence if the job J_i in Figure 8–16 belongs to task T_i, for $i = 1, 2, \ldots, 6$, and the tasks are indexed in order of increasing relative deadlines, then the worst-case blocking times $b_i(rc)$ are 6, 6, 5, 4, 4, and 0 when the tasks are scheduled in the EDF basis.

*8.7.3 Applicability of the Basic Priority-Ceiling Protocol in Job-Level Dynamic-Priority Systems

As discussed in Chapter 6, jobs do not have fixed priorities when scheduled according to some job-level dynamic-priority algorithm. As an example, we consider a system that contains three tasks $T_1 = (2, 1.0)$, $T_2 = (2.5, 1.0)$, and $T_3 = (0.8, 10, 0.5)$ and is scheduled according to the nonstrict LST algorithm. Initially, $J_{1,1}$ has priority 1 while $J_{2,1}$ has priority 2. However, at time 0.8 when $J_{3,1}$ is released and the slacks of all the jobs are updated, the slack of $J_{1,1}$ is still 1.0, but the slack of $J_{2,1}$ is only 0.7. Hence, $J_{2,1}$ has the highest priority, while the priority of $J_{1,1}$ drops to 2.

Another example is where the tasks are scheduled in a round-robin manner. This scheduling discipline can be implemented by giving the highest priority to jobs in turn, each for a fixed slice of time.

The allocation rule of the basic priority-ceiling protocol remains effective as a means to avoid deadlock and transitive blocking. To see that deadlock between two jobs J_i and J_k

can never occur, let us suppose that both jobs require X and Y. As soon as either X or Y is granted to one of the jobs, the ceiling of the system becomes π_i or π_k whichever is higher. As a consequence, it is no longer possible for the other job to acquire any resource. For this reason, it is not possible for J_i and J_k to circularly wait for one another, even though their priorities may change.

To see why it is not possible for any three jobs to block each other transitively, let us suppose that at time t, J_i is granted some resource X. Moreover, sometime afterwards, J_k is granted another resource Y. This is possible only when J_k does not require X. Therefore, it is not possible for J_k to be directly blocked by J_i, while it blocks some other job J_j.

A remaining question is whether priority inheritance is still effective in preventing uncontrolled priority inversion and keeping the delay suffered by every job due to priority inversion bounded from above. Clearly the statement of the priority-inheritance rule given in Section 8.4 needs to be modified in order to make sense. While the priority of the job J requesting and being denied a resource is higher than the priority of the job J_l blocking J at the time, the assigned priority of J_l may become higher than the priority of J at some later time. One way to take this fact into account is to let the blocking job J_l execute at the highest of the priority ceilings of all resources it holds.

8.8   PREEMPTION-CEILING PROTOCOL

We can avoid paying the time or storage overhead of the dynamic-priority-ceiling protocol described above for a class of dynamic-priority systems, which includes deadline-driven systems. We call systems in this class fixed preemption-level systems and will define this term shortly. For a fixed preemption-level system, Baker [Bake91] has a simpler approach to control resource accesses. The approach is based on the clever observation that the potentials of resource contentions in such a dynamic-priority system do not change with time, just as in fixed-priority systems, and hence can be analyzed statically. The observation is supported by the following facts:

1. The fact that a job J_h has a higher priority than another job J_l and they both require some resource does not imply that J_l can directly block J_h. This blocking can occur only when it is possible for J_h to preempt J_l.

2. For some dynamic priority assignments, it is possible to determine a priori the possibility that jobs in each periodic task will preempt the jobs in other periodic tasks.

Because of fact 1, when determining whether a free resource can be granted to a job, it is not necessary to be concerned with the resource requirements of all higher-priority jobs; only those that can preempt the job. Fact 2 means that for some dynamic priority systems, the possibility that each periodic task will preempt every other periodic task does not change with time, just as in fixed-priority systems. We have already seen that in a deadline-driven system, no job in a periodic task with a smaller relative deadline is ever preempted by jobs in periodic tasks with identical or larger relative deadlines, despite the fact that some jobs in the latter may have higher priorities.

8.8.1   Preemption Levels of Jobs and Periodic Tasks

The possibility that a job J_i will preempt another job is captured by the parameter *preemption level* ψ_i of J_i. The preemption levels of jobs are functions of their priorities and release times. According to a *valid preemption-level assignment*, for every pair of jobs J_i and J_k, the preemption level ψ_i of J_i being equal to or higher than the preemption level ψ_k of J_k implies that it is never possible for J_k to preempt J_i. Stated in another way,

Validity Condition: If π_i is higher than π_k and $r_i > r_k$, then ψ_i is higher than ψ_k.

Given the priorities and release times of all jobs, this condition gives us a partial assignment of preemption levels, that is, the preemption levels of a subset of all jobs. The preemption levels of jobs that are not given by the above rule are valid as long as the linear order over all jobs defined by the preemption-level assignment does not violate the validity condition.

As an example, we return to the system of jobs in Figure 8–8. Since jobs with higher priorities are released later, it is possible for every job to preempt all the jobs with lower priorities than itself. In this case, the preemption levels of the jobs dictated by the the validity condition give us a complete assignment. For these jobs, we can simply let the preemption levels of the jobs be equal to their respective priorities.

Figure 8–19 gives another example. As usual, the five jobs are indexed in decreasing priorities. Their release times are such that $r_4 < r_5 < r_3 < r_1 < r_2$. We note that J_1, the job with the highest priority, has a later release time than J_3, J_4, and J_5. Hence, J_1 should have a higher preemption level than these three jobs. However, it is never possible for J_1 to preempt J_2 because J_1 has an earlier release time, and it is never possible for J_2 to preempt J_1, because J_2 has a lower priority. We therefore give these two jobs the same preemption level. Similarly, J_3 should have a higher preemption level than J_4 and J_5, and we can give J_4 and J_5 the same preemption level. In summary, we can assign ψ_i for $i = 1, 2, 3, 4,$ and 5 the values 1, 1, 2, 3, and 3, respectively; it is easy see that this is a valid preemption level assignment. (Again, a smaller integer represents a higher preemption level.) Alternatively, we can assign preemption levels according to the release times of the jobs: the earlier the release time, the lower the preemption level. This assignment also satisfies the validity condition. The resultant preemption levels are 2, 1, 3, 5, and 4, respectively.

Let us now return to periodic tasks. When periodic tasks are scheduled on the EDF basis, a valid preemption-level assignment is according to the relative deadlines of jobs: the smaller the relative deadline, the higher the preemption level. (An assumption here is that

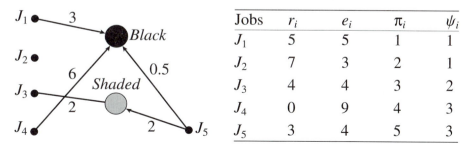

Jobs	r_i	e_i	π_i	ψ_i
J_1	5	5	1	1
J_2	7	3	2	1
J_3	4	4	3	2
J_4	0	9	4	3
J_5	3	4	5	3

FIGURE 8–19   A schedule according to the preeption-ceiling protocol.

either release-time jitters are negligible or the relative deadlines of all jobs remain fixed despite release-time jitters.) For this preemption-level assignment, all the jobs in every periodic task in a deadline-driven system have the same preemption level. This is an example of fixed preemption-level systems. A system of periodic tasks is a *fixed preemption-level system* if there is a valid assignment of preemption levels to all jobs such that all the jobs in every task have the same preemption level. Clearly, all fixed-priority systems are also fixed preemption-level systems. Indeed, an obvious preemption-level assignment in a fixed-priority system is to make the preemption level of each job equal to its priority.

When there is no chance of confusion, we call the preemption level of all the jobs in a fixed preemption-level task T_i the *preemption level of the task* and denote it by ψ_i. We index periodic tasks in a fixed preemption-level system according to their preemption levels: the higher the level, the smaller the index. For example, suppose that the system of periodic tasks in Figure 8–16 are scheduled on the EDF basis. The preemption levels of the tasks T_1, T_2, T_3, and T_4 are 1, 2, 3 and 4, respectively, because the relative deadlines of the tasks are 2, 2.2, 5, and 10, respectively.

In Chapter 6, we pointed out that when priorities are assigned on the FIFO basis or the LIFO basis, periodic tasks have dynamic priorities. In a FIFO system, no job is ever preempted. This is a degenerate fixed preemption-level system where all periodic tasks have the same preemption level. In contrast, periodic tasks scheduled on the LIFO basis have varying preemption levels. To illustrate, let us consider the system of three tasks T_1, T_2, and T_3 in Figure 8–18. Suppose that the priorities of jobs in them are assigned on the LIFO basis. $J_{1,1}$ is released later than $J_{2,1}$ and $J_{3,1}$, has a higher priority than they and hence can preempt these jobs. Also, $J_{2,2}$ can preempt $J_{1,2}$ and $J_{3,1}$, and $J_{3,2}$ can preempt $J_{1,3}$ and $J_{2,2}$. Suppose that we let the preemption level of each task at any time in a period equal the preemption level of the job released at the beginning of the period. For this system, we find that the preemption levels of the three tasks are 1, 2, and 3, respectively, in (0, 3); 2, 1, and 3 in (3, 4.5); 1, 2, and 3 in (4.5, 5); 2, 3, and 1 in (5, 6) and so on. In other words, this system has dynamic preemption levels.

8.8.2 Definitions of Protocols and Duration of Blocking

A *preemption-ceiling protocol* makes decisions on whether to grant a free resource to any job based on the preemption level of the job in a manner similar to the priority-ceiling protocol. This protocol also assumes that the resource requirements of all the jobs are known a priori. After assigning preemption levels to all the jobs, we determine the preemption ceiling of each resource. Specifically, when there is only 1 unit of each resource, which we assume is the case here, the *preemption ceiling* $\Psi(R)$ of a resource R is the highest preemption level of all the jobs that require the resource. For the example in Figure 8–19, the preemption ceiling of *Black* is 1, while the preemption ceiling of *Shaded* is 2.

The *(preemption) ceiling of the system* $\hat{\Psi}(t)$ at any time t is the highest preemption ceiling of all the resources that are in use at t. When the context is clear and there is no chance of confusion, we will simply refer to $\hat{\Psi}(t)$ as the ceiling of the system. We again use Ω to denote a preemption level that is lower than the lowest preemption level among all jobs since there is no possibility of confusion. When all the resources are free, we say that the ceiling of the system is Ω.

Like the priority-ceiling protocol, the preemption-ceiling protocol also has a basic version and a stack-based version. The former assumes that each job has its own stack and the latter allows the jobs to share a common stack. Basic versions of priority-ceiling and preemption-ceiling protocols differ mainly in their allocation rules. For this reason, only the allocation rule of the basic preemption-ceiling protocol is given below. You can see that the principle of this rule for both protocols is the same, the only difference being the parameters (i.e., priority or preemption levels and ceilings) used by the rule.

Rules of Basic Preemption-Ceiling Protocol

> **1 and 3.** The *scheduling rule* (i.e., rule 1) and *priority inheritance rule* (i.e., rule 3) are the same as the corresponding rules of the priority-ceiling protocol.
>
> **2.** *Allocation Rule*: Whenever a job J requests resource R at time t, one of the following two conditions occurs:
>
> **(a)** R is held by another job. J's request fails, and J becomes blocked.
>
> **(b)** R is free.
>
> > **(i)** If J's preemption level $\psi(t)$ is higher than the current preemption ceiling $\hat{\Psi}(t)$ of the system, R is allocated to J.
> >
> > **(ii)** If J's preemption level $\psi(t)$ is not higher than the ceiling $\hat{\Psi}(t)$ of the system, R is allocated to J only if J is the job holding the resource(s) whose preemption ceiling is equal to $\hat{\Psi}(t)$; otherwise, J's request is denied, and J becomes blocked.

The stack-based preemption-ceiling protocol is called the Stack-Based Protocol (SBP) by Baker [Bake91]. It is defined by the following rules. Rules 0, 1, and 2 are essentially the same as the corresponding rules of the stack-based priority-ceiling protocol; again, the difference is that priority levels/ceilings are replaced by preemption levels/ceilings. In addition, the stack-based preemption-ceiling protocol has an inheritance rule. We will show the need for this rule shortly.

Rules of Basic Stack-Based, Preemption-Ceiling Protocol

> **0.** *Update of the Current Ceiling*: Whenever all the resources are free, the preemption ceiling of the system is Ω. The preemption ceiling $\hat{\Psi}(t)$ is updated each time a resource is allocated or freed.
>
> **1.** *Scheduling Rule*: After a job is released, it is blocked from starting execution until its preemption level is higher than the current ceiling $\hat{\Psi}(t)$ of the system and the preemption level of the executing job. At any time t, jobs that are not blocked are scheduled on the processor in a priority-driven, preemptive manner according to their assigned priorities.
>
> **2.** *Allocation Rule*: Whenever a job J requests for a resource R, it is allocated the resource.
>
> **3.** *Priority-Inheritance Rule*: When some job is blocked from starting, the blocking job inherits the highest priority of all the blocked jobs.

Obviously, when the preemption levels of jobs are identical to their priorities, these versions of the preemption-level protocol are the same as the corresponding versions of the priority-ceiling protocol. For this reason, if the jobs in Figure 8–8 are scheduled according to the preemption-ceiling protocol, the resultant schedules are the same as those shown in Figures 8-10 and 8-17.

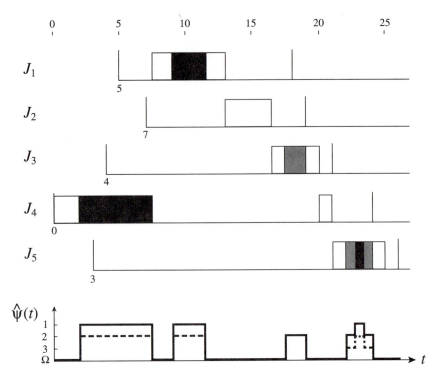

FIGURE 8–20   Example of priority ceilings of multiple-unit resources.

To see the necessity of the priority-inheritance rule of the stack-based preemption-ceiling protocol when preemption levels are assigned on the basis of jobs's relative deadlines, let us examine Figure 8–20. This figure gives an EDF schedule of jobs in Figure 8–19. (The deadline of each job is indicated by the second vertical bar on its time line. Specifically, the deadlines of J_1 and J_2 are at 18 and 18.5, respectively.) The preemption levels of the jobs are 2, 1, 3, 5 and 4, respectively, which are chosen based on the relative deadlines of the jobs.[3] The preemption ceiling of *Black* is 2, while the preemption ceiling of *Shaded* is 3. Hence, the preemption ceiling of the system is given by the dotted line in the graph. Because of the priority-inheritance rule, J_4 inherits the priority of J_1 when it blocks J_1 from starting execution at time 5. Consequently, J_4 can continue to execute and completes its critical section. Without this rule, J_1 would be blocked because of rule 1, but J_2, whose preemption level is 1, could start execution at time 7. Consequently, it would complete before J_4 completes its

---

[3]We note that the stack-based preemption-ceiling protocol without the priority-inheritance rule would produce the schedule in Figure 8–20 if the preemption levels of jobs are 1, 1, 2, 3, and 3, respectively. (The ceiling of the system for this set of preemption levels is given by the solid line in the graph below the schedule.) Nevertheless, we may not want to use this set of preemption levels and choose the set based on jobs' relative deadlines, despite the need for priority inheritance. You recall that this set of preemption levels was obtained by analyzing both the priorities and release times of the jobs. If each of these jobs is the first job of a periodic task, the preemption levels of the second jobs in the tasks containing J_1 and J_2, respectively, must be 2 and 1 in order to meet the validity condition. Now, undesirably, the preemption levels of these tasks vary with time.

critical section. In other words, without the inheritance rule, J_1 would be blocked first by J_4 and then by J_2. This uncontrolled priority inversion is prevented by the inheritance rule.

It is not surprising that both versions of the preemption-ceiling protocol prevent deadlock and transitive blocking and ensure that every job is blocked for at most the duration of one critical section. Like priority ceilings, preemption ceilings of resources impose an order on all the resources. The preemption ceiling $\hat{\Psi}(t)$ of the system tells us the subset of all jobs which we can safely grant available resources at time t. This subset contains all the jobs whose preemption levels are higher than the ceiling $\hat{\Psi}(t)$ of the system. Such a job J can be granted any resource R that is available at t because it does not require any resource that is in use at the time. Moreover, none of the jobs that are holding any resources at t can later preempt J.

8.9   CONTROLLING ACCESSES TO MULTIPLE-UNIT RESOURCES

Both versions of the priority-ceiling protocol and preemption-ceiling protocol described in the previous sections assume that there is only one unit of each resource. We now describe an extension to these protocols so that they can deal with the general case where there may be more than one unit of each resource (type).

8.9.1   Priority (Preemption) Ceilings of Multiple-Unit Resources

The first step in extending the priority-ceiling protocol is to modify the definition of the priority ceilings of resources. We let $\Pi(R_i, k)$, for $k \leq v_i$, denote the priority ceiling of a resource R_i when k out of the v_i (≥ 1) units of R_i are free. If one or more jobs in the system require more than k units of R_i, $\Pi(R_i, k)$ is the highest priority of all these jobs. If no job requires more than k units of R_i, $\Pi(R_i, k)$ is equal to Ω, the nonexisting lowest priority. In this notation, the priority ceiling $\Pi(R_j)$ of a resource R_j that has only 1 unit is $\Pi(R_j, 0)$.

Let $k_i(t)$ denote the number of units of R_i that are free at time t. Because this number changes with time, the priority ceiling of R_i changes with time. The (current) priority ceiling of the system at time t is equal to the highest priority ceiling of all the resources at the time.

Figure 8–21 gives an example. The resource requirement graph gives the numbers of units of the resources X, Y, and Z required by the five jobs that are indexed in decreasing order of their priorities. The table below the graph gives the priority ceilings of each resource for different numbers of free resource units. For example, there are 2 units of X. When 1 unit of X is used, only J_3 is directly blocked. Therefore, $\Pi(X, 1)$ is π_3. J_1 is also directly blocked when both units of X are in use. For this reason, $\Pi(X, 0)$ is π_1, the higher priority between π_1 and π_3. When both units of X are free, the ceiling of the resource is Ω. Similarly, since J_2, J_3, and J_5 require 2, 3, and 1 unit of Y, which has 3 units, $\Pi(Y, 0)$, $\Pi(Y, 1)$, and $\Pi(Y, 2)$ are equal to π_2, π_2, and π_3, respectively. Suppose that at time t, 1 unit of each of X, Y, and Z is free. The priority ceilings of the resources are π_3, π_2, and Ω, respectively, and the priority ceiling of the system is π_2.

The preemption ceilings of resources that have multiple units can be defined in a similar manner: The preemption ceiling $\Psi(R_i, k)$ of the resource R_i when k units of R_i are free is the highest preemption level of all the jobs that require more than k units of R_i. Hence, if the jobs in Figure 8–21 were indexed in decreasing order according to their preemption levels and we replaced π_i and $\Pi(*, k)$ in the table by ψ_i and $\Psi(*, k)$, respectively, we would get the preemption ceilings of the three resources. The preemption ceiling of the system at time t is equal to the highest preemption ceiling of all the resources at the time.

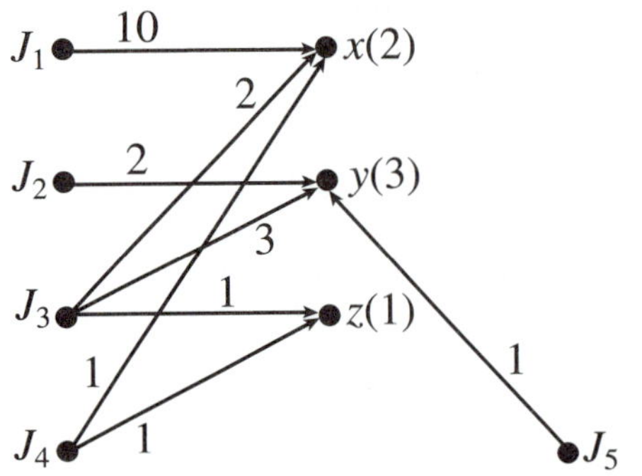

Units Required by	Resources	$x(2)$	$y(3)$	$z(1)$
	J_1	1	0	0
	J_2	0	2	0
	J_3	2	3	1
	J_4	1	0	1
	J_5	0	1	0
	$\Pi(*, 0)$	π_1	π_2	π_3
	$\Pi(*, 1)$	π_3	π_2	Ω
	$\Pi(*, 2)$	Ω	π_3	Ω
	$\Pi(*, 3)$	Ω	Ω	Ω

FIGURE 8–21   Example of priority ceilings of multiple-unit resources.

8.9.2 Modified Rules

It is straightforward to modify the ceiling-priority protocol so it can deal with multiple-unit resources. In essence, the scheduling and allocation rules remains unchanged except for the new definition of priority ceiling of resources. However, since more than one job can hold (some units of) a resource, scheduling rule 1b needs to be rephrased for clarity. It should read as follows:

Scheduling Rule of Multiple-Unit Ceiling-Priority Protocol

> Upon acquiring a resource R and leaving $k \geq 0$ free units of R, a job executes at the higher of its priority and the priority ceiling $\Pi(R, k)$ of R.

Similarly, the allocation rule of the priority-ceiling (or preemption-ceiling) protocol for multiple units of resources is a straightforward modification of the allocation rule of the basic priority-ceiling (preemption-ceiling) protocol.

Allocation Rule of Multiple-Unit Priority-(Preemption-) Ceiling Protocol

> Whenever a job J requests k units of resource R at time t, one of the following two conditions occurs:
>
> **(a)** Less than k units of R are free. J's request fails and J becomes directly blocked.
> **(b)** k or more units of R are free.
> > **(i)** If J's priority $\pi(t)$ [preemption level $\psi(t)$] is higher than the current priority ceiling $\hat{\Pi}(t)$ [preemption ceiling $\hat{\Psi}(t)$] of the system at the time, k units of R are allocated to J until it releases them.
> > **(ii)** If J's priority $\pi(t)$ [preemption level $\psi(t)$] is not higher than the system ceiling $\hat{\Pi}(t)$ [$\hat{\Psi}(t)$], k units of R are allocated to J only if J holds the re-

source(s) whose priority ceiling (preemption ceiling) is equal to $\hat{\Pi}(t)$ $[\hat{\Psi}(t)]$; otherwise, J's request is denied, and J becomes blocked.

You can see that this rule is essentially the same as the allocation rule of the basic version. The only change is in the wording to accommodate multiple-unit requests.

8.9.3 Priority-Inheritance Rule

In the case where there is only 1 unit of each resource, we have shown that when a job J is blocked, only one lower-priority job is responsible for this blocking and this lower-priority job inherits J's priority. This may no longer be true in a system containing multiple resource units. More than one lower-priority job may be responsible. The question is which one of these jobs should inherit J's priority.

To illustrate, let us examine a system where there are 3 units of resource R, and there are four jobs, each requiring 1 unit of R. Suppose that at the time when the highest priority job J_1 requests a unit of R, all 3 units are held by the other three jobs. Now, all three lower-priority jobs block J_1. In this case, it is reasonable to let J_2 (i.e., the job with the highest priority among the three lower-priority jobs) inherit J_1's priority until it releases its units of R.

Indeed, an important special case is when a job can request and hold at most 1 unit of every resource at a time. (An example is counting semaphores.) In this case, the following priority-inheritance rule proposed by Chen [Chen] works well, that is, each job is blocked at most once for the duration of one critical section.

Priority-Inheritance Rule

> When the requesting job J becomes blocked at t, the job with the highest priority among all the jobs holding the resource R that has the highest priority ceiling among all the resources inherits J's priority until it releases its unit of R.

In general, a job may request and hold arbitrary numbers of resources. The example in Figure 8–22 illustrates that a straightforward generalization of the priority-ceiling protocol and the above priority-inheritance rule ensures that each job is blocked at most once. The system in this example has five jobs indexed in decreasing order of their priorities. (In the description below, the priorities are 1, 2, 3, 4 and 5.) There are two resources *Black* and *Shaded*. The numbers of units are 5 and 1, respectively. The resource requirements of the jobs and priority ceilings of the resources are listed in Figure 8–22(a).

1. At time 0, J_5 starts to execute. When it requests 1 unit of *Black* at time 0.5, the ceiling of the system is Ω; therefore, it is granted 1 unit of *Black* and continues to execute. The ceiling of the system stays at Ω because there still are sufficient units of *Black* to meet the demand of every job.

2. At time 1, J_4 becomes ready. It preempts J_5 and, later, requests and is granted 1 unit of *Black*. Now, J_2 would be directly blocked if it requests *Black*, and the ceiling of *Black*, and consequently of the system, becomes 2, the priority of J_2.

3. At time 2, J_3 preempts J_4, and at time 2.5, J_2 preempts J_3. J_2 becomes blocked when it requests *Shaded* at time 3 because its priority is not higher than the ceiling of the system. J_4 now inherits priority 2 and executes.

	no. of units	units required					$\Pi(*, k), k =$					
		J_1	J_2	J_3	J_4	J_5	0	1	2	3	4	5
Black	5	2	4	0	1	1	1	1	2	2	Ω	Ω
Shaded	1	1	1	0	0	1	1	Ω	Ω	Ω	Ω	Ω

(a)

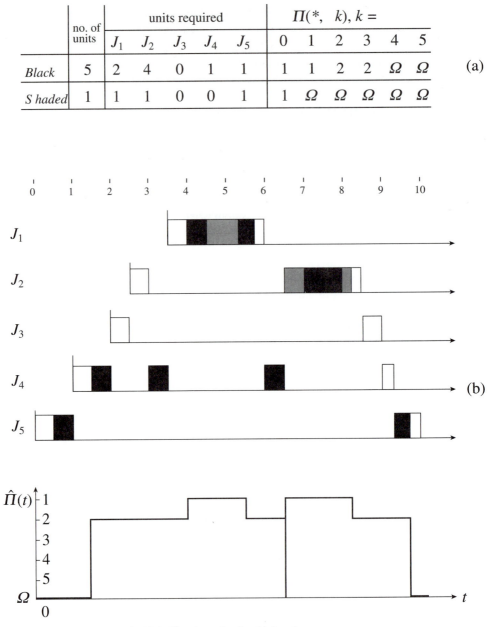

(b)

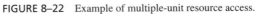

FIGURE 8–22 Example of multiple-unit resource access.

4. At time 3.5, J_1 preempts J_4. Since its priority is higher than the ceiling of the system, J_1 is allocated both resources when it requests them.

5. At time 6, J_1 completes, and J_4 continues to execute until it releases its 1 unit of *Black* at time 6.5. The ceiling of the system returning to Ω, J_2 is allocated *Shaded*. After *Shaded* is allocated, the ceiling of the system becomes 1.

6. At time 7, when J_2 requests 4 units of *Black*, the units are available. The ceiling of the system is 1, but J_2 holds the resource with this priority ceiling. Hence it is allocated 4 units of *Black*.

7. When J_2 completes, J_3 resumes. When J_3 completes, J_4 resumes, and it is followed by J_5. The system becomes idle at time 10.

From this example, we can see that Chen's priority-inheritance rule works for the general case as well. Specifically, we let R denote the resource whose priority ceiling is the highest among all resources in the system at time t. Let J' denote the job that has acquired the resource latest among all jobs holding R. If a requesting job J becomes blocked at t, J' inherits the priority of J. The fact that the priority-ceiling protocol defined by the rules stated in this section ensures that every job is blocked at most once can be proved in a manner similar to the proof of Theorem 8.2.

*8.10   CONTROLLING CONCURRENT ACCESSES TO DATA OBJECTS

Data objects are a special type of shared resources. When jobs are scheduled preemptively, their accesses to (i.e., reads and writes) data objects may be interleaved. To ensure data integrity, it is common to require that the reads and writes be serializable. A sequence of reads and writes by a set of jobs is *serializable* if the effect produced by the sequence on all the data objects shared by the jobs is the same as the effect produced by a serial sequence (i.e., the sequence of reads and writes when the jobs execute according to a nonpreemptive schedule).

8.10.1   Convex-Ceiling Protocol

The resource access-control protocols described in earlier sections do not ensure serializability. For example, both the NPCS and PC (Priority- and Preemption-Ceiling) protocols allow a higher-priority job J_h to read and write a data object X between two disjoint critical sections of a lower-priority job J_l during which J_l also reads and writes X. The value of X thus produced may not be the same as the value produced by either of the two possible serial sequences (i.e., all the reads and writes of J_l either proceed or follow that of J_h).

Motivation and Assumptions.   A well-known way to ensure serializability is Two-Phase Locking (2PL). According to the 2PL protocol, a job never requests any lock once it releases some lock. Hence, the critical sections of J_1 and J_3 in Figure 8–1 satisfy this protocol, but the critical sections of J_2 do not. Under the 2PL protocol, J_2 would have to hold the locks on R_2 and R_3 until time 16. (This is because we also require the critical sections be properly nested.)

We can easily get concurrency-control protocols that not only ensure serializability but also prevent deadlock and transitive blocking by augmenting the protocols described in earlier sections with the two-phase locking rule. As a result, we have the NPCS-2PL and the PCP-2PL protocols. The augmented protocols have an obvious shortcoming: prolonged blocking. Following the 2PL rule, a job may hold a data object even when it no longer require the object. As a consequence, it may block other jobs for a longer duration.

The convex-(priority-) ceiling protocol [Naka] described below is another extension of the priority-ceiling protocol. It is an improvement over the PCP-2PL protocol because it reduces the duration of blocking. In the description below, we assume that there is only one of each data object.

Priority-Ceiling Function.   As with the PCP-2PL protocol, the convex-ceiling protocol assumes that the scheduler knows a priori the data objects require by each job and, therefore, the priority ceiling of each data object. In addition, each job notifies the scheduler immediately after it accesses each of its required objects for the last time. We call a notification sent by a job J_i after it accesses R_k for the last time the *last access notification* for R_k by J_i and the time of this notification the *last access time of R_k by J_i*.

For each job J_i in the system, the scheduler generates and maintains the following two functions: the *remainder priority ceiling*, $RP(J_i, t)$ and the *priority-ceiling function*, $\Pi(J_i, t)$. $RP(J_i, t)$ is the highest priority ceiling of all data objects that J_i will require after time t. When J_i is released, $RP(J_i, t)$ is equal to the highest priority ceiling of all data objects required by the job. The scheduler updates this function each time when it receives a last access notification from J_i. When the job no longer requires any object, its remainder priority ceiling is Ω.

When each job J_i starts execution, its priority-ceiling function $\Pi(J_i, t)$ is equal to Ω. When J_i is allowed to access an object R_k for the first time, $\Pi(J_i, t)$ is set to the priority ceiling $\Pi(R_k)$ of R_k if the current value of $\Pi(J_i, t)$ is lower than $\Pi(R_k)$. Upon receiving a last access notification from J_i, the scheduler first updates the function $RP(J_i, t)$. It then sets the priority-ceiling function $\Pi(J_i, t)$ of the job to $RP(J_i, t)$ if the remainder priority ceiling is lower.

Figure 8–23 gives an example. The job J_i requires three data objects: *Dotted*, *Black*, and *Shaded*. Their priority ceilings are 1, 2, and 3, respectively. Figure 8-23(a) shows the time intervals when the job executes and accesses the objects. The two functions of the job are shown in Figure 8–23(b). At time 0, $RP(J_i, 0)$ is 1. The job sends last access notifications at times 4, 6, and 8 when it no longer needs *Dotted*, *Black*, and *Shaded*, respectively. The scheduler updates $RP(J_i, t)$ at these instants; each time, it lowers the remainder priority ceiling to the highest priority ceiling of all objects still required by the job in the future.

Initially, $\Pi(J_i, t)$ is equal to Ω. At time 2 when J_i accesses *Black* for the first time, its priority ceiling function is raised to 2, the priority ceiling of *Black*. $\Pi(J_i, t)$ stays at 2 until time 3 and is raised to 1 at time 3 when J_i accesses *Dotted* for the first time. At time 4 when the last access notification for *Dotted* is received, $\Pi(J_i, t)$ is set to 2, the updated value of $RP(J_i, t)$. Similarly, $\Pi(J_i, t)$ is lowered to 3 and Ω at the last access times 6 and 8 of *Black* and *Shaded*, respectively.

By definition, $RP(J_i, t)$ is a nonincreasing function of t. The priority-ceiling function $\Pi(J_i, t)$ first raises as the job is allowed to access more and more data objects. Its value, once lowered, never rises again. In other words, the priority-ceiling function of every job is "two-phase"; it has only one peak.

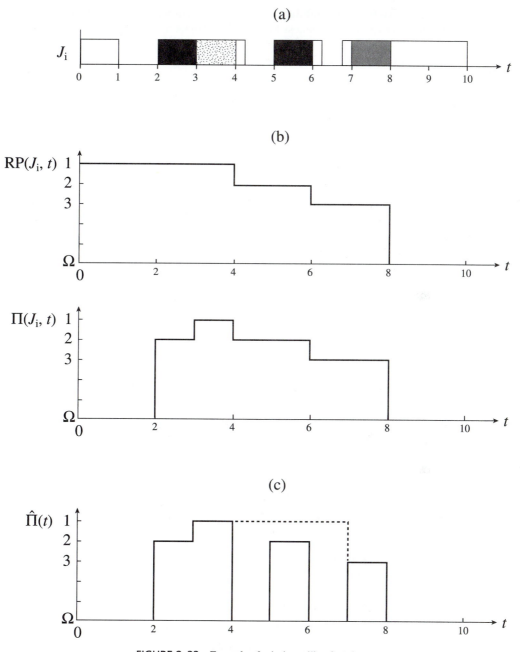

FIGURE 8–23   Example of priority-ceiling functions.

Definition and Capability.   As with the priority-ceiling protocol, at any time t when the scheduler receives a request to access an object R for the first time from any job J, it computes the system ceiling $\hat{\Pi}(t)$. $\hat{\Pi}(t)$ is equal to the highest priority of the priority-ceiling functions of all the jobs in the system. The convex-ceiling protocol defined by the following rules.

Rules of Convex-Ceiling Protocol

1. *Scheduling Rule*: At any time, jobs that are not suspended are scheduled on the processor in a preemptive, priority-driven manner. Upon its release, the current priority of every job J_i is its assigned priority π_i. It executes at this priority except when the inheritance rule is applied.

2. *Allocation Rule*: When a job J_i requests to access a data object R for the first time,
   (a) if J_i's priority is higher than the system ceiling $\hat{\Pi}(t)$, J is allowed to continue execution and access R;
   (b) if J_i's priority is not higher than $\hat{\Pi}(t)$,
       i. if $\hat{\Pi}(t)$ is equal to $\Pi(J_i, t)$, J_i is allowed to access R;
       ii. otherwise, J is suspended.

3. *Priority-Inheritance Rule*: When J_i becomes suspended, the job J_l whose priority-ceiling function is equal to the system ceiling at the time inherits the current priority $\pi_i(t)$ of J_i

By definition, the priority-ceiling function of any job J (and hence the ceiling of the system) never falls below the priority ceiling of any data object already read and written by J until J no longer requires the object. In this way, the convex-ceiling protocol prevents other jobs from reading and writing the objects required by J between the reads and writes of J. The formal proof that the protocol ensures serializability can be found in [Naka].

In principle, the convex-ceiling protocol is the same as the basic priority-ceiling protocol. (The system ceiling used by the basic priority-ceiling protocol can also be defined as the highest priority of the priority-ceiling functions of all the jobs: The priority-ceiling function of a job is equal to the highest priority ceiling of all the resources being used by the job.) That the convex-ceiling protocol prevents deadlock and transitive blocking follows straightforwardly from this fact.

From its definition, we see that that the convex-ceiling protocol can be implemented entirely in the application level. An application-level object manager can serve as the scheduler. It maintains the priority-ceiling functions of jobs and controls the concurrent accesses to data objects. It can do so without relying on a locking mechanism. Since the basic priority-ceiling and PCP-2PL protocols can also be defined in the same manner, the same can be said for these protocols as well.

Comparison with Basic and PCP-2PL Protocols.   To illustrate the differences between this protocol and the basic priority-ceiling protocol, we return to the example in Figure 8–23. Suppose that after J_i accesses *Black*, a job J_2 with priority 2 were to request access to a data object. According to the convex-ceiling protocol, this request would be denied and J_2 would be suspended until time 6 when the system ceiling is lowered to 3. In contrast, according to the basic priority-ceiling protocol, the system ceiling is given by the solid line in Figure

8–23(c). J_2 would be allowed to access its required data object starting from time 4. J_2 would be blocked for a shorter amount of time at the expense of potential violation of serializability.

On the other hand, according to the PCP-2PL protocol, the system ceiling would be given by the dotted line in Figure 8–23(c) because J_i does not release any data object until it no longer requires additional objects. As a consequence, J_2 would be blocked for 1 more unit of time when compared with the convex-ceiling protocol. A job with priority 1 can be blocked by J_i for only 1 unit of time under the convex-ceiling protocol, but can be blocked for 5 units of time under PCP-2PL protocol.

8.10.2 Other Real-Time Concurrency Control Schemes

One way to improve the responsiveness of soft real-time jobs that read and write multiple data objects is to abort and restart the lower-priority job whenever it conflicts (i.e., contends for some data object) with a higher-priority job. A policy that governs which job proceeds at the expense of which job is called a *conflict resolution policy*.

Well-Known Conflict Resolution Policies.   To explain conflict resolution policies that have been proposed for database transactions, we note that each transaction typically keeps a copy of each object it reads and may write in its own memory space. When it completes all the reads, writes, and computations, it writes all data objects it has modified back to the global space. This last step is called commit. So, until a transaction commits, no shared data object in the database is modified, and it is safe to abort and restart a transaction and take back the data objects allocated to it.

Abbott, *et al.* [AbMo] showed that the 2PL-HP schemes perform well for soft real-time transactions compared with Optimistic Concurrency Control (OCC) schemes, which we will explain shortly. According to the 2PL-HP scheme, all transactions follow a two-phase policy in their acquisitions of (locks of) data objects. Whenever two transactions conflict (i.e., they want to access the same object), the lower-priority transaction is restarted immediately (i.e., the executing instance is aborted and new instance is made ready immediately). In essence, this scheme allocates data objects to transactions preemptively. Therefore, priority inversion cannot occur.

The results of a soft real-time transaction remains useful to some extent even when the transaction completes late. In contrast, the result of a late transaction with a firm deadline is useless and hence is discarded. The 2PL-HP scheme does not work well for firm real-time transactions compared with OCC schemes. The reason is that 2PL-HP can cause wasted restart and wasted wait [HoJC]. The former refers to a restart of a lower-priority transaction which turns out to be unnecessary because the conflicting higher-priority transaction completes late. A way to reduce wasted restarts is by simply suspending a conflicting lower-priority transaction when a conflict occurs. If the conflicting higher-priority transaction completes in time, the suspended transaction is aborted and restarted. On the other hand, if the conflicting transaction completes late, the suspended transaction can resume. Unfortunately, the stop and wait may cause the lower-priority transaction to be late, and thus incurs wasted wait.

Optimistic Concurrency Control Schemes.   Optimistic concurrency control is an alternative approach to two-phase locking. Under the control of an OCC scheme, whether a transaction conflict with other executing transactions is checked immediately before the transaction commits. This step is called validation. If the transaction is found to conflict with other transactions at the time, one of them is allowed to proceed and commit, while the conflicting transactions are restarted. Different OCC schemes differ in the choices of these transactions. A priority-based OCC scheme allows a conflicting lower-priority scheme to proceed until validation time and then is restarted if it is found to conflict with some higher-priority transaction at validation time.

Most performance evaluation studies (e.g., [HaCL, LeSo] found that OCC schemes perform better than 2PL-based schemes in terms of on-time completions of real-time transactions. However, when the performance criterion is temporal consistency, OCC schemes tend to give poorer performance, especially when the transactions are periodic. In particular, Song, *et al.* [SoLi] found that the age and dispersion of data read by transactions tend to be larger under an OCC scheme than under lock-based schemes. (The terms temporal consistency, age and dispersion were defined in Section 1.4.1.) This is because both blocking and preemption can cause temporal inconsistency (i.e., age and dispersion of data being large). Blocking due to resource contention can cause higher-priority update transactions to complete late and data to be old. However, preempted transactions may read data that are old and have large age dispersion as well. When transactions are periodic, a transaction restarted in one period is likely to restart again in other periods. The repeated restarts lead to a large variance in the age and dispersion of data.

8.11 SUMMARY

This chapter described several protocols for controlling accesses to shared resources in systems where jobs are scheduled on a processor in a preemptive, priority-driven manner. This section first summarizes them and then discusses the effect of resource contention with aperiodic jobs and rules for safe mode changes.

8.11.1 Resource Access-Control Protocols

Because every unit of resource can be used by at most one job at a time without preemption, priority inversions may occur. The primary design objective of resource access control protocols is to control priority inversion, that is, to keep the duration of every priority inversion (and hence the blocking time suffered by the higher-priority job) bounded from above. Among the protocols described above,

1. the NPCS and priority-inheritance protocols do not require prior knowledge on the resources required by jobs, while all other protocols do;
2. the priority-inheritance protocol does not prevent deadlock, while all other protocols do; and
3. all protocols except the priority-inheritance protocol ensures that every job is blocked at most once.

Nonpreemptive Critical Section (NPCS) Protocol.   The NPCS protocol described in Section 8.3 offers the simplest means to ensure that every job is blocked at most once if it does not self-suspend. According to this protocol, the scheduler allows the executing job to use any resource at any time and never preempts a job when the job is using any resource.

A job can be blocked only if it becomes ready when some lower-priority job is in a critical section (i.e., using some resource). The blocking time thus incurred is at most equal to the execution time of the critical section. Simplicity is the major advantage of this protocol. Its disadvantage is that every job can be blocked by all lower-priority jobs.

Priority-Inheritance Protocol.   According to the priority-inheritance protocol described in Section 8.4, the request for a resource is denied and the requesting job becomes blocked only if the resource is in use. When this occurs, the job that directly blocks the requesting job (i.e., is using the requested resource) inherits (i.e., executes at) the requesting job's priority. Because of priority inheritance, a job may also be priority-inheritance blocked when a lower-priority job inherits a higher priority. The priority-inheritance protocol keeps the blocking time bound from above by the maximum execution time of critical sections of lower-priority jobs each time a job is blocked. However, a job that conflicts with more than one job over more than one resource can be blocked a multiple number of times. Again, this protocol does not prevent deadlock.

Basic Priority-Ceiling Protocol.   Section 8.5 described a version of the priority-ceiling protocol. This protocol prevents deadlock and transitive blocking among jobs. When it is used, a job that never self-suspends is blocked at most once, and the duration of blocking is bounded from above by the maximum execution time of critical sections of lower-priority jobs.

The scheduler finds a priori the priority ceiling of each resource (i.e., the highest priority of all jobs that require the resource). When a job J requests a resource, say at time t, the scheduler first finds the system ceiling $\hat{\Pi}(t)$, which is the highest of the priority ceilings of all resources in use at the time. The requesting job can use the resource only when the job's priority is higher than the system ceiling or when the job has the resource whose priority ceiling is equal to $\hat{\Pi}(t)$. When the requesting job becomes blocked, the job holding the resource with priority ceiling $\hat{\Pi}(t)$ inherits the priority of the requesting job.

The priority-ceiling protocol is nongreedy: a requesting job may be denied a resource and becomes priority-ceiling blocked even when the resource is free. Every time a job requests a resource, the scheduler must update the system ceiling. The complexity of this operation is $O(\log \rho)$ where ρ is the number of resource types. The priority-ceiling protocol is better suited for a fixed-priority system of periodic tasks than dynamic-priority systems.

Ceiling-Priority (Stack-Based Priority-Ceiling) Protocol.   According to the ceiling-priority protocol, which is identical to the stack-based version of the priority-ceiling protocol, each job executes at its assigned priority when it does not hold any resource, and at the highest of priority ceilings of all resources held by the job whenever the job holds any resource. Another way to implement the protocol is to have the scheduler update the system ceiling each time the status (i.e., in use or free) of a resource changes. Upon release, a job whose priority is no higher than the system ceiling is blocked until the system ceiling becomes lower than its priority. Once a job is unblocked and scheduled for execution, it is never blocked because all its required resources are available.

The stack-based version of the priority-ceiling protocol is described in Section 8.6. It allows the jobs to share the run-time stack if the jobs never self-suspend. The stack-based version has the same worst-case blocking time as the basic version. It is much simpler to implement. For this reason, it is preferred over the basic priority-ceiling protocol even for jobs that do not share stack space.

Preemption-Ceiling Protocols.   In principle, the priority-ceiling protocol can be used in a dynamic-priority system. However, the high overhead due to the updates of priority ceilings of resources upon the releases of new jobs makes it unattractive. The preemption-ceiling protocol described in Section 8.8 is a better alternative. The protocol is motived by the observation that the potential for a job to preempt other jobs depends not only on its priority but also on its release time. Therefore, rather than than working with priorities of jobs, the preemption-ceiling protocol assigns each job a preemption level based on its priority and release time: the higher the preemption level of a job, the larger the possibility of its preempting other jobs. So, a job that has a higher priority and later release time should have a higher preemption level. For example, the preemption levels of jobs in a deadline-driven system can be assigned on the basis of their relative deadlines: the shorter the deadline, the higher the preemption level.

The preemption ceiling of a resource is the highest preemption level of all jobs that require the resource. The basic and stack-based versions of the preemption-ceiling protocol are essentially the same as the corresponding versions of the priority-ceiling protocol except that in place of priority ceilings, the schedulers works with the preemption ceiling of resources.

Periodic tasks in many dynamic-priority systems (e.g., those scheduled on the EDF or LST basis) have fixed preemption levels. The preemption-ceiling protocol is a better option because it should have lower run-time overhead than the priority-ceiling protocol.

Priority- and Preemption-Ceiling Protocols for Multiple-Unit Resources.   The priority-ceiling (and preemption-ceiling) protocols were extended in Section 8.9 so they can deal with multiple-unit resources. The priority ceiling $\Pi(R, k)$ of a resource R that has $v \geq 1$ units when k ($v \geq k \geq 0$) are available is the highest priority of all jobs that require more than k units of R. The system ceiling at any time is equal to the highest of priority ceilings of all resources in the system. Except for this modification, the multiple-unit priority-ceiling protocol is the same as the basic version.

Implementation Issue.   The most straightforward implementation of the priority-ceiling (or preemption-ceiling) protocol makes use of a locking mechanism: A job locks a (unit of a) resource when the scheduler allows it to use the resource and releases the lock to free the resource. The definition of the protocol makes this assumption.

This protocol can also be implemented without relying a locking mechanism. An implementation without locking requires that each job notifies the scheduler when it is no longer requires a resource, in addition to requesting the use of a resource. The scheduler keeps a priority-ceiling function $\Pi(J, t)$ for each job J. At any time t, $\Pi(J, t)$ is the highest priority ceiling of all resources which J is allowed to use at time t. This function is updated each time the scheduler allows J to access a resource and when a notification from the job is received. The system ceiling at time t is equal to the highest ceiling of priority-ceiling functions of all jobs at time t. You can find in Section 8.10.1 reworded allocation and inheritance rules of the protocol that assume the information used by the scheduler is kept in this form and jobs do not lock resources.

Protocols for Controlling Accesses to Data Objects.   Section 8.10 discussed the additional concern about serializability when jobs share data. A way to ensure serializable accesses to data objects is to augment the priority-ceiling and preemption-ceiling protocols with a two-phase locking rule. The augmented protocol is called the PCP-2PL protocol. This is also the basic principle of the convex-ceiling protocol described in Section 8.10.1. This protocol improves on the PCP-2PL protocol by reducing the blocking times. Optimistic concurrency control are well-known alternatives to locking-based protocols described above.

Computing the Total Blocking Time.   Finally, let us denote the number of times each job J_i self-suspends by K. Moreover, each job J_i has resource conflict over different resources with v_r lower-priority jobs and v_n lower-priority jobs have nonpreemption segments. Let $b_i(ss)$, $b_i(rc)$, and $b_i(np)$ denote the blocking times of J_i due to self-suspension, resource contention, and nonpreemptivity, respectively. Then the total blocking time b_i suffered by J_i is given by

$$b_i = b_{i,k}(ss) + (K + 1)\max(b_i(rc), b_i(np))$$
$$b_i = b_{i,k}(ss) + \max(K + 1, v_r)b_i(rc) + \min(K + 1, v_n)b_i(np)$$
$$b_i = b_{i,k}(ss) + (K + 1)b_i(rc) + (K + 1)b_i(np)$$

when resource accesses are controlled according to the NPCS, priority-inheritance, and priority-ceiling (or preemption-ceiling) protocols, respectively.

8.11.2   Resource Contention with Aperiodic Jobs

Aperiodic (and sporadic) jobs may also use resources. Their resource requirements must be taken into account when we compute the blocking time due to resource contention of any job (or task). The techniques for computing blocking time described earlier can be used for this purpose as well, provided that an aperiodic job is never suspended while it is in a critical section because the server executing it runs out of budget.

To prevent prolonged blocking, the deferrable and sporadic server algorithms must be modified as follows so the server will not be suspended because it runs out of budget when the aperiodic job being executed is holding some resource. (1) When the server exhausts its budget, the scheduler suspends the server immediately if the aperiodic job being executed is not in a critical section, but if the job is in a critical section, the scheduler waits until the job exits from the critical section and then suspends the server. In other words, the server is nonpreemptable while it is in a critical section. (2) Whenever the scheduler has allowed the server to execute after the server budget is exhausted (i.e., allows the server to overrun its allocated time), the scheduler deducts the length of the overrun from the server budget when it replenishes the server budget. As a consequence of this overrun, a lower-priority task may suffer additional delay. When we compute the time demand of the lower-priority task, we need to add the execution time of the longest critical section of the aperiodic task as a blocking term into the time demand function [e.g., given by the expression in Eq. (7.1)] of the task.

An advantage of a total bandwidth, constant utilization, or weighted fair-queueing server is that such a server never runs out of budget before the completion of the aperiodic job being executed. Consequently, when some job in the aperiodic task executed by such a server requires resources, we can simply treat the aperiodic task in the same way as a periodic task in our computation of blocking time. A slight complication is the choice of preemption level for the server in a system that uses a preemption-ceiling protocol, since the "relative deadline" of the server changes with time. The server should be given a high preemption level for the sake of the system's aperiodic response. If the server has a low preemption level (e.g., based on the longest relative deadline it may have), it in effect executes in the background of periodic tasks.

8.11.3   Mode Changes

We conclude this chapter by returning to the question that was last discussed in Section 5.7.2: how to carry out mode change. In other words, when it is safe to add new (periodic and sporadic) tasks into a priority-driven system and delete existing tasks from it. Earlier chapters mentioned admissions of tasks after they pass acceptance, but do not explicitly say when. During a mode change, that is, when the system changes from one operation mode to another, not only *new tasks* (i.e., tasks that do not run in the current mode but will run in the new mode) need to be added, but also *old tasks* (i.e., tasks that run in the current mode but will not run in the new mode) need to be deleted. As we did in Section 5.7.2, we focus here on periodic tasks. This subsection provides a brief summary of rules governing the deletion and addition of these tasks; you can find details on mode-change protocols in [SRLR].

Task Deletions and Admissions.   In the simpler case, tasks' resource accesses are controlled by the NPCS and priority-inheritance protocols. The scheduler does not maintain, and therefore does not need to update, resource usage information. In the task deletion phase, the scheduler deletes every old task T and reclaims the processor time allocated to the task. Specifically, it deletes T immediately if at the start t of the mode change, the current job of T has not begun to execute. However, it waits to do so until the beginning of the next period of T or when the current job completes, whichever is later, if the job has executed at time t. Therefore, the length of time the scheduler takes to complete the task-deletion phase is at most equal to the longest of the periods of all old tasks.

In principle, new tasks can be added one by one as sufficient processor time becomes available and the new task becomes schedulable with existing tasks. This does not speed up the completion of mode change, however, and it is much simpler for the scheduler to wait until the task-deletion phase completes and then adds all the new tasks at once.

Updates of Resource Usage Information.   In a system that uses priority-ceiling, ceiling-priority, or preemption-ceiling protocols, priority (preemption) ceilings of resources must be updated before new tasks can be added into the system. The scheduler raises the priority ceiling of a resource whose new priority ceiling (i.e., the ceiling in the new mode) is higher than the old after the start t of the mode change as soon as the resource is free. It waits until all the tasks that use a resource R whose new priority ceiling is lower than the old have been deleted and then lowers the priority ceiling of R to the new value.

A new task that will use a resource R whose priority ceiling must be raised can be added into the system only after the priority ceiling of R has been raised. All the updates of priority (or preemption) ceilings are surely complete shortly after the task-deletion phase completes or all the resources are released, whichever is later.

EXERCISES

8.1 A system contains five jobs. There are three resources X, Y, and Z. The resource requirements of the jobs are listed below.

$$
\begin{array}{ll}
J_1: & [X; 2] \\
J_2: & \text{none} \\
J_3: & [Y; 1] \\
J_4: & [X; 3\ [Z; 1]] \\
J_5: & [Y; 4\ [Z; 2]]
\end{array}
$$

The priority J_i is higher than the priority of J_j for $i < j$. What are the maximum blocking times of the jobs under the nonpreemptable critical-section protocol and under the priority-ceiling protocol?

8.2 A system contains the following four periodic tasks. The tasks are scheduled by the rate-monotonic algorithm and the priority-ceiling protocol.

$$
\begin{array}{ll}
T_1 = (3, 0.75) & b_1 = 0.9 \\
T_2 = (3.5, 1.5) & b_2 = 0.75 \\
T_3 = (6, 0.6) & b_3 = 1.0 \\
T_4 = (10, 1) &
\end{array}
$$

b_i is the blocking time of T_i. Are the tasks schedulable? Explain your answer.

8.3 Consider a fixed-priority system in which there are five tasks T_i, for $i = 1, 2, 3, 4,$ and 5, with decreasing priorities. There are two resources X and Y. The critical sections of T_1, T_2, T_4, and T_5 are $[Y; 3]$, $[X; 4]$, $[Y; 5\ [X; 2]]$, and $[X; 10]$, respectively. (Note that T_3 does not require any resource.) Find the blocking times $b_i(rc)$ of the tasks.

8.4 A fixed-priority system contains four tasks T_i, for $i = 1, 2, 3, 4,$ and 5, with decreasing priorities and uses the ceiling-priority protocol to control resource access. There are three resources X, Y, and Z; each has 1 unit. The critical sections of the tasks are $[X; 4]$, $[Y; 6]$, $[Z; 5]$, and $[X; 3\ [Y; 2\ [Z; 1]]]$, respectively. Suppose that T_2 may self-suspend once, and $b_2(ss)$ is 1. The other tasks never self-suspend. What are the blocking times of the tasks?

8.5 Sections 8.6.1 and 8.6.2 give two different implementations (and two different names) of the ceiling-priority protocol.
  (a) Discuss the pros and cons of the implementations.
  (b) The definitions of the stack-based, priority-ceiling protocol and ceiling-priority protocol do not say whether jobs are allowed to self-suspend. Do protocols still limit the duration of blocking if jobs may self-suspend? If yes, give an intuitive argument to support your answer. If no, give an illustrative example.
  (c) Oftentimes, jobs of equal priority are scheduled on the round-robin basis. Modify the definition of priority ceilings of resources and the scheduling rule of the ceiling-priority protocol to make the protocol work for such jobs. (*Hint*: Consider restricting the priorities of all jobs to even integers. Define the priority ceiling of each resource to be the highest of the priorities of all jobs that require the resource minus one. In other words, the ceiling priorities of all resources are odd integers.)

8.6 A fixed-priority system contains five tasks. There are two kinds of resources X and Y. The resource X has 3 units and Y has 2 units. The resource requirements of the tasks are as follows:

$$T_1 : [X, 1; 3]$$
$$T_2 : [Y, 1; 4]$$
$$T_3 : [Y, 1; 4 [X, 3; 2]]$$
$$T_4 : [X, 1; 4] [Y, 2; 2]]$$
$$T_5 : [Y, 1; 3]$$

The priority of T_i is higher than the priority of T_k if $i < k$.

(a) Suppose that the system uses the stack-based priority-ceiling protocol. What are the maximum blocking times of the jobs?

(b) Suppose that these periodic tasks have the following parameters: $T_1 = (40, 5, 20)$, $T_2 = (30, 5, 25)$, $T_3 = (35, 5, 30)$, $T_4 = (60, 6, 40)$, and $T_5 = (55, 5, 50)$. Are these tasks schedulable? Explain your answer.

8.7 A system contains the following five periodic tasks. The tasks are scheduled rate-monotonically.

$$T_1 = (6, 3, [X; 2])$$
$$T_2 = (20, 5, [Y; 1])$$
$$T_3 = (200, 5, [X; 3 [Z; 1]])$$
$$T_4 = (210, 6, [Z; 5 [Y; 4]])$$

Compare the schedulability of the system when the priority-ceiling protocol is used versus the NPCS protocol.

8.8 A system contains six jobs, J_i, for $i = 1, \ldots, 6$. Jobs J_2 and J_3 have the same priority. Otherwise, the smaller the index, the higher the priority. There are three resources X, Y, and Z in the system; each resource has 1 unit. The stack-based priority-ceiling protocol is used to control resource access. The amounts of time the jobs use the resources are given by the following table. (A blank means zero.)

Jobs	X	Y	Z
J_1	1		
J_2		7	
J_3			1
J_4			
J_5			2
J_6	3	4	

(a) Find the blocking times of all jobs.

(b) Suppose that all the jobs except J_5 are released at the same time t. At time t, J_5 holds Z. Which jobs are ready for execution and which ones are not? Explain your answers.

8.9 A system contains three periodic tasks (T_1, T_2 and T_3) and three resources (X, Y, and Z). There are 3 units of resource X, 2 units of resource Y, and 3 units of resource Z. The resource requirements of the tasks are as follows:

$$T_1: [Y, 1; 4 [X, 3; 2]]$$
$$T_2: [Z, 3; 5 [Y, 1; 1]]$$
$$T_3: [Z, 1; 7 [X, 1; 3]]$$

(a) Draw the resource requirement graph for the task system.

(b) Suppose that the periods and execution times of the tasks are given by

$$T_1 = (20, 5)$$
$$T_2 = (15, 6)$$
$$T_3 = (35, 8)$$

Construct a table of preemption ceilings for the resources, assuming that the tasks are scheduled according to the earliest-deadline-first algorithm. Are the tasks schedulable? Why?

(c) What are the blocking times of the tasks if the tasks are scheduled rate-monotonically? Are the tasks schedulable according to the rate-monotonic algorithm? Why?

8.10 Given a system consisting of the following tasks whose periods, execution times, and resource requirements are given below.

$$T_1 = (2, 0.4, [X, 3; 0.3])$$
$$T_2 = (3, 0.75, [X, 1; 0.3][Y, 1; 0.4])$$
$$T_3 = (6, 1.0[Y, 1; 0.4][Z, 1; 0.5[X, 1; 0.4]])$$
$$T_4 = (8, 1.0[X, 1; 0.5][Y, 2; 0.1][Z, 1; 0.4])$$

There are 3 units of X, 2 units of Y, and 1 unit of Z. The tasks are scheduled by the EDF algorithm and the stack-based protocol.

(a) Find the preemption ceiling of each resource and the the maximum blocking time for each task.

(b) Are the tasks schedulable according to the earliest-deadline-first algorithm? Why?

8.11 Rule 3 of the basic priority-inheritance protocol assumes that when a job J becomes blocked, the job which directly blocks it has an equal or lower priority. Prove that this is assumption is valid in the absence of a deadlock. Given an example to show that this assumption is not true when there is a deadlock.

8.12 Show that under the control of the priority-inheritance protocol, a job can be blocked directly by any lower-priority job for at most once for the duration of one outermost critical section, in the absence of a deadlock.

8.13 As defined in Section 8.4, three jobs J_1, J_2, and J_3 are said to be *transitively blocked* when J_3 blocks J_2 which in turn blocks J_1. Show that priority-ceiling protocol prevents transitive blocking of three or more jobs and, hence prevents deadlock among three or more jobs.

8.14 You are given a system of n periodic tasks that are scheduled on a fixed-priority basis and under the basic priority-ceiling protocol and the resource requirement graph of the system. Write a pseudocode description of an algorithm that computes the blocking set **BS**$_i$ and the worst-case blocking time b_i of each task.

8.15 Suppose that periodic tasks are scheduled according to a fixed-priority scheduling algorithm and there is only 1 unit of resource of each type. We can, therefore, choose to use either the Stack-Based Protocol (SBP) or Priority-Ceiling Protocol (PCP). Give examples to illustrate that (a) PCP is better than SBP and (b) SBP is better than PCP, when performance is measured in terms of blocking times. Explain why such an example (or examples) cannot exist if you cannot find one (or both) of the examples.

CHAPTER 9

Multiprocessor Scheduling, Resource Access Control, and Synchronization

Thus far, we have ignored several realistic facts: Almost every system contains more than one processor,[1] control and data dependencies impose precedence constraints among jobs, and timing constraints of jobs are usually not independent. Ignoring these realistic but complicating factors has allowed us to focus on the basic principles of scheduling, resource access control, and schedulability analysis. We now understand these principles and are ready to discuss how the algorithms based on them can be applied to real-life systems containing more than one processor and what other algorithms are needed to deal with problems that do not arise in uniprocessor systems.

An example of the problems that arise in multiprocessor environments is the task assignment problem. As discussed earlier, most hard real-time systems built to date are static, that is, jobs or tasks are partitioned and statically bound to processors. The task assignment problem is concerned with how to partition the system of tasks and passive resources into modules and how to assign the modules to processors. Another example is the interprocessor synchronization problem. Some kind of synchronization protocol is needed to ensure that precedence constraints of jobs on different processors are always satisfied. We want to achieve a good performance according to some appropriate criteria, while minimizing the amount of work the schedulers of the individual processors have to do to coordinate for this purpose. As yet another example, oftentimes we are given only the overall deadline of each chain of jobs (i.e., a set of jobs whose precedence graph is a chain) on different processors and, hence, the freedom to choose intermediate deadlines of individual jobs in the chain. The problem here is how to derive the intermediate deadlines of jobs in the midst of each chain from the given deadline of the job at the end of the chain.

This chapter describes solutions to these problems. In order to establish a common framework for our discussion, Section 9.1 provides details on the model of multiprocessor and

---

[1] According to our model, even a PC has two processors: a CPU and a disk, which we call "processors." Earlier chapters assume that there is no disk activities when the system is running. Hence, it suffices to model only the CPU. If we want to study the performance of disk scheduling algorithms, we need to include the disk and disk controller explicitly in our model.

distributed systems that we skipped in Chapter 3. Unavoidably, we will need some additional terms and notations. Section 9.1 also introduces them and the assumptions that we will make throughout the chapter.

9.1 MODEL OF MULTIPROCESSOR AND DISTRIBUTED SYSTEMS

The common feature that is shared by the diverse systems studied in this chapter is that each system contains more than one processor. Some systems are commonly known as multiprocessor systems and others as distributed systems. A multiprocessor system is *tightly coupled* so that global status and workload information on all processors can be kept current at a low cost. The system may use a centralized dispatcher/scheduler. When each processor has its own scheduler, the decisions and actions of the schedulers of all the processors are coherent. In contrast, a distributed system is *loosely coupled*; in such a system, it is costly to keep global status and workload information current. The schedulers on different processors may make scheduling and resource access control decisions independently. As a consequence, their decisions may be incoherent as a whole.

Throughout this chapter, we assume that *each processor has its own scheduler*. Among the criteria we will use to evaluate each scheduling, resource access-control, or synchronization algorithm is how much the algorithm relies on current global information, how much coordination among schedulers is required and, therefore, how suitable the algorithm is for loosely coupled systems. Except for occasional reminders of this issue, we do not distinguish multiprocessors from distributed systems and call them all multiprocessors or multiprocessor systems (as opposed to uniprocessors and uniprocessor systems studied earlier.)

9.1.1 Identical versus Heterogeneous Processors

In Chapter 3, we discussed briefly the necessity of dividing processors into different types. We say that processors are of the same type, or they are *identical*, if the processors can be used interchangeably. For example, each of the CPUs in a parallel machine can execute every computation job in the system; therefore the CPUs are identical. If any message from a source to a destination can be sent on any of the data links connecting them, then the links are identical.

In contrast, processors of different types cannot be used interchangeably. Different types of processors may be functionally different. For example, CPUs, file disks, and transmission links are functionally different. Obviously, they cannot be used interchangeably. In addition, processors may be of different types for many other reasons. For example, if the designer decides to use some CPUs for some components of the application system but not others, then the CPUs are divided into different types according to the components that can execute on them. In a static system, the application system is partitioned into μ components and jobs in each component execute on a fixed CPU; we view the CPUs as μ different processors. Here, we are not concerned with why processors are different but simply assume that the types of processors are given to us.

The model of heterogeneous processors used here is known as the *unrelated processor* model in scheduling theory literature [Blas]. According to this model, each job can execute on some types of processor but, in general, not on all types. Different types of processors may have different speeds. The execution times of each job on different types of processors are "unrelated," hence the name of the model. For example, the execution time of a computation-intensive job may be one second on CPU1 but is five seconds on a less powerful CPU2. On the other hand, because CPU2 has better interrupt handling and I/O capabilities, the execution time of an I/O-intensive job is ten seconds on CPU1 but is only three seconds on CPU2. Both of these jobs cannot execute on a transmission link and signal processor, so their execution times on these types of processors are infinite. You can see that the unrelated processor model allows us to characterize all systems.

We will consistently use the letter P to denote processor(s). In general, the system contains μ types of processors. There are a total of m_i processors of type i. The total number m of processors is $\sum_{i=1}^{\mu} m_i$. In most of our discussion, the types of processors are not relevant, and we call the processor simply by P_i for $i = 1, 2, \ldots, m$. We need to keep in mind at all times, however, that the processors may be different even when this fact is not stated explicitly.

9.1.2 End-to-End Jobs and Tasks

In the previous four chapters, we viewed jobs as individual units of work. They have their own given release times and deadlines and are independent except for resource conflicts. In practice, a system function is often provided by a set of related jobs, that is, a task. The jobs in each task may have precedence constraints. Here, we focus our attention on the special case where the precedence graph of each task is a chain. This simplifies our discussion and covers a wide range of situations of practical interest. Moreover, most of the algorithms and protocols described later generalize straightforwardly to tasks whose precedence graphs are trees and forests.

For example, in an air surveillance system, a collision avoidance task may consist of a sequence of jobs that execute when an aircraft first enters its coverage area. The first job processes the radar data on a signal processor to generate a track record on the target's location and velocity. The second job transmits the track record to a data processor. The third job correlates the track record with tracks and track records of other targets on the data processor to detect potential collisions. These jobs may be followed by jobs that display the target, decide the corrective action to deal with the target, and so on. Similarly, a task in a real-time monitor system may consists of three jobs: sampling, encoding, and processing the reading of a sensor on a field processor; sending the sensor data by a communication processor to the central control processor; and correlating and displaying the data with other sensor data on the control processor.

Job Shops and Flow Shops.   From these examples, we see that concurrency in a multiprocessor arises naturally as jobs of different tasks sequencing through different processors in a pipeline fashion. The classical *job shop* and *flow shop* models [GaJS, Fren] capture this type of concurrency. According to the job shop model, each task T_i in the system is a chain of $n(i)$ jobs, denoted by $J_{i,k}$ for $k = 1, 2, \ldots, n(i)$. For all $1 \leq k < n(i)$, adjacent jobs $J_{i,k}$ and $J_{i,k+1}$ on the chain execute on different processors. $J_{i,k+1}$ becomes ready for execution when $J_{i,k}$ completes. We denote the (maximum) execution time of job $J_{i,k}$ by $e_{i,k}$. The real-time monitor task, for example, is a chain of three jobs. The air surveillance task is a chain of more than four jobs. A task to transmit a packet in a packet-switched network consists of jobs which model the transmissions of the packet by the switches en route from the source to the destination.

We specify the processors on which the $n(i)$ jobs in each task T_i execute by the *visit sequence* $\mathbf{V}_i = (V_{i,1}, V_{i,2}, \ldots, V_{i,n(i)})$ of the task [Bett]. The kth entry $V_{i,k}$ in this sequence gives the name of the processor on which the job $J_{i,k}$ executes. So, the visit sequence of the real-time monitor task is (*field processor, communication processor, control processor*). Visit sequences $\mathbf{V}_1 = (P_1, P_3)$ and $\mathbf{V}_2 = (P_2, P_3, P_4, P_3, P_1)$ of tasks T_1 and T_2 in a system of four processors tell us that T_1 has two jobs, $J_{1,1}$ on P_1 followed by $J_{1,2}$ on P_3, while T_2 has five jobs and they execute in turn on P_2, then on P_3, P_4, P_3, and finally on P_1.

A *flow shop* is a special job shop in which all tasks have the same visit sequence. For example, suppose that all the tasks in a real-time monitor system are similar to the monitor task mentioned above; each task samples, processes, and displays the reading of a different sensor. The visit sequences of all the monitor tasks are (*field processor, communication processor, control processor*) if the system has only one processor of each of the three types. This system can be modeled as a flow shop.

End-to-End Timing Constraints.   The job shop model of multiprocessor systems we adopt here differs from the classical model in two ways. The first difference is a substantive one. The classical job shop model assumes that all tasks are ready for execution at the same time. Typically, the objective of classical job shop scheduling is to maximize the throughput (i.e., the number of tasks completed per unit time) of the system or to minimize the average response time of the tasks. In contrast, our tasks have arbitrary release times and deadlines, and some tasks have hard deadlines. Meeting hard deadlines is always our primary objective.

The timing constraints that can be derived directly from the high-level requirements of the application are typically end-to-end in nature. They give the release time and deadline of each task as a whole. For example, suppose that the surveillance system mentioned earlier is required to issue a command for an evasive action whenever a collision is detected. The high-level requirement that a correct evasive action be taken in time imposes an overall relative deadline on the collision avoidance task associated with each target monitored by the system.

Formally, we let the release time r_i of a task T_i in a job shop be the release time of the first job $J_{i,1}$ in the task. The deadline d_i of the task is the deadline of its last job $J_{i,n(i)}$. As long as the last job completes by the task's deadline, it is not important when the other jobs in the task complete. The executions of these jobs are constrained only by the dependencies between them and by the fact that they must complete sufficiently early to allow the on-time completion of the last job. Because the timing constraints of such a task are imposed on the jobs at the two ends of the task, we call them *end-to-end release time* and *end-to-end deadline* when we want to emphasize this point. A task that has an end-to-end release time and deadline is an *end-to-end task*. We will use the term end-to-end task hereafter, since it is more informative than "task in a job shop."

Periodic End-to-End Tasks.   The second difference between the classical job shop model and ours is mostly a matter of notation. Just like periodic tasks in a uniprocessor environment, end-to-end tasks in a multiprocessor system may be periodic. An end-to-end task T_i is periodic with period p_i if a chain of $n(i)$ jobs is released every p_i (or more) units of time and the jobs in the chain execute in turn on processors according to the visit sequence $(V_{i,1}, V_{i,2}, \ldots, V_{i,n(i)})$. We call the infinite sequence of jobs that executes on processor $V_{i,k}$ the kth subtask $T_{i,k}$, for $k = 1, 2, \ldots, n(i)$, of T_i. As an example, we return to the real-time monitor tasks mentioned earlier. Each task is a periodic end-to-end task because during each sampling period, a chain of three jobs are released to sample and process a sensor reading, to transmit the sensor data, and to correlate and display the data. So, this task consists of three subtasks; they are the sequences of jobs that execute on the field processor, the communication processor, and the control processor, respectively.

To be exact, the first subtask $T_{i,1}$ of an end-to-end periodic task T_i is a periodic task with period p_i. Following the completion of the jth job of the first subtask $T_{i,1}$ on processor $V_{i,1}$, the jth job of the second subtask $T_{i,2}$ can be released on processor $V_{i,2}$. Similarly, following the completion of the jth job of the kth subtask $T_{i,k}$ on processor $V_{i,k}$, the jth job in the $(k+1)$st subtask $T_{i,k+1}$ can be released on processor $V_{i,k+1}$. As you will see later in Section 9.4, the subsequent subtasks $T_{i,k}$ for $k > 1$ may or may not be periodic tasks, depending on the protocol used to synchronize the jobs on different processors.

We call the end-to-end periodic task T_i the parent task of the $n(i)$ subtasks, and subtasks in the same parent task are sibling (sub)tasks. The *period of an end-to-end periodic task* is the period of its first subtask. For the sake of convenience, we say that the period of a parent task is also the periods of all the subtasks in it, even when some of its subtasks are not periodic. By the phase ϕ_i of an end-to-end periodic task T_i, we mean the release time of the first job of its first subtask. The execution time $e_{i,k}$ (for $k = 1, 2, \ldots, n(i)$) of the subtask $T_{i,k}$ is the maximum amount of time required to complete any job in $T_{i,k}$.

Parallelism.   In addition to pipelined executions of jobs on different types of processors, parallel executions are possible whenever there is more than one processor of the same type. In an air traffic control system, for example, there may be an array of signal processors, making it possible to execute many FFTs in parallel. Similarly, multiple links and switches between a sender and receiver pair provide parallel paths that can be used to increase the throughput or reduce delays of messages between them. The traditional multiprocessor models (e.g., [Blas, EaLA]) used in studies on parallel and distributed scheduling, task assignment, and load balancing capture this parallelism.

To exploit parallelism, we may want to dispatch and schedule jobs on processors dynamically (i.e., make the system dynamic). As it will be become evident later in Section 9.7, while the advantage of parallel execution of jobs with soft timing constraints is obvious, serious difficulties in the validation of hard timing constraints remain. We do not know how to determine in a robust, efficient, and accurate way whether a dynamic system of hard real-time jobs can meet all the deadlines. For this reason, we adopt the dynamic approach only in some special cases, such as signal processing, where either validation is easy or jobs have soft timing constraints.

9.1.3   Local versus Remote Resources

We assume that each resource resides on a processor. By a resource R residing on a processor, we mean that the scheduler of the processor controls the access to the resource R and when a job uses the resource, its critical section executes on the processor. We now describe two resource models: the MPCP model and the end-to-end model; they give us two somewhat different views of a multiprocessor system.

MPCP Resource Model.   An extension of the priority-ceiling protocol to control resource access in multiprocessor systems is called the *Multiprocessor Priority-Ceiling Protocol* (MPCP) [ShRL88], which we will describe in Section 9.3. We call the model used by this protocol the MPCP model. This model calls the processor on which each resource resides its *synchronization processor*. The processor on which each job is released and becomes ready for execution is the *local processor* of the job. From the perspective of a job, a resource that also resides on the local processor of the job is a *local resource*, and a resource that resides on another processor is a *remote resource*. A *global resource* is required by jobs that have different local processors.

Figure 9–1 gives an example. The system shown here has three jobs, two processors, P_1 and P_2, and two resources, *printer* and *fileServer*. Processor P_1 is the synchronization processor of *printer*, and processor P_2 is the synchronization processor of *fileServer*. The jobs J_1 and J_2 are local to P_1, while J_3 is a local job on P_2. Suppose that J_1 is a text formating and printing job. It executes on P_1 and uses only the local resource *printer*. In other words, it has only a *local critical section*, which is shown as a shaded box in the figure. Similarly, the backup job J_3 requires only *fileServer*. Since *fileServer* resides on its local processor, this resource is local to J_3. (Critical sections during which the *fileServer* is used are shown as black boxes.) On the other hand, during the execution of J_2, it requires a file maintained by the *fileServer*. *fileServer* is a global resource. During the remote *global critical section* while J_2 uses this resource, the file server executes on the behalf of J_2 on P_2. (Later, we will simply say that the global critical section of J_2 executes on P_2.) After the global critical section of J_2 completes, it returns to execute on P_1 and uses the *printer* before it completes.

In summary, according to the MPCP model, a job may require both local and remote resources. The access to each resource is controlled by the scheduler of the synchronization processor of the resource. The critical section during which the job uses a resource executes on the synchronization processor of the resource. Hence, a job that has κ_r (outermost) remote critical sections gives up its local processor κ_r times and become eligible for execution on its

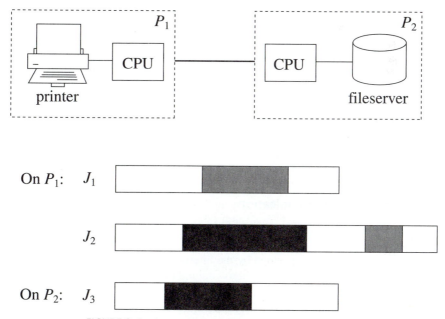

FIGURE 9–1   A system containing local and remote resources.

local processor $\kappa_r + 1$ times. Requests for resources on each processor may be from local jobs and remote jobs, and the resource access-control protocol used on the processor may handle these requests in different ways.

In general, local and remote critical sections of a job may be nested. A job may hold a resource on one processor and then request resources on another processor. The MPCP model allows such nested critical sections. However, the multiprocessor priority-ceiling protocol described later in Section 9.3 no longer ensures bounded blocking time, and the performance of any straightforward modification of the protocol can be very poor if such critical sections are allowed.

End-to-End Resource Model. A reasonable restriction is that no job makes nested requests for resources that reside on different processors. Stated another way, all the resources used by every job during every nested critical section reside on the same processor. In a system that satisfies this assumption, we can view each job that requires resources on more than one processor as an end-to-end job.

For example, job J_2 in Figure 9–1 consists of three component jobs. The first one executes on its local processor and does not require any resource. Its remote critical section is the second component, and this component executes on the remote processor P_2. The third component job is the portion after the remote critical section and executes on P_1. Since J_1 and J_3 do not require any remote resource, each of them consists of only one component.

In general, each job that requires only local resources has only one component, which, of course, executes on the local processor. Each remote outermost critical section of a job is a component job which executes on the synchronization processor of the remote resources guarded by the critical section and the critical sections nested in it. A portion of a job is a component job on its local processor if the portion (1) is before or after a remote critical section (or a sequence of contiguous remote critical sections) and (2) either requires no resource or only local resources. Hence, a job that has κ_r remote outermost critical sections can have up to $2\kappa_r + 1$ component jobs, and they execute alternately on the local processor, then on a remote processor, then back on the local processor, and so on until the last component job completes on the local processor. By this definition, every component job requires only resources on the processor on which the component job executes. The scheduler of each processor can treat all requests for resources controlled by it as local requests.

This resource model fits naturally within the end-to-end job (task) model. In our subsequent discussion, we do not distinguish jobs from component jobs and call them all jobs. Each job in an end-to-end task requires only resources on its local processor. From the above discussion, we know that this assumption leads to no loss of generality.

9.1.4 Interprocessor Communication

In Section 9.2, we will describe algorithms that we can use to partition an application system into components, called modules, and assign modules to processors. These algorithms make use of the information provided by the interconnection parameters of jobs defined in Section 3.4. (You recall that these parameters include the volume of shared data exchanged between each pair of dependent jobs.) However, you will see that in all sections of this chapter except Section 9.2, we seem to ignore the time required to synchronize jobs and transmit data among them. The reason is that it is not necessary to account for the cost of interprocessor communication separately in an ad hoc manner. The task and resource models used here allow us to take this cost into account in several ways. We now examine some of these ways.

A special case of practical interest is where interprocessor communication is via shared memory. Sometimes, we treat shared memory as a plentiful resource and do not include this resource in our model. The implication is that the execution of a job is never adversely affected by memory contention; therefore, the cost of interprocessor communication is negligible. This assumption is clearly not true in general. When the assumption is not true, we can model shared memory explicitly either as a resource or as a processor.

As an example, Figure 9–2(a) shows a possible configuration of a real-time monitor system that has many field processors. The producer jobs that collect and process sensor data execute on these processors. Consumer jobs that correlate and display the data execute on the control processor. The jobs communicate via a shared dual-port memory. Each field processor

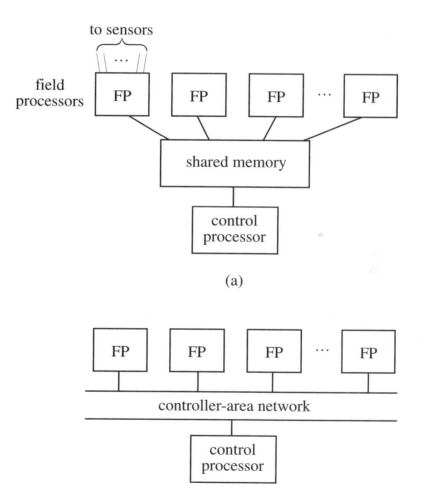

(a)

(b)

FIGURE 9–2   Examples of interprocessor communication architectures.

is connected via a dedicated link to a port of the memory that is shared by all field processors. To take into account the effect of memory contention, we can model the shared memory as a processor. The system contains three types of processors: field processors, shared-memory "processor," and the control processor. The workload consists of end-to-end jobs, each containing a memory-access job. (Specifically, each producer is an end-to-end job whose first component executes on a field processor and whose memory-access component executes on the shared memory. Each consumer job is an end-to-end job which first executes on the shared memory and then on the control processor.) In this way, the delay in the completion of each job caused by memory contention is taken into account by the response time of the memory-access component of the job. Alternatively, you can model the shared memory as a global resource whose synchronization processor is the shared-memory "processor," and both the producer and consumer jobs require this resource.

Figure 9–2(b) shows another configuration where all the processors are connected via a network. Specifically the network is a Controller Area Network (CAN) [ISO93], which we will describe in Section 11.4. The results produced by each job on the field processor are sent via the network to the control processor. Such a network can be modeled as a processor on which message transmission jobs are scheduled nonpreemptively on a fixed-priority basis. You can see that we do not need to include the interprocessor communication costs in our model because they are taken into account by the response times of the message-transmission jobs on the network.

In general, communication networks can be modeled naturally as processors. The scheduling algorithms used on some networks, such as the IEEE 802.5 token ring [Stal] and CAN, more or less resemble priority-driven algorithms used for CPU scheduling. Other types of networks, such as the FDDI network [Stal], may use very different scheduling algorithms. In all cases, we can take into account interprocessor communication costs by including network processor(s) and message-transmission jobs in our model. There is no need to consider this factor separately in some ad hoc manner.

Finally, CPUs may be connected via dedicated links. When message transmissions between a pair of CPUs are under program control (e.g., in polling or synchronized message transfer), each simplex link can be modeled as single-unit resource on the sending CPU. When a job sends a message, it is in a critical section using this resource. When message transmissions are done via a DMA (Direct Memory-Access) interface, we can take into account the time required for sending each message by lengthening the execution time(s) of job(s) that execute concurrently with DMA-controlled message transmissions. In both cases, we can take into account the effect of interprocessor communication by adjusting the execution time and blocking time parameters of all the jobs in the system accordingly. In subsequent sections, we will assume such adjustments have already been made.

9.1.5 Structure of Distributed Scheduler for End-to-End Tasks

To conclude this lengthy section, we remind ourselves that the primary objective of scheduling in a multiprocessor system is to ensure that all the end-to-end timing constraints are met. The end-to-end scheduling problem differs fundamentally from the problems on multiprocessor and distributed scheduling. The latter are concerned with scheduling jobs on interchangeable processors so as to maximize the likelihood of on-time completion, to equalize resource utilization, to provide redundancy, to increase availability, and so on. Many excellent multiprocessor and distributed scheduling algorithms can be found in the literature. They can be used with end-to-end scheduling algorithms when appropriate to improve the overall performance of a multiprocessor system, but by themselves, are not solutions to the end-to-end scheduling problem.

Most of the scheduling algorithms described in this chapter are for scheduling end-to-end tasks. A common assumption made by all of them is that each processor has its own scheduler. The scheduler uses a uniprocessor scheduling algorithm or an extension of such an algorithm to schedule the jobs on the processor. Schedulers on different processors may use different scheduling algorithms.

In addition, the schedulers on all the processors synchronize dependent jobs on different processors according to a (*execution*) *synchronization protocol*. This protocol governs when a job $J_{i,k}$ on a processor $V_{i,k}$ is released and ready for execution after its immediate predecessor $J_{i,k-1}$ completes on $V_{i,k-1}$, which scheduler makes this determination, and whether and how the actions of the schedulers are coordinated.

9.2 TASK ASSIGNMENT

If the system is static, as most current hard real-time systems are, the application system is partitioned into modules, and modules are assigned and bound to processors. We call this step *task assignment*. Oftentimes, task assignment is done off-line. At some stage in the design and development process of a real-time system, the execution times, resource requirements, data and control dependencies, and timing constraints of all the tasks become known. Task assignment is then done to determine how many processors of each type are needed, how the tasks should be partitioned, and on which processor each application module executes. Sometimes, task assignment is done on-line. In a system where application tasks may be created and admitted to the system at any time, task assignment to decide where to execute each new task is the first step of an acceptance test on a multiprocessor application.

This section describes three increasingly more complex formulations of the task assignment problem and task assignment algorithms based on these formulations. The first one ignores both the costs of communication and the placements of resources. The second one considers communication costs only while the third one considers both communication costs and resource-access costs. A system may use all three approaches at one time or the other. Except for trivial cases, the problem of finding an optimal assignment of tasks to processors is NP-hard in the strong sense [GaJo79]. Finding an optimal assignment is usually impractical, even when assignment is done off-line. The formulations presented here have good heuristics and software packages which give suboptimal solutions in reasonable amounts of time.

9.2.1 Task Assignment Based on Execution-Time Requirements

Sometimes, it is appropriate to consider only the processing time requirements of the jobs and tasks and ignore communication costs. An example is when all tasks communicate via a shared memory; so, the communication costs of individual tasks are independent of where the tasks execute. For some applications (e.g., signal processing), it is possible to provide a sufficient number of memory modules and carefully lay out the address spaces of tasks to minimize memory contention. For these applications, the cost of communication can be made negligibly small.

During the early design stage, we may want to ignore communication and resource-access costs despite the fact that they may be significant and depend on where the tasks execute. At this stage, most parameters of the tasks are still unknown, but it may be possible to estimate roughly the execution times of the tasks from the complexities of the algorithms executed by them. The simple task assignment algorithms described below can then be used to determine whether the number and kinds of processors planned for the system are likely to be adequate. The number and characteristics of the tasks in some applications may change during run time. These algorithms are efficient enough for the purposes of on-line acceptance test and load balancing.

Simple Bin-Packing Formulation. In its simplest form, the task assignment problem can be stated as follows. We are given the utilizations of n periodic tasks. We are asked to partition the system into modules in such a way that the tasks in each module are schedulable by themselves on a processor according to a uniprocessor scheduling algorithm of a given class. A task assignment is defined by the subset of tasks in every module, that is, the tasks assigned to each processor. We say that an assignment requires m processors if it partitions the n tasks into m schedulable modules. The quality of a task assignment is measured solely by the number of processors required by the assignment. The smaller the number of processors required by an assignment, the better the assignment.

As an example, suppose that we want to schedule n independent, preemptable periodic tasks whose relative deadlines are equal to their respective periods according to the EDF algorithm. The total utilization of all the tasks exceeds 1; so it is impossible to feasibly schedule them on one processor. To determine how to partition the tasks so they are schedulable on a minimum number of processors, it suffices for us to know the utilization u_i, for $i = 1, 2, \ldots, n$, of all the tasks. We know that the tasks in each module are schedulable if their total utilization is no greater than 1. However, we may constrain the total utilization of all tasks in each module to be equal to or less than some value $\hat{U} < 1$. In this way, we leave some spare capacity on each processor for sporadic and aperiodic tasks and future extensions. It is straightforward to formulate this task assignment problem as the simple bin-packing problem [CoGJ]: the sizes of all the bins are equal to $\hat{U}$, and sizes of the items to be packed into the bins are u_i, for $i = 1, 2, \ldots, n$. The number of bins required to pack all the items is the number of processors required to feasibly schedule all n tasks. The tasks represented by the items packed in each bin are in a module assigned on a processor. We can use one of the well-known bin-packing algorithms to find an optimal or suboptimal packing.

Many other task assignment problems are also equivalent to this simple *uniform-size bin-packing problem*. For example, we can work with densities of tasks if the periodic tasks have relative deadlines that are shorter than their respective periods or when some tasks are sporadic. Partitioning rate-monotonically scheduled periodic tasks is the same bin-packing problem if we use ln 2 as the schedulability criterion. As another example, suppose that we are given a set of independent jobs that are released at the same time and have the same relative deadline and we are asked to schedule the jobs nonpreemptively on a minimum number of identical processors to meet the deadline. We again have this bin-packing problem, where the bin size is equal to the relative deadline of the jobs and the sizes of the items to pack are equal to the execution times of the jobs.

More generally, tasks may need to execute on different types of processors. If every task can only execute on one type of processor, then all the tasks in the system are partitioned into

μ disjoint subsets according to the types of processors on which they can execute. Therefore, we can find the assignment of tasks in one subset at a time. Each time, we focus on the tasks that require type i processors and find an assignment of these tasks on type i processors. The bin-packing formulation cannot deal with the general case where tasks can execute on more than one type of processor, but the two more complex approaches to be described later can.

The bin-packing problem is NP-complete, but there are many simple and good heuristic algorithms to solve it. An example is the first-fit algorithm. According to this algorithm, tasks are assigned one by one in turn in an arbitrary order. The first task is assigned to processor P_1. After $i - 1$ tasks have been assigned, the ith task T_i is assigned to the processor P_k if the total utilization of T_i and the tasks already assigned to P_k is equal to or less than $\hat{U}$, but assigning T_i to any of the processors $P_1, P_2, \ldots, P_{k-1}$ would make the total utilization of tasks on the processor larger than $\hat{U}$. The number of processors required by the assignment is the number of processors on which some task is assigned.

It is common to measure the worst-case performance of a heuristic bin-packing algorithm by the ratio of the number of processors required by an assignment produced by the algorithm to the number m_o of processors required by an optimal assignment in the limit as m_o approaches infinity. (A large m_o means a large total utilization of the system.) This ratio is never more than 1.7 for the first-fit algorithm [CoGJ]. Simulation results show that when the utilizations of tasks are uniformly distributed in $[0, \hat{U}]$, the total utilization per processor achievable by the first-fit algorithm is $0.93\hat{U}$ on average.

Sometimes, we are given a fixed number m of processors. In this situation, a more meaningful question is how large can the total utilization of the periodic tasks be for the existence of a feasible assignment, that is, an assignment according to which the tasks on every processor are schedulable? Oh and Baker [OhBa] showed that in a system containing m identical processors, each scheduled on a fixed-priority basis, the first-fit algorithm can always find a feasible assignment if the total utilization U of the independent, preemptable periodic tasks is no greater than

$$U_{FF} = m(2^{1/2} - 1) = 0.414m \tag{9.1a}$$

In other words, U_{FF} is the schedulable utilization of the first-fit assignment algorithm for a fixed-priority system containing m processors. Oh and Baker also found that if the total utilization of the periodic tasks exceeds $(m + 1)(1 + 2^{1/(m+1)})$, the first-fit algorithm may not find a feasible assignment on m processors. For m equal to 2, the lower bound $0.414m$ is slightly larger than 60 percent of this upper bound, and for large m, the lower bound is more than 80 percent of the upper bound.

Many well-known off-line heuristics have even better worst-case and average performances. The first-fit decreasing algorithm is an example. This algorithm is the same as the first-fit algorithm except that the tasks are first sorted in nonincreasing order according to their utilizations and are assigned in turn in that order. The ratio of the number of processors required by the first-fit decreasing algorithm to the number m_o of processors required by an optimal algorithm is only 1.22 in the limit as m_o approaches infinity. On the average, the total utilization of tasks assigned to each processor is 98 percent of the total allowed utilization $\hat{U}$.

The existence of simple heuristic bin-packing algorithms and the knowledge of their average and worst-case performance make the uniform-size bin-packing formulation of the task assignment problem a good approach. Again, we can use this simple method to estimate the number of processors of each type needed to feasibly schedule all the tasks and to determine on-line whether a new task can be accepted and which processor should be used to execute the task if it is accepted.

Variable-Size Bin-Packing Formulation. There are more accurate schedulability conditions for fixed-priority tasks than that their total utilization is no greater than ln 2. The performance of a bin-packing algorithm may be improved if it uses one of these conditions as the schedulability criterion of fixed-priority tasks on each processor. For example, suppose we choose to schedule the periodic tasks on each processor rate-monotonically. We can use the schedulable utilization $U_{RM}(n(i))$ given by Eq. (6.10) as the schedulability criterion: $n(i)$ tasks can be assigned to a processor P_i if their total utilization is no more than $U_{RM}(n(i))$. Since $U_{RM}(n(i))$ is larger than ln 2, we may find an assignment that requires fewer processors and, hence a better assignment.

However, because the total utilization of tasks that can be put on a processor is now a function of the number of tasks, the size of the bin corresponding to each processor P_i depends on the number of items placed in the bin. We now have a more complex bin-packing problem: a variable-size bin-packing problem. Most known heuristic algorithms require some other parameter of all the tasks in addition to their utilizations and are not suited for on-line task assignment.

RMFF Algorithm. The Rate-Monotonic-First-Fit (RMFF) algorithm [DhLi] is such a heuristic algorithm. According to this algorithm, tasks are first sorted in nondecreasing order according to their periods. We assign each task in turn, starting from task T_1, until all tasks are assigned in the first-fit manner. A task T_i can be assigned to a processor if the total utilization of T_i and the x tasks already assigned to the processor is equal to or less than $U_{RM}(x + 1)$.

As an example, we consider the periodic tasks whose parameters are listed in the table in Figure 9–3. Their total utilization is 1.903. The assignment produced by the RMFF algorithm

T_i	u_i	T_i	u_i	T_i	u_i
(2, 1)	0.500	(4.5, 0.1)	0.022	(8, 1)	0.125
(2.5, 0.1)	0.040	(5, 1)	0.200	(8.5, 0.1)	0.012
(3, 1)	0.333	(6, 1)	0.167	(9, 1)	0.111
(4, 1)	0.250	(7, 1)	0.143		

P_1: (2, 1), (2.5, 0.1), (4.5, 0.1), (6, 1), (8.5, 0.1)
P_2: (3, 1), (4, 1), (7, 1)
P_3: (5, 1), (8, 1), (9, 1)

(a)

P_1: (2, 1), (3, 1), (6, 1)
P_2: (4, 1), (5, 1), (7, 1), (8, 1), (9, 1)
P_3: (2.5, 0.1), (4.5, 0.1), (8.5, 0.1)

(b)

FIGURE 9–3 Example of task assignments. (a) The RMFF assignment. (b) An optimal assignment.

is given in Figure 9–3(a). The tasks listed after each processor name are assigned to that processor. The RMFF assignment requires three processors. The number turns out to be the minimum. (To see why three processors are required, we look at the assignment in Figure 9–3(b). The tasks on each of the processors P_1 and P_2 fully utilize the processor, making the third processor necessary.)

Unfortunately, the worst-case performance of the RMFF algorithm is far from that indicated by the above example. The ratio of number of processors required by an assignment produced by the RMFF algorithm to the number m_o of processors required by an assignment produced by an optimal algorithm is never less than 2.0 and never more than 2.23 in the limit as m_o approaches infinity.

The RMST and RMGT Algorithms.   The RMFF algorithm does not exploit the fact that the schedulable utilization of tasks on a processor is higher when the tasks are closer to being simply periodic. From Theorem 6.13, we know that when tasks are scheduled rate-monotonically on a processor, their schedulable utilization is significantly higher if the tasks can be partitioned into a small number of subsets each of which contains simply periodic tasks. Hence, a good approach to task assignment is to first partition the given set of periodic tasks into such subsets. Each subset of simply periodic tasks is schedulable as long as the total utilization of the subset is no greater than one. If more than one subset is assigned to a processor, their schedulable utilization is a function of the number of subsets, not the number of tasks.

The Rate-Monotonic Small Tasks (RMST) algorithm proposed by Burchard, *et al.* [BLOS] uses a similar principle. It is for systems in which tasks assigned to each processor are scheduled rate-monotonically. The algorithm is based on Theorem 6.14. It first sorts the periodic tasks in nondecreasing order according to their parameters X_i's which are calculated from their periods according to Eq. (6.14b). (For a task with period p_i, $X_i = \log_2 p_i - \lfloor \log_2 p_i \rfloor$.) It then assigns the tasks in this order on processors in the first-fit manner. The schedulability condition

$$u_i + U_k \leq \max(\ln 2, 1 - \zeta_k \ln 2)$$

used to check whether a task T_i can be assigned to a processor P_k is a corollary of Theorem 6.14. In this inequality, U_k is the total utilization of the tasks that have already been assigned to P_k when T_i is being assigned. The parameter ζ_k is equal to $\max_l X_l - \min_l X_l$ where the max and min functions are taken over T_i and the tasks already assigned to P_k. You recall that the value of ζ defined by Eq. (6.14a) for the given subset of periodic tasks is smaller when the period of every task T_l in the subset is closer to being equal to $y2^{x_l}$ for some constant y common to all tasks and a positive integer x_l. Theorem 6.14 says that the schedulable utilization of a subset of periodic tasks is a nonincreasing function of ζ. The complexity of the algorithm is $O(n \log n)$ for a system containing n periodic tasks.

To illustrate, Figure 9–4 lists the tasks in Figure 9–3 in nondecreasing order according to the parameter X_i. Clearly, tasks with periods 2, 4, and 8 can be assigned to one processor (P_1). The task with period 8.5 can also be assigned to this processor. The total utilization of the tasks on this processor is 0.887, which is less than $1 - 0.087 \times \ln 2 = 0.94$. However, the task with period 4.5 cannot be assigned to P_1 because if we were to assign this task to P_1, ζ_1 would be 0.170 and the total utilization of the first five tasks would have to be less than $1 - 0.170 \times \ln 2 = 0.882$, while the total utilization of the five tasks is 0.920. So, the task with

T_i	u_i	X_i	T_i	u_i	X_i
(2, 1)	0.500	0	(2.5, 0.1)	0.040	0.322
(4, 1)	0.250	0	(5, 1)	0.200	0.322
(8, 1)	0.125	0	(3, 1)	0.333	0.585
(8.5, 0.1)	0.012	0.087	(6, 1)	0.167	0.585
(4.5, 0.1)	0.033	0.170	(7, 1)	0.143	0.807
(9, 1)	0.111	0.170			

P_1: (2, 1), (4, 0), (8, 1), (8.5, 0.1)
P_2: (4.5, 0.1), (9, 1), (2.5, 0.1), (5, 1), (6, 1)
P_3: (3, 1), (7, 1)

FIGURE 9–4 An RMST assignment of tasks in Figure 9–3.

period 4.5 is assigned on P_2. You may want to check for yourself that none of the other tasks can be assigned on P_1 and the tasks with periods 3 and 7 cannot be assigned to P_2.

Let u_{max} denote the maximum of the utilizations of the periodic tasks in the system. Burchard, *et al.* showed that in a system containing $m \geq 2$ processors, the schedulable utilization of the RMST algorithm is

$$U_{RMST} = (m - 2)(1 - u_{max}) + 1 - \ln 2 \qquad (9.1b)$$

that is, this algorithm can always find a feasible assignment if the total utilization U of the tasks is no greater than U_{RMST}. The ratio of the number of processors required by an assignment produced by the RMST algorithm to the number m_o of processors required by an optimal algorithm is $1/(1 - u_{max})$ in the limit as m_o approaches infinity.

Comparing Eqs. (9.1a) and Eq. (9.1b), we see that for large m, the RMST algorithm performs better than the RMFF algorithm only when u_{max} is smaller than 0.586. The performance of the Rate-Monotonic General Task (RMGT) algorithm, also by Burchard, *et al.*, does not depend on the utilizations of the individual tasks. It can produce a feasible assignment on m processors whenever the total utilization of all periodic tasks is no greater than

$$U_{RMGT} = 0.5 \left(m - \frac{5}{2} \ln 2 + \frac{1}{3} \right) = 0.5(m - 1.4) \qquad (9.1c)$$

The RMGT algorithm first partitions all periodic tasks into two subsets according to their utilization. Tasks whose utilization is equal to or smaller than 1/3 are in one subset. These tasks are first assigned to processors according to the RMST algorithm. Then, the large tasks whose utilization is larger than 1/3 are assigned on the first-fit basis to processors each of which has at most one task assigned by the RMST algorithm. The time-demand analysis method is used to check whether a large task can be assigned on a processor that already has a task.

9.2.2 Task Assignment to Minimize Total Communication Cost

When CPUs are connected via some kind of network, the cost of communication between a pair of tasks is usually significantly lower when they are on the same CPU than when they are on different CPUs. In this situation, we want to take into account communication cost when we partition the tasks into modules and assign them to CPUs. The goal of task assignment is, therefore, to partition all the tasks in the system into modules and assign each module to a processor in such a way that the number of required processors to feasibly schedule all the tasks is minimum and some function of communication costs among tasks in different modules is minimum. In the literature on real-time systems and on multiprocessor and distributed systems, you can find numerous approaches (e.g., simulated annealing [TiBW], branch-and-bound [PeSh], network flow, bin packing, and heuristic search) to different variants of this task assignment problem. Most of these approaches are for off-line task assignment; so is the approach presented here.

Below, we first focus on the special case of homogeneous systems. We then consider the general case of unrelated heterogeneous systems.

Homogeneous Systems.   The cost of communication between two tasks on different processors depends on both the volume of data exchanged between them during their execution and the bandwidth of the communication link connecting the processors. The former is an interconnection parameter of the tasks, and the latter is a parameter of the underlying system. Rather than taking into account both types of parameters at the same time and solving for a task assignment in one step, we divide the problem into two subproblems: task partition and module assignment. The task partition step divides the given system of tasks into modules based solely on the task parameters. The module assignment step assigns modules to processors; this step also takes into account the characteristics of the underlying network used to support interprocessor communication.

The Partition Problem.   For the purpose of deciding which tasks should be put in the same module, we characterize the cost of communication between any pair of tasks T_i and T_k by a single *communication cost* $C_{i,k}$. $C_{i,k}$ can be the total volume of data exchanged during the execution of the jobs in the tasks. For example, if the tasks T_i and T_k are periodic, $C_{i,k}$ can be the total volume of data exchanged between the tasks during any hyperperiod. This measure is sufficiently general because communication overhead (e.g., message processing time and transmission time) are functions of the data volume.

Let $\iota_{i,j}$ denote the *interference cost* that is incurred when tasks T_i and T_j are placed on the same processor. This factor can sometimes be used to account for the effect of memory contention. We can also use it to take into account external constraints on the assignment. If we do not want T_i and T_j to be in the same module for some reason, we can take care of this constraint by letting $\iota_{i,j}$ equal infinity. Otherwise, if T_i and T_j can be in the same module, we let $\iota_{i,j}$ be 0 or some finite cost.

We assume here that the number of processors m and, hence, the number m of modules into which the tasks are to be partitioned are given. The problem of partitioning n periodic tasks into m modules can be formulated as an integer (0/1) linear programming problem. There are research and commercial integer linear programming packages which you can use to solve this problem. You can find them by searching the Web.

In the integer linear program definition given below, $\delta_{i,k}$ is equal to 1 when $i = k$ and is equal 0 when $i \neq k$. The variable $A_{i,k}$ is equal to 1 if the task T_i is placed in the kth module and is equal to zero if T_i is in any other module. The task partition we find by solving the integer linear program is given by the values of $A_{i,k}$, for $i = 1, 2, \ldots, n$ and $k = 1, 2, \ldots, m$.

Integer Linear Programming Formulation of the Partition Problem

We are given, for $i, j = 1, 2, \ldots, n$,

- the utilization u_i of each periodic task T_i;
- the communication cost $C_{i,j}$ for T_i and T_j, which is incurred when the tasks are in different modules;
- the interference cost $\iota_{i,j}$ for T_i and T_j, which is incurred when the tasks are in the same modules; and
- the maximum allowed total utilization $\hat{U}_k$ of all tasks in the kth module.

We are to find $A_{i,k}$, for all $i = 1, 2, \ldots, n$ and $k = 1, 2, \ldots, m$, that satisfy the constraints

$$A_{i,k} = 0, 1 \qquad \text{for } i = 1, 2, \ldots, n \text{ and } k = 1, 2, \ldots, m \qquad (9.2a)$$

$$\sum_{k=1}^{m} A_{i,k} = 1 \qquad \text{for } i = 1, 2, \ldots, n \qquad (9.2b)$$

$$\sum_{i=1}^{n} u_i A_{i,k} \leq \hat{U}_k \qquad \text{for } k = 1, 2, \ldots, m \qquad (9.2c)$$

and minimize the cost function

$$C_{\text{total}} = \sum_{i=1}^{n} \sum_{j=1}^{n} \sum_{k=1}^{m} \sum_{l=1}^{m} (1 - \delta_{i,j}) A_{i,k} A_{j,l} [C_{i,j}(1 - \delta_{k,l}) + \iota_{i,j} \delta_{k,l}] \qquad (9.2d)$$

Eq. (9.2a) restates the definition of the variables $A_{i,k}$'s: The value of each variable $A_{i,k}$ is either 0 or 1. Eq. (9.2b) states that every task must be in one and only one module. Eq. (9.2c) states that the total utilization of all the tasks in the kth module must not exceed the maximum allowed total utilization of that module. The first term in each product term in Eq. (9.2d) makes it unnecessary for us to say that the sum over j includes only values of j not equal to i. Every pair of tasks T_i and T_j contributes $C_{i,j}$ to the total cost function C_{total} if they are placed in different modules (i.e., both $A_{i,k}$ and $A_{j,l}$ are equal to 1 for some $k \neq l$). They contribute $\iota_{i,j}$ if they are placed in the same module (i.e., $A_{i,k}$ and $A_{j,l}$ are equal to 1 for some $k = l$).

For a given m, it is possible that no feasible solution (i.e., a partition satisfying all the constraints) exists. (This would be the case for sure when $\sum_{i=1}^{n} u_i$ is larger than $\sum_{k=1}^{m} \hat{U}_k$.) To find the minimum number of modules required for a feasible solution to exist, we have to solve this integer linear programming problem repeatedly for increasingly larger values of m.

Figure 9–5 gives a simple example. The system has eight tasks, and their parameters are listed in the table in Figure 9–5(a). The total utilization of the tasks is 1.66. Suppose that after the tasks are partitioned and assigned to processors, they will be scheduled on the EDF basis. Hence, the total utilization of tasks in each module can be as large as 1, and $m = 2$ may suffice. For simplicity, we let the interference cost every pair of tasks be equal to 0. The weight of an edge between two vertices T_i and T_j in the task graph in Figure 9–5(b) gives the communication cost between tasks T_i and T_j. Edges with zero weights are omitted from the graph. (In the figure, the weight of each edge is given by number next to the edge.) For $m = 2$, the cost function C_{total} is the sum of the following terms:

i	T_i	u_i	i	T_i	u_i
1	(2, 1)	0.50	5	(6, 1)	0.17
2	(3, 1)	0.33	6	(10, 1)	0.10
3	(4, 1)	0.25	7	(15, 1)	0.07
4	(5, 1)	0.20	8	(25, 1)	0.04

(a)

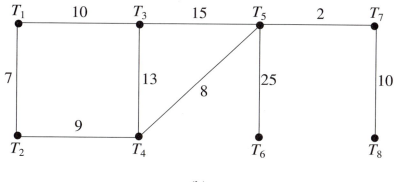

(b)

FIGURE 9–5   Example of task partitioning.

$7(A_{1,1}A_{2,2} + A_{1,2}A_{2,1})$, $10(A_{1,1}A_{3,2} + A_{1,2}A_{3,1})$, $9(A_{2,1}A_{4,2} + A_{2,2}A_{4,1})$, $13(A_{3,1}A_{4,2} + A_{3,2}A_{4,1})$, $15(A_{3,1}A_{5,2} + A_{3,2}A_{5,1})$, $8(A_{4,1}A_{5,2} + A_{4,2}A_{5,1})$, $25(A_{5,1}A_{6,2} + A_{5,2}A_{6,1})$, $2(A_{5,1}A_{7,2} + A_{5,2}A_{7,1})$, and $10(A_{7,1}A_{8,2} + A_{7,2}A_{8,1})$.

(In other words, there is a term $C_{i,j}(A_{i,1}A_{j,2} + A_{i,2}A_{j,1})$ in the right-hand side of Eq. (9.2d) for each nonzero $C_{i,j}$. This cost is incurred if either term in the parentheses is nonzero.)

A solution of the above integer programming problem is given by

$$A_{1,1} = A_{2,1} = A_{3,2} = A_{4,2} = A_{5,2} = A_{6,2} = A_{7,1} = A_{8,1} = 1$$

and all other $A_{i,k}$'s are 0. These values tell us that T_1, T_2, T_7, and T_8 are in module 1, and the remaining four tasks are in module 2. The total utilization of tasks in these modules are 0.94 and 0.72, respectively. Of terms listed above, only $10A_{1,1}A_{3,2}$, $9A_{2,1}A_{4,2}$, and $2A_{5,2}A_{3,1}$ are nonzero. Hence, C_{total} is equal to $10 + 9 + 2 = 21$.

Module Assignment.   If the processors are connected by a broadcast network, the costs of interprocessor communication among all processors are the same. The modules of tasks produced in the partition step can be assigned to processors in an arbitrary manner. Otherwise, the module assignment problem solved in the second step can be stated as follows.

We are given a task graph and a resource graph, and are asked to embed the task graph of modules on the resource graph of processors.

Specifically, in the task graph, there is a vertex for each module T_i in the system. There is an edge between two modules T_i and T_j if the total communication cost of all tasks between the modules is nonzero, and the weight of this edge gives the cost. In the example in Figure 9–5, the task graph obtained after the task partitioning step consists of only two modules. The weight of the edge between them is equal to 21.

In the resource graph, there is a vertex P_i for each processor P_i in the system. An edge between two vertices P_i and P_j represents a direct link between processors P_i and P_j. The weight $b_{i,j}$ of the edge represents some performance measure of the link. An example is the bandwidth of the link. The bandwidth $b_{i,k}$ of a communication path between two processors P_i and P_k that are not directly connected by a link is the minimum (or average, maximum, etc.) bandwidth of all the edges along the path. A path between two processors P_i and P_k, and hence between the modules assigned to the processors, is x hops in length if the minimum (or average, maximum, and so on) length of all the paths between the processors is x.

Our problem is to assign modules to processors such that every module is assigned to a processor and at most one module is assigned to any processor. Moreover, we want the assignment to optimize some cost function or to keep the cost function below an acceptable threshold. Examples of cost functions are

- the average (or maximum) number of hops between modules;
- the average (or maximum) weighted number of hops, which is the average (or maximum) of the number of hops between a module pair times the communication cost between the pair; and
- the average (sum, or maximum) of some function of the communication cost between a pair of modules and the bandwidth of the path between the processors to which the modules are assigned;

where the average (sum, or maximum) is taken over all pairs of modules in the system.

The problem stated above is a graph-embedding problem, that is, the embedding of the task graph into the resource graph. Even in its simplest form, graph embedding is computationally difficult [LiSt].

Unrelated Heterogeneous Systems. We can also formulate the problem of assigning periodic tasks to unrelated processors as a integer linear programming problem. This time, we combine task partitioning and module assignment into one single step. Here, the variable $A_{i,k}$ is equal to 1 if the task T_i is assigned to kth processor and is equal to 0 if T_i is assigned to another processor. (Rather than introducing a new set of symbols, we overload the ones introduced earlier.) The solution, $A_{i,k}$ for $i = 1, 2, \ldots, n$ and $k = 1, 2, \ldots, m$ of the following integer linear program gives us an assignment of n tasks to m unrelated processors.

Integer Linear Programming Formulation of Periodic Task Assignment to Unrelated Processors: We are given

- the utilization $u_i(P_k)$ of every periodic task T_i if the task is assigned to processor P_k, for $i = 1, 2, \ldots, n$ and $k = 1, 2, \ldots m$;
- the maximum allowed total utilization $\hat{U}_k$ of all tasks assigned to processor P_k, for $k = 1, 2, \ldots m$;
- the communication cost $C_{i,j}$, which gives the volume of data exchanged between tasks T_i and T_j, for $i, j = 1, 2, \ldots, n$;
- the communication bandwidth $b_{k,l}$ of the path between processors P_k and P_l, for $k, l = 1, 2, \ldots m$; and
- the interference cost $\iota_{i,j;k}$, which is incurred when both tasks T_i and T_j, for $i, j = 1, 2, \ldots, n$, are assigned to the processor P_k, for $k = 1, 2, \ldots, m$.

We are to find $A_{i,k}$, for all $i = 1, 2, \ldots, n$ and $k = 1, 2, \ldots, m$, that satisfy the constraints

$$A_{i,k} = 0, 1 \qquad \text{for } i = 1, 2, \ldots, n \text{ and } k = 1, 2, \ldots, m \qquad (9.3a)$$

$$\sum_{k=1}^{m} A_{i,k} = 1 \qquad \text{for } i = 1, 2, \ldots, n \qquad (9.3b)$$

$$\sum_{i=1}^{n} u_i(P_k) A_{i,k} \leq \hat{U}_k \qquad \text{for } k = 1, 2, \ldots, m \qquad (9.3c)$$

and minimize the cost function

$$C_{\text{total}} = \sum_{i=1}^{n} \sum_{j=1}^{n} \sum_{k=1}^{m} \sum_{l=1}^{m} (1 - \delta_{i,j}) A_{i,k} A_{j,l} (C_{i,j}/b_{k,l} + \iota_{i,j;k} \delta_{k,l}) \qquad (9.3d)$$

The first three equations state essentially the same constraints as Eq. (9.2a), (9.2b), and (9.2c), respectively. The constraint that some task T_i cannot be assigned to some processor P_k can be expressed as $u_i(P_k) = \infty$ and, therefore, need not be treated separately. Comparing Eq. (9.3d) with Eq. (9.2d), we note that every pair of tasks T_i and T_j contributes $C_{i,j}/b_{k,l}$ to the total cost function C_{total}. The fact that the communication cost among tasks on the same processor is negligible can be stated as $b_{k,l} = \infty$ when $k = l$. Again, tasks T_i and T_j contribute $\iota_{i,j;k}$ if they are both assigned to processor P_k (i.e., $A_{i,k}$ and $A_{j,l}$ are equal to 1 for some $k = l$). Finally, in the special case when the processors are identical, the utilization $u_{i,k}$ of every task T_i is independent of the processor P_k to which it is assigned.

9.2.3   Integration of Task and Resource Assignments

The problem of deciding where to place resources in relation to the tasks that use them differs depending on the resource model. While a simple modification of the previous formulation suffices for the end-to-end model, a more extensive modification is required for the MPCP model. We consider here only the case of homogeneous processors.

End-to-End Model.   Suppose we are given a task graph description of the system in which what resources each periodic task uses and when the task uses them are specified by the resource parameters of the task. To determine the placements of resources simultaneously with the assignments of periodic tasks, we expand the task graph in the way described below to capture the resource usage constraints and costs and end-to-end nature of the tasks. We then apply the integer linear programming technique to the system of end-to-end tasks described by the expanded task graph, working with individual subtasks instead of the given tasks. Except for an increase in size of the problem, the definition of the integer linear programming problem given above remains the same.

Decomposing Tasks into Chains of Subtasks.   You recall that according to the end-to-end model, each periodic task that uses resources is an end-to-end task, that is, a chain of subtasks. So, we begin by decomposing each task into an end-to-end task. In this decomposition, each (outermost) critical section of the given task is a subtask, and each of the portions before the first critical section, after the last critical section and between critical sections, is a subtask.

As a result of the decomposition, each periodic task T_i in the given task graph is expanded into a chain of $n(i)$ subtasks $T_{i,1}, T_{i,2}, \ldots, T_{i,n(i)}$. The utilization $u_{i,k}$ of the subtask $T_{i,k}$ is equal to $e_{i,k}/p_i$, where $e_{i,k}$ is the maximum execution time of $T_{i,k}$. In the task graph, there is an edge from the predecessor $T_{i,(k-1)}$ to the successor $T_{i,k}$ for each $k = 2, 3, \ldots, n(i)$ (i.e., each job in the latter subtask is the successor of the corresponding job in the former).

We can influence the decision on where sibling subtasks are placed by adjusting the weights of edges between (vertices representing) the subtasks. For example, suppose that it is more desirable to place sibling subtasks in the same module. In this case, we give the edge between each of the adjacent sibling subtask pairs in the expanded task graph a large weight. As an example, the weight may be some constant β_{sibling} plus $\max_{i \neq j} C_{i,j}$ or the actual communication cost between the subtasks, whichever is larger. $\beta_{\text{sibling}} \geq 0$ is a design parameter; the larger it is, the more likely adjacent sibling subtasks will be placed in the same module. On the other hand, if it does not matter whether sibling subtasks are in the same module, we make the weights of the edges between adjacent sibling subtasks equal to the actual communication costs between the subtasks. In any case, the weights of edges in the expanded task graph give the communication costs in the integer linear program defined by Eq. (9.2).

Specifying Resource Usage Constraints and Interpreting the Solution.   Subtasks that use a resource must be assigned to the same processor as the resource. To take into account this constraint, we focus on the subset $\mathbf{T}(R_k)$ containing all the subtasks that use the resource R_k for each resource R_k at a time. In the expanded task graph, we add an edge between every pair of subtasks in the subset and make the weight of the edge infinite. In other words, the "communication cost" between any pair of subtasks that use the same resource is infinity if the tasks are in different modules.

The integer linear program defined by the expanded task graph may not have a feasible solution, which occurs when m is too small. We may get a solution, but the total communication cost is infinite. We get this solution when it is not possible to place all the subtasks that require some resource on the same processor. When this occurs, we must redesign the application system, adding redundant resources, or shortening the execution times of critical sections, and so on in order to make the system schedulable.

MPCP Model.   Tia, *et al.* [TiLi] formulated the problem of simultaneous assignment of periodic tasks and resources in the MPCP model as a graph partitioning problem. As in the previous formulation, the cost of communication between any pair of tasks T_i and T_j assigned to different processors is given by a single value $C_{i,j}$, the communication cost of the task pair. Similarly, the usage of a resource R_j by a task T_i is given by a single value $Y_{i,j}$, called the resource utilization. (For example, $Y_{i,j}$ can be the fraction of time per period of T_i the task uses R_j.)

Graph Partitioning Formulation.   The graph used for this purpose is called an assignment graph. In the assignment graph, each task, processor, or resource in the system is represented by a vertex. The graph contains the following three types of edges.

- There is a task-task edge between two task vertices T_i and T_j if the tasks T_i and T_j communicate. The weight of the edge between them is their communication cost $C_{i,j}$.
- There is a task-processor (or resource-processor) edge between a task T_i (or resource R_i) vertex to a processor vertex P_j if the task (or resource) is constrained to be assigned to the processor, and the weight of this edge is infinity.
- There is a task-resource edge between a task vertex T_i and a resource vertex R_j if the task uses the resource. The weight of this edge is a function of the resource utilization $Y_{i,j}$ and the priority π_i of the task T_i. We will discuss the choice of this function and the effect of the choice shortly.

An m-way cut of a graph is a minimal subset of edges whose removal causes the graph to be partitioned into m disjoint subgraphs. An m-way cut of an assignment graph gives us a task and resource assignment when each disjoint subgraph contains exactly one processor vertex: The tasks and resources represented by the task and resource vertices in each subgraph are assigned to the processor represented by the processor vertex in the subgraph. Hereafter, by an m-way cut, we mean specifically a cut that gives us an assignment. The cut size of an m-way cut is the sum of the weights of all the edges in the cut. With the weights given above, the cut size is equal to the sum of the total communication cost and total resource usage cost.

Once we have defined the assignment graph, the problem is then that of finding an m-way cut of the assignment graph that satisfies the schedulability constraints of the processors and has the minimum cut size. This problem is NP-hard. A good heuristic is by Kernighan and Lin [KeLi70]. The heuristic is robust, can deal with arbitrary edge weights, and can accommodate additional constraints on each disjoint subset.

Resource Usage Costs versus Communication Costs.   A remaining question is what weights we should give to task-resource edges. As you will see in the next section, according to the MPCP model the end-to-end response times of tasks depend not only on where they execute but also on whether the resources they use are local and remote. In particular, a higher-priority task assigned on the synchronization processor of some global resource may be preempted by remote lower-priority tasks that require the resource. As a consequence, the higher-priority task may suffer a long blocking time. To minimize this blocking time, we should assign tasks that share a resource to the same processor as the resource whenever possible. When this is not possible, the following objectives seem reasonable.

1. The larger the fraction $Y_{i,j}$ of time a task T_i uses a resource R_j, the more T_i and R_j should be assigned to the same processor.

2. When choosing between two tasks of different priorities that do not use a global resource, we want to have the lower-priority task assigned to the same processor as the resource.

A way to bias the choice of the m-way cut so that the corresponding assignment meets the above objectives as much as possible is to make the weight of each edge between a task T_i and a resource R_j an increasing function of the resource utilization $Y_{i,j}$ and the task priority π_i. (You recall that the larger the integer π_i, the lower the priority of T_i.)

Finally, by multiplying the weights of all task-resource edges by a proportional constant, we can adjust the relative importance of communication costs and resource usage costs: The larger this design parameter, the larger the weights of task-resource edges, and the more importance placed on the total resource usage cost.

9.3 MULTIPROCESSOR PRIORITY-CEILING PROTOCOL

This section describes the *Multiprocessor Priority-Ceiling Protocol* (MPCP) [ShRL88]. This protocol assumes that tasks and resources have been assigned and statically bound to processors and that the scheduler of every synchronization processor knows the priorities and resource requirements of all the tasks requiring the global resources managed by the processor. For most of this section, we assume that all the resources used by every job during every nested critical section reside on the same processor. At the end of the section we will discuss the case without this restriction.

According to the multiprocessor priority-ceiling protocol, the scheduler of each processor schedules all the local tasks and global critical sections on the processor on a fixed-priority basis and, except for the modification described below, controls their resource accesses according to the basic priority-ceiling protocol described in Section 8.5. To motivate this modification, we recall that according to the MPCP model, when a task uses a global resource, its global critical section executes on the synchronization processor of the resource. If the global critical section of a remote task were to have a lower priority than some local tasks on the synchronization processor, these local tasks could delay the completion of the global critical section and prolong the blocking time of the remote task. To prevent this, the multiprocessor priority-ceiling protocol schedules all global critical sections at higher priorities than all local tasks on every synchronization processor. This can easily be implemented in a system where the lowest priority π_{lowest} of all tasks is known: The scheduler of each synchronization processor schedules the global critical sections of a task with priority π_i at priority $\pi_i - \pi_{\text{lowest}}$. (Just as a smaller positive integer represents a higher priority, a more negative integer represents a higher priority.)

For example, in a system where tasks have priorities 1 through 5, π_{lowest} is 5. A global critical section of a task with priority 5 is scheduled at priority 0, which is higher than priority 1. Similarly, the priority of a global critical section of a task with priority 1 is -4, which is the highest priority in the system.

9.3.1   Blocking Time Due to Resource Contention

Figure 9–6 gives a simple example to illustrate the types of blocking a job may suffer under the multiprocessor priority-ceiling protocol. The system contains two processors. Jobs J_2, J_4 and J_5 are local to processor P_1, which is the synchronization processor of the resource *dotted*. *Dotted* is a local resource because it is only required by local jobs J_2 and J_4. Jobs J_1 and J_3 are local to processor P_2, which is the synchronization processor of the resource *black*. *Black* is a global resource required by J_1, J_2, and J_3. As usual, we index the jobs in decreasing priorities. The short vertical bar on the time line of each job marks the release time of the job.

As in uniprocessor systems, a job may be blocked by low-priority jobs on the same processor. In this example, J_2 is directly blocked by J_4 when J_2 requests *dotted* at time 4,

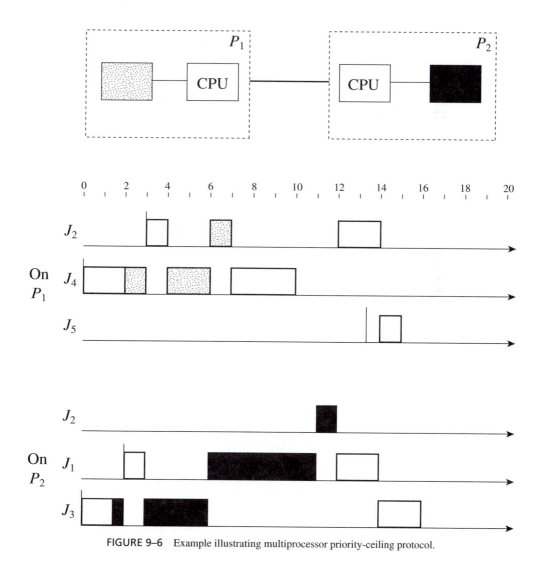

FIGURE 9–6   Example illustrating multiprocessor priority-ceiling protocol.

and J_1 is directly blocked by J_3 when J_1 requests *black* at time 3. A job may also be priority-inheritance blocked or avoidance blocked by lower-priority jobs on its local processor; these conditions do not occur in this simple example.

In addition, the execution of a global critical section may be delayed by global critical sections of other jobs on the synchronization processor. In this example, the global critical section of J_2 on P_2 is delayed by the global critical section of the higher-priority job J_1 in the time interval $(7, 11]$. The preemption delay thus suffered by J_2 must be taken into account when we want to determine the schedulability of J_2. We treat this delay as a factor of J_2's blocking time.

At time 11, J_1 exits from its (global) critical section. Its priority is lower than the priority of the global critical section of J_2. Consequently, J_2 preempts J_1 on P_2 in the interval $(11, 12]$. The total delay experienced by a job due to preemption by global critical sections of lower-priority jobs is also a factor in the total blocking time of the job.

Finally, a job may be delayed by a local higher-priority job whose execution is suspended on the local processor when the higher-priority job executes on a remote processor. This delay is another factor of the blocking time of a job. In this example, J_2 is suspended at time 7. As a consequence, it is still not completed in $(13, 14]$, and J_5, which is released at time 13.2, cannot start execution until time 14.

9.3.2 Upper Bounds to Factors of Blocking Time $b_i(rc)$

We now confine our attention to one task T_i at a time and try to bound the total blocking time $b_i(rc)$ of (each job in) T_i due to resource contention in a multiprocessor system under the multiprocessor priority-ceiling protocol. Each job in T_i (or simply T_i) may have both local and remote critical sections. Specifically, by a critical section, we mean an outermost critical section, except when it is stated otherwise. By local (or remote), we mean local (or remote) with respect to the target task T_i (i.e., the task of interest).

In general, $b_i(rc)$ is the sum of the following five terms:

1. *local blocking time*, which is due to its contention for resources on its local processor;
2. *local preemption delay*, which is due to the preemption of T_i by global critical sections that belong to remote tasks but execute on its local processor;
3. *remote blocking time*, which is due to its contention with some lower-priority tasks for remote resource(s) on the synchronization processor(s) of the resource(s);
4. *remote preemption delay*, which is due to preemptions by higher-priority global critical sections on synchronization processors of the remote resources required by T_i; and
5. *deferred blocking time*, which is due to the suspended execution of local higher-priority tasks.

The upper bounds of the factors of $b_i(rc)$ described below assume that every job in every task completes within one period of the task. These bounds are stated in terms of the notations listed in Table 9–1. To keep them simple, we suppress the subscript i; these parameters and variables are all of the target task T_i.

Local Blocking Time (*LBT*).   According to the priority-ceiling protocol, after each job in T_i is released, it may be blocked once by a lower-priority local task. Moreover, each

TABLE 9–1   Notations used to express upper bounds of blocking factors

κ_r:	the number of remote critical sections of T_i
P_L:	the local processor of T_i
P_j:	for $1 \leq j \leq \kappa_r$, the synchronization processor of the jth remote critical section of each job in T_i
$\mathbf{T}(P_L, \text{gcs})$:	the subset of all tasks that have global critical sections on P_L
$\mathbf{T}(P_L, \text{gcs}, \text{remote})$:	the subset containing all the remote tasks in $\mathbf{T}(P_L, \text{gcs})$
$\mathbf{T}(P_L, \text{gcs}, \text{lower})$:	the subset containing all the lower priority local tasks in $\mathbf{T}(P_L, \text{gcs})$
$\mathbf{T}(P_j, \text{gcs}, \text{lower})$:	the subset of all tasks that have global critical sections on processor P_j and have lower priorities than T_i
$\mathbf{T}(\text{gcs}, \text{higher})$:	the subset of all equal or higher priority remote tasks that have global critical sections on any remote synchronization processor P_j, for $j = 1, 2, \ldots, \kappa_r$, on which T_i executes
$\mathbf{T}(\text{local}, \text{higher})$:	the subset containing all higher priority local tasks
$\hat{c}_L$:	the blocking time of T_i caused by lower priority local tasks on the local processor P_L
$\hat{c}_{k,\text{total}}(P_L)$:	the total execution time of all global critical sections that belong to another task T_k and execute on processor P_L
$\hat{c}_{k,\text{max}}(P_L)$:	the maximum execution time of all global critical sections that belong to T_k and execute on processor P_L
$\hat{c}_{k,\text{max}}(P_j)$:	the maximum execution time of all the global critical sections of T_k on processor P_j
$\hat{c}_{k,\text{total}}$:	the total execution time of all global critical sections of T_k that execute on any P_j, for $j = 1, 2, \ldots, \kappa_r$
$e_{k,L}$:	the maximum execution time of the portion of each job in local task T_k that is executed on the local processor P_L
suspension_time_of_T_k:	the total maximum amount of time for which any job in a local task T_k may be suspended on P_L while it waits for its remote global critical sections to complete.

time when it uses a remote resource, it gives up the local processor. When it resumes on the local processor, it may be blocked again by some lower-priority local task. Therefore, the local blocking time of task T_i is bounded from above by

$$LBT = (\kappa_r + 1)\hat{c}_L \tag{9.4a}$$

If P_L is the only processor in the system, κ_r is 0, and the blocking time of T_i due to resource contention is at most equal to $\hat{c}_L$. We can find $\hat{c}_L$ in the way described in Section 8.5 by ignoring all global resources and remote tasks. We can also bound $\hat{c}_L$ loosely by the maximum execution time of all the local critical sections of lower-priority tasks on P_L.

Local Preemption Delay (*LPD*).   In addition to higher-priority local tasks on P_L, T_i may also be preempted by global critical sections of tasks in $\mathbf{T}(P_L, \text{gcs}, \text{remote})$ and $\mathbf{T}(P_L, \text{gcs}, \text{lower})$. During each period of T_i, each global critical section of a task T_k in $\mathbf{T}(P_L, \text{gcs}, \text{remote})$ may execute $\lceil p_i/p_k \rceil + 1$ times. (This can happen because the global critical section of T_k does not become ready for execution on P_L periodically. A global critical section of T_k may be ready for execution shortly after a period of T_i begins, $\lfloor p_i/p_k \rfloor$ times in the period and then once more before the period ends.) On the other hand, each task T_k in $\mathbf{T}(P_L, \text{gcs, lower})$ has a lower priority than T_i and can delay the current job of T_i only if it is in a global critical section at the time when the current job in T_i is released. Once T_k exits from the global critical section, it cannot enter another global critical section before the current job of T_i completes, unless the job gives up the local processor to access a remote resource. In other words, the current job of T_i can be delayed by each job in $\mathbf{T}(P_L, \text{gcs, lower})$ at most $\kappa_r + 1$ times. Hence, the local preemption delay factor in the blocking time of T_i is bounded from above by

$$LPD = \sum_{T_k \in \mathbf{T}(P_L, \text{gcs,remote})} (\lceil p_i/p_k \rceil + 1)\hat{c}_{k,\text{total}}(P_L)$$

$$+ \sum_{T_k \in \mathbf{T}(P_L, \text{gcs,lower})} (k_r + 1)\hat{c}_{k,\text{max}}(P_L) \qquad (9.4b)$$

You may have noticed that local tasks with equal or higher priorities than T_i and global critical sections on P_L are not included in the sum in Eq. (9.4b). Hence the execution times of their global critical sections are not included in the local preemption delay of T_i. The reason is that we will include these times in the time-demand function of T_i as parts of the execution times of these tasks and, thus correctly take into account these global critical sections when we want to determine whether T_i is schedulable. We will return to this point shortly.

Remote Blocking Time (*RBT*).   Each time when T_i requests a global resource on a remote synchronization processor, its global critical section may be blocked once by a task that also requires some global resource on the processor and has a lower priority than π_i. This factor of the blocking time of T_i is bounded from the above by

$$RBT = \sum_{j=1}^{\kappa_r} \max_{T_k \in \mathbf{T}(P_j, \text{gcs,lower})} (\hat{c}_{k,\text{max}}(P_j)) \qquad (9.4c)$$

Remote Preemption Delay (*RPD*).   The global critical sections of each task T_k in $\mathbf{T}(\text{gcs, higher})$ may execute $\lceil p_i/p_k \rceil + 1$ times during a period of T_i. Hence the total remote preemption delay suffered by T_i is bounded from above by

$$RPD = \sum_{T_k \in \mathbf{T}(\text{gcs,higher})} (\lceil p_i/p_k \rceil + 1)\hat{c}_{k,\text{total}} \qquad (9.4d)$$

Deferred Blocking Time (*DBT*).   Finally, the total amount of time each job in T_i can be blocked due to deferred execution of a local higher-priority task is bounded from the above by

$$DBT = \sum_{T_k \in \mathbf{T}(\text{local,higher})} \min(e_{k,L}, suspension\_times\_of\_T_k)$$

suspension_time_of_T$_k$ is often unknown; we simply bound this delay by

$$DBT = \sum_{T_k \in \mathbf{T}(\text{local,higher})} e_{k,L} \qquad (9.4e)$$

9.3.3   An Illustrative Example

Figure 9–7 gives an illustrative example. The system has three processors and seven tasks. G_1, G_2, and G_3 are global resources; their synchronization processors are P_3, P_3, and P_1, respectively. We want to find the blocking time $b_3(rc)$ of task T_3. The local processor of this task is P_1, and X is a local resource on the processor. P_1 is also the local processor of T_1 and T_4. P_2 is the local processor of T_2, T_5, and T_7; and P_3 is the local processor of T_6. The critical sections and other relevant parameters of the tasks are listed below:

T_1: $[X; 0.5] [G_1; 2.0] [G_3; 0.4]; e_{1,L} = 1.0$
T_2: $[G_1; 0.1] [G_1; 0.5]; 14p_2 = p_3$
T_3: $[X; 2] [G_2; 1.0] [X; 0.1] [G_2; 1.0] [X; 0.1] [X; 0.1]$
T_4: $[X; 1.0] [X; 2.0] [X; 8.0] [G_3; 0.7]; 1.5p_4 = p_3$
T_5: $[G_3; 0.6] [G_3; 1.0]; p_5 = 1.5p_3$
T_6: $[G_1; 5.0] [G_2; 0.3]$
T_7: $[G_2; 1.0]$

We want to find the blocking time $b_3(rc)$ of T_3 due to resource conflict.

1. T_3 has two global critical sections, that is, $\kappa_r = 2$. The maximum execution time of all local critical sections of the lower-priority task T_4 is 8.0. Hence, the local blocking time of T_3 is $(2 + 1) \times 8.0 = 24.0$ according to Eq. (9.4a).
2. To compute the local preemption delay, we note that the subset $\mathbf{T}(P_L, \text{gcs})$ contains the local lower priority task T_4 and the remote task T_5. Hence, the right-hand side of Eq. (9.4b) contains two terms. Since κ_r is 2 and the execution time of the global critical section of T_4 is 0.7, the local preemption delay contributed by T_4 is $3 \times 0.7 = 2.1$.

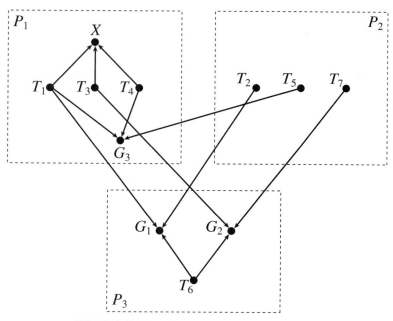

FIGURE 9–7   Example of blocking times under MPCP.

Similarly, since $\lceil p_3/p_5 \rceil$ is equal to 1 and the total execution time of the global critical sections of T_5 on P_1 is $1.0 + 0.6 = 1.6$, the preemption delay contributed by global critical sections of T_5 is $2 \times 1.6 = 3.2$. The total preemption delay of T_3 is, therefore, bounded by $2.1 + 3.2 = 5.3$. For the reason discussed earlier, we do not include the execution time of the global critical section $[G_3, 0.4]$ of T_1 in the local preemption delay.

3. To find the remote blocking time of T_3, we note that both remote global critical sections of T_3 execute on P_3. The tasks in the subset $\mathbf{T}(P_3, \text{gcs}, \text{lower})$ of lower-priority tasks that have global critical sections on P_3 are T_6 and T_7. The sum on the right-hand side of Eq. (9.4c) has two identical terms. The value of the max function in each term is 5.0. Hence the remote blocking time of T_3 is 10.

4. The subset $\mathbf{T}(\text{gcs}, \text{higher})$ of all remote tasks that have equal or higher priority than T_3 and have global critical sections on the remote synchronization processor P_3 contains only T_2. Since the total execution time of the global critical sections of this task is 0.6, the remote preemption delay of T_3 is $(\lceil p_3/p_2 \rceil + 1) \times 0.6 = (14 + 1) \times 0.6 = 9.0$.

5. The only higher-priority task on the local processor P_1 is T_1. The deferred blocking time of T_3 is never more than 1, the maximum execution time of T_1 on the local processor.

Summing up these five factors, $b_3(rc)$ is equal to $24 + 5.3 + 10 + 9.0 + 1.0 = 49.3$.

From the example in Figure 9–7, we can see that the upper bound of the blocking time of any task T_i given by Eq. (9.4) is a loose one. A reason is that the upper bounds of the individual factors do not make use of many parameters of the tasks. The bound of each individual blocking factor assumes the worst-case scenarios which give that factor its maximum value. Some of these scenarios may never occur in some systems, and they can never all occur in most systems. Given a system and the parameters of the tasks, we often can tighten the bound considerably by making use of these parameters to eliminate some scenarios from consideration.

To illustrate, we examine the above example more closely. The upper bound to local blocking time given by Eq. (9.4a) assumes the worst-case scenario that a job of T_3 may be blocked by the same critical sections $[X, 8.0]$ of T_4 all three times. These critical sections must be in three different jobs of T_4. Because Eq. (9.4a) does not use any information on the periods and other characteristics of local critical sections in this computation, it cannot eliminate this scenario from consideration. In reality, if p_4 is larger than the maximum response time of T_3, each job in T_3 can be blocked only by critical sections of one job in T_4. In this case, the local blocking time suffer by T_3 is at most equal to 11 (i.e., the total execution time of the three critical sections of T_4). We can get this tighter bound only when we take into account the periods and (upper bounds of) response times of the tasks.

For a similar reason, if T_2 were a local task on P_3 (rather than being local on P_2 as in this example) and each of its jobs were not consisting entirely of global critical sections, each global critical section of T_2 could only execute once during the time when a global critical section of T_3 is ready for execution on processor P_3. This is because once T_2 exits from a global critical section, its priority is lower than the priority of the global critical section of T_3. Until the global critical section of T_3 completes, T_2 cannot execute. In that case, the remote preemption delay would only be 0.6, but Eq. (9.4d) would give us 9.0. Again, by being general, Eq. (9.4d) is overly conservative sometimes.

9.3.4   Schedulability Tests

Once the blocking time due to resource contention of each task in a multiprocessor system is found, either the time-demand analysis method described in Section 6.6, or, if the task priorities are assigned on the rate-monotonic basis, an appropriate schedulable utilization bound described in Section 6.7 can be used to determine whether the system scheduled according to the multiprocessor priority-ceiling protocol can meet all its deadlines. In the computation of the time-demand function of T_i, we use its total execution time e_i but exclude from the (total) execution time of each equal or higher-priority task T_k the total execution time of T_k's global critical sections that are executed on remote processors where T_i does not execute. In other words, rather than the execution time e_k of T_k, we use $e_{k,L} + \hat{c}_{k,\text{total}}$

We also need to modify the computation of the total blocking time b_i of each task T_i accordingly. Because each job in the task is suspended κ_r number of times, the blocking time b_i of T_i must include an additional $\kappa_r b_i(np)$ units; this is the amount of time each job in T_i may be delayed by nonpreemptive lower-priority tasks when it resumes on the local processor after the completion of its global critical sections.

To illustrate, we return to the previous example. Suppose that the local execution times of T_1 and T_4 on processor P_1 are 1.0 and 15, respectively, and the execution time e_3 of T_3 is 5.0. The periods of the tasks are $p_1 = 20$, $p_3 = 100$, and $p_4 = 160$. Moreover, T_4 has a nonpreemptable portion and the execution time of this portion is 1.0. Hence, the total blocking time of T_3 due to nonpreemptivity is $(2 + 1) \times 1.0 = 3.0$ and its blocking time b_i is $49.3 + 3.0 = 52.3$. The time-demand function $w_3(t)$ of T_3 is given by Eq. (6.18). The execution time of T_1 used in the expression is 3, which is equal to T_1's local execution time $e_{1,L}$ (i.e., 1) plus the execution time of T_1's global critical section on P_3 (i.e., 2). T_3's time demand function is $w_3(t) = 5.0 + 52.3 + \lceil t/20.0 \rceil 3.0$. Solving $w_3(t) = t$ iteratively, we find that the maximum response time of T_3 is 69.3.

9.3.5   Effect of Nested Requests for Resources on Different Processors

Before concluding this section, let us use the previous example to examine the effect of nested requests for resources that reside on different processors. Specifically, let us suppose that the third critical section of T_4 were a nested one involving X and G_2: $[X, 8.0 [G_2, 0.5]]$. The completion of the inner critical section may be delayed by T_6 and T_7 (due to remote blocking) and by T_2 (due to remote preemption). The former is equal to the maximum execution time of the critical sections of T_6 and T_7 on P_3, which is equal to 5.0. The latter is at least equal to $(\lceil p_4/p_2 \rceil + 1) \times 0.6$, which is 6.6. In other words, the completion of the outer critical section and the release of X can be delayed by at least $5.0 + 6.6 = 11.6$ additional units of time. Hence the local blocking time of T_3 can be as large as $3 \times (8.0 + 11.6) = 58.8$. In general, the total blocking times of some tasks can become unacceptably large.

Much more seriously, when tasks make nested requests for resources residing on different processors, the multiprocessor priority-ceiling protocol described above no longer prevents deadlock. To illustrate, suppose that the second critical section of T_3 is also nested, for example, it is $[G_2, 1.0 [X, 0.5]]$. Now a deadlock may occur if the scheduler on each processor applies the uniprocessor priority-ceiling protocol to control accesses to the resources managed by it independently of the schedulers of the other processors. (It will be possible for T_3 to hold G_2 on P_3 and then request X on P_1 while T_4 holds X and requests G_2.) To avoid deadlocks, the schedulers on all processors must have available the state of all the resources in the system and apply the priority-ceiling rule on a global basis. (In this example, the scheduler on P_3 would have denied the request by T_3 for G_2 after X is allocated to T_4 on P_1.) This degree of coordination would make this version of the multiprocessor priority-ceiling protocol unsuitable for all but the most tightly coupled systems.

9.4 ELEMENTS OF SCHEDULING ALGORITHMS FOR END-TO-END PERIODIC TASKS

As we discussed in Section 9.1.3, when nested requests for resources on different processors are disallowed, each periodic task that requires resources on more than one processor can be thought of as an end-to-end periodic task. Each job of the task consists of a chain of component jobs which execute in sequence on different processors. Each component job requires only resources local to the processor on which the job executes.

Specifically, the system contains m processors, P_j for $j = 1, 2, \ldots, m$, and n periodic tasks, T_i for $i = 1, 2, \ldots, n$. Each task T_i has $n(i)$ subtasks, $T_{i,k}$, for $k = 1, 2, \ldots, n(i)$. These subtasks execute in turn on different processors according to its visit sequence $\mathbf{V}_i = (V_{i,1}, V_{i,2}, \ldots, V_{i,n(i)})$ where $V_{i,k} = P_j$ means that the kth subtask $T_{i,k}$ executes on processor P_j. The first subtask $T_{i,1}$ is a periodic task with period p_i, the period of the parent task T_i. We denote the jth job of subtask $T_{i,k}$ by $J_{i,k;j}$. $J_{i,k;j}$ is the immediate predecessor of $J_{i,k+1;j}$ for $k = 1, 2, \ldots, n(i) - 1$ and, hence, the latter cannot be released on processor $V_{i,k+1}$ until the former completes on processor $V_{i,k}$. In our subsequent discussion, we will say that $T_{i,k}$ is the immediate predecessor of $T_{i,k+1}$, when we mean that each job in $T_{i,k}$ is the immediate predecessor of the corresponding job in $T_{i,k+1}$.

For example, according to the end-to-end task model, the task T_1 in Figure 9–7 consists of three subtasks and its visit sequence is (P_1, P_3, P_1). The first subtask $T_{1,1}$ has period 20 if the period of its parent task T_1 is 20. $T_{1,1}$ requires the resource X. The second subtask $T_{1,2}$ executes on P_3 and requires G_1. The final portion $T_{1,3}$ again executes on P_1 and requires the resource G_3.

The two essential components of any end-to-end scheduling scheme are (1) protocol(s) for synchronizing the execution of sibling subtasks on different processors so that precedence constraints among subtasks are maintained and (2) algorithms for scheduling subtasks on each processor. This section describes choices for these elements and their pros and cons. It focuses on the special case where subtasks on every processor are scheduled in a priority-driven manner. Doing so allows us to compare the end-to-end approach with the MPCP approach, which requires all tasks be scheduled on a fixed-priority basis.

However, *according to the end-to-end approach, the fact that no subtask in the system ever requires remote resources makes it possible for the scheduler on each processor to use any of uniprocessor scheduling algorithms and resource-access protocols to schedule subtasks on the processor and control their accesses to resources.* It is even possible for the system to use a mixture of scheduling strategies (e.g., use dynamic-priority schemes on some processors while using fixed-priority schemes on the others, or make some processors priority-driven while making others clock-driven.) Indeed, most real-life systems use mixed scheduling strategies on different types of processors. (As an example, we look at an end-to-end task whose subtasks compress video images periodically on a computer, transmit the video stream across a network, and decompress and display the video on another computer. The computers at the two ends invariably schedule the compression and decompression subtasks differently from the way the network schedules the transmission of the video stream.) We will return in Section 9.6 to discuss the general case.

9.4.1   Interprocessor Synchronization Protocols

Just like a periodic task in a uniprocessor system, the jobs of the first subtask $T_{i,1}$ of every end-to-end periodic task T_i are released no less than p_i units of time apart. A question is when should the jobs in the subsequent sibling subtasks be released? This question does not arise in uniprocessor systems, but as we will see shortly, is important in multiprocessor systems because how jobs in sibling subtasks are released critically affects the schedulability, completion-time jitter, and average response time of end-to-end tasks. We call a protocol that governs when the schedulers on different processors release the jobs of sibling subtasks an *(interprocessor) execution synchronization protocol*. Since there is no ambiguity, we call it simply a synchronization protocol in this section.

A synchronization protocol is *correct* if it (1) never releases jobs in any first subtask before the end-to-end release times of the jobs and (2) never allows the violation of any precedence constraint among sibling subtasks. Except for these criteria, the scheduler of each processor has the freedom to advance or delay the releases of the jobs on the processor. Hereafter, we assume that the scheduler on every processor always works so that (1) is always true and focus our attention on ways to ensure that (2) is also always true.

There are two types of synchronization protocols: greedy (or work-conserving) and nongreedy (or nonwork-conserving). When sibling subtasks are synchronized according to the *greedy synchronization protocol*, the jth job $J_{i,k+1;j}$ of a subtask $T_{i,k+1}$ is released on $V_{i,k+1}$ as soon as its immediate predecessor $J_{i,k;j}$ completes on $V_{i,k}$, for every $k = 1, 2, \ldots, n(i) - 1$. On the other hand, if the subtasks are synchronized according to a *nongreedy synchronization protocol*, the completion time of $J_{i,k;j}$ is the earliest possible release time of $J_{i,k+1;j}$. For reasons which we will discuss soon, the scheduler may delay the release of $J_{i,k+1;j}$ even though its immediate predecessor has already completed.

The remainder of this subsection describes and compares four synchronization protocols: the greedy protocol, the phase-modification protocol, the modified phase-modification protocol, and the release-guard protocol [Bett, Sun]. From the standpoint of the application, a protocol is good if its leads to a small maximum end-to-end response time, maximum end-to-end completion-time jitter, and average end-to-end response time. It will become evident shortly that a protocol usually achieves a small maximum end-to-end response time and completion-time jitter of each individual task at the expense of the average end-to-end response time of all the tasks. From the standpoint of the underlying system, a protocol is good if it is easy to implement, has low run-time overhead, and permits simple acceptance tests. Some protocols require global clock and global load information. Obviously, such a protocol is not as well suited for loosely coupled systems as a protocol that does not have these requirements.

Greedy Synchronization Protocol.   By far, the greedy synchronization protocol is more commonly used, especially in nonreal-time systems. An example can be found in video communication; we often see that the transmission of each newly compressed video frame (i.e., a job of the transmission subtask over a network) is made ready as soon as the compression of the frame (i.e., the corresponding job of the compression subtask on the sending computer) completes. In a connection-oriented packet-switched network, each subtask is the transmission of the packets over a connection by a switch. A packet is ready for transmission at a switch as soon as it arrives, that is, its transmission by the previous switch completes. Similarly, an interrupt handler is ready for execution on the CPU as soon as a DMA controller completes the transfer of a block of data, and the processing of a file is ready as soon as the retrieval of the file completes.

These examples illustrate the fact that the greedy synchronization protocol can be implemented in many different ways. For the sake of concreteness, we speak of the protocol as if it is implemented as follows. When the jth job of $T_{i,k}$ completes on $V_{i,k}$, the scheduler of $V_{i,k}$ sends a "synchronization signal" to the scheduler of $V_{i,k+1}$ on which the successor subtask $T_{i,k+1}$ executes. (In the above examples, the synchronization signal is in the form of a send system call, a packet arrival, a hardware interrupt, and an I/O complete notification, respectively.) Upon receiving the synchronization signal, the scheduler of $V_{i,k+1}$ releases the corresponding job $J_{i,k+1;j}$ immediately. As you recall from our discussion in Section 9.1.4, because the multiprocessor system model used here already takes into account interprocessor communication costs, we let the delay in the delivery of the synchronization signal be zero.

The greedy synchronization protocol is simple. It does not require global clock synchronization. The only global information required by the scheduler of each processor is the identities of the immediate upstream processor and the next downstream processor in the visit sequence of each task that executes on the processor. Our intuition tells us that since every job is released and becomes ready for execution at the earliest possible instant, the greedy synchronization protocol yields the shortest average end-to-end response time of all tasks, compared with nongreedy protocols. This conjecture was substantiated by the simulation results in [Sun]. However, the interrelease intervals of consecutive jobs in a later subtask (i.e., a subtask other than the first one) can be shorter than the period of the subtask. We should not be surprised that the bursty nature of the later subtasks has some undesirable effect on the schedulability of end-to-end tasks in a priority-driven system.

An example from [Sun] illustrates this point. The system in this example contains two processors and three periodic tasks. Tasks $T_1 = (6, 3)$ and $T_3 = (6, 10, 4)$ do not have subtasks, and they execute on P_1 and P_2, respectively. The task T_2 has two subtasks: $T_{2,1} = (9, 3)$ executes on P_1, and $T_{2,2} = (9, 3)$ executes on P_2. The relative end-to-end deadlines of the tasks are equal to their respective periods. The tasks are given fixed priorities on both processors: T_1 has a higher priority on P_1, and $T_{2,2}$ has a higher priority on P_2. Figure 9–8(a) shows the schedule of the tasks when they are synchronized according to the greedy protocol. The dashed vertical arrows at times 6 and 12 represent synchronization signals between processors. Because the interrelease times of jobs in $T_{2,2}$ can be as short as 6, T_3 cannot meet its deadlines. In contrast, the schedule in Figure 9–8(b) shows that if the jobs in $T_{2,2}$ are released periodically, T_3 always meets its deadlines.

Indeed, as we will discuss in detail in Section 9.5, the greedy synchronization protocol is unsuitable for hard real-time applications because tasks thus synchronized may have extremely large end-to-end response times when scheduled on a fixed-priority basis. Furthermore, there is yet no schedulability analysis method that can give sufficiently tight upper bounds to end-to-end response times of greedily synchronized, fixed-priority tasks. As a consequence, response time guarantees in fixed-priority systems are sometimes unduly pessimistic.

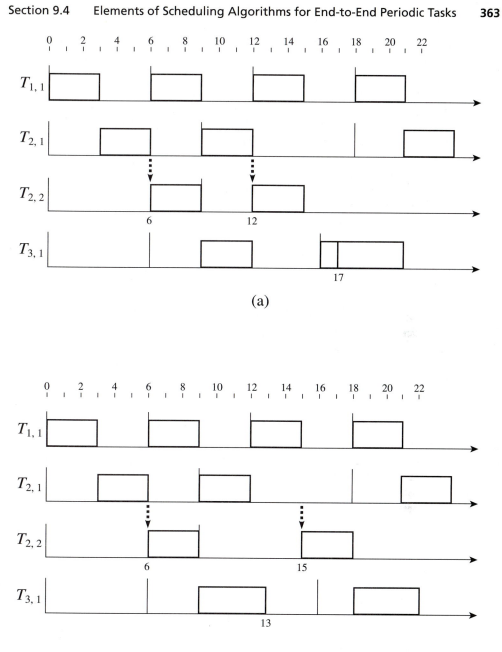

(a)

(b)

FIGURE 9–8   Effect of synchronization on fixed-priority end-to-end periodic tasks. (a) Greedy synchronization. On $P_1 : T_{1,1} = (6, 3)$, $T_{2,1} = (9, 3)$. On $P_2 : T_{2,2} = (9, 3)$, $T_{3,1} = (6, 10, 4)$. (b) Nongreedy synchronization.

The problem exemplified by tasks in Figure 9–8 does not arise if the jobs on P_2 are scheduled on the EDF basis; both tasks are schedulable despite the interrelease-time jitter of $T_{2,2}$. However, the completion-time jitter of $T_{2,2}$ is bigger because its release-time jitter is bigger. From Figure 9–8, you can see that the end-to-end response time of T_2 can be as large as 9. [The EDF schedule in the first period of T_2 is the same as that segment of the schedule in Figure 9–8(a).] However, the release-time jitter and, consequently, the completion-time jitter, of a subtask grows with the number of predecessors it has. In order to control completion-time jitter and keep the queue length (and required buffer space) at each processor small, the nongreedy approach has also been proposed for synchronizing task execution in deadline-driven systems [FeVe]. We will return in Chapter 11 to describe how nongreedy synchronization protocols are implemented in switched networks for this purpose.

Phase-Modification Protocols. Again, according to a nongreedy synchronization protocol, the scheduler may delay the releases of jobs. Nongreedy protocols are usually time-driven to some extent. The objective is not only to enforce precedence constraints but also to shape the release-time pattern of every successor subtask so that the subtask behaves like a periodic task if its first sibling subtask is a periodic task. (By *release-time pattern* of a task (or subtask), we mean the sequence of release times of jobs in the task.) There are two approaches. The first approach is to maintain minimum temporal distances between the release times of jobs in sibling subtasks. According to this approach, the earliest release time of each job in a later subtask is some fixed amount of time after the release of the corresponding job in the immediate predecessor subtask. Another approach is to make each subtask periodic; hence, the earliest release time of every job is equal to the release time of the previous job in the same subtask plus the period of the subtask. For both approaches, the release time of every job is either its earliest release time thus determined or the completion time of its immediate predecessor, whichever is later.

The *phase-modification protocol* [Bett] takes the first approach. The protocol requires the knowledge of an upper bound $W_{i,k}$ to the response time of every subtask $T_{i,k}$; $W_{i,k}$ is computed either a priori before the system begins to execute or during the acceptance test when the task T_i is admitted to the system. According to this protocol, the release time of the jth job of the subtask $T_{i,k+1}$ is $W_{i,k}$ time units after the release time of the jth job of the subtask $T_{i,k}$, for $k = 1, 2, \ldots, n(i) - 1$. In other words, the jth job $J_{i,k+1;j}$ of $T_{i,k+1}$ is released on processor $V_{i,k+1}$ at time $\phi_i + (j - 1)p_i + \sum_{l=1}^{k} W_{i,l}$. [You recall that ϕ_i is the phase of T_i, and hence, the release time of the jth job in $T_{i,1}$ is $\phi_i + (j - 1)p_i$.]

The phase-modification protocol would produce the schedule in Figure 9–8(b). The response time of $T_{2,1}$ is never more than 6. Consequently, the jobs in $T_{2,2}$ are released 6 units of time after the release times of the corresponding jobs in $T_{2,1}$.

The conceptual simplicity of the phase-modification protocol is an advantage. It requires that (1) the clocks of different processors be synchronized, (2) the jobs of every first subtask indeed be released periodically, and (3) an upper bound $W_{i,k}$ on the response time of every subtask $T_{i,k}$ be available to the schedulers of all processors on which successors of $T_{i,k}$ execute. In a system where these requirements can be met at a sufficiently low cost, the protocol is particularly simple to implement. No interaction among the schedulers is necessary for the synchronization purpose. As long as every job $J_{i,1;j}$ of the first subtask $T_{i,1}$ is released at $\phi_i + (j - 1)p_i$ and the response time of every subtask $T_{i,k}$ never exceeds its upper bound $W_{i,k}$, no job is released prior to the completion of its immediate predecessor, and the protocol works correctly.

By definition of the protocol, every subtask $T_{i,k}$ is indeed a periodic task if the first subtask of T_i is a periodic task. An upper bound $W_{i,k}$ on the response time of $T_{i,k}$ can be computed by using a schedulability test for uniprocessor systems on the subtasks that execute together with $T_{i,k}$ on $V_{i,k}$ without regard to subtasks on other processors. The end-to-end response time of the parent task T_i is bounded by the sum $W_i = \sum_{l=1}^{n(i)} W_{i,l}$. That the scheduler can validate the schedulability of end-to-end tasks and provide end-to-end response time guarantee with relative ease is an important advantage of this protocol.

Our intuition tells that the average end-to-end response time of all tasks is longer in a system that uses this protocol when compared with the average response time in a system that uses the greedy synchronization. The results of a simulation study in [Sun] indeed support this conjecture on average end-to-end response time. However, the maximum end-to-end response time of each task may be shorter. The example in Figure 9–8 gives us some insight into why this is true.

The shortcomings of the phase-modification protocol are obvious. It requires global clock synchronization as well as global information on upper bounds to response times. These requirements make it unsuitable for loosely coupled systems. More seriously, even in a tightly coupled system where these requirements can be met at a reasonable cost, it may not work correctly. The release times of jobs in the first subtasks may be jittered, and some jobs may overrun and execute for longer than their respective execution times. These conditions are unavoidable for all but purely deterministic applications. Under these conditions, the completion time of a predecessor job $J_{i,k;j}$ may be later than the computed upper bound $\phi_i + (j - 1)p_i + \sum_{l=1}^{k} W_{i,l}$, which, according to the protocol, is the release time of the successor job $J_{i,k+1;j}$. The precedence constraint between $J_{i,k;j}$ and $J_{i,k+1;j}$ is violated when this happens.

Modified Phase-Modification Protocol.   We can overcome the shortcomings of the phase-modification protocol, while retaining its advantages, in two ways. Both require synchronization signals among schedulers, in addition to the use of timers. The *Modified Phase-Modification Protocol* (or the MPM protocol for short) is one way. Like the phase-modification protocol, the MPM assumes that the response time of each subtask $T_{i,k}$ is bounded by $W_{i,k}$, and this bound is computed by the scheduler of $V_{i,k}$ when $T_{i,k}$ is admitted to the system. Each successor job $J_{i,k+1;j}$ is released either at $W_{i,k}$ units of time after the release of its predecessor $J_{i,k;j}$ or at the actual completion time of $J_{i,k;j}$, whichever is later. This is the only difference between the phase-modification and MPM protocols.

A way to implement the MPM protocol is as follows. The scheduler of $V_{i,k}$ sends a synchronization signal to the scheduler of $V_{i,k+1}$ immediately after each job $J_{i,k;j}$ completes only if the job completes at or later than its computed latest completion time $r_{i,k;j} + W_{i,k}$. ($r_{i,k;j}$ is the release time of $J_{i,k;j}$.) If $J_{i,k;j}$ completes early (i.e., the response time of $J_{i,k;j}$ is shorter than $W_{i,k}$), the scheduler waits until the latest completion time of the job and then sends the synchronization signal. The scheduler of $V_{i,k+1}$ releases the successor job $J_{i,k+1,j}$ upon receipt of this signal.

In the example in Figure 9–8, $W_{2,1}$ is 6. $J_{2,1;1}$ is released at time 0. Its latest completion time is 6. Hence scheduler of P_1 sends a synchronization signal as soon as it completes at 6. The second job $J_{2,1;2}$ of $T_{2,1}$ is released at time 9, and its latest completion time is $9 + 6 = 15$. The scheduler of P_1 waits until time 15 and then sends a synchronization signal. Similarly, the subsequent signals are sent at 24, 33, and so on. The scheduler of P_2 releases the jobs in $T_{2,2}$ at these instants. Consequently, $T_{2,2}$ is a periodic task.

The MPM protocol does not require a global clock. Since each scheduler requires only information on the release times and bounds on the response times of local jobs, global load information is also not required. By definition, the MPM protocol works correctly even when the jobs of the first subtask are released sporadically and some job overruns. Moreover, as long as there is no overrun (and hence the response times of all jobs are within the respectively upper bounds), the scheduler of $V_{i,k}$ sends the synchronization signal and the scheduler of $V_{i,k+1}$ releases a job of $T_{i,k+1}$ at $\sum_{l=1}^{k} W_{i,l}$ time units after the release of each job in $T_{i,1}$. Under this condition, the release-time pattern of $T_{i,k+1}$ is the same as that of $T_{i,1}$ for all $k = 1, 2, \ldots, n(i) - 1$.

Because of this property, this protocol is used as a means to control end-to-end completion-time jitters in packet-switched networks. Specifically, the jitter-EDD algorithm proposed by Verma, *et al.* [VeZF] incorporates the MPM protocol with EDF scheduling at each switch along the route used for each connection. To enable the scheduler of the next downstream switch to shape the release-time pattern, each scheduler puts in the header of each packet an ahead time. The *ahead time* is equal to the difference between the latest possible completion time and the actual completion time of the transmission of the packet. Upon the arrival of a packet on a connection, each scheduler delays the release of the packet by an amount equal to the value of the ahead time in the packet header.[2] Using our terminology, we would describe the algorithm as follows. The upstream processor $V_{i,k}$ sends a synchronization signal containing the ahead time as soon as each immediate predecessor job $J_{i,k;j}$ completes. The downstream processor $V_{i,k+1}$ releases the successor job $J_{j,k+1;j}$ at the time instant equal to the arrival time of the synchronization signal plus the ahead time. You can see that except for the difference in implementation, this algorithm is the same as the MPM protocol.

However, two limitations of the MPM protocol make it less than ideal. First, the successor subtask $T_{i,k+1}$ may no larger behave like a periodic task whenever an overrun on some processor upstream causes the response time of some job in a predecessor subtask to be larger than the corresponding computed upper bound. As an example, suppose that the first job $J_{2,1;1}$ of $T_{2,1}$ in Figure 9–8 were to overrun and execute for 4 units of time, instead of 3, and the second job $J_{2,1;2}$ were to execute for 2 units of time. Then the first two synchronization signals would be sent at times 10 and 15. The first two jobs of $T_{2,2}$ would be released 5 time units apart, rather than the minimum interrelease time of 9 units.

Second, the scheduler on each processor $V_{i,k}$ is insensitive to the load condition of the downstream processor $V_{i,k+1}$. As a consequence, the system cannot take advantage of idle times on its processors to reduce the average end-to-end response time of all tasks. This is a shortcoming for tasks which have no end-to-end completion-time jitter requirements while a short average end-to-end response time is desirable. To illustrate, let us examine the schedule in Figure 9–8(b), which is also the schedule produced by the MPM protocol in the absence of any release-time jitter and overrun. P_2 becomes idle at time 13. At this time, $J_{2,2;2}$ can be released without affecting the schedulability of the subtasks on P_2 or increase their maximum response time. According to the MPM protocol, the scheduler must wait until time 15 to release $J_{2,2;2}$.

---

[2]According to the rate-control algorithm described in [VeZF], the scheduler further delays the release of the packet by the difference between the per-hop relative deadline and the maximum allowed per-hop completion-time jitter of the packet if this difference is positive. This additional delay is not necessary if the deadline for transmitting each packet is equal to its release time plus the minimum of its relative deadline and maximum completion-time jitter.

Release-Guard Protocol.   The Release-Guard protocol (or the RG protocol for short), which we will define in the next paragraph, is another way to improve the phase-modification protocol. It is also an improvement over the MPM protocol as it does not have the limitations of the MPM protocol. It differs from the phase-modification protocols in a fundamental way: Rather than trying to maintain a minimum temporal distance between the release times of every immediate predecessor/successor pair, the RG protocol makes sure that the intervals between release times of jobs in any subtask are never less than the period of the subtask whenever it is necessary to do so in order to ensure the schedulability of the lower-priority subtasks or to keep completion-time jitter small.

In essence, according to the *RG protocol* [Sun], the scheduler of the processor $V_{i,k}$ sends a synchronization signal to the scheduler of the next downstream processor $V_{i,k+1}$ upon the completion of every job in $T_{i,k}$. For each local subtask $T_{i,k+1}$, the scheduler of $V_{i,k+1}$ releases the first job $J_{i,k+1;1}$ when its receives the first synchronization signal for the subtask. For every $j > 1$, the scheduler of $V_{i,k+1}$ records the release time $r_{i,k+1,j-1}$ of the latest released job $J_{i,k+1,j-1}$. It releases the subsequent job $J_{i,k+1;j}$ according to one of the two rules stated below. It follows rule 1 if the processor never idles since $r_{i,k+1,j-1}$. It releases $J_{i,k+1;j}$ according to rule 2 if the processor becomes idle sometime in the interval $(r_{i,k+1,j-1}, r_{i,k+1,j-1} + p_i)$.

1. For every $j > 1$, the scheduler releases the jth job $J_{i,k+1;j}$ of $T_{i,k+1}$ either when it receives the synchronization signal indicating the completion of $J_{i,k;j}$ or at time $r_{i,k+1;j-1} + p_i$, whichever is later.
2. The scheduler releases $J_{i,k+1;j}$ either when it receives the synchronization signal indicating the completion of $J_{i,k;j}$ or when the processor becomes idle, whichever is later.

A way to implement this protocol is to let the scheduler of $V_{i,k+1}$ maintain a piece of data, called the *release guard*, for each local subtask $T_{i,k+1}$. Initially the release guard for every subtask is 0. The release guard of $T_{i,k+1}$ is set to $r_{i,k+1,j} + p_i$ at the time $r_{i,k+1,j}$ when the jth job of the subtask is released for all $j \geq 1$ and is set to the current time whenever the processor becomes idle. The scheduler releases the next job of $T_{i,k+1}$ either at the release guard of the subtask or at the time when the jth synchronization signal for the subtask is received, whichever is later. (Another way to implement the RG protocol is to synchronize sibling subtasks greedily but use a sporadic server to execute jobs in each subtask. Problem 9.9 gives more detail on this alternative.)

If the RG protocol is used in the system described in Figure 9–8(b), the scheduler of P_2 releases the job $J_{2,2;1}$ as soon as it receives the signal at time 6 because the release guard of $T_{2,2}$ is 0 at the time. At time 6, the scheduler sets the release guard of $T_{2,2}$ at 15. When it receives the second synchronization signal at time 12, the scheduler records the receipt of the signal but does not release $J_{2,2;2}$. When the processor becomes idle at time 13, the release guard is set to 13. Since the synchronization signal has been received earlier, the scheduler releases $J_{2,2;2}$ and updates the release guard to 22.

That the RG protocol works correctly in the presence of release-time jitters and task overruns is evident from its definition. If rule 2 is never applied, the jobs in every subtask $T_{i,k+1}$ are never released closer than p_i units of time apart. Rule 2 is applied only when the processor becomes idle. If the schedulability of the system is determined based on one of the schedulability tests for uniprocessor systems that is insensitive to the phases of tasks, a system found schedulable by the test remains schedulable even when a job of every subtask on the processor is released at the same time. The advance in the release of the next job in $T_{i,k+1}$ will not adversely affect the schedulability of the system. On the other hand, if completion-time jitter of any subtask must be controlled, the scheduler can simply ignore rule 2 for that subtask.

Because it does not rely on synchronized clocks and global load information and requires only minimal interaction among the schedulers, the RG protocol is as equally suited for loosely coupled systems as tightly coupled systems. Unlike the phase-modification protocols, it does not require a computed upper bound on the response time of every subtask. Hence, the scheduler can use a simpler schedulability test, such as one based on a schedulable utilization, when deciding whether to admit a new task into the system. In addition, the RG protocol can easily be integrated with the tick scheduling mechanism mentioned in Section 6.8.5; we will describe how in Section 12.2.2.

Relative Performance of Synchronization Protocols.   In a series of simulation experiments, Sun [Sun] showed that the performance of a synchronization protocol depends primarily on the number of subtasks in each end-to-end task and the total utilization of each processor. The greedy synchronization protocol usually yields a much smaller (e.g., by a factor of 2 to 4) average end-to-end response times compare with the phase-modification protocols. On the other hand, it outperforms the release guard protocol significantly in this respect only when the total utilization of each processor exceeds 70 percent. Under this condition, the ratio of the average end-to-end response time under the release guard protocol and the average end-to-end response time under the greedy protocol grows almost linearly with the number of subtasks per task. (At 70 percent total utilization, the growth is almost negligible but at 90 percent total utilization, the ratio grows from near 1 for 2 subtasks per task to 3 for 8 subtasks per task.)

However, in terms of the maximum end-to-end response time they can guarantee, the disadvantage of the greedy synchronization protocol often more than offsets its advantage in terms of average performance. For example, Sun found that the ratio of the upper bound to end-to-end response times achievable by the greedy synchronization to that achievable by any of the nongreedy synchronization protocol ranges from 1.9 for systems in which each task has 6 subtasks and the total utilization of each processor is 60 percent to 17 for systems when these parameters are 8 and 80 percent. In terms of worst-case performance, the greedy protocol performs comparably only when the number of subtasks per task is small (e.g., 2 or 3) and the processors are relatively lightly loaded (e.g., total utilization is 50 percent or less).

As we will see in Section 9.5, a more serious disadvantage of the greedy synchronization protocol for hard real-time applications where tasks are added and deleted dynamically is that there exists no fast schedulability analysis algorithm for the protocol. The schedulability analysis algorithm for greedy protocol described in Section 9.5.2, as well as the Tindell and Clark algorithm [TiCl], is too complex to be used as an on-line acceptance test. Moreover, it requires global knowledge of all parameters of all subtasks. Even when high run-time overhead and global knowledge are tolerable, the schedulability analysis algorithm is not good because it can produce very loose, and sometimes infinite, bounds. For these reasons, the greedy synchronization protocol is unsuitable for hard real-time applications. The release-guard protocol offers a better alternative.

9.4.2 Scheduling of Subtasks on Each Processor

Again, we focus here on multiprocessor systems in which subtasks on every processor are scheduled according to some priority-driven algorithm and leave the discussion on problems in mixing scheduling strategies to Section 9.6. Even with this restriction, there are many alternative approaches to scheduling subtasks on each processor. An alternative is to schedule the subtasks on each processor according to some fixed-priority algorithm, e.g., the (uniprocessor) priority-ceiling protocol. Since the priorities of subtasks on each processor are assigned, used, and manipulated only by the local scheduler, there is no reason that sibling subtasks on different processors cannot have different priorities. We can use a mixture of fixed-priority and dynamic-priority algorithms (e.g, scheduling subtasks on CPUs on a fixed-priority basis while scheduling subtasks on network links using dynamic-priority algorithms). Similarly, we can use different resource access-control protocols on different processors.

Heuristics for Priority Assignment.   The problem we have here is how to assign priorities to subtasks or jobs so as to feasibly schedule all the tasks if they can be feasibly scheduled. That this problem is NP-hard for all but a few special cases of little practical interest follows straightforwardly from the fact that the job-shop scheduling problem is NP-hard in general. We can use computational intensive techniques such as branch-and-bound and simulated annealing to find feasible priority assignments off-line if all the tasks executed in every mode are known a priori. For systems where tasks are created and added on-line, we must rely on simple heuristics, which are our focus here.

Most heuristic priority-assignment schemes solve the priority-assignment problem in two steps. The first step computes an intermediate relative deadline $D_{i,k}$ of every subtask $T_{i,k}$ from the end-to-end relative deadline D_i of its parent task T_i and the parameters of some or all of the tasks in the system. We call this step the *deadline-assignment* step and an algorithm for this purpose a *deadline-assignment* or *slack-distribution* algorithm.

Once each subtask $T_{i,k}$ has a local relative deadline, the scheduler of $V_{i,k}$ uses this intermediate relative deadline as the (virtual) local relative deadline of the subtask and makes its scheduling decision based on this local relative deadline. Thus the problem of assigning priorities to end-to-end tasks is reduced to that of assigning priorities to subtasks on each processor. This is what the second step does. No new algorithms are needed; uniprocessor scheduling algorithms discussed in previous chapters can be used for this purpose.

Deadline-Assignment Algorithms.   There are many deadline-assignment algorithms [KaGa93, KaGa94, Sun]. Among them are the four algorithms defined below in order of increasing complexity. $UD_{i,k}$, $ED_{i,k}$, $PD_{i,k}$, and $NPD_{i,k}$ are the local relative deadlines assigned to subtask $T_{i,k}$ according to the four algorithms, respectively. Again, D_i is the relative deadline of its parent task T_i. $e_{i,k}$ is the execution time of subtask $T_{i,k}$, and $e_i = \sum_{l=1}^{n(i)} e_{i,l}$ is the total execution time of all the subtasks in T_i. $U(V_{i,k})$ is the total utilization of the all the subtasks that execute on the processor $V_{i,k}$. The equations below hold for every subtask $T_{i,k}$ [$k = 1, 2, \ldots, n(i)$] in every task T_i ($i = 1, 2, \ldots, n$).

- *Ultimate Deadline (UD) Algorithm*

$$UD_{i,k} = D_i \qquad (9.5a)$$

- *Effective Deadline (ED) Algorithm*

$$ED_{i,k} = D_i - \sum_{l=k+1}^{n(i)} e_{i,l} \qquad (9.5b)$$

- *Proportional Deadline (PD) Algorithm*

$$PD_{i,k} = D_i e_{i,k}/e_i \qquad (9.5c)$$

- *Normalized Proportional Deadline (NPD) Algorithm*

$$NPD_{i,k} = D_i \frac{e_{i,k}U(V_{i,k})}{\sum_{l=1}^{n(i)} e_{i,l}U(V_{i,l})} \qquad (9.5d)$$

The subtask $T_{i,n(i)+1}$ does not exist. For the sake of convenience, we let its execution time $e_{i,n(i)+1}$ equal 0 and include it in the sum in Eq. (9.5b).

We use the example from [Sun] to illustrate. The system contains four tasks. Table 9–2 lists their relevant parameters. The end-to-end relative deadline of every task is equal to its period. T_2, T_3, and T_4 have only one subtask each. T_1 has three subtasks. The execution of T_1 starts and ends on P_1. These two segments are called $T_{1,1}$ and $T_{1,3}$; they execute with T_2 (called $T_{2,1}$ in the table) on P_1. The middle subtask $T_{1,2}$ of T_1 may model a remote procedure call. $T_{1,2}$ executes with $T_{3,1}$ (i.e., T_3) and $T_{4,1}$ (i.e., T_4) on P_2. The total utilization of P_1 and P_2 are 0.4 and 0.88, respectively. The local relative deadlines calculated according to the algorithms are as listed. (The system also has two resources: DB, a database, and PR, a printer. The critical sections of the subtasks are listed, but we do not need this information right now.)

To see the rationales of the algorithms, we keep in mind that most priority assignments for real-time applications tend to give jobs with shorter relative deadlines higher priorities. The simplest algorithm, the UD algorithm, requires no information about the tasks except their end-to-end deadlines. However, it ignores the fact that an earlier subtask must be completed before its later sibling(s) can start and hence is more urgent than later subtasks. Similarly, a subtask that has successors with a larger total execution time is more urgent than a subtask that has successors with a smaller total execution time. The ED algorithm takes into account these factors. A subtask whose successors have a total execution time of x units must complete at least x units of time before the deadline of the parent task; otherwise, its last sibling subtask has no chance to complete in time.

TABLE 9–2   An example on deadline assignment.

$T_{i,k}$	$V_{i,k}$	p_i	$e_{i,k}$	Crit. Sec.	$UD_{i,k}$	$ED_{i,k}$	$PD_{i,k}$	$NPD_{i,k}$
$T_{1,1}$	P_1	15	1		15	11	3	2.0
$T_{1,3}$	P_1	15	2	$[PR; 1]$	15	15	6	4.1
$T_{2,1}$	P_1	20	4	$[PR; 1]$	20	20	20	20
$T_{3,1}$	P_2	2	1		2	2	2	2
$T_{1,2}$	P_2	15	2	$[DB; 2]$	15	13	6	8.9
$T_{4,1}$	P_2	20	5	$[DB; 1]$	20	20	20	20

The scheduler of $V_{i,k}$ computes the effective deadline of a subtask $T_{i,k}$ based on the execution times of $T_{i,k}$'s successor subtasks. This information can be made available to the scheduler at the time when the task T_i is admitted to the system. However, if the execution times of all the sibling subtasks are known to the schedulers of all the processors in the visit sequence V_i of T_i, the PD algorithm can also be used. In essence, this algorithm distributes the slack of each parent task to its subtasks in proportion to their execution times so that their amounts of slack per unit of execution time are the same. (In the example in Table 9–2, the amounts of slack per unit of execution time of subtasks in T_1 are all equal to 2.) In contrast, the ED algorithm gives all the slack of the parent task to the first subtask in the system.

Since the amount of slack per unit execution time gives a good measure of how urgent each subtask is, we expect that the PD deadline assignment is the best if the processors in the visit sequence of T_i have identical workloads and use the same priority assignment. Invariably, the loads on different processors are different. A subtask executing on a more heavily loaded processor needs more slack, if it is to be equally schedulable as a sibling subtask on a more lightly loaded processor. This is rationale of the NPD algorithm. According to this algorithm, the amount of slack a subtask has is proportional to the product of its execution time and the utilization of the processor on which it executes. Therefore, although $T_{1,2}$ and $T_{1,3}$ in our example have the same execution time, the relative deadline (and hence the slack) of the former is more than twice that of the latter because the utilization of P_2 is more than twice the utilization of P_1.

As expected, simulation results in [KaGa93, Sun] show that when priorities of subtasks are based on their NPD deadlines, the subtasks are more likely to be schedulable when compared with other deadline assignments. These studies assume up-to-date global information on the utilization of all processors and the execution times of all subtasks in the system and ignore the overhead required to maintain this information. In a system where tasks are added and deleted frequently, the utilization values available to the schedulers may be out of date, introducing inaccuracy in slack distribution. This inaccuracy, together with the possibly high overhead incurred to maintain global load information, may very well negate any advantage of the NPD algorithm. For example, the NPD algorithm is not a good choice in a packet-switched network. Connections in such a network are established and torn down frequently, and the NPD algorithm would require all the switches to broadcast their load conditions upon these events. In comparison, the PD algorithm can be implemented easily at connection establishment time.

9.5 SCHEDULABILITY OF FIXED-PRIORITY END-TO-END PERIODIC TASKS

In this section, we suppose that every subtask $T_{i,k}$ in the system is assigned a fixed priority $\pi_{i,k}$ and ask whether every task can meet its end-to-end deadlines. To answer this question, we need to consider two cases: when tasks are synchronized nongreedily and greedily.

9.5.1 Schedulability of Nongreedy Synchronized Tasks

By far, it is easier to determine the schedulability of tasks synchronized according to one of the nongreedy protocols described in Section 9.4. Indeed, this is the primary design objective of these protocols.

Upper Bounds to End-to-End Response Times.   When sibling subtasks are synchronized according to any of the nongreedy synchronization protocols described above, we can treat each subtask $T_{i,k}$ like a periodic task when trying to find its maximum possible response time. The period of this subtask is equal to the period p_i of its parent task T_i, and its execution time is $e_{i,k}$. The end-to-end response time of each task can be bounded according to following theorem.

THEOREM 9.1.   An upper bound W_i to the end-to-end response time of any periodic task T_i in a fixed-priority system synchronized according to the MPM protocol or the RG protocol is given by

$$W_i = \sum_{k=1}^{n(i)} W_{i,k} \tag{9.6}$$

where $n(i)$ is the number of subtasks in T_i and the upper bound $W_{i,k}$ to the response time of every subtask $T_{i,k}$ is obtained by considering only subtasks on the same processor as $T_{i,k}$ and by treating every such subtask $T_{j,l}$ as a periodic task whose period is equal to the period p_j of the parent task T_j.

That the theorem is true when the MPM protocol is used follows directly from the definition of the protocol. However, when the RG protocol is used, a job in a subtask $T_{i,k}$ may be released some time after the completion time of the corresponding job in its immediate predecessor $T_{i,k-1}$ since the release guard may be later. [Figure 9–8(b) gives an example: $J_{2,1;2}$ completes at time 12, but the release of its successor $J_{2,2;2}$ is postponed until 13.] Consequently, when sibling subtasks are thus synchronized, that every job in every subtask $T_{i,k}$ is released no later than $\sum_{l=1}^{k-1} W_{i,l}$ units of time after the release of the corresponding job in the first sibling subtask $T_{i,1}$ is no longer obvious. Lemma 9.2 says that this is true nevertheless. That Theorem 9.1 is true when the RG protocol is used follows directly from this lemma.

LEMMA 9.2.   When subtasks are synchronized according to the RG protocol and there is no overrun, every job of every subtask $T_{i,k}$ for $k = 2, 3, \ldots, n(i)$ is released no later than $\sum_{l=1}^{k-1} W_{i,l}$ units of time after the release time of the corresponding job in its first sibling subtask $T_{i,1}$.

*Proof.   We show by induction that this lemma is true when rule 2 of the RG protocol is never applied. Since rule 2 never delays the release of any job and never lengthens the maximum response time of any job, the lemma remains true when the rule is applied.

According to the definition of the RG protocol, for every $l = 2, 3, \ldots, k$, the first job $J_{i,l;1}$ is released immediately when the scheduler of $V_{i,l}$ receives a synchronization signal, and this signal is surely received within $W_{i,l-1}$ units of time after the release time of the first job in the immediate predecessor $T_{i,l-1}$. Hence, for any $2 \leq k \leq n(i)$, the first job in $T_{i,k}$ is released by $\sum_{l=1}^{k-1} W_{i,l}$ units of time after the release of the first job in $T_{i,1}$, that is, the lemma is true for the first jobs of all subtasks of T_i.

The lemma is also true for all the jobs in the second sibling subtask $T_{i,2}$. To prove this statement, let us suppose that the lemma is true for the xth job, for some $x > 1$, and all the jobs before the xth in this subtask. Let t_l and t_l' denote the release times of the xth job $J_{i,l;x}$ and the $(x + 1)$st job $J_{i,l;x+1}$, respectively, for $l = 1, 2, \ldots n(i)$. We note that (1) $t_2 - t_1$ (i.e, the difference between the release times of the xth jobs of $T_{i,2}$ and $T_{i,1}$) is never larger than $W_{i,1}$, and (2) $t_1' - t_1$ (i.e., the difference in the release times of the $(x + 1)$st and the xth jobs in $T_{i,1}$) is never less than p_i. Hence, the release guard governing the release of $J_{i,2;x+1}$ is no later than $t_1' + W_{i,1}$. (This fact is illustrated by Figure 9–9. In this figure, solid arrows above each time line indicate the release times of the jobs in the subtask named at the left of the time line, and the dashed arrows indicate synchronization signals.) Moreover, the $(x+1)$st synchronization signal from the scheduler of $V_{i,1}$ is also never later than this time when there is no overrun. Consequently, at $W_{i,1}$ units of time after the release time of the $(x + 1)$st job of $T_{i,1}$, the $(x + 1)$st job of $T_{i,2}$ has certainly been released.

Now suppose that the lemma is true for the all the jobs in all the predecessor sibling subtasks of $T_{i,k}$ for any k in the range $2 < k \leq n(i)$ and it is also true for the xth job and all the jobs before the xth of $T_{i,k}$. To show that the lemma is true for the $(x+1)$st job of $T_{i,k}$ as well, we examine Figure 9–9 again. Because $t_k - t_1$ is never larger than $\sum_{l=1}^{k-1} W_{i,l}$, and $t_1' - t_1$ is never less than p_i, the release guard governing the release of $J_{i,k;x+1}$ is no later than $t_1' + \sum_{l=1}^{k-1} W_{i,l}$. Moreover, because the $(x+1)$st synchronization signal from the scheduler of $V_{i,k-1}$ is also never later than this time, $J_{i,k,x+1}$ is released for sure by this time.   □

Upper Bounds to Response Times of Subtasks.   Because of Theorem 9.1, the problem of finding an upper bound to the end-to-end response time of a task T_i whose subtasks are synchronized nongreedily is just the problem of finding upper bounds to the response times of its subtasks on all processors in its visit sequence. The most straightforward approach to bounding the response time of each subtask $T_{i,k}$ is to treat all the subtasks on the processor $V_{i,k}$ where $T_{i,k}$ execute as independent periodic tasks. Then, $W_{i,k}$ can be found by doing a time-demand analysis (as described in Chapter 6) on the subtask $T_{i,k}$. The complexity of this

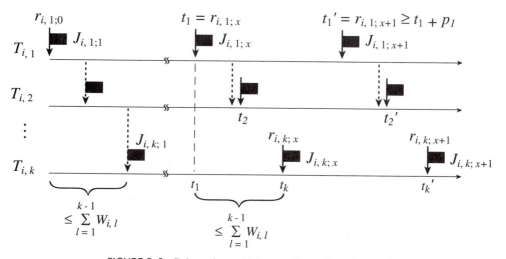

FIGURE 9–9   Release times of jobs according to the RG protocol.

computation is the complexity $O(np_{max})$ of the general schedulability test, where p_{max} is the maximum period of all tasks in the system. Alternatively, if the computation of $W_{i,k}$ is done on-line, we can reduce the run-time overhead at the expense of the accuracy of the upper bound by computing it according to [Bett]:

$$W_{i,k} = \frac{e_{i,k} + b_{i,k} + \sum_{T_{j,l} \in \mathbf{T}_H(V_{i,k})} e_{j,l}}{1 - \sum_{T_{j,l} \in \mathbf{T}_H(V_{i,k})} u_{j,l}} \tag{9.7}$$

$\mathbf{T}_H(V_{i,k})$ denotes the subset of subtasks, excluding $T_{i,k}$, that execute on processor $V_{i,k}$ and have equal or higher priorities than $T_{i,k}$.

As an example, Table 9–3 lists a set of priorities of the subtasks in the system described by Table 9–2. It also lists the upper bounds of their response times computed according to these two methods. It is evident that while the accuracy of Eq. (9.7) is adequate for higher-priority subtasks, it is quite poor for lower-priority subtasks. This is especially true for low-priority subtasks that execute on a heavily loaded processor. The reason is that the denominator can be very small under this condition. $T_{4,1}$ is an example. The upper bound of $W_{4,1}$ computed according Eq. (9.7) is 21.8, indicating that the task T_4 cannot meet its deadlines since its relative deadline is 20. In contrast, the upper bound on its response time computed according to the general schedulability test (listed as GST) shows that it in fact can.

Similarly, $W_{1,1}$ of subtask $T_{1,1}$ in the system is 3 according to the general schedulability test. $W_{1,2}$ and $W_{1,3}$ are 6 and 4, respectively. Hence the end-to-end response time of their parent task T_1 is never more than 13. If we were to compute the upper bounds of the response times of its subtasks according to Eq. (9.7), the upper bound to the end-to-end response time of this task would be 15.

*Effect of Precedence Constraints among Sibling Subtasks. In some systems, sibling subtasks never execute on the same processor. (An example is a packet-switched network: Sibling subtasks are packet transmissions at different switches.) For such a system, subtasks on each processor are indeed independent of each other, and the upper bounds W_i computed in ways described above are as accurate as the upper bounds for uniprocessor systems. In general, however, two or more sibling subtasks may execute on the same processors. (Such a task is said to be *recurrent* [Bett, Sun].) The system described by Table 9–3 is an example: Both $T_{1,1}$ and $T_{1,3}$ execute on P_1. For such a system, upper bounds found by the method described above are inaccurate for two reasons. First, the method ignores the dependency between sibling subtasks. Second, the method ignores the effect of lower-priority subtasks. We describe

TABLE 9–3 Upper bounds to the response times of subtasks in Table 9-2.

$T_{i,k}$	$V_{i,k}$	p_i	$e_{i,k}$	$\pi_{i,k}$	$b_{i,k}$	$W_{i,k}$ (9-7)	$W_{i,k}$ (GST)
$T_{1,1}$	P_1	15	1	15	0	3	3
$T_{1,3}$	P_1	15	2	15	1	4	4
$T_{2,1}$	P_1	20	4	20	0	8.75	7
$T_{3,1}$	P_2	2	1	2	0	1	1
$T_{1,2}$	P_2	15	2	15	1	8	6
$T_{4,1}$	P_2	20	5	20	0	21.8	14

now methods to take these factors into consideration and thus improve the accuracy of the upper bounds. Unfortunately, these improved methods only work when the end-to-end relative deadline of every task is no greater than its period.

Specifically, the method described above ignores the dependencies among sibling subtasks that execute on the same processor and assumes that jobs in these subtasks can be released simultaneously. This assumption may introduce inaccuracies in the time-demand functions of low-priority jobs. To illustrate, we look at the simple system of two tasks whose parameters are listed in Figure 9–10. In particular, we focus on $T_{2,1}$ which executes on P_1 together with two subtasks $T_{1,1}$ and $T_{1,3}$ of T_1 and has a lower priority than both of these

$T_{i,k}$	$V_{i,k}$	p_1	D_1	$e_{i,k}$	$\pi_{i,k}$
$T_{1,1}$	P_1	15	15	3	1
$T_{1,3}$	P_1	15	15	5	1
$T_{2,1}$	P_1	8	8	1	2
$T_{1,2}$	P_2	15	15	3	2
$T_{1,4}$	P_2	15	15	2	2

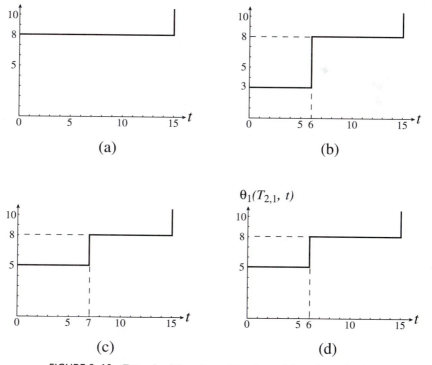

FIGURE 9–10   Example of time-demand functions of dependent subtasks.

subtasks. If jobs in $T_{1,1}$ and $T_{1,3}$ can be released at the same time, the total processor time demanded by these subtasks in any time interval of length t can be as large as the function shown in Figure 9–10(a). Based on this total time demand of T_1 on processor P_1, the upper bound $W_{2,1}$ found by the time-demand analysis is equal to 9. This bound would lead us to the conclusion that $T_{2,1}$ is not schedulable.

In reality, it may be impossible for jobs in $T_{1,1}$ and $T_{1,3}$ to be released at the same time if the end-to-end response time of T_1 never exceeds its period. If the xth job in $T_{1,1}$ is released at the same time (say at t_0) with the target job J in $T_{2,1}$ whose maximum response time we are computing, then the xth job of $T_{1,3}$ can never be released before $t_0 + 3 + 3$ (i.e., the earliest possible time instant when the xth job in $T_{1,2}$ can complete). In this case, the contribution of T_1 to the time-demand function $w_{2,1}(t)$ of $T_{2,1}$ is never more than that shown in Figure 9–10(b), where the horizontal axis gives the time t since t_0. On the other hand, if the xth job in $T_{1,3}$ is released at time t_0, then the $(x + 1)$st job in $T_{1,1}$ is never ready for execution before $t_0 + 5 + 2$. In this case, the contribution by T_1 to $w_{2,1}(t)$ is never more than that shown in Figure 9–10(c). The time demand of T_1 on P_1 since t_0 is never more than the function shown in Figure 9–10(d), which is obtained by taking the larger value of the functions in Figures 9–8(b) and (c) at every t. The time-demand function $w_{2,1}(t)$ of the task $T_{2,1}$ in the range $(0, 8]$ can be obtained by adding one unit of time (i.e., the execution time of $T_{2,1}$) to this function. When we solve $w_{2,1}(t) \leq t$, we find that the upper bound $W_{2,1}$ to the response time of $T_{2,1}$ is 6 and $T_{2,1}$ is schedulable.

Let $\mathbf{T}_H(V_{i,k})$ denote the subset of all subtasks, not including $T_{i,k}$, that execute on $V_{i,k}$ and have priorities equal to or higher than $T_{i,k}$. The above example tells us that when we want to compute an upper bound $W_{i,k}$ to the response time of a subtask $T_{i,k}$ in a system where some tasks are recurrent, we need to consider as a whole each task which has subtasks in $\mathbf{T}_H(V_{i,k})$, not the subtasks in the subset individually. Specifically, let $\Theta_j(T_{i,k}, t)$ denote the *interference function* of $T_{i,k}$ by the task T_j. The value of $\Theta_j(T_{i,k}, t)$ at time t is an upper bound of the total amount of processor time demanded in any time interval of length t by the task T_j which has one or more subtasks in $\mathbf{T}_H(V_{i,k})$. (In the previous example, the function in Figure 9–10(d) is, therefore, $\Theta_1(T_{2,1}, t)$.) The time-demand function $w_{i,k}(t)$ of the subtask $T_{i,k}$ can be written in term of its interference functions:

$$w_{i,k}(t) = e_{i,k} + b_{i,k} + \sum_{T_j \in \mathbf{T}_H(V_{i,k})} \Theta_j(T_{i,k}, t) \tag{9.8}$$

When we assume that all sibling subtasks on $V_{i,k}$ of each task T_j in $\mathbf{T}_H(V_{i,k})$ are independent, $\Theta_j(T_{i,k}, t)$ is simply equal to the maximum time demand in any time interval of length t of a periodic task whose period is p_j and whose execution time is equal to the sum of the execution times of all sibling subtasks of T_j in $\mathbf{T}_H(V_{i,k})$. This upper bound is correct no matter what the end-to-end response time of the task is. However, the method used in the previous example to find the more accurate interference function $\Theta_1(T_{2,1}, t)$ in Figure 9–10(d) works only when the end-to-end response time of the task T_1 is no greater than its period. In particular, the function in Figure 9–10(c) is a correct upper bound because every job in T_1 completes before the next job is released, and it takes at least 7 units of time to complete the xth jobs in $T_{1,3}$ and $T_{1,4}$. In contrast, suppose that there were a task with priority 1 on P_2 and this task can cause the response time of $T_{1,2}$ to be large. Then it would be possible for the xth job of $T_{1,3}$ to become ready for execution just when the $(x + 1)$st job of $T_{1,1}$ was released. In this case, only the function in Figure 9–10(a) is a correct interference function by T_1.

Input: Parameters of all y subtasks [called $T(1), T(2), \ldots, T(y)$] that are of T_j and are in the subset $\mathbf{T}_H(V_{i,k})$; the precedence relation among them is $T(1) < T(2) < \ldots < T(y)$.

Output: The interference function $\Theta_j(T_{i,k}, t)$ of target task $T_{i,k}$ by T_j.

1. Set each possible interference function $X_l(t)$, for $l = 1, 2, \ldots, y$, to 0.
2. Find each possible interference function $X_l(t)$, for $l = 1, 2, \ldots, y$, as follows:
   (a) Set the phase of the subtask $T(l)$ to 0.
   (b) For each $x > l$, set the phase of $T(x)$ to the sum of execution times of $T(l)$ and all subtasks of T_j which are successors of $T(l)$ and predecessors of $T(x)$.
   (c) For each $x < l$, set the phase of $T(x)$ to the phase of $T(y)$ plus the sum of execution times of $T(y)$, all successors of $T(y)$ in T_j and all predecessors of $T(x)$ in T_j.
   (d) $X_l(t)$ is equal to the total amount of time demanded by subtasks $T(1), T(2), \ldots, T(y)$ in the time interval $(0, t]$ when the phases of the subtasks are set as described above.
3. The interference function $\Theta_j(T_{i,k}, t)$ is equal to $\max(X_1(t), X_2(t), \ldots, X_y(t))$.

FIGURE 9–11   Computation of interference function of subtask $T_{i,k}$ by T_j.

Figure 9–11 describes how to find the interference function $\Theta_j(T_{i,k}, t)$ of $T_{i,k}$ by a task T_j, for $j \neq i$, which has subtasks in $\mathbf{T}_H(V_{i,k})$. Again, the interference function thus computed is correct only when the end-to-end response time of the task T_j is no greater than its period p_j.

When we want to find an upper bound to the end-to-end response time of a target task T_i, we should first bound the end-to-end response time of each recurrent task T_j which has subtasks in the subset $\mathbf{T}_H(V_{i,k})$ for some subtask $T_{i,k}$ of T_i. If the end-to-end response time of T_j is never greater than p_j, we calculate the interference function of each subtask in $T_{i,k}$ by T_j in the manner described in Figure 9–11; otherwise, we use the more pessimistic interference function based on the assumption that subtasks in T_j are independent. This procedure does not work when T_i is also recurrent and has subtasks in some subset $\mathbf{T}_H(V_{j,l})$. One way is to first assume that the end-to-end response time of every recurrent task is never greater than its period, calculate the interference function by this task as described in Figure 9–11 for every target subtask, and compute an upper bound to the end-to-end response time of every task in the system. If the upper bound for every recurrent task thus computed is equal to or less than its period, the upper bounds of all tasks thus computed are correct. If the upper bound for some recurrent task turns out to be greater than its period, the upper bounds for all tasks that execute on some processor with this recurrent task are not correct and must be recomputed.

*Effect of Lower-Priority Subtask.   Thus far, we have ignored lower-priority sibling subtasks of subtasks in the set $\mathbf{T}_H(V_{i,k})$ when we try to bound the response time of a target subtask $T_{i,k}$. Table 9–4 gives an example to illustrate why inaccuracy in the resultant upper bound may be introduced in this way. The table lists the parameters of subtasks on a processor. The subtasks $T_{1,3}$ and $T_{1,7}$ have higher priorities than the target subtask $T_{2,1}$ but the other subtasks of T_1 has lower priorities than $T_{2,1}$. Subtasks $T_{1,2}$, $T_{1,4}$, and $T_{1,6}$ (not listed here) execute on other processors.

TABLE 9–4   Parameters of subtasks on a processor

$T_{i,k}$	p_i	$e_{i,k}$	$\pi_{i,k}$
$T_{1,1}$	30	3	4
$T_{1,3}$	30	5	1
$T_{1,5}$	30	7	4
$T_{1,7}$	30	2	2
$T_{2,1}$	75	1	3

Both methods for calculating the interference function $\Theta_1(T_{2,1}, t)$ described above assume that jobs in $T_{1,3}$ and $T_{1,7}$ can be released and ready for execution during the time the target job J of $T_{2,1}$ is waiting to complete. This of course is impossible if the end-to-end response time of T_1 is never greater than its period. If the xth job of $T_{1,3}$ is released at the same time as the target job J, before J completes, the xth job of $T_{1,5}$ cannot start because it has a lower priority. Hence, the xth job of $T_{1,7}$ cannot be released before J completes. Moreover, because $T_{1,1}$ has a lower priority, none of the subsequent jobs in $T_{1,3}$ and $T_{1,5}$ can be released before J completes. Similarly, if the xth job of $T_{1,7}$ is released at the same time as the target job, the $(x + 1)$st job of $T_{1,3}$ and all the subsequent jobs in $T_{1,3}$ and $T_{1,5}$ cannot be released before the target job completes. In this case, the interference function $\Theta_1(T_{2,1}, t)$ is equal to 5 [i.e., $\max(5, 2)$] for all t.

Again, this kind of improvement does not work when the end-to-end response time of any recurrent task is larger than its period. Suppose that in this example, the end-to-end response time of T_1 is larger than 30. Then it is possible for target job J to be released after the completion of xth job in $T_{1,5}$ and one or more later jobs in $T_{1,3}$. Consequently, it is possible for the xth job of $T_{1,7}$ and one or more later jobs of $T_{1,3}$ to be released at the same time with the target job J.

As an exercise, Problem 9.7 asks you to modify the algorithm in Figure 9–11 so it can take advantage of the presence of lower-priority subtasks in T_j that also execute on $V_{i,k}$ with target subtask $T_{i,k}$ in order to reduce the interference function $\Theta_j(T_{i,k}, t)$. However, in this case, some improvement over treating all subtasks independently can still be realized even when the end-to-end response times of recurrent tasks can be greater than their respective periods. You should exploit this possibility in your solution.

*9.5.2   Schedulability of Tasks under Greedy Synchronization

This subsection describes an algorithm that can be used to compute upper bounds to end-to-end response times of tasks synchronized according to the greedy synchronization protocol. This algorithm, called algorithm SA/DS (Schedulability Analysis for Direct Synchronization Protocol) in [Sun], differs from the schedulability analysis methods described above in that it does not attempt to bound the response times of individual subtasks. Rather, to find an upper bound W_i to the end-to-end response time of each task T_i, algorithm SA/DS first tries to find an upper bound $IW_{i,k}$ to the intermediate end-to-end response time of each subtask $T_{i,k}$ of the task. The *intermediate end-to-end response time* of $T_{i,k}$ is the maximum length of time between the release of a job in $T_{i,1}$ in the first subtask to the completion of the corresponding job in $T_{i,k}$. By definition, end-to-end response time of T_i is the intermediate end-to-end response time of its last subtask $T_{i,n(i)}$. Hence, $W_i = IW_{i,n(i)}$.

Specifically, algorithm SA/DS is an iterative algorithm. It takes as input a set $\{IW_{i,k}^{(0)}\}$ of initial estimates of intermediate end-to-end response times of of all subtasks in the system. During each iteration, say the $(x+1)$st, the algorithm uses the set $\{IW_{i,k}^{(x)}\}$ of estimates produced in the xth iteration as input and produces as output a new set of estimates $\{IW_{i,k}^{(x+1)}\}$. If the output estimate for every subtask is equal to the input estimate for the subtask, then the bound $IW_{i,k}^{(x+1)}$ produced during the iteration is a correct upper bound $IW_{i,k}$ to the intermediate end-to-end response time of $T_{i,k}$, and an upper bound W_i to the end-to-end response time of the task T_i is equal to $IW_{i,n(i)}$. If the input and output estimates for some subtask are not equal, another iteration is carried out using the output estimates just produced as input. We will return shortly to discuss how to choose the initial estimates and the correctness, complexity, and accuracy of algorithm SA/DS.

Upper Bounds to Intermediate End-to-End Response Times of Subtasks.   The core of algorithm SA/DS is an algorithm called algorithm IEERT (Immediate End-to-End Response Time) [Sun], which is invoked during each iteration [say the $(x+1)$st for some $x \geq 0$] to find an upper bound $IW_{i,k}^{(x+1)}$ to the intermediate end-to-end response time of one target subtask $T_{i,k}$ at a time. We note that to find $IW_{i,k}^{(x+1)}$, we must be able to bound from above the amount of processor time demanded by every subtask in $\mathbf{T}_H(V_{i,k})$ in any time interval of length t. To be concrete, we focus on such a subtask $T_{j,g}$ for some $g > 1$ and let this time interval be $(t_0, t_0 + t]$ for some arbitrary t_0 after the phase of T_j. The problem of finding this upper bound is the same as the problem of finding an upper bound to the number of jobs in $T_{j,g}$ that can possibly be released in this interval. During the $(x+1)$st iteration, we compute this number based on the input estimate $IW_{j,g}^{(x)}$.

Figure 9–12 shows the possible release times of the jobs in $T_{j,g}$ and in its first sibling subtask $T_{j,1}$. For the sake of concreteness, we call the first and the last jobs of $T_{j,g}$ that are released in the time interval $(t_0, t_0 + t]$ $J_{j,g;1}$ and $J_{j,g;y}$, respectively. The arrows labeled $r_{j,g;1}$ and $r_{j,g;y}$ above the time line of $T_{j,g}$ indicate the release times of these jobs, respectively, and the arrows labeled $r_{j,1;1}$ and $r_{j,1;y}$ above the time line of $T_{j,1}$ indicate the release times of the corresponding jobs in the first subtask $T_{j,1}$. From Figure 9–12, we see that

$$r_{j,1;y} - r_{j,1;1} \leq t + IW_{j,g}^{(x)}$$

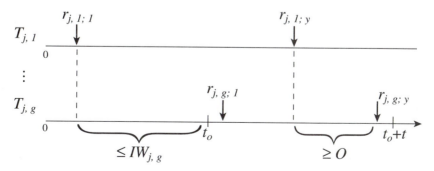

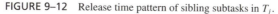

FIGURE 9–12   Release time pattern of sibling subtasks in T_j.

when we use 0 as the lower bound on the minimum intermediate end-to-end response time of $T_{j,g}$. Since $T_{j,1}$ is a periodic task with period p_j, the number y of jobs of $T_{j,1}$ whose successor jobs in $T_{j,g}$ are released in the interval $(t_0, t_0 + t]$ is never more than $\lceil (t + IW_{j,g}^{(x)})/p_j \rceil$. It follows that the total amount of time on processor $V_{i,k}$ demanded by jobs in $T_{j,g}$ during any time interval of length t is never more than $\lceil (t + IW_{j,g}^{(x)})/p_j \rceil e_{j,g}$.

This fact is the theoretical basis of algorithm IEERT. When the algorithm is invoked during the $(x + 1)$st iteration to compute the intermediate end-to-end response time $IW_{i,k}^{(x+1)}$ for any target subtask $T_{i,k}$, it carries out the following steps.

Step 1:   Algorithm IEERT first computes for the target subtask $T_{i,k}$ an upper bound Y to the length of any level-$\pi_{i,k}$ busy interval on the processor $V_{i,k}$. Y is the minimum of the solutions to the equation

$$t = \left\lceil \frac{t + IW_{i,k}^{(x)}}{p_k} \right\rceil e_{i,k} + \sum_{T_{j,g} \in \mathbf{T}_H(V_{i,k})} \left\lceil \frac{t + IW_{j,g}^{(x)}}{p_j} \right\rceil e_{j,g}$$

and this solution can be found in an iterative manner similar to the way described in Section 6.5.3.

Step 2:   Algorithm IEERT then calculates an upper bound $N_{i,k}$ to the number of jobs in $T_{i,k}$ that can possibly be released and completed in a level-$\pi_{i,k}$ busy interval according to

$$N_{i,k} = \left\lceil \frac{Y + IW_{i,k}^{(x)}}{p_i} \right\rceil$$

Step 3:   The third step computes upper bounds to the intermediate end-to-end response times of the $N_{i,k}$ jobs in the busy interval. The output estimate $IW_{i,k}^{(x+1)}$ for the target subtask $T_{i,k}$ is the maximum of the intermediate end-to-end response times of these $N_{i,k}$ jobs.[3] Specifically, the completion time $f(J_{i,k;l})$ of the lth job $J_{i,k;l}$ in this busy interval is bounded from above by the sum of t_0, the beginning of this busy interval, and the minimum of the solutions of

$$t = le_{i,k} + \sum_{T_{j,g} \in \mathbf{T}_H(V_{i,k})} \left\lceil \frac{t + IW_{j,g}^{(x)}}{p_j} \right\rceil e_{j,g}$$

A lower bound to the release time of the corresponding job $J_{i,1;l}$ in the first subtask $T_{i,1}$ is $t_0 - IW_{i,k-1}^{(x)} - (l - 1)p_i$. An upper bound $IW_{i,k-1}^{(x+1)}$ to the intermediate end-to-end response time of $J_{i,k;l}$ is the difference between $f(J_{i,k;l})$ and this lower bound.

We note that an estimate of the intermediate end-to-end response time ($IW_{i,k}^{(x)}$ or $IW_{j,g}^{(x)}$) appears in each of the ceiling functions above. This is because 0 is used as the lower bound

---

[3] Gutierrez, *et al.* [GuGH] pointed out that the Tindell and Clark algorithm [TiCl] is faster. The reason is that Tindell and Clark's algorithm does not compute the intermediate end-to-end response times of all $N_{i,k}$ jobs in a level-$\pi_{i,k}$ busy interval. The proof of correctness of Tindell and Clark's algorithm is too lengthy to be included here; it can be found in [GuGH].

on the minimum intermediate end-to-end response time of $T_{i,k}$ (or $T_{j,g}$). When the minimum execution times of subtasks are nonzero, we can improve the accuracy of the bound $IW_{i,k}$ by replacing $IW_{i,k}^{(x)}$ (or $IW_{j,g}^{(x)}$) by the maximum jitter of the subtask $T_{i,k}$ (or $T_{j,g}$), which is equal to $IW_{i,k}^{(x)}$ (or $IW_{j,g}^{(x)}$) minus the sum of the minimum execution times of all predecessors of $T_{i,k}$ (or $T_{j,g}$) and the minimum execution time of $T_{i,k}$ (or $T_{j,g}$).

Initial Estimates, Termination Condition, and Correctness of Algorithm SA/DS.
You recall that in solving Eq. (6.7) iteratively to find an upper bound to the response time of a task, we can start with an initial estimate that may be too optimistic and hence is not a correct upper bound. Similarly, during the first iteration of algorithm SA/DS, we can use as the initial estimate $IW_{i,k}^{(0)}$ for every subtask $T_{i,k}$ the sum $\sum_{g=1}^{k} e_{i,g}$ of execution times of $T_{i,k}$ and all of its predecessor subtasks. The initial estimate may not be a correct upper bound to the intermediate end-to-end response time of $T_{i,k}$. As stated earlier, the iterative process of algorithm SA/DS terminates when the output estimate $IW_{i,k}^{(x+1)}$ is equal to the input estimate $IW_{i,k}^{(x)}$ for every subtask in the system.

Sun showed in [Sun] that when algorithm SA/DS terminates, the output estimate $IW_{i,n(i)}^{(x+1)}$ produced during the last iteration is a correct upper bound W_i of the end-to-end response time of the task T_i for every $i = 1, 2, \ldots, n$. However, algorithm SA/DS sometimes does not terminate even when the total utilization of every processor is reasonably small. Intuitively, we can see from the description of the algorithm IEERT why this can happen. The upper bound to the completion time of each job in each target subtask $T_{i,k}$ tends to grow with the input estimates $IW_{j,g}^{(x)}$'s, and the lower bound to the release time of the corresponding job in the first subtasks tends to decrease with the input estimates. Consequently, it is possible for some output estimates to grow with each iteration, and the growth may never slow down.

The example given in [Sun] to illustrate this phenomenon consists of six processors and two tasks. Each task has six subtasks, and its period is 3. The execution times of all subtasks are 1. The visit sequences of the two tasks are $(P_1, P_2, P_3, P_4, P_5, P_6)$ and $(P_6, P_5, P_4, P_3, P_2, P_1)$. The first three subtasks of each task have higher priority than the later three subtasks of the other task. (This can be the model of a network of six packet switches in which two streams of packets transverse the switches in opposite directions. Each stream is given a higher priority during the first three hops.) The total utilization of every processor is 2/3, and the response times of all subtasks would be no greater than 2 if all subtasks were periodic. However, when the subtasks are synchronized greedily, the estimates of intermediate end-to-end response times of subtasks grow without bound as algorithm SA/DS iterates. For such a system, algorithm SA/DS can tell us that the system is not schedulable. However, since the upper bounds produced by the algorithm are not tight, we do not know whether the system is in fact not schedulable.

Figure 9–13 summarizes the operations of algorithm SA/DS. The algorithm terminates either when a correct upper bound W_i to the end-to-end response time of every task T_i is found or when the bound for task T_i found during an iteration exceeds the relative end-to-end deadline D_i of the task, whichever is sooner. The complexity of this algorithm is high: The complexity of algorithm IEERT is linear in the number of subtasks in the system and the maximum period of all tasks, and the number of iterations required for its termination depends on the parameters of the subtasks. This algorithm is clearly unsuitable if the schedulability of any task is done on-line, for example, during the acceptance test of the task.

Input: Parameters of all subtasks in the system **T** of n tasks.

Output: A set W_i of end-to-end response times of all tasks T_i's in **T** or the declaration that the system is unschedulable.

1. For each subtask $T_{i,k}$, set $IW_{i,k}$ to $\sum_{g=1}^{k} e_{i,g}$ and $IW'_{i,k}$ to 0.
2. Invoke algorithm IEERT to compute $IW'_{i,k}$ for every subtask $T_{i,k}$ using $IW_{i,k}$ as input.
3. If $IW'_{i,k}$ is equal to $IW_{i,k}$ for every subtask $T_{i,k}$ in **T**, $W_i = IW_{i,n(i)}$ for every $i = 1, 2, \ldots, n$. Stop.
4. If $IW'_{i,n(i)}$ becomes larger than the relative deadline D_i of T_i, for some $1 \le i \le n$, declare the system unschedulable and stop.

FIGURE 9–13   Pseudocode description of algorithm SA/DS.

9.5.3   Relative Performance of End-to-End and MPCP Approaches

We are now ready to compare the performance of the end-to-end approach and the multiprocessor priority-ceiling protocol approach to scheduling periodic tasks in multiprocessor systems. In particular, we want to answer the question when one should use one approach rather than the other in systems where fixed priority scheduling can be used on all processors?

For illustrative purposes, Table 9–5(a) lists again the parameters of the end-to-end task system described earlier by Table 9–2. We suppose that the intermediate deadlines of the subtasks are assigned according to the Proportional Deadline (PD) algorithm described in Section 9.4.2, and the priorities of subtasks are assigned on the deadline monotonic basis.

TABLE 9–5   Comparison between end-to-end and MPCP approaches.

$T_{i,k}$	$V_{i,k}$	p_i	$e_{i,k}$	Crit. Sec.	$PD_{i,k}$	$\pi_{i,k}$	$b_{i,k}(rc)$	$W_{i,k}$
$T_{1,1}$	P_1	15	1		3	3	0	1
$T_{1,3}$	P_1	15	2	$[PR; 1]$	6	6	1	3
$T_{2,1}$	P_1	20	4	$[PR; 1]$	20	20	0	7
$T_{3,1}$	P_2	2	1		2	2	0	1
$T_{1,2}$	P_2	15	2	$[DB; 2]$	6	6	1	6
$T_{4,1}$	P_2	20	5	$[DB; 1]$	20	20	0	14

(a) The parameters and response times of tasks in the end-to-end model

T_i	Local Proc	p_i	e_i	Crit. Sec.	π_i	$b_i(rc)$	W_i
T_1	P_1	15	5	$[DB; 2]\ [PR; 1]$	15	3	8
T_2	P_1	20	4	$[PR; 1]$	20	3	12
T_3	P_2	2	1		2	5	6
T_4	P_2	20	5	$[DB; 1]$	20	6	22

(b) The parameters and response times of tasks in the MPCP model

One of the nongreedy protocols is used to synchronize subtasks in T_1. Since all resource accesses are local, the blocking times due to resource contention $b_{i,k}(rc)$'s of all the subtasks are as listed. Using the time-demand method described earlier, we find that the end-to-end response time W_i of the parent task T_i, for $i = 1, 2, 3, 4$ are 10, 7, 1, and 14, respectively. If the end-to-end relative deadlines of the tasks are equal to their respectively periods, these tasks are all schedulable.

Table 9–5(b) describes the same four tasks T_1, T_2, T_3 and T_4, this time in parameters of the MPCP model. The former two tasks are local on P_1, while the latter two are local on P_2. PR is a local resource on P_1, and DB is a global resource on P_2. T_1 requires DB, its global critical section is $[DB, 2]$. T_4 also requires DB, but only for 1 unit of time. Tasks on both processors are scheduled rate-monotonically. The blocking time $b_1(rc)$ of T_1 arises solely due to local and remote blocking which contribute 2 and 1 time units, respectively, according to Eqs. (9.4a) and (9.4c). Therefore, $b_1(rc)$ is equal to 3. The blocking time $b_2(rc)$ consists solely of the deferred blocking time; it is 3, according to Eq. (9.4e). On processor P_2, T_3 can be preempted by global critical sections of T_1 and T_4. Hence, the blocking time $b_3(rc)$ of this task is equal to its local preemption delay which, according to Eq. (9.4b), can be as large as 5. Finally, the blocking time of T_4 is also equal to its local preemption delay, and it is 6. The upper bounds of response times of the four tasks are 8, 12, 6, and 22, respectively. Therefore, T_3 and T_4 are not schedulable.[4]

The above example points out that when tasks are scheduled according to the multi-processor priority-ceiling protocol, the local tasks on a synchronization processor of a global resource can be adversely affected by tasks that use this resource. The reason is that global critical sections are scheduled at higher priorities than local tasks, even when local tasks have very short relative deadlines. In contrast, the end-to-end approach does not have this shortcoming. It is usually a better alternative whenever many local tasks run on synchronization processors of global resources.

Similarly, in a system where some processors are heavily loaded and others are lightly loaded, the end-to-end approach may perform better. The reason is that it is possible to schedule subtasks of each end-to-end task according to different priorities. For instance, the NPD algorithm gives larger relative deadlines to subtasks on more heavily loaded processors and, thus, allocate them more slack than subtasks on relatively lightly loaded processors. Priorities of subtasks assigned on the basis of this kind of relative deadline take into account the load conditions of different processors implicitly.

Sun [Sun] compared the performance of the end-to-end and MPCP approaches when they are applied to a system of five processors; each has five tasks and one resource. The system parameters he varied include processor utilization, number of critical sections per task, the total execution time of critical sections, and the total execution time of each task. Whether each task can meet its deadline is determined by comparing the task's worst-case response time, which is computed according to the schedulability analysis methods described above, with the task's relative deadline. His results indicate that the end-to-end approach is

---

[4]One may argue that Eq. (9.4a) is too loose for this system. Because T_2 has only one critical section, T_1 cannot be blocked twice, once when it request for PR and once more when it return after using the remote resource. Hence the local blocking time of T_1 is only 1 and $b_1(rc)$ is 2. Similarly, the deferred blocking time of T_2 cannot be as large as 3; it is at most equal to 2, the execution time of the critical section $[DB, 2]$ of T_1. However, these reductions in blocking times of T_1 and T_2 do not alter the conclusion that T_3 and T_4 are not schedulable.

more likely to feasibly schedule all tasks than the MPCP approach when tasks have a small number of long critical sections. (For example, for processor utilization ranging from 0.5 to 0.7, each task has no more than three critical sections and the total execution time of the critical sections of each task is 5 percent or more of the task's execution time.) A reason for the poorer performance the MPCP approach is that the bounds on task blocking times become overly pessimistic under this condition. Sun's effort to tighten the blocking time bounds under MPCP failed to change this conclusion.

It should not be a surprise that the end-to-end approach is not always better than the MPCP approach. Sun found that the MPCP performs better when each task has a large numbers of short critical sections (e.g., four or more critical sections with a total execution time no more than 1 percent of the task execution time.) The primary reason for the poorer performance of the end-to-end approach is the loose bound to end-to-end response time. When bounding the response times of sibling subtasks, the interference from some other tasks may be counted repeatedly, while in reality, repeated interference may never occur. Unfortunately, the repeated counting cannot be safely eliminated. When a task has a large number of global critical sections, this problem becomes more serious, leading us to conclude that a task is not schedulable when in fact it may be.

9.6   END-TO-END TASKS IN HETEROGENEOUS SYSTEMS

Thus far, our discussion on end-to-end scheduling has assumed that a priority-driven scheme is used to schedule every processor. We now remove this restrictive assumption. It is not valid for most real-life systems. All but the simplest embedded systems contain different types of processors (e.g, CPUs, disks, and networks). Typically, a variety of approaches are taken to scheduling tasks on these processors. Rather than digressing here to describe some of them (e.g., network scheduling algorithms), we postpone their descriptions until later chapters and focus here on end-to-end scheduling issues.

Exactly which scheduling algorithms are used on individual processors and how these algorithms work are unimportant here. Whatever the choice is, it is essential is that the scheduling algorithm used on every processor keeps the response time of every subtask on the processor bounded from above as long as the processor time demands (i.e., release-time patterns and execution times of jobs) of the subtasks on the processor satisfy the design constraint of the algorithm. Most algorithms described in previous chapters meet this requirement for periodic subtasks that never overrun and sporadic tasks that satisfy some release-time pattern constraint (e.g., a leaky bucket constraint).

Hereafter, by a *real-time scheduling algorithm*, we mean specifically one that meets this requirement. Moreover, when the processor time demand of every subtask $T_{i,k}$ on a processor meets the design constraint of the scheduling algorithm used by the processor, we can obtain an upper bound $W_{i,k}$ to the subtask's response time on the processor without considering tasks that execute on other processors. Without loss of generality, we assume that the scheduler on every processor uses a real-time scheduling algorithm.

The previous section pointed out that in a system of end-to-end periodic tasks, a way to keep the worst-case end-to-end response time of every periodic task small and end-to-end schedulability analysis (hence acceptance test) simple is to use a nongreedy interprocessor synchronization protocol that reshapes the release-time pattern of every subtask to make the subtask periodic. The MPM and RG protocols are such protocols. They do not require priority-driven scheduling be used on individual processors. Indeed, the proof of Theorem 9.1 remains correct for a much broader class of systems. To emphasize this fact, we restate it in the corollary below. In contrast, we cannot generalize the schedulability analysis of end-to-end periodic tasks that are synchronized greedily.

> **COROLLARY 9.3.** In a system where a real-time algorithm is used to schedule subtasks on every processor, an upper bound W_i to the end-to-end response time of any periodic task T_i synchronized according to the MPM protocol or the RG protocol is given by

$$W_i = \sum_{k=1}^{n(i)} W_{i,k} \qquad (9.9)$$

where $n(i)$ is the number of subtasks in T_i and the upper bound $W_{i,k}$ to the response time of every subtask $T_{i,k}$ is obtained by considering only subtasks on the same processor as $T_{i,k}$ and by treating every such subtask $T_{j,l}$ as a periodic task whose period is equal to the period p_j of the parent task T_j.

It is still appropriate to divide the end-to-end relative deadline of each parent task into local relative deadlines of its subtasks (i.e., to distribute the total slack of the task among its subtasks). The schedulers of the processors in the visit sequence of the task then aim at meeting the respective local relative deadlines. The deadline assignment algorithms presented in Section 9.4.2 can be used for this purpose. The NPD algorithm is especially good when deadline assignment is done at configuration time.

When deadline assignment is done during acceptance test and admission control time, an alternative is to let the scheduler of each processor in the visit sequence of the new task determine and propose a feasible local relative deadline. As an example, in a switched network that allows the applications to request real-time connections, each request for connection specifies the end-to-end relative deadline of packets on the connection. Upon receiving a request, the network first chooses a route (i.e., all the switches used to relay packets on the connection). The request is then sent from switch to switch along the route. Upon receiving a request, each switch computes an upper bound to the local response time of packets on the connection, based on the release-time pattern declared in the request and the current load on the switch. It then offers a local relative deadline that is equal to or larger than this upper bound; if the switch accepts the connection, it will guarantee the offered relative deadline. As the request propagates to the destination, the destination adds all the relative deadlines offered by the switches en route. If the total relative deadline is equal to or less than the requested end-to-end relative deadline, the connection is acceptable. During the acknowledgement pass, each switch used by the connection commits to guarantee the local relative deadline it offered or a larger relative deadline chosen for the switch by the destination. At all times, each switch schedules the packets it relays aiming to meet the local relative deadline thus determined.

In general, during an acceptance test to determine whether to admit a new end-to-end periodic task, one or more schedulers choose the processors used to execute its subtasks, that is, the visit sequence of the task. Then the schedulers of the processors in the visit sequence determine the local relative deadlines of its subtasks either sequentially, as in switched networks, or in parallel. The task is acceptable if the sum of the individual local relative deadlines is no greater than the end-to-end relative deadline requested by the new task. Once the new task is admitted, each scheduler on each processor aims at meeting the relative deadline of the local subtask, using a uniprocessor scheduling algorithm suited for the processor and tasks executing on it. Again, it is not required that the scheduling algorithms used on all processors be the same, only that they all provide bounded response times.

*9.7 PREDICTABILITY AND VALIDATION OF DYNAMIC MULTIPROCESSOR SYSTEMS

Thus far, we have confined our attention to static systems. The technology for validating the timing constraints of static systems is relative mature. You have seen many provably correct, efficient, and accurate methods for determining the schedulability of tasks in static systems. In contrast, we know very little about how to validate dynamic systems in a rigorous and efficient manner. This section summarizes the few available schedulability conditions and validation algorithms. In general, their accuracy is poor. You will see that much work remains to be done.

We first introduced the notion of predictable execution in Chapter 4. Predictable execution of a set $\mathbf{J}$ of jobs is defined in terms of three possible schedules of $\mathbf{J}$ according to the given scheduling algorithm: the maximal, minimal, and actual schedules. If every job in $\mathbf{J}$ were to execute for as long as its maximum execution time (or as short as its minimum execution time), the resultant schedule of $\mathbf{J}$ would be the maximal (or the minimal) schedule. As long as the range of execution time of every hard real-time job is known, we can easily construct these schedules. The actual execution times of jobs are unknown, and the actual schedule of $\mathbf{J}$ is, therefore, unknown.

The example in Figure 4–8 illustrates that in a dynamic system, the actual start time $s(J_i)$ of a job J_i according to the actual schedule of $\mathbf{J}$ can be later (or earlier) than its start time $s^+(J_i)$ [or $s^-(J_i)$] according to the maximal schedule (or minimal schedule). The start time of J_i is said to be unpredictable when this condition occurs. Similarly, the actual completion (finishing) time $f(J_i)$ of J_i according to the actual schedule of $\mathbf{J}$ can be later (or earlier) than its completion time $f^+(J_i)$ [or $f^-(J_i)$] according to the maximal schedule (or minimal schedule); the completion time of J_i is unpredictable if this is true. On the other hand, if $s^-(J_i) \leq s(J_i) \leq s^+(J_i)$, then J_i is *start-time predictable*, and if $f^-(J_i) \leq f(J_i) \leq f^+(J_i)$, then J_i is *completion-time predictable*. The execution of J_i is predictable (or simply J_i is predictable), if J_i is both start-time and completion-time predictable. The execution behavior of the entire set $\mathbf{J}$ is predictable if every job in $\mathbf{J}$ is predictable.

The existence of examples such as the one in Figure 4–8 demonstrates that the execution of jobs in dynamic, priority-driven multiprocessors is unpredictable in general. However, such a system has predictable execution under several conditions. When one of these conditions is satisfied, the response time of each job according to the maximal and minimal schedules, respectively, give us tight upper and lower bounds of the response time.

Validation of Preemptable/Migratable Systems.   A preemptable/migratable system is a dynamic system in which jobs are scheduled in a priority-driven manner on m processors. Every job can be dispatched to execute on any processor, can be preempted at any time, and, when preempted, can be resumed on any processor. In other words, the job can migrate among processors. A condition for predictability of a preemptable/migratable system is that jobs have no precedence constraints and do not contend for resources.

THEOREM 9.4. The execution of a system of preemptable/migratable jobs is predictable if all the jobs have fixed release times, are independent, and do not contend for resources.

The proof and practical implication of this theorem are similar to that of Theorem 4.4. In particular, this theorem tells us we can validate a preemptable and migratable system in ways similar to those used to validate static systems. Because of Theorem 4.4, validation algorithms for static systems can work solely with maximum execution times of all jobs when computing upper bounds of their response times. Similarly, when we want to compute an upper bound to the completion time of a job J_i in a preemptable/migratable system of jobs that have no precedence constraints, we can begin by computing its maximal completion time $f^+(J_i)$ using an extended time-demand analysis method, which ignores release-time jitters, nonpreemptivity, and resource contention. We then add the additional delay the job may suffer due to these factors. Unfortunately, algorithms that take into account the effects of these factors are far more inaccurate than schedulability analysis algorithms for static systems.

Other Conditions for Predictability. The system in Figure 4–8 is a preemptable/nonmigratable system. Jobs in such a system are scheduled in a priority-driven manner, and every job can be dispatched to execute on any processor. However once a job starts on a processor, it is constrained to execute on that processor. This scheduling strategy is commonly used because job migration is too costly in most multiprocessor and distributed systems. Figure 4–8 illustrates that if jobs are not allowed to migrate, their execution is no longer predictable even when the jobs are independent. However, under the conditions stated in Theorems 9.5 and 9.6, the execution of preemptable/nonmigratable, independent jobs is predictable. The proofs of the theorems can be found in [Ha].

THEOREM 9.5. If in a system of preemptable/nonmigratable, independent jobs, preemption can never occur, then the execution of the jobs is predictable.

THEOREM 9.6. If according to the maximal schedule of a system of preemptable/nonmigratable independent jobs, no job is preempted and the jobs start in the same sequence according to the maximal and minimal schedules, then their execution is predictable.

The condition of Theorem 9.5 is satisfied by jobs scheduled on a FIFO basis. Also, when all the jobs have the same release time and their precedence constraint graph is an in-forest (i.e., every job has at most one successor), no job is ever preempted. In both of these cases, the execution of the system is predictable.

9.8 SUMMARY

This chapter described how uniprocessor scheduling and schedulability analysis algorithms are extended to schedule hard real-time tasks in static multiprocessor systems. In a static system, scheduling involves the following steps.

1. Task assignment: The first step is to choose a processor to execute every task. When the task has subtasks, this means choosing a processor for each of its subtasks.

2. Interprocessor synchronization: When tasks have precedence constraints, their executions are synchronized according to some execution synchronization protocol(s).

3. Task scheduling: If the processor on which the task (or subtask) executes is scheduled in a priority-driven manner, the jobs in the task (or subtasks) are assigned a priority (or priorities). If the processor is scheduled on the clock-driven basis, the time slots during which the task is scheduled are chosen. In general, a processor may use any real-time scheduling algorithm, that is, an algorithm can provide a local response time guarantee.

4. Schedulability analysis: An appropriate schedulability analysis method is used to validate that the task always meets its deadline. When tasks are added on-line, this analysis is done as an acceptance test.

Task Assignment.   Section 9.2 described three approaches to task assignment. All of them are computational difficult. For each approach, the section formulates the task assignment problem in terms of one or more frequently encountered problems that have good heuristics and software packages. You can find numerous other formulations in the literature on task assignment and load balancing.

When communication and resource usage costs are ignored, the problem of assigning periodic and sporadic tasks to processors is a bin-packing problem. Well-known heuristics such as first-fit and next-fit algorithms and their extensions are good solutions. We measure the performance of an algorithm for assigning tasks on m processors by the schedulability utilization achievable by the algorithm. Equation Eq. (9.1) gives the schedulability utilizations on m processors for the FF, RMST, and RMGT algorithms. The latter two algorithms extend the first-fit algorithm to achieve higher schedulable utilizations. However, unlike the first-fit algorithm, they are off-line algorithms.

When the objective of task assignment is to minimize the total communication cost, as well as finding a feasible assignment using as few processors as possible, the task assignment problem can be formulated as a integer linear programming problem. Section 9.2.2 contains the definitions of integer linear programs whose solutions give assignments of communicating periodic tasks to processors in homogeneous and heterogeous systems.

By expanding the given task-graph description of the system to capture the end-to-end nature of tasks and to take into account resource usage costs, we can effectively modify the integer linear programs defined in Section 9.2.2 so their solutions give simultaneous assignments of tasks and resources in a system based on the end-to-end model. Section 9.2.3 gives a graph-partitioning formulation of the simultaneous task and resource assignment problem for systems based on the MPCP (multiprocessor priority-ceiling protocol) model.

Interprocessor Synchronization.   Section 9.4.1 described two approaches to synchronizing the execution of end-to-end tasks in multiprocessor systems: the greedy and nongreedy approaches. The objectives of an interprocessor synchronization protocol are to enforce the precedence constraints among sibling subtasks and, if the protocol is nongreedy, to also shape the release time patterns of later subtasks.

Greedy synchronization is simple: Each scheduler releases each successor job as soon as the immediate predecessor job completes. Since these jobs execute on different processors, when a job completes on a processor, the scheduler of the processor must notify the scheduler(s) of processor(s) on which the immediate successor(s) of the job execute. Except for this minimal amount of interaction, the schedulers on different processors can be independent. The advantages of this approach are that global clock and load information are not required and that the average end-to-end response time of all tasks is minimum. However, unless the completion-time jitter on each processor is kept small by some other means, interrelease time intervals of a later subtask can be arbitrarily small. The sporadic nature of later subtasks may adversely affect the maximum end-to-end response times and the schedulability of the system. As another consequence, the schedulability analysis algorithm for greedy synchronized end-to-end tasks in a fixed-priority system is complex and is unsuitable as an on-line acceptance test. For greedy synchronized systems using mixed types of scheduling algorithms, there is no good (i.e., efficient, robust, and accurate) schedulability analysis algorithms with which we can bound the end-to-end response times of tasks.

The nongreedy synchronization protocols reshape the release-time patterns of later subtasks. Both the MPM protocol and the RG protocol can keep the release-time pattern of any later subtask the same as that of its first sibling subtask despite release-time jitters. These protocols do not require globally synchronized clocks or global load conditions. In the presense of overruns, the RG protocol never allows interrelease time intervals of any subtask to be shorter than its period, but the MPM protocol may fail to do so. The MPM protocol requires that an upper bound to the response time of every subtask of a task be computed when the task is admitted to the system, because it requires this information to operate. In contrast, the RG protocol does not require this information. Except under heavy load, the average end-to-end response time achieved by the RG protocol is close to that achieved by the greedy protocol, but the maximum end-to-end response time achieved by the RG protocol is much better.

Scheduling Subtasks on Each Processor.   In a system based on the MPCP model, every task must be scheduled according to a fixed-priority algorithm. However, in a system based on the end-to-end model, the only restriction on the choice of the scheduling algorithm and resource access-control protocol for each processor is that they can guarantee each task executing on the processor a bounded response time as long as the release-time pattern and execution-time distribution of every task meet specified constraints.

A way to transform the problem of scheduling tasks that execute in turn on multiple processors into uniprocessor scheduling problems is to first divide the overall end-to-end relative deadlines into local relative deadlines of subtasks on individual processors. The scheduler on each processor then aims at meeting the local relative deadline of each subtask executing on the processor without consideration to its sibling subtasks. Section 9.4.2 gives four hueristics for this purpose. They are the UD, ED, PD, and NPD algorithms.

*Validation of Dynamic Multiprocessor Systems.   The literature on parallel and distributed computing is full of excellent scheduling and load balancing algorithms for use in dynamic multiprocessor systems. They are not used for hard real-time applications not because their performance is poor but because there is no robust and accurate schedulability analysis algorithms with which we can validate dynamic systems. Only systems in which preemption and migration of jobs are allowed at all times are predictable. When the execution of jobs are predictable, we can determine their schedulability based on their maximum execution times. This is exactly what schedulability analysis algorithms for static systems do. Restrictions on migration and preemption introduce scheduling anomalies and unpredictable execution behavior. As a consequence, the bounds on response times computed based on maximum and minimum execution times may not be correct bounds on worst-case and best-case response times. This fact makes schedulability analysis and validation difficult. Even for preemptable/migratable systems, existing algorithms designed to bound the effects of non-preemptivity, resource contention, and precedence constraints in dynamic systems are far too pessmistic to be useful.

EXERCISES

9.1 In Section 9.1, we described how a shared memory can be modeled as a processor. It is more natural to view the memory and memory ports as a resource. This resource is managed by a synchronization processor on which there is no local job. Develop a MPCP model of a real-time monitor system that contains two field processors and a control processor, which communicate via a shared memory.

9.2 Section 9.2.1 presented the Oh and Baker's [OhBa] schedulable utilization for a fixed-priority system containing m processors and independent periodic tasks: The minimum achievable utilization of the first-fit algorithm is in the range $(0.414m, (m + 1)(1 + 2^{1/(m+1)}))$.

    (a) To get some insight into why the upper bound is true, consider the set of m periodic tasks $T_i = (p_i, e_i)$, for $i = 1, 2, \ldots, m$, whose parameters are as follows: e_i is equal to $2^{i/(m+1)}$, and $p_i = 2^{1/(m+1)} e_i$. In other words, the utilization of every task is equal to $1/2^{1/(m+1)}$. Show that if the execution time of any task is larger than the value given above by some arbitrarily small $\varepsilon > 0$, the first-fit algorithm may not find a feasible assignment on m processors.

    (b) Based on the Oh and Baker's lower bound, find the minimum number of processors so that the independent periodic tasks listed in Table P9-1 are schedulable preemptively according to the rate-monotonic algorithm.

TABLE P9–1   Parameters of 12 periodic tasks for the problem on FF algorithms.

p_i	2.5	3.0	4.5	6.0	7.0	8.5	10.0	15.0	21.0	24.0	26.0	29.0
e_i	1.0	0.6	1.0	1.0	1.0	0.5	1.0	3.0	3.0	2.0	2.0	2.0

    (c) Using the rate-monotonic first-fit algorithm, find a feasible assignment of the tasks in part (b) on as many processors as necessary.

    (d) Using the RMST algorithm, find a feasible assignment of the tasks in part (b).

9.3 A system contains 10 independent periodic tasks. Their periods and execution times are listed in Table P9-2.

    (a) Using the first-fit algorithm, find an assignment of these tasks to processors.

    (b) Using the RMST algorithm, find an assignment of these tasks to processors.

TABLE P9–2   Parameters of 10 periodic tasks for the problem on the RMST algorithm.

p_i	7	21	29	49	64	66	160	235	260	450
e_i	2	3	9	15	20	16	32	72	25	120

9.4 In Section 9.2.2, we described the integer linear programming formulation of the task partitioning problem. This problem can also be formulated as a minimum m-way cut problem, which also has many good heuristic solutions. The formulation is as follows. For the given system, we have a (task partition) graph in which there is a vertex T_i for each task T_i in the system. The weight of each vertex is u_i. There is an undirected edge between every pair of vertices T_i and T_j, and the weight of the edge is equal to $C_{i,j}$. We want to find an m-way cut which partitions all the vertices in this graph into m disjoint subsets which is such that (1) the sum of all the weights of vertices in each subset is less than $\hat{U}$ and (2) the sum of all the weights of edges each of which connects vertices in different subsets is minimized. You can see that (1) is imposed to ensure the schedulability of tasks in each subset (i.e., module). The sum (2) is the total communication cost among tasks in different modules.

  (a) Draw the task partition graph of the system in Figure 9–5. What is the 2-way cut which represents the solution of the linear integer program?
  (b) In this formulation, we have not provided a way to put external constraints on not placing tasks in the same module explicitly in the graph specifying the system. Suggest a way to modify the graph so it will allow us to take care of these constraints.

9.5 Consider a processor P in an end-to-end system that uses the release-guard protocol to synchronize subtasks on different processors. There are only two subtasks $T_{i,j} = (4, 2)$ and $T_{k,1} = (10, 4)$ on P, and they are scheduled rate-monotonically. Moreover, suppose that

  • $T_{k,1}$ is the first subtask in the task T_k (i.e., it has no predecessors), and
  • The first three synchronization signals from the predecessor of $T_{i,j}$ come at times 1, 2, and 3.

  When are the first three jobs in $T_{i,j}$ released on P?

9.6 There are three periodic tasks T_1, T_2, and T_3 executing on a CPU: $T_1 = (5, 0.5)$, $T_2 = (11, 1.0)$, and $T_3 = (14, 1.0)$. The tasks are scheduled on a processor rate-monotonically. During each period, each task accesses a file server to retrieve a file after it executes for 0.1 unit of time, is blocked until its data transfer is complete, and then becomes ready for execution again. Suppose that the file transfer is done under DMA control and requires a negligible amount of CPU time. The file server takes 0.5, 1, and 2 units of time, respectively, to complete the file transfers for the tasks. The disk is a nonpreemptive resource; the disk controller schedules disk accesses by the tasks nonpreemptively according to the priority-driven algorithm which gives each task a priority identical to its priority on the processor. Are these tasks schedulable according to the priority ceiling protocol? Explain your answer fully.

9.7 Modify the algorithm described by Figure 9–11 so it can take advantage of the presence of lower-priority subtasks of a task T_j that executes on the same processor as the target subtask $T_{i,k}$ in order to reduce the interference function $\Theta_j(T_{i,k}, t)$.

9.8 The end-to-end task model used in this chapter assumes that each subtask is a simple task that executes on a processors. Kao and Garcia-Molina [KaGa] generalized the simple end-to-end task model to include serial-parallel tasks. According to their model, each subtask $T_{i,k}$ may be complex, meaning that it is composed of $n_{i,k}$ parallel subtasks $T_{i,k,l}$, for $l = 1, 2, \ldots, n_{i,k}$; each $T_{i,k,l}$ being simple means that it is not further decomposed into parallel subtasks. The subtask $T_{i,k}$ completes when all its parallel subtasks complete.

  (a) The synchronization protocols described in Section 9.4.1 clearly must be modified if some subtasks are complex. Give a brief description of the modification needed for the greedy, the MPM, and the RG protocols to work correctly if some end-to-end tasks contain complex subtasks. (In other words, the precedence graph of the system is a serial-parallel graph.)
  (b) In this part, we assume that every task has a given release time and deadline. Each task is either complex or simple. An algorithm proposed by Kao and Garcia-Molina for assigning virtual local relative deadlines to parallel subtasks of a complex task T_i is called the DIV-x algorithm. According to this algorithm, the relative deadline D_i of a complex task

T_i is divided among its parallel subtasks. Specifically, the virtual local relative deadline of each parallel subtask $T_{i,k}$ of a complex task T_i that has $n(i)$ parallel simple subtasks is equal to $xD_i/n(i)$ where x is a design parameter that can be adjusted. After the local relative deadlines are computed, the parallel subtasks on each processor are scheduled on the EDF basis.

   i. Let x equal to one, so it has no effect on the deadline assignment. Discuss the possible advantage and disadvantage of dividing the relative deadline of a complex task among its parallel subtasks. Why not simply give each parallel subtask the relative deadline of the parent task?

   ii. Suppose that there are two identical complex tasks T_1 and T_2, and each parallel subtask of each task executes on the same processor with the corresponding subtask of other task. What is the effect if the parameter x is the same for both task? What is the effect if the parameter x is twice as large for T_1 as for T_2.

9.9 Section 9.4.1 pointed out that the major shortcoming of the greedy synchronization protocol is due to the fact that the minimum interrelease time of jobs in a subtask $T_{i,k}$ is no longer equal to the period p_i of its parent task. As a consequence, in a fixed-priority system, the subtask may interfere with lower-priority subtasks and delay their jobs more severely than a periodic task. One way to minimize the effect of bursty releases of jobs in $T_{i,k}$ on lower-priority subtasks on the same processor $V_{i,k}$ as $T_{i,k}$ is to use a sporadic server with period p_i and execution budget $e_{i,k}$ to execute jobs in $T_{i,k}$.

   (a) Suppose that the subtask of T_2 in Figure 9–8 are synchronized greedily. Rather than scheduling each job in $T_{2,2}$ immediately after it released, the scheduler of P_2 uses a SpSL sporadic server of period 9 and budget 3 to execute the jobs in this subtask. Draw the schedule of the subtasks on P_2. If your schedule is correct, no job on this processor completes late.

   (b) You recall that the execution times of jobs in each subtask $T_{i,k}$ can be less $e_{i,k}$. Therefore, a SpSL server used to execute the subtask may have multiple chunks of budget at times. For the purpose of executing subtasks, this kind of server is unnecessarily complicated. A simple sporadic server whose budget is set to $e_{i,k}$ at each replenishment time and is consumed instantaneously when each job in $T_{i,k}$ completes may work as well. Compare and contrast these two kinds of sporadic servers for the purpose of executing subtasks on each processor when sibling subtasks are synchronized greedily.

   (c) The combination of the greedy synchronization protocol and the simple sporadic server algorithm in part (b) resembles the RG protocol. Is this combination a way to implement the RG protocol? If yes, explain why; if not, discuss the differences.

9.10 Table 9–4 lists upper bounds to the response times of subtasks defined in Table 9–3. Compute these upper bounds yourself.

9.11 This problem compares the merits of the end-to-end scheduling and the MPCP protocol for scheduling tasks with a shared resource in a multiprocessor real-time monitoring system shown in Table P9-3. The system contains two processors, the field processor P_f and the host processor P_h, and three resources, SD and C on P_f and SM on P_h. Each of the sensor-processing tasks T_{s_i}, for $1 \leq i \leq 4$, periodically reads a sensor and, under the control of the shared data server SD, places its reading in a shared data structure on the field processor P_f. In addition, there is a communication server C on P_f. T_{d_i}, for $i = 1, 2$, are two display tasks. They are local to the host processor P_h. T_{d_1} periodically communicates with the servers on P_f, retrieves the sensor data, and displays the data with the help of the screen manager SM on P_h. T_{d_2} also generates and displays data but does not need any of the resources modeled here other than the screen manager. The parameters of the tasks are listed in Table 9P-3.

T_k	Local Proc	p_k	e_k	Critical Sections
T_{s_1}	P_f	7	1.0	[SD; 0.5]
T_{s_2}	P_f	11	1.0	[SD; 0.5]
T_{s_3}	P_f	15	1.5	[SD; 1.0]
T_{s_4}	P_f	40	3.0	[SD; 2.5]
T_{d_1}	P_h	30	10	[SD; 1.5] [C; 0.5] [SM; 1.0]
T_{d_2}	P_h	40	10	[SM; 5.0]

(a) Suppose that the tasks are scheduled rate-monotonically and resource access control is under the MPCP protocol.

    i. Find the blocking time of each task.

    ii. Compute the maximum possible response time of each task.

(b) Suppose that the end-to-end scheduling approach is used. All the tasks execute entirely on one processor, except T_{d_1}.

    i. Decompose T_{d_1} into subtasks and find their normalized proportional relative deadlines.

    ii. Suppose that the subtasks of T_{d_1} are scheduled with the other tasks on each processor deadline-monotonically according their relative deadlines or normalized proportional relative deadlines. Find the maximum possible end-to-end response time of T_{d_1} and the maximum possible response times of the other task. According to your calculation here and in part (a), which of the approaches is better?

(c) Suppose that instead accessing sensor data once each period, the task T_{d_1} breaks up this work into five pieces. In other words, the segments of lengths 1.5 and 0.5 are broken up into five segments each of lengths 0.3 and 0.1, respectively. Each pair of consecutive segments are separately by a 1-unit length segment on P_h. How does this change affect the conclusion you have reached in part (b)? Explain how?

CHAPTER 10

Scheduling Flexible Computations and Tasks with Temporal Distance Constraints

Thus far, our primary focus has been on the scheduling, resource access-control, and validation algorithms based on the classical periodic task model. This short chapter describes two other workload models and associated classes of scheduling algorithms and thus wraps up our discussion on real-time scheduling.

Specifically, Section 10.1 describes flexible computation techniques. The term *flexible computation* (or application) refers to a broad class of applications that are designed and implemented to trade off at run-time the quality of the results (services) they produce for the amounts of time and resources they use to produced the results. In particular, a flexible application can reduce its time and resource demands at the expense of the quality of its result. For as long as the user finds its result quality acceptable, a flexible application can degrade gracefully when resources are scarce and the demands of competing workloads are high. In recent years, the flexible computation approach has been proposed as a means for handling overload and increasing availability of applications in domains as diverse as Artificial Intelligence (AI), signal processing and tracking, real-time communication, and databases [HoZi]. Section 10.1 describes workload models that capture the characteristics and requirements of flexible applications and algorithms that have been developed to schedule them.

Section 3.5.1 mentioned that the timing constraints of many applications can be characterized more conveniently and naturally by temporal distances rather than deadlines. An example is the sound and visual display jobs in a passive sonar system. The associated sound and image must be presented to the operator within 100 milliseconds of one another. In a radar signal processing and tracking system, the completion times of consecutive jobs that monitor and track a target are required to be no more than a certain time apart for the system to track the target. The updates of a replicated file on different machines must be no more than a certain time apart in order to ensure mutual consistency among copies. In each of these cases, the requirement in temporal distance between the completion times of the jobs is important, even more so than the absolute times at which the jobs complete. Section 10.2 first gives a precise definition of temporal distance constraints and then describes algorithms for scheduling tasks with this type of timing constraints.

10.1 FLEXIBLE APPLICATIONS

We divide existing flexible computation techniques into two broad categories, depending on whether they are designed for graceful degradation in result quality or in timeliness. For many real-time applications, a timely result of a poorer quality is better than a late result of the desired quality. An example is surveillance and collision avoidance: It is better for the system to issue a timely warning, together with an estimated location of the conflict traffic, than a late command for evasive action. Another example is voice transmission. While a poorer quality voice encoded with fewer bits may be tolerable, long pauses due to large transmission delay may not be. One way to increase the likelihood of their on-time completion is to make the jobs flexible. By design and implementation, a flexible job contains an *optional component* (or components) which can be discarded (i.e., left unexecuted) when necessary in order to reduce the job's processor time and resource demands by its deadline. In the literature (e.g., [BoDe, ChLL, DeKT, FeLi, GrZi, KaGS, ShLi95, VrLi]), the term flexible computation (or imprecise computation) approach usually means techniques for the design, implementation, and scheduling of such jobs and tasks and the analysis of flexible applications containing them.

Applications with firm deadlines (e.g., [HaRa, BeBu]) are in another category. A real-time application with firm deadlines does not have optional jobs. Nevertheless, it has flexibility because the lateness of some of its jobs is acceptable, provided that some on-time criteria are met. Specifically, a task is said to have the (l, L) *firm deadline* constraint if at least $l \geq 0$ jobs among any consecutive $L \geq l$ jobs in the task must complete in time. The parameter L is the *failure window* of the task. So, a hard real-time task has $(1, 1)$ deadlines, while a soft real-time task has $(0, L)$ deadlines. At the risk of abusing the term, we also call techniques for scheduling tasks with firm deadlines flexible computation techniques. The failure of a task to meet its firm deadline requirement is called a *dynamic failure*.

To distinguish applications of the two categories, we call them applications with firm quality versus those with firm deadlines. The former have flexible resource demands but hard timing constraints; they degrade gracefully by reducing their demands and result quality. The latter have fixed resource demands; they degrade gracefully by relaxing their timeliness.

10.1.1 Characterization of Flexible Applications

Except for their timing constraints, flexible applications with firm deadlines do not differ from classical real-time applications. Their demands can be characterized by classical workload models. We ignore them for now. In this subsection, we first look at ways to implement flexible applications with firm quality and workload models to characterize these applications. We then introduce performance measures which algorithms for scheduling flexible applications stride to optimize.

Implementation Methods.   As stated earlier, one way to make an application adaptable to fluctuations in resource availability and competing demands is to structure each time-critical job so that its has an optional component. The optional component does not have to be executed for the job to produce an acceptable result. In contrast, the part of the job that must be completed in time is *mandatory*. When there are sufficient resources, the optional component is also completed by the job's deadline, and the result of the job has the desired quality. This result is *precise*. If the optional component, or a portion of the optional component, is discarded, the result quality of the job degrades. A result of an acceptable but degraded quality is an *imprecise result*.

Sieve Method.   From the perspective of implementation, the simplest flexible tasks are those containing optional jobs that can be discarded in their entirety. An example of such flexible tasks is the transmission of an MPEG-encoded video. The transmissions of I-frames are mandatory. On the other hand, B- and P-frames can be dropped when necessary if a lower frame rate is acceptable. Hence, the transmissions of B- and P-frames are optional. Another example is the job that estimates the current level of background noise at the receiver in a radar signal processing system. An old estimate can be used at the expense of a higher false alarm rate or lower detection rate. Therefore, this job can be discarded when the system is resource poor. Similarly, in a flight management system, the job that updates the estimated time of arrival can be discarded when the system is busy flying the plane amid heavy turbulence and traffic.

We call a discardable optional function a *sieve*. In a flexible system containing seives, these functions are identified by the application, and the scheduler is designed to take advantage of the possibility of discarding them during overloads.

Milestone Method.   A job is *monotone* if its optional component can be terminated anytime and the quality of the result produced by the job does not decrease as its optional component executes longer.[1] A monotone computation job is based on an incremental algorithm whose result converges monotonically to the desired result with increasing running time. Iterative algorithms are monotone by design. Many algorithms for numerical computation, statistical estimation and prediction, heuristic search (e.g., [Korf]), approximate query processing (e.g., [BuDW, VrLi]) and incremental information gathering, planning and reasoning [BoDe, GrZi, ZiRu] are monotone. Similarly, transmissions of voices, images, and videos can be made monotone by using layered encoding techniques. When we browse the Web, we often see a partial or fuzzy image at the start, and the image gradually clears up and completes as we wait (i.e., as more data arrive). The retrieval of the image is monotone. This implementation method is called the *milestone method*.

At appropriate instants during its execution, the program implementing a monotone job saves the immediate result produced at the time, together with some indicators of the quality achieved. When the program terminates, the latest saved results and quality indicators are returned. Programming languages such as FLEX [KeLi91] allow a programmer to specify the parts of a program that are optional. The run-time system can integrate the process of saving immediate results under program control with a systemwide checkpointing process to reduce the frequency and sizes of checkpoints [HuFL].

When tasks are monotone, the decision on which optional components and what portions of the optional components to schedule can be made dynamically. Because the scheduler can terminate a monotone job any time after its mandatory component completes, we have the maximum flexibility in scheduling when flexible applications are implemented using this method.

---

[1] In general, the result quality of a job may also depend on the amounts of other resources (e.g., memory, network bandwidth, etc.) allocated to the job. The job is monotone if its result quality is a nondecreasing function of the amount of every resource allocated to it. Here, we ignore all other resources except processor time for the sake of simplicity.

Multiple Version Method.   Almost all applications can be made flexible using the multiple-version method. In a multiversion application, each flexible job has a primary version and one or more alternate version(s). The primary version produces the precise result of the desired quality but has a larger execution time and require more resources. An alternate version has a small execution time and uses few resources, but produces an imprecise result. When it is not possible to complete the primary version of every job by its deadline, the scheduler may choose to schedule alternate versions of some jobs.

The feasibility and effectiveness of the multiple-version method has been demonstrated for both real-time computing and communication. Performance data show that there is little additional advantage beyond what can be gained with two versions [KiTo]. Therefore, we consider only the two-version case.

Workload Models.   Similar to the classical deterministics models, models of flexible applications (with firm quality) also characterize the workload on a processor by a set of preemptable, possibly dependent jobs. Each job J is characterized by its release time r, absolute deadline d, and execution time e.

Basic Imprecise Computation Model.   The basic imprecise computation model [LLSC] used to characterize flexible applications is a straightforward generalization of the classical models. Each flexible job J is decomposed logically into a chain of two jobs M and O, which are the mandatory and optional components of J, respectively. (We will use the term mandatory and optional components and jobs interchangeably.) The mandatory component M is the predecessor of the optional component O. Their release times and deadlines are the same as those of their parent job J. e_m and e_o denotes the execution times of M and O, respectively, and $e = e_m + e_o$. In our subsequent discussion, we will call e_m and e_o the mandatory execution time and optional execution time, respectively, of the parent job J.

You may have noticed that the chain consisting of components M and O is just a special case of end-to-end jobs. A job J in the classical workload model is a special case of a flexible job whose optional component has zero execution time, that is, $e_m = e$. Many algorithms in AI are anytime (e.g.,[BoDe, Korf]). If allowed, an anytime algorithm runs forever, and the longer it runs, the better its result. The IRIS (Increasing Reward with Increasing Service) model used to characterize anytime jobs is also a special case of the imprecise computation model. An anytime job does not have a mandatory component, and the execution time of its optional component is equal to the difference between its deadline and release time.

According to a *valid schedule* of a flexible application, the amount of processor time allocated to every job J is at least equal to its mandatory execution time e_m and at most equal to its execution time e. We say that a job completes when its mandatory component completes. Hence, a valid schedule is a *feasible* one if according to the schedule, every mandatory job completes in time; in other words, the amount of processor time allocated by the schedule to every job J by its deadline is no less than e_m. When we say that an optional component completes, we mean that it completes by its deadline, and by the completed portion of an optional component, we mean the portion completed by its deadline. Furthermore, our discussion assumes that no optional component executes beyond its deadline, as if the scheduler terminates every optional component at its deadline if the component is not complete at the time. (In practice, one may not want to terminate a job for the fear that this action may leave the system in some inconsistent state. Rather, the scheduler preempts the job at its deadline and allows the job to execute to completion in the background when there is no ready job with future deadlines. However, only the result produced by the job before its deadline is of use.)

Imprecise Periodic Task Model.   A variation of the basic imprecise computation model is the imprecise periodic task model [ChLL]. The system **T** consists of periodic tasks T_i for $i = 1, 2, \ldots, n$. Each job $J_{i,k}$ in T_i is a chain of its mandatory component $M_{i,k}$ and its optional component $O_{i,k}$. Therefore, we can also think of of each task $T_i = (\phi_i, p_i, e_i, D_i)$ as an end-to-end task that is a chain of two periodic tasks: $T_{m,i} = (\phi_i, p_i, e_{m,i}, D_i)$ and $T_{o,i} = (\phi_i, p_i, e_{o,i}, D_i)$. The ratios e_i/p_i and $e_{m,i}/p_i$ are the utilization and *mandatory utilization* of the task T_i, respectively. The *total mandatory utilization* of the system is the sum of mandatory utilizations of all the tasks in the system.

Flexible Tasks with 0/1 Constraints.   Typically, there is no benefit by completing a sieve in part. We want to either execute a seive to completion before its deadline or discard it entirely. This constraint on the way optional jobs are scheduled is called the *0/1 constraint*.

From the view point of scheduling, two-version jobs are the same as jobs that have 0/1 constraints. We can view the alternate version of each two-version job as the mandatory component and the primary version as the mandatory component plus an optional component. The mandatory execution time of the job is the same as that of the alternate version, and the optional execution time is equal to the difference between the execution times of the two versions. The optional component must be either scheduled and completed by its deadline, corresponding to the primary version being scheduled, or discarded entirely, corresponding to the alternate version being scheduled. Consequently, scheduling jobs that have two versions is the same as scheduling jobs with the 0/1 constraint. Hereafter, we will not mention multi-version jobs but bear in mind that everything said about scheduling jobs with 0/1 constraint also applies to multiversion jobs.

Model of Dependent Flexible Jobs.   A key assumption of all the models described above is that the quality of the result produced by a flexible job depends only on the amounts of resources allocated to the job. This assumption is not valid when jobs are dependent. If the result produced by a predecessor is imprecise, a successor job may need to execute longer in order to compensate for the degradation in input quality. As an example, in a signal processing and tracking application, the tracker uses the result produced by the signal processor. The result of the signal processors being imprecise means that there may be more false tracks and/or missed targets. The tracker may need to compute longer in order to achieve an acceptable tracking accuracy and the desired accuracy.

Feng, *et al.* [FeLi] uses an extended end-to-end model to capture this kind of dependency. According to this model, the execution times of both the mandatory and optional components of a successor job depend on the result quality of its immediate predecessor(s), that is, the quality of its input. Specifically, each job has a mandatory extension and an optional extension which model the extra work the job must do to compensate for a poorer input. (The job is a chain containing its mandatory component, followed by its mandatory extension, which is in turned followed by its optional component and optional extension.) When the input is precise, the execution times of both extensions are zero. The execution times of both extensions are nonincreasing functions of the quality of the job's input.

When all the jobs are well behaved (e.g., when they are monotone), the execution times of extensions of a successor job are nonincreasing functions of the amount of processor time allocated to its predecessor(s). This dependency of jobs' demands for resources on the amounts of resources allocated to other jobs significantly complicates the scheduling problem. To date, there are no good algorithms for scheduling such jobs in the sense that they are simple to implement and their performance well understood. For this reason we will ignore this dependency between execution times and input quality hereafter.

Criteria of Optimality.   Algorithms for scheduling flexible applications have two objectives. The first is the objective of all classical hard real-time scheduling algorithms: To ensure that each job will produce an acceptable result on time. This means that all the mandatory jobs complete by their deadlines. We will keep this objective in mind at all times when we describe algorithms for scheduling flexible applications. A criterion of optimality for such an algorithm is that it can find a feasible schedule whenever the given set of jobs (tasks) has a feasible schedule.

The second objective is to maximize the result quality of each flexible application, or more concretely, to schedule as much as possible optional jobs in the application. There are many ways to quantify the result qualities of individual jobs, tasks containing the jobs, and the application as a whole, and different quantifications give us different performance criteria.

Errors and Rewards.   The quality of a result of a flexible job is typically measured in terms of the error in the result (or reward attained by the job). Roughly speaking, the error in a result is the distance between the result and the desired, precise result. Application developers work with domain-specific error measures (e.g., confidence interval, least mean square error, and tracking error). For the sake of scheduling, however, what the precise result is and what the distance means are irrelevant. It suffices to measure this distance in terms of the amount of work done by the job (or equivalently, the amounts of resources allocated to the job) to obtained the result versus the precise result.

The definition of error introduced by Chung, *et al.* [ChLL] was thus motivated. The definition assumes that the mandatory component of every job completes on time; otherwise, the system has a hard timing failure. (This implies that the operating system has the capability to do admission control and hard real-time scheduling. Hence, the results produced by all jobs are acceptable in absence of timing failure.) The error in the result of a job is maximum when its optional component is discarded entirely. For the sake of convenience, we let this maximum equal 1 for every job. Let x denote the amount of processor time allocated to the optional component of a job J by the job's deadline. x is called the (*length of the*) *completed optional portion*. Let $\varepsilon(x)$ be the error in the result produced by a job whose completed optional portion has length x. We have just said that $\varepsilon(0) = 1$ for all jobs. On the other hand, the error in a precise result is 0. Hence, $\varepsilon(e_o) = 0$ for all jobs. For a job with 0/1 constraints, these two error values completely characterizes the behavior of its result quality.[2]

The error in the result of a monotone job typically decreases in discrete steps as the length of its completed optional portion increases. In other words, the error function is dis-

---

[2]This 0/1 error is analogous to *value*, the metric used to measure the performance of on-line scheduling algorithms, which was defined in Section 4.9. Analogously, we can define the value of a job to be x and x is either 0 or e_o.

continuous. Because it is difficult to work with discontinuous error functions, they are approximated by continuous error functions exemplified by the ones shown in Figure 10–1. The linear error function

$$\varepsilon(x) = 1 - \frac{x}{e_o} \tag{10.1}$$

is simply the normalized length (i.e., the execution time) of the discarded optional portion. When the error behavior of a job (i.e., the convergence behavior of the underlying algorithm) is not known, this is a reasonable characterization of error.

Well-behaved monotone algorithms are designed to yield a good result early; such an algorithm has a faster rate of convergence to the desired result earlier, and the convergence rate slows as the algorithm runs longer. The error function of a monotone job based on such an algorithm behaves like the convex function in Figure 10–1. The concave error function is applicable when the error convergence rate of the underlying algorithm is slow at the start but increases as the algorithm runs longer. A concave error function gives a continuous family of error measures that approach the 0/1 constraint.

Rather than error functions, some scheduling algorithms work with reward functions of jobs. The reward of a job is complementary to its error. So, a job with 0/1 constraint achieves its maximum reward when its optional component completes in time and no reward otherwise. The reward of a monotone job increases as its optional component executes longer. If we were to normalize the reward of a job so that its maximum reward is 1 when its optional component completes in time, then the reward of a job is equal to $1 - \varepsilon(x)$ when the length of its completed optional component is x. Rather than switching between the terms, we will drop the term reward function and stick with error function in our discussion.

Static Quality Metrics.   Many algorithms for scheduling flexible applications attempt to minimize total error, average error, or maximum error of all the jobs in the system. We call these performance measures *static quality metrics*. The reason for this name will be become evident shortly.

When the workload consists of a finite number of jobs, say $J_1, J_2, \ldots, J_n$, the *total error* E_{total} produced by a schedule that allocates x_i units of processor time to the optional

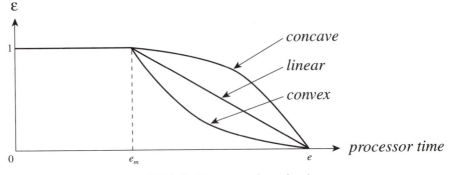

FIGURE 10–1   Three types of error functions.

component of the job J_i by its deadline, for all $i = 1, 2, \ldots, n$, is

$$E_{\text{total}}(x_1, x_2, \ldots, x_n) = \sum_{i=1}^{n} wt_i \, \varepsilon_i(x_i) \qquad (10.2a)$$

Similarly, the *maximum error* of the system is

$$E_{\max}(x_1, x_2, \ldots, x_n) = \max_{1 \le i \le n} (wt_i \, \varepsilon_i(x_i)) \qquad (10.2b)$$

In these expressions, $0 \le wt_i$ is a weight associated with the job J_i. By choosing the weights, we can account for the different degrees to which the errors in the results produced by the individual jobs impact the overall quality of the result produced by the system.

The total error is not appropriate for a system of periodic tasks, since there are an infinite number of jobs. An analogous performance measure is the average error. The *average error* E_i of a periodic task T_i is computed over a window of $L_i \ge 1$ periods. Let $x_{i,k}$ denote the amount of processor time allocated to the optional component of $J_{i,k}$ in T_i by the deadline of the job. The average error of T_i is given by

$$E_i = \frac{1}{L_i} \sum_{k=j}^{j+L_i-1} \varepsilon_i(x_{i,k}) \qquad (10.3a)$$

and the average error of the system containing n periodic tasks $T_1, T_2, \ldots, T_n$ is

$$E_{\text{ave}} = \sum_{i=1}^{n} wt_i \, E_i \qquad (10.3b)$$

where $0 \le wt_i$ is the weight of the task T_i, and $\sum_{i=1}^{n} wt_i = 1$.

Dynamic Failures and Firm Deadlines.   Chung, *et al.* pointed out that the quality metrics defined above are *static*. They are applicable for applications in which no optional component is required to complete in time. This is not true if the effects of errors in results produced by jobs in a periodic task are cumulative. If the optional components of jobs in a number of consecutive periods do not complete, the optional component of a subsequent job may no longer be optional. Such a periodic (or sporadic) task is called an *error-cumulative task*. An example is a location update task in which each job updates the current position of an object. The mandatory component produces a rough estimate; together, the mandatory and optional components produces an accurate estimate. When the optional components of several consecutive jobs do not complete, the error in the location estimate cumulates. Once the cumulated error reaches a threshold, the optional component of the next job becomes mandatory; it must also be completed in time in order to bring the location error back to an acceptable level.

A timing requirement of an error-cumulative task T_i is that one job out of every L_i consecutive jobs in T_i be complete in its entirety, that is, both its mandatory and optional components must complete in time. In the simplest case, the optional components of all other jobs can be discarded entirely. (We have this case if the tolerable error cumulation interval L_i is independent of the errors in the results produced by jobs whose optional components are left incomplete.) This requirement is the same as the $(1, L_i)$-firm deadline requirement. The tolerable error cumulation interval of the task is its failure window.

Indeed, error cumulation is one of the reasons for the general (l, L)-firm deadline requirement. All jobs in a task T_i with a (l_i, L_i)-firm deadline requirement have the same execution time e_i. l_i jobs out of any consecutive L_i jobs (i.e., in its failure window) are mandatory while the others are entirely optional. Thus, the (l_i, L_i)-firm deadline dynamic failure model fits in the general framework of flexible computation models.

10.1.2 Algorithms for Scheduling Flexible Applications

This subsection gives an overview of algorithms for scheduling flexible applications on a processor. Some of these algorithms are off-line, and others are on-line. Off-line algorithms aim at finding an *optimal static schedule*. This term refers to a schedule of the given system that (1) is feasible whenever the mandatory components of the system are schedulable and (2) minimizes one of the static quality metrices (i.e., average error, total error, and maximum error) of the system. Most on-line algorithms are priority-driven. Some are also designed to minimize a static quality metric, while others are designed to prevent dynamic failures.

Constrained Optimization Formulation.   When all the parameters of all jobs in the system are known, it is possible to compute an optimal static schedule off-line at design time or configuration time. The problem of finding such a schedule is typically formulated as a constrained optimization problem.

Illustrative Example.   To illustrate, we consider the problem of scheduling a system of flexible periodic tasks $T_i = (p_i, e_i)$, for $i = 1, 2, \ldots, n$, to minimize the average error of the system. The tasks are truly periodic. The average error is given by Eq. (10.3), and the window L_i over which the average error of T_i is computed is equal to H/p_i, where H is the length of a hyperperiod of the system. Aydin, *et al.* [AMMM] showed that when the error functions are linear or convex and feasible schedules of the system exist, there is always an optimal static schedule which allocates the same amount of processor time to all optional jobs of each task by their respective deadlines. In other words, we can confine our search for an optimal schedule among those feasible schedules according to which the length $x_{i,k}$ of the completed portion of every optional job $J_{i,k}$ in task T_i is equal to x_i, for every $i = 1, 2, \ldots, n$. Because $x_{i,k} = x_i$, the average error of T_i is simply equal to $\varepsilon_i(x_i)$.

Thus the problem of finding an optimal static schedule of the system is reduced to the problem of finding the set $\{x_1, x_2, \ldots, x_n\}$ of processor allocations to jobs in the optional tasks that satisfies the following constraints:

$$0 \le x_i \le e_o; \qquad \text{for } i = 1, 2, \ldots, n \tag{10.4a}$$

$$\sum_{i=1}^{n} \frac{e_{m,i} + x_i}{p_i} \le 1 \tag{10.4b}$$

and minimizes the objective function

$$E_{\text{ave}} = \sum_{i=1}^{n} wt_i \, \varepsilon_i(x_i) \tag{10.4c}$$

(or any of the static quality metrics). The first constraint follows from the definition of a valid schedule. The second constraint is the necessary and sufficient condition for the existence of a feasible schedule that allocates $e_{m,i} + x_i$ units of processor time by the deadline of the job to every job in every task T_i. A system of periodic tasks $(p_i, e_{m,i} + x_i)$, for $i = 1, 2, \ldots, n$, is schedulable by the EDF algorithm if the above constraints are met. By definition, the solution of the problem yields the minimum average error among all feasible schedules of the given systems.

When the error functions of all tasks are linear, these three expressions define a linear program. For a system containing tens or even hundreds of tasks, the running time of a linear program solver may be low enough for use at run time as an acceptance test. (When a task requests admission, the scheduler first checks for the acceptability of the new task based on its mandatory execution time and if the task is acceptable, solves the linear program to obtain a new optional processor time allocation.)

The problem is considerably more complex when the error functions of the tasks are nonlinear, especially if the tasks have different error functions, as these functions typically are in practice. In particular, when the error functions of some tasks are concave, we cannot no longer confine our search for an optimal static schedule among schedules that allocate the same amount of processor time to all jobs in each task. Aydin, et al. showed that when the error functions are concave, the problem of finding an optimal static schedule is NP-hard, just like the problem of scheduling jobs with 0/1 constraints is.[3]

General Constrained Optimalization Formulation.
To describe the constrained optimization formulation in general, we suppose that the given system consists of n jobs J_i, for $i = 1, 2, \ldots, n$. (For periodic tasks, n is the number of jobs in each hyperperiod.) The known parameters of each job J_i are its release time r_i, deadline d_i, mandatory execution time $e_{m,i}$, and optional execution time $e_{o,i}$. The error of the job J_i is $\varepsilon_i(x_i)$ when its optional component is allocated x_i units of processor time by the job's deadline.

The release times and deadlines of all the jobs partition the time interval from the earliest release time to the latest deadline of all jobs into disjoint intervals, each of which does not contain any release time or deadline. Let I_k, for $k = 1, 2, \ldots, K$ ($K \leq 2n - 1$), denote these time intervals. (For example, suppose there are two jobs and their release times and deadlines are 0, 2, 5, and 6. These time instants partition the time interval from 0 to 6 into three intervals $(0, 2]$, $(2, 5]$, and $(5, 6]$.) For the sake of convenience, we let t_k and t_{k+1} denote the beginning and the end of the interval I_k, respectively. In other words, $I_k = (t_k, t_{k+1}]$. Each of these instants is either a release time or a deadline of some job in the system.

Let $a_{i,k}$ denote the amount of processor time in interval I_k that is allocated to job J_i. The problem of finding an optimal static schedule of the n jobs can be stated as follows: We want

---

[3]To give us some insight into why the problem of scheduling jobs with concave error functions resembles the problem of scheduling jobs with the 0/1 constraint, let us look at the simplest case when all jobs have the same weight and same error function. Suppose that we were to allocate processor time to each optional job in small quanta, each of length z for a small $z > 0$. Let y_k denote the reduction in the result error of a job when its optional component is given kz units of processor time for some $k \geq 0$. The fact that the error function of the job is linear or convex and nonincreasing implies that $y_{k+1} - y_k$ is the a nonincreasing function of k. Therefore, it makes sense to distribute the processor time available to all the optional jobs evenly among them. This is why we can let $x_{i,k} = x_i$ in our search for an optimal static schedule. In contrast, when their error functions are concave and nonincreasing, $y_{k+1} - y_k$ is the a nondecreasing function of k. The available processor time should be distributed unevenly among optional jobs; some optional jobs should be given as much processor time as they can use at the expense of other optional jobs. This resembles the way to distribute processor time among jobs with 0/1 constraints.

to find allocations $a_{i,k}$, for $i = 1, 2, \ldots, n$ and $k = 1, 2, \ldots K$, subjected to the constraints

$$a_{i,k} \geq 0 \qquad\qquad \text{for } i = 1, 2, \ldots, n; \ k = 1, 2, \ldots, K \qquad (10.5a)$$

$$a_{i,k} = 0 \text{ if } t_k \geq d_i \text{ or } t_{k+1} \leq r_i \qquad \text{for } i = 1, 2, \ldots, n; \ k = 1, 2, \ldots, K \qquad (10.5b)$$

$$0 \leq \sum_{i=1}^{n} a_{i,k} \leq t_{k+1} - t_k \qquad \text{for } k = 1, 2, \ldots, K \qquad (10.5c)$$

and

$$\qquad\qquad (10.5d)$$

$$e_{m,i} \leq \sum_{k=1}^{K} a_{i,k} \leq e \qquad \text{if \textit{the job} } J_i \text{ \textit{is monotone}} \qquad (10.5e)$$

or

$$\sum_{k=1}^{K} a_{i,k} = e_{m,i} \text{ or } e \qquad \text{if \textit{the job} } J_i \text{ \textit{has 0/1 constraint}} \qquad (10.5f)$$

Equation (10.5a) states the obvious fact that $a_{i,k}$ must be nonnegative. The constraint of Eq. (10.5b) follows from the fact that a job can be scheduled only in time intervals that are within its feasible interval $(r_i, d_i]$. (By construction each of the time intervals I_k either is disjoint from or is included in the feasible interval.) Equation (10.5c) ensures that the total amount of processor time within any time interval I_k allocated to all the jobs is no more than the length of the interval. The processor allocations of each monotone job must satisfy Eq. (10.5d), which makes sure that the total amount of processor time in all intervals that is allocated to the job is no less than its mandatory execution time and no greater than its execution time. The processor allocations of each job with 0/1 constraint must satisfy Eq. (10.5e).

The optimal static schedule is given by the allocation $a_{i,k}$'s that satisfy the above constraints and minimize the objective function, which is either the total error E_{total} or the maximum error $E_{\max}$ given by Eq. (10.2) or is the average error

$$E_{\text{ave}} = \frac{1}{n} \sum_{i=1}^{n} wt_i \, \varepsilon_i(x_i) \qquad (10.5g)$$

where the amount x_i of processor time allocated to the optional component of J_i is given by

$$x_i = \sum_{k=1}^{K} a_{i,k} - e_{m,i} \qquad (10.5h)$$

Again, the complexity of this optimization problem depends on the error functions and weights of jobs. The simplest case is when jobs have identical weights. When jobs have identical weights and error functions are linear, an optimal static schedule that minimizes the total (average) error of n monotone jobs can be found by a simple $O(n \log n)$ algorithm [ShLC]. When jobs have convex error functions and identical weights, the total error of all jobs can be kept small by making the ratio $x_i/e_{o,i}$ of the processor time allocation x_i of each optional job to its execution time equal to this ratio of every other optional job as much as possible. In other words, we want to minimize $\max_{1 \leq i \leq n}(1 - x_i/e_{o,i})$. An optimal schedule can be found in $O(n^2)$ time when optional jobs have identical execution times and in $O(n^3)$ time when the jobs have arbitrary execution times [ShLi96].

When jobs have arbitrary weights, we have a linear program to solve in the simple case when all the error functions are linear. In general, the constrained optimization problem ranges from a quadratic programming problem (when all error functions are convex and quadratic) to an NP-hard problem (when some or all error functions are concave or some jobs have 0/1 constraint).

The constrained optimization problem can be generalized in a straightforward manner to take into account the dependency of result qualities on the allocations of other resources in addition to processor time. The added dimensions in the resource versus quality trade-off increases the number of constraints the solution must meet. The complexity of the problem can be kept tractable only by keeping the error functions simple (e.g., linear) and the constraints linear.

Priority-Driven Scheduling to Minimize Errors.   Most heuristic algorithms for scheduling flexible periodic tasks are preemptive and priority-driven. All of them adjust the priority of each task based on the amount of progress its current job has already made toward completion and/or the history of missed deadlines within the current failure window.

Mandatory-First Algorithms.   Many algorithms designed to minimize one of the static quality metrics use the following strategy: Optional tasks are executed in the background of mandatory tasks. Aydin, *et al.* [AMMM] calls this strategy the *mandatory-first strategy*.

As examples, the family of algorithms for scheduling periodic flexible tasks proposed by Chung, *et al.* [ChLL] are mandatory-first algorithms. The objectives of these algorithms are, first, to ensure that all mandatory jobs complete on time and, second, to keep the average error of the system small. Given a system of n periodic tasks, each consisting of a chain of a mandatory task and an optional task, such an algorithm gives all mandatory tasks higher priorities than the optional tasks. Moreover, the priorities of mandatory tasks are assigned according to some fixed-priority algorithm (e.g., the rate-monotonic algorithm).

The algorithms in this class differ only in how they assign priorities to optional tasks. Some of the algorithms make priority assignments to optional tasks based on the characteristics of error functions. Examples of these algorithms include the least-utilization algorithm, which assigns fixed priorities to optional tasks: The smaller the weighted optional utilization $wt_i \, e_{o,i}/p_i$ of an optional task, the higher the task's priority. In contrast, the least-attained-time algorithm is a dynamic-priority algorithm; it assigns the highest priority at any time to the optional job that has attained the least processor time among all ready optional jobs at the time. The former tends to perform well when the error functions of all tasks are linear, while the latter performs well when the error functions are convex. When the error functions are concave, optional jobs should be scheduled on the first-in-first-out basis. The best-incremental-return algorithm assumes complete knowledge of error functions. When there is no mandatory job ready for execution, the scheduler gives the highest priority to the ready optional job whose error will decrease by the largest amount (when compared with what other ready optional jobs can achieve) if the job is given the next quantum of processor time.

In practice, the exact behavior of the error functions is unknown, and different tasks may have different types of error functions. An algorithm that ignores the error functions but attempts to minimize the average error by assigning higher priorities to more urgent optional jobs is more suitable. Examples of such algorithms are the *shortest-period algorithm*, which assigns fixed priorities to optional tasks on the rate-monotonic basis, and the *earliest-deadline algorithm*, which assigns priorities to optional jobs on the earliest-deadline-first basis. The earliest-deadline algorithm is optimal among mandatory-first algorithms in the sense that this algorithm can always find a schedule that achieves zero average error whenever any algorithm in this class can.

Aydin, *et al.* [AMMM] showed that mandatory-first algorithms are not optimal: These algorithms may fail to find a feasible schedule with the smallest possible total or average error. This fact can be illustrated by a simple example: a system of two periodic tasks of equal weights. The mandatory and optional components of T_1 are $M_1 = (3, 1)$ and $O_1 = (3, 1)$. The error in the result produced by a job in T_1 is $1 - x/e_{o,1}$ when the optional component is allocated x units of processor time by its deadline. The task $T_2 = (6, 2)$ is entirely mandatory. We note that the minimum average error achievable by any mandatory-first algorithm is $1/2$ because the first optional job in T_1 in each hyperperiod is discarded entirely. On the other hand, an algorithm that treats all optional jobs as mandatory and schedules all jobs on the EDF basis yields zero average error.

In general, the performance of mandatory-first algorithms is poor (e.g., average error being more than twice of the possible minimum), especially when the mandatory utilization of the system is large (e.g., larger than 70 percent). It is not surprising that among all the mandatory-first algorithms, the best-incremental-return algorithm has the best performance, but the implementation of this algorithm is complicated, and the assumption that all error functions are known is unrealistic.

A major advantage of the mandatory-first strategy (and hence algorithms using this strategy) is that it is more robust in the presence of overruns. (Here, by an overrun, we mean that a job's mandatory component runs longer than its mandatory execution time. An overrun can occur when a transient fault causes a recovery action during the execution of a mandatory job.) This strategy is preferred if a late mandatory job has serious consequences while good result quality is relatively unimportant. In a system that contains functionally critical sporadic jobs, a scheduler increases the chance of these jobs being accepted by completing periodic mandatory jobs as soon as possible. The mandatory-first strategy makes a clear separation of guaranteed services and best-effort services as most schemes for supporting these services do.

Slack Stealing Approach. The alternative to the mandatory-first strategy is to execute optional components whenever mandatory components have slack. In essence, the solutions of the constrained optimization problems described above give us the amount of slack each optional component can use. We can also use the slack-stealing algorithms described in Chapters 5 and 7 to schedule optional components by treating optional components as aperiodic jobs.

The on-line algorithms for scheduling monotone jobs with arbitrary release times and deadlines proposed by Shih, *et al.* are slack-stealing algorithms [ShLi96]. The algorithms consider both off-line jobs, whose parameters are known a priori before the system starts to execute, and on-line jobs, whose parameters become known when they arrive after the system has started to execute. (Examples of off-line jobs are jobs in periodic tasks with fixed release times; on-line jobs are sporadic jobs.) There are four cases depending on whether on-line jobs are ready for execution when they arrive and whether there are off-line jobs: (1) There are no off-line jobs, and every on-line job is ready for execution when it arrives; (2) there are off-line jobs, and every on-line job is ready for execution when it arrives; (3) there are no off-line jobs, and on-line jobs have arbitrary ready times; and (4) there are off-line jobs, and on-line jobs have arbitrary ready times.

The on-line algorithms for all four cases assume that the mandatory components of all off-line and on-line jobs are schedulable. (In other words, some other scheme is used to do an acceptance test.) Given that feasible schedules of the jobs exist, these algorithms produce feasible schedules that yield the minimum total error. The operations of the algorithms are described by the pseudocode in Figure 10–2. Rather than computing a numerical table of slacks of all mandatory components in the system as the slack-stealing algorithms in Chapters 5 and 7 do, these algorithms maintain a data structure, called the reservation list for the purpose of keeping track of when mandatory components have slack. The reservation list contains a reservation for each of the jobs that has arrived but is not completed. Specifically, the reservation of each job J_i consists of one or more reserved (time) intervals in its feasible interval $(r_i, d_i]$. When the scheduler makes a reservation for a job J_i, it inserts reserved intervals of the job in the reservation list. At any time, the reserved intervals of a job are found by scheduling the mandatory component of the job, together with yet-to-be-completed mandatory components of all jobs, according to the Latest-Ready-Time (LRT) algorithm. (The algorithm was described in Section 4.6.) Each mandatory component is scheduled at or before its deadline,

---

0. Generate the reservation list containing reservations of all off-line jobs if any. Put all ready jobs in the job queue ordered on the earliest-deadline-first basis.

1. For as long as the job queue is not empty and no event occurs, execute the job at the head of the job queue, the job with the earliest deadline among all ready jobs.

2. When one of the following events occurs, do as described:

    2.1 When a job becomes ready:

        – update the reservation of the current job;

        – put the newly ready job in the job queue;

        – goto step 1.

    2.2 When the mandatory component of the current job completes:

        – cancel the reservation of the current job;

        – goto step 1.

    2.3 When the optional component of the current job completes or its deadline is reached:

        – terminate the job and remove the job from the job queue;

        – goto step 1.

    2.4 When a new on-line job arrives:

        – if the current job is mandatory, update the reservation of the current job;

        – make reservation for this new job;

        – if this job is ready, insert it into the job queue;

        – goto step 1.

    2.5 When the beginning of a reserved interval is reached:

        – if the interval is reserved for the current job, then goto step 1; else update the reservation of the current job;

        – put the job assigned to the reserved interval at the head of the job queue;

        – goto step 1.

FIGURE 10–2   Description of on-line, slack-stealing algorithms.

and mandatory components are scheduled in the latest-ready-time-first order. An interval is reserved for a mandatory component if the interval is assigned to the component in the LRT schedule. In this way, each mandatory component is scheduled as late as possible according to the reservation, leaving as much slack as possible to execute optional components.

Initially, when a reservation is first made, the total length of all reserved intervals of J_i is equal to its mandatory execution time $e_{m,i}$. The on-line scheduling algorithms use the reservation list as a guide (just as the slack-stealing algorithms described in earlier chapters use the slack information). They never schedule any optional component in a reserved interval. In this way, the algorithms ensure that a sufficient amount of time is allocated to every mandatory job for it to complete by its deadline. The reservation list is updated as the execution of each mandatory job M_i progresses to completion. At each update, the length of its reservation is reduced to the execution time of the to-be-completed portion, and the reservation is eventually deleted when M_i completes.

All the on-line algorithms schedule jobs on the Earliest-Deadline-First (EDF) basis. The scheduler maintains a prioritized job queue in which jobs are ordered on the EDF basis. The scheduler makes a reservation for each on-line job as it arrives, puts the job into the job queue when it becomes ready, and fetches the first job from the job queue for execution. For every job, the processor always executes the mandatory component first and then executes the optional component. Within each reserved interval, the scheduler lets ready mandatory components execute in EDF order. The scheduler lets the optional job execute as long as time remains before the beginning of the earliest reserved interval among all reserved intervals. If an optional component is executing when the beginning of a reserved interval is reached, the scheduler stops executing the optional component.

The algorithms for the different cases differ in the data structures they use to maintain the reservation list and the complexities of the steps to make new reservations and to update and cancel existing reservations. The simplest is case (1) where all jobs are on-line and ready upon arrival. In this case, there is no need to keep track of the identities of the jobs assigned to individual reserved intervals, only when the intervals begin and end and the total amount of time reserved for each job. New reserved intervals can be added and existing reserved intervals can be shortened and deleted in constant time. The complexity of the on-line algorithm for this case, called the NORA Algorithm, is $O(n \log n)$. The algorithm for case (2), where there are off-line jobs with arbitrary ready-times but on-line jobs are ready upon arrival, also has this complexity. Cases (3) and (4), where the ready times of all jobs are arbitrary, are more complex. The scheduler needs to keep track of where the reserved intervals of every job are. Making a new reservation or canceling an existing reservation requires $O(\log^2 n)$ time. The on-line algorithm for these cases, called the ORA algorithm, has time complexity $O(n \log^2 n)$.

Algorithms for Preventing Dynamic Failures.   Most algorithms designed to prevent dynamic failure of periodic (and sporadic) tasks are dynamic-priority algorithms. We begin here by looking at algorithms for scheduling error-cumulative tasks; these tasks have the least stringent firm deadline requirement.

Algorithms for Scheduling Error-Cumulative Flexible Tasks.   As stated earlier, a periodic error-cumulative task T_i is required to meet the $(1, L_i)$-firm deadline (i.e., one out every L_i consecutive jobs in it must complete in time) if its tolerable interval of error cumulation is L_i periods. The primary objective of algorithms for scheduling such tasks is to ensure that all mandatory components and at least one out of every L_i consecutive optional components in every task T_i complete in time. The simplest variant of this scheduling problem is when all tasks have identical periods and error functions. Even this simple variant is NP-hard [ChLL]. An approximate algorithm with bounded performance is known only for this simple case.

Heuristic algorithms for scheduling error-cumulative periodic tasks proposed by Cheong [Cheo] also use the mandatory-first strategy and schedule all mandatory tasks on a fixed-priority basis. All optional jobs have lower priorities, except those optional jobs that are promoted by the scheduler to mandatory status. When the scheduler promotes an optional job of a task T_i to mandatory, it gives the optional job the priority of the mandatory task M_i.

Cheong's algorithms differ from each other in the rules they use to decide when to promote an optional job. The first-period (or the last-period) algorithm statically segments time into L_i-period error cumulation windows and promotes the optional job in the first period (or the last period) in each window to mandatory. According to the random algorithm, the scheduler decides randomly in each period of each task T_i whether to promote its optional job to mandatory with a probability γ_i. The probability that none of L_i consecutive jobs is promoted is equal to $(1 - \gamma_i)^{L_i}$. This is the probability of a dynamic failure of T_i. A variation of this algorithm is random increasing. According to the random-increasing algorithm, the scheduler increases the promotion probability γ_i of an optional job in a task T_i whenever the cumulative error of the task increases. By adjusting the promotion probability γ_i or rate of increase in this probability, the random strategies can ensure that a sufficient number of optional jobs are made mandatory.

An error-cumulative periodic task T_i scheduled according to the first-period or the last-period algorithm is a multframe task. (Multiframe tasks and their schedulability were described in Section 6.7.5.) T_i consists of a peak frame with execution time e_i followed by $L_i - 1$ normal frames with execution time $e_{m,i}$. The schedulability of the system thus scheduled can be determined using the analysis scheme for multiframe tasks. When the average error is also important, a scheduler may dynamically adjust the L_i-period window. (Using the last period strategy, the scheduler monitors the optional jobs in T_i. If an optional job in a period k before the last period in an L_i-period window completes in time, the scheduler may simply start a new L_i-period window from period $k + 1$.) In this way, the scheduler makes use of background time unused by mandatory jobs to complete as many optional jobs as possible.

Algorithms for Scheduling to Meet (l, L)-Firm Deadlines. An algorithm proposed by Ramanatham [Rama], called algorithm Sched_mkfirm, for scheduling n periodic tasks with firm deadlines uses a strategy that is a generalization of the first-period (or last-period) strategy. At the release time of each job $J_{i,k}$ in periodic task $T_i = (p_i, e_i)$ with the (l_i, L_i)-firm deadline constraint, the scheduler classifies the entire job as mandatory or optional according to the rule described below. The stream of mandatory jobs in T_i are given the fixed priority of the task. (Algorithm Sched_mkfirm assigns priorities to tasks on the rate-monotonic basis, but as you will see shortly you can use any fixed-priority scheme.) Optional jobs of all tasks are given the lowest priority; hence, they execute in the background of mandatory jobs.

The classification rule works as follows. Based on the parameters L_i and l_i that specify the firm deadline requirement of each task T_i, the scheduler checks at the release time of the kth job $J_{i,k}$, for $k = 1, 2, \ldots$, whether

$$k = \lfloor L_i \lceil (k - 1)l_i/L_i \rceil / l_i \rfloor + 1 \qquad (10.6)$$

It classifies $J_{i,k}$ mandatory if k satisfies this equality; otherwise, it classifies $J_{i,k}$ optional. As an example, suppose that T_i is a hard real-time task. Both L_i and l_i are equal to 1, and every positive integer value of k satisfies this expression. Every job in the task is mandatory as it should be. If $L_i = 2$ and $l_i = 1$, Eq. (10.6) is satisfied by $k = 1, 3, 5, \ldots$. Hence, the first, third, fifth and all subsequent odd numbered jobs are mandatory. If $L_i = 5$ and $l_i = 3$, then the values of k that satisfy Eq. (10.6) are 1, 2, 4, 6, 7, 9, and so on.

Ramanatham showed that among every consecutive L_i jobs in each task T_i, at least l_i jobs are classified mandatory. (Moreover, when $l_i \geq L_i/2$, no two consecutive jobs in T_i are classified optional.) Hence, if all mandatory jobs in T_i complete in time, the task satisfies the (l_i, L_i)-firm deadline requirement.

To check whether $T_i = (p_i, e_i)$ indeed meets this requirement when its mandatory jobs are scheduled at a priority lower than the priorities of mandatory jobs in tasks T_j for $j = 1, 2, \ldots, i-1$, we compute the time demand function of T_i according to

$$w_i(t) = e_i + b_i + \sum_{j=1}^{i-1} \left\lceil \frac{l_j}{L_j} \left\lceil \frac{t}{p_j} \right\rceil \right\rceil e_j$$

where b_i is the blocking time of T_i. The sum in the right-hand side of this expression gives the maximum processor time demands of mandatory jobs in higher-priority tasks when the jobs of each higher-priority task T_j are classified based on T_j's (l_j, L_j)-firm deadline requirement in the manner described above. If $w_i(t) = t$ has a solution for some $t \leq p_i$, then all mandatory jobs in T_i surely complete in time and T_i meets the (l_i, L_i)-firm deadline requirement. We can extend the general time-demand analysis method described in Section 6.6 in a straightforward manner so it can be used to determine the schedulability of tasks with firm relative deadlines that are larger than their respective periods.

One way to enhance the performance of algorithm Sched_mkfirm in terms of on-time completions of optional jobs is to use it with slack stealing. Bernat, et al. [BeBu] suggested the dual-priority algorithm [DaWe] be used for this purpose. This algorithm is defined in Problem 7.19.

We note that the classification decisions made by algorithm Sched_mkfirm are independent the execution history of the tasks. Indeed, the sequence of mandatory jobs in each task can be computed off-line or at admission control time. Other algorithms for scheduling jobs with firm deadlines adjust the priorities of jobs in each task T_i based on the history of the task's execution. For example, according to the distance-based priority assignment algorithm [HaRa], the scheduler monitors the response times of jobs in each task T_i and records a miss ("0") for each late job and a meet ("1") for each on-time job. The state of the task at the beginning of any period is defined by the string of length L_i of 1's and 0's that indicates the number and occurrence times of late jobs. [For example, for $L_i = 3$, the possible states of the task T_i are (111), (110), (101), and so on.] The scheduler increases the priority of T_i when the task is closer to failing its (l_i, L_i)-deadline requirement. [For example, if l_i is 1, then the failure distance of T_i is 1 when it is in state (100), because the task will fail if one more job completes late, but is 3 when T_i is in state (111), because T_i will fail if the next three jobs complete late.] The smaller its failure distance, the higher the task's priority. Such an algorithm is considerably more complicated to implement than the algorithm Sched_mkfirm. There is no analysis method with which one can determine the schedulability of thus scheduled tasks.

Algorithms for Scheduling Jobs with the 0/1 Constraint.   We conclude this section by looking at the problem of scheduling jobs with 0/1 constraint. When their optional components have identical execution time and weights, n jobs with the 0/1 constraint can optimally be scheduled to yield minimum total error in $O(n \log n)$ time or $O(n^2)$ time depending on whether the jobs have identical or different release times. These algorithms can be found in [ShLC].

However, the general problem of scheduling jobs with the 0/1 constraint to minimize the total error is NP-complete when their optional components have arbitrary execution times. A heuristic algorithm for scheduling jobs with identical weights is the largest-execution-time-first algorithm. According to this algorithm, the larger the execution time of an optional component, the higher its priority with respect to other optional components. Let $E_{\text{total},h}$ and $E_{\text{total},o}$ denote the total error of schedules of the flexible jobs produced using this algorithm and an optimal algorithm respectively. Ho, *et al.* showed that $E_{\text{total},h} \leq 3E_{\text{total},o}$ [HoLW].

Another reasonable performance metric is the number of discarded jobs. For example, when scheduling jobs with multiple versions, we want to minimize the number of jobs whose alternate versions are scheduled, that is, the number of discarded optional components. The shortest-execution-time-first algorithm is a reasonable algorithm when the objective is to minimize the number of discarded optional jobs. This algorithm gives higher priorities to optional components with smaller execution times. Let $n_{d,h}$ and $n_{d,o}$ be the numbers of discarded optional components in a schedule produced using this heuristic and in an optimal schedule, respectively. Ho, *et al.* also showed that $n_{d,s} \leq 2n_{d,o}$.

10.2   TASKS WITH TEMPORAL DISTANCE CONSTRAINTS

This section describes algorithms for scheduling tasks that are required to meet temporal distance constraints [HaLH]. We need a few definitions before we can proceed.

10.2.1   Temporal Distance Model

To define the term distance constraint precisely, we consider a task T_i that is a chain of jobs $J_{i,k}$, for $k = 1, 2, \ldots$. Let ϕ_i denote the release time of T_i. This means that the first job $J_{i,1}$ in T_i is ready for execution at ϕ_i, and each subsequent job $J_{i,k+1}$ ($k \geq 1$) becomes ready when its immediate predecessor $J_{i,k}$ completes. In this sense, the task T_i is an end-to-end task, and ϕ_i is its phase.

Let $f_{i,k}$ denote the completion time of the kth job $J_{i,k}$ according to some schedule. The *temporal distance* (or simply distance) between this job $J_{i,k}$ and the next job $J_{i,k+1}$ in T_i is the difference $f_{i,k+1} - f_{i,k}$ between their completion times. The (temporal) *distance constraint* of task T_i is C_i if the completion times of any two consecutive jobs in the task are required to satisfy the inequalities

$$f_{i,1} - \phi_i \leq C_i \tag{10.7a}$$

$$f_{i,k+1} - f_{i,k} \leq C_i \qquad \text{for } k = 1, 2, \ldots \tag{10.7b}$$

If the completion times of all the jobs in T_i according to a schedule satisfy these inequalities, then T_i meets its distance constraint C_i.

A schedule of a system **T** consisting of tasks $T_1, T_2, \ldots, T_n$ with distance constraints $C_1, C_2, \ldots, C_n$, respectively, is *feasible* if every task in **T** meets the task's distance constraint. A system is *schedulable* according to an algorithm if the algorithm surely produces a feasible schedule.

Analogous to the convention used in earlier chapters, we index the tasks in order of their distance constraints. In other words, if $i < j$, then $C_i < C_j$. We said that the distance constraints $C_1, C_2, \ldots, C_n$ of the n tasks are harmonic if C_i divides C_j for every pair of $i < j$. The *density*[4] δ_i of a task T_i with execution time e_i and distance constraint C_i is e_i/C_i. The density Δ of the system is equal to the sum $\sum_{i=1}^n \delta_i$.

Just like periodic and sporadic tasks studied in previous chapters, tasks with distance constraints are preemptable. However, it is reasonable to disallow arbitrary preemption. In particular, the scheduler is not allowed to preempt a job $J_{i,k}$ just before its completion, leaving an infinitesmally small portion (say a portion with execution time negligibly small compared with e_i) to be completed later. If the scheduler is allowed this preemption, then the problem of scheduling T_i to meet its distance constraint C_i is trivial: The scheduler simply schedules the last infinitesmally small portions of the jobs in T_i periodically C_i units apart and then schedules the remaining portions of the jobs as if they were released periodically with period C_i.

10.2.2 Distance Constraint Monotonic (DCM) Algorithm

The *Distance Constraint Monotonic* (DCM) *algorithm* [HaLH] does not preempt jobs arbitrarily. The algorithm has two elements: priority assignment and separation constraint.

Priority Assignments and Separation Constraints. Analogous to the Deadline Monotonic (DM) algorithm, the DCM algorithm is priority-driven and assigns fixed priorities to tasks on the basis of their temporal distance constraint: The smaller the distance constraint C_i of a task T_i, the higher the task's priority. Therefore, tasks with indices $i - 1$ or less have higher priorities than T_i, for all $i = 1, 2, \ldots, n$.

The DCM algorithm is only partially defined by the its priority assignment rule. The second element of the algorithm is the rule it uses to shape the ready time pattern of jobs in each task. You recall that in Section 9.4.1 we discussed the necessity of delaying the readiness of later jobs in each higher-priority end-to-end task in order to increase the schedulability of lower-priority tasks in a fixed-priority system. Analogously, if the scheduler were to let each successor job $J_{i,k+1}$ ($k \geq 1$) in a task T_i with distance constraints be ready for execution as soon as its immediate predecessor job $J_{i,k}$ completes, it might leave no time for lower-priority tasks. This is why the scheduler imposes a separation constraint between consecutive jobs in each task T_i. The *separation constraint* between two consecutive jobs $J_{i,k}$ and $J_{i,k+1}$ ($k \geq 1$) in T_i is the minimum length of time between the completion time $f_{i,k}$ of a job $J_{i,k}$ and the ready time $r_{i,k+1}$ of its immediate successor $J_{i,k+1}$.

Specifically, according to the DCM algorithm, the separation constraint imposed by the scheduler on jobs in each task T_i is equal to $C_i - W_i$, where W_i is the maximum response time

---

[4]Since C_i is not equal to the interrelease time between jobs in T_i in general, the term density may not have the same meaning as the same term used in previous chapters.

of jobs in T_i. In other words, the scheduler computes the ready times of jobs in T_i according to

$$r_{i,1} = \phi_i \qquad\qquad (10.8a)$$

$$r_{i,k+1} = f_{i,k} + C_i - W_i \qquad \text{for } k \geq 1 \qquad (10.8b)$$

An implicit assumption here is that $W_i \leq C_i$. This condition must hold; otherwise it is impossible for T_i to meet its distance constraint C_i.

Given a system **T** that is schedulable according to the DCM algorithm, the maximum response time W_i of all jobs in each task T_i can be obtained as follows:

1. Find the maximum response time W_1 of the highest priority task T_1.
2. For each task T_i for $i > 1$, find W_i after the maximum response times of all higher-priority tasks have been found by constructing a DCM schedule of i tasks $T_1, T_2, \ldots, T_i$, assuming that every task were released at time 0, that is, $\phi_k = 0$ for all $1 \leq k \leq i$. W_i is equal to the response time of the first job in T_i according to this schedule.

As a summary, we note that the DCM algorithm can be implemented using the same mechanism as the release-guard protocol for scheduling end-to-end tasks. (The protocol was described in Section 9.4.1.) A distance constraint task is similar to an end-to-end task in the sense that it consists of a chain of jobs. The DCM scheduler gives each task a fixed priority; according to the DCM algorithm, a task with a smaller distance constraint has a higher priority. The ready times of all jobs in a task other than the first job are in fact their release guards. Rather than setting the release guard of the next job in a task when it releases the current job, the DCM scheduler sets the release guard according to Eq. (10.8) when the current job of the task completes.

Schedulability of Tasks with Harmonic Distance Constraints.   We observe that the temporal distance between a job $J_{i,k+1}$ and its immediate predecessor is

$$C_i - W_i + y$$

when the response time of $J_{i,k+1}$ is y. By definition $y \leq W_i$; hence, this distance is no greater than C_i.

Again, the critical assumption is that $W_i \leq C_i$. This condition must hold; otherwise it is impossible for T_i to meet its distance constraint C_i. The question now is, under what condition is a system **T** with distance constraints schedulable by the DCM algorithm? The following theorem gives the answer for the special case when tasks in **T** have harmonic distance constraints.

THEOREM 10.1.   A system **T** of tasks whose distance constraints are harmonic and separation constraints are given by Eq. (10.8) is schedulable on a distance constraint monotonic basis if its density Δ is no greater than 1.

This theorem is true because under the conditions stated here, tasks in **T** behave just like simply periodic tasks. This claim can be proven by induction; you can find the formal

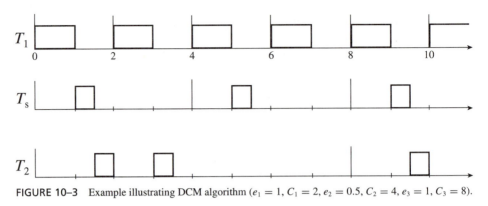

FIGURE 10–3   Example illustrating DCM algorithm ($e_1 = 1, C_1 = 2, e_2 = 0.5, C_2 = 4, e_3 = 1, C_3 = 8$).

proof in [HaLH]. Rather than repeating it here, we look at the illustrative example in Figure 10–3. The distance constraints of the tasks T_1, T_2, and T_3 are 2, 4, and 8, respectively, and their execution times are 1, 0.5, and 1. They are all released at time 0. $W_1 = 1$, $W_2 = 1.5$, and $W_3 = 3.5$. These response times are all less than the respective distance constraints. According to Eq. (10.8), $r_{1,1} = 0$, $r_{1,2} = 1+2-1 = 2$, and for $k > 1$ in general, $r_{1,k} = 2(k-1)$. Similarly, jobs in T_2 become ready at 0, 4, and so on, and jobs in T_3 become ready at 0, 8, 16, and so on. In short, tasks T_1, T_2, and T_3 behave just like periodic tasks $(2, 1.0)$, $(4, 0.5)$, and $(8, 1.0)$, respectively. The density e_i/C_i of each task T_i are equal to the utilization of the periodic task (C_i, e_i), for $i = 1, 2, 3$.

We can generalize from this example. When distance constraints of tasks in a system **T** are harmonic and the system is scheduled according to the DCM algorithm, every task T_i with distance constraint C_i and execution time e_i behaves exactly the same as the periodic task (C_i, e_i). Theorem 10.1 follows directly from Theorem 6.3.

10.2.3 Scheduling Tasks with Arbitrary Distance Constraints

A task T_i in a system of tasks with arbitrary distance constraints no longer behaves like a periodic task (C_i, e_i) when scheduled according to the DCM algorithm. Indeed, the time interval between the ready times of consecutive jobs in it can be as small as $e_i + C_i - W_i$. (To illustrate, suppose that the distance constraint of T_3 in Figure 10–3 is 7 instead. The maximum response time of the task is 3.5. The second job $J_{3,2}$ is ready at time 7 and completes at 8. Therefore, the third job is ready at $8 + 7 - 3.5$, which is 11.5.) Of course, we can treat T_i as a periodic task $(C_i + e_i - W_i, e_i)$ when we want to determine whether it and lower-priority tasks are schedulable. (For example, we would treat the task T_3 as the periodic task $(4.5, 1)$.) Unfortunately, because $C_i + e_i - W_i$ can be significantly smaller than C_i, the performance of this approach can be poor.

Specialization.   A way to improve the schedulability of tasks with arbitrary distance constraints is to first transform them into tasks with harmonic distance constraints. The operation carried out for this purpose is called *specialization*.

Parameters of Accelerated Tasks.   When given a system of tasks $T_1, T_2, \ldots, T_n$ with distance constraints $C_1, C_2, \ldots, C_n$, respectively, a specialization operation transforms the tasks into *accelerated tasks*[5] $T_1', T_2', \ldots, T_n'$ with distance constraints $C_1', C_2', \ldots, C_n'$, respectively. For every $i = 1, 2, \ldots, n$, the parameters of the accelerated task T_i' are related to the parameters of the corresponding original task T_i and the other accelerated tasks as follows:

1. The execution time of T_i' is the execution time e_i of T_i.
2. The distance constraint C_i' of T_i' is no greater than the distance constraint C_i of T_i.
3. The new distance constraints $C_1', C_2', \ldots, C_n'$ are harmonic.

Clearly, if the accelerated tasks meet their distance constraints, so do the given tasks. Because their distance constraints are harmonic, the accelerated tasks can meet their distance constraints when scheduled according to the DCM algorithm if their total density $\sum_{i=1}^{n} e_i / C_i'$ is no greater than 1.

As an example, suppose that the distance constraints of the given tasks are 4, 5, 11, and 18. The distance constraints of the accelerated tasks produced by specialization are 4, 4, 8, and 16.

Algorithm Sr.   We now describe an algorithm for specialization [HaLH] and call this algorithm Sr (rather than the specialization operation Sr). The goal of the algorithm is to find a set of distance constraints of accelerated tasks that satisfies relations 2 and 3 and gives the accelerated tasks the smallest total density. We call this set of accelerated tasks the *minimally accelerated set*.

During specialization, algorithm Sr first computes all the possible bases. A number b is a *base* if the distance constraint of every accelerated task T_i' can be expressed as $b \cdot 2^{j_i}$ for some integer j_i satisfying $b \cdot 2^{j_i} \leq C_i$.

Han, *et al.* showed that

$$b_i = \frac{C_i}{2^{\lceil \log_2(C_i/C_1) \rceil}} \tag{10.9a}$$

for $i = 1, 2, \ldots, n$ are the only possible bases. The distance constraint $C_i'(b_k)$ of the accelerated task C_i' computed from base b_k is given by

$$C_i'(b_k) = b_k \cdot 2^{\lfloor \log_2(C_i/b_k) \rfloor} \tag{10.9b}$$

We say that the accelerated task $T_i'(b_k)$ with this distance constraint is obtained by specializing T_i with respect to b_k.

Among all the possible bases, algorithm Sr chooses the base $\hat{b}$ which yields the smallest total density Δ' of the accelerated tasks. In other words,

---

[5]We use here the same term as Section 6.7.3 did. Theorem 6.15 stated there gave a sufficient condition for the schedulability of rate-monotonically scheduled periodic tasks that have arbitrary periods. To determine whether a system of periodic tasks is schedulable based on this condition, one first finds an accelerated set of periodic tasks: The period of each accelerated task is no greater than the period of the corresponding task in the given system and the periods of all accelerated tasks are harmonic. A transformation of the given tasks into accelerated tasks is exactly a specialization. The algorithms developed by Han [Han] for finding an accelerated set can be used for the purpose of specialization.

Input: Parameters of n given tasks $T_1, T_2, \ldots, T_n$.

Outputs:

(i) The total density Δ' of a set of n accelerated tasks which have the minimum total density among all accelerated sets that satisfy (1)–(3). (Say this set is specialized with respect to $\hat{b}$),

(ii) The distance constraints $C_1', C_2', \ldots, C_n'$ of the accelerated tasks specialized with respect to the base $\hat{b}$.

1. For $i = 1, 2, \ldots, n$, compute the base $b_i = C_i / 2^{\lceil \log_2(C_i/C_1) \rceil}$.
2. Sort the list of bases $b_1, b_2, \ldots, b_n$ in nondecreasing order and remove duplicates from the list.
3. For every base b_i remaining in the list, compute the total density $\Delta(b_i) = \sum_{k=1}^{n} e_k / b_i 2^{\lfloor \log_2(C_k/b_i) \rfloor}$ of the accelerated tasks specialized with respect to b_i.
4. Find the base $\hat{b}$ such that $\Delta(\hat{b})$ is the smallest among $\Delta(b_i)$ for all i.
5. Return $\Delta' = \Delta(\hat{b})$ and $C_i' = \hat{b} \cdot 2^{\lfloor \log_2(C_i/\hat{b}) \rfloor}$ for all i.

FIGURE 10–4   Specialization operation.

$$\Delta' = \sum_{i=1}^{n} \frac{e_i}{C_i'(\hat{b})} = \min_{\text{all } b_k} \left(\sum_{i=1}^{n} \frac{e_i}{C_i'(b_k)} \right) \tag{10.9c}$$

The accelerated tasks obtained by algorithm Sr are specialized with respect to $\hat{b}$. Their distance constraints are given by

$$C_i' = \hat{b} \cdot 2^{\lfloor \log_2(C_i/\hat{b}) \rfloor} \tag{10.9d}$$

Figure 10–4 summarizes in pseudocode the specialization operation. The complexity of the algorithm is $O(n \log n)$. The algorithm also provides the minimum total density Δ' of all sets of accelerated tasks that satisfy relations 1–3.

Table 10–1 gives an illustrative example. The system has four tasks. Their distance constraints, being 6, 10, 16, and 24, are not harmonic. To find a minimally accelerated set for these tasks, algorithm Sr first computes all the possible bases according to Eq. (10.9a). C_1 for this system is 6. $b_1 = C_1$. $C_2/C_1 = 10/6 = 1.67$. Since $\lceil \log_2 1.67 \rceil$ is 1, $b_2 = 10/2 = 5$.

TABLE 10–1   An Example Illustrating Specialization

	e_i	C_i	δ_i	b_i	$C_i'(b_1)$	$C_i'(b_2)$	$C_i'(b_3)$	$C_i'(b_4)$
T_1	2	6	0.33	3	6	5	4	6
T_2	3	10	0.30	5	6	10	8	6
T_3	2	16	0.13	4	12	10	16	12
T_4	1	24	0.04	6	24	20	16	24
Δ or Δ'			0.77		1.04	0.95	1.11	1.04

Similarly, $b_3 = 4$ and $b_4 = 6$. The distance constraints of accelerated tasks obtained by specializing the corresponding original tasks with respect to these bases are listed in the table. Since the base $b_2 = 5$ yields the minimum total density of 0.95, Algorithm Sr chooses this base. The minimally accelerated tasks obtained by the algorithm have distance constraints $C_i' = 5$, $C_2' = 10$, $C_3' = 10$, and $C_1' = 20$. Theorem 10.1 says that these tasks are schedulable according to the DCM algorithm.

Schedulability.   In short, a procedure for scheduling a system **T** of tasks with arbitrary distance constraints is as follows:

1. Apply algorithm Sr to find a minimally accelerated system **T′** from the given system **T**.
2. Schedule the tasks in **T′** according to the DCM algorithm if **T′** thus found is feasible.

By **T′** being feasible, we mean that its total density is no greater than 1 and hence can be feasibly scheduled by the DCM algorithm. If the minimally accelerated system found by algorithm Sr is not feasible, then the procedure fails. We do not know whether the system **T** is schedulable for sure.

The question now is under what condition does a system **T** have a feasible minimally accelerated system **T′**. The following theorem gives a sufficient condition. Its proof can be found in [HaLH].

THEOREM 10.2.   Algorithm Sr can surely find a feasible accelerated set $\{(C_i', e_i)\}$ of tasks with harmonic distance constraints if the total density Δ of the given system of n tasks is such that

$$\Delta \leq n(2^{1/n} - 1)$$

The expression on the right-hand side of the equation is exactly $U_{RM}(n)$, the schedulable utilization of a system of n periodic tasks.

This condition is sufficient but not necessary. (This fact is illustrated by the example in Table 10–1. The total density of the system is 0.77. It is larger than than $U_{RM}(4) = 0.757$. Nevertheless, the system is schedulable.) There is no known necessary and sufficient schedulability condition for tasks with arbitrary distance constraints.

10.3 SUMMARY

This chapter described the flexible computation and distance-constraint workload models and algorithms for scheduling applications that fit these models.

10.3.1 Flexible Computations

A flexible task with firm quality has optional components which can be discarded when necessary so that mandatory components of the task and other tasks can complete on time. Algorithms for scheduling flexible tasks can be divided into two broad categories: algorithms designed to optimize static quality metrics and algorithms designed to prevent dynamic failures. The former are for applications in which no optional components are ever required to complete on time. These algorithms aim at completing all mandatory components on time while optimizing some static measure of result quality. The latter deal with applications in which mandatory jobs may change dynamically with the execution history of the tasks. An algorithm designed to prevent dynamic failures makes sure that optional components which have become mandatory also complete on time.

Optimization of Static Quality Metrics.   Metrics used to measure result quality include average, maximum, and total error in results produced by all tasks. These metrics are defined in Eqs. (10.2) and (10.3). Some algorithms that aim at minimizing such a metric schedule optional components in the background of mandatory components. These algorithms tend to be more stable and robust and can accommondate sporadic jobs better. The cost of their robustness is performance. The (average, total, or maximum) error achievable by mandatory-first algorithms can be significantly larger than when slacks of mandatory components are effectively used to complete more of the optional components.

In contrast to mandatory-first algorithms, slack-stealing algorithms postpone the execution of mandatory components as much as possible without causing them to be late and use the slack to execute as many optional components as possible. A slack-stealing algorithm may compute the amounts of slack (and hence the portions of optional components to be scheduled and completed) off-line when the temporal parameters of all jobs are known and fixed. These amounts can be determined by solving a constrained optimization problem, exemplified by the ones defined by Eq. (10.4) and (10.5). Such a problem can be solved in polynominal time when the error functions are linear and convex but is difficult when the error functions are concave and when optional jobs have 0/1 constraints. Algorithms that determine on-line when mandatory components have slacks can deal only with error functions that are linear or convex.

Prevention of Dynamic Failures.   A task T with a (l, L) firm deadline is required to complete l or more jobs in every consecutive L jobs. Algorithms designed to meet firm deadlines typically classify jobs in each task as mandatory or optional depending whether their late completions will cause the task to miss the task's firm deadline. Eq. (10.6) gives a criterion for this classification. Jobs classified as optional are then scheduled in the background of jobs classified as mandatory. This strategy can also be combined with slack-stealing as suggested by Bernat, *et al.* [BeBu].

10.3.2 Tasks with Distance Constraints

The completion times of jobs in a task with distance constraints must satisfy the inequalities in Eq. (10.7). The first step in scheduling a system of tasks with distance constraints checks whether the distance constraints are harmonic. If the distance constraints are harmonic, the system can be feasibly scheduled by the DCM algorithm if their total density is no greater than 1.

The DCM algorithm assigns fixed priorities to tasks according to their distance constraints; the smaller the distance, the higher the priority. In addition, the DCM scheduler adds temporal separation between the completion time of each job and the ready time of the job's immediate successor. Specifically, the ready time of each job is computed from the completion time of its immediate predecessor according to Eq. (10.8).

If the distance constraints of the tasks are not harmonic, they are transformed into more stringent but harmonic distance constraints. This process is called specialization. The accelerated tasks obtained by specialization are then scheduled according to the DCM algorithm. n tasks with arbitrary distance constraints can be specialized into n accelerated tasks that have harmonic distance constraints and a total density no greater than 1 if the total density Δ of the given tasks is no greater than $U_{RM}(n) = n(2^{1/n} - 1)$. In other words, a system of tasks with arbitrary distance constraints is schedulable by specialization followed by DCM algorithm if its total density Δ of no greater than $U_{RM}(n)$.

EXERCISES

10.1 Instead of formulating the problem of finding an optimal static schedule as a constrained optimization problem, we can also formulate it as a network-flow problem when the tasks have identical weights and error functions are linear.

(a) Suppose that you are given a system of two periodic flexible tasks: $T_1 = (4, 3)$ and $T_2 = (7, 2)$. T_1 consists of $M_1 = (4, 1)$ and $O_1 = (4, 2)$, and T_2 consists of $M_2 = (7, 1)$ and $O_2 = (7, 1)$. The periodic tasks are truly periodic, and they have equal weights.

   i. Construct a network-flow graph of this system which you can use to determine whether the system can be feasibly scheduled. (*Hint*: Similar to the network-flow graph described in Section 5.8.1, your graph contains a source vertex, a sink vertex, and a job vertex for each job in a hyperperiod. Rather than frame vertices, your graph has interval vertices: All release times in the hyperperiod partition the hyperperiod into disjoint time intervals, and there is an interval vertice for each of these intervals.) Find a maximum flow that gives you a schedule of the mandatory tasks.

   ii. Modify the network-flow graph you obtained in part (i) and use the modified network-flow graph to find an optimal schedule that minimizes the average error of the system. Assume that the average error of every task is taken over a hyperperiod.

(b) Describe a general procedure you can follow to (1) determine whether a system of jobs with known and fixed parameters can be feasibly scheduled and (2) if it can be, find an optimal static schedule of the system when jobs have identical weights and linear error functions.

10.2 Bernat, *et al.* [BeBu] suggested the use of the dual-priority scheme described in Problem 7.19 for scheduling periodic tasks with firm deadlines. Suppose that the periodic task T_1 described in that problem has $(1, 3)$-firm deadlines. What are the relative priority promotion times of the tasks?

CHAPTER 11

Real-Time Communication

This chapter and the next chapter discuss communication and operating system support for real-time applications. They do not provide a comprehensive treatment of these topics, as it is impossible to do so, even with seemingly an unlimited amount of space in each chapter. Rather, they focus on issues that do not arise in nonreal-time systems, in general, and, in particular, features and capabilities that are needed to meet performance objectives of real-time applications.

This chapter is devoted to network services for multiprocessor and distributed real-time applications. Section 11.1 describes a general model of real-time communications; the model helps us point out where interfaces between components usually are and where access and flow control may be exercised. This section also presents assumptions made in most of the chapter, terms needed in later sections, and characteristics and performance requirements of real-time traffic. *Quality of service* is a term commonly used to mean a collection of figures of merits, such as performance, reliability, and reconfigurability. We are concerned mainly with real-time performance and will use the terms performance and quality of service interchangeably.

With the exception of Section 11.7, the chapter focuses on real-time communication in distributed systems. Sections 11.1–11.6 approach the issues from bottom up. Sections 11.2, 11.3, and 11.4 describe schemes for flow control and scheduling in packet-switched networks and protocols to control medium access in broadcast networks. These schemes have been proposed in recent years to ensure timely delivery of real-time messages. Sections 11.5 and 11.6 describe well-known resource reservation, Internet, and transport protocols designed to support real-time communication. Section 11.7 focuses on communication in tightly coupled multicomputer systems. Section 11.8 summarizes the chapter. We defer discussions on networking software to the next chapter, which is on operating systems.

The discussion here assumes background knowledge on widely used protocols for traditional data communication. You can find information on these protocols in texts on networks and Internet communication. Examples are texts by Stallings [Stal] for a general treatment of networking issues and local area networks and books by Comer and Steven [CoSt] for TCP, UDP, and IP. This chapter intends to complement the coverage of these and similar texts.

11.1   MODEL OF REAL-TIME COMMUNICATION

Figure 11–1 shows the well-known model of distributed systems, which we assume in most of this chapter. The hosts are connected by a communication network (or several interconnected networks). We simplify the top layers and call all entities above the transport-layer applications.

11.1.1   Architectural Overview

We focus on messages exchanged among applications on different hosts. In other words, the source and destination(s) of every message are application tasks (or end users) residing on different hosts. The network interface of each host contains an input queue (or a system of input queues) and an output queue (or a system of output queues). In later sections, we will also refer to these queues as input/output buffers or simply buffers. For the sake of concreteness, we assume that these queues are jointly maintained by two (local) servers: the Transport Protocol (TP) handler and Network-Access-Control (NAC) handler. The former interfaces with local applications and provides them with message transport services. The latter interfaces with the network below and provides network-access and message-transmission services to the TP handler. (The client/server architecture assumed here may introduce more delay and unpredictability than necessary and other networking software structures may be more suitable for real-time communication. We will return to these issues in Chapter 12 when we discuss networking software.)

Figure 11–1 shows the data paths (indicated by heavy arrows) traversed by messages in and out of two hosts. The circles marked TPH and NACH are the TP and NAC handlers,

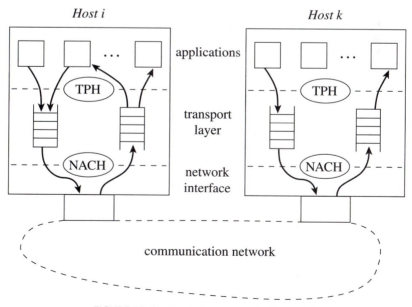

FIGURE 11–1   A real-time communication model.

respectively. When requested to send a message by a local application task, the source TP handler places the message in the output queue. From there, each outgoing message is delivered to the network under the control of the source NAC handler. After the message has traversed the network, the destination NAC handler places the message in the input queue and notifies the destination TP handler. The destination TP handler then moves the message to the address space of the destination application task and notifies the application task of the arrival of the message.

When there is no possibility of ambiguity or when there is no need to be specific, we use the terms source and destination endpoints (or simply source and destination) to mean either the source and destination application tasks, or the TP handlers, or the NAC handlers, or the entry and exit points of the network. The activities of sending a message can naturally be represented in the end-to-end model by a chain of jobs. The source and destination applications are the predecessor and successor of this chain, respectively. At the beginning and end of the chain are the source and destination TP processing jobs. In between them, each job that accesses the network or transmits the message becomes ready for execution after its immediate predecessor completes, possibly with some delay in its readiness introduced by the execution synchronization protocol used along the path. This model is the one which we worked with in Chapter 9.

11.1.2 Packets, Network Bandwidth, and Physical Size

Messages are typically fragmented into segments for their transmission through the communication network. Each segment is handled by the network as a basic transmission unit, and the transmission of the unit is nonpreemptable. Such a unit is called a frame, a packet, a cell, and the like, in different types of networks. We use the name *packet* to refer to all these basic transmission units. As an example, a packet is a 53-byte cell in an ATM network. In an IEEE 802.5 token ring [IEEE89], it is a frame of tens of kilobits. (The maximum length of a data frame in a token ring is limited by the length of time a station is allowed to transmit each time it is polled.)

For convenience, we take as the basic time unit the length of time required to transmit a maximum length packet at a switch or network interface over the data link on which we focus our attention. (We include in this time the processing overhead, that is, the time required for packet header processing and other operations performed on the packet in order to transmit it.) For example, the time required to transmit a 53-byte packet over a 100-MHz link is 4.24 microseconds and, hence, a time unit is 4.24 microseconds (plus processing overhead). If the transmission rate of the link is 1 GHz, then a time unit is 424 nanoseconds. Similarly, we measure the length of each message by the number of (maximum length) packets. For example, a message of length 100 has $100 \times 53 = 5.3$ Kbytes if each packet has 53 bytes, and the length of time to transmit the message is 100 time units. On the other hand, if the length of each packet is 10,000 bytes, then a message of length 100 has 1 Mbyte; still, its transmission time is 100 time units.

We also measure queueing and propagation delay in terms of this time unit: The length of delay is measured in terms of the number of packets that can be transmitted in that length of time. Furthermore, we measure the length of each transmission link by the number of packets that can be transmitted within the length of time they take to traverse the link. So, each 100 microseconds of delay over a 100-MHz link where each packet is 53 bytes in length is $100/4.24 = 23.6$ time units because in 100 microseconds, we can transmit this many 53-byte packets over the link, but this delay is only one time unit if the packet size is 10,000 bits. Over a 1 GHz link, the same 100 microseconds is 236 or 10 time units, respectively. The use of this basic time unit allows us to take into account the transmission rate and packet size of each network implicitly and eliminates the need to have separate units for distance and time.

Similarly, when our discussion focuses on one input or output link, the absolute value of its bandwidth is irrelevant; only how this bandwidth is allocated among the message streams on the link is. We therefore say that the link bandwidth is one (one packet per unit time). When we say that a message stream is allocated a bandwidth of $\tilde{u}$, we always mean that the message is given the fraction $\tilde{u}$ of the link bandwidth.

11.1.3 Real-Time Traffic Models

In real-time communications literature, the term real-time traffic typically means *isochronous* (or synchronous) traffic, consisting of message streams that are generated by their sources on a continuing basis and delivered to their respective destinations on a continuing basis. Such traffic includes periodic and sporadic messages, which require some degree of guarantee for on-time delivery. In addition, there are also aperiodic (or asynchronous) messages. Aperiodic messages have soft timing constraints and expect the system to deliver them on a best-effort basis.

In our discussion, we also refer to each of these types of messages as a message stream and denote it by M_i for some index i when it is necessary to distinguish it from other message streams. We use interchangeably the expressions that a message instance or packet arrives and that it is released for transmission. A message instance or packet arrives (or departs) at a point in time when the last bit in it arrives (or departs).

Periodic and Aperiodic Messages.   Periodic message streams, or simply *periodic messages*, are generated and consumed by periodic tasks, and their characteristics are similar to the characteristics of their respective source tasks. Specifically, the transmission of a periodic message is a periodic task. Examples are message streams carrying sensor data and actuator commands generated and consumed by data acquisition tasks and digital controllers. Constant Bit-Rate (CBR) digitized voices and videos are accurately modeled by periodic messages.

Adopting the notation used in earlier chapters, we denote a periodic message M_i by the tuple (p_i, e_i, D_i). This means that the interarrival (interrelease) times of instances in M_i are never less than the *period* p_i of the message, the maximum length of the instances in M_i is equal to e_i packets, and each instance must be delivered to the destination within D_i units of time from its arrival at the source. D_i is the (end-to-end) relative deadline of M_i. This traffic model is called the *peak rate* model in real-time communication literature [AKRS].

There are also aperiodic message streams; the transmission of an aperiodic message stream is an aperiodic task. Like aperiodic tasks, an aperiodic message stream does not have a relative deadline. However, it is desirable to keep the average delay suffered by aperiodic message instances as small as possible.

Sporadic Messages.   You recall that a periodic task is a poor model for some applications. Similarly, a periodic message is an inaccurate model of any sporadic message stream whose instances have widely varying lengths and/or interarrival times. Examples include a MPEG-compressed video stream, because the lengths of frames in it vary widely, and command and control messages generated in response to unexpected events, because the interarrival times of message instances vary widely. In general, we can characterize a sporadic message stream M_i in the same way we characterizes a sporadic task. Section 7.8.1 described three models that are commonly used in real-time communication literature: the FeVe model [FeVe], the (λ, β) model [Cruz], and the leaky bucket model [Turn, ClSZ].

According to the FeVe model, a sporadic message M_i is characterized by a 5-tuple $(p_i, \overline{p}_i, I_i, e_i, D_i)$. The parameters p_i, e_i and D_i are the minimum interarrival time, maximum length, and relative deadline of the instances in M_i, just like these parameters of a periodic message. $\overline{p}_i$ is the average interarrival time of the instances of M_i where the average is taken over an interval of length I_i. In a switched network, a switch typically transmits each packet without waiting for the arrivals of later packets in the same message instance. The FeVe model in this case simplifies to $M_i = (p_i, \overline{p}_i, I_i, D_i)$. The packets in M_i never arrive less than p_i units of time apart, and their average interarrival time over any time interval of length I_i is $\overline{p}_i$. The maximum length of each "instance" of M_i is 1 and is omitted in the tuple.

A message stream meets the (Λ, E) leaky bucket constraint if it can be produced by a (Λ, E) leaky bucket filter. The example in Figure 7–22 illustrates that a periodic message stream satisfies this constraint. Many sporadic messages that have seemingly very different characteristics may satisfy this constraint. Among their common characteristics is that the length of any instance never exceeds E and the total length of all instances arriving in any time interval of length t never exceeds $E + \Lambda t$. Similarly, according to the (λ, β) model, the number of packets that arrive in any time interval of length t never exceeds $\beta + \lambda t$.

11.1.4   Performance Objectives and Constraints

We want to measure the performance of scheduling, synchronization, and flow-control algorithms used for real-time communication and the performance of the resultant communication system along two dimensions: from the points of view of the user and the system. The user is concerned with the on-time delivery of periodic and sporadic messages and the average response time of aperiodic messages. (Hereafter, we use the term *delay* of a message instead of response time because delay is the term used in communication literature.) The system, on the other hand, wants to meet users' demands and requirements with minimum amounts of resources and good utilization of every resource. As always, the best algorithms are those that can achieve the desired balance among these oftentimes conflicting performance objectives.

Miss, Loss, and Invalid Rates.   Of course, the user wants all instances of periodic and sporadic messages to be delivered on time. However, absolute guarantee of on-time delivery in a communication system where a significant fraction of messages is sporadic incurs a high cost in resource utilization. Moreover, such a guarantee may not be required for the bulk of real-time traffic, for example, those from multimedia and video-on-demand applications. Therefore, algorithms and protocols for real-time communications are typically designed to allow some deadline misses, provided that the miss rate is below some acceptable threshold. The miss rate of a message stream or a set of message streams is the fraction of all message instances or packets that are delivered to their destinations too late. As we discussed in Chapter 3, miss rate is not a hard constraint. The user rarely requires a rigorous demonstration that some threshold miss rate is never exceeded; some statistics and histograms on miss rate usually suffice.

In earlier chapters, we assumed that no job is ever blocked or lost because there is no space in the ready job queue for it when it becomes ready for execution. This assumption is usually valid for computation tasks but often not valid in communication systems. It is not economically sound to put so many input/output buffers in all the network-access interfaces and switches that buffer overflow never occurs and hence this assumption holds. When a queue is full or when the queue length reaches a certain (drop) threshold, some packet(s) destinated for the queue are dropped (i.e., discarded). As a consequence, some packets may be lost. The loss rate of a message stream or a set of message streams gives the fraction of all message instances (or packets) in the stream(s) that are dropped en route for flow and congestion control reasons. (Some packets and messages may also be discarded because they are found erroneous. We do not consider this factor since it does not depend on the algorithms and protocols discussed here.)

Delay Jitter, Buffer Requirement, and Throughput.   While it is important that the end-to-end delay experienced by messages of interactive applications (e.g., teleconferencing) be acceptably small, this performance objective is relative unimportant for some isochronous traffic. For example, the performance of a video-on-demand system is not seriously affected by the end-to-end delay suffered by packets in each video stream. In contrast, delay jitter and throughput are important.

The *delay jitter* of a message stream is the variation (e.g., the maximum or average absolute difference) in the delays suffered by different message instances or packets in the stream. In earlier chapters, we talked about, and made use of, the fact that there is no advantage to completing a job in a periodic or sporadic task early. We gain no advantage by delivering packets in a periodic or sporadic message early. In fact, it may be disadvantageous to do so. A packet that arrives too early to be processed by the destination must be buffered. Hence, a larger delay jitter of a message stream means that more buffers must be provided by the stream. For this reason, many algorithms and protocols for real-time communication are designed to keep not only the worst-case delay small but also delay jitter small. Fortunately, these performance measures can be minimized simultaneously by using some nongreedy synchronization protocol such as those described in Chapter 9.

Finally, the *rate* of each message stream measures the throughput of the stream. Most of the scheduling and flow-control algorithms described in subsequent sections are *rate-based* [ZhKe], meaning that they are designed to provide each message stream with a guaranteed minimum throughput independent of the demands of the other message streams.

11.1.5 Real-Time Connections and Service Disciplines

It is common to adopt the connection-oriented approach for real-time traffic. According to the connection-oriented approach, a logical simplex connection from the source to the destination is set up for the transmission of each message stream (or set of message streams). In most parts of this chapter, we assume that all the packets on each connection are sent along a fixed route. The chosen route remains in use until the connection is torn down or when some adaptation mechanism is invoked to alter the route. Furthermore, we confine our attention to communication between a source and destination pair, postponing the discussion on multicast communication to Section 11.5.

Admission Control and Connection Establishment.   There are good reasons for using a fixed route for traffic on each connection. As examples, high speeds of modern networks make it impractical to route individual packets independently. More importantly, the use of a fixed route for each connection allows each switch en route, in addition to the endpoints, to set aside the required bandwidth and buffer space for the connection so the network can provide some form of performance guarantee. This also enables control over packet transmission (e.g., traffic shaping) to be done on a per connection basis.

To request a connection, the requesting client (or clients) declares the characteristics of the message stream and the required performance of the connection. The former are defined by parameters of the message stream to be carried on the connection, for example, by the parameters of a leaky bucket filter that constrains the message stream. Collectively, these parameters are called the *flow specification*. The required performance is stated in terms of *quality-of-service parameters* such as end-to-end delay, jitter, and so on. The admission controller of each handler and switch along the chosen route uses these parameters as the basis of an acceptance test to determine whether to admit the connection. The connection is admitted if the requested quality of service can be delivered to the new connection without causing any deterioration of the quality of service of existing connections serviced by the handler or switch.

Packet-Switched Networks.   The next two sections discuss packet-switched networks. They make several assumptions, which are valid for most switched, multihop networks. The diagram in Figure 11–2(a) illustrates such a network. The circles in the diagram represent switches. Figure 11–2(b) shows a $m \times m$ switch; it has m input links and m output links, both called links $1, 2, \ldots, m$. The switch routes packets on its input links to its output links.

We can represent every switching (i.e., routing) pattern by a permutation of the m-tuple $(1, 2, \ldots, m)$. A number i at position k means that the switch is configured to route a packet coming on the input link i to (the queue of) the output link k at the same time when it is routing packets on the other input links to other output links as specified by the permutation. As an example, for a 4×4 switch, the 4-tuple $(2, 4, 1, 3)$ means that a packet on input link 2 goes to the queue of output link 1, a packet on input link 4 goes to the queue of output link 2, and so on. This is the switching pattern depicted by Figure 11–2(b). The switch is *nonblocking*, meaning that every permutation represents a possible switching pattern.

Without loss of generality, we assume that switches are output buffered. At each switch, there is a buffer pool for each of its output links, holding packets that are queued for transmission on the link. Once the switch routes a packet to this queue, the packet waits in the queue until the scheduler schedules it for transmission, and then it is transmitted to the next hop at the other end of the output link. The amount of time the switch takes to route packets from its input links to its output links is negligibly small. Consequently, the time a packet takes passing through a switch is essentially equal to its waiting time at the output queue (i.e., its output queueing delay) plus the packet transmission time (i.e., the time required to transmit the packet onto the output link and hence the length of the packet). We call this sum the *per hop delay* of the packet.

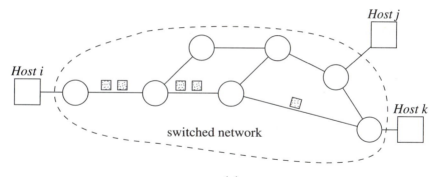

(a)

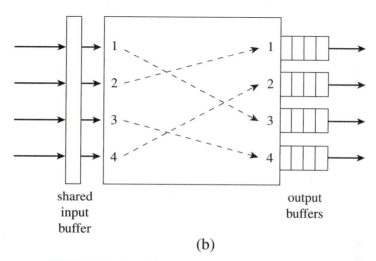

(b)

FIGURE 11–2   A multihop switched network and a 4 × 4 switch.

The end-to-end delay of each packet through a switched network is equal to the sum of the per hop delays it suffers passing through all the switches en route plus the total time it takes to propagate along all the links between the switches. Since the propagation time is independent of the scheduling and synchronization algorithms used by switches, we will ignore it in our subsequent discussion and focus solely on per hop delay. Moreover, the delay of a packet on an output link is independent of how the transmissions of packets on other output links are scheduled. Therefore, when we talk about scheduling packet transmissions, we mean specifically scheduling packets on all the connections that make use of the same output link, and when we say all packets, we mean only these packets.

Taxonomy of Service Disciplines.   The combination of an acceptance test and admission control protocol, an (execution) synchronization protocol and a scheduling algorithm used for the purposes of rate control, (delay) jitter control and scheduling of packet transmissions is called a *service discipline*. In essence, rate control and jitter control serve the purpose of flow-control for real-time traffic. Flow control is applied at endpoints and within the communication network to prevent an entity upstream from overloading entities downstream. (Up- and downstream follow the convention of river flow: The direction of traffic flow away from the source is downstream.) Traditional flow-control schemes, such as the sliding-window protocol [Stal], are inappropriate for real-time traffic for many reasons. For example, they can introduce large variations in the flow rate and delay. As you will see in subsequent sections, rate- and jitter-control mechanisms for real-time traffic are integral parts of a service discipline, rather than being separated from scheduling and buffer management functions. In this way, they differ fundamentally from the traditional flow-control mechanisms for data traffic.

Specifically, the term *rate control* is used in the communications literature to mean load management; the purpose is to ensure that the bursty traffic and resulting overloads on any connection do not adversely affect the performance of other connections. From the discussion in Section 9.4, we can see that even if the message stream on a connection is periodic (i.e., never bursty) when it enters a switched network, variations in delay at upstream switches may cause the arrivals at downstream switches to be bursty. Overloads that arise can be managed by exercising rate control at individual switches.

However, as we will see later, a better way is to apply rate control at the first switch but (delay) *jitter control* at subsequent switches along the route of each connection whenever the delay through every switch can be bounded. Jitter control is usually done by preserving the traffic pattern of the first switch at every switch. (The term traffic pattern refers to the spacings between the time instants at which packets become ready for transmission.) As a result of jitter control, not only the end-to-end delay jitter and required buffer space at each switch en route are kept constant, rather than growing linearly with the number of hops from the source when there is no jitter control, but also overloads at downstream switches and the destination are managed as byproducts.

Service disciplines are divided into two types in the literature. Some are *rate-allocating*, and some others are *rate-controlled* [ZhKe]. Rate-allocating disciplines allow packets on each connection to be transmitted at higher rates than the guaranteed rate (i.e., the minimum rate required to meet the guaranteed delay and throughput of the connection), provided the switch can still meet the guarantees to all other connections. A service discipline is rate-controlled if it ensures each connection the guaranteed rate but never allows packets on any connection to be sent above the guaranteed rate. In general, a bandwidth-preserving server that claims all the background time is rate-allocating. The sporadic/background server and the total bandwidth server described in Chapter 7 are examples. The constant utilization server is rate-controlled. So, you see that rate-allocating algorithms are work-conserving (i.e., greedy), while rate-controlled algorithms are nonwork-conserving (i.e., nongreedy).

The subsequent sections divide the service disciplines according to the types of algorithms used for scheduling packet transmissions in switched networks: priority-based and the weighted round-robin approaches. In the next section, we first describe several well-known priority-based service disciplines. These disciplines should sound familiar to you because they are essentially the same or strongly resemble the general scheduling and synchronization algorithms described in earlier chapters. We then describe well known weighted round-robin service disciplines for scheduling the transmissions of real-time messages.

11.2 PRIORITY-BASED SERVICE DISCIPLINES FOR SWITCHED NETWORKS

According to a priority-based service discipline, the transmissions of ready packets are scheduled in a priority-driven manner. Among this class of disciplines, the most well known are weighted fair-queueing [DeKS, PaGa93, StVa98a], Delay Earliest-Due-Date (Delay-EDD) [FeVe], jittered-EDD [VeZF], and Rate-Controlled Static Priority (RCSF) [ZhFe]. The performance of these disciplines are listed in Table 11-1, which appears in Section 11.8. Here, we describe how these disciplines work and why they have the listed performance.

11.2.1 Weighted Fair-Queueing Discipline

In Section 7.4.5 we described the preemptive version of the Weighted Fair-Queueing algorithm and discussed how it can be used for scheduling aperiodic jobs in general. The original version of Weighted Fair-Queueing (WFQ) algorithm, which is nonpreemptive, was proposed by Demers, *et al.* [DeKS] for scheduling packet transmissions in switched networks. It is also known as the packet-by-packet generalized processor-sharing algorithm. Hereafter in this chapter, by WFQ algorithm, we always mean the nonpreemptive version.

To describe the nonpreemptive version, this time in terms how it may be implemented in a switch, we focus on an output link. Let n denote the number of established connections on the link. Each connection i is allocated a fraction $\tilde{u}_i$ of the link bandwidth. (For the sake of clarity, we sometimes say connection i and packet j, i.e., the jth packet on the connection, when we mean any connection and any packet on the connection. We also call a packet on connection i a connection-i packet.) Let $U = \sum_{i=1}^{n} \tilde{u}_i$ denote the total link bandwidth allocated to all n connections. Without loss of generality, $U \leq 1$. (The implicit assumption is that the switch subjects each new connection request to an acceptance test and rejects the request whenever the requested bandwidth exceeds the available bandwidth.)

Scheduling Packets.   As stated earlier in Section 11.1.5, we assume that the switch is output buffered. The buffer space that holds all packets on connection i being transmitted or waiting to be transmitted is in essence a FIFO queue for the connection. Each connection-i packet is placed at the end of this queue upon arrival without scheduler attention. A packet becomes *ready* for transmission when it reaches the head of the queue, that is, when all connection-i packets that arrived before it have been transmitted. Each packet is removed from the queue when its transmission completes. We say that a connection i is idle when no connection-i packet is waiting or is being transmitted; otherwise, the connection is backlogged.

For the purpose of scheduling ready packets on backlogged connections, the scheduler keeps a priority queue. Each backlogged connection (say connection i) has an entry (fn_i, i) in this queue. The entry gives the *finish number* fn_i of the connection, or more precisely, the finish number of the ready packet on the connection. It also gives the ID i of the connection. (You can find the definition of finish number in Section 7.4.5. We will describe again how this number is computed shortly.) The entries are sorted in order of finish numbers: the smaller the number, the earlier in the queue. Therefore, we call this queue the SFN (Smallest Finish Number first) queue. The only exception to this order is the entry of the packet currently being transmitted. Since scheduling is nonpreemptive, the scheduler keeps this entry at the head of the SFN queue, even when the finish numbers of new entries inserted during the packet's transmission are smaller. Ready packets on backlogged connections are transmitted in the order given by this queue.

Scheduling according to the WFQ algorithm is done as follows:

- When the first packet in a busy interval of the output link arrives, the scheduler computes its finish number and enters this number and connection ID in the SFN queue. It commences the transmission of the packet immediately.
- During a link busy interval, the scheduler computes the finish number of each packet that arrives on an idle connection and inserts the corresponding entry into the SFN queue.
- For as long as the link is busy, whenever the transmission of a packet (say a connection-i packet) on the link completes, the packet is removed from the connection's FIFO queue and the entry containing the finish number of this packet is removed from the head of the SFN queue. The scheduler chooses the next packet to transmit in the following manner.

    (i) If connection i is still backlogged, the scheduler computes the finish number of its new ready packet and inserts this number and connection ID in the SFN queue.

    (ii) It then commences the transmission of the ready packet on the connection identified by the first entry in the SFN queue.

Computing Finish Numbers.   We now restate the rules governing the computation of the finish numbers, which were stated in terms of server budget replenishment in Section 7.4.5. You recall that it is necessary for the scheduler to maintain the current values of the total bandwidth U_b of all backlogged connections and the finish number FN of the link. t denotes the current time, and t_{-1} denotes the previous time instant when FN and U_b were updated. There are n existing connections on the output link of interest here. By the *length* of a packet, we mean the time required to transmit the packet at the transmission rate of the output link. You recall that we normalize time so that the maximum length of all packets transmitted over the link is 1.

Rules for Computing the First Finish Number of a Link Busy Interval

I1 For as long as the link is idle, $FN = 0$, $U_b = 0$, $t_{-1} = 0$, and finish number fn_i of connection i, for every $i = 1, 2, \ldots, n$, is 0.

I2 When the first packet of length e arrives and starts a busy interval of the link,

   (a) set $t_{-1} = t$; and

   (b) the packet being a connection-i packet, increment U_b by $\tilde{u}_i$, compute $fn_i = fn_i + e/\tilde{u}_i$, and insert the entry (fn_i, i) in the *SFN* queue.

Rules for Computing Subsequent Finish Numbers during a Link Busy Interval

R1 For every i, when a connection-i packet arrives at t during a link busy interval, if connection i was idle prior to this arrival,

   (a) increment FN by $(t - t_{-1})/U_b$, compute $fn_i = \max(FN, fn_i) + e/\tilde{u}_i$, and insert the entry (fn_i, i) in the *SFN* queue; and

   (b) set $t_{-1} = t$ and increment U_b by $\tilde{u}_i$.

R2 For every i, when the transmission of a connection-i packet completes,

    (a) if the connection remains backlogged, increment fn_i by $e/\tilde{u}_i$, where e is the length of the new ready connection-i packet, and insert the entry (fn_i, i) in the *SFN* queue;

    (b) if connection i becomes idle,

        i increment the link finish number *FN* by $(t - t_{-1})/U_b$; and

        ii set $t_{-1} = t$, and decrement U_b by $\tilde{u}_i$.

The schedule in Figure 7–14(d) contains no preemption and hence also illustrates this version of the WFQ algorithm. (You recall that the numbers under the time lines in the figure give the real time instants corresponding to the finish numbers of the connections as time progresses.)

Maximum Delay and Queue Length at the First Switch.   The delay between when a packet becomes ready (i.e., when it reaches the head of the FIFO queue of its connection) and when its transmission completes is called its *latency*. Corollary 7.9 allows us to conclude that the latency of a packet on connection i that is allocated the fraction $\tilde{u}_i$ of link bandwidth is bounded from above by

$$L_i = e_i/\tilde{u}_i + 1 \tag{11.1a}$$

where e_i is the maximum length of all connection-i packets. The first term in the right-hand side gives the amount of time required to transmit the largest connection-i packet on a slower link of bandwidth $\tilde{u}_i$ times that of the physical link. The second term accounts for the effect of nonpreemptivity, and the maximum blocking time due to nonpreemptivity is equal to 1. Because of the rate-control function provided by a WFQ scheduler, this upper bound holds independent of the arrival rates of all other connections.

The per hop delay suffered by a packet is equal to the sum of the queueing delay and latency. We now examine the maximum per hop delay $W_i(1)$ that can be incurred by any packet on connection i as the packet transverses the first switch. From queueing theory, we know that this delay is unbounded if there is no constraint on the arrival pattern, even when the fraction $\tilde{u}_i$ of link bandwidth allocated to connection i is equal to the average fraction u_i of link bandwidth required by the connection. (u_i is the utilization of connection i.) Therefore, upper bounds on per hop delay for a connection are usually derived based on some flow specification that constrains the traffic pattern. We suppose here that the arrivals of packets on connection i satisfy the (u_i, E_i) leaky bucket constraint, the connection is allocated the fraction $\tilde{u}_i$ of output link bandwidth, and $\tilde{u}_i = u_i$. From the arguments given in the derivation of Eq. (7.16) and by Parekh and Gallager [PaGa93], the maximum delay per hop incurs when packets of total length E_i arrive at the beginning of a busy interval of connection i[1] and then packets of total length $\tilde{u}_i$ arrive every unit of time.

---

[1]Parekh and Gallager examined what they call "all-greedy GPS system" in which the total length of packets arriving on every connection at the start of a link busy is the maximum possible and showed that per hop delay of each connection is maximum under this condition. This argument, which is similar in spirit to the critical-instant argument we used in earlier chapters, is necessary without the benefit of Corollary 7.9. The corollary allows us to reason about the maximum delay for each connection without regard to the arrivals on other connection. This is why we look at a busy interval of the connection alone.

The total time required to complete the transmission of all packets that arrive at the start of the busy interval is no more than $E_i/\tilde{u}_i + 1$. (This is because the transmission of the first connection-i packet in the busy interval can be blocked for 1 unit of time, but subsequent connection-i packets are never blocked as long as the connection remains backlogged.) From this observation, we see that the per hop delay of any connection-i packet through the first switch suffered by a packet of length e is bounded from above by

$$W_i(1) = (e + E_i)/\tilde{u}_i + 1 \tag{11.1b}$$

It follows that the maximum queue length at the first switch is $E_i + \tilde{u}_i$. Since each packet is held in the buffer until its last bit is transmitted, the required buffer size is $E_i + e_i + \tilde{u}_i$ when $\tilde{u}_i$ is equal to u_i.

Maximum End-to-End Delay and Delay Jitter.   We now look at a connection i that transverses ρ switches. Suppose that only the traffic into the first switch en route is shaped to meet the (u_i, E_i) leaky bucket constraint. The intermediate switches do not do any traffic shaping.

Let us first look at the simple case where the output links transversed by the connection at all switches have the same bandwidth and the connection is allocated the same fraction $\tilde{u}_i = u_i$ of bandwidth. We can deduce the end-to-end delay suffered by a packet through ρ switches from the arrival and departure rates of connection-i packets shown in Figure 11–3. The dashed line in the figure shows the maximum arrival rate of a (u_i, E_i) leaky bucket constrained connection. The departure rate of packets at the first switch is bounded by the two solid lines in the figure. The fastest departure rate occurs when all other connections on the output link are idle, while the slowest departure rate occurs when the total allocated bandwidth of all connections is 1 and all connections are backlogged. The 1 extra unit of delay at each switch is due to the nonpreemptivity of the WFQ algorithm. Since the arrival rate at each subsequent switch is the departure rate of the previous switch, the slowest departure rate of connection-i packets at subsequent switches is as shown. In short, the end-to-end delay of a packet of length e through ρ homogeneous switches under the WFQ algorithm is given by

$$W_i(\rho) = \frac{E_i + \rho e}{\tilde{u}_i} + \rho$$

when the bandwidth allocation $\tilde{u}_i$ is equal to the utilization u_i of the connection.

In general, the output links of switches transversed by connection-i packets may have different transmission rates. To be explicit, for each switch j transversed by the connection i, for $j = 1, 2, \ldots, \rho$, we let $e_{\max}(i, j)$ denote the time required to transmit the largest packet of all connections sharing the same output link with connection i at the switch. Suppose that connection-i arrivals to the first switch satisfy the (λ_i, E_i) leaky bucket constraint with the average arrival rate λ_i measured in terms of bits per unit time, and e and E_i are measured in numbers of bits. Without loss of generality, we assume that the output link bandwidth allocated to connection i at each switch is equal to λ_i. (An allocation smaller than this rate would make the connection unstable, leading to unbounded queueing delay and packet loss. An allocation larger than this rate would lead to a waste in bandwidth.) Then, in terms of these notations, the maximum ρ hop end-to-end delay of a connection-i packet of length e bits is

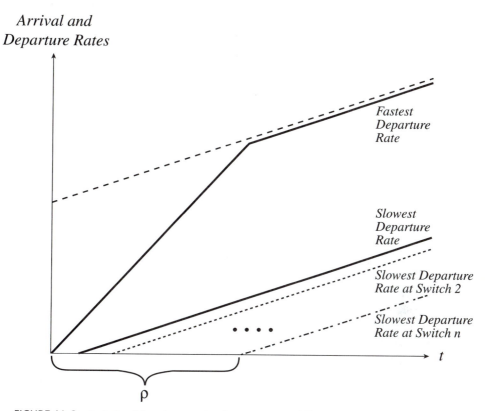

FIGURE 11–3   Arrival and departure rates in a homogeneous multihop network under WFQ algorithm.

equal to

$$W_i(\rho) = \frac{E_i + \rho e}{\lambda_i} + \sum_{j=1}^{\rho} e_{\max}(i, j) \tag{11.2a}$$

Since a packet may be transmitted immediately after it arrives at every switch, the minimum delay is $\rho e/\lambda_i$. Hence, the maximum delay jitter at the ρth switch is

$$\frac{E_i}{\lambda_i} + \sum_{j=1}^{\rho} e_{\max}(i, j)$$

This means that the buffer space BS_i required by connection i grows with the number of switches from the source and is equal to

$$BS_i = E_i + e + \sum_{j=1}^{\rho} \lambda_i e_{\max}(i, j) \tag{11.2b}$$

11.2.2 Rate-Proportional Server (RPS) Model and Algorithm

While the WFQ algorithm offers advantages in delay and fairness, its implementation is complex: the link finish number may be updated up to $O(n)$ times per finish-number computation (and hence scheduling decision). In contrast, a virtual clock computation according to the virtual clock algorithm takes $O(1)$ time, but that algorithm is unfair. In their effort to find approximate implementations of WFQ that retain the merits of WFQ but have complexity $O(1)$, Stiliadis, *et al.* [StVa98a, StVa98b] developed a characterization of algorithmic features that yield bounded delay and fairness. They call it the Rate-Proportional Server (RPS) model. We now define RPS and describe an algorithm, called the frame-based WFQ, which approximates WFQ but has scheduling complexity $O(1)$.

Connection Potentials and Link Potential.   Algorithms that more or less emulate the GPS algorithm all order ready packets for transmission based on some time-varying values of individual connections. These values are called by different names, such as finish number and virtual clock (or deadlines). Stiliadis, *et al.* refer to them all as *potential*.

Generally speaking, potentials of individual connections and the link have the following properties.

1. Within a link busy interval, the potential $\pi_i(t)$ of each backlogged connection i is a nondecreasing function of time t.

2. The link potential $\pi(t)$ at time t is a function of time t and of potentials of existing connections immediately prior to t.

3. When a connection is idle, its potential remains constant. When a packet (say a connection-i packet) arrives at time t while the connection (i.e., connection i) has been idle, the potential $\pi_i(t)$ of the connection is $\max(\pi_i(t^-), \pi(t^-))$, where t^- denotes the instant immediately before t.

Algorithms differ in the ways they compute link potential. To achieve bounded delay, however, link potential must satisfy the following constraints:

$$\pi(t_2) - \pi(t_1) \geq t_2 - t_1 \qquad (11.3a)$$

where both t_1 and t_2 are time instants in the current link busy interval and $t_1 < t_2$. Moreover, for every backlogged connection i,

$$\pi(t) \leq \pi_i(t) \qquad (11.3b)$$

As examples, according to the GPS algorithm, the potentials of all backlogged connections and of the link are equal. In contrast, according to the virtual clock algorithm, the link potential $\pi(t)$ is equal to the current time t while the potentials (i.e., the virtual clocks or deadlines) of individual connections are equal to or larger than t and can be arbitrarily larger than t.

RPS Algorithm.   Like the GPS algorithm, the Rate-Proportional Server (RPS) is an idealized algorithm that cannot be implemented in practice. It also assumes that every connection i is allocated a fraction $\tilde{u}_i$ of the link bandwidth and $\sum_{i=1}^{n} \tilde{u}_i \leq 1$. The scheduler maintains potentials of individual connections and the link as described above. Specifically, the link potential satisfies Eqs. (11.3a) and (11.3b). Moreover, when a connection i is backlogged throughout an interval $(t_1, t_2]$, for $t_1 < t_2$,

$$\pi_i(t_2) - \pi_i(t_1) = \frac{\tilde{w}_i(t_1, t_2)}{\tilde{u}_i} \tag{11.3c}$$

where the attained time $\tilde{w}_i(t_1, t_2)$ of connection i is the amount of time within $(t_1, t_2]$ used to transmit connection-i packets. This equation says that the difference in connection-i potentials at these time instants is equal to the normalized service attained by connection i during the time interval between the instants.

The way in which backlogged connections are scheduled resembles the FB (i.e., preemptive least-attained-time-first) algorithm [Klie]. RPS can be called the least-potential-first algorithm. At any time, packets on backlogged connections with the smallest potential are transmitted on an infinitesmally fine-grain weighted round-robin basis, each connection i attaining service at a rate proportional to its bandwidth allocation $\tilde{u}_i$. It is easy to see that GPS is a special case of the RPS algorithm, when the normalized services $\tilde{w}_i(t_1, t_2)/\tilde{u}_i$, and hence $\pi_i(t)$, for all backlogged connections $i = 1, 2, \ldots, n$ are equal and $\pi(t) = \pi_i(t)$.

11.2.3   Frame-Based Weighted Fair Queueing

The frame-based WFQ (FWFQ) algorithm proposed by Stiliadis, *et al.* [StVa98b] makes use of the above described properties of potential. You recall that a WFQ scheduler updates the link potential (i.e., link finish number) whenever a connection changes from being idle to backlogged and vice versa. In the worst case, this update needs to be done upon each packet arrival and departure and leads to the high complexity of the algorithm. In contract, a FWFQ scheduler time stamps and queues each packet in much the same way as the virtual clock algorithm. Therefore, its scheduling overhead is $O(1)$. The mechanism used by FWFQ to prevent starvation is *recalibration*; the scheduler "periodically" increases the link potential in order to keep it close to the potentials of backlogged connections.[2] Between recalibrations, the link potential increases at the rate of 1 per unit time, just like the link potential of the virtual clock algorithm.

The FWFQ algorithm provides the same latency as the WFQ, but is not as fair. The key parameter that determines fairness is the frame period F. Each recalibration (say the kth) increases the link potential to kF if the link potential is smaller than this value at the recalibration time. The larger the frame period, the less frequent the recalibration and the less fair the FWFQ, but the lower the recalibration overhead. Let $y_i = e_i/\tilde{u}_i$ denote the length of time required to transmit the largest packet on connection i when packets are transmitted according to the GPS algorithm and the connection has the fraction $\tilde{u}_i$ of the link bandwidth. The description of FWFQ below assumes that the frame period F is no less than y_i for every connection i.

Recalibration of Link Potential.   A FWFQ scheduler recalibrates the link potential for the kth time ($k > 0$) when the following conditions become true for the first time since the

---

[2]As you will see shortly, the work done by the scheduler to determine when a recalibration should take place is also of order $O(n)$. However, this work is done on a per recalibration basis.

last recalibration. (It is convenient here to think that there is a recalibration at the start of the current link busy interval and this recalibration is the zeroth.) Again, we take the start of the current link busy interval as the time origin and call the time of the kth recalibration t_k.

1. The potential of every backlogged connection (say connection i) satisfies the following inequality:

$$\pi_i(t_k) \geq kF \tag{11.4a}$$

2. The potentials of all connections are such that

$$\pi_i(t_k) < (k+1)F \tag{11.4b}$$

At recalibration time t_k, the scheduler sets the link potential according to

$$\pi(t_k) = \max(\pi(t_k^-), kF) \tag{11.4c}$$

Between recalibrations, the link potential increases at the rate of one per unit time. In other words,

$$\pi(t) = \pi(t_k) + (t - t_k) \qquad \text{for } t_k < t \leq t_{k+1} \tag{11.4d}$$

By recalibrating link potential $\pi(t)$ in this manner, the scheduler makes sure that the link potential never lags more than F from the link potentials of backlogged connections.

A parenthetical remark is in order here. You will see shortly that we use the terms the potential of a ready packet on a backlogged connection and the potential of the connection interchangeably. This is all right because each backlogged connection has only one ready packet, whose potential is computed when the packet is queued for transmission. The potential of an idle connection is either 0, when the connection has never been backlogged during the current link busy interval, or equal to the potential of the last transmitted packet on the connection.

Scheduling Ready Packets.   Before describing algorithmically how link potential recalibration is done, we first look at how packet transmissions in a link busy interval are scheduled. The scheduler keeps a priority queue in which each ready packet (say on connection i) has an entry (π_i, i). This entry gives the potential π_i of (the ready packet) of the connection and the ID i of the connection. We call this priority queue the SP (Smallest Potential) queue because the entries are in the smallest-potential-first order. (Again, the only exception is the entry of the packet being transmitted at the time; because the scheduler keeps the entry at the head of the SP queue until the transmission completes, this entry may be out of order.) When a packet (say on connection i) becomes ready, the scheduler computes its potential π_i according to the rules described below. It then inserts the entry (π_i, i) in the SP queue. Ready packets are sent in the order that their entries appear in this queue.

Computing Connection Potentials and Link Potential.   The FWFQ algorithm is a packet-by-packet algorithm, which computes the potentials of backlogged connections in a way similar to the virtual clock algorithm, except for the link potential recalibration. The scheduler determines when conditions Eqs. (11.4a) and (11.4b) are true by examining the potential stamps of departing packets. This is done as described below. In the description, t denotes the current time, t_{-1} denotes the time of the last recalibration, and k denotes the next recalibration. e denotes the length of the ready packet being discussed. As you will see, the scheduler marks some packets for the purpose of determining when Eqs. (11.4a) and (11.4b) hold and, therefore, when it needs to recalibrate link potential. It keeps track of the number of marked packets yet to be transmitted using a counter X. The Boolean variable *Flag* is true when some packet has been marked since the last recalibration and is false otherwise.

Rules for Computing the Potential of the First Packet

I1 For as long as the link is idle, $k = 0$, $t_{-1} = 0$, $X = 0$, *Flag* is false, the connection-i potential $\pi_i = 0$, for $i = 1, 2, \ldots, n$, and the link potential $\pi = 0$.

I2 When the first packet of length e arrives and starts a busy interval of the link,

   (a) set $t_{-1} = t$ and increment k by 1;

   (b) the packet being a connection-i packet, compute $\pi_i = e/\tilde{u}_i$;

   (c) if $\pi_i > kF$, mark the packet, set *Flag* to true, and increment X by 1; and

   (d) insert the entry (π_i, i) in the SP queue.

Rules for Computing Subsequent Potentials and Recalibration

R1 For every i, when a connection-i packet arrives at t in a link busy interval, if connection i were idle prior to this arrival,

   (a) compute $\pi_i = \pi + t - t_{-1} + e/\tilde{u}_i$;

   (b) if $\pi_i > kF$, mark the packet, set *Flag* to true, and increment X by 1; and

   (c) insert the entry (π_i, i) in the SP queue.

R2 For every i, when the transmission of a connection-i completes,

   (a) if the packet is marked, decrement X by 1;

   (b) If $X = 0$ and *Flag* is true, do recalibration, that is, set $\pi = \max(\pi + t - t_{-1}, kF)$, increment k by 1, set $t_{-1} = t$, and set the *Flag* to false; and

   (c) if the connection remains backlogged,

   i. compute $\pi_i = \pi_i + e/\tilde{u}_i$;

   ii. if $\pi_i > kF$, mark the packet, set the *Flag* to true, and increment X by 1; and

   iii. insert the entry (π_i, i) in the SP queue.

An Illustrative Example.   Figure 11–4 gives an example to illustrate the recalibration process. The example is similar to the one in Figure 7–14. There are four connections on the output link, called C_i for $i = 1, 2, 3, 4$, in the figure. Their bandwidth allocations are $1/4$, $1/8$, $1/4$ and $3/8$, and the lengths of packets on the connections are 1, 1, 1.5 and 3, respectively. C_4 remains backlogged at all times in the current busy interval. The other three connections become idle after transmitting 5, 4, and 2 packets, respectively. Later at time 31, C_1 becomes backlogged again.

The figure shows the FWFQ schedule when frame period F is 10. The graph below the schedule shows how the link potential varies with time; the arrows above the schedule give the times of recalibration and the value of the link potential immediately after each recalibration.

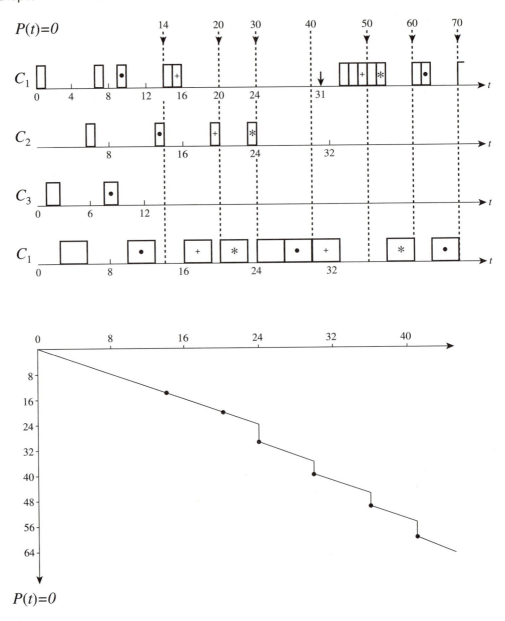

There is a line of mathtext here that would be better done in emacs or TeX.

FIGURE 11–4   Example illustrating frame-based WFQ algorithm: $\hat{u}_1 = 1/4$, $e_1 = 1$; $\hat{u}_2 = 1/8$, $e_2 = 1$; $\hat{u}_3 = 1/4$, $e_3 = 1.5$; $\hat{u}_4 = 3/8$, $e_3 = 3$.

1. When the second packet on C_1 departs, the potential of C_1, which is the potential stamp of the third packet, is equal to 12. Since it is greater than 10 (i.e., F), the third packet is marked. (In the figure, we mark the packet by a dot.) The second packets on each of the other connections are marked (by dots) for the same reason.

2. At time 14, the second packet of C_2 has been transmitted, and there are no more marked packets, that is, X becomes 0. This fact tells the scheduler that Eq. (11.4a) is now true [and Eq. (11.4b) is true as well]. It, therefore, recalibrates link potential. At this time kF is equal to 10. Since the link potential immediately before 14 is 14 (i.e., $t - t_{-1} = 14$), which is larger than 10, the recalibrated link potential is equal to 14.

3. At time 20, the scheduler again finds all the packets marked (by + in the figure) since the last recalibration have been transmitted. It does recalibration; this time the link potential just before recalibration is 20 (i.e., $14 + t - t_{-1} = 20$), which is equal to kF.

4. At time 24, the scheduler finds that all packet marked (by * in the figure) since the recalibration at time 20 have been transmitted, and hence condition [Eq. (11.4a)] is true again. This time, it sets the link potential to 30 as indicated by the figure.

5. After 24, only C_4 is backlogged. Each recalibration increases the link potential. Then at time 31, C_1 becomes backlogged again.

You may want to trace the remaining segment of the schedule yourself as an exercise. We expect that the increases in link potential at each recalibration to be somewhat smaller after time 31 than before time 31 for the same reason that recalibration at time 14 and 20 has no effect on link potential. (Since all connections are backlogged initially and they full utilize the link, the round number according to the GPS algorithm increases at the same rate with real time.)

11.2.4   Delay-EDD and Jitter-EDD Service Disciplines

Delay-EDD [FeVe] and jitter-EDD [VeZF] service disciplines are also well known priority-based service disciplines. These service disciplines rely on the EDF algorithm to schedule the transmissions of packets on each output link. The operations of each switch k according to the delay-EDD discipline are described in Figure 11–5.

Both the delay-EDD and jitter-EDD service disciplines characterize the message stream on each connection by the periodic message model. In other words, the message stream to be transmitted on connection i is $(p_i, 1, D_i)$; the declared peak rate of the connection is one packet per p_i units of time and the end-to-end relative deadline for their delivery is D_i.

Connection Establishment.   The source client requests a connection i by declaring parameters p_i and D_i of the packets on the connection in the request-for-connection message. As the request message is routed from the source to the destination, each switch en route determines whether to accept the connection and if it accepts the connection, what maximum delay it can guarantee and, hence, what local relative deadline to offer to clients. Each switch temporarily sets aside the link bandwidth and buffer space required to guarantee its offered local relative deadline. It then puts the local relative deadline in the request message and forwards the message to the switch downstream.

Upon receiving the request message, the destination client checks whether the sum of the local relative deadlines offered by all switches en route is no greater than the end-to-

Operations of switch k according to Delay-EDD Service Discipline:

- Information maintained by the scheduler for each output link:
  - the total density Δ of all existing connections using the link (initially $\Delta = 0$),
  - the total buffer space BS committed to existing connections (initially, $BS = 0$), and
  - the minimum value $p_{\min}$ of the periods of all existing connections using the link (initially $p_{\min} = \infty$).
- Upon receiving a request message for a connection carrying message stream $(p_i, 1, D_i)$, rejects the connection if $\Delta + 1/p_i \geq 1 - 1/p_{\min}$; otherwise, do the following:
  - computes an offered local relative deadline LD_i (i.e., $min(p_i, 1/(1 - \Delta - 1/p_{\min}))$) and the required bandwidth (i.e., $1/LD_i$) to guarantee this deadline; and increment Δ by $1/LD_i$;
  - computes offered buffer space SB_i and increments BS by SB_i; and
  - puts the values of offered local relative deadline and buffer space in the request message and sends the message to the switch downstream.
- Upon receiving a positive acknowledge message for the establishment of connection i containing values of local relative deadline $D_{i,k}$ and buffer space $bs_{i,k}$ chosen by the destination,
  - sets the local relative deadline of packets on connection i to $D_{i,k}$,
  - decrements Δ by $1/LD_i - 1/min(D_{i,k}, p_i)$,
  - decrements total allocated buffer space BS by $SB_i - bs_{i,k}$
  - updates $p_{\min}$ to $min(p_{\min}, p_i)$.
- Upon receiving a negative acknowledge message for the establishment of connection i, free bandwidth and buffer space set aside for the connection, that is, decrement Δ by $1/LD_i$ and decrement BS by SB_i.
- Upon receiving the jth packet on connection i,
  - stamps the packet with its deadline ($= \max(a_{i,j}, (j - 1)p_i) + D_{i,k}$), and
  - places the packet in the FIFO queue for the connection.
- As long as the FIFO queue for any connection is not empty, transmits the packet with the earliest deadline among the packets at the heads of all the queues.

FIGURE 11–5   Operations of a switch according to delay-EDD service discipline.

end relative deadline D_i of the connection. If this sum is greater than D_i, the connection establishment fails. If this sum is no greater than D_i, the destination client allocates to each switch a local relative deadline that is never less than the local relative deadline offered by the switch. The destination puts the local relative deadline it allocates to each switch in the establishment acknowledgment message. As the acknowledgement message is returned to the source along the same route traversed by the request message, each switch k en route is informed of the local relative deadline $D_{i,k}$ of packets on the new connection i. The switch allocates to the connection the output link bandwidth and buffer space required to meet this relative deadline and frees any extra resources set aside earlier. In this way, the local relative deadline at the switch is determined at connection establishment time.

Rate Control and Scheduling.   At switch k, each packet is transmitted with other packets on the same output link on the EDF basis according to its local deadline. Unlike the WFQ algorithm, the EDF algorithm by itself cannot provide timing protection to any connection against overloads on other connections. The rate-control scheme used in the delay-EDD discipline for the purpose of timing protection works as follows. The deadline $d_{i,j}$ for the transmission of each newly arrived packet (say the jth) on any connection i is not calculated based on its actual arrival time $a_{i,j}$. Rather, it is based on its effective arrival time.[3] The *effective arrival time* $a_{i,1}^e$ of the first packet on each connection i is equal to its actual arrival time $a_{i,1}$. The effective arrival time of the jth packet (for $j > 1$) is given by

$$a_{i,j}^e = \max(a_{i,j-1}^e + p_i, a_{i,j}) \tag{11.5a}$$

The local deadline for the transmission of the jth packet at switch k is

$$d_{i,j} = a_{i,j}^e + D_{i,k} \tag{11.5b}$$

It is easy to see that the deadlines for the transmissions of two consecutive packets on connection i are never less than p_i time units apart. In effect, it is as if the packets were transmitted by a sporadic server $(p_i, 1)$ whose budget is always set to 1 at each replenishment and is consumed in one chunk. That other connections are protected from any overload on connection i follows straightforwardly from principles of such servers. As long as arrivals of packets on connection i do not exceed the declared peak rate, the deadline for the transmission of every packet is equal to $D_{i,k}$ plus its actual arrival time. Since the switch has allocated sufficient output link bandwidth to guarantee this delay, the transmission of the packet surely completes by its deadline, and the delays of packets on connection i through the switch is surely no greater than $D_{i,k}$.

Jitter Control.   According to the delay-EDD discipline, the maximum end-to-end delay of a packet from the source through switch k on connection i can be as large as $\sum_{j=1}^{k} D_{i,k}$. On the other hand, because each packet is queued for transmission as soon as it arrives, its end-to-end delay through the first k switches can be as small as k. Consequently, the delay jitter at the kth switches can be as large as $\sum_{j=1}^{k} D_{i,k} - k$ even when the traffic on connection i is periodic. The jitter grows with the number of hops k from the source, and so is the amount of buffer space required of switch k to prevent packet loss on the connection.

The jitter-EDD discipline [VeZF] is an enhancement of the delay-EDD discipline designed to keep the end-to-end delay jitter at switch k under $D_{i,k}$. Hence, the amount of buffer space required for connection i at the switch constant is independent of how many hops the switch is from the source. The jitter-EDD is a nongreedy discipline. For the sake of shaping the arrival time pattern of packets on each connection, the scheduler holds incoming packets in a holding queue and releases them for transmission at more regularly spaced time instants. To enable the scheduler of switch k to do this, the scheduler of the upstream switch $k - 1$ puts in the header of each packet the ahead time of the packet. The *ahead time* of a packet sent

---

[3]Comparing their definitions, we see that the effective arrival time of the next packet is the same as the release guard, when we view of the transmissions of packets at switch k as instances of a subtask of an end-to-end task. The delay-EDD discipline is greedy: A packet is ready for transmission upon arrival. In contrast, the release-guard protocol is nongreedy: If the transmissions of packets were governed by the release-guard protocol, each packet would become ready for transmission at its effective arrival time. This is the major difference between this rate-control scheme and the release-guard protocol. The release-guard protocol not only provides rate control but also delay jitter control, while delay-EDD scheme does not provide jitter control.

by switch $k - 1$ is equal to the difference between the local relative deadline $D_{i,k-1}$ of the connection and the actual delay of the packet at switch $k - 1$. Upon receiving a packet j with ahead time $ah_{i,j}$, the scheduler calculates the ready time $r_{i,j}$ of the packet according to

$$r_{i,j} = \max(a^e_{i,j}, a_{i,j} + ah_{i,j}) \tag{11.6a}$$

$a^e_{i,j}$ is given by Eq. (11.5a); it is included in the calculation of $r_{i,j}$ for the sake of rate control. The scheduler holds the packet in the holding queue until its ready time. At $r_{i,j}$, the scheduler stamps the packet with the deadline

$$d_{i,j} = r_{i,j} + D_{i,k} \tag{11.6b}$$

and moves it to the ready queue. Once in the ready queue, the packet is scheduled and transmitted with other packets on the EDF basis.

Separation of the Rate-Control and Jitter-Control Functions.   From the description of the jitter-EDD discipline above, it appears that rate-control and jitter-control actions are interwined and exercised at every switch. In fact, the schedulers can compute the ready times of packets in the following simpler way

$$r_{i,j} = \begin{array}{ll} a^e_{i,j} & \text{at the first switch} \\ a_{i,j} + ah_{i,j} & \text{at each of the downstream switches} \end{array} \tag{11.6c}$$

because the values thus obtained are equal to the ones given by Eq. (11.6a) when the end-to-end delay of the connection is guaranteed. This expression tells us that rate control is applied only at the first switch and the downstream switches apply only jitter control.

To see why this simpler implementation is correct, we note that at the first switch, the ahead time of every packet is 0. (We assume here that the source client of any connection i does not use the jitter-EDD discipline to schedule its delivery of packets to the network.) Hence, at the first switch, every packet is ready for transmission at its effective arrival time according to both Eqs. (11.6a) and (11.6c). In effect, the jitter-EDD discipline behaves just like the release-guard protocol when rule 2 of the protocol is never applied. As a consequence, the stream of packets ready for transmission on the connection fits the periodic message model $(p_i, 1, D_i)$.

On a connection whose end-to-end delay is guaranteed, rate control is not necessary at downstream switches, provided that jitter control is applied. Specifically, the scheduler at each switch k simply keeps each packet for $ah_{i,j}$ units of time (i.e., its ahead time) in the holding queue and gives the packet the deadline $a_{i,j} + ah_{i,j} + D_{i,k}$[4] when it moves the packet to the ready queue. We see that the jitter-EDD discipline behaves like the MPM protocol at subsequent switches. Section 9.4.1 showed that this protocol preserves at each switch downstream the pattern of ready times at the first switch when the delays of packets at all switches indeed never exceed the respective local relative deadlines. The end-to-end jitter is always less than the local relative deadline of the connection at the last switch. The advantage of this simpler

---

[4]As it turns out, when the delay of every packet at all the upstream switches never exceeds the respective local relative deadlines, Eqs. (11.6a) and (11.6c) give the same ready time for every packet. Problem 11.3 asks you to prove the truth of this statement by induction.

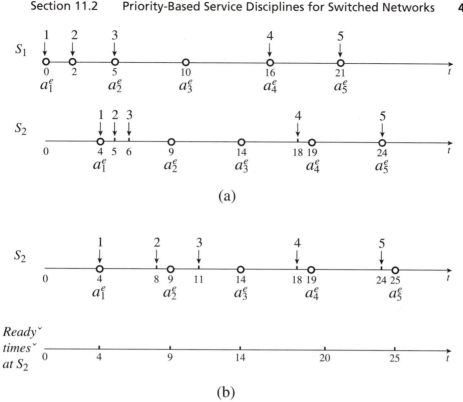

FIGURE 11–6   Example illustrating the delay-EDD and jitter-EDD discipliens.

computation of packet ready times is that there is no need for the scheduler at any downstream switch to maintain the state information needed to compute the effective arrival times of the packets on every connection.

Figure 11–6 gives an example. The declared message stream on the connection is $(5, 1, D)$, where D is satisfiable when every switch guarantees the local relative deadline 4. The arrows above the time line labeled S_1 show the arrivals of five packets at the first switch on the connection. The arrival of packet 1 starts the current busy interval. We take as the time origin the arrival time of this packet. If the delay-EDD discipline is used, the effective arrival times of the packets are 0, 5, 10, 16, and 21, and their local deadlines are 4, 9, 14, 20, and 25, respectively. Since the packets are ready for transmission upon arrival, the arrival pattern at the second switch shown by the time line labeled S_2 in part (a) is possible; the delays of the packets are 4, 3, 1, 2, and 3, respectively. (Here, the constant propagation delay between switches is taken to be 0. To account for this delay, we can simply shift these times by this constant delay.) At the second switch, the packets are ready for transmission when they arrive at times 4, 5, 6, 18, and 24. However, their effective arrival times are 4, 9, 14, 19, and 24.

Now suppose that the jitter-EDD discipline is used at all switches. At the first switch, the packets are ready for transmission at their effective arrival times 0, 5, 10, 16, and 21. If the packets have the same delays of 4, 3, 1, 2 and 3, their arrival times at the second switch are 4, 8, 11, 18, and 24. These time instants are marked by arrows above the time line labeled

S_2 in Figure 11–6(b). The packets are held in the holding queue for 0, 1, 3, 2 and 1 units of time (i.e., their ahead times), respectively. As a result, they become ready for transmission at 4, 9, 14, 20, and 25. The traffic patterns at both switches are the same: The ready time of each packet at the second switch is equal to 4 (the local relative deadline) plus its ready time at the first switch. As we expect, both Eqs. (11.6a) and (11.6c) give the same values, and it is unnecessary for the scheduler at the second switch to compute the expected arrival times of the packets (which, by the way, are 4, 9, 14, 19, and 24, respectively.)

Scheduling Overhead and Buffer Requirement.   To compute the ready times and deadlines of packets on each connection, the scheduler at the first switch on each connection must maintain for the connection the effective arrival time of the next packet. This information is not necessary at the subsequent switches since the schedulers at these switches need not compute the effective arrival times.

The scheduler may maintain one queue for each output link. In that case, the complexity of inserting each packet into this queue is $O(\log BS)$, where BS is number of buffers (and therefore the maximum length of the output queue) allocated to all connection. Figure 11–5 says that the scheduler maintains a FIFO queue of maximum length $bs_{i,k}$ for each connection, where $bs_{i,k}$ is the number of buffers allocated to the connection. Since packets on the same connection have the same relative deadline, they are sorted among themselves according to their absolute deadlines in the FIFO queue. Thus, the selection of the packet with the earliest deadline can be done in $O(\log n)$ time, where n is the number of connections sharing the output link.

By design of the jitter-EDD discipline, the delay jitter of packets on each connection at any switch is never more than the local relative deadline. Consequently, the number of buffers required for the connection i at switch k (for $k > 1$) is equal to $D_{i,k-1}$ (or $\lceil D_{i,k-1} \rceil$ when $D_{i,k-1}$ is not an integer).

11.2.5   Fixed-Priority Discipline

All the algorithms described so far in this section are dynamic-priority scheduling algorithms. An alternative is to schedule packets on each connection according to a fixed priority. This is what the RCSP discipline [ZhFe] does.

The RCSP discipline characterizes the message stream on each connection i according to the FeVe model [i.e., the message stream on each connection i is $(p_i, \overline{p}_i, I_i, D_i)$]. At connection establishment time, the scheduler at each switch along the route of the connection request message first chooses a priority for the connection. In order to increase the success rate of connection establishment, the switch gives the requested new connection as high a priority as it can feasibly support, that is, none of the existing connections will be adversely affected by the new connection. In general, if the information on the chosen route is available, this choice could be based on one of the priority-assignment algorithms described in Section 9.4.2. It can also be based other considerations, such as the importance of the connection and the type of message stream carried on it. It may even be chosen or suggested by the source or destination client of the connection.

After choosing the priority for the requested connection i, the scheduler at switch k computes the local relative deadline $D_{i,k}$ that the switch can offer to the connection; $D_{i,k}$ is the maximum possible delay of packets on the connection at switch k. Zhang and Ferrari

[ZhFe] propose that the scheduler use the time-demand analysis method for the purpose of determining $D_{i,k}$.

The end-to-end relative deadline that can be guaranteed for each connection is simply the sum of the local relative deadlines offered by all switches on the route used by the connection request message. Again, the destination client can choose to relax the guarantee and handle this relaxation and the acknowledgement of the connection request in the same way as it is done according to the delay-EDD and jitter-EDD disciplines.

The complex of the admission scheme based on time-demand analysis is high. An alternative is to schedule the connections on the rate-monotonic or deadline-monotonic basis and compute the local relative deadline based on one of the schedulable utilizations in Section 6.7. In addition to being simpler to implement, an important advantage of this alternative is that the scheduler can allocate a fraction of the output link bandwidth to each connection at establishment time, knowing that the guarantee to existing connections will not be violated later when it accepts a new connection provided there is sufficient spare output link bandwidth to give to the new connection.

From the discussion on synchronization protocols in Section 9.4.1, we know that it is essential for every switch on the route of a connection scheduled on a fixed-priority basis to exercise rate or jitter control even when the input traffic on each connection is well behaved at the first switch. Otherwise, the delay at the switch may not be bounded. One way is to apply the release-guard protocol at the first switch, with rule 2 of the protocol disabled, for the purpose of regulating the rate of the traffic entering the network and apply the MPM protocol at downstream switches to preserve the traffic pattern shaped at the first switch. This is just what the jitter-EDD discipline does.

11.3 WEIGHTED ROUND-ROBIN SERVICE DISCIPLINES

Except for defining the term in Chapter 4, we have thus far ignored *Weighted Round-Robin* (WRR) algorithms. The reason is that these algorithms are unsuitable for scheduling precedence-constrained jobs, which were our primary focus. However, messages in a switched network are pipelined through the switches; earlier packets in a message are sent from a switch without having to wait for the arrivals of later packets. For scheduling message transmissions through switches, and for pipelined jobs in general, the WRR scheme offers an excellent alternative to time-driven and priority-driven schemes. Its major advantage over the time-driven scheme when used for end-to-end scheduling in a network or distributed system is that it does not require globally synchronized clocks. The major advantage of the WRR scheme over priority-driven schemes is that it does not require any sorted queue. These advantages make the WRR scheme a good practical choice, especially for constant bit-rate traffic such as uncompressed voices. Indeed, some forms of the WRR scheme have been implemented in ATM networks (e.g., [SaKK]).

This section describes four variants of the WRR scheme that have been proposed for scheduling message transmissions in packet-switched networks. The section focuses on constant bit-rate messages. These messages fit the periodic message model, so the message stream on each connection i is $M_i = (p_i, e_i, D_i)$. Here, the parameters in the tuples are parameters of instances of M_i, not those of individual packets as in the previous section. So, p_i is the minimum interarrival time of message instances on connection i, e_i is the maximum number of packets in each message (instance), and D_i is the end-to-end relative deadline for delivery of every message. The summary section (Section 11.8) of this chapter lists the performance of WRR algorithms for scheduling constant bit-rate message streams.

11.3.1 Greedy WRR Discipline

In its simplest form, the WRR scheduling algorithm works as follows. During connection establishment, the scheduler at each switch assigns to the new connection i a weight wt_i. This means that that connection i is allocated wt_i slots in each *round* during which packets on all existing connections sharing the same output link are transmitted in turn. Each *slot* has length 1, the time to transmit a maximum-size packet.

Throughput and Delay Guarantees.   Specifically, during each round, if more than wt_i packets on connection i are waiting, wt_i packets are transmitted. If wt_i or fewer packets are waiting, all packets on the connection are transmitted. After the scheduler completes the transmission of packets on connection i, it proceeds to transmit packets on connection $i + 1$ in the same manner; except, of course, the maximum number of packets on connection $(i + 1)$ transmitted per round is wt_{i+1}. In this way, each connection i is guaranteed wt_i slots in each round.

A design parameter of each switch is the maximum number of slots RL per round. We call this parameter the *round length* (of the output link). At all times, the sum of weights of all n connections on the output link is no greater than RL, that is, $\sum_{i=1}^{n} wt_i \leq RL$. Each connection i is guaranteed the throughput rate of wt_i / RL, and this guarantee is never violated due to overloads on other connections.

The upper limit on the round length RL (and consequently the maximum weight assigned to any connection) is imposed by the delay guarantee that the switch provides to each connection. A packet may have to wait for an entire round even when there is no other packet on the connection waiting at the switch when it arrives. Hence, to guarantee that every instance of every message be transmitted within a period of the message, RL must satisfy

$$RL < p_{\min} \tag{11.7a}$$

where $p_{\min}$ is the minimum of the periods of messages on all existing connections. Moreover, the weight wt_i of each connection i must satisfy the following constraint.

$$wt_i \geq \left\lceil \frac{e_i}{\lfloor p_i / RL \rfloor} \right\rceil \tag{11.7b}$$

That each instance of M_i is transmitted within one period follows directly from the fact that there are at least $\lfloor p_i / RL \rfloor$ rounds within each period of M_i and at least e_i packets are transmitted within this many rounds. On the other hand, if connection i were assigned a smaller weight than the lower bound in (11.7b), the throughput provided to connection i would be lower than the declared peak rate e_i / p_i of its message. The delay of packets on the connection may grow without bound.

Since each message in M_i takes at most $\lceil e_i / wt_i \rceil$ rounds to complete, the delay of the message through a switch is at most equal to $\lceil e_i / wt_i \rceil RL$. A packet sent in a round at a switch is eligible for transmission at the next downstream switch. Therefore, the message suffers this delay only at the first switch but only one more additional round of delay through each of the subsequent switches. Therefore, the end-to-end delay W_i of a message on a connection i that traverses ρ switches is bounded from above by

$$W_i \leq (\lceil e_i / wt_i \rceil + \rho - 1)RL \leq p_i + (\rho - 1)RL \qquad (11.8)$$

when the round lengths at all ρ switches en route are RL.

Connection Establishment.   Because weights of all connections on an output link depend on the round length used for the link, a change of the latter may require changes of the weights. It would be too costly for the scheduler to adjust the round length dynamically as a part of acceptance test and admission of new connections. For this reason, the round length used at each switch is chosen a priori based on the characteristics of all types of traffic the switch is designed to carry. In particular, the round length used for each output link satisfies the constraint Eq. (11.7a) for all anticipated connections.

Admission control and connection establishment in a network that uses the WRR discipline are simple. Again, the request for each new connection provides as part of the flow specification the parameters p_i, e_i, and D_i of the message stream M_i to be carried by the new connection i. The scheduler of each switch computes the weight wt_i required by the connection according to the expression in the right-hand side of Eq. (11.7b). If the sum of weights assigned to all existing connections is no more than $RL - wt_i$, the scheduler accepts the connection and allocates wt_i slots per round to the connection. Otherwise, the scheduler rejects the connection. If all ρ switches on the route selected for the connection accept the connection and the end-to-end delay computed according to Eq. (11.8) does not exceed the end-to-end relative deadline D_i of M_i, the connection is admitted and established. Otherwise, the connection establishment fails and the schedulers at switches en route free the slots assigned to the connection when informed of the failure.

Delay Jitter and Buffer Requirements.   The WRR discipline is greedy and, hence, rate allocating. The actual throughput of a connection can exceed its guaranteed rate. Like all other greedy disciplines, the greedy WRR discipline does not control delay jitters. The end-to-end delay of a message can be as small as $e_i + \rho - 1$. (This occurs when every packet is transmitted in 1 unit of time after its arrival at all ρ switches en route.) Therefore, the end-to-end delay jitter of can be as large as $p_i - e_i + (\rho - 1)(RL - 1)$.

At the kth switch from the source of a connection i, the end-to-end delay jitter is $p_i - e_i + (k - 1)(RL - 1)$. Because of this delay jitter, the amount of buffer required at switch k for connection i to prevent packet loss is $(1 + \lceil (k - 1)(RL - 1)/p_i \rceil)e_i$ packets. As expected, this amount grows linearly with the number of hops from the source. Again, the way to fix this problem is to do some form of traffic shaping at each switch, and this is the motivation of the various nongreedy variants of the WRR discipline.

11.3.2   Time-Driven WRR Disciplines

This and the next subsection describe three nongreedy WRR disciplines, which use different mechanisms to control delay jitters. They are the Stop-and-Go (S&G) algorithm [Gole], Hierarchical Round-Robin (HRR) algorithm [KaKK], and the Budgeted Weighted Round-Robin (BWRR) algorithm [Phil]. The former two are purely time-driven, while the BWRR algorithm is not.

S&G Algorithms.   We note that according to the greedy WRR algorithm, the actual length of a round varies with the amounts of traffic on the connections sharing the link. In contrast, the S&G algorithm fixes the lengths of rounds by dividing the time into intervals, called *frames*, that have fixed length *RL*. If a connection i is allocated wt_i slots per frame, the scheduler transmits up to wt_i packets in each frame, just as it would according to the WRR algorithm. However, because frames begin at fixed-time instants, the number of packets transmitted per *RL* units of time is never more than wt_i, even when some slots are idle and more packets on connection i are waiting. In this way, the S&G algorithm controls the transmission rate of every connection.

Specifically, at a switch that uses the S&G algorithm, the scheduler divides the time into frames of length *RL*. A packet arriving at the switch during the jth ($j \geq 1$) frame is eligible for transmission during the $(j+1)$st frame. This can be accomplished by having the scheduler maintain two queues (also called frames) for each output link: the input queue and the output queue. During any frame, the former holds the arriving packets that will be transmitted on the output link in the next frame, and the latter holds the packets being transmitted on the output link during the current frame. The scheduler swaps the input and output queues at end of each frame. Hence these queues are usually called the *next* and *current* queues, respectively. On a well-behaved connection i that is allocated a weight equal to the lower bound given by Eq. (11.7b), the delay of each message at the first switch is bounded from the above by $p_i + RL$. The end-to-end delay of messages on connection i through ρ switches is bounded from the above by $p_i + \rho RL$.

A packet that arrives at the first switch during the jth frame is eligible for transmission at the switch during the $(j + 1)$st frame, during the $(j + 2)$nd frame at the second switch, during the $(j + 3)$rd frame at the third switch, and so on. Hence the end-to-end delay jitter at every switch consists solely of the delay jitter introduced at the switch, which is less than $2RL$. Because there must be wt_i spaces in the input queue and an equal amount in the output queue for each connection i, the total buffer space required per connection is $2wt_i$. There is no packet loss if the flow rate of each connection is regulated at the source so that no more than wt_i packets arrive at the first switch in any frame.

An implicit assumption in the argument above is that the clocks (and hence frames) of the switches are synchronized, so when we factor out the constant propagation delay between switches, the frame in which a packet is transmitted from a switch k begins at the same time as the frame in which it arrives at the next downstream switch $k + 1$ for every $k \geq 1$. If the frames of different switches are not synchronized, the end-to-end delay through ρ switches can be as large as $p_i + (2\rho - 1)RL$, and the amount of buffer space required for a connection with weight wt_i at each switch is $3wt_i$.

Hierarchical Round-Robin Algorithm.   We note that the maximum end-to-end delay and delay jitter achievable by the S&G algorithm depends solely on the round length *RL*. It is necessary to use different round lengths for different types of connections requiring different end-to-end relative deadline and delay-jitter guarantees. This is the rationale of the HRR algorithm.

The HRR algorithm uses different round lengths for different levels of guaranteed service: the higher the level, the shorter its round length (called frame time in [KaKK]). It is convenient to think of a switch that provides X levels of guaranteed services as having X servers for each output link, one per service level. Each server has a pair of input and output queues. Incoming packets on a connection serviced at level x are placed in the input queue of server x. The scheduler allocates weights to servers and schedules the servers according to this weight. When server x is scheduled, it transmits packets on the connections serviced by it in the stop-and-go round-robin manner. There is also a best-effort server, which transmits nonreal-time packets when scheduled.

To be specific, we let service level 1 be the highest and service level x be higher than level y if $x < y$ for $x, y = 1, 2, \ldots, X$. For each service level x, the scheduler divides the time into frames of fixed length RL_x. The frame lengths for the X service levels are such that $RL_x < RL_y$ if $x < y$. Each server x has weight sw_x: The scheduler schedules the server for sw_x slots of time in each frame of length RL_x. Kalmanek, et al. [KaKK] use a time-driven, hardware implementation of the HRR algorithm. The implementation requires three counters per service level and some combinational logic circuits to transfer of the control among service levels.[5] The best-effort server is scheduled in the background at leftover time not used by the X guaranteed server.

To guarantee that each service level x has the constant fractional bandwidth sw_x / RL_x, the frame lengths and weights of the servers must be chosen so that all the servers are schedulable. To guarantee the declared rate of a real-time connection i that has the message stream (p_i, e_i, D_i) and is serviced at level x, the weight wt_i allocated to the connection must be at least equal to $\lceil e_i / (\lfloor p_i / RL_x \rfloor) \rceil$. Therefore, during connection establishment, a new connection i can be accepted and serviced at level x if the sum of its required weight and the weights of all the existing connections serviced at level x are no greater than the weight sw_x of server x. The end-to-end delay of a connection i with this weight wt_i is at most equal to $p_i + \rho RL_x$ and the end-to-end delay jitter of the connection never exceeds $2RL_x$. Finally, the amount of buffer space required for the connection is $2wt_i$ when the frames are synchronized.

11.3.3   Budgeted Weighted Round-Robin Algorithm

Like the S&G and HRR algorithms, the Budgeted Weighted Round-Robin (BWRR) algorithm [Phil] is nongreedy and rate-controlling. It is designed to achieve the performance of synchronized S&G and HRR algorithms. Unlike these algorithms, however, the BWRR algorithm does not divide time into fixed-length frames and hence does not require a synchronized clock.

Budget and Budget Consumption.   Rather, the BWRR algorithm controls the transmission rate of each connection using a budgeting mechanism similar to that used by sporadic servers. For the purpose of describing this mechanism, we focus on a connection i. We assume that the flow rate of the connection is such that no more than wt_i packets per round (of length RL) are delivered to the first switch on the connection, where wt_i is the weight assigned to the

---

[5]It is not necessary to schedule the servers in a time-driven manner. We can view each server x as a periodic task, whose period is RL_x, execution time is sw_x, and relative deadline is RL_x. The scheduler schedules the servers rate-monotonically.

connection by all switches en route to the connection.[6] The objective of the BWRR algorithm is that wt_i packets can be transmitted per RL units of time at each switch but no more than wt_i packets.

Initially when a connection i is established, the scheduler at each switch sets the budget bgt_i to the weight wt_i of the connection and the next replenishment time nrt_i of the connection at 0. (The nrt_i being 0 may sound strange, but we will clarify this point shortly.) The connection is eligible when its budget is nonzero. The scheduler transmits packets on all eligible connections on the WRR basis. It decrements the budget bgt_i of connection i each time it transmits a packet on the connection. A connection i is no longer eligible when the budget of the connection is exhausted (i.e., $bgt_i = 0$) and becomes eligible again when its budget is replenished.

Rationales of Budget Replenishment Procedure.   It may help us to understand the budget replenishment procedure of the BWRR algorithm better if we keep in mind the following similarity and difference between this algorithm and the sporadic server algorithm(s). You recall that the sporadic server algorithm(s) determines when to replenish the budget of a sporadic server based on when sporadic jobs arrive and when their executions begin. Similarly, the times at which the budget of a connection is replenished depend on arrivals and transmissions of packets on the connection. According to the BWRR algorithm, the scheduler keeps track of the reception of each group of wt_i packets on connection i and sets the replenishment time upon the arrival of the last packet in each group. (We will describe how below.)

The budget of a sporadic server is replenished at computed replenishment times, and to do this, the processor must have a timer for each sporadic server. This is reasonable because there is only one or a few sporadic servers on a CPU. In contrast, replenishing the budget of each connection at the computed replenishment times of the connection would incur an unreasonable amount of overhead. Philp [Phil] pointed out that this overhead can be saved if the scheduler does budget replenishments for connection i only at times when it stops transmitting packets on connection $i - 1$, the one serviced before connection i in each round. In other words, whenever it is the turn of connection i, the scheduler replenishes the budget of the connection if the budget is supposed to be replenished at or earlier than the current time. We will see shortly that replenishment times are set at RL or more units apart. Because of this and the fact that the scheduler does this checking every round, the amount of budget the connection has when the scheduler is servicing the connection is the same as when the budget is replenished at the computed next replenishment time nrt_i.

Because the actual budget replenishment may take place later than the time given by nrt_i, at any time after nrt_i, the replenishment at nrt_i may or may not be pending. In order to be able to determine which is the case, the scheduler maintains a pending flag pg_i which it sets to true after each update of the next replenishment time nrt_i of connection i and to false when it replenishes the budget of the connection i. Initially this flag is false, indicating that the budget was set to wt_i at $nrt_i = 0$, and this replenishment is not pending.

---

[6]This assumption is made to simplify the description of the BWRR algorithm. (Because of this assumption, the schedulers of all switches operate in the same manner). In reality, on a connection i whose flow rate is (p_i, e_i), a message of length e_i may be delivered as a whole every p_i units of time to the first switch. The operations of the scheduler at the first switch differ from that of schedulers at downstream switches. The replenishment procedure presented here must be modify for the first switch. This is left to you as an exercise in Problem 11.7.

Finally, we need to keep in mind that even when no more than wt_i packets per round enter the network and no more than wt_i packets per RL units of time are transmitted by upstream switches, a switch downstream may received two groups of wt_i packets within a time interval of length RL. (This occurs when the earlier group is transmitted late in the earlier round and the later group is transmitted early in the later round.) To keep track of the arrival of a later group of wt_i packets that arrive before a pending replenishment has taken place, the scheduler also maintains a variable srt_i (second replenishment time). srt_i keeps the value of the replenishment time following the next pending replenishment time nrt_i.

Budget Replenishment Procedure.   In summary, the information the scheduler maintains for each connection i are the budget bgt_i, the next replenishment time nrt_i, the second replenishment time srt_i, and the pending flag pg_i. When the connection is established, these variables are set to wt_i, 0, 0, and false, respectively. The scheduler keeps track of the reception of each group of wt_i packets on connection i. The budget bgt_i of connection i is replenished only at times when the scheduler gets ready to transmit packets on the connection. The scheduler updates the information on the connection at these times as well as upon the receipt of the last packet in each group of wt_i packets following the two rules below.

1. Upon the receipt of the last packet in each group of wt_i packets on connection i, the scheduler sets nrt_i to the current time plus RL and the pending flag pg_i to true, if pg_i is false (and hence the budget has been replenishment since nrt_i). If the pending flag pg_i is true, the scheduler sets srt_i to max($current\ time$, nrt_i) plus RL.
2. Whenever the scheduler stops transmitting packets on connection $i - 1$ and the pending flag pg_i is true, it sets the budget bgt_i to wt_i if the current time is later than nrt_i. If $srt_i > nrt_i$, it sets nrt_i to srt_i; otherwise, it sets the flag pg_i to false because there is no more pending replenishment.

After taking care of budget replenishment, the scheduler transmits packets on connection i for as long as bgt_i is nonzero or there are packets on the connection to transmit.

Figure 11–7 illustrates the operations of the scheduler at the second switch S_2 of a connection i according to the BWRR algorithm. A group of wt_i is transmitted in every one of the first three rounds from the first switch S_1. The last packets of the three groups arrive at the second switch S_2 at times a_1, a_2 and a_3; these times are indicated by arrows marked by the variables in the figure. The arrows marked by rt_j and t_j for $j = 1$, 2 and 3 indicate, respectively, the jth value of nrt_i and the jth time when the scheduler checks on behalf of the connection whether there is a budget replenishment pending and replenishes the budget if there is. The bottom two diagrams give the values of bgt_i and pg_i as functions of time.

1. At time a_1, the budget bgt_i is wt_i and flag pg_i is false. The scheduler sets nrt_i to the current time plus RL, indicated by rt_1, and the flag pg_i to true.
2. At time a_2, the second group of wt_i packets arrives, the flag pg_i is true. nrt_i being later than a_2, the scheduler sets the srt_i to nrt_i plus RL, which is indicated by rt_2
3. At time t_1 when the scheduler stops transmitting packets on the previous connection, it sees pg_i being true, but nrt_i is rt_1, that is, the pending replenishment is supposed to take place later. Hence the scheduler does nothing. However bgt_i is wt_i at the time, so

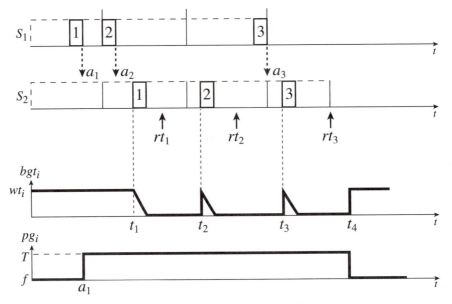

FIGURE 11–7   Example illustrating the BWRR algorithm.

the scheduler commences to transmit packets on connection i and continue to transmit them until bgt_i becomes 0.

4. In the next round, when it is the turn of connection i (at t_2), the scheduler sees that pg_i is true. Now the value of nrt_i (being rt_1) is earlier than current time. The scheduler sets the budget to wt_i. Because srt_i is larger than nrt_i, the scheduler sets nrt_i to srt_i ($= rt_2$). After thus taking care of the budget, the scheduler proceeds to transmit packets on the connection.

5. At time a_3 when the third group of packets arrives at S_2, the scheduler again sees that the replenishment at $nrt_i = rt_2$ is pending. It sets srt_i to a_3 plus RL because a_3 is later than rt_2.

6. At time t_3, the scheduler sets the budget bgt_i to wt_i and nrt_i to srt_i, which is shown as rt_3 in the figure. The third group of packets is transmitted and the budget of the connection is zero afterwards.

7. At time t_4, the budget bgt_i is set at wt_i again. This time, srt_i is equal to nrt_i. The scheduler sets to the flag pg_i to false. The connection becomes idle. Hereafter, until the arrivals of new packets, the values of bgt_i and pg_i remain unchanged.

Performance of BWRR Algorithm.   To find the per hop and end-to-end delay of a connection i, we look at the delay of any packet in each group of wt_i packets on the connection through a switch. Because when the connection is established its budget bgt_i is set to wt_i, each packet in the first group is transmitted within RL units of time from its arrival. After the last packet of the group is transmitted, the budget of the connection is exhausted, and the scheduler turns its attention to the next connection. However, upon the arrival (say at time t)

of the last packet in each group, the next replenishment time is set at no later than RL units after t. Therefore, packets in the subsequent group are surely transmitted within RL units after their arrivals. The per hop delay is bounded from above by RL, and Eq. (11.8) also gives an upper bound to the end-to-end delay of packets on connection i through ρ switches scheduled according to the BWRR algorithm. In other words, the BWRR algorithm can guarantee the same maximum end-to-end delay as the greedy WRR algorithm.

To see how large the delay jitters of messages transmitted according to the BWRR algorithm can be, we note that the delay of any message at the first switch is never less than $wt_i + (\lceil e_i/wt_i \rceil - 1)RL$. If the output links at switches downstream are idle upon the arrival of every packet in the message, the delay suffered by the packet at each downstream switch is 1. Consequently, the end-to-end delay of message is bounded from below by $wt_i + (\lceil e_i/wt_i \rceil - 1)RL + \rho - 1$. The maximum end-to-end delay jitter of the message is $(\rho - 1)RL - wt_i + 1$.

Although the end-to-end delay jitter bound of the BWRR algorithm grows with the number of switches on the route used by a connection, the number of buffers required per connection is $2wt_i$ at all switches. To see why, let us look at the transmissions of two consecutive groups of wt_i packets through two consecutive switches. Suppose that the first group is transmitted at switch k at time t. The second group can be transmitted as early as $t + wt_i$. Since the switch $k + 1$ downstream may transmit the earlier group as late as $t + RL$, it requires at least $2wt_i$ buffers for the connection. Now, let us look at the third group following these two groups. The earliest time at which there is budget to transmit the third group at switch k is $t + wt_i + RL$. When this group arrives at switch $k + 1$, the first group has already left. Therefore, $2wt_i$ buffers are sufficient for the connection.

The extra overhead required by the BWRR algorithm over that of the greedy WRR algorithm is the time required to maintain the variables nrt_i, srt_i and pg_i for each connection i. This overhead is constant, independent of the number n of connections sharing the same output link.

11.4 MEDIUM ACCESS-CONTROL PROTOCOLS OF BROADCAST NETWORKS

In our terminology, the transmission medium of a broadcast network is a "processor." A Medium Access-Control (MAC) protocol is a discipline for scheduling this type of processor. Scheduling the transmission medium is done distributedly by network interfaces of hosts in the network. This is why MAC protocols typically either look different or are in fact different from the scheduling algorithms described earlier. (Thus far, the scheduling algorithms we have described are for centralized scheduling by a single scheduler or by a set of distributed schedulers emulating a global scheduler.) Indeed, some MAC protocols are designed for distributed scheduling by loosely coupled schedulers, and they are fundmentally different from centralized scheduling algorithms.

This section first describes briefly the protocols used in Controller Area Networks (CANs) [ISO93] and IEEE 802.5 [IEEE89] token rings. In essence these protocols are ways to implement centralized scheduling in a distributed manner. It then describes two MAC protocols that are based on a distributed scheduling model and designed for distributed scheduling. They are the timed-token MAC protocol [ACZD] and the priority-based reservation scheme [ShSS]. The former is used in several network standards (including the Fiber Distributed Data Interface (FDDI) [ANSI], IEEE 802.4 [IEEE85], and the Survivable Adaptable Fiber Optic Embedded Network (SAFENET) [KoPa]). The latter was proposed for the IEEE 806.6 Distributed Queue Dual Bus (DQDB) metropolitan area network standard [IEEE90a]. These protocols are no longer as important as they were because of the declined usage of the networks for which they were developed. However, the algorithmic aspects of these protocols are relevant to distributed scheduling in general and worthy of our attention.

Hereafter, we call the transmission medium of a network simply the network. A *station* on the network is the network interface of a host on the network. We continue to call each basic unit of data transmitted nonpreemptively over the network a packet. (Such a unit is usually called a frame, but we have already used the term earlier to mean something else.) The statement that a station *listens* means that it monitors the data on the network, and that it *hears* or *sees* means that it senses the presence of data or some special bit patterns on the network.

Each station maintains its own outgoing and incoming queues as shown in Figure 11–1. Except for where it is stated otherwise, we assume that the header of each packet contains the address of the destination station (or the ID of the message). When a station is not transmitting, it listens on the network. It copies the packet into its buffer (i.e., it receives the packet) when it hears its own address in the packet header (or the ID of a message it is prepared to receive). We focus here on the real-time aspects of the MAC protocols.

11.4.1   Medium Access Protocols in CAN and IEEE 802.5 Token Ring

We measure the size of a broadcast network in term of the ratio of the network round-trip delay to the transmission time of a maximum length packet. If this ratio is small (say on the order of 10^{-2} or smaller), every station can hear the transmission of every other station almost immediately after the transmission starts. We say that the network is small when this ratio is small. In a small network, circulating control information among the stations takes a small fraction of packet transmission time. The stations on the network can coordinate their decisions and actions without incurring significant performance penalty. By so doing, they can carry out a centralized scheduling algorithm in a distributed manner.

Fixed-Priority Scheduling in CAN.   Controller Area Networks (CANs) [ISO93] are examples of very small networks. CANs are used to connect components of embedded controllers. An example is an automotive control system, whose components control the engine, the brakes, the environment, and so on, of a car. At the transmission rate of one Mbits (or 500 Kbits) per second, the end-to-end length of a CAN must be no greater than 50 meters (or 100 meters). This means that within a fraction of a bit-time (i.e., the length time required to transmit one bit) after a station starts to transmit, all the stations on the network can hear the transmission. Therefore, functionally, the network behaves like a local bus. In particular, the outputs of all stations are wire-ANDed together by the bus: The bit on the network during a bit-time is a logical "0" if the output of any station is a "0" and a logical "1" only when the outputs of all stations are "1." The MAC protocol for CANs takes advantage of this feature.

Each message stream transmitted in the network has a unique message ID. Each packet in the stream begins with this ID, with the most significant bit first. A station on the network determines whether to receive a packet based on the ID number of the packet. (The packet does not contain the source and destination addresses.) Finally, a packet contains 1 to 8 bytes of data.

In principle, the CAN MAC protocol is a CSMA/CD (Carrier-Sense Multiple Access/Collision Detection) protocol. A station with a packet to send waits until it hears that the network is idle and then commences to transmit the ID number of the packet. At the same time, the station listens. Whenever it hears a "0" on the network while it is transmitting a "1", it interrupts its own transmission. In this way, network contention is resolved in favor of the packet with the smallest ID among all contending packets.

As a consequence, packets in each message stream are given a fixed priority that is equal to the ID of the message: the smaller the ID, the higher the priority. Packets are transmitted nonpreemptively according to their priorities. As the ID number is 11 bits, the network supports 2048 priority levels. This is a sufficiently large number of priority levels; we do not need to be concerned with schedulability loss due to the finiteness of priority levels. The schedulability of the message streams can be determined using existing methods for fixed-priority scheduling.

Prioritized Access in IEEE 802.5 Token Rings.   In an IEEE 802.5 token ring network [IEEE89], packets are transmitted in one direction along a circular transmission medium. A station transmits a packet by breaking the network and placing its packet on the output link to the network. As the packet circulates around the network, the station(s) identified by the destination address in the packet header copies the packet. When the packet returns to the source station, the station removes the packet from the network.

Polling.   Network contention is resolved by a polling mechanism called *token passing*. For the purpose of polling, each packet has in its header an 8-bit Access Control (AC) field. One of the bits in an AC field is called the token bit. By examining this bit in the current packet on the network, a station can determine whether the network is busy (i.e., some station is using the network and the packet is a data packet from the station) or the network is free (i.e., the packet is a polling packet). As a polling packet circulates around the ring, the stations are polled in a round-robin manner in the order of their physical locations on the ring. The polling packet is called the *free token* and, when there is no possibility of confusion, simply the *token*.

When a free token reaches a station that has outgoing packets waiting, it can seize the token (i.e., stop it from circulating) under the condition described in the next paragraph. After it seizes the token, it changes the token bit to mark the token busy and transmits packet(s) in its outgoing queue. When the station completes its transmission, it generates a free token and transmits the free token downstream. Afterwards, it continues to relay the token and data packets of other stations as long as its outgoing queue is empty.

Priority Scheduling.   Prioritized access is made possible by using the two groups of 3 bits each in the AC field: Their values represent the token priority Π_T and the reservation priority Π_R. Specifically, the 3 token priority bits give the priority of the token. A station can seize the free token only when its outgoing packet has an equal or higher priority than the token priority Π_T. When a station seizes the token, it leaves the token priority unchanged but sets the reservation priority to the lowest priority of the network. It then marks the token busy and puts the token in the header of the packet and transmits the packet.

Reservation for the next turn to use the network is done distributedly during the transmission of a data packet in the following manner. As a data packet circulates around the ring, a station with outgoing packets can make a reservation for future use of the network by setting the reservation priority bits in the AC field to the highest priority π of its outgoing packets, if π is higher than Π_R. When the data packet returns to the source station, the reservation priority Π_R is equal to the highest priority of all packets waiting at all stations to be transmitted on the network.

When a source station removes its own packet from the network, it saves the reservation priority carried in the packet. Suppose that when the source station transmits a free token, it sets the token priority of the token to this reservation priority or the highest priority of its outgoing packets, whichever is higher.[7] In this case, the priority arbitration mechanism allows the stations to jointly carry out any fixed-priority scheduling algorithm. [As an example, it is common to divide messages into classes, depending on whether they are synchronous (i.e., periodic) or asynchronous (i.e., aperiodic), urgent or not urgent. Packets in messages of any class can be given the same priority.] Even the EDF algorithm is possible with this priority arbitration mechanism if the round-trip delay of the network is small and the clocks of the stations are synchronized.

Schedulability Analysis.   Strosnider, *et al.* [StML] demonstrated how existing schedulability analysis methods can be applied to determine the schedulability of message transmissions on an IEEE 802.5 token ring. The amount of time each packet occupies the network is equal to its transmission time plus the round-trip delay it takes to return to the source station. For the purpose of schedulability analysis, we use this amount as the "execution time" of the packet transmission. The round-trip delay includes the propagation delay of the transmission medium itself, plus the delays introduced by stations on the network. This delay is usually on the order of 10^{-2} or less of the packet transmission time. By including this delay and the time used to transmit the packet header, the checksum, and the delimiting bits in the execution time, the overhead introduced by framing the user data according the MAC protocol can be taken into account.

In addition, we need to take into account the following three factors.

1. Context switching: A context-switch time is equal to the amount of time required to transmit a free token, plus the round-trip delay of the network, which is an upper bound of the time the token takes to reach the station whose outgoing packet(s) has the highest priority among all outgoing packets during the transmission of the latest data packet.

2. Blocking: Since packets are transmitted nonpreemptively, we also need to take into account the blocking time due to nonpreemptivity. Moreover, a high-priority packet that arrives at a station just after the header of the current data packet passed the station may need to wait for a lower-priority packet. (The lower-priority packet is from a station upstream, and the priority of the next free token is set at the priority of this lower-

---

[7]According to the IEEE 802.5 protocol, the source sets the priority of the free token at the maximum of the token priority, the reservation priority, and the highest priority of its own outgoing message. Because of this action, it is possible for a free token to remain unclaimed. The protocol allows a station whose outgoing packets have lower priorities than the priority of a free token to set the reservation priority to the highest priority π of all its outgoing packets if the reservation priority carried in the free token is lower. If a free token remains unclaimed and returns to the source station, the source station lowers the token priority to the reservation priority before sending the free token back to the network again.

priority packet.) The blocking delay caused by this priority inversion must also be taken into account. Hence, the total blocking time is equal to twice the maximum execution time.

3. Limited priority levels: Since the network provides only eight priority levels, schedulability loss should also be taken into account.

*11.4.2 Timed-Token Medium Access-Control Protocol

When the transmission medium is a bus, stations can poll each other by circulating a polling packet (also called a token) according to a token circulation list. The list gives the polling order. Each station polls the next station downstream according to the circulation list by broadcasting a token that has the address of the next station in the header. A station may transmit its data packet(s) only when polled. When it completes its transmission, it transmits the token to the next station downstream. Many bus networks, such as the IEEE 802.4 token bus [IEEE85], use this token-passing scheme. Even networks (such as FDDI [ANSI]) in which the transmission medium is a ring can use it, rather than the fixed circulation list determined by the physical locations of the stations on the ring.

The prioritized medium access-control method in IEEE 802.4 and FDDI standards is called the *timed-token MAC method*. Conceptually, it resembles the weighted round-robin approach. However, because scheduling decisions are made distributedly by all stations without close coordination, the timed-token method differs from the WRR scheme significantly in behavior.

The timed-token MAC protocol divides all messages on the network into two major classes: the *synchronous class* and the *asynchronous class*.[8] Synchronous messages are periodic messages and have deadlines, and asynchronous messages are aperiodic messages. Each station sets aside some network bandwidth for the transmission of synchronous messages and transmits asynchronous messages on a time available basis.

Protocol Parameters.   The amount of the bandwidth allocated to synchronous messages by a station depends on the values of two protocol parameters. A protocol parameter is the *Target Token Rotation Time* (*TTRT*) of the network. This is a global parameter; all stations have the same *TTRT*. It is chosen at network initialization time. *TTRT* is the expected amount of time the token takes to circulate around the network, that is, the expected length of the interval between two consecutive times a station is polled. (A commonly used expression is two consecutive token visits of a station.) *TTRT* is analogous to the round length *RL* of the WRR scheme. While the actual round length never exceeds *RL* according to the WRR scheme, the actual token rotation time may exceed *TTRT*, because each station decides on how long it keeps the token. The timed-token MAC protocol is designed to take this possibility into account.

Each station k has a local protocol parameter SA_k, called the the *synchronous allocation* of the station. The station k can transmit synchronous messages for as long as SA_k units

---

[8]The protocol further divides asynchronous messages into classes depending on the urgency of the messages. This division is not relevant to the discussion here.

of time each time it receives the token. So, the expected synchronous network bandwidth allocated to synchronous messages from station k is equal to $SA_k/TTRT$. However, because the actual token rotation time can exceed $TTRT$, the actual synchronous network bandwidth of the station can be smaller.

The protocol parameters are not independent. The synchronous allocations of different stations can be arbitrary provided their sum does not exceed $TTRT$, that is,

$$\sum_{i=1}^{m} SA_k \leq TTRT \tag{11.9a}$$

where m is the number of stations on the network. We again ignore the propagation delay τ of the token around the network. When we want to take into account this factor, we can subtract the factor from $TTRT$ in our calculations. The fraction of time wasted due to propagation delay is $\tau/TTRT$, and the maximum total utilization of all messages schedulable on the network is $1 - \tau/TTRT$.

The target token rotation time in turn must be bounded from above by the periods of synchronous messages on the network. When these messages are periodic, that is, $M_i = (p_i, e_i)$, for $i = 1, 2, \ldots, n$, we must have

$$TTRT \leq p_i/2 \qquad \text{for } i = 1, 2, \ldots, n \tag{11.9b}$$

This constraint arises from the fact that a station with a message (p_i, e_i) can transmit every instance of the message within one period only if the token visits the station at least once during every period. The time between two consecutive visits of the token at any station is bounded from above by $2TTRT$. (We will return to explain the reason shortly.) In general, the relative deadline D_i of a message may not be equal to its period p_i. The term p_i in Eq. (11.9b) should be replaced by D_i when $D_i < p_i$.

Operations and Behavior.   Again, according to the timed-token MAC protocol, a station with packets to transmit waits until it receives the token. When it receives the token, it can transmit synchronous messages for no more than SA_k units of time.

Whether a station can transmit asynchronous messages after transmitting its synchronous messages depends on whether the token returns to the station early or late. For the purpose of determining whether the token is early or late, each station keeps track of the arrival time t_{-1} of the token during the previous visit. Let t_0 denote the arrival time of the token at the station during the current visit. If $t_0 - t_{-1} \geq TTRT$, the token is late, and the station transmits the token immediately after its synchronous messages. When the token is not late, the station transmits asynchronous messages for at most $TTRT - t_0 + t_{-1}$ units of time.

To implement the timed-token MAC method, each station k maintains a timer, called the *token rotation timer TRT_k*, and uses it to keep track of the elapsed time since the last arrival of the token at the station. The timer is set to $TTRT$ upon the first arrival of the token. Once set, the TRT_k timer counts down until either the token arrives again or the timer expires (i.e., the count zeros), whichever is sooner. If the token arrives before the expiration of the timer, the remaining count of the timer upon the token arrival gives the amount time the station can transmit asynchronous messages. After saving this count so it can use the count to time the duration of asynchronous message transmission, the station sets the timer TRT_k again to $TTRT$. If the timer expires before the arrival of the token, the timer is set to $TTRT$ upon expiration. In this case, the token is late. A flag LC is set to indicate this fact. The station does not send any asynchronous messages and does not set the timer TRT_k if the flag LC is set when it receives the token. It simply resets the flag, sends its synchronous messages for SA_k or less units of time and transmits the token to the station downstream. The station repeats this procedure upon subsequent arrivals of the token.

In short, the stations jointly try to keep the time between two consecutive visits to any station within $TTRT$. When no station transmits any asynchronous message and the synchronous allocations of all stations satisfy Eq. (11.9), the token indeed visits each station every $TTRT$ or less units of time. The timed-token method behaves just like the greedy WRR scheme. Because asynchronous messages are transmitted sometimes, however, the time between consecutive visits of the token to a station k can exceed $TTRT$. In the worst case, the length of time between the consecutive arrival times of the token at any station can be as large as $2TTRT$ [SeJo]. [One way this can occur is if (1) the token leaves a station k at time t, (2) because there is no traffic on the network, the token returns to the station k immediately after t, (3) the station transmits asynchronous messages until time $t + TTRT$, and then (4) because every station now has synchronous messages waiting, the token takes another $TTRT - SA_k$ units of time to return to the station.]

The Synchronous Bandwidth Allocation Problem.   An important question is how to choose the synchronous allocations of stations so that all synchronous messages can be delivered on time. For the purpose of this discussion, it is more convenient for us to focus on synchronous messages and ignore the stations from where they originate. We speak of the synchronous allocation assigned to each message and token visits to (the station transmitting) the message. This view leads to no loss of generality, because the synchronous allocation of a station is equal to the sum of the synchronous allocations of all its synchronous messages. When there is no possibility of ambiguity, we call synchronous messages simply messages.

The synchronous bandwidth allocation problem can be stated follows: We are given a set of n messages in the network, and they are $M_i = (p_i, e_i)$, for $i = 1, 2, \ldots, n$. The total utilization U of all messages on the network is $\sum_{i=1}^{n} e_i/p_i$. We are also given the target token rotation time $TTRT$ of the network, and it satisfies the constraints in Eq. (11.9). The problem is to choose the synchronous allocation SA_i of each message M_i in such a way that all the deadlines of the messages are met whenever it is feasible to do so. An algorithm which determines the synchronous allocations of all messages based on the parameters of the messages is called a *Synchronous Bandwidth Allocation* (SBA) *scheme*. An SBA scheme is *valid* only if it satisfies the protocol constraint in Eq. (11.9a). It is *feasible* if it is valid and it guarantees that all instances of all messages are transmitted by their deadlines.

Deadline Constraint on Synchronous Allocations.   Clearly, for a scheme to be feasible, the amount of time available to transmit every message M_i in any period of length p_i must be at least equal to e_i. This requirement imposes a lower bound on the synchronous allocation SA_i of every message M_i.

To determine this lower bound, we examine Figure 11–8 which shows the worst-case condition from the point of view of message M_i; under this condition, the amount of time available for the transmission of M_i is minimum. The time origin on the horizontal axis is

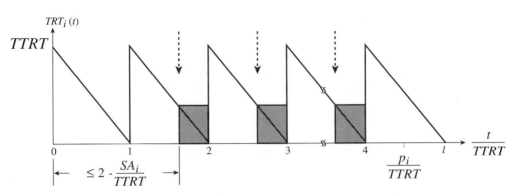

FIGURE 11–8   The worst-case condition under which the time avaiable to M_i is minimum.

the beginning of a period of the message. The vertical axis is labeled $TRT_i(t)$; it gives the remaining time in the token rotation timer of (the sending station of) message M_i as a function of time t since the beginning of the period. The heavy dashed arrows mark the times of token arrival. The shaded boxes indicate the time available for the transmission of message M_i. Shortly before time 0, the token rotation timer TRT_i was set to $TTRT$. The time at which the token arrives for the first time since time 0 can be as late as $2TTRT - SA_i$. This is what is shown in the figure. Subsequently, the token returns every $TTRT$ units of time. Because the TRT_i timer alway expires before the token arrives, no asynchronous message is transmitted. From this figure, we see that the number of token visits within a period of the message can be as small as $\lfloor p_i/TTRT \rfloor - 1$. The synchronous allocation SA_i for message M_i must be satisfy the following constraint:

$$SA_i \geq \frac{e_i}{\lfloor \min(D_i, p_i)/TTRT \rfloor - 1} \tag{11.10}$$

so that at least e_i units of time are available to transmit M_i within every period of M_i or, if the relative deadline D_i of M_i is less than p_i, within D_i units of time. Agrawal, *et al.* [ACZD] calls this constraint the *deadline constraint* for message M_i. *The set* $\{SA_i\}$ *of the synchronous allocations chosen by a feasible SBA scheme must satisfy the constraints in Eqs. (11.9) and (11.10).*

Performance of Simple SBA Schemes.   Agrawal, *et al.* [ACZD] suggested that we measure the performance of SBA schemes the same way we measure the performance of algorithms for scheduling periodic tasks in general, that is, by their schedulable utilizations. As long as the total utilization U of all synchronous messages is no greater than the schedulable utilization U_X of an SBA scheme X, all deadlines are met when the synchronous allocations of all messages are determined according to scheme X. The higher the schedulable utilization of an SBA scheme, the better the scheme.

At a quick glance, the SBA problem may appear to be as simple as the problem of assigning weights to periodic messages in the WRR schemes. Several simple schemes seems to be reasonable; examples are the full-length allocation scheme, the equal allocation scheme, the proportional allocation scheme, and the normalized proportional allocation scheme. The synchronous allocation SA_i assigned to the message M_i according to these schemes are, e_i,

$TTRT/n$, $u_i TTRT$, and $(u_i/U)TTRT$, respectively, where $u_i = e_i/p_i$ is the utilization of message M_i, U is the total utilization of all messages, and the relative deadline of every message is equal to its period. The former three schemes use only local information, while the normalized proportional scheme requires information on U, which is global.

Unfortunately, all of these simple schemes have very low schedulable utilizations. Agrawal, *et al.* [ACZD] showed that the schedulable utilizations of the full-length allocation and proportional allocation schemes asymptotically approach 0, and the schedulable utilization of the equal allocation scheme is $1/(3n - 1)$, which is also small when there are a large number n of messages. Even the schedulable utilization of the normalized proportional scheme is only $1/3$.

To gain some insight into why these schemes work so poorly, we look at some of the examples developed by Agrawal, *et al.* for this purpose. Without loss of generality, let us suppose that the minimum period of synchronous messages is 1. Equation (11.9b) constrains the target token rotation time $TTRT$ to be no greater than $1/2$. ε denotes an arbitrarily small positive number, which is less than $TTRT$

Now, suppose that the network has two synchronous messages; they are $M_1 = (1, (1 - TTRT)\varepsilon)$ and $M_2 = ((2 - \varepsilon)/\varepsilon, (2 - \varepsilon)TTRT)$. The total utilization U is ε, that is, arbitrarily small. Yet, the full-length allocation scheme is invalid because the sum of the synchronous allocations of the messages thus assigned is at least equal to $2TTRT$; the protocol constraint of Eq. (11.9a) is violated.

Similarly, suppose that the network has two messages $M_1 = (1, (1 - TTRT)\varepsilon)$ and $M_2 = (1 + TTRT - \varepsilon, (1 + TTRT - \varepsilon)\varepsilon TTRT)$. Their total utilization U is equal to ε. If their synchronous allocations are assigned according to the proportional allocation scheme, SA_1 is equal to $(1 - TTRT)TTRT\varepsilon$ and SA_2 is equal to $TTRT^2\varepsilon$. The amount of time allocated to M_2 during any of its periods cannot exceed $\lfloor p_2/TTRT \rfloor SA_2$. Substituting into this expression the values of p_2 and SA_2, bounding $\lfloor x \rfloor$ by x and observing that $TTRT \leq 1/2$, we find that this amount is less than e_2, the execution time of M_2. In other words, despite the arbitrarily small total utilization of the messages, the proportional allocation scheme is not feasible.

Finally, suppose that the network has three messages $M_1 = (1, \varepsilon)$, $M_2 = (1.5 - \varepsilon, \varepsilon)$, and $M_3 = (3, 1 - 3\varepsilon)$ for some small positive number ε that is less than $1/3$, and $TTRT$ is equal to $1/2$. The total utilization of the messages is $1/3 + \varepsilon/(1.5 - \varepsilon)$, which is less than $1/3 + \varepsilon$. The synchronous allocation SA_2 of M_2 according to the normalized proportional scheme is equal to $e_2/(1 + 4\varepsilon/3)$, which is less than e_2. Since the token is available for the transmission of M_i only once within one period of the message in the worst case, the message may misses some of its deadlines. This example illustrates that the normalized proportional allocation scheme may be infeasible when the total utilization of messages exceeds $1/3$. Agrawal, *et al.* proved that as long as the total utilization is less than $1/3$, this scheme is feasible. You can find the proof for this schedulable utilization in [ACZD] and the citations in the paper.

Global versus Local SBA Schemes.   Because the performance of simple SBA schemes is poor, it is necessary to use a more complex scheme. Since synchronous allocation of each message is computed only during acceptance test time when a new message stream is inserted into the network, a higher complexity of the SBA scheme is tolerable, if the SBA scheme is a local scheme. By *local SBA scheme*, we mean one according to which the synchronous allocation of each message is chosen based only on the parameters of the message or the parameters of the subset of synchronous messages from the same station. So, the full-length, equal allocation and proportional allocation schemes are local schemes.

In contrast, a *global SBA scheme* chooses synchronous allocation of each message based on the parameters of all messages. The normalized proportional allocation scheme is an example. The overhead of admitting a new synchronous message into the network and guaranteeing the timely delivery of all existing synchronous messages according to a global scheme is high. It includes, of course, the overhead of maintaining global information and the time required to compute synchronous allocations. Arguably, this overhead may be tolerable. More seriously, however, the synchronous allocations of all existing messages (and hence all stations in the network) must be changed upon the admission of each new message. The management overhead thus incurred can be prohibitive. For this reason, global SBA schemes (such as the one based on the linear programming formulation [HaSH]) is suitable only for closed systems which do not allow new synchronous messages to be added on-line.

Although no local SBA scheme can be optimal [HaSH], some do perform reasonably well. (Here by a scheme being optimal, we mean that the scheme surely finds a feasible set of synchronous allocations if such a set exists.) An example is the KaMZ SBA scheme developed by Kamat *et al.* [KaMZ]. Given a message $M_i = (p_i, e_i, D_i)$ and the target token rotation time *TTRT*, the KaMZ scheme first computes the integer $x_i = \lfloor D_i/TTRT \rfloor$. The synchronous allocation SA_i is equal to

$$SA_i = \frac{\max(x_i TTRT/p_i, 1)e_i}{\lfloor D_i/TTRT - 1 \rfloor}$$

Kamat *et al.* showed that the set of synchronous allocations satisfies the protocol and deadline constraints and, therefore, is feasible provided the total utilization of all messages is no greater than

$$\hat{U}_{\text{KaMZ}} = \frac{\lfloor D_{\min}/TTRT - 1 \rfloor}{\lfloor D_{\min}/TTRT + 1 \rfloor}$$

where $D_{\min}$ is the minimum relative deadline of all the messages on the network. Moreover this schedulable utilization is tight, that is, there is a set of messages whose total utilization is slightly larger than the bound and for which this set of synchronous allocation is not feasible. Since *TTRT* should be no more than $D_{\min}/2$ is this case, the schedulable utilization of this scheme is at least equal to 1/3, the schedulable utilization of the normalized proportional-allocation scheme.

Choice of Target Token Rotation Time.   Thus far, we have assumed that the target token rotation time *TTRT* is given. We now ask what choice of *TTRT* may work better. To answer to this question, we must take into account the propagation delay τ of the token round the network, which we have ignored thus far. Since the fraction $\tau/TTRT$ of the time (and network bandwidth) is lost, we must multiply all the expressions of schedulable utilization discussed above by $1 - \tau/TTRT$ when $\tau/TTRT$ is not negligibly small.

We note that Eq. (11.10) follows from the fact that in any time interval of length t, the number of token visits to any station can be as small as $\lfloor t/TTRT - 1 \rfloor$. The term minus one in this expression is due to the delayed first visit of the token; it is the major factor contributing to the poor performance of the SBA schemes described earlier. We can reduce the effect of this factor by making the target token rotation time *TTRT* smaller. On the other hand, to keep the fraction of lost bandwidth due to a token circulating the network small, we want to make *TTRT* as large as possible.

*11.4.3   Medium-Access Control in DQDB Networks

Figure 11–9 shows a Distributed-Queue Dual Bus (DQDB) network, the type of network for which the IEEE 806.6 metropolitan area network standard [IEEE90a] was developed. As its name implies, a DQDB network has two undirectional buses, called bus A and bus B. The slot generator at the head end of each bus generates 53 octet slots on the bus; a station places its outgoing data for stations downstream using these slots. Together, the buses provide the stations with full-duplex capability.

There are two types of slots on the network: preallocated (PA) slots and Queue-Arbitrated (QA) slots. PA slots are for isochronous traffic. Allocation to bandwidth provided by PA slots is done centrally by the bandwidth manager and virtual circuit server (BMVS). QA slots are for asynchronous traffic. As an example, during connection establishment and tear down, stations and the BMVS communicate via QA slots. Access to these slots is scheduled distributedly by individual stations and the BMVS.

Centralized Allocation of Isochronous Bandwidth.   We now focus on how PA slots on one bus are allocated to isochronous connections using the bus. These slots are divided into groups; the slot generator generates a slot every 125 microseconds periodically for each

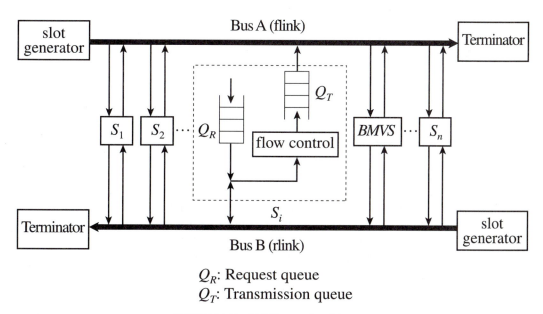

Q_R: Request queue
Q_T: Transmission queue

FIGURE 11–9   DQDB network architecture.

group. Each slot group is identified by its Virtual Circuit Identifier (VCI). The header of every PA slot contains the VCI of the group to which the slot belongs.

Connection Establishment.   The basic unit of bandwidth allocation is a 64-kbits/sec channel. The 64-kbits/sec bandwidth of a channel is provided by one octet in every slot of a PA slot group (i.e., 8 bits per slot times 8 kilo-slots per second). Since the data field of each PA slot contains 48 octets, each PA slot group provides 48 isochronous channels. Each of these channels is identified by a 2-tuple of group number and offset; the latter specifies the octet within the slot used by the channel. As examples, channels $(33, 7)$ and $(177, 42)$ are the seventh octet of the slots in group 33 and the forty-second octet of the slots in group 177, respectively.

A connection consists of one or more isochronous channels. A source station requests connection by sending the BMVS a request containing the source and destination IDs of the new connection and the requested number of channels. The BMVS accepts the request when there are sufficient free isochronous channels to meet the request; otherwise, it rejects the request. When it accepts a request, the BMVS first finds and allocates to the new connection the octets to be used by the connection. (If the BMVS finds that the current PA slot group does not provide a sufficient number of usable octets to satisfy the new request, it chooses a new VCI and requests the slot generator to generate a new PA slot group with this VCI.) The BMVS then sends to the source station the VCI(s) and offset(s) which identify the corresponding isochronous channel(s) it has just allocated to the connection. The source station passes this information to the destination(s). Hereafter, the source sends data on the connection via the channel(s), and the destination copies the data carried on the channel(s). The channel(s) used by a connection is freed when the connection is torn down.

Sharing Isochronous Channels among Connections.   The utilization of a bus critically depends on how the BMVS uses available isochronous channels to meet the demands of connections. To illustrate, we consider the example in Figure 11–10. The network has eight stations. Suppose that there are two connections on bus A; they are called $x_1(1, 3; 2)$ and $x_2(5, 8; 3)$. These connections are represented by solid arrows labeled by their names. The parameters of each connection give the IDs of the source and destination stations and the number of isochronous channels used by the connection. (So, the first two parameters of $x_1(1, 3; 2)$ tell us that x_1 is from station 1 to station 3, and the last parameter tells us that it uses two channels.)

We say that two connections *intersect* if the bus segment connecting the source and destination of one connection overlaps with the bus segment connecting the source and destination of the other connection. The connections are *disjoint* if they do not intersect. From Figure 11–10, it is evident that connections x_1 and x_2 are disjoint. Disjoint connections can use the same channels. The BMVS can minimize bandwidth utilization by exploiting this fact. In our example, the total number of isochronous channels required by both connections x_1 and x_2 is 3, not a total of 5. (Station 5 simply overwrites the data from station 1 when the octets they share pass by.) On the other hand, suppose that rather than x_2, the second connection were $x_3(2, 6; 4)$, which is represented by the dashed arrow. x_1 and x_3 are not disjoint and cannot share any channel. Consequently, the total number of isochronous channels required by x_1 and x_3 is 6.

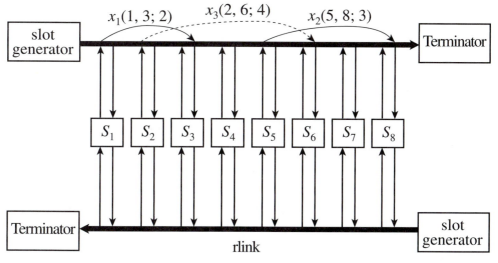

FIGURE 11–10   Example of isochronous channel reuse.

If the BMVS exploits channel sharing, but makes no attempt to maximize sharing, then it can use a simple $O(n)$ algorithm (where n is the number of connections) such as the following one. Upon receiving a request for connection $x_i(src_i, dest_i; m_i)$, the BMVS (1) finds the subset $\mathbf{X}_{\text{disj}}$ of existing connections that are disjoint from x_i and the total number l of channels allocated to connections in $\mathbf{X}_{\text{disj}}$. (2) If $l \geq m_i$, the BMVS meets the new request by allocating to the new connection m_i of the channels used by $\mathbf{X}_{\text{dist}}$; if $l < m_i$, the BMVS makes up the shortfall with free channels. The BMVS can find the subset $\mathbf{X}_{\text{dist}}$ with the aid of an interval graph. In an interval graph $(\mathbf{X}, \mathbf{Y})$, there is a vertex x_j in the vertex set $\mathbf{X}$ for every existing connection. There is an edge $y_{j,k} = (x_j, x_k)$ in edge set $\mathbf{Y}$ between vertices x_j and x_k if the connections represented by them intersect. When servicing a request, the BMVS first adds the new connection x_i and edges adjacent to the vertexes into the graph. A vertex is in $\mathbf{X}_{\text{disj}}$ if it is not adjacent to x_i.

Optimal Channel Allocation.   The problem of how to maximize sharing of isochronous channels by disjoint connections, and thus maximizing the utilization of the channels, is known as the *(isochronous) channel reuse problem* [HuLi]. Stating it generally, we are given a set of k existing connections $x_1, x_2, \ldots, x_k$ and a set of l requests for new connections $x_{k+1}, x_{k+2}, \ldots, x_{k+l}$. We want to find an allocation of isochronous channels to all connections in such a way that (1) the existing connections continue to use the channels already allocated to them and (2) the requirements of the new connections are met with a minimum number of additional isochronous channels.

In a special case of the channel reuse problem, all connections require an identical number of channels. Huang, *et al.* [HuLi] formulated the case as an interval graph coloring problem. In this formulation, the vertex set $\mathbf{X}$ of the interval graph contains a vertex for every existing or new connection. A coloring of a graph is a mapping from $\mathbf{X}$ onto a set $\mathbf{C}$ of integers, in such a way that every pair of adjacent vertexes are mapped onto different integers in $\mathbf{C}$. (Intuitively, the integers represent available channels, and a mapping of a vertex x_i to an integer

j represents an allocation of the channel represented by j to connection x_i. The restriction on coloring reflects the restriction that intersecting connections cannot share channels. The cardinality of **C** is the total number of isochronous channels used by connections in **X**.) In the problem given here, the vertexes representing existing connections are already colored. The objective is to color the vertexes representing new connections with a minimum number of additional colors. This problem is a generalization the vertex coloring problem. (The vertex coloring problem is the special case where none of the vertexes are already colored and can be solved in polynominal time.) Huang, *et al.* showed that the general problem of coloring partially colored interval graphs is NP-complete and proposed a near-optimal algorithm to solve the problem. Unfortunately, the time complexity $O(n^3)$ of the algorithm is high, where n is the number of connections.

IEEE 802.6 Distributed Scheme for Scheduling Queue-Arbitrated Slots.   In contrast to centralized scheduling of PA slots, access to QA slots is scheduled in a distributed manner by the stations and BMVS. (BMVS is a station also; hereafter, we will not mention it separately.) To describe how, we return to Figure 11–9 and focus on scheduling data transmission on one of the buses, say bus A. Each unit of data is carried by a QA slot generated by the slot generator at the head end of the bus. A distributed reservation scheme is used to provide all stations with priorized access to QA slots. To reserve QA slots, the stations send requests piggybacked on data slots on bus B. (These buses are also called *flink* and *rlink*, respectively, in the figure. Since the longer names are more informative than A and B, we now call the buses by these names.)

Priority-Based Reservation.   To facilitate priority-based reservation of QA slots on the flink, each slot on rlink has a request field. According to IEEE 802.6, this field contains 4 request (REQ) bits, one for each of the four priority levels supported by the protocol. A station makes a request by setting the REQ bit corresponding to the priority of its request. In the discussion below, we call a slot on rlink containing a "1" at one of the REQ-bit positions a request, and the priority of the request is indicated by which of the 4 REQ bits is "1."

Each station maintains a prioritized request queue Q_R as shown in Figure 11–9. (The figure shows only the queues for access QA slots on flink by station S_i. There is an identical set of queues for the station's access to QA slots on rlink. For the moment, we ignore the transmission queue which is also shown in the figure. As you will see shortly, IEEE 802.6 protocol does not use this queue. Later, we will use the queue to explain desired properties of reservation schemes.) The request queue holds not only the station's own requests waiting to be sent, but also preempted requests from stations upstream on the rlink. The latter arise because the reservation request is preemptive. By this, we mean that a station lets a request from a station upstream on rlink passes only if it has no request to make or its requests have lower priorities. If the station has an equal or higher-priority request waiting to be sent, it copies the passing request, replaces the passing request by the waiting request, and inserts the copied request in its own request queue. (In other words, the station sets the higher priority REQ bit in the passing slot, resets the REQ bit that was set, and queues a request of the priority of the preempted request.) It then repeats this process in order to send the preempted request on rlink, either using an empty request slot (i.e., one containing no request) or by preempting a passing request.

We say that a request is serviced when the requesting station gets to use a QA slot and thus satisfies the request. A request is outstanding after it is sent until it is serviced. According to IEEE 802.6 reservation scheme, a station can make only one request at a time; hence each station has at most one outstanding request at any time. This restriction is for the sake of fairness.

A QA slot is busy when its BUSY bit is set, indicating that the slot carries data; otherwise, the slot is free. In order to determine when it can use a free QA slot to satisfy its outstanding request, each station maintains a count of the number of outstanding higher-priority requests from stations upstream on rlink (i.e., downstream on the flink). It increments the counter whenever it sees a higher-priority request pass by and decrements the count when it lets a free QA slot pass by. All outstanding higher-priority requests have been serviced when this count becomes 0.[9] The station refrains from using a free QA slot to satisfy its own outstanding request until the count becomes 0. For as long as the count is 0, the station can use free slots arriving at the station even when it has not made any request to use them. In essence, the protocol allows the stations to use unreserved QA slots for background asynchronous data when the network is not fully loaded and these slots are available.

Shortcomings of IEEE 802.6 Reservation Scheme.   Sha, *et al.* [ShSS] pointed out that the IEEE 802.6 priority-based reservation scheme has three major shortcomings when used to support real-time communication. The most obvious one is the small number (namely four) of priority levels. Four priority levels would lead to significant loss of schedulable utilization for applications whose asynchronous messages have a large number of priority levels.

Another shortcoming is unbounded priority inversion. This is partially due to the restriction that each station can have only one outstanding request. Hence, reservations cannot be made independently of the traffic on flink. The undesirable effect of this restriction is illustrated by the following example from [ShSS]. Suppose that a station S_1 upstream on the flink has l slots of data to send every $100l$ slot times and the end-to-end delay of the network is very small compared with l slot times. After S_1 has been sending for some time, another station S_2 at a distance z slot-time downstream from S_1 wants to send one slot of data every 10 slot times. Because S_2's data have a shorter relative deadline (say 10), requests from S_2 have a higher priority than requests from S_1. In the absence of priority inversion, S_2 should get 1 slot every 10 slots. However, each request from S_2 takes z slot time to reach S_1, each free QA slot allowed passed by S_1 takes another z slot time to reach S_2, and S_2 is not allowed to send another request until it gets the free slot. As a result, S_2 can make at most one request and get one free slot every $2z$ slot times. S_2 would not be able to meet its throughput and deadline requirements if $z > 5$ despite the fact that its requests have a higher priority and total utilization of the network is only 0.11. This priority inversion can persist for an arbitrary length of time because it persists as long as S_1 has data to send.

The third shortcoming is due to the fact that a station is allowed to use free QA slots, even when the station did not make any request, whenever its count of outstanding higher-priority requests from downstream stations is 0. This introduces additional unpredictability in when a request from a downstream station will be serviced, much like the unpredictability

---

[9]We note that there is no need for a station to keep track the number of outstanding higher-priority requests from stations upstream on flink. Upstream stations see free QA slots before the station and exercise the same control in their use of the slots.

in token arrival time introduced by the timed-token method's allowing stations to send asynchronous data when the token arrives early. This unpredictability makes it difficult to predict which station will miss deadlines when the network becomes overloaded.

System Coherence.   Sha, *et al.* pointed that the shortcomings of the IEEE 802.6 protocol arise from the fact that the protocol does not provide system coherence. For a distributed priority-based reservation scheme to be free of these serious shortcomings, it must approximate a centralized scheme. In particular, it must have the following properties to achieve system coherence.

> *Losslessness:* Every request is registered correctly.
>
> *Consistency:* All stations perceive the same order in which their own outstanding requests and requests of downstream stations will be serviced.
>
> *Bounded priority inversion:* In a dual-bus network with end-to-end delay W, the duration of priority inversion is said to be bounded when the duration never exceeds $2W$.

(The notion of system coherence is more general than it is applied here on DQDB networks. In general, one may be willing to accept a longer duration of priority inversion, for example, a duration of no greater than $2kW$ for some positive bounded weight k when control information takes at most W units of time to propagate throughout the system.)

The necessity of the losslessness property is self-evident. This means that *each station can always reliably copy requests onto the rlink*. The scheme cannot possibly work correctly if some request can be lost.

Self-Entry and Tie-Breaking Rules to Achieve Consistency.   To describe the rules needed to achieve consistency and bounded priority inversion, we look at a scheme that supports a larger number of priority levels. We also back off from the above described IEEE 802.6 implementation. For the sake of clarity, we assume that each slot on rlink carrying a request is marked by a request bit, followed by a priority field that gives the priority level of the request. Rather than using a counter to keep track of outstanding requests, each station maintains a transmission queue, as shown in Figure 11–9. The queue keeps track of the order in which free QA slots arriving at the station are to be used. Specifically, the queue contains entries for all the outstanding requests known to the station (i.e., its own outstanding requests and outstanding requests from stations downstream on flink.) These entries are in the order of their priorities. To maintain this queue, the station puts its own outstanding requests in this queue. It also copies each request that passes by and inserts the request in the queue.

In terms of the states of transmission queues, we say that a reservation scheme is consistent if, when two or more requests are in the transmission queues of more than one station, they appear in the same order in these queues. The consistency property is achieved whenever the reservation scheme satisfies the self-entry and tie-breaking rules. The former says that a station never enters a request into its transmission queue before it successfully places the request on the rlink. By following this rule, a station prevents itself from having in its transmission queue any request that it may fail to send.

According to the tie-breaking rule, when a station wants to put on rlink a request of the same priority as a passing request, the tie is broken in favor of the station's request. In other words, equal-priority requests on rlink are preempted. (This is the tie-breaking rule we used earlier in the description of the IEEE 802.6 protocol.) Furthermore, the station sends preempted requests in FIFO order. To see the necessity of this rule, suppose that two equal-priority requests, RQ_1 and RQ_2, are on rlink and RQ_1 is ahead of RQ_2. Seeing these requests, a station S enters them in its transmission queue in this order. Suppose that a station S' downstream on rlink preempts RQ_1 in order to send a higher-priority request. If S' could not preempt RQ_2 when it wants to put RQ_1 back on rlink, the transmission queues of S' and downstream stations on rlink would have RQ_2 ahead of RQ_1 and would be inconsistent with the transmission queue in S. By allowing a station to preempt equal-priority requests, these requests appear in the stations' transmission queues in the same order as they appear on rlink.

Rules to Keep Priority Inversion Bounded.   The rules for a priority-based reservation scheme to achieve bounded priority inversion are the request preemption rule, autonomous request rule, and flow-control rule. The need for the request preemption rule is self-explanatory: A station can put its higher-priority request on rlink ahead of an equal- or lower-priority request. Earlier, in our description of the shortcomings of the IEEE 802.6 protocol, we illustrated that if a station can have at most one outstanding request, the duration of priority inversion cannot be bounded. Generally speaking, that restriction makes the request traffic on rlink dependent on the data traffic on flink and hence not autonomous. The *autonomous request rule* simply says this dependence is not allowed: A station must be able to send requests independent of when its outstanding requests are serviced. Thus, the rule makes it possible for each station to inform stations upstreams of its own demand in a timely fashion.

Finally, the flow-control rule makes sure that every station waits a sufficient amount of time before it commences its transmission on a new connection. To give stations upstream from it on flink enough time to hear and act upon its requests, it should wait $2z$ slot times when the propagation delay from the station to the slot generator is z slot time.

11.5   INTERNET AND RESOURCE RESERVATION PROTOCOLS

In earlier sections we saw that rate and jitter control is an integral part of good service disciplines for real-time traffic in switched networks. If every switch reserves resources (i.e., link bandwidth and buffer space) for every connection routed through it and exercises rate and jitter control of traffic on the connection, congestion within the network and at the destination can be prevented and real-time performance guaranteed. Similarly, in order to deliver the desired quality of service to users through interconnected networks, hosts and routers must reserve resources needed to ensure quality. While the onset of congestion in networks carrying only data traffic tends to be gradual, allowing time for congestion-control mechanisms to react and adapt, congestion of real-time (video and audio) traffic can build up quickly in integrated service networks. Traditional congestion-control mechanisms do not work well, whereas admission control and resource reservation provide an effective means to prevent congestion.

How hosts and routers (and switches) operate and interact for the purpose of resource-reservation is governed by a *resource-reservation protocol*. This section first discusses issues in resource reservation and then describes the well-known resource-reservation protocol RSVP protocol [ZDES, BZBH] that was designed to deal with these issues. The ST-II protocol [Topo] is an Internet protocol as well as a resource-reservation protocol. We conclude this section with an overview of ST-II as a contrast to RSVP.

11.5.1   Issues in Resource Reservation

Before we describe these protocols, let us pause to discuss four closely related issues that a resource-reservation protocol must deal with but we have ignored thus far. They are the multicast nature of communication, heterogeneity of the destinations, the dynamics of multicast group membership, and the relationship between resource reservation and routing and admission-control functions.

Multipoint-to-Multipoint Communication.   Thus far, we have confined our attention to unicast communication, that is, communication between a source and destination pair. In applications such as video-on-demand and teleconferencing, messages from a source are broadcast to multiple destinations. The hosts participating in the communication form a *multicast group*. In the former case, there is one source: The communication is one-to-many. In the latter case, there are many sources: The communication is many-to-many. Many distributed applications and fault-tolerance mechanisms also require multicast capabilities among entities.

Giving each source an independent point-to-point connection to each destination is usually an unacceptable approach because of the potential waste in resources. The common approach is to give each source a multicast tree connection to all destinations. A *multicast tree connection*, or simply a multicast tree, from a source host in a switched network or interconnected network is a set of point-to-point simplex connections between pairs of routers (or switches) and hosts that form a spanning tree; the tree is rooted at the source and connects all the destinations. Figure 11–11(a) gives an example. The graph represents a multicast tree from the source host H_1. Each vertex represents a router R_i (shown as a circle) or a host H_i (shown as a square). Each directed edge in the tree represents a simplex connection. At each entity represented by a vertex adjacent to the edge, resources required to carry messages from the source host over the connection have been reserved, and these messages are transmitted according to some connection-oriented service discipline.

When there is more than one source host in a multicast group and all sources may transmit at the same time, the only viable approach is to have a multicast tree for every host. (An example is a distributed monitoring and control system, where every host exchanges commands with all the other hosts in each round of interaction.) Oftentimes, however, only a subset of hosts in the group transmits simultaneously. (For example, in an audio teleconferencing, only one or a few people talk at a time.) One can save a great deal of resources by having the sources share resources whenever possible. As an example, Figure 11–11(b) shows a multicast group for which multicast trees from some sources traverse some common routers and transmission links. We use an undirected edge between a pair of endpoints to represent one or more pairs of simplex connections in both directions between the endpoints. So, the graph in Figure 11–11(b) represents three multicast trees rooted at H_1, H_3, and H_4. Hosts H_2 and H_5 receive messages but never send any of their own. The connections to them are simplex. H_1 never receives, and H_4 sends and receives via different routers. The connections to and from them are simplex also. We can sometimes reduce the bandwidth and buffer space reserved for a multicast group at routers and links traversed by more than one multicast tree of

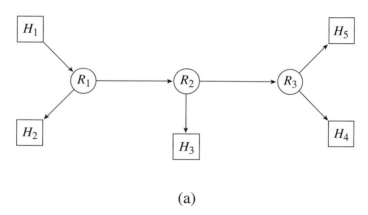

(a)

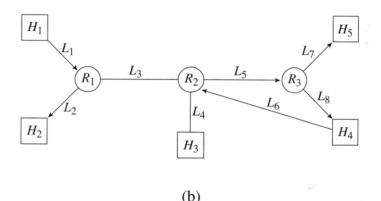

(b)

FIGURE 11–11   Multicast trees of a multicast group.

the group by using a resource-reservation protocol that considers the aggregate requirements of the multicast group as a whole. Indeed, this is what RSVP protocol does.

Heterogeneity of Destinations.   In general, some destination hosts may not be able or willing to set aside the communication and computing resources needed to achieve the quality of service provided by the source and demanded by some other destinations. A method to accommodate different quality of service requirements of destinations is to have the source use a layered scheme to encode its messages. Examples of these schemes for image, video, and audio messages can be found in [SuTa, WoOn]. A message carrying layered encoded video or audio can be divided into a mandatory part that gives an acceptable quality followed by one or more optional parts that improve the quality. A destination may choose to receive only packets that give it a poorer quality video and audio, rather than all the packets that the source uses to encode high-resolution and -fidelity video and audio. This reduction in the desired quality in turn leads to a reduction in the amounts of transmission bandwidth and buffer space that routers en route must reserve on behalf of the destination and the destination must have itself.

As an example, suppose that the hosts H_4 and H_5 in Figure 11–11(a) can only receive and process a low-resolution video stream. Then some network bandwidth and buffer space can be saved by reserving downstream to the right of router R_2 only the bandwidth and buffer space needed to guarantee the delivery of the low-resolution video stream. The other hosts demand a high-resolution video transmitted by H_1, and resources required to guarantee the timely delivery of the high-resolution video must be reserved at entities represented by the subtree at and to the left of R_2.

Dynamic Multicast Group Membership.   Another behavior of many multicast applications is that participants may join and leave a multicast group. Take video-on-demand for example. A viewer may preview or order a movie at any time. A new destination joins the multicast group when this happens, and the destination may leave the group after previewing.

When there is more than one source in a multicast group, the destination may choose to receive from different sources and make this choice dynamically. As an example, in a multimedia teleconference, a destination with limited resources may choose to receive only videos from a subset of the multicast group. The destination may dynamically change the sources in this subset.

Relation to Routing and Admission Control.   The establishment of a multicast tree connection involves routing, that is, the choices of routers and links spanning the tree, as well as resource reservation. One can easily argue that good utilization of network resources can be achieved only if the resources required by the connection are taken into account in the choice of the route. This is the rationale of some routing and real-time connection establishment protocols. The ST-II protocol described below takes this approach and provides routing and admission control along with resource reservation.

An alternative is to treat resource reservation as a separate function from routing and admission control. This is the approach taken by RSVP protocol. Modularity is an obvious advantage. The protocol itself is not concerned with the establishment and maintenance of the underlying multicast tree. Rather, it makes use of the routing and admission-control functions provided by the network or interconnected networks. As a result, RSVP protocol is "portable." With this approach, the routers used by each multicast tree are chosen by the routing protocol based on partial knowledge of the resource requirement (e.g., maximum and average demands) of the multicast group. This can lead to poorer resource utilization. However, resources reserved for a multicast group can be reclaimed if they are not needed later, so it is not obvious that modularity can be gained only at the expense of significant performance penalty. There are yet no evaluation and measurement data to tell us how large the penalty is.

Design Objectives.   In summary, a resource-reservation protocol should accommodate heterogeneous destinations in a multicast group whose membership may change dynamically. At any time, the total resource demand of the multicast group as whole is usually smaller than the sum of the demands of individual members because the members may not use their resources at the same time. Ideally, the amounts of resources reserved at any time for the multicast group should approximate the total amounts demanded by the group as a whole.

11.5.2   RSVP (Resource-Reservation Protocol)

Among the distinguishing features of the RSVP protocol, the most important ones are receiver-initiated reservation and multiple reservation styles,. A means to accomplish them is based on the concept of "soft state," which we will explain shortly. Because destinations in a multicast group may want different qualities of service and know the qualities they want, it is better to let them be responsible for reserving the resources necessary to achieve the desired qualities. This is the rationale behind *receiver-initiated reservation*. According to this design principle, each destination requests and helps to maintain the resource reservation needed to guarantee its desired quality of service.

We now give an overview of how the RSVP protocol works. After this overview, we can better appreciate the notion of reservation styles, so we defer the explanation of this notion until then.

Multicast and Sink Trees.   Figure 11–12 shows where RSVP fits in hosts and routers [BZBH]. Again, each source in a multicast group has a multicast tree to all destinations. Both data message streams and control messages from the source are transmitted along this tree. RSVP is concerned solely with resource reservation. It assumes that the routers used to support the multicast tree of every source are chosen according to the routing protocol(s) of the network or interconnected networks. The output links used by each router to multicast messages from the source are given by a routing table, which is maintained by the routing module. During network reconfigurations or outages, the routing table of the router is kept up-to-date by that module. Similarly, admission of new multicast connections and mapping between application and network quality of service parameters are handled by an admission-control module and packet classifier, respectively, in a lower layer.

The resource-reservation protocol establishes and maintains a *sink tree* for each destination and uses it to send control messages from the destination. A sink tree is a spanning tree that is rooted at the destination and connects all the sources in the multicast group. It is ob-

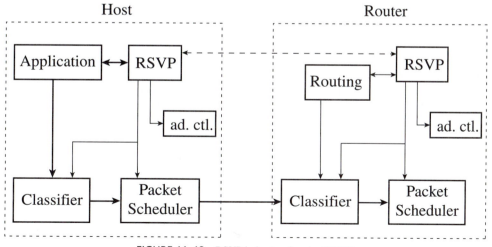

FIGURE 11–12   RSVP in host and router [BZFJ].

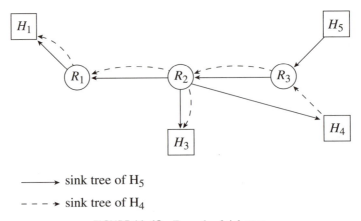

sink tree of H_5

- - - → sink tree of H_4

FIGURE 11–13   Example of sink trees.

tained by tracing in the reverse direction from the destination to every source along the paths in the multicast tree of the source. So, if the multicast trees of sources have some routers and links in common, the sink trees of destinations may also have routers and links in common. As an example, Figure 11–13 shows the sink trees of H_4 and H_5 in the multicast group of Figure 11–11.

Again, each destination is responsible for the initiation and maintenance of resource reservation on its own behalf. Resource-reservation messages for this purpose from the destination are sent along its sink tree to all the sources.

Protocol Operations   The operations of the RSVP protocol are described by the pseudocode in Figure 11–14. As a result of these operations, resources are reserved at routers (and switches) to guarantee the quality of service desired by each destination. The description, which intends to give an overview, leaves out details that are not essential for the understanding of the RSVP protocol. An example of what is omitted are the specification and handling of reservation style, which we will explain shortly.

Path and Reservation States.   Each router used by a multicast group maintains two types of information, called the path state and the reservation state. The *path state* for each source is concerned with the path used by the source; it includes information about the input link on which messages from the source arrive and output links on which these messages are transmitted. The RSVP protocol uses this information to maintain the sink trees of destinations. The *reservation state* for each destination is concerned with resources set aside for the destination to support the quality of service desired by the destination; the name of the destination (i.e., the *reserver*) for whom resources are reserved and the amount reserved are among the information provided by the reservation state.

Hosts in each multicast group help the routers used by them to maintain the path and reservation states for the group through the use of path and reservation messages. A *path message* is a control message sent by a source and forwarded by the routers in its multicast tree. Each source sends its first path message no later than when it commences transmission and sends subsequent path messages periodically. Among the information carried in each path

RSVP Operations

- Information created and maintained for each multicast group:
  - the multicast tree of each source by the routing module, and
  - sink tree of each destination by RSVP.
- Each source in each multicast group
  - sends a path message containing its own flow specification and a time value before commencing transmission, and
  - periodically sends a new path message.
- Each destination in each multicast group
  - sends a reservation message containing a flow specification and a time value upon receipt of a path message,
  - periodically sends a new reservation message, and
  - upon the receipt of an RSVP reject message, carries out an application specified action.
- Each router used by each multicast group does the following:
  - Upon the receipt of a path message carrying the flow specification of a source,
    - ∗ if no path state for the source exists, creates a new path state; otherwise updates an existing path state;
    - ∗ resets timer of the path state to the time value in the path message;
    - ∗ if the path message caused a new path state be created or indicates a route change, forwards the message immediately downstream on the multicast tree; otherwise, discard the message.
  - Upon the receipt of a reservation message carrying the flow specification of a destination,
    - ∗ if the requested resources are available,
      - + reserves resources and creates a new reservation state if the destination does not have and cannot share an existing reservation, otherwise updates an existing reservation state;
      - + resets timer of the reservation state to the time value in the reservation message; and
      - + forwards the reservation message downstream on the sink tree according to the rules defined by the protocol;
    - ∗ if the requested resources are not available, rejects the reservation request and sends an RSVP reject message on the multicast tree to the destination.
  - Upon the receipt of an RSVP reject message, forwards the message downstream to the destination.
  - Periodically sends to all routers downstream on multicast trees of the group a path message containing information carried in path messages which the router has received since its previous periodic path message.
  - Whenever the timer of a path or reservation state expires, deletes the state.

FIGURE 11–14   Overview of RSVP operations.

message of a source is the flow specification of its message stream. A router updates the path state of the source upon receiving a path message from the source.

Each destination sends *reservation request messages*, or reservation messages for short, which are forwarded along the sink tree of the destination. Each reservation message is a request to the routers receiving it for a new reservation of resources on behalf of the destination or an update of an existing reservation. Among the information contained in each reservation message is a flow specification giving the quality of service desired by the reserver. A destination sends its first reservation message when it receives a path message from a source whose message streams it wishes to receive and, afterwards, sends reservation messages periodically to maintain the reservation.

Suppose that a router has sufficient resources. Upon receiving the first reservation message from a destination, the router reserves the resources needed to support the quality of service defined by the flow specification in the message and creates a new reservation state for the destination if the destination cannot share an existing reservation established earlier for another destination in the multicast group. If the destination can share an existing reservation, the router updates the existing reservation state to include this destination. It then forwards the reservation message to routers downstream on the sink tree. Upon receiving subsequent reservation messages from a destination, the router updates the reservation state of the destination and forwards the message to routers downstream on the sink tree.

A router may reject a reservation request, due to insufficient resources, for example. In this case, an RSVP reject message is sent back to the requesting destination. The action taken by the destination upon the receipt of a reject message is application dependent.

Soft States. According to most protocols, a connection once established is maintained until its endpoints explicitly request the connection be torn down. The state information on the connection is maintained by all the routers used by the connection until disconnect time.

According to the RSVP protocol, on the other hand, each router maintains the reservation (and path) state(s) of a host for only a certain length time. The host must explicitly request that the state be maintained before the timer associated with each state expires; otherwise the router deletes the state. This is the so-called "soft state" [Clar88] and is the preferred design choice for applications that have long lifetimes and are dynamic in nature. During the lifetime of such an application, hosts are likely to join and leave multicast groups, their quality of service demands may change, and the condition of the underlying network may change. These changes may require changes in the multicast and sink trees of the application and the amounts of resources reserved on its behalf. With the use of soft states, the network can adapt to these changes more automatically.

Specifically, each reservation (or path) message carries a time value for the purpose of timing when the corresponding reservation (or path) state is to be refreshed. Upon receiving a reservation message and an update of the corresponding reservation state, each router sets its timer of the reservation state to the time value carried in the reservation message. If no reservation message to refresh the reservation state arrives before the timer expires, the router deletes the reservation state. The router treats each path state similarly; the length of time the state is maintained without refreshment is dedicated by the time value in the associated path messages. From the description in Figure 11–14, we see that the loss of state information will not cause any problem since path and reservation states are automatically re-created upon receipt of path and reservation messages associated with them.

The need for each host to periodically transmit messages for the purpose of refreshing its states maintained by routers leads to a higher protocol overhead. However, both types of control messages (i.e., path and reservation messages) require much smaller amounts of bandwidth and buffer space compared with what are required for data messages. Moreover, by merging the control messages from all hosts and forwarding them periodically whenever there is no new state information to warrant immediate forwarding, the protocol overhead can be kept small. Indeed, this is the reason for the periodical forwarding of path messages and the merging of reservation messages. We leave out the rules governing the merging and forwarding of control messages. You can find them in [BZBH].

Reservation Styles.   Another important concept of the RSVP protocol is *reservation style*. We have already seen that as a result of propagating its reservation messages through the sink tree of a destination, resources required by message streams to the destination are reserved. In addition to this mechanism, the protocol also allows each destination to specify which source or sources in the multicast group may use the resources reserved on its behalf and to dynamically change this specification if it so desires. The function provided by routers for this purpose is called a filter. A *filter* is a list of names of sources whose message streams can use the resources reserved for the destination; the destination wants to receive messages only from sources named in its filter. A destination that wants a filter includes the filter in its reservation messages. Alternatively, a destination may choose to have no filter applied to its reservation, meaning that all sources in the multicast group may use its resources.

So, depending on whether a filter is to be applied or not by the routers, the reservation for a destination is either a *filter reservation* or a *no-filter reservation*. The former is further divided into two styles: *fixed-filter reservation*, if the filter of the destination is fixed, or *dynamic-filter reservation*, if the filter may change. The destination specifies the reservation style it wants by putting one of these names (and, if it is a filter reservation, a filter) in its reservation messages.

To see how the utilization of network resources can be improved by taking advantage of reservation styles, we recall the possibility for two or more destinations in the same multicast group to share a reservation at a router. Clearly, destinations that are in the same group and always receive the same message streams sent to them via the same output link of a router can share resources and hence, a reservation state. (If one destination wants a higher quality of service than the other, then sufficient resources to guarantee the higher quality are reserved.) On the other hand, destinations that want to receive message streams from different sources or change among sources cannot share resources and reservations. By letting each destination inform the routers on its sink tree of its reservation style in its reservation messages, the routers can decide whether the destination can share a reservation with some other destinations in the multicast group and, therefore, can merge its reservation state with the reservation state of other destinations.

No-Filter Reservation.   In particular, a router can merge the reservations of destinations that use the no-filter reservation style whenever messages to the destinations are sent on the same output link. As an example, suppose that all the hosts in Figure 11–11 choose the no-filter reservation style. The destinations H_3, H_4, and H_4 have different quality of service requirements for messages from H_1 and require bandwidths $BW_{1,3}$, $BW_{1,4}$, and $BW_{1,5}$, respectively, to meet the requirements. ($BW_{j,k}$ denotes the bandwidth required for messages from source H_j to destination H_k.) The amounts of bandwidth of links L_3 and L_5 reserved by routers R_1 and R_2 for messages from H_1 are $\max(BW_{1,3}, BW_{1,4}, BW_{1,5})$, and $\max(BW_{1,4}, BW_{1,5})$, respectively, not the sums of the $B_{j,k}$'s. Similarly, the bandwidth of link L_5 reserved for messages from all sources to H_4 and H_5 is $\max(BW_{1,4}, BW_{1,5}) +$

$\max(BW_{3,4}, BW_{3,5}) + BW_{4,5}$. This amount of bandwidth is required because router R_2 is told by the destinations that they may want to receive from all three sources in the multicast group simultaneously. R_2 maintains one reservation state for all these destinations. Obviously, at R_1 and R_2, H_2 cannot share the reservation state of the other destinations because messages to H_2 are sent via a different output links.

Fixed-Filter Reservation. If a destination chooses the fixed-filter reservation style, it provides the set of sources permitted to use the resources reserved on its behalf. A router can merge the reservation states of destinations only if the intersection of their source sets is nonempty. So, suppose that H_4 and H_5 both choose fixed-filter reservation style and their filters are (H_1) and (H_3), respectively. R_2 is asked to reserve on link L_5 bandwidth $BW_{1,4}$ for messages from H_1 to H_4 and bandwidth $BW_{3,5}$ for messages from H_3 to H_5. Clearly, the router must maintain separate reservation states for the destinations. On the other hand, if the filters of these destinations are (H_3), a reservation state for both destinations suffices.

Dynamic-Filter Reservation. By specifying the dynamic-filter reservation style, a destination informs the router that it wishes to receive only messages from the hosts named in its filter, but it may change the filter from time to time. In this case, each router reserves the required resources and creates a separate reservation state for the destination. In our example, suppose that the reservation style chosen by H_5 is dynamic. Even if the filters of both H_4 and H_5 are the same, say (H_1), R_2 must maintain separate reservation states for them, because the filter of H_5 may later be changed to (H_3, H_4).

11.5.3 ST-II, Internet Stream Protocol

ST-II [Topo] is an enhanced version of the ST (stream) protocol. Like RSVP, ST-II is an element of an Integrated Service Packet Network (ISPN) architecture, supports multicast and resource reservation, and allows the specification of traffic characteristics and quality of service requirements. (Figure 11–15 shows how the ST-II protocol fits in an ISPN architecture.[10]) It differs from RSVP in several important aspects, however. For example, ST-II integrates multicast routing, connection establishment, and data transmission functions, while RSVP is not concerned with these functions. Unlike RSVP, resource reservation is source initiated and does not accommodate heterogeneous receiver quality of service requirements. Whereas multiple sources in a multicast group may share resource reservations according to RSVP, each source has its own multicast tree and resource reservation according to ST-II.

Stream and Multicast Routing. As its name implies, ST-II supports streams across networks. The term *stream* (ST) refers to

1. a set of simplex data paths (i.e., routes) from a source application entity to one or more destination application entities,
2. resources allocated to support the transmission of data from the source, and

---

[10]We will not discuss in this chapter the standard protocols IP (Internet Protocol), UDP (Unreliable Datagram Protocol) and TCP (Transmission Control Protocol) that have long been used to support nonreal-time applications such as e-mail and file transfer. They are described extensively in the literature (e.g., [CoSt]).

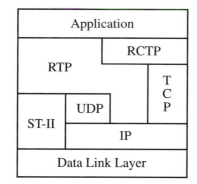

FIGURE 11–15   ST-II protocol in midst of other protocols.

3. the state information on data transmission and resource allocation maintained by routers along the data paths and by destinations.

(Earlier, we called the entities at the endpoints of data paths sources and destinations.) In short, a stream is a simplex one-to-many multicast connection that is maintained by ST-II at the IP layer. (In contrast, IP provides connectionless communication, leaving the establishment and maintenance of connections among applications to TCP at the transport layer. Whereas IP packets are handled independently, ST-II data packets on a stream are not independent.)

The ST-II protocol assumes that some routing module can be called upon to generate unicast routing tables, each of which gives a path from the source to a destination in a multicast group. During stream setup, ST-II obtains these tables and builds the multicast tree of the stream from these tables. (This is because ST-II protocol was developed before the advent of Internet multicast routing.) At each router where unicast paths to different destinations diverge, the ST-II module replicates data packets from the source and forwards the replicated packets on the diverging paths. This is why we said earlier that ST-II also deals with routing and data transmission.

Stream Setup and Resource Reservation.   Each stream is identified by a global name. Both stream establishment and resource reservation are initiated by the source. A source initiates this by sending a CONNECT message. Among the parameters of this message is the flow specification, which describes the desired and minimal sizes and flow rates of packets from the source.

The CONNECT message also specifies the destinations at the endpoints of the multicast stream. When a router receives a CONNECT messages, it maps each of the destinations to a next-hop router or host based on the unicast routing tables from the routing module. It then determines the amounts of local and network resources required to support the stream. If it has sufficient resources, it allocates the resources to the stream and forwards the CONNECT message to the next-hop router or host on the route to each destination.

Each ST-II multicast tree consists of homogeneous data paths, meaning that the amounts of resources at all points on the tree are identical. In other words, the quality of service provided by a stream is determined by the most resource poor router or destination. If the router does not have enough resources to support the flow specification in the CONNECT message, it can allocate smaller amounts. In this case, it updates the flow specification to reflect the reduction in quality of service of the stream and then forwards the modified CONNECT message, containing the updated flow specification, to the next hop.

In order to support the flow specification of a new stream, a router may break some established stream that is less important (i.e., with lower precedence) in order to free some resources. If the router cannot provide sufficient resources, it refuses the stream. It breaks an established stream or refuses a new connect request by sending a REFUSE message to the previous hop, giving the reason for its refusal in the message.

The process of choosing the next hop, reserving resources, and possibly downgrading the flow specification is repeated at each hop until the CONNECT message reaches all destinations. When a destination receives a CONNECT message, it can determine the resources it needs to participate in the multicast from the message's flow specification. If the destination wants to accept the stream but does not have (or does not want to commit) sufficient resources, it can further downgrade the flow specification. It then returns an ACCEPT message containing the name and updated flow specification of the stream.

When the source receives an ACCEPT message from a destination, it either downgrades its own flow specification to accommodate the destination, or it rejects the participation of the destination. This rejection is indicated by a DISCONNECT message to the destination.

Changes in Group Membership and Exchange of Control Messages.   Unlike the RSVP path and reservation states which must be refreshed periodically, an ST-II multicast group membership, as well as route and resource allocation, once set up for a stream, remains until it is changed explicitly. A source may add a new destination to an established multicast stream by sending a CONNECT message. A destination can leave a multicast group by sending a REFUSE message, and an established multicast stream can be torn down in part or in whole by the source sending DISCONNECT messages. Similarly, a stream can be modified by changing its resource allocations.

ST-II control messages such as CONNECT, DISCONNECT, ACCEPT, and REFUSE are sent using the the ST Control Message Protocol (SCMP), which is a part of ST-II. Reliable exchange of control messages is accomplished by requiring hop-by-hop acknowledgement. A control message not acknowledged within a timeout interval is retransmitted.

11.6 REAL-TIME PROTOCOL

Since their advent, the transport protocols TCP and UDP and the Internet protocol IP have served nonreal-time applications well [CoSt]. Yet these protocols are unsuitable for real-time applications for many reasons. IP is connectionless. Previously, we have argued that the connection-oriented approach is more advantageous for real-time applications because of the ability to reserve resources, manage quality of service, and provide isolation in an end-to-end manner for each flow. Therefore, one way to enhance the real-time capabilities of the Internet is to have a connection-oriented alternative to IP. ST-II is such an alternative. TCP is a connection-oriented transport protocol. However, its error-control, flow-control, and sequencing mechanisms are designed to provide users with reliable, sequenced data delivery; they can introduce large delay and jitter and severely limit end-to-end throughput. Unlike data, many real-time applications are more tolerant of erroneous and lost data. For these applications, the cost in real-time performance is too high for the gain in reliability.

This section gives a brief overview of the Real-time Protocol (RTP) and Real-Time Control Protocol (RTCP) [SCFJ]. RTP is a data transport protocol for real-time applications. RTCP is the control protocol accompanying RTP. Other transport-layer protocols for multimedia applications include the older protocols: Packet Video Protocol (PVP) and network voice protocol [Cole]. We leave them for you to investigate.

11.6.1   Data Transport

RTP is designed to support multicast communication in interactive multimedia applications, such as audio and video teleconferencing and distributed simulation. It deals solely with data delivery and uses services (e.g., multicast routing, resource reservation and quality of service guarantee) provided by lower-layer protocols. In particular, RTP can run on the unreliable datagram protocol UDP. It uses UDP's multiplexing and error-control services and compensates UDP with its own sequencing function. Monitoring, control, and identification functions are provided by RTCP.

RTP is designed to be scalable from a few participants to thousands of participants in multicast communication and to be able to accommodate heterogeity of sources, receivers, and networks. Like RSVP, RTP also assumes that multicast group membership may change dynamically. In contrast with TCP, which is separate from applications, RTP is often integrated with applications. By providing headers that can be modified and expanded, the protocol can be tailored by applications.

To explain its main features, we look at a multicast group participating in a video teleconferences supported by RTP and UDP. According to RTP, their audio and video data are transmitted separately. Each medium uses a separate multicast network address and a pair of UDP ports,[11] one for data packets and one for control packets. The combination of the network address and a port is a *destination transport address*, so each medium uses a pair of transport destination addresses. (We assume here that the IP multicast is used and all participants have the same destination transport address pair. In the case where the underlying layer supports only unicast, each participant has its own transport destination address.) Before the start of the teleconference, one of the participants obtains from a resource manager the transport address pairs to be used by the group and distributes this information to all participants. Thus their multicast session is established.

RTP Packets.   During the conference, each chunk of audio or video data (e.g., a segment of audio or an image) from each participant is framed by an RTP header to form an RTP packet. Our example assumes that RTP runs on UDP; hence RTP packets are framed in UDP packets and sent by UDP. A participant may have multiple microphones and cameras. These devices are called synchronization sources. (In general, the term *synchronization source*, or SSRC or source for short, refers to an entity that generates and sends an RTP data stream. We

---

[11]A port of a transport protocol is an abstraction (e.g., a positive integer) that the protocol uses to distinguish destinations within a host. Specifically, each destination is identified by a unique 2-tuple, consisting of the host's network address and the destination's port number.

will discuss other types of SSRC shortly.) Headers of data packets from the same SSRC have the same SSRC identifier; the identifier helps a receiver separate data packets from the SSRC from data packets generated by other SSRCs.

Data packets from each SSRC are sequenced and time stamped consecutively. The header of each RTP packet contains the time stamp and sequence number of the packet. The former gives the sampling instant of the first octet of the packet. The latter gives the order of the packet with respect to other packets in the same data stream. The need for sequence and timing information arises from the fact that RTP packets on a session may be lost and delivered out of order. (UDP packets are routed through the network independently of each other, so, if RTP runs on top of UDP, there is no guarantee against lost and out-of-sequence packets.) Timing information also makes it possible for the destination to synchronize the associated audio and video (to achieve lip synchronization, e.g.).

Another type of information contained in an RTP packet header is the method used to encode the data. Examples of encoding methods are PCM (Pulse Code Modulation) for audio and JPEG for image. Each SSRC can change the encoding method during the conference. The flexibility of using different encoding methods enables the applications to trade off between quality and resource demands. For example by changing to an encoding scheme that requires a lower bandwidth but produces poorer voice, image, or video, a source can lessen its bandwidth demand during network congestion at the expense of the quality of its data. This is also a way for a multicast group to accommodate a new participant who is resource poor and is constrained to use a lower-quality/required bandwidth scheme.

Mixers and Translators. In addition to hosts, there are also mixers and translators; both are RTP relays. Such a relay connects two or more networks (or interconnected networks) at the transport level. To a relay, each network is defined by its network and transport layer protocols (e.g., IP/UDP), a multicast address, and a transport-layer destination port.

Each *translator* relays streams of RTP packets from different sources separately, that is, without altering their SSRC identifiers. Some translators may alter the encoding of data in data packets. Translators may be used as filters that forward packets to destinations protected by firewalls for security reasons. Translators are also needed to connect hosts that support different protocols (e.g., some hosts only IP/UDP while other hosts only ST-II) and to replicate from multicast to unicast.

In contrast to translators, a *mixer* receives data streams from one or more sources, combines the streams in some manner, possibly changes the data encoding, and then forwards the combined stream onward. Because its input data streams are from different sources and the streams are not synchronized, a mixer first adjusts the timing of packets in each stream and generates its own time stamps of packets in the combined stream. The mixer is the SSRC of the combined stream. The SSRCs of original data streams are called contributing sources (CSRC). Each packet in the combined stream contains in its header a CSRC list, which gives the identifiers of the contributing sources of the data contained in the packet. With this information, a receiver can identify the original source of the data even after it is mixed with other data streams by a mixer.

Often, mixers are used to support heterogeity among destinations. For example, some destinations may be connected through a network with a lower bandwidth. To accommodate such a destination without forcing all destinations to accept poorer quality, a mixer may be used to forward the lower-bandwidth audio stream on low bandwidth links. A video mixer may be used to scale images from separate sources and compose them into one video stream (e.g., putting smaller images of participants in an image to simulate a conference scene.)

11.6.2 RTCP Control Protocol

As stated earlier, there is a control port associated with each data port. Control packets carrying control and monitoring information on data transmission to the data port are sent under the control of RTCP to the control port using the same multicast route as the associated data packets.

Specifically, reception quality is fed back to every participant in a multicast group, as well as to a network service provider or monitor when there is one. Distributing this feedback information is the primary function of RTCP. This information is needed to support adaptive encoding and congestion control. It also helps in fault diagnosis, since a monitor can easily determine from reports of all participants whether a problem in data distribution is local or global.

Transmission of Reception Quality Reports.   Each receiver (i.e, a destination) periodically sends RTCP report packets, simply called reports hereafter. Such a report contains a reception block for each of the sources from which the receiver has received data since the previous report. This block provides the values of performance measures (e.g., fraction and cumulative number of packets lost, interarrival jitter, and delay) used to measure the quality of the data from the source. A report may be a receiver report or a sender report. A receiver report contains only reception blocks. A receiver sends a receiver report if it has not sent any data since the transmission of its previous report. Otherwise, if it has sent some data, it sends a sender report, which contains a sender information section, in addition to reception blocks. The sender section provides transmission statistics and source description items (SDES); we will return shortly to describe some of the items.

We note that multimedia data traffic is self-limiting. For example, usually only one or two people talk and only a few images are sent and displayed at a time during a teleconference independent of the group size. In contrast, control traffic can grow linearly with group size if each participant sends its reception report at a rate independent of group size. To constrain the growth in control traffic, RTCP keeps the total bandwidth consumed by control packets from all participants in a multicast group constant. In particular, the recommended fraction of bandwidth allocated to RTCP for each multicast session is 5 percent of the total RTP bandwidth of the session. This 5 percent is further divided among senders (i.e., those sending sender reports) and nonsenders, with 1.25 percent for senders and the remaining 3.75 percent for nonsenders. In this way, the protocol ensures that sufficient bandwidth is available for the transmission of sender reports which, as we will see shortly, are more time critical.

Computation of Reception Report Retransmission Interval.   To maintain a constant total rate, each participant must estimate the group size (i.e., the number of participants) of its multicast session and calculate the interval p between consecutive RTCP packet transmissions based on the estimated number. The information it maintains for the purpose of this computation include the following:

t_p: the previous transmission time of a RTCP packet;

t_n: the next scheduled transmission time of a RTCP packet;

members: the most recent estimate of group size;

senders: the most recent estimate of the number of senders in the session;

rtcp_bw: the total bandwidth to be used for RTCP packets by all participants; and

avg_rtcp_size: the average RTCP packet size, in octets, over all RTCP packets sent and received by participants.

The rules used by each participant to compute its retransmission interval p are rather complicated. We give only highlights below, leaving out most of the details for you to find out from [SZFJ].

While the average retransmission interval of each participant is chosen deterministically, the next transmission time t_n is chosen randomly. Thus, control packets from all participants tend to spread out over time, rather than arriving deterministically and possibly bunched together in time.

Specifically, the value of the retransmission interval p is computed in two steps.

1. The average retransmission interval p_d is computed deterministically according to $p_d = \max(p_{\min}, nC)$ with the parameters $p_{\min}$, C and n determined according to the rules given below.

2. The retransmission interval p is computed from p_d by first randomly choosing a number x from a uniform distribution in the range $[0.5 p_d, 1.5 p_d]$. The retransmission interval p is equal to $x/1.21828$.[12]

After a participant computes the retransmission interval p, it sets the next transmission time t_n of its reception report to the previous transmission time t_p plus p.

The parameter $p_{\min}$ used in step 1 is the minimum average retransmission interval. This parameter is normally five seconds. However, it is desirable to enable a participant (an application) to quickly send a sender report when it starts up and begins to send data. (The report provides the SDES needed by receivers.) For this reason, when a participants just starts, its average minimum retransmission interval is only half the normal minimum value, that is, 2.5, before the participant sends its first report.

The value of the parameter C is a function of *members*, *senders*, and *avg_rtcp_size*. Depending on the percentage of members who are senders, there are two cases. When $0 < senders < 0.25\ members$, the senders share 25 percent of the RTCP bandwidth *rtcp_bw*, leaving the rest of this bandwidth to nonsenders. Hence, the average retransmission interval of a participant depends on whether the participant is a sender. If the participant is a sender, the constant C is equal to *avg_rtcp_size* divided by 25 percent of the RTCP bandwidth, and n is equal to the number of senders. On the other hand, for a participant which is not a sender, the constant C is equal to *avg_rtcp_size* divided by 75 percent of the RTCP bandwidth, and n is equal to the number of nonsenders. When $sender > 0.25\ members$, all participants are treated equally. C is equal to *avg_rtcp_size* divided by *rtcp_bw*, and n is equal to *member*.

---

[12]1.21828 is equal to $e - 1.5$, where e is the constant 2.71828. Because of this fudge factor, p has the intended average.

To estimate the number of participants, each participant keeps a member table containing the SSRCs of participants known to it. Each time the participant receives an RTP or RTCP packet from a source whose SSRC is not in the table, it enters the SSRC into the table and increments *member*. It deletes the SSRC of a participant and decrements *member* when it receives a BYE packet from the participant. The BYE packet indicates that the participant has left the multicast group. Similarly, each participant keeps a sender table and updates the table and the estimate *sender* each time it receives an RTP packet from the sender.

Collision Resolution and Intermedia Synchronization.   One of the functions of RTCP is to support collision resolution and intermedia synchronization. An SSRC identifier carried in RTP headers of packets from a source and in the associated RTCP packets is a 32-bit number that is unique within an RTP session. This identifier is chosen randomly by the source when the source starts. Because each source makes this choice independently, it is possible for sources to collide (i.e., the SSRC identifiers chosen by them are identical). Although the probability of a collision is small (less than 10^{-4} when there are 1000 sources), the fact that it can occur makes it necessary for all the sources to be able to detect collisions. When a source detects that its own SSRC identifier is the same as that of other source(s), it sends a BYE RTCP packet containing the identifier, indicating that it ceases to participate and then chooses a new SSRC identifier for itself and uses the new identifier in its packets.

In addition to the above reason, the SSRC identifier of a source also changes when the source restarts. The fact that the SSRC identifier of a source may change makes it necessary to provide another means for receivers to identify each source. This function is provided by RTCP. RTCP packets from each source carry a persistent transport-level identifier called CNAME. When a source starts, its CNAME is sent to all participants in its sender reports. This identifier allows receivers to associate multiple data streams from the source. Intermedia synchronization also requires that the network time-stamp and RTP time-stamps be included in the RTCP packets of data senders.

*11.7   COMMUNICATION IN MULTICOMPUTER SYSTEMS

Before concluding this chapter, we return to the subject of scheduling and flow control in switched networks, this time focusing on those that are used in multicomputer systems. Like packet-switched networks, multihop networks used to interconnect processors in massively parallel machines also consist of crossbar switches connected by full-duplex links. (Each full-duplex link is a pair of simplex input and output links). Unlike packet-switched networks, however, these networks typically adopt a simpler routing and flow-control scheme called *wormhole routing* [BaOz, FeRU, LiMu, ReHS]. This section gives a brief overview of the subject.

11.7.1   Wormhole Networks

In a wormhole network (i.e., one that uses wormhole routing), messages are segmented into very small flow-control units, called *flits*. In the simplest wormhole networks, each switch provides only enough buffer space to hold one flit per input link. The buffer is there in order to decouple the input link from the output links.

Routing and Transmission.   Only one flit can occupy a link at each time step; while a message is using a link, another message that also needs the link must wait. Therefore, the transmission of a message may be blocked from starting. Specifically, when the header (i.e., the first flit) of a message reaches a switch, the switch selects an output link for the message based on the information provided in the header. If the output link is free at the time, the header moves forward on that link to the next switch, leaving the input link it used to reach the current switch to the second flit in the message. Similarly, the third flit follows, using the link freed by the second flit, and so on. On the other hand, if an output link chosen for a message is in use, the header is buffered and waits at the switch until the output link becomes free. In the meantime, subsequent flits that have reached upstream switches occupy the flit buffers there, one per switch. The associated input links (i.e., output links of the corresponding upstream switches) are not available to other messages.

We call this phase of message transmission the routing phase. The routing of a message starts when its header leaves the source processor and completes when the header reaches the destination processor. Hereafter, the message has all the links along the path between its source and destination. Each link is occupied by one of the message's flits. The flits shift downstream by one link (i.e., one switch) in each time step without intervention of the switches. Thus, the message "worms" its way nonpreemptively through the network without being queued at any switch. Its transmission completes when its last flit is delivered to the destination processor.

In short, the message delay through a wormhole network is the sum of its routing time and transmission time. The latter is essentially the total propagation delay of all links on its transmission path. The time required to route a message depends on the overall network traffic and is the nonpredictable component of message delay.

Path Selection and Scheduling.   To make the network scalable with the number of processors in the system, algorithms used to select paths for messages are typically simple. As an example, in a two-dimensional mesh network, each switch is connected to four neighboring switches. It is common to use one-bend paths for unicast messages. A one-bend path between two processors in a mesh consists of a segment of column links and a segment of row links. If the path of every message traverses a column segment first and then a row segment (or vice versa), there is no deadlock [DaSe, DaAo, Duat]. There are equally simple, deadlock-free routing algorithms for high-dimensional interconnection networks.

Typically, algorithms used to schedule nonreal-time messages do not prioritize messages. They can be divided into two categories: greedy and throttling. According to a greedy algorithm, each message is routed along a deadlock-free path as soon as it is ready for transmission at the source. In contrast, according to an algorithm that does throttling, a message may wait at the source. This intentional delay to start routing serves a purpose similar to traffic shaping in packet-switched networks, that is, to reduce the worst-case delay.

Studies on wormhole routing of nonreal-time messages are primarily concerned with an average case bound on message delay. As an example, Felperin, *et al.* [FeRU] proposed a delayed greedy algorithm for scheduling transmissions of equal-length messages through an $m \times m$ mesh. After a message becomes ready, the source holds it for a random number of time steps. At the end of the random interval, the message is routed without prioritization greedily along a one-bend path. The number of time steps a source i holds each message is equal to $x_i(b^2l\log^2 m + bl\log m + 2m^{1/2})$, where b is a fixed constant, l is the length of all messages, and x_i is an integer chosen from a uniform distribution from 0 to $2y^{1/2}/\log m - 1$. (y is a design constant.) Felperin, *et al.* showed that the algorithm can deliver (i.e., route and transmit) all messages in $O(lm^{1/2}\log m + m/\log m)$ time steps with a high probability when the destinations of messages are chosen randomly. Here a high probability means a probability larger than $(1 - e^{-cy})$ where c is a positive constant and e is the base of natural logarithms.

We note that the larger y is, the longer on the average each source delays routing its messages, but the higher the probability for its messages to be delivered within the upper bound number of time steps. (The probability exponentially approaches 1 within increasing y.) It is not surprising that the delay bound can be tightened if after traversing the row segment of its one-bend path, the header flit waits for a number of steps before it traverses the column segment. For example, every message can be delivered within $lm^{1/2}(b\log m + 2)$ time steps with high probability if all messages are routed according to a slightly more complicated delayed greedy algorithm that holds the header flit for $blm^{1/2}\log m$ time steps after the header has traversed the row segment.

11.7.2 Priority-Driven Flow Control

Schemes for scheduling real-time messages through wormhole networks are typically priority-based. Each switch may provide a number of flit buffers per link to facilitate time multiplexing of the link. A connection may be set up for messages between a source and destination pair. Such wormhole networks, sometimes called flit-buffered networks, start to resemble packet-switched networks. The differences, however, are not just that flits are much smaller than packets and that there is only buffer for one flit or one message per connection at each switch. More importantly, dropping flits in wormhole networks is not acceptable, whereas flow-control and sequencing schemes for packet-switched networks allow switches to drop packets when the buffer overflows (and thus keep the traffic moving). A flit simply waits at the switch when it cannot move forward, causing subsequent flits in the message to wait at upstream switches. The problem then is how to adaptively route the messages so as to minimize the probability and duration of this wait.

Assumptions and Rationale of the PPCS-RT Scheme.   As an example of real-time flow-control schemes, we look at the preemptive circuit switching (PPCS-RT) scheme proposed by Balakrishnan, *et al.* [BaOz]. This scheme assumes that real-time messages are periodic. Each message has a fixed priority. An implicit assumption is that the lengths of message instances are long compared with the transmission time along the longest path in the network. (The scheme would perform poorly for short messages, e.g., each contains a few flits.) When every message is routed along a fixed path, the blocking time of each message can be bounded. Consequently, the schedulability of each message can be determined.

In our description, we refer to an instance of a periodic message simply as a message when it is not necessary to be specific, as we did in earlier sections. We assume that every message uses a fixed path. By competing messages, we mean messages whose transmission paths intersect and therefore may compete either directly or indirectly for some link.

To see the rationale behind the PPCS-RT scheme, we note again that messages are transmitted nonpreemptively. A message M can be blocked by a competing lower-priority message M_l whose transmission has commenced when M becomes ready (say at time t). The blocking time thus incurred can be as large as the maximum transmission time e_{max} of all lower-priority competing messages. This amount of blocking is unavoidable. To keep the blocking time suffered by each message M as close to this minimum as possible, competing lower-priority messages that are still being routed at time t should not delay the transmission of M. In other words, if it is at all possible, the routing of competing lower priority messages should be stopped and the links occupied by them freed for M. Otherwise, if another lower-priority competing message is routed to its destination ahead of M while M_l is being transmitted, M will be blocked by this message as well as M_l.

Path Establishment and Data Delivery.   According to the PPCS-RT scheme, a path (i.e., a connection) for each message instance is established first. The instance is transmitted in the data delivery phase when path establishment succeeds. The scheme minimizes blocking by making the allocation of flit buffers (hence the associated links) to messages preemptable during path establishment.

Successful Path Establishment.   During path establishment, only the header flit is routed through the network. The header serves as a request. When the header reaches a switch, it is allocated a Virtual Channel (VC), which is a flit buffer and associated flow-control state. (There is only one VC per link; hence the message that is allocated the VC is also allocated the link.) If the output link selected for the message is free, the header continues and is allocated a VC at each switch it reaches. When the header flit reaches the destination, path establishment succeeds. From this point in time until the data delivery phase ends, the VCs and associated links are allocated to the message. A *success* control flit is then routed from the destination back to the source along the reverse path. After receiving the *success* flit, the source commences to transmit the message. The VCs and associated links are freed when the transmission of the entire message instance completes.

Preemption of VCs.   Suppose that during the path establishment phase of a lower-priority message M_l, a higher-priority competing message M is also being routed. Moreover, suppose that the header of M reaches a switch where a VC has been allocated to M_l and as a consequence, the header of M cannot proceed. In this case, the switch generates and sends a *preempt* flit to the next switch along M_l's path, and each of the switches on M_l's path forwards the *preempt* flit to the next downstream switch. Preemption of M_l's VCs takes place if the *preempt* flit catches up with the header of M_l at a switch before the header reaches its destination. (This can happen if M_l's header is stopped somewhere en route because some link on its path is being used by a competing message.) A *free* flit is routed from the switch backward along the M_l's path; each switch along the way frees the VC (and the associated link) that is allocated to M_l. The *free* flit informs the source of M_l that the path establishment fails and must be retried.

On the other hand, the header of M_l may be routed without interference. The *preempt* flit may not be able to catch up with the header before the header reaches M_l's destination. The preemption attempt fails when this happens, and the higher-priority message M must wait until the data delivery phase of M_l completes. While M waits, higher-priority messages may preempt M and take the VC's and links allocated to M thus far.

Preemption Stack and Handling of Control Flits.   In order to eliminate the need for a preempted message to retry path establishment and, more importantly, the possibility for some lower-priority message to acquire the VCs freed by the preempted message before the retry, each switch maintains a preemption stack. When a switch receives a *free* flit to preempt the VC held by a message, the priority of the message is pushed on the top of the stack. Later on, when the switch receives a header flit to request the VC, the switch allocates the VC to the header only if the VC is free and the priority of the header is higher than the priority on the top of preemption stack.

The PPCS-RT scheme is considerably more complicated than the simple schemes for nonreal-time messages. In addition to a preemption stack for each link, the switch needs to maintain the state of each active path (i.e., an establishing, preempted, or established path) through it. It also needs to properly handle the exchange of control flits and possible race conditions. As examples of factors that complicate the implementation, *success* has a higher priority than *preempt*. (Once a *success* starts to return on a path, the associated VCs must not be preempted.) It is possible for the *success* and *preempt* flits of a path to cross one another. (This can happen when the flits are being exchanged by a pair of switches.) When a switch detects a *preempt* arriving after the *success* flit on the same path, it deletes the *preempt*. This is possible only when the switch has a record of the *success* flit on the same path.

Schedulability Analysis.   What is gained at the expense of complexity is the bounded duration of priority inversion. For the purpose of determining the schedulability of each message M_i, the execution time of a periodic message M_i whose path contains ρ_i links is equal to

$$e_i = \rho_i(e_{he} + e_{\text{suc}}) + \rho_i - 1 + l_i/BW$$

where l_i (in bits) is the maximum length of instances of M_i, e_{he} and e_{suc} are the times per hop required to send a header flit and *success* flit, respectively, and BW is the bandwidth of the links.

For the blocking time b_i of a message M_i, it is safe to use the largest execution time of all messages in $\mathbf{M}_{l,i}$, where $\mathbf{M}_{l,i}$ is the set of lower-priority messages that compete with M_i. In addition to $\mathbf{M}_{l,i}$, one must also find the set $\mathbf{M}_{h,i}$ of competing equal- and higher-priority messages. The time demand function of M_i should include the time demand of messages in $\mathbf{M}_{h,i}$, the execution time of M_i and its blocking time.

11.8 SUMMARY

This chapter focused on algorithms and protocols for real-time communication. Specifically, it devoted most of its pages to service disciplines for packet-switched networks, medium-access control protocols for broadcast networks, and high-level protocols for voice and video traffic in interconnected networks and distributed systems. Only the previous section is concerned with scheduling and flow-control in multicomputer systems.

11.8.1 Service Disciplines for Switched Networks

We described several service disciplines for scheduling packet transmissions in packet-switched networks. Some of them are priority-based and others are weighted round-robin schemes.

Priority Based Disciplines. Among the well known priority-based schemes are the Weighted Fair-Queueing (WFQ) discipline, delay-EDD, and jitter-EDD disciplines and the RCSP discipline. The priority assignment used by the former three is dynamic, while that used by RCSP discipline is fixed. Section 11.2 described these disciplines. Table 11.1 lists their performance and complexity. n is the number of connections sharing an output link. The number of switches (i.e., hops) between the source and destination of the connection is ρ. e is the maximum length of packets on the connection.

The weighted fair-queueing discipline has many advantages. Most important is timing isolation for each connection, hence the independence of latency and rate of each connection on the demand of other connections. Its scheduling complexity can be reduced to $O(1)$ by updating the system finish number periodically according the frame based WFQ scheme. The performance of the weighted fair-queueing discipline listed in Table 11.1 is for a connection whose traffic meets the (E, u) leaky bucket constraint, and bandwidth allocation is equal to the average rate u. D denotes the end-to-end deadline of the messages.

According to the delay-EDD, jitter-EDD, and RCSP disciplines, a connection is accepted only when its end-to-end delay D is achievable. This is why Table 11.1 lists D as their achievable end-to-end delay. The schedulable link utilization achievable by these algorithms can be determined using methods described in Chapters 6 and 7.

WFQ and delay-EDD are rate allocating; under these disciplines, both end-to-end delay jitter and buffer requirements grow with the number ρ of hops from the source. In contrast, the jitter-EDD discipline succeeds in keeping the end-to-end delay jitter equal to the delay jitter of a single hop. The buffer requirement stays independent of the number of hops as well under the jitter-EDD scheme. The RCSP discipline can use some release-guard-like rate-control scheme with a fixed-priority assignment to keep the worst-case end-to-end response time bounded. As a byproduct, delay jitter and buffer requirements do not grow with the number of hops.

Weighted Round-Robin Disciplines. The major disadvantage of priority-based disciplines is that they require priority queues. The Weighted Round-Robin (WRR) disciplines do not. The four variants of the weighted round-robin approach are the greedy WRR algo-

TABLE 11–1 Performance of Priority-Based Service Disciplines

Performance Measures	WFQ	Delay-EDD	Jitter-EDD	RCSP
Acceptance Test	$O(1)$	$O(1)$	$O(1)$	$O(1)$
Scheduling Complexity	$O(n)$	$O(\log n)$	$O(\log n)$	$O(\log n)$
End-to-End Delay Bound	$E/u + \rho(e+1)$	$\leq D$	$\leq D$	$\leq D$
End-to-End Jitter	$const \times \rho$	$const \times \rho$	$const$	$const$
Buffer Space Requirement	$const \times \rho$	$const \times \rho$	$const$	$const$

rithm, the Stop-and-Go (S&G) algorithm, the Hierarchical Round-Robin (HRR) algorithm, and the Budgeted Weighted Round-Robin (BWRR) algorithm. Sections 11.3 described these disciplines.

Table 11.2 summarizes their performance when used to schedule the transmissions of constant bit-rate messages. Such a message on a connection i is characterized by its period p_i and execution time e_i. The weight assigned to the connection is wt_i at all switches; and the round length used by all switches is RL. These disciplines are simple to implement and perform well for constant bit-rate traffic.

11.8.2   Medium Access Protocols of Broadcast Networks

Section 11.4 described several Medium Access-Control (MAC) protocols for scheduling packet transmissions on broadcast networks. They are the Controller Area Network (CAN) MAC scheme, token-passing schemes used in token rings and buses, and the dual-queue dual-bus protocol.

Fixed-Priority Scheduling in Broadcast Network.   Both the contention-resolution protocols used in CANs and the token-passing scheme used in IEEE 802.5 token rings emulate centralized priority scheduling of a single processor. CANs are bus networks. They are very small networks: The end-to-end propagation delay is a fraction of time required to transmit a bit. Hence, the bus acts like a wired-AND logic circuit. The contention-resolution scheme used in CAN is like CSMA/CD. It makes use of the wire-AND function provided by the bus for priority arbitration. Priorities of messages are their IDs: The smaller the ID, the higher the priority. When all instances in each periodic message have the same ID, the network behaves like a nonpreemptive, fixed-priority system. Since message IDs are 11 bits long, there are 2048 priority levels.

In an IEEE 802.5 token ring, contention is resolved according to a token-passing scheme which polls stations on a ring in the order of their physical locations on the ring. A station can piggyback a reservation for use of the ring on the data frame circulating on the ring. The station that has the highest priority message waiting gets to use the network if the station makes a reservation in time (i.e., the message is ready before the header of the current data frame reaches the station). The token-passing scheme conveniently supports any fixed-priority scheme. Since there are only eight priority levels, schedulability loss due to nondistinct priorities can be significant when the priority-assignment algorithm requires a large number of priorities.

*Timed-Token Scheme.   Section 11.4.2 described the timed-token medium access-control protocol in a token bus, FDDI, and SAFENET networks. According to the timed-token protocol, stations poll each other by circulating among themselves a polling packet called a token. Traffic on the networks is divided into synchronous (i.e., periodic) and asynchronous classes. Each station in the network has a synchronous allocation SA. When polled, the station can send synchronous messages for no more than SA units of time. The station sends asynchronous messages after its synchronous allocation is exhausted only when the token returns to the station earlier than a threshold time, indicating that the network traffic is light. If there were only synchronous messages, the timed-token scheme would be like a distributed weighted round-robin scheme. Because of the presence of asynchronous messages and the

TABLE 11-2 Performance of WRR Service Disciplines

Performance Measures	Greedy WRR	Synchronized S&G and HRR	S&G and HRR	BWRR
Acceptance Test	$O(1)$	$O(1)$	$O(1)$	$O(1)$
Scheduling Complexity	$O(1)$	$O(1)$	$O(1)$	$O(1)$
End-to-End Delay Bound	$p_i + (\rho - 1)RL$	$p_i + \rho RL$		$p_i + (\rho - 1)RL$
End-to-End Jitter Bound	$p_i - e_i + (\rho - 1)(RL - 1)$	$2RL$	$2RL$	$(\rho - 1)RL - wt_i + 1$
Buffer Space Requirement	$(1 + \lceil (k - 1)(RL - 1)/p_i \rceil)e_i$	$2wt_i$	$3wt_i$	$2wt_i$

way the spare network bandwidth is used for their transmission, the timed-token scheme behaves completely differently, however.

Local Synchronous Bandwidth Allocation (SBA) schemes are practical, since the amount of synchronous allocation of each station is determined solely on the basis of the parameters of its own messages. Unfortunately, local SBA schemes typically work poorly, meaning they cannot guarantee the timely delivery of synchronous messages even when the total synchronous demand of all stations is low. Global schemes are not practical for networks in which new synchronous messages may be added on-line since the addition of each new message requires changes of synchronous allocations of all stations.

*Dual-Queue Dual-Bus (DQDB) Scheme.   Section 11.4.3 described DQDB networks. Such a network consists of two unidirectional buses. The slot generator at the head end of each bus generates slots on the bus; a station places its outgoing data for stations downstream on that bus using these slots. With head ends at opposite ends, the buses together provide the stations with full-duplex capability.

Some slots are preallocated by the network's bandwidth manager in the form of 64-kbps isochronous (i.e., periodic) channels to connections at connection establishment time. The problem then is how to take advantage of the fact that nonoverlapping connections can share channels to maximize channel usage. This problem, called the channel reuse problem, is typically solved using graph theoretical techniques.

Some slots are queue arbitrated. They are called QA slots and are for sporadic and aperiodic messages. Access to QA slots is controlled and distributed by all stations according to a priority-based reservation scheme. A station requests a QA slot on one bus (flink) by putting its request on the other bus (rlink). Based on all the requests it sees, the station keeps track of the order in which free QA slots on the flink will be used by itself and stations downstream. Since each station knows only a subset of all requests, the transmission queues of difference stations may become inconsistent. When this happens, the distributed reservation scheme does not approximate a centralized scheme and is said to be incoherent. Incoherence may lead to unbounded priority inversion. Section 11.4.3 gave the rules that must be obeyed to achieve coherence.

11.8.3 Resource-Reservation and Real-Time Transport Protocols

Section 11.5 described resource-reservation protocols which govern how hosts and routers interact for the purpose of setting aside bandwidth and buffer space to ensure some quality of service. Section 11.6 described a transport protocol for video and audio traffic.

Resource Reservation and Internet Protocols.   Both the RSVP and ST-II protocols support multicast communication among members that may join and leave their multicast groups any time. While the RSVP protocol is separate from routing, admission control, connection establishment, and data transmission, these functions are part of the ST-II protocol.

RSVP Protocol is a receiver-initiated protocol designed to accommodate heterogeous receivers which may desire different service qualities. An implicit assumption is that not only the group membership may change anytime, but also the service quality (hence the resources needed to support the quality) desired by each individual member may change. Rather than requiring an explicit request to change reservation, resource reservations under RSVP must be renewed at frequencies specified by the group members. Both path and reservation states maintained by each router are soft, meaning that the states are deleted if not renewed within specified time intervals.

Another unique feature of RSVP is reservation style. It allows each receiver to specify which source or sources in the multicast group may use the resources reserved on its behalf and to dynamically change this specification if it so desires. This specification is provided to the routers in the form of a filter. A filter names the sources whose message streams can use the resources reserved for the receiver.

Internet Stream Protocol (ST-II) is an enhanced stream protocol. Unlike RSVP, resource reservation is source initiated. Unlike RSVP which allows sources in a multicast group to share resource reservations, under ST-II, each source has its own multicast tree and resource reservation. The amounts of resources at all points on each multicast tree are identical. In other words, the quality of service provided by a stream is determined by the most resource-poor router or receiver. An ST-II multicast group membership and resource reservation are changed only when explicitly requested by group members.

Real-Time Protocol.   The Real-Time Protocol (RTP) is a data-transport protocol for multimedia application such as audio and video teleconferencing and distributed simulation. It provides data delivery service solely, uses UDP's multiplexing and error-control services and compensates UDP with its own sequencing function. The accompanying control protocol RTCP provides monitoring, control, and identification functions.

RTP and RTCP are scalable from a few participants to thousands of participants per multicast group and can accommodate heterogeity of sources, receivers, and networks. RTP can be integrated with applications.

EXERCISES

11.1 Consider a connection that is allocated a fraction BW of the total bandwidth, and packet transmissions on all connections are scheduled according to the virtual clock algorithm (i.e., nonpreemptive total-bandwidth server algorithm).

(a) Suppose that the connection first becomes busy at time t_{-1} and remains busy until time t. Show that if the total length of all packets arriving on the connection in the busy interval $(t_{-1}, t]$ is no greater than $BW(t - t_{-1})$, the virtual clock of the connection is no greater than t, and the virtual clock of the connection is greater than t if the total length of all packets arriving in the interval exceeds $BW(t - t_{-1})$.

(b) Suppose that the time t_{-1} was the last time instant when the virtual clock of the connection was equal to current time. How large can the virtual clock of the connection be at some time t after t_{-1} if the total length of all packets arriving on the connection in the interval $(t_{-1}, t]$ is no greater than $BW(t - t_{-1})$?

11.2 The description of the jitter-EDD discipline in Section 11.2.4 is the one given in [ZhKe]. It differs from the one given in [VeZF]. According to [VeZF], a packet with ahead time $ah_{i,j}$ arriving at switch k at time $a_{i,j}$ is held in the holding queue for $ah_{i,j}$ units of time. It becomes ready and is moved to the ready queue at time

$$r_{i,j} = a_{i,j} + ah_{i,j}$$

and its deadline is set at

$$d_{i,j} = \max(r_{i,j} + D_{i,k}, d_{i,j-1} + p_i)$$

where $d_{i,j-1}$ is the deadline of the previous packet, the deadline of the first packet on the connection being $r_{i,1} + D_{i,k}$.

(a) Using this definition of the jitter-EDD discipline, calculate at the second switch the ready times and the deadlines of the packets whose arrival times at the first switch are given in Figure 11–6. Note that according to this version of the jitter-EDD discipline, a packet may be ready for transmission earlier than when its ready time is calculated according to Eq. (11.6a). Discuss the consequence of this difference.

(b) According to [VeZF], a connection may request, in addition to an end-to-end relative deadline, an end-to-end jitter bound. As a consequence, each connection i has a local jitter bound $J_{i,k}$ as well as a local relative deadline $D_{i,k}$ at each switch k. When $J_{i,k} < D_{i,k}$, the ready time of a packet is equal to

$$r_{i,j} = a_{i,j} + ah_{i,j} + D_{i,k} - J_{i,k}$$

and the deadline is set at

$$d_{i,j} = \max(r_{i,j} + J_{i,k}, d_{i,j-1} + p_i)$$

Note that the ready time of the packet is further delayed by $D_{i,k} - J_{i,k}$ and $J_{i,k}$ is used in the calculation of the packet deadline. It appears that a connection i can request the same delay and jitter guarantee by simply requesting the end-to-end relative deadlines being equal to the end-to-end jitter bound, if the latter is smaller. Moreover, the switches can guarantee the end-to-end jitter bound only if they can guarantee the smaller end-to-end deadline. Hence, the jitter bound is a redundant parameter for this discipline. Is this statement true or false? Explain your answer.

11.3 Section 11.2.4 states that when the jitter-EDD discipline is applied at switches en route to a real-time connection i, at every switch except the first switch, the two arguments of the max function in the right-hand side of Eq. (11.6a) are equal. Therefore there is no need for the switch to maintain information the effective arrival time of the next packet on each connection. Prove that the statement is true by induction.

11.4 Eq. (11.8) gives the maximum delay experience by a message (p_i, e_i, D_i) through ρ switches which use the greedy WRR discipline and the same round length RL. How should this equation be modified if the round lengths used by different switches are different; at the kth, the round length is RL_k.

11.5 The discussion in Section 11.3 on WRR algorithms assumes that each connection carries a periodic message stream. This is often not the case, for example, a connection may carry a video stream and an accompanied audio stream. We can logically divide the connection that carries multiple periodic message streams into multiple subconnections each carrying a single periodic message stream and calculate the weight to assign to each subconnection and thus the total weight assigned to all the connections. Using a pseudocode, describe the procedure for establishing such multiple-message connections.

11.6 When we described the S&G algorithm in Section 11.3.2, we assumed that the frames of different switches are synchronized so the packets arriving by the end of the $j-1$th frame becomes eligible for transmission immediately after the end of the frame, which is the beginning of the next frame. If the frames of different switches are not synchronized, the end-to-end delay of a message on connection i serviced at level x through ρ switches can be as large as $p_i + (2\rho - 1)RL$ and the number of buffers required for the connection at each switch is $3wt_i$. Prove this statement is true.

11.7 The description of the BWRR algorithm assumes that on each connection i no more than wt_i packets per RL units of time are delivered to the first switch. This assumption is made for convenience (so the schedulers of all switches operate in the same manner). In reality, on a connection i whose flow rate is declared by (p_i, e_i), a message of length e_i may be delivered as a whole every p_i units of time to the first switch. How should the scheduler of the first switch replenish the budget of the connection?

11.8 We consider here a token ring in which reservation and token priorities are set in the way described in Section 11.4.1. We measure all times in terms of bit-times, each being the time required to transmit 1 bit over the transmission medium. An active station listens on the network and participates in priority arbitration; the delay it introduces is 27 bit-times. (The delay introduced by each station is equal to 2 bit-times when the station is passive.) The total number of bits used to frame the user data in each packet is 104 bits (i.e., a packet containing x information bits is $x + 104$-bits long.

(a) In this part, you are asked to compute the parameters of the network and traffic that you will need in parts (b) and (c).

   i. Suppose there are 10 stations on the ring, all are active. If the distance between every pair of adjacent stations is equal to 100 feet and the transmission rate is 20 Megabits/sec, what is the total round-trip delay of the network? What is the execution time (i.e., the amount of time the packet occupying the network) of a packet which contains x information bits?

   ii. Suppose message M_i from every station i is synchronous. In particular, every message M_i is a periodic message (p_i, e_i). The periods of messages are either 33.3 msec, 66.7 msec, 75 msec, or 100 msec. What are the lengths of these periods in terms of bit-times?

(b) Suppose that the priorities of the messages are assigned on the rate-monotonic basis. If the execution times of the messages are equal, what is the largest execution time at which some message will not be schedulable? The answer you will get is the maximum packet size schedulable on the network.

(c) What is your answer to the question in part (b) if

   i. Each station has two message streams to transmit?

   ii. The transmission rate is 100 Megabits/sec?

11.9 Section 11.4.1 pointed out that according to the IEEE 802.5 protocol, the token priority of a free token is set at the higher value of the token priority and reservation priority of the latest data packet. Because of this, the token priority may become higher with time. According to the protocol, the token priority is lowered only after the free token has circulated the network, remained unclaimed, and returned to the source station. The time thus lost can be considered to be a part of context-switch time. Discuss how to take this factor into account schedulability analysis as accurately as possible.

Operating Systems

This chapter describes operating systems services and mechanisms. A good real-time operating system not only provides efficient mechanisms and services to carry out good real-time scheduling and resource management policies, but also keeps its own time and resource consumptions predictable and accountable. The chapter first discusses how to implement operating system functions to accomplish these objectives. It then examines how well several widely used real-time operating systems and general-purpose operating systems perform in this respect.

There are numerous texts and survey articles on operating systems principles in general and on real-time systems in specific (e.g., [Bute, Crow, Gall, SiGa, NiFB, TaWo]). In particular, Gallmeister [Gall] gives insightful discussions on effective approaches to programming real-time applications and selection of real-time operating systems, as well as capabilities of existing UNIX operating systems and Application Program Interfaces (APIs). Rather than duplicating their treatment of these topics, this chapter complements their coverage. It emphasizes those services and mechanisms that are easy to implement, have low overhead, can make the implementation of many algorithms described in previous chapters significantly simpler but are not provided by most existing operating systems.

Following the introduction, Section 12.1 begins by introducing the terminology used here and relates the terms to the terms used in previous chapters. More than general-purpose operating systems, a real-time operating system should be modular and extensible. In embedded systems, the kernel must be small because it is often in ROM and RAM space may be limited. Some systems are safety critical and require certification, including the operating system. Simplicity and smallness are advantageous from this perspective as well. This is why a real-time operating system may have a microkernel that provides only essential services, such as scheduling, synchronization, and interrupt handling. Section 12.1 describes a general structure of an operating system microkernel and the services it typically provides. Sections 12.2 and 12.3 discuss the quality of these services and point out where timing unpredictability is typically introduced. They also describe operating system primitives that can drastically simplify user-level implementation of many scheduling algorithms (e.g., the sporadic-server algorithm and release-guard protocol).

Continuing the thrust of Sections 12.2 and 12.3, Sections 12.4 and 12.5 describe two desirable architectural features that are not yet found in most existing systems. Some real-time applications (e.g., air traffic control) require all the functionalities (e.g., I/O, files, and networking) of general-purpose operating systems. A real-time operating system typically provides these services by adding to the kernel optional components, which we call (System) Service Providers (SSPs).[1] Section 12.4 presents the processor reserve abstraction proposed by Mercer, *et al.* [MeST], together with the associated architecture of SSPs. This abstraction supports accurate monitoring and control of resource consumption of each SSP when the SSP executes on behalf of its clients.

Most operating systems (even those that support multiple scheduling policies) schedule all applications according to the same scheduling algorithm at any given time. Whether each application can meet its timing requirements is determined by a global schedulability analysis based on parameters of every task in the system. The necessity of detailed timing and resource usage information of all applications that may run together often forces the applications to be developed together and, thus, keeps the system closed. Section 12.5 describes an operating system architecture that offers real-time applications an open environment. Hard real-time applications can run with soft real-time and nonreal-time applications in this environment. It makes use of the two-level scheduling scheme described in Section 7.9. This scheme enables each real-time application to be scheduled in a way best suited for the application and the schedulability of the application to be determined independent of other applications that may run with it on the same hardware platform.

Sections 12.6 and 12.7 get back to the reality of existing operating systems. Specifically, Section 12.6 compares and contrasts several widely used real-time operating systems. Section 12.7 describes the shortcomings of Windows NT and Linux, two commonly used general-purpose operating systems and ways to make real-time applications run more predictably on these operating systems. Section 12.8 summarizes the chapter. Throughout the chapter, we often refer to *Real-Time POSIX*. By this, we mean the real-time and thread extensions [IEEE98] of the POSIX Application Program Interface (API) standard [IEEE90b, Zlot]. You can find a brief overview of Real-Time POSIX in the appendix of this chapter.

12.1 OVERVIEW

We now switch over to use the terms commonly used in operating system literature. This section adds a few important ones to the terms we used in earlier chapters. We make several assumptions about the implementation of the applications and the architecture of the operating system. These assumptions help keep our discussion concrete. They lead to no loss of generality for most of the chapter.

12.1.1 Threads and Tasks

A *thread* implements a computation job and is the basic unit of work handled by the scheduler. In earlier chapters, we spoke of the admission of a job (or a task) into the system after an acceptance test; this step encompasses the creation of a thread that implements the job.

---

[1]The term *server* is commonly used to refer to a system service provider. We use the uncommon term SSP here in order to avoid further overloading the term server, which was used in earlier chapters to mean a user-level task that executes one or more aperiodic and sporadic tasks. We will use the term server again later in this chapter to mean something similar.

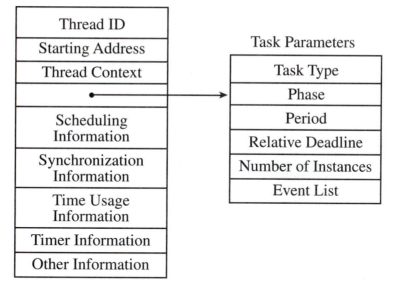

FIGURE 12–1   Thread Control Block.

When the kernel *creates* a thread, it allocates memory space to the thread and brings the code to be executed by the thread into memory. In addition, it instantiates a data structure called the *Thread Control Block* (TCB) and uses the structure to keep all the information it will need to manage and schedule the thread. Figure 12–1 shows a general structure of thread control blocks. The information kept in the TCB of a thread includes the ID of the thread and the starting address of thread's code. The context of a thread refers to the values of registers (e.g., program counter and status register) and other violatile data that define the state and environment of the thread. When a thread is executing, its context changes continuously. When the thread stops executing, the kernel keeps its context at the time in the thread's TCB. We will explain the other types of information later as the need for the information becomes apparent.

When we say that the operating system inserts a thread in a queue (e.g., the ready or suspend queue), we mean that it inserts (a pointer to) the TCB of the thread into a linked list of TCBs of other threads in that queue. The kernel *destroys* a thread by deleting its TCB and deallocating its memory space.

Periodic Threads.   A periodic (computation) task is a thread that executes periodically. It is clearly inefficient if the thread is created and destroyed repeatedly every period. In an operating system that supports periodic tasks (e.g., Real-Time Mach [ToNR] and EPIQ [DLZS]), the kernel reinitializes such a thread and puts it to sleep when the thread completes. The kernel keeps track of the passage of time and releases (i.e., moves to the ready queue) the thread again at the beginning of the next period. We call such a thread a *periodic thread*.

The parameters of a periodic thread include its phase (i.e., the interval between its creation and its first release time), period, relative deadline, and the number of instances. A periodic thread with a finite number of instances terminates and may be destroyed by the kernel after it has executed for the specified number of times. These parameters are given by the application[2] when its requests the creation of the periodic thread. They are kept in the TCB of the thread.

Most commercial operating systems do not support periodic threads. We can implement a periodic task at the user level as a thread that alternately executes the code of the task and sleeps until the beginning of the next period. (In other words, the thread does its own reinitialization and keeps track of time for its own next release.) We will return to describe this implementation in Section 12.2.1. The difference in the implementation is unimportant in our discussion. For the sake of concreteness, we assume that the operating system supports periodic threads in this section.

Aperiodic, Sporadic, and Server Threads.   Analogously, we can implement a sporadic or aperiodic task as a *sporadic thread* or *aperiodic thread* that is released in response to the occurrence of the specified types of events. The events that cause the releases of these threads occur sporadically and may be triggered by external interrupts. Upon its completion, a sporadic thread or aperiodic thread is also reinitialized and suspended. We assumed this implementation of aperiodic (and sporadic) tasks in Figures 5–7 and 5–10, which describe a cyclic executive in a multithreaded time-driven system. An aperiodic task is the same as a periodic task, except for the types of events that causes their releases.

We call a thread that implements a bandwidth-preserving server or a slack stealer a *server thread*. In Chapter 7 we talked about a "server queue." Such a queue is simply a list of pointers which give the starting addresses of functions to be executed by the server thread. Each aperiodic (or sporadic) job is the execution of one of these functions. Upon the occurrence of an event that triggers the release of an aperiodic job, the event handler (frequently an interrupt service routine) inserts into this list a pointer to the corresponding function. Thus, the aperiodic job is "released" and queued. When the server is scheduled, it executes these functions in turn. In our discussion of bandwidth-preserving servers, we assume that this is how aperiodic and sporadic jobs are implemented.

Major States.   Our subsequent discussion focuses primarily on priority-driven systems. We will mention five major states of a thread.

- *Sleeping*: A periodic, aperiodic, or server thread is put in the *sleeping* state immediately after it is created and initialized. It is released and leaves the state upon the occurrence of an event of the specified types. Upon the completion of a thread that is to execute again, it is reinitialized and put in the sleeping state. A thread in this state is not eligible for execution.
- *Ready*: A thread enters the ready state after it is released or when it is preempted. A thread in this state is in the ready queue and eligible for execution.
- *Executing*: A thread is the *executing* state when it executes.

---

[2]We use the term application here to mean a group of threads that jointly deliver some services to the end user. Threads in the group communicate and synchronize with each other, while threads in different applications communicate relatively rarely if at all. You may question why we do not call such a group a process. According to its common definition, different processes execute in different address spaces; hence, threads in different processes execute in different address spaces. We call our thread groups applications to avoid this implication because there may be only a single address space for all threads in the system. Later, when we say a process, we mean a process.

- *Suspended (or Blocked)*: A thread that has been released and is yet to complete enters the suspended (or blocked) state when its execution cannot proceed for some reason. The kernel puts a suspended thread in the suspended queue.
- *Terminated*: A thread that will not execute again enters the terminated state when it completes. A terminated thread may be destroyed.

You recall from our earlier discussion that a job (and hence a thread) can be suspended or blocked for many reasons. For example, it may be blocked due to resource-access control; it may be waiting to synchronize its execution with some other thread(s); it may be held waiting for some reason (e.g., I/O completion and jitter control), and so on. A bandwidth-preserving server thread enters the suspended state when it has no budget or no aperiodic job to execute. The operating system typically keeps separate queues for threads suspended or blocked for different reasons (e.g., a queue for threads waiting for each resource). For the sake of simplicity, we call them collectively the suspended queue. Similarly, the kernel usually keeps a number of ready queues. For example, to support fixed-priority scheduling, there may be a queue for ready threads of each priority level. We often call all these queues collectively the ready queue.

12.1.2 The Kernel

Again, with a few exceptions, a real-time operating system consists of a microkernel that provides the basic operating system functions described below. Figure 12–2 shows a general structure of a microkernel.[3] There are three reasons for the kernel to take control from the executing thread and execute itself: to respond to a system call, do scheduling and service timers, and handle external interrupts. The kernel also deals with recovery from hardware and software exceptions, but we ignore those activities here.

System Calls.   The kernel provides many functions which, when called, do some work on behalf of the calling thread. An application can access kernel data and code via these functions. They are called Application Program Interface (API) functions. Figure 12–2 lists several examples.

A *system call* is a call to one of the API functions. In a system that provides memory protection, user and kernel threads execute in separate memory spaces. Upon receiving a system call, the kernel saves the context of the calling thread and switches from the user mode to the kernel mode. It then picks up the function name and arguments of the call from the thread's stack and executes the function on behalf of the thread. When the system call completes, the kernel executes a return from exception. As a result, the system returns to the user mode. The calling thread resumes if it still has the highest priority. If the system call causes some other thread to have the highest priority, then that thread executes.

We have just described what happens when a thread makes a *synchronous system call*. The calling thread is blocked until the kernel completes the called function. When the call is *asynchronous* (e.g., in the case of an asynchronous I/O request), the calling thread continues

---

[3]Many small embedded applications (e.g., home appliances and traffic light controllers) require only a nano-kernel. A nanokernel provides only time and scheduling services and consists of only the clock interrupt part of the figure.

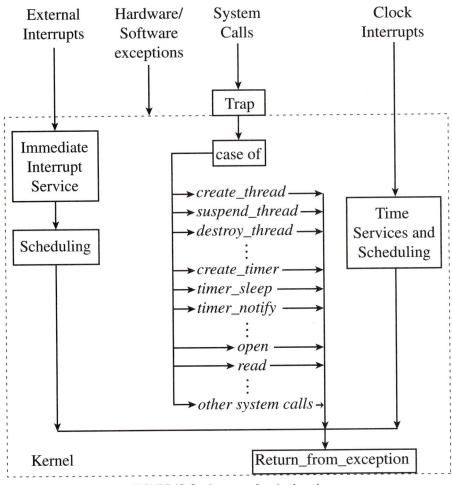

External Interrupts
Hardware/ Software exceptions
System Calls
Clock Interrupts

Trap

Immediate Interrupt Service

case of

create_thread
suspend_thread
destroy_thread
⋮
create_timer
timer_sleep
timer_notify
⋮
open
read
⋮
other system calls

Time Services and Scheduling

Scheduling

Kernel

Return_from_exception

FIGURE 12–2   Structure of a microkernel.

to execute after making the call. The kernel provides a separate thread to execute the called function.

Many embedded operating systems do not provide memory protection; the kernel and user execute in the same space. Reasons for this choice are the relative trustworthiness of embedded applications and the need to keep overhead small. (The extra memory space needed to provide full memory protection is on the order of a few kilobytes per process. This overhead is more serious for small embedded applications than the higher context-switch overhead that also incurs with memory protection.) In such a system, a system call is just like a procedure or function call within the application.

Figure 12–2 shows examples of *thread management* functions: create thread, suspend thread, resume thread and destroy thread.[4] The timer functions listed below them exemplify

---

[4]A *fork( )* function, which creates a duplicate process, is another means to create threads: all the threads in the calling process.

the time services a real-time operating system provides. From the user's point of view, a (software) *timer* is an object used to keep track of time. In addition to systemwide timers, most operating systems allow threads (or processes) to have their own timers. A per thread (or per process) timer is created by the kernel on behalf of a thread (or process) when the thread calls the create timer function. In a system that contains more than one clock, the calling thread specifies the clock to which the timer is to be bound; by this, we mean that the timer will keep track of time according to that clock. A *clock* is a hardware device that contains a counter. At any time, the content of the counter gives a representation of the current time.

A set-timer function call specifies the ID of the timer to be set and an expiration time. By calling this function, a thread asks the kernel to carry out an action at the timer expiration time. The action may be the execution of a specified function, or the waking up of a suspended thread, or the placement of a message in a message queue, and so on. We say that a *timer event* occurs at the timer's expiration time; when a timer event occurs, the kernel carries out the specified action. As a consequence, the calling thread carries out its own action or synchronizes with other threads at the specified time. In a system that supports periodic tasks, the kernel uses such a function to take care of the releases of periodic thread instances. We will return to discuss clocks and timers in more detail in Section 12.2.1.

Time Services and Scheduling.   The scheduler is a central part of the kernel. In most operating systems, the scheduler executes periodically, as well as whenever the state of any thread changes. To trigger the scheduler into action, the system clock device raises interrupts periodically. A *clock interrupt* refers to an interrupt from the device. In Section 6.8.5, which describes how to determine the schedulability of applications that run on an operating system whose scheduler only executes periodically, we called the period of clock interrupts the tick size. The tick size used by most operating systems is 10 milliseconds.[5]

At each clock interrupt, the kernel does the following chores.

1. *Processes timer events*: A clock device has a timer queue. The pending expiration times of all the timers that are bound to the clock are stored in time order in this queue. By checking this queue, the kernel can determine whether some timer events have occurred since the previous time it checked the queue. This is what the kernel does first when servicing a clock interrupt. As we said earlier, when the kernel finds that a timer event did occur, it is to carry out a specified action. The kernel processes in turn all the timer events that have occurred and queues the specified actions. It carries out the actions before returning control to the user.

2. *Updates execution budget*: Most real-time operating systems (including all Real-Time POSIX-compliant systems) provide the user with the choice of round-robin or FIFO scheduling of threads of equal priority. (These policies are called *SCHED_RR* and *SCHED_FIFO*, respectively.) To schedule equal-priority threads in a round-robin manner, the scheduler gives such a thread a *time slice* when it schedules the thread for execution. We can think of the time slice as the execution budget of the executing thread. At each clock interrupt, the scheduler decrements the budget of the thread by

---

[5]In a clock-driven system that uses a cyclic scheduler, clock interrupts occur only at the beginnings of frames.

the tick size. If the thread is not complete when the budget (i.e., its remaining time slice) becomes 0, the kernel decides to preempt the thread. The same mechanism can be used for the FIFO policy. The scheduler simply gives a thread that chooses the FIFO policy an infinite time slice or does not decrement the budget of such a thread, thus making the thread nonpreemptable by equal-priority threads.

3. *Updates the ready queue and returns control*: As a result of the above actions, some threads may become ready (e.g., released upon timer expiration) and the thread that was executing at the time of the clock interrupt may need to be preempted. The scheduler updates the ready queue accordingly and then gives control to the thread at the head of the highest priority queue.

In addition, the kernel may also update monitoring information, such as interval timers which keep track of the total processor time consumption of the thread and the time spent by the kernel on behalf of the thread.

We can see from what it does at each clock interrupt that the periodical execution of the scheduler is necessary. However, if the scheduler executes only at clock interrupts, the responsiveness and schedulability of the system depend critically on the tick size. The typical 10-millisecond tick size is sufficiently short for round-robin scheduling of time-shared applications but may severely degrade the schedulability of applications with stringent timing requirements. A smaller tick size can improve the system in this respect but means more frequent service of clock interrupts and a higher scheduling overhead. For this reason, most operating systems do not rely on tick scheduling (sometimes called time-based scheduling) alone. Rather, it is used in combination with event-driven scheduling. The kernel invokes the scheduler to update the ready queue whenever it wakes up or releases a thread, finds a thread unblocked, or creates a new thread, and so on. Thus a thread is placed in the proper place in the ready queue as soon as it becomes ready.

External Interrupts.   Hardware interrupts provide an effective mechanism for notifying the application of the occurrences of external events and dealing with sporadic I/O activities. For applications that have such activities, handling external interrupts is an essential function of the kernel.

Depending on the source of the interrupt, the amount of time required to handle an interrupt varies. In particular, handling interrupts from DMA (Direct Memory Access) interfaces may take significant amounts of time. A network interface is an example. When there is an incoming message to be delivered, the interface raises an interrupt. In response to this interrupt, the protocol handler executes to identify the thread that is to receive the message, move the message to the address space of the receiving thread, perform handshakes, and so on. The required time can be large and varied. Service routines for disk and network devices can take hundreds of microseconds to tens of milliseconds to complete. For this reason, in most operating systems, interrupt handling is divided into two steps.

Immediate Interrupt Service.   The first step of interrupt handling is executed at an interrupt priority level. All modern processors support some form of priority interrupt. The relationship between interrupt priority levels and normal thread priorities (i.e., software priorities) are depicted by Figure 12–3: The higher the box, the higher the priority. The number of interrupt priority levels depends on the hardware and is unimportant to our discussion here. It

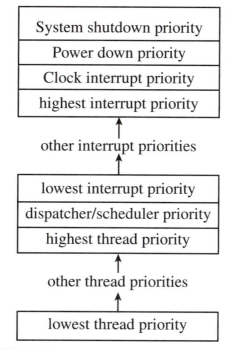

FIGURE 12–3   Hardware and software interrupt priorities.

suffices for us to note that all interrupt priority levels are higher than all thread priorities. In fact, interrupt priorities are higher than the priority at which the scheduler executes.

When an interrupt occurs, the processor pushes the program counter and status register on the interrupt stack and branch to the starting address of the kernel's interrupt handling code. When the kernel executes, it disables interrupts temporarily so it can safely modify data structures that might otherwise also be modified by interrupt service routines. It then saves the processor state on the interrupt stack, enables interrupts, and calls the interrupt service routine of the interrupting device to service the device (e.g., reload registers in the device interface). When more than one device is attached to the same interrupt request line and hence may have raised the interrupt, the kernel calls their interrupt service routines in turn. (When polled, the interrupt service routine of a device that did not raise the interrupt returns immediately.) If during the execution of an interrupt service routine a higher-priority interrupt is raised, the processor and the kernel take care of the higher-priority interrupt in the same manner.

In Figure 12–2, the first step of interrupt handling is called *immediate interrupt service*. Again the immediate interrupt service routine executes at an interrupt priority. The total delay experienced by a device from the time it raises an interrupt to the time its interrupt service routine begins to execute (and hence the device begins to be serviced) is the sum of the following factors:

1. the time the processor takes to complete the current instruction, do the necessary chores (e.g., flush the instruction pipeline and read the interrupt vector), and jump to the trap handler and interrupt dispatcher part of the kernel;

2. the time the kernel takes to disable external interrupts;

3. the time required to complete the immediate interrupt service routines of higher-priority interrupts if any;

4. the time the kernel takes to save the context of the interrupted thread, identify the interrupting device, and get the starting address of the interrupt service routine; and

5. the time the kernel takes to start the immediate interrupt service routine of the interrupting device.

The sum of the above factors is called the *interrupt latency*. It measures the responsiveness of the system to external events. We note that the first factor is very small because the operations are done by the interrupt handling hardware. Similarly, factors 2, 4, and 5 are relatively small (i.e., in order of a few or a few tens of microseconds) and deterministic. Factor 4 is typically shorter when the application and kernel execute in the same address space. By far, factor 3 can be the largest among these factors and contributes to variation in interrupt latency. This factor can be kept small only by making immediate interrupt handling routines as short as possible.

We pause to note three points here. First, the term interrupt service routine refers specifically to the device-dependent portion of the routine provided by the device driver. Many operating systems provide the portion of interrupt service code that are device-independent (i.e., the code for saving processor state before the device-dependent code executes). A bare-bone operating system for embedded applications may not provide such code. We must have this part of the code in the interrupt service routine. The advantage is speed; the processor jumps directed to interrupt service routines without going through the kernel.

Second, we assume here that the operating system polls all the devices that may raise interrupts at the same priority and thus identifies the interrupting device or devices. In embedded systems, numerous I/O devices may be attached to the same interrupt request line. A more effective alterative to polling (also called autovectoring) is vector interrupt: The interrupting device identifies itself by giving the processor an interrupt vector (i.e., the starting address of its interrupt service routine or its identifier) when its interrupt request is granted by the processor. The processor then branches to the address indicated by the vector after saving the program counter and status register. Not all I/O buses support vector interrupt. Hence your choice of vector interrupt limits your choice of I/O bus (e.g., to VME bus) and portability of your interrupt handling mechanism. For the sake of portability, an operating system typically polls even when the I/O bus supports vector interrupt. Ignoring an interrupt vector and polling the requesting device do no harm, while an interrupt handling mechanism that relies on vector interrupt capability does not work when the I/O bus and interrupting device do not have the capability.

Third, rather than getting ready to accept interrupt again as soon as possible as described here, operating systems provide the application with control over when interrupt is enabled again. Thus, the application can control the rate at which external interrupts are serviced and the amount of time spent in interrupt handling.

Scheduled Interrupt Service.   Except for the simplest devices, the immediate step does not complete interrupt handling. Rather, it invokes another service routine to complete interrupt handling. We call the function executed in the second step of interrupt handling a *scheduled interrupt handling routine.* The execution of this routine is typically preemptable and should be scheduled at a suitable (software) priority in a priority-driven system. (As an example, in the real-time operating system LynxOS [Bunn], the priority of the kernel thread that executes a scheduled interrupt handling routine is the priority of the user thread that opened the interrupting device.) This is why Figure 12–2 shows that following immediate interrupt service, the scheduler executes and inserts the scheduled interrupt handling thread in the ready queue. The scheduler then lets the highest priority thread have the processor.

Since scheduled interrupt handling routines may modify kernel data, they are executed by kernel threads in operating systems that provide memory protection. LynxOS and SunOS are examples. When a device driver is created in LynxOS, a kernel thread comes into existence. At its creation, the thread has the lowest priority in the system. Whenever a user thread opens the device driver, the kernel thread inherits the current priority of the user thread. When the I/O operation of the user thread completes, the priority of the kernel thread returns to the level immediately before the priority inheritance. The LynxOS literature refers to this priority inheritance as priority tracking and points out that this mechanism gives us accountability of the delay incurred by threads due to interrupt handling. (Problems 6.24 and 6.30 are about how to analyze the schedulability of such a system.) In SunOS, the kernel thread, called the interrupt thread, is created at interrupt time and is terminated when interrupt handling completes. However unlike kernel threads in LynxOS, an interrupt thread executes immediately after creation. Without priority tracking, the execution of interrupt threads can lead to uncontrolled priority inversion.[6]

We can think of the scheduled interrupt handling step as an aperiodic or sporadic thread. When the immediate interrupt service routine completes, an aperiodic thread is released to execute the scheduled interrupt service routine or inserts the routine into the queue of a bandwidth-preserving server. The scheduler can use some of the bandwidth-preserving or slack-stealing algorithms described in Chapter 7 for this purpose. Unfortunately, existing operating systems not only do not provide such servers but also do not provide good hooks with which we can customize the scheduler for this purpose. It is expensive to implement most of these algorithms in the user level without help from the kernel. In Section 12.2.2, we will describe minor modifications of the scheduling mechanism that simplify the implementation of bandwidth-preserving servers both in the user level and within the kernel.

Hereafter, we will refer to the strategy of dividing interrupt handling into two steps as *split interrupting handling.* As we will see in Sections 12.6 and 12.7, most modern operating systems use this strategy in one form or the other.

12.2 TIME SERVICES AND SCHEDULING MECHANISMS

This and the next sections discuss the basic operating system functions that the previous section either did not mention or treated superficially. Specifically, this section discusses time services and scheduling mechanisms, leaving interprocess communication and synchronization, software interrupts, memory management, and I/O and networking to the next section.

---

[6]A way to reduce the effect of this incorrect prioritization is to have the interrupt thread sets its own priority to the priority of the thread causing the interrupt as soon as that thread is identified.

12.2.1 Time Services

Obviously, good time services are essential to real-time applications. To provide these services and support its own activities, every system has at least one clock device. We have been calling it the system clock. In a system that supports Real-Time POSIX, this clock is called CLOCK_REALTIME.

Clocks and Time. Again, a clock device contains a counter, a timer queue, and an interrupt handler. The counter is triggered to increment monotonically by a precise periodic sequence of pulses. At any time, the content of the counter gives a representation of the current time. We have been calling this counter a (hardware) clock and the triggering edge of each pulse a clock tick. The timer queue contains the pending expiration times of timers bound to the clock.

A system may have more than one clock device and uses them for different purposes. For example, a real-time monitor system may use a clock device to trigger the sampling and digitization of sensor readings and initialize the input of sensor data. A digital control system may use one or more clock devices to time the control-law computations of a rate group or commands to embedded plants.

Resolution. The *resolution* of a clock is the granularity of time provided by the clock. Today's technology makes it possible to have hardware clocks with resolution on an order of nanoseconds. However, the clock resolution available to applications is usually orders of magnitude coarser, on an order of hundreds of microseconds or milliseconds.

To see why there is such disparity, let us look at how an application finds what the current time is. Typically, the kernel maintains a software clock for each clock device it supports. It programs the clock device to raise interrupts periodically. Whenever it gets an interrupt from the clock device, it updates the software clock, and hence the current time according to the clock. Therefore, the resolution of the software clock is equal to the period of these interrupts. A thread gets the current time according to a clock by calling a get time function, such as the POSIX function *clock_gettime( )*, and providing as an argument the ID of the clock to be read. In response to the request, the operating system returns the current time according to the corresponding software clock. Therefore, the resolution of time seen by the calling thread is resolution of the software clock.

In Sections 6.8.5 and 12.1.2, we called the interrupts from the system clock that triggers the scheduler into action clock interrupts. We said that the typical period of clock interrupts is 10 milliseconds. If an operating system updates the system clock only at these interrupts, its clock resolution is 10 milliseconds. A 10-millisecond resolution is too coarse for many applications. For this reason, most modern operating systems support, or allow applications to request, a finer clock resolution. To support a finer resolution, the system clock device is set to interrupt at a higher frequency. At each of the higher-frequency interrupts, the kernel merely updates the software clock and checks the clock's timer queue for timer expirations. Typically, the period of these interrupts, hence the resolution of the software clock, ranges from hundreds of microseconds to tens of milliseconds. It is more convenient if the resolution divides the tick size, so the kernel does tick scheduling at one interrupt out of an integer x number of interrupts from the clock, where x is the ratio of tick size to clock resolution. For the sake of clarity, we will call the higher-frequency interrupts from the clock device *time-*

service interrupts and continue to call the one-out-of-*x* subsequence of interrupts at which the scheduler executes *clock interrupts*.

The resolution of each (software) clock is a design parameter of the operating system. The finer the resolution, the more frequent the time-service interrupts and the larger the amount of processor time the kernel spends in responding to these interrupts. This overhead places a limitation on how fine a resolution the system supports. Moreover, the response time of the get time function is not deterministic, and the variation in the response time introduces an error in the time the calling thread gets from the kernel. This error is far greater than a few nanoseconds! A software clock resolution finer than this error is not meaningful.

High Resolution.   A way to provide a finer resolution than hundreds of microseconds and more accurate time to an application is to map a hardware clock into the address space of the application. Then, the application can read the clock directly. On a Pentium processor, a user thread can read the Pentium time stamp counter.[7] This counter starts at zero when the system is powered up and increments each processor cycle. At today's processor speed, this means that counter increments once a few nanoseconds. By computing from the cycle count provided by the counter, an application can get more precise and higher-resolution time than that provided by the operating system.

However, an operating system may not make the hardware clock readable for the sake of portability, and processors other than those in the Pentium family may not have a high-resolution time stamp counter. Using its own clock/timer device and device driver, an application can maintain its own high-resolution software clock. A higher overhead is a disadvantage of this scheme: The overhead incurred by an application in the maintenance of its own software clock is invariably larger than when the software clock is maintained by the kernel.

Timers and Timer Functions.   Most operating systems (including all Real-Time POSIX compliant systems, Windows NT, and Solaris) allow a thread or process to have its own timers.[8] Specifically, by calling the create timer function, a thread (or process) can create a per thread (or per process) timer and, in a system containing multiple clocks, bind the timer to a specified clock. Associated with each timer is a data structure which the kernel creates in response to the create timer call. Among the information kept in the data structure is the expiration time of the timer. The data structure may also have a pointer to a handler; the handler is a routine that the calling thread wants to be execute when a timer event occurs. A thread destroys its own timer by calling the destroy timer function.

We say that a thread *sets* (or arms) a timer when it asks the kernel to give the timer a future expiration time. A timer is *canceled* (or disarmed) if before the occurrence of the timer event, it is set to expire at or before the current time. (In effect, the kernel does not act when it finds this expiration time.) Every operating system provides timer functions with

---

[7]Some operating systems also use this counter to improve clock resolution. At each time-service interrupt, the kernel reads and stores the time stamp. When servicing a *clock_gettime( )* call, the kernel reads the counter again. From the difference in the two counter readings, the kernel can compute the elapse of time since the last time-service interrupt. By adding this time to the clock reading, the kernel gets and returns a more accurate time.

[8]Operating systems, such as Linux, that do not support per process timers provide one or more systemwide timers. Processes cannot destroy these timers but can set them and use them for alarm purposes.

which a thread can set and cancel timers. Similarly, various forms of set-timer functions allow a thread to specify an action to take upon timer expiration. The types of action include calling a specified function, waking up a thread, and sending a message to a message queue.

The expiration time can be either *absolute* or *relative*. The former is a specific time instant. The latter is the length of the delay from the current time to the absolute expiration time. There are two kinds of timers: one-shot or periodic. When set, a *one-shot timer* expires once at the specified expiration time or when the specified delay has elapsed. In contrast, a thread sets a *periodic timer* by giving it a first expiration time and an interval between consecutive expiration times. Starting from the first expiration time, the periodic timer expires periodically until it is cancelled.

Asynchronous Timer Functions.   As an example, we look at the set watchdog timer function *wdStart( )* provided by VxWorks [Wind]. A watchdog (or alarm) timer is a one-shot timer that supports relative time. After a timer is created, a thread can use it by calling the *wdStart( )* function and specifying as arguments the timer ID, the delay to the expiration time, the function to call at the expiration time, and an argument to be passed to the specified function. A thread can cancel a timer before its expiration by calling *wdCancel( )*.

A watchdog timer mechanism is useful for many purposes. Figure 12–4 gives an example: An implementation of a timing monitor. The timing monitor logs the deadlines missed by input tasks. Each of these tasks processes sporadic sensor readings collected by an input device. Whenever the input device presents a sensor reading by raising an interrupt, its input task must process the reading within the relative deadline of the task. The example assumes that the driver code for each device *device_k* consists of a short interrupt service routine *ISR_k* followed by a data processing routine *DPR_k*. When the *ISR_k* completes, it

---

- During system initialization: The application process creates sporadic thread *S_k* to execute the data processing routine *DPR_k* for each input device *device_k* and sets the *late* flag of the device to false.
- The sporadic thread *S_k*
  - After being created, creates watchdog timer *wdTimer_k* and then suspends itself.
  - When awaked and scheduled, executes *DPR_k*.
  - At the end of *DPR_k*, calls *wdTimercancel(wdTimer_k)* if *late* is false, and then enables interrupt from *device_k* and suspends itself.
- Input device *device_k*: When sensor data become available, raises an interrupt if interrupt is enabled.
- Immediate interrupt handling step:
  - After identifying the interrupting device *device_k*, disables interrupt from *device_k*.
  - Calls *wdTimerSet (wdTimer_k, relativeDeadline_k, timingMonitor, device_k)* so that the watchdog timer will expire at current time plus *relativeDeadline_k*.
  - Services *device_k*.
  - Sets *late* to false and wakes up sporadic thread *S_k*.
- Timing Monitor function *timingMonitor( )*: When called, sets *late* to true and increments by 1 the number of deadlines missed by the specified device.

FIGURE 12–4   Example illustrating the use of watchdog timers.

wakes up a sporadic thread S_k to execute *DPR_k*. The operating system schedules sporadic threads according to some suitable algorithm. During the immediate interrupt handling step, the *ISR_k* routine sets the watchdog timer. The watchdog function *wdTimerSet( )* in Figure 12–4 is similar to the VxWorks's *wdStart( )*. The first argument of the function identifies the watchdog timer. The specified delay is equal to the relative deadline *relativeDeadline_k* of the input task; the function to be called when the timer expires is the timing monitor, and the argument to be passed to the timing monitor is the ID *device_k* of the input device. After setting the watchdog timer, the interrupt service routine wakes up the sporadic thread S_k, which, when scheduled, executes the data processing routine *DPR_k*. If the thread completes before the timer expires, it cancels the timer before suspending itself again. On the other hand, if the timer expires before the thread completes, the timing monitor is called, which increments by one the number of sensor readings from the input device that are not processed in time.

The above watchdog timer function uses a function call as a means to notify the application of the occurrence of a timer event. The other mechanisms commonly used for this purpose are messages and signals. As an example, the *timer_arm( )* function in Real-Time Mach [StTo] takes as arguments the timer expiration time and a port. At the specified time, the kernel sends a notification message containing the current time to the specified port. Thus, such a timer function enables the calling thread to synchronize and communicate with the thread or threads that will receive the message at that port.

Signal is the notification mechanism used by Real-Time POSIX timer function *timer_settime( )*. When a thread calls the *timer_create( )* function to request the creation of a timer, it specifies the clock to which the timer is to be bound, as well as the type of signal to be delivered whenever the timer expires. If the type of signal is not specified and the clock to which the timer is bound is CLOCK_REALTIME, the system will deliver a SIGARLM (alarm clock expired) signal by default.

After creating a timer, a thread can set it by calling *timer_settime( )*. The parameters of this function include

1. the ID of the timer to be set;
2. a flag indicating whether the new expiration time is relative or absolute;
3. the new timer setting, which gives the delay to the expiration time or the absolute value of the expiration time, depending on value of the flag; and
4. the period between subsequent timer expiration times.[9]

Again, when the timer expires, the system delivers a signal of the specified type to the calling thread.

Earlier in Section 12.1, we mentioned that a periodic thread can be implemented at the user level. This can be done using a timer as shown in Figure 12–5(a). In this example, a thread named *thread_id* is created at configuration time to implement a periodic task. The intended behavior of the task is that it will be released for the first time at 10 time units after *timer_create*(CLOCK_REALTIME, NULL, timer_id);

block SIGALRM and other signals;

instancesRemaining = 200;

timer_settime(timer_id, relative, 10, 100);

while (instancesRemaining > 0)

    sigwaitinfo(SIGALRM);

    statements in the program of the periodic tasks;

    instancesRemaining = instancesRemaining - 1;

endwhile;

timer_delete(timer_id);

thread_destroy(thread_id);

(a) Implementation 1

instancesRemaining = 200;

nextReleaseTime = $clock + 10$;

while (instancesRemaining > 0)

    NOW = $clock$;

    if (NOW < nextReleaseTime), do

        timer_sleep_until (nextReleaseTime);

        statements in the program of the periodic task;

        nextReleaseTime = nextReleaseTime +100;

    else

        statements in the program of the periodic task;

        nextReleaseTime = NOW +100;

    instancesRemaining = instancesRemaining −1;

endwhile;

thread_destroy(thread_id);

(b) Implementation 2

FIGURE 12–5   User level implementations of periodic tasks. (a) Implementation 1. (b) Implementation 2.

its creation and afterwards, periodically once every 100 time units. The task has only 200 jobs; so the thread will be deleted after it has executed 200 times. After the thread is created, it first creates a timer and specifies that the timer is bound to the system clock, indicated by the argument CLOCK_REALTIME. The NULL pointer argument indicates that the timer will deliver the default timer expiration signal SIGALRM whenever it expires. The *timer_create( )* function returns the ID (*timer_id*) of the timer. The thread then blocks SIGALRM signal, as well as other signals that it does not want to process, except when it synchronously waits for the signal. After it thus initializes itself, the thread sets the timer to expire periodically starting from 10 time units from the current time and then once every 100 time units. After this, the thread calls *sigwaitinfo( )*[10] to wait for SIGALRM. This function returns immediately if a SIGALRM is waiting; otherwise, the thread is blocked until the signal arrives. When the function returns, the thread "is released" to execute the code of the periodic task. After it has been released and executed 200 times, the thread asks operating system to delete the timer and itself.

It is important to note that *such a periodic task may not behave as intended*. There are many reasons; we will discuss them at the end of this subsection.

Synchronous Timer Functions.   The set-timer functions in the previous examples are asynchronous. After being set, the timer counts down while the calling thread continues to execute. Consequently, a thread can set multiple timers to alarm at different rates or times. In contrast, after calling a synchronous timer function, the calling thread is suspended.

As an example, we look at the *timer_sleep( )* function provided by Real-Time Mach. The function causes the calling thread to be suspended either until the specified absolute time or for the specified time interval. When the specified time is relative, the timer function is similar to the Real-Time POSIX *nanosleep(t)*; the parameter *t* specifies the length of the interval the calling thread sleeps.

We can implement the periodic task in Figure 12–5(a) using the *timer_sleep( )* function as well. After a thread is created, it executes the code in Figure 12–5(b). For clarity, we refer to the timer function as *timer_sleep_until( )* to indicate that the argument is absolute, and this timer function uses the system's timer. We assume here that the thread can get the current time by reading the clock directly, and the value of *clock* is the current time. When this assumption is not true, the thread must call a function [e.g., *clock_gettime( )*] to get the current time from the operating system.

Timer Resolution.   We measure the quality of timers by their resolution and accuracy. The term resolution of a timer usually means the granularity of the absolute time or the time interval specified as an argument of a timer function. We call this granularity the *nominal timer resolution*. If the nominal timer resolution is x microseconds, then the operating system will not mistake two timer events set x microseconds apart as a single timer event. However, this does not mean that the granularity of time measured by the timer, as seen by application threads, is this fine.

Periodic Timer Interrupts.   To illustrate, we recall that in most operating systems, the kernel checks for the occurrences of timer events and handles the events only at time-service interrupts and these interrupts occur periodically. Now let us suppose that the nominal timer resolution is 10 microseconds and the period of time-service interrupts is 5 milliseconds. A threads sets a timer to expire twice 10 microseconds apart and reads the current time at the occurrence of each timer event. Suppose that the first timer event occurs at 5 microseconds

---

[10]*sigwaitinfo( )* is a Real-Time POSIX function for synchronous signal waiting. When a signal arrives, the function does not call the signal handler. Rather, it returns the number of the signal to the thread. If a SIGARLM signal arrives while it is blocked and the thread is not waiting, the overrun count of the timer is incremented by one. By processing this count, the thread can determine the number of times the system has delivered SIGALRM. The example does not include the step to process the overrun counter.

before an interrupt and the second one at 5 microseconds after the interrupt. The kernel handles the first one at the interrupt and the second at the next time-service interrupt. The time values read by the thread are approximately 5 milliseconds apart.

We call the granularity of time measured by application threads using timers the *actual timer resolution*. In a system where the kernel checks for timer expirations periodically, this resolution is no finer than the period of time-service interrupts. We can get a finer actual resolution only by having the kernel check the timer queue more frequently.

One-Shot Timer Interrupts.   Alternatively, some operating systems (e.g., QNX) program the clock device to raise an interrupt at each timer expiration time. In other words, the clock interrupts in the one-shot mode. As a part of timer interrupt service, the kernel finds the next timer expiration time and sets the clock to interrupt at that time. Thus, the kernel carries out the requested action as soon as a timer expires. With this implementation, the actual timer resolution is limited only by the amount of time the kernel takes to set and service the clock device and to process each timer event, since the kernel cannot respond to timer events more frequently than once per this amount of time. This time is in order of microseconds even on today's fast processors.

Since the clock device no longer interrupts periodically, some other mechanism is needed to maintain the system clock and to time the kernel's periodic activities. (Section 12.7.2 gives an example: UTIME [HSPN], a high-resolution time service on Linux. UTIME reads the Pentium time stamp counter at each timer interrupt and computes time based on the cycle counts.) This means that more work needs to be done upon each timer interrupt and the execution time of the the timer interrupt service routine is larger. (With UTIME, the execution time of timer interrupt service routine is several time larger than in standard Linux where timer expiration is checked periodically.) Moreover, each timer expiration causes an interrupt. As a consequence, the overhead of time services can be significant higher than when the occurrences of timer events are checked only periodically, especially when there are many timers and they expire frequently.

Timer Accuracy.   By timer error, we mean the difference between the absolute time (or time interval) specified by the calling thread and the actual time at which the specified action starts. Timer error depends on three factors. The first is the frequency at which timer expirations are checked. This factor is the period of time-service interrupts in most operating systems since they check for timer expirations periodically.

The second source of error arises from the fact that timer events may not be acted upon by the kernel in time order. In some operating systems (e.g., Windows NT 4.0 and Linux), when more than one timer is found expired at a clock interrupt, the kernel takes care of the timer with the latest expiration time first and in decreasing time order. In other words, it services timer events in LIFO order. Therefore, if the order of occurrences of timer events is important, you will need to take care of this matter. For example, if two timer expiration times are within the same clock interrupt period, you need to give the timer that is supposed to trigger an earlier activity a later expiration time.

The time spent to process timer events is the third and the most unpredictable source of error in the absolute time or delay interval the calling thread gets from the kernel. Just as lengthy interrupt service routines cause large variation in interrupt latency, lengthy timer-service routines increase timer error. By minimizing the amount of time spent processing each timer event, the error introduced by this factor can be kept negligibly small compared with the period of time-service interrupts.

Release-Time Jitters of Periodic Tasks.   We conclude our discussion on timers by looking closely at the user-level implementations of a periodic task in Figure 12–5. In particular, we ask what can cause jitters in the release times of the periodic thread. Suppose that the kernel finishes creating the thread and places it in the ready queue at time t. The programmer's intention is for the thread to be released for the first time at time $t + 10$. We see that the actual first release time can be later than this time because (1) the thread may be preempted and not scheduled until a later time and (2) it takes some time to create a timer (and to get the current time) when the thread starts to execute. If our time unit is millisecond, the delay due to factor (2) is small and can be neglected, but the delay due to factor (1) is arbitrary. Therefore, the implementations are correct only if we accept that $t + 10$ is the earliest release time of the first instance, while the actual release time of this instance may be much later.

Similarly, 100 time units are the minimum length of time between the release times of instances of this task. The subsequent instances of the thread will be released periodically only if the while loop always completes within 100 time units. According to implementation 2, if the response time of an instance of the thread exceeds 100, the next instance is released as soon as the current instance completes. (Again, the next release can be delayed since the thread can be preempted between iterations of the loop.) In contrast, the timer in implementation 1 continues to signal every 100 time units. If a signal arrives while the thread is executing its program, the signal is blocked. The pseudocode in Figure 12–5(a) does not describe a correct implementation of a periodic task because it neglects this situation. In general, Real-Time POSIX signals that arrive while blocked are queued, but not SIGARLM signals. Instead, the number of times the SIGARLM signal has arrived while the signal is blocked is indicated by the timer overrun count. By examining this count, the thread can determine when the code of the periodic task should be executed again. How to do so is left for you as an exercise in Problem 12.6. In any case, the periodic task is not truly periodic. Moreover, because the thread can be preempted for an arbitrary amount of time, the interrelease time of consecutive instances can be arbitrarily large.

12.2.2   Scheduling Mechanisms

This section discusses several aspects regarding the implementation of algorithms for scheduling periodic tasks and aperiodic tasks. In particular, we call attention to those scheduling services that the kernel can easily provide which can significantly simplify the implementation of complex algorithms for scheduling aperiodic tasks in the user level.

Fixed-Priority Scheduling.   All modern operating systems support fixed-priority scheduling. Many real-time operating systems provide 256 priority levels. As discussed in Section 6.8.4, a fixed-priority system with this many priority levels performs as well as an ideal system that has an infinite number of priority levels. (The loss in schedulable utilization of a rate-monotonically scheduled system due to nondistinct priorities is negligible.) In contrast, a general-purpose operating system may provide fewer levels. For example, there are only 16 real-time priority levels in Windows NT.

A parameter of the create thread function is the priority of the new thread; the priority of each new thread is set at the *assigned priority*, that is, the priority chosen for the thread according to the algorithm used to schedule the application. (This is sometimes done in two steps: The thread is first created and then its priority is set.[11]) Once created, the assigned priority of the thread is kept in its TCB. In a system that supports priority inheritance or the ceiling-priority protocol, a thread may inherit a higher priority than its assigned priority. In Sections 8.4 and 8.6 where these protocols were described, we called the time varying priority which a thread acquires during its execution its *current priority*. The current priority also needs to be kept in the thread's TCB.

To support fixed-priority scheduling, the kernel maintains a ready queue for each priority level. Whenever a thread is ready to execute, the kernel places it in the ready queue of the thread's current priority. For this reason, the current priority of a thread is often called its dispatch priority.

Real-Time POSIX-compliant systems provide the applications with the choice between round-robin or FIFO policies for scheduling equal-priority threads. Having all equal-(current-) priority threads in one queue makes it convenient for the kernel to carry out either policy. We already described how to do this in Section 12.1.2.

Finding the highest priority ready thread amounts to finding the highest priority nonempty queue. The theoretical worst-case time complexity of this operation is $O(\Omega)$, where Ω is the number of priority levels supported by the operating system. In fact, the number of comparisons required to scan the queues is at most $\Omega/K + \log_2 K - 1$, where K is the word length of the CPU. (How this is done is left to you as an exercise in Problem 12.7.) Therefore, on a 32-bit CPU, the scheduler takes at most 12 comparisons to find the highest priority threads when there are 256 priority levels.

EDF Scheduling.   Most existing operating systems supposely support dynamic priority. This claim typically means that the operating system provides a system call by which a thread can set and change its own priority or the priority of some other thread. This mechanism is adequate for mode-change and reconfiguration purposes but is too expensive to support dynamic scheduling policies such as the EDF algorithm. [We note that to change the priority of a thread that is ready to run, the thread must be removed from the queue for its current priority, the value of its priority (in TCB) changed, and then the thread inserted into the queue for its new priority.]

A better alternative is for the kernel to provide EDF scheduling capability. As it turns out, the kernel can support both fixed-priority and EDF scheduling using essentially the same queue structure, in particular, the queues for deadline-monotonic scheduling. In addition to the small modification of the queue structure, which we will describe below, some of the kernel functions need to be modified as follows.

---

[11]An example is a thread is created by a *fork( )* function. It inherits the priority of the parent thread in the parent process. If the system supports EDF scheduling, the absolute and relative deadlines of each thread should also be included in the TCB of the thread.

1. The create thread function specifies the relative deadline of the thread. (Earlier, we mentioned that if the operating system supports periodic threads, the relative deadline should be a parameter of each periodic thread. To support EDF scheduling, the operating system needs this parameter of every thread, not just periodic threads.)

2. Whenever a thread is released, its absolute deadline is calculated from its release time and relative deadline. This can the done by either a timer function or the scheduler.

In short, both the relative and absolute deadlines of each ready thread are known, and they are kept in the TCB.

Rather than maintaining a single EDF queue, the scheduler keeps a FIFO queue for threads of each relative deadline. The scheduler places each newly released thread at the end of the queue for threads which have the same relative deadline as the new thread, as if the threads were scheduled on the deadline-monotonic basis. Clearly, the threads in each queue are ordered among themselves according to their absolute deadlines. Therefore, to find the thread with the earliest absolute deadline, the scheduler only needs to search among the threads at the heads of all the FIFO queues.

To minimize the time for dequeueing the highest priority thread, the scheduler can keep the threads at the heads of the FIFO queues in a priority queue of length Ω', where Ω' is the number of distinct relative deadlines supported by the system. This queue structure is shown in Figure 12–6. The time to update the queue structure is the time required to insert a new thread into the priority queue. The time complexity of this operation is $O(\log \Omega')$, and it occurs only when a thread completes and when the scheduler inserts a new thread into an empty FIFO queue. The scheduler can dequeue the highest priority thread in $O(\log \Omega')$ time as well. The schedulable utilization of a large number of threads depends on Ω'. This dependency was discussed in Section 6.8.4.

Preemption Lock.   Some kernel activities leave the system in inconsistent states if preempted. Consequently, it is necessary to make some portions of some system calls nonpreemptable. In a good operating system, system calls are preemptable whenever possible, and

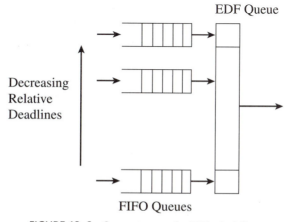

FIGURE 12–6   Queue structure for EDF scheduling.

each nonpreemptable section is implemented efficiently so its execution time, and hence the blocking time due to nonpreemptivity, is as small as possible.

Almost all real-time operating systems allow a thread to disable preemption. We use the name *preemption lock*, which is the name used by VxWorks [Wind] for this mechanism. [In VxWorks, a task can call *taskLock( )* to disable preemption; no other task can preempt it until it completes or executes the unlock routine *taskUnlock( )*.] You recall that the Nonpreemptable Critical Section (NPCS) protocol is a simple way to control access to shared resources (e.g., mutex objects and reader/writer locks). With preemption lock, this protocol is simple to implement at the user level. Each thread makes itself nonpreemptable immediately prior to entering a critical section and makes itself preemptable when it no longer holds any resource. Because the resource requested by the thread is always available and the thread has the highest priority just before it becomes nonpreemptable, the thread always acquires the lock successfully. Of course, a thread should never self-suspend when it holds any lock and is therefore nonpreemptable.

Preemption lock is often achieved by locking or disabling the scheduler. Alternatively, an operating system (e.g., pSOS+ [Moto]) may provide a task with a choice of running in preemptive or nonpreemptive mode. A task can disable preemption by setting a mode-control bit; task switching occurs only when a nonpreemptive running task blocks or reenables preemption. Since hardware interrupt service routines execute at priorities higher than the scheduler, as shown in Figure 12–3, interrupts are not disabled while some thread is preemption locked.

Aperiodic Thread Scheduling.   None of the commercial real-time operating systems support bandwidth-preserving servers. The implementation of such a server as a user thread requires the ability to monitor the duration of the server's execution (i.e., the consumed server budget) at the user level. Timer functions of the kind described above are cumbersome, expensive, and inaccurate for this purpose. To replenish the budget of a sporadic server in a fixed-priority system, the thread that maintains the server (called the user-level scheduler below) needs to know when busy intervals of higher-priority threads begin and end. To get this information at the user level, the user-level scheduler needs the cooperation of those threads, and even with their cooperation, incurs large overhead. On the other hand, as we will see shortly, it is easy and inexpensive for the kernel to get and provide this information.

Monitoring Processor Time Consumption.   Specifically, to maintain a server in the user level, we must monitor the server budget consumption at the user level. What we need for this purpose is an interval timer (a stop watch) that can be reset at the replenishment time of each server. The timer counts whenever the server executes. The timer signals the user-level scheduler when the count reaches the server budget. Such a timer is similar to the UNIX interval timer ITIMER_VIRTUAL[12] in the sense that it counts only at times when the server executes. Indeed, if ITIMER_VIRTUAL were more accurate, it could be used for this purpose.

---

[12]Interval timers ITIMER_VIRTUAL and ITIMER_PROF are used by performance monitoring and profiling tools. The former keeps track of the CPU time consumed by the thread itself. The latter gives the total CPU time consumed by the thread plus the time consumed by the kernel while working on behalf of the thread.

Unfortunately, ITIMER_VIRTUAL has two major shortcomings. The first is its resolution, and the second is its accuracy.

In most UNIX systems, the kernel updates ITIMER_VIRTUAL only at times when it services clock interrupts. As a consequence, the resolution of the timer is coarse and the consumed budget measured by the timer may be erroneous.

The coarse resolution is not a problem, since we can take into account the effect of (actual) timer resolution as we take care of the effect of tick scheduling in our choice of server size. If we use ITIMER_VIRTUAL to measure the consumed budget, the measured value has two kinds of errors. At each clock interrupt, the kernel increments ITIMER_VIRTUAL of a thread by a tick size if it finds the thread executing. If the kernel treats a server thread in this manner, the interval timer may give an overestimation of the consumed budget since the server may not have executed throughout the clock interrupt period. On the other hand, when the kernel finds a thread not executing at the time of the clock interrupt, it does not increment ITIMER_VIRTUAL, even when the thread has executed during part of the clock interrupt period. If the thread is the server, the interval timer may underestimate the consumed budget as a consequence. An overestimation is not a serious problem; the server may be less responsive because it may be suspended when in fact it should still be eligible for execution. In contrast, an underestimation of the consumed budget may cause the server to overrun and therefore does not work correctly.

We can easily modify the tick scheduling mechanism to monitor server budget consumption correctly, if not accurately. For this purpose, the kernel needs to keep the current budget of each server thread (and in the case of a SpSL server, the current budget chunks) in the TCB of the thread. The scheduler sets the time slice of a server to the current server budget whenever it schedules the server to run. The scheduler decrements the budget by the tick size during every clock interrupt period in which the server has executed.[13] Figure 12–7 shows a way to do so. As a consequence, the scheduler never underestimates the consumed budget. Whenever the scheduler preempts a server or suspends a server, it writes the server's current budget (i.e., the remaining time slice) back to the TCB of the server. When the budget becomes 0, the server is no longer eligible for execution, and the scheduler moves the server back to the suspended queue.

The kernel can keep track of server budget consumption much more accurately if it takes advantage of a high-resolution hardware clock (or Pentium time counter). The scheduler reads the clock and updates the current budget of each server thread at each context switch that involves the thread. Indeed, the kernel can more accurately monitor the processor time consumption of every thread in the same manner.

Tracking Busy Intervals.   Similarly, in a fixed-priority system, it is simple for the kernel to monitor and detect the beginnings and ends of busy intervals of threads with priorities higher than that of a server (or any thread). In Chapter 7, we called this set of threads $\mathbf{T}_H$, server priority π_s, and a busy interval of $\mathbf{T}_H$ a level-(π_{s-1}) busy interval. You recall that the beginning of a busy interval of $\mathbf{T}_H$ is an instant prior to which no thread in the set is ready for

---

[13]The scheme described here is sufficient for SpSL or deferrable servers because the budget of a SpSL or a deferrable server is consumed only when the server executes. In contrast, according to the consumption rule of simple sporadic servers stated in Section 7.3.1, after the server begins to execute, its budget should also be decremented when lower-priority threads execute. A more complex monitoring scheme is required to support this rule.

Input information maintained by kernel:

- *currentBudget*: Set to server budget at replenishment time.
- *decremented*: FALSE if the budget has not been decremented in current clock interrupt period; TRUE if otherwise.
- server priority π_s.
- *level-π_iBusy*: TRUE if the current time is in a level-π_s busy interval; FALSE otherwise
- *BEGIN* and *END*: Beginning and end of the current level-π_s busy interval.

Monitoring consumed server budget:

- When scheduling the server,
  - set time slice to *currentBudget*;
  - set *decremented* to FALSE;
- When preempting or suspending the server in the midst of a clock interrupt period,
  - if *decremented* is FALSE,
    * decrement (remaining) time slice by tick size;
    * if time slice is 0, suspend server;
    * otherwise, set *decremented* to TRUE and *currentBudget* = remaining time slice;
- At a clock interrupt when the server is executing,
  - if *decremented* is TRUE, set *decremented* to FALSE;
  - Otherwise,
    * decrement time slice by tick size;
    * if time slice is 0, suspend server.

Tracking level-π_s busy interval:

- Upon clock interrupt,
  - if *level-π_sBusy* is TRUE,
    * if the queues for priorities π_s or higher are empty,
      + set *END* to current time and *level-π_sBusy* to FALSE;
      + service timer events;
      + if a thread in $\mathbf{T}_H$ is released, set *BEGIN* to current time and *level-π_sBusy* to TRUE;
    * otherwise (i.e., if the queues are not empty), service timer events;
  - otherwise (i.e., if *level-π_sBusy* is FALSE),
    * service timer events;
    * if a thread in $\mathbf{T}_H$ is released, set *BEGIN* to current time and *level-π_sBusy* to TRUE;
- When releasing a thread at times other than clock interrupts,
  - if *level-π_sBusy* is FALSE and the newly released thread is in $\mathbf{T}_H$, set *BEGIN* to current time and *level-π_sBusy* to TRUE;
- When a thread of priority π_s or higher completes,
  - if *level-π_sBusy* is TRUE and queues for priorities π_s and higher become empty, set *END* to current time and set *level-π_sBusy* to FALSE.

FIGURE 12–7 Monitoring budget consumption and tracking busy intervals by kernel.

execution and at which a thread in the set is released. The end of the busy interval is the first instant when all threads in $\mathbf{T}_H$ that were released before the instant have completed. Since a new busy interval may begin immediately after a busy interval ends, the processor may be continuously busy executing threads in $\mathbf{T}_H$ for the entire duration. This is why the boundaries of busy intervals cannot be detected by simply monitoring the idle/busy state of the thread set $\mathbf{T}_H$.

The kernel can check for the end of a busy interval at each clock interrupt as follows. When servicing a clock interrupt or releasing a thread upon the occurrence of a signal or interrupt, the kernel first checks whether the queues for priorities higher than π_s are empty. The current time is the end *END* of a busy interval if some of these queues were not empty the last time the kernel checked them but are all empty at the current time.

After the kernel checks the queues, it checks timer events if it is responding to a clock interrupt. The current time is the beginning *BEGIN* of a busy interval if the previous busy interval has ended and a thread in $\mathbf{T}_H$ is released at the time. Figure 12–7 also gives a pseudocode description of this scheme. *BEGIN* and *END* are information needed for determining the next replenishment time of a bandwidth-preserving server. (The replenishment rules of different servers are described in Sections 7.2 and 7.3.)

Hook for User-Level Implementation.   In summary, the modified tick scheduling mechanism described above is only slightly more complicated than the existing one. The additional overhead is small. With this modification, it is relatively straightforward to implement bandwidth-preserving servers, as well as a slack stealer.

However, for modularity and customizability reasons, it is better for the operating system to provide good hooks so that bandwidth-preserving servers and slack stealers can be implemented efficiently in the user level. The minimum support the operating system should provide for this purpose is an ITIMER_VIRTUAL-like timer that never underestimates the processor time consumption of the specified thread. Better yet is for the operating system to also support server threads and provides a system call for a user thread to set the server thread budget.

Busy-interval tracking is essential. Again, this can be done with only a small modification to the standard scheduling mechanism. It would be most convenient if the operating system provides an API function which a thread can call if the thread wants to be notified when the current busy interval of the specified priority ends and when a new busy interval begins.

Static Configuration.   As Chapter 9 pointed out, we want multiprocessor or distributed real-time applications to be statically configured so we can validate their end-to-end timing constraints. In a static system, computation tasks are partitioned into modules, each module is bound to a processor, and the tasks and threads on each processor are scheduled according to a uniprocessor scheduling algorithm. Over a network, each message stream is sent over a fixed route. Many real-time operating systems are uniprocessor, multitasking systems, so if we run our application on multiple networked machines on any of these operating systems, our application is naturally statically configured.

In contrast, modern general-purpose operating systems and some real-time operating systems (e.g., such as QNX [QNX]) are Symmetrical Multiprocessor (SMP) systems. Multiprocessor operating systems are designed to support dynamically configured applications. In a dynamic system, the dispatcher/scheduler puts all the ready threads in a common queue and schedules the highest priority thread on any available processor. This is what the scheduler in an SMP operating system does unless you tell it to do otherwise. The mechanism for this purpose is called *processor affinity* [Solo, QNX]. Among the scheduling information maintained in the TCB of each thread, there is an affinity mask. There is a bit for every processor in the system. By default, the affinity mask of a thread is set to all 1's, telling the scheduler that the thread can run on every processor. By using a set affinity mask system call, a thread can set its own affinity mask or that of another thread (or process) so there is only one "1" among all bits. This value of the mask tells the scheduler to schedule the thread only on the processor indicated by the "1" in the mask. In this way, a real-time application can bind its threads and processes to processors.

pSOS+m [Moto] is a multiprocessor kernel that supports the MPCP (Multiprocessor Priority-Ceiling) and end-to-end multiprocessor models in a natural way. We postpone this discussion until Section 12.6 when we describe this operating system.

Release Guard Mechanism.   In Chapter 9 it was also pointed out that simply binding computation tasks to CPUs is not sufficient. If the tasks are scheduled on a fixed-priority basis, we should synchronize the releases of periodic tasks on different CPUs according to one of the nongreedy protocols discussed in Section 9.4.1. Similarly, sending message streams through fixed routes is not sufficient. Traffic shaping at the network interfaces is needed. By doing so, the worst-case response time of each end-to-end task can be computed by the sum of worst-case response times of the subtasks on individual CPUs and networks.

Among nongreedy protocols, the Release-Guard (RG) protocol is best, because it not only keeps the worst-case response time of every subtask small but also keeps the average response time of all subtasks small. Moreover, in any operating system that supports periodic threads, it is straightforward to integrate rule 1 of the protocol into the mechanism for releasing periodic threads. Specifically, the kernel maintains for each periodic thread a release guard, which the kernel sets to the current time plus the period of the thread whenever it releases the thread. The kernel releases the thread at that time only if it has received notification (in the form of a message, or an I/O complete notification, etc.) from the predecessor; otherwise, it waits until the notification is received. This rule is also simple to implement in the user level. (The implementations of periodic threads in Figure 12–5 can be modified straightforwardly to incorporate a release guard for the thread; the modification is left to you as an exercise.)

According to rule 2 of the protocol, the release guard of every thread is set to the current time at the end of each busy interval of the entire system. This rule is expensive to implement in the user level unless the kernel helps. If the kernel detects the end of each busy interval and provides a notification of some form, it is also simple to integrate rule 2 with the maintenance of periodic threads and bandwidth-preserving servers. At the end of each busy interval, which can be detected in the way shown in Figure 12–7, the kernel (or a user-level scheduler) can set the release guard of every periodic thread to the current time and release all those threads for which the notifications for the completion of their predecessors have already been received.

12.3   OTHER BASIC OPERATING SYSTEM FUNCTIONS

This section continues our discussion on operating system services that are essential for all but the simplest embedded applications. Specifically, it discusses real-time issues in communication and synchronization, software interrupt, memory management, I/O, and networking.

12.3.1   Communication and Synchronization

As they execute, threads *communicate* (i.e., they exchange control information and data). They *synchronize* in order to ensure that their exchanges occur at the right times and under the right conditions and that they do not get into each other's way. Shared memory, message queues, synchronization primitives (e.g., mutexes, condition variables, and semaphores), and events and signals are commonly used mechanisms for these purposes.[14] Almost all operating systems provide a variety of them in one form or the other. (The only exceptions are single-threaded executives intended solely for small and deterministic embedded applications.)

This subsection discusses message queues and mutexes and reader/writer locks, leaving events and signals to the next subsection. We skip shared memory entirely. Shared memory provides a low-level, high-bandwidth and low-latency means of interprocess communication. It is commonly used for communication among not only processes that run on one processor but also processes that run on tightly coupled multiprocessors. (An example of the latter is radar signal processing. A shared memory between signal and data processors makes the large number of track records produced by signal processors available to the tracking process running on the data processor or processors.) We gloss over this scheme because we have little that is specific to real-time applications to add to what has already been said about it in the literature. (As an example, Gallmeister [Gall] has a concise and clear explanation on how to use shared memory in general and in systems that are compliant to POSOX real-time extensions in specific.) The little we have to add is the fact that real-time applications sometimes do not explicitly synchronize accesses to shared memory; rather, they rely on "synchronization by scheduling," that is, threads that access the shared memory are so scheduled as to make explicit synchronization unnecessary. Thus, the application developer transfers the burden of providing reliable access to shared memory from synchronization to scheduling and schedulability analysis. The cost is that many hard real-time requirements arise from this as a result and the system is brittle. Using semaphores and mutexes to synchronously access shared memory is the recommended alternative.

Message Queues.   As its name tells us, a message queue provides a place where one or more threads can pass messages to some other thread or threads. Message queues provide a file-like interface; they are an easy-to-use means of many-to-many communication among threads. In particular, Real-Time POSIX message queue interface functions, such as *mq_send( )* and *mq_receive( )*, can be implemented as fast and efficient library functions. By

---

[14]We skip over pipes, UNIX FIFOs, and NT named pipes. These are efficient mechanisms for communication among equal-priority processes, but their lack of prioritization is an obvious shortcoming as a means of interprocess communication in general. Gallmeister [Gall] compares UNIX pipes, FIFOs, and message queues and Hart [Hart] compares UNIX FIFOs with NT named pipes.

making message queues location transparent, an operating system can make this mechanism as easy to use across networked machines as on a single machine.

As an example of how message queues are used, we consider a system service provider. Message queues provide a natural way of communication between it and its clients. The service provider creates a message queue, gives the message queue a name, and makes this name known to its clients. To request service, a client thread opens the message queue and places its Request-For-Service (RFS) message in the queue. The service provider may also use message queues as the means for returning the results it produces back to the clients. A client gets the result by opening the result queue and receiving the message in it.

Prioritization.   You can see from the above example that message queues should be priority queues. The sending thread can specify the priority of its message in its send message call. (The parameters of the Real-Time POSIX send function *mq_send( )* are the name of the message queue, the location and length of the message, and the priority of the message.) The message will be dequeued before lower-priority messages. Thus, the service provider in our example receives the RFS messages in priority order.

Messages in Real-Time POSIX message queues have priorities in the range [0, MQ_MAX_PRIO], where the number MQ_MAX_PRIO of message priorities is at least 31. (In contrast, noncompliant operating systems typically support only two priority levels: normal and urgent. Normal messages are queued in FIFO order while an urgent message is placed at the head of the queue.) It makes sense for an operating system to offer equal numbers of message and thread priorities.[15] Some systems do. For the sake of simplicity, our subsequent discussion assumes equal numbers of threads and message priorities.

Message-Based Priority Inheritance.   A message is not read until a receiving thread executes a receive [e.g., Real-Time POSIX *mg_receive( )*]. Therefore, giving a low priority to a thread that is to receive and act upon a high-priority message is a poor choice in general, unless a schedulability analysis can show that the receiving thread can nevertheless complete in time. (Section 6.8.6 gives a scheme: You can treat the sending and receiving threads as two job segments with different priorities.)

A way to ensure consistent prioritization is to provide message-based priority inheritance, as QNX [QNX] does. A QNX server process (i.e., a service provider) receives messages in priority order. It provides a work thread to service each request. Each work thread inherits the priority of the request message, which is the priority of the sender. Real-Time POSIX does not support message-based priority inheritance. A way suggested by Gallmeister [Gall] to emulate this mechanism is to give the service provider the highest priority while it waits for messages. When it receives a message, it lowers its priority to the message priority. Thus, the service provider tracks the priorities of the requests.

---

[15] A question here is whether 32 message priority levels are sufficient if the system provides a larger number of thread priorities. To answer this question, we suppose there are 256 thread priorities, and these priorities are mapped uniformly to the 32 message priorities: A thread of priority x sets its message priority to $\lfloor x/8 \rfloor$. (As we did in earlier chapters, a smaller integer represents a higher priority.) Its message may experience priority inversion only when threads of priorities $1 + 8\lfloor x/8 \rfloor, 2 + 8\lfloor x/8 \rfloor, \ldots, 8 + 8\lfloor x/8 \rfloor$ are sending messages via the same message queue at the same time.

Traditional service providers in microkernel systems are single threaded and service one request at a time. Since its execution is preemptable, uncontrolled priority inversion can still occur even with message-based priority inheritance. To control priority inversion in this case, we want the service provider to inherit the highest priority of all the threads requesting services at the time. In a system where message-queue send and receive functions are implemented as system calls, this priority inheritance can be done by having the kernel raise the priority of the service provider to the message priority (i.e., the sender's priority) whenever it places a message at the head of the service provider's request message queue if the priority of the service provider is lower at the time. The kernel adjusts the priority of the service provider as indicated by the priority of the message at the head of its (RFS) message queue each time the service provider executes a receive. A service provider is suspended when its message queue is empty. A suspended thread consumes no processor time; hence there is no harm leaving the service provider at its current priority. When the kernel puts a message in an empty queue, it sets the service provider's priority accordingly.

No Block and Notification.   A useful feature is nonblocking. The Real-Time POSIX message-queue send function *mq_send( )* is nonblocking. As long as there is room in a message queue for its message, a thread can call the send function to put a message into the queue and continue to execute. However, when the queue is full, the *mq_send( )* may block. To ensure that the send call will not block when the message queue is full, we set the mode of the message queue to nonblocking (i.e., O_NONBLOCK). (The mode is an attribute of the message queue which can be set when the message queue is opened.) Similarly, by default, a thread is blocked if the message queue is empty when it calls *mq_receive( )*. We can make the receive call nonblocking in the same manner.

Notification means that a message queue notifies a process when the queue changes from being empty to nonempty. (A Real-Time POSIX message queue notifies only one process.) The service provider in the above example can arrange to be notified; thus it saves itself the trouble of having to poll its request message queue periodically after the queue becomes empty. Notification also enables a receiving process to respond quickly. As an example, suppose that a user-level bandwidth-preserving server uses a message queue as its ready queue. When an aperiodic thread is released, a message is placed in the message queue. The capability of the message queue to notify the server is essential.

Synchronization Mechanisms.   Threads (and processes) synchronize using mutexes, reader/writer locks, condition variables, and semaphores. Chapters 8 and 9 already discussed extensively protocols for controlling priority inversion that may occur when threads contend for these resources. This subsection describes a way to implement priority inheritance primitives for mutexes and reader/writer locks in a fixed-priority system. As you will see, the overhead of priority inheritance is rather high. Since the priority-ceiling protocol uses this mechanism, its overhead is also high (although not as high as simple priority inheritance since there is no transitive blocking). We will conclude the subsection by comparing priority inheritance protocol with the Ceiling-Priority Protocol (CPP). CPP is sometimes called a poor man's priority-ceiling protocol; you will see why it is so called.

Basic Primitives.   In the remainder of this subsection, the term resource refers solely to either a mutex or reader/writer lock. We assume here that the operating system provides two functions: *inherit_pr( )* and *restore_pr( ).*[16] A resource manager within the operating system or at the user level can use them to raise and restore the priorities of threads, respectively, as threads acquire and release resources. Since each resource request or release may lead to the invocation of one of these functions, it is essential that they be implemented efficiently.

The function *inherit_pr(TH)* is called when a thread (named *TH* here) is denied a resource *R* and becomes blocked. The effect of this function is that all threads directly or indirectly blocking *TH* inherit *TH*'s priority. (We say that these threads inherit *TH*'s priority through resource *R*.) You may have noticed that this statement assumes that the current priorities of all these threads are lower than *TH*'s priority. This assumption is true when there is only one processor, there is no deadlock, and threads never self-suspend while holding any resource, so immediately before it becomes blocked, *TH* has the highest priority of all ready and blocked threads.

The function *restore_pr( )* is called when a resource is released. It has two parameters: The name of the resource that has just been released and the ID of the thread which releases the resource. The effect of the function is that the current priority of the specified thread is restored to a level π_r.

Inheritance Function.   Figure 12–8 describes in pseudocode how the *inherit_pr( )* function works. Again, the function is called when a thread named *TH* is denied a resource *R* and becomes blocked. As the first step, the function looks up the thread holding *R* at the time. The owner TH_1 of *R* may itself be blocked waiting for another resource R_1, which may be held by yet another thread TH_2, and so on. In Chapter 8, we represented the blocking relationship by a chain in the wait-for graph, as shown in Figure 12–9. In this blocking chain, all the threads except the thread TH_i at the end is blocked. Figure 12–8 assumes that every blocking chain ends at a thread which is not blocked. If resource access is controlled according to the priority-ceiling protocol, a blocking chain may end at a resource node as well because a thread may be denied a resource even when the resource is free. The pseudocode description of *inherit_pr( )* does not take care of this case.

Tracking down threads on a blocking chain can be done easily if (1) in the date structure maintained for each resource that is in use, there is a pointer to the thread holding the resource and (2) in the TCB of each blocked thread, there is a pointer to the resource for which the thread waits. The pseudocode of *inherit_pr( )* assumes that these pointers are maintained and calls them owner and wait-for pointers, respectively. By following these pointers, *inherit_pr( )* finds each thread on the blocking chain, starting from the newly blocked thread. After finding a thread, the function changes the priority of the thread to that of the newly blocked thread. To ensure the consistency of scheduling and synchronization information, *inherit_pr( )* first locks the scheduler; it unlocks the scheduler when it completes.

Priority Restoration.   A thread may hold multiple resources at the same time and may inherit different priorities as other threads become blocked when they contend for these resources. Historical information on how the thread inherited its current priority is needed to

---

[16]The implementation of these primitives is similar to that of the SunOS 5.0 priority inheritance mechanism [KhSZ]. The SunOS 5.0 names them *pi_willto( )* and *pi_waive( )*.

Information maintained by the kernel:

- A circular linked list, called Inheritance Log (IL), for every thread;
- For each resource R that is in use, a data structure consisting of
  - a priority queue for threads that will be blocked when they request R, and
  - an owner pointer to the thread TH holding R.

When called after a thread TH, whose current priority is π, is denied resource R, the function *inherit_pr(TH)*

1. locks scheduler;

2. adds a wait-for pointer to R in the thread's TCB;

3. starting from TH to the end of the blocking chain, finds the next thread, *nextThread*, on the chain as follows:

   (a) *thisThread = TH*;

   (b) follows *thisThread*'s wait-for pointer to the resource X *thisThread* is waiting for;

   (c) follows the owner pointer of X to find the ID, *nextThread*, of the thread holding X;

   (d) if a record on X is not in the IL of *nextThread*, inserts the record (resource name X, *nextThread*'s current priority) in the IL;

   (e) sets the current priority of *nextThread* to π;

   (f) if *nextThread* is not blocked, goes to step 4;

       otherwise, sets *thisThread = nextThread* and goes back to step 3(b);

4. unlocks scheduler.

When *restore_pr(R, TH)* is called, if the record (R, π) is in IL of TH,

1. locks scheduler;

2. computes the new priority π_r of the thread TH based on records in IL;

3. sets the priority of TH to π_r and removes (R, π) from IL;

4. unlocks scheduler.

FIGURE 12–8   Priority inheritance primitives.

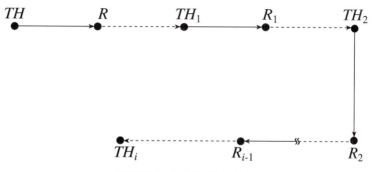

FIGURE 12–9   Blocking chain.

facilitate the determination of the thread's new current priority after it releases each resource. The pseudocode description of *inherit_pr( )* and *restore_pr( )* assumes that this information is maintained for each thread in its TCB as a linked list of records, one for each resource which the thread holds and through which the thread has inherited some priority. The list is called an Inheritance Log (IL).

When *restore_pr(TH, R)* is called, it searches the IL of the specified thread *TH* for the record on the specified resource *R*. The absence of a record on *R* indicates that the thread has not blocked any thread while it holds *R*. Hence, when the thread releases *R*, *restore_pr( )* does not change its priority. If a record on *R* exists, the function *restore_pr( )* computes the new thread priority, called π_r, based on the information provided by all records in the IL, restores the thread's priority to π_r, and then deletes the record on *R*. The computation of π_r is left for you as an exercise.

Ceiling-Priority Protocol. The overhead of the ceiling-priority protocol can be considerably lower than the priority inheritance protocol because each resource acquisition and release requires the change of the priority of at most the executing thread. CCP can be implemented easily by the system or at the user level in a fixed-priority system that supports FIFO within equal policy. (Problem 8.5 discussed how to implement this protocol if the system supports only round-robin within equal priority.) You recall that CCP requires prior knowledge of resource requirements of all threads. The resource manager generates from this knowledge the priority ceiling $\Pi(R)$ of every resource *R*. In addition to the current and assigned priorities of each thread, the thread's TCB also contains the names of all resources held by the thread at the current time.

Whenever a thread requests a lock on *R*, the resource manager locks the scheduler; looks up $\Pi(R)$; if the current priority of the requesting thread is lower than $\Pi(R)$, sets the thread's current priority to $\Pi(R)$; allocates *R* to the thread; and then unlocks the scheduler. Similarly, when a thread unlocks a resource *R*, the resource manager checks whether the thread's current priority is higher than $\Pi(R)$. The fact that the thread's current priority is higher than $\Pi(R)$ indicates that the thread still holds a resource with a priority ceiling higher than $\Pi(R)$. The thread's priority should be left unchanged in this case. On the other hand, if the thread's current priority is not higher than $\Pi(R)$, the priority may need to be lowered when *R* is released. In this case, the resource manager locks the scheduler, changes the current priority of the thread to the highest priority ceiling of all resources the thread still holds at the time, or the thread's assigned priority if the thread no longer holds any resource, and then unlocks the scheduler.

12.3.2 Event Notification and Software Interrupt

Event notification, exception handling, and software interrupts are essential for multitasking systems. Responsive mechanisms are needed to inform threads of the occurrences of timer events, the receipt of messages, the completion of asynchronous I/O operations, and so on. In UNIX systems, signal is the general mechanism for these purposes. Most of this subsection is devoted to the Real-Time POSIX signal as its features exemplify what are good and practical for real-time applications.

Signal and Similar Mechanisms. We saw earlier that in a UNIX system, interrupt handlers and the kernel use signals as a means to inform threads of the occurrences of exceptions (e.g., divide by zero and bad system call) or waited for events (e.g., the expiration of a timer and arrival of a message). A thread may signal another thread to synchronize and communicate. (For example, a predecessor thread may signal a successor thread when it completes.) A thread has a service function, called a signal handler. When the kernel delivers a signal to the thread, the signal handler executes. Thus, the signal mechanism provides asynchrony and immediacy, just as hardware interrupts do.

Non-UNIX systems typically provide these capabilities using more than one mechanism. As an example, in Windows NT [Solo, Hart], events and Asynchronous Procedure Calls (APCs) serve the same purposes as signals in UNIX systems. Events are set by threads for the purpose of notification and synchronization. They are synchronous. In other words, a thread must explicitly wait for an event for the event to have effect, and the thread is suspended while it waits. When a thread sets an event (object) to the signaled state, the thread(s) that is waiting on the event is awakened and scheduled. An NT event is an efficient and powerful notification and synchronization mechanism. Being synchronous, NT event delivery does not have the relatively high overhead of asynchronism. It is many-to-many in the sense that multiple threads can wait on one event and a thread can wait for multiple events. In contrast, each UNIX signal is targeted to an individual thread or process, and each signal is handled independently of other signals.

As its name implies, NT APCs are asynchronous.[17] The kernel and device drivers use kernel-mode APCs to do work in the address spaces of user threads (e.g., to copy data from kernel space to the space of the thread that initiated the I/O). Environment subsystems (i.e., the POSIX subsystem) uses APCs as software interrupts (e.g., to suspend a thread). Indeed, the POSIX subsystem on NT implements the delivery of POSIX signals to user processes using APCs. We will discuss this mechanism further in Section 12.7.1.

Similarly, the pSOSystem [Moto] provides events and asynchronous signals. The former are synchronous and point-to-point. An event is sent to a specified receiving task. The event has no effect on the receiving task if the task does not call the event receive function. In contrast, an asynchronous signal forces the receiving task to respond.

More on Signals.   Internal to UNIX operating systems, signals used for different purposes are identified by numbers. In programs and in the literature, they are referred to by their symbolic names. The correspondence between the number and the symbolic name of each signal is given in the header file *<signal.h>*. Most POSIX signals (i.e., signal numbers) are used by the operating system; what they do is defined by the system. (We have already seen SIGALRM for signaling upon timer expiration. Other examples are SIGTERM for terminating a process, SIGFPE for floating-point exception, and SIGPIPE for writing a pipe with no readers.) There are also signal numbers which are to be used solely for application-defined purposes. A Real-Time POSIX compliant system provides at least eight application-defined signals. An application-defined signal (with one of the numbers reserved for applications) is defined by the function (i.e., the signal handler) which the application sets up for the operating system to call when a signal with that number arrives. [Specifically, the action to be taken upon

---

[17]More precisely, NT kernel-mode APCs are asynchronous; a kernel-mode APC interrupts a thread without the thread's cooperation. There are also user-mode APCs. A user-level APC queued for a thread is delivered to the thread only when the thread is in a wait state (e.g., by having previous executed a *SleepEx* to test whether it has a pending APC).

the occurrence of a signal is specified by the data structure *sigaction* on the signal. Among the information provided by this data structure is a pointer to the signal handler, a mask *sa_mask* and a flag field *sa_flag*. A process (thread) can ask the operating system to set these members by calling *sigaction( )* and providing these and other arguments of the function.]

By default, when a signal arrives, it is handled, meaning that the signal handler set up for the signal is executed. A process (thread) may ignore any signal, except those (e.g, SIGKILL) used by the operating system to stop and destroy an errant process. The operating system ignores a signal when the pointer to the associated signal handler has the system-defined constant SIG_IGN as its value.

Just as it is necessary to be able to disable interrupts, it is essential that signals can be blocked selectively from delivery. This is done via signal masks. Some signals may need to be blocked from delivery while a signal handler is executing. One specifies the signals blocked by the handler of a signal by putting their numbers in *sa_mask* in the data structure *sigaction* of that signal. The operating system does not deliver a signal thus blocked while the signal handler is executing. Each process (thread) also has a signal mask containing numbers of signals the process (thread) wants blocked. A signal thus blocked is delivered by the operating system but remains pending until the process (thread) unblocks the signal by removing its number from the signal mask.

Signal delivery is on per process basis, so if a thread ignores a signal, all threads in the process do also. On the other hand, each thread has its own signal mask. Therefore, threads in a process can choose to block or unblock signals independent of other threads. Some signals (e.g., SIGTERM for terminating a process) are intended for the entire process. Such a signal, if not ignored, is delivered to any thread that is in the process and does not block the signal. The signal is blocked only when all threads in the process blocks it.

Real-Time POSIX Signals. POSIX real-time extensions [IEEE98] change the POSIX signals to make the mechanism more responsive and reliable. To distinguish signals conforming to POSIX real-time extensions from POSIX and traditional UNIX signals, we call the former real-time signals. First, as we mentioned earlier, there are at least eight application-defined real-time signals versus only two provided by POSIX. These signals are numbered from SIGRTMIN to SIGRTMAX.

Second, real-time signals can be queued, while traditional UNIX signals cannot. Queueing is a per signal option; one chooses the queueing option for a real-time signal by setting bit SA_SIGINFO in the *sa_flags* field of the *sigaction* structure of the signal. If not queued, a signal that is delivered while being blocked may be lost. Hence, queueing ensures the reliable delivery of signals.

Third, a queued real-time signal can carry data. A traditional signal handler has only one parameter: the number of the signal. In contrast, the signal handler of a real-time signal whose SA_SIGINFO bit is set has as an additional parameter a pointer to a data structure that contains the data value to be passed to the signal handler. This capability increases the communication bandwidth of the signal mechanism. As an example, a server can use this mechanism to notify a client of the completion of a requested service and pass the result back to the client at the same time.

Fourth, queued signals are prioritized: The smaller the signal number, the higher the priority. They are delivered in priority order.

Fifth, POSIX real-time extensions provide a new and more responsive synchronous signal-wait function called *sigwaitinfo*. When a signal arrives for a process that is blocked after calling the POSIX synchronous signal-wait function *sigsuspend*, the signal handler executes before the process returns from the blocked state. In contrast, upon the arrival of the signal, the *sigwaitinfo* function does not call the signal handler; it merely unblocks the calling process. Figure 12–5(a) gives an example of how this function may be used.

Overhead and Timing Predictability.   The down side of the signal mechanism is the slow speed and high overhead of signal delivery. Like a hardware interrupt, a signal also causes a trap out of the user mode, complicated operations by the operating system, and a return to user mode. The time taken by these activities is high in comparison with other communication and synchronization mechanisms.

Signal handler are executed ahead of threads of all priorities. (Typically, the kernel executes signal handlers prior to returning control to the user.) Hence, it is important that the execution times of signal handlers be kept small, just as it is important that execution times of interrupt service routines small.

12.3.3   Memory Management

Thus far, we have ignored memory and memory management. An underlying assumption throughout previous chapters is that all the real-time applications that may run together fit in memory. Indeed, a task is not admitted into the system if there is not enough memory to meet its peak memory space demand. A mode change cannot complete unless the operating system can find sufficient memory for the codes, data, and run-time stacks of the threads that execute in the new mode. We now discuss those aspects of memory management that call for attention. They are virtual memory mapping, paging, and memory protection. Whereas all general-purpose operating systems support virtual memory and memory protection, not all real-time operating systems do, and those that do typically provide the user with the choice of protection or no protection. Unlike nonreal-time applications, some real-time applications do not need these capabilities, and we do not get these capabilities without penalty.

Virtual Memory Mapping.   We can divide real-time operating systems into three categories depending on whether they support virtual memory mapping (i.e., virtual contiguity) and paging (i.e., demand paging or swapping). Real-time operating systems designed primarily for embedded real-time applications such as data acquisition, signal processing, and monitoring,[18] may not support virtual memory mapping. The pSOSystem is an example [Moto]. Upon request, the system creates physically contiguous blocks of memory for the application. The application may request variable size segments from its memory block and define a memory partition consisting of physically contiguous, fixed-size buffers.

---

[18]The lack of virtual memory mapping is not a serious problem when the application has a small code and relatively small number of operating modes (and hence configurations). The application may be data intensive and its data come in fixed-size chunks. A radar signal processing application is an example. It needs fixed-size buffers to hold digitized radar returns from range bins, and the space required for its FFT code and run time stack is small by comparison. During a mode change, for example, from searching to tracking, it may request more buffers or free some buffers. The number of buffers required in each mode is usually known.

Memory fragmentation is a potential problem for a system that does not support virtual mapping. After allocating variable-size segments, large fractions of individual blocks may be unused. The available space may not be contiguous and contiguous areas in memory may not be big enough to meet the application's buffer space demand. The solution is to provide virtual memory mapping from physical addresses, which may not be contiguous, to a contiguous, linear virtual address space seen by the application.

The penalty of virtual address mapping is the address translation table, which must be maintained and hence contribute to the size of the operating system. Moreover, it complicates DMA-controlled I/O. When transferring data under DMA control, it is only necessary to set up the DMA controller once if the memory addresses to and from which the data are transferred are physically contiguous. On the other hand, when the addresses are not physically contiguous, the processor must set up the DMA controller multiple times, one for each physically contiguous block of addresses.

Memory Locking.   A real-time operating system may support paging so that nonrealtime, memory demanding applications (e.g., editors, debuggers and performance profilers) needed during development can run together with target real-time applications. Such an operating system must provide applications with some means to control paging. Indeed, all operating systems, including general-purpose ones, offer some control, with different granularities.

An examples, Real-Time POSIX-compliant systems allow an application to pin down in memory all of its pages [i.e., *mlockall( )*] or a range of pages [i.e., *mlock( )* with the starting address of the address range and the length of the range as parameters]. So does Real-Time Mach. In some operating systems (e.g., Windows NT), the user may specify in the create thread system call that all pages belonging to the new thread are to be pinned down in memory. The LynxOS operating system controls paging according to the demand-paging priority. Memory pages of applications whose priorities are equal to or higher than this priority are pinned down in memory while memory pages of applications whose priorities are lower than the demand-paging priority may be paged out.

Memory Protection.   As we stated in Section 12.1.2, many real-time operating systems do not provide protected address spaces to the operating system kernel and user processes. Argument for having only a single address space include simplicity and the light weight of system calls and interrupt handling. For small embedded applications, the overhead space of a few kilobytes per process is more serious. Critics points out a change in any module may require retesting the entire system. This can significantly increase the cost of developing all but the simplest embedded systems. For this reason, many real-time operating systems (e.g., QNX and LynxOS) support memory protection.

A good alterative is to provide the application with the choices in memory management such as the choices in virtual memory configuration offerred by VxWorks [Wind] and QNX [QNX]. In VxWorks, we can choose (by defining the configuration in *configAll.h*) to have only virtual address mapping, to have text segments and exception vector tables write protected, and to give each task a private virtual memory when the task requests for it.

12.3.4 I/O and Networking

Three modern features of file system and networking software are (1) multithreaded-server architecture, (2) early demultiplexing and (3) lightweight protocol stack. These features were developed to improve the performance of time-shared applications, high-performance applications and network appliances. As it turns out, they also benefit real-time applications with enhanced predictability.

Multithreaded Server Architecture.   Servers in modern operating systems are typically multithreaded. In response to a request, such a server activates (or creates) a work thread to service the request. By properly prioritizing the work thread, we can minimize the duration of priority inversion and better account for the CPU time consumed by the server while serving the client.

As a example, we consider a client thread that does a read. Suppose that the file server's request queue is prioritized, the request message has the same priority as the client, and the work thread for each request inherits the priority of the request message. (Section 12.3.1 described a way to do this.) As a consequence, the length of time the client may be blocked is at most equal to the time the server takes to activate a work thread. I/O requests are sent to the disk controller in priority order. For the purpose of schedulability analysis, we can model the client thread as an end-to-end job consisting of a CPU subjob, which is followed by a disk-access subjob, and the disk-access job executes on the disk system (i.e., the controller and the disk) and is in turn followed by a CPU subjob. Both CPU subjobs have the same priority as the client thread, and their execution times include the lengths of time the work thread executes. Since the time taken by the server to activate a work thread is small, the possible blocking suffered by the client is small. In contrast, if the server were single-threaded, a client might be blocked for the entire duration when the server executes on behalf of another client, and the blocking time can be orders of magnitude larger.

Early Demultiplexing.   Traditional protocol handlers are based on layered architectures. They can introduce a large blocking time. For example, when packets arrive over a TCP/IP connection, the protocol module in the network layer acknowledges the receipts of the packets, strips away their headers, reassembles them into IP datagrams, and hands off the datagram to the IP module after each datagram is reassembled. Similarly, the TCP and IP modules reassemble IP datagrams into messages, put the messages in order and then deliver the messages to the receiver. Because much of this work is done before the identity of the receiver becomes known, it cannot be correctly prioritized. Typically, the protocol modules execute at a higher priority than all user threads and block high-priority threads when they process packets of low-priority clients.

The duration of priority inversion can be reduced and controlled only by identifying the receiver of each message (i.e., demultiplexing incoming messages) as soon as possible. Once the receiver is known, the execution of the protocol modules can be at the priority of the receiver.

Traditionally, incoming messages are first moved to the buffer space of the protocol modules. (Figure 11-1 is based on this assumption.) They are then copied to the address space of the receiver. Early demultiplexing also makes it possible to eliminate the extra copying. Some communication mechanisms [e.g., Illinios FM (Fast Message] [PaLC]) for high-speed local networks take this approach. The fact that messages are copied directly between the network interface card and the application is a major reason that these mechanisms can achieve an end-to-end (i.e., application-to-application) latency in the order of 10 to 20 microseconds.

Lightweight Protocol Stack.   Protocol processing can introduce large overhead and long latency. This is especially true when the protocol stack has the client/server structure: Each higher-level protocol module uses the services provided by a protocol module at a layer below. This overhead can be reduced by combining the protocol modules of different layers into a single module and optimizing the module whenever possible. A challenge is how to provide lightweight, low overhead protocol processing and still retain the advantages of the layer architecture.

An example of operating systems designed to meet this challenge is the Scout operating system [MMOP, MoPe]. Scout is based on the Path abstraction. Specifically, Scout uses paths as a means to speed up the data delivery between the network and applications. Conceptually, a path can be thought of as a bidirectional virtual connection (channel) which cuts through the protocol layers in a host to connect a source and a sink of data to the network. From the implementation point of view, a path is an object that is obtained by glueing together protocol modules (called routers) to be used to process data between an application and network.

At configuration time, a path consisting multiple stages is created one stage at a time starting from one end of the path (e.g., the network layer router). A stage is created by invocating the function *pathCreate( )* on the router specified by one of the arguments of the function. (The other argument of the function specifies the attributes of the path.) As the result of the invocation of *pathCreate( )* and the subsequent invocation of *createStage* function, the router creates a stage of the path and identifies the next router, if any, on the path. Similarly, the next stage is created by the next router, and if the next router is to be followed by yet another router, that router identified. This process is repeated until the entire sequence of stages is created. The stages are then combined into a single path object and initialized. Whenever possible, Scout applies path transformation rules to optimize the path object.

At run time, each path is executed by a thread. Scout allows these threads to be scheduled according to multiple arbitrary scheduling policies and allocates a fraction of CPU time to threads scheduled according to each policy. As you will see shortly, this features complements ideally resource reserves that we will present in the next section.

Still, priority inversion is unavoidable because when a packet arrives, it may take some time to identify the path to which the packet belongs. Scout tries to minimize this time by giving each router a demultiplexing operation. A router asks the next router to refine its own decision only when it cannot uniquely decide to which path a packet belongs.

*12.4 PROCESSOR RESERVES AND RESOURCE KERNEL

One can easily argue that a real-time operating system should support as options admission control, resource reservation, and usage enforcement for applications that can afford the additional size and complexity of the option. By monitoring and controlling the workload, the operating system can guarantee the real-time performance of applications it admits into the system. This is the objective of the CPU capacity-reservation mechanism proposed by Mercer, *et al.* [MeST] to manage quality of services of multimedia applications. Rajkumar, *et al.* [RKMO] have since extended the CPU reserve abstraction to reserves of other resources and used it as the basis of *resource kernels*. In addition to Real-Time Mach, NT/RK[19] also provides resource kernel primitives. Commercial operating systems do not support this option.

12.4.1   Resource Model and Reservation Types

A resource kernel presents to applications a uniform model of all time-multiplexed resources, for example, CPU, disk, network link. We been calling these resources processors and will continue to do so.

An application running on a resource kernel can ensure its real-time performance by reserving the resources it needs to achieve the performance. To make a reservation on a processor, it sends the kernel a request for a share of the processor. The kernel accepts the request only when it can provide the application with the requested amount on a timely basis. Once the kernel accepts the request, it sets aside the reserved amount for the application and guarantees the timely delivery of the amount for the duration of the reservation.

Reservation Specification.   Specifically, each reservation is specified by parameters e, p, and D: The reservation is for e units (of CPU time, disk blocks, bits or packets, and so on) in every period of length p, and the kernel is to provide the e units of every period (i.e., every instance of the reservation) within a relative deadline D. Let ϕ denote the first time instant when the reservation for the processor is to be made and L denote the length of time for which the reservation remains. The application presents to the kernel the 5-tuple (ϕ, p, e, D, L) of parameters when requesting a reservation.

In addition to the parameters of individual reservations, the kernel has an overall parameter B for each type of processor. As a consequence of contention for nonpreemptable resources (such as buffers and mutexes), entities executing on the processor may block each other. B is the maximum allowed blocking time. (B is a design parameter. It is lower bounded by the maximum duration of time entities using the processor holding nonpreemptable resources. Hence, the larger B is, the less restriction is placed on applications using the processor, but the larger fraction of processor capacity becomes unavailable to reservations.) Every reservation request implicitly promises never to hold any nonpreemptable resources so long as to block higher-priority reservations on the processor for a duration longer than B, and the kernel monitors the usage of all resources so it can enforce this promise.

As an example, let us look at CPU reservation. From the resource kernel point of view, each CPU reservation (p, e, D) is analogous to a bandwidth-preserving server with period p and execution budget e whose budget must be consumed within D units of time after replenishment. Any number of threads can share a CPU reservation, just as any number of jobs may be executed by a server. In addition to the CPU, threads may use nonpreemptable resources. The kernel must use some means to control priority inversion. The specific protocol it uses is unimportant for the discussion here, provided that it keeps the duration of blocking bounded.

Maintenance and Admission Control.   If all the threads sharing each CPU reservation are scheduled at the same priority (i.e., at the priority of the reservation), as it is suggested

---

[19]NT/RK is a middleware that runs on top of Windows NT. NT 5.0 allows processes to set execution and memory usage limits for a process or group of processes. This capability can be exploited to support CPU and memory resource reserves; it is described in Section 12.7.1.

in [RKMO], each CPU reservation behaves like a bandwidth-preserving server. The kernel can use any bandwidth-preserving server scheme that is compatible with the overall scheduling algorithm to maintain each reservation. The budget consumption and busy interval tracking mechanisms described in Figure 12–7 are useful for this purpose.

The simplest way is to replenish each CPU reservation periodically. After granting a reservation (p, e, D), the kernel sets the execution budget of the reservation to e and sets a timer to expire periodically with period p. Whenever the timer expires, it replenishes the budget (i.e., sets the budget in the reserve back to e). Whenever any thread using the reservation executes, the kernel decrements the budget. It suspends the execution of all threads sharing the reservation when the reservation no longer has any budget and allows their execution to resume after it replenishes the budget. You may have noticed that we have just described the budget consumption and replenishment rules of the deferrable server algorithm. (The algorithm was described in Section 7.2.) In general, threads sharing a reservation may be scheduled at different fixed priorities. This choice may make the acceptance test considerably more complicated, however. If budget replenishment is according to a sporadic server algorithm, budget replenishment also becomes complicated.

The connection-oriented approach is a natural way to maintain and guarantee a network reservation. A network reservation with parameters p, e, and D is similar to a connection on which the flow specification is (p, e, D). After accepting a network reservation request, the kernel establishes a connection and allocates the required bandwidth to the connection. By scheduling the message streams on the connection according to a rate-based (i.e., bandwidth-preserving) algorithm, the kernel can make sure that the message streams on the connection will receive the guaranteed network bandwidth regardless of the traffic on other connection.

In summary, the resource kernel for each type of processor schedules competing reservations according to an algorithm that provides isolation among reservations if such algorithms exist. Previous chapters give many such algorithms for CPU and network scheduling. The kernel can use the schedulability conditions described in those chapters as the basis of its acceptance test when deciding whether to accept and admit a reservation.

An exception is disk. Clearly, the kernel needs to use a real-time disk-scheduling algorithm that allows the maximum response time of each disk access request to be bounded from the above.[20] However, most real-time disk scheduling algorithms are not bandwidth-preserving. For this reason, the kernel must provide this capability separately from scheduling.

Types of Reservation.   In addition to parameters p, e, and D, Real-Time Mach also allows an application to specify in its reservation request the type of reservation: hard, firm,

---

[20]Real-time disk scheduling algorithms typically combine EDF and SCAN strategies. According to the SCAN algorithm, the read/write head scans the disk, and the next request to service is the one closest to the head in the direction of scan. This strategy minimizes average seek and latency times but ignores timeliness. According to real-time scheduling algorithms such as EDF-SCAN and "just-in-time," when a request completes, the head moves to the request with the earliest deadline among all pending requests. A pure EDF scheme may yield poor average seek and latency. To improve this aspect of performance, requests on tracks between the just completed request and the request with the earliest deadline may also be serviced. Different algorithms make the decision on whether to service the in-between requests based on different criteria, for example, whether the request with the earliest deadline has slack, or whether its deadline is within a certain window of time.

or soft. Thus, it specifies the action it wants the kernel to take when the reservation runs out of budget.

The execution of all entities sharing a *hard reservation* are suspended when the reservation has exhausted its budget. In essence, a hard reservation does not use any spare processor capacity. A hard network reservation is rate controlled; its messages are not allowed to transmit above the reserved rate even when spare bandwidth is available. We make hard reservations for threads, messages, and so on, when completion-time jitters need to be kept small and early completions have no advantage.

In contrast, when a *firm reservation* (say a CPU reservation) exhausts its budget, the kernel schedules the threads using the reservation in the background of reservations that have budget and threads that have no reservation. When a *soft reservation* runs out of budget, the kernel lets the threads using the reservation execute along with threads that have no reservation and other reservations that no longer have budget; all of them are in the background of reservations that have budget. A firm or soft network reservation is rate allocated. We make firm and soft reservations when we want to keep the average response times small.

Rajkumar, *et al.* [RKMO] also suggested the division of reservations into *immediate reservations* and normal reservations. What we have discussed thus far are normal reservations. An immediate reservation has a higher priority than all normal reservations. We will return shortly to discuss the intended use of immediate reservations.

12.4.2   Application Program Interface and SSP Structure

The API functions Real-Time Mach provides to support resource reservation include *request( )* and *modify( )* for requesting and modifying reservations. There are also functions for binding threads to a reservation and specifying the type of a reservation. In addition, an application may create a port for a reservation and request the kernel to send a notification message to that port whenever the budget of the reservation is exhausted.

Mercer, *et al.* [MeST] pointed out that a System Service Provider (SSP) executes mostly in response to requests from clients. If each SSP were to reserve sufficient resources to ensure its responsiveness, most of its reserved resources would be left idle when there is no request for its service. A better alternative is to have the client pass the client's reservations needed by the SSP to do the work along with the request for service.

In a microkernel system adopting this approach, each SSP has only a small CPU reservation. Only its daemon thread executes using this reservation. When a client requests service from an SSP, it allows the SSP to use its own reservations. When the SSP receives a request, the daemon thread wakes up, executes using the SSP's CPU reservation, creates a work thread to execute on the client's behalf, and suspends itself. This work thread uses the client's CPU reservation, as well as reservations of other types of processors. In this way, the resources used by the SSP to service each request are charged to the requesting client. The SSP structure described in the next section is an extension, and we will provide more detail on this structure when we describe the extension.

To explain the use of the immediate reservation type, we consider the example given by [RKMO]: A stream of packets from the network is stored on the disk. The application clearly needs both network bandwidth and disk bandwidth; hence, it may have reservations for both types of processors. Moreover, CPU time is also needed for processing incoming packets and writing them to disk. If the application's CPU reservation were used to do this work, the receive buffer might not be drained sufficiently fast to prevent overflow, since the application's CPU reservation may have a low priority and large relative deadline. The alternative proposed by Rajkumar, *et al.* is to have a separate (immediate) CPU reservation for processing incoming packets and writing the packets to disk and give the reservation the highest priority to ensure its immediate execution. However, immediate reservation introduces priority inversion. It is the same as executing a scheduled interrupt service routine immediately rather than properly prioritizing it. The execution times of threads using immediate reservations must be kept very small.

To conclude this section, we note that the above example illustrates an end-to-end task. Its subtasks execute on the network, on the CPU, and the disk. Providing guaranteed resource reservation for each processor type is a way to ensure that each subtask has a bounded response time and the response time of the end-to-end task is bounded by the sum of the maximum response times of its subtasks.

*12.5   OPEN SYSTEM ARCHITECTURE

For most of this book, we have assumed that all the hard real-time applications running on the same platform form a monolithic system. Their tasks are scheduled together according to the same algorithm. When we want to determine whether any application can meet its timing requirements, we carry out a global schedulability analysis based on the parameters for each combination of tasks from all applications that may run together. In essence, the system is closed, prohibiting the admission of real-time applications whose timing characteristics are not completely known.

12.5.1   Objectives and Alternatives

Ideally, a real-time operating system should create an open environment. Here, by an *open environment*, we mean specifically one in which the following development and configuration processes are feasible.

1. Independent Design Choice: The developer of a real-time application that is to run in an open environment can use a scheduling discipline best suited to the application to schedule the threads in the application and control their contention for resources used only by the application.

2. Independent Validation: To determine the schedulability of an application, its developer can assume that the application runs alone on a virtual processor that is the same as the target processor but has a speed that is only a fraction $0 < s < 1$ of the speed of the target processor. In other words, if the maximum execution time of a thread is e on the target processor, then the execution time used in the schedulability analysis is e/s. The minimum speed at which the application is schedulable is the *required capacity* of the application.[21]

---

[21] We note that the notion of the required capacity s here is essentially the same as that in the processor reserve model. As we will see shortly, it is not necessary for an application in the open system to specify the period p in real time over which ps units of processor time are to be allocated to the application. Instead, the application informs the operating system the shortest relative deadline of all of its threads.

3. Admission and Timing Guarantee: The open system always admits nonreal-time applications. Each real-time application starts in the nonreal-time mode. After initialization, a real-time application requests to execute in the real-time mode by sending an admission request to the operating system. In this request, the application informs the operating system of its required capacity, plus a few overall timing parameters of the application. (In the open environment described below, the parameters are the shortest relative deadline, the maximum execution time of all nonpreemptable sections, the presence or absence of sporadic threads and, if its periodic tasks have release-time jitters, an upper bound on release-time jitters.) The operating system subjects the requesting application to a simple but accurate acceptance test. If the application passes the test, the operating system switches the application to run in real-time mode. Once in real-time mode, the operating system guarantees the schedulability of the application, regardless of the behavior of the other applications in the system.

In short, independently developed and validated hard real-time applications can be configured at run time to run together with soft real-time and nonreal-time applications.

We recall that the fixed-time partitioning scheme discussed in Section 6.8.7 is a way to achieve the above goal and has been used to allow safety-critical applications to run together with nonsafety-critical applications. According to that scheme, we partition time into slots and confine the execution of each application in the time slots allocated to the application. We saw in Section 6.8.7 that if applications do not share any global resource (i.e., resources shared by tasks in different applications) and the time slots are assigned to applications on the TDM (Time-Division Multiplexing) basis, we can determine the schedulability of each application independently of other applications. The number of slots per round an application requires to be schedulable is then its required capacity. An application can be admitted into the system whenever the system has enough spare time slots per round to meet the required capacity of the application. The key parameter of the fixed-time partitioning scheme is the length of the time slots. Obviously, this length should be smaller than the shortest relative deadline of all applications. The shorter the time slots, the closer the system emulates a slower virtual processor for each application, but the higher the context-switch overhead. Hence, using the fixed-time partitioning scheme, we cannot accommodate stringent response time requirements without paying high overhead. Modern operating systems typically provide priority-driven scheduling. Some kind of middleware is needed to put the time-driven scheme on them.

The remainder of this section describes a uniprocessor open system architecture that uses the two-level priority-driven scheme described in Section 7.9. That scheme emulates infinitesmally fine-grain time slicing (often called fluid-flow processing sharing) and can accommodate stringent response time requirements. Deng, *et al.* [DLZS] implemented a prototype open system based on the architecture by extending the Windows NT operating systems. The prototype demonstrates that the architecture can easily be incorporated into any modern operating system to make the operating system open for real-time applications and still remain backward compatible for existing nonreal-time applications. By using a two-level scheme in a similar way to schedule messages to and from networks (e.g., Zhang, *et al.* [ZLDP] give a scheme for scheduling periodic messages over Myrinet), the architecture can be extended into a distributed one.

12.5.2 Two-Level Scheduler

According to the two-level priority-driven scheme described in Section 7.9, each real-time application (denoted by $\mathbf{T}_k$ for some $k \geq 1$) is executed by a bandwidth-preserving server S_k, which in essence is a constant utilization or total bandwidth server, and all the nonreal-time applications are executed by a total bandwidth server S_0. At the lower level, the *OS scheduler* maintains the servers and schedules all the ready servers. (A server is ready when it has ready threads to execute and budget to execute them.) At the higher level, the *server scheduler* of each server S_k schedules the ready threads in the application(s) executed by the server.

Scheduling Hierarchy. At each scheduling decision time, the OS scheduler schedules the server with the earliest deadline among all ready servers. When a server is scheduled, it executes the thread chosen by its own server scheduler according to the scheduling algorithm Σ_k used by the application(s) executed by the server. The block diagram in Figure 12–10 depicts this scheduling hierarchy. To highlight the fact that the scheduling disciplines used by the real-time applications may be different, the block diagram shows two different real-time scheduling disciplines. Nonreal-time applications are scheduled according to a time-shared scheduling discipline. The block diagram also suggests that we put all the schedulers in the

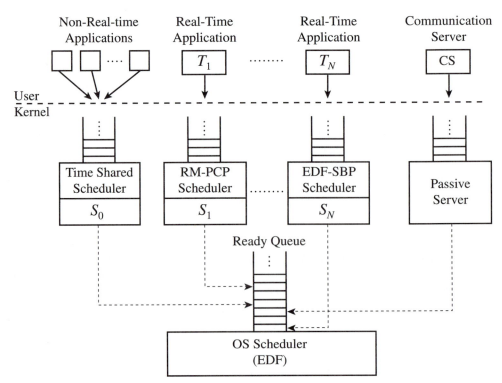

FIGURE 12–10 A two-level scheduler.

kernel; thus, only one context switch occurs at each scheduling decision time, just as in a one-level scheduling scheme.

An application can use any protocol to control access to its local resources. In this section, by a local resource, we mean one that is used by only one application. A resource shared by multiple applications is a global resource. In the open system, global resource contention is resolved according to the Nonpreemptable Critical Section (NPS) protocol or the ceiling-priority protocol. Consequently, a section of a thread may be nonpreemptable. In general, a thread or a section of a thread may be nonpreemptable for reasons other than global resource access control. There is no need for us to distinguish the reasons. Hereafter, we simply say that some applications have nonpreemptable sections, lumping applications that use global resources into this category.

Without loss of generality, we assume that the required capacity s_k of every real-time application $\mathbf{T}_k$ is less than 1. (Otherwise the application cannot share the processor with other applications.) The maximum execution time of every thread in each real-time application becomes known when the thread is released. One of the parameters a real-time application declares to the operating system when it requests to execute in the real-time mode is the maximum execution time of the nonpreemptable sections of all its threads. After admitting the application, the operating system never allows any thread in the application to be nonpreemptable for more than the declared amount of time. Similarly, the operating system ensures that no nonreal-time thread is nonpreemptable for longer than a certain length of time. (This length is a design parameter.) Consequently, at any time the maximum execution time of the nonpreemptable sections of all threads in the system is known.

In Section 7.9, we called an application that is scheduled according to a preemptive, priority-driven algorithm and contains threads whose release times are not fixed a *nonpredictable* application. It is so called because the OS scheduler needs to know the next event time of such an application at each server budget replenishment time but the server scheduler for the application cannot compute this time accurately. (At any time, the *next event time* of an application is the occurrence time of the earliest of all events in the applications that may cause a context switch.) Applications whose threads have fixed and known release times and applications that are scheduled nonpreemptively are *predictable*. An application of the former kind is predictable because its server scheduler can compute the next event time accurately. Similarly, an application that is scheduled in the clock-driven manner is predictable. A nonpreemptively scheduled application is predictable, even when it contains aperiodic and sporadic threads, because this computation is not necessary.

Operations of the OS scheduler.   Figure 12–11(a) describes the operations of the OS scheduler and its interaction with the server schedulers. At initialization time, the OS scheduler creates a total bandwidth server S_0 to execute all the nonreal-time applications and a server for each service provider. The size of S_0 is $\tilde{u}_0$, and the total size of the servers for all system service providers is $\tilde{u}_p$. The total size $U_t = \tilde{u}_0 + \tilde{u}_p$ (< 1) of these servers is the processor utilization that is no longer available to real-time applications.

Scheduling NonReal-Time Applications.   Again, the server scheduler of S_0 schedules all the nonreal-time threads according to a time-sharing scheduling algorithm. We let x denote

Initialization

- Create a total bandwidth server S_0 with size $u_0 < 1$ for nonreal-time applications and a passive server for each service provider in the system.
- Set U_t to the total size of S_0 and all passive servers.

Acceptance test and admission of a new real-time application T_k:

- Upon request from the application, do the acceptance test as described in Figure 12–11(c).
- If T_k passes the acceptance test, create server S_k of size u_k, following the rules described in Figure 12–11(c).

Maintenance of each server S_k: Replenish the budget and set the deadline of server S_k according to Figure 12–11(b).

Interaction with server scheduler of each server S_k:

- When a thread in the application T_k becomes ready, invoke the server scheduler of S_k to insert the thread in S_k's ready queue.
- If T_k uses a preemptive scheduling algorithm, before replenishing the budget of S_k, invoke the server scheduler of S_k to update the next event time t_k of T_k.
- When a thread in T_k enters its nonpreemptable section, mark the server S_k nonpreemptable until the thread exits the nonpreemptable section, and mark the server preemptable when the nonpreemptable section exceeds the declared maximum length.
- When a thread in T_k requests a global resource, grant the thread the resource and mark the server S_k nonpreemptable until the thread releases the global resource.

Scheduling of all servers: Schedule all ready servers on the EDF basis, except when a server is marked nonpreemptable; when a server is nonpreemptable, it has the highest priority among all servers.

Termination of a real-time application T_k:

- Destroy server S_k.
- Decrease U_t by u_k.

(a) Operation of the OS scheduler

FIGURE 12–11   Acceptance test, admission, and server maintenance. (a) Operations of OS scheduler. (b) Server maintenance rules. (c) Acceptance test and choice of server size.

the length of the time slices used by the time-sharing scheduler. The OS scheduler sets the budget of S_0 to x when the first nonreal-time thread is ready to execute (say at time 0) and sets the deadline of the server at $x/\tilde{u}_0$. Hereafter, at each time t when the budget of S_0 is exhausted and there are threads ready to be executed by S_0, the OS scheduler sets the budget to x and the corresponding deadline to either $t + x/\tilde{u}_0$ or the current deadline of the server plus $x/\tilde{u}_0$ whichever is later. Moreover, whenever a busy interval ends, the OS server gives the server x units of budget and sets the server deadline at the current time plus $x/\tilde{u}_0$.

As long as the server S_0 is schedulable (meaning that its budget is always consumed before the current deadline), the open system offers nonreal-time applications a virtual slower processor with speed $\tilde{u}_0$. As you will see later, the acceptance test of the open system is such that S_0 is always schedulable. Hereafter, we will keep in mind the existence of server S_0 and processor utilization $\tilde{u}_0$ committed to the server. Other than this, we will not be concerned with nonreal-time applications any further.

Passive Server. The server created by the OS scheduler for each service provider is a passive server. A *passive server* is a sporadic server. Its execution budget comes from two sources. The first is the server's processor time allocation; the server has a very small size. (This is analogous to processor reservation of a system service provider.) The OS scheduler treats the passive server as a total bandwidth server of its size and replenishes its budget according to the rules described in Section 7.4.3. The only "aperiodic task" executed by the server using this budget is the daemon thread of the service provider. The daemon thread is created during initialization (or when a service provider is admitted into the system). It is suspended immediately after it is created and wakes to run whenever the service provider receives a request for service. When the daemon thread runs, it creates a work thread to service the request and puts itself back to the suspended state again.

In addition, a passive server also gets execution budget from client applications of the SSP executed by the server. When a client application requests a service, it passes to the service provider its own budget and the associated deadline for consuming the budget.[22] The work thread created by the daemon to service the client's request executes with this budget and has this deadline. (Conceptually, we can think of the budget/deadline passed to the passive server as a CPU reservation. This reservation is not replenished periodically, however; rather it is under the control of the server scheduler of the client application.) We will return to provide more details on how the scheduler of a passive server works.

Admission, Termination, and Scheduler Interactions. To request admission, that is, to execute in the real-time mode, a new real-time application $\mathbf{T}_k$ provides in its request to the OS scheduler the information needed by the scheduler to do an acceptance test. If the application passes the test, the OS scheduler creates a server S_k of size $\tilde{u}_k$ to execute the new application. (The information the OS scheduler needs to do an acceptance test and the rules used by the scheduler to do the test and select the server type and size are described below.) Whenever a real-time application terminates, the OS scheduler destroys its server.

When a thread in a real-time application $\mathbf{T}_k$ becomes ready, the OS scheduler invokes the server scheduler of the server S_k to insert the thread into the server's ready queue. The server scheduler orders the ready threads according to the scheduling algorithm Σ_k of the real-time application $\mathbf{T}_k$.

12.5.3 Server Maintenance

Again, the OS scheduler maintains (i.e., replenishes its budget and sets its deadline) the server S_k for each real-time application $\mathbf{T}_k$ with the help of the scheduler of S_k. Figure 12–11(b) summarizes the rules the OS scheduler uses. In the figure, $\tilde{u}$ denotes the size of the server being maintained. For simplicity, we take as the time origin the time instant immediately after the server is created; this is the instant when the application executed by the server begins to execute in real-time mode.

---

[22]In the prototype in [DLZS], the budget and deadline are passed by the server scheduler of the client application to the scheduler of the passive server. In this way, the number of context switches is kept small.

Inputs: Server size$= \tilde{u}$, scheduling quantum$= q$, start time of the application$= 0$.

- If the application is cyclically scheduled with frame size f,
  - server type: Constant utilization
  - replenishment rule: At time $0, f, 2f, \ldots$, set budget to $\tilde{u} f$ and deadline to $f, 2f, 3f, \ldots$, respectively.
- If the application is nonpreemptively scheduled:
  - server type: Constant utilization.
  - replenishment rule: The constant utilization server algorithm.
- If the application is unpredictable,
  - server type: Total bandwidth server-like.
  - replenishment rule:
    * replenishment time t:
      (1) when the ready queue is empty and a thread is released, or
      (2) when the ready queue is nonempty,
        (i) t is the current server deadline d, or
        (ii) the budget is exhausted at t and the next event time is not the release time of a thread with priority higher than the thread at the head of the server ready queue.
    * budget replenished: $\tilde{u}(t_n + q - max(t, d))$, where t_n is a lower bound to the next event time and q is the scheduling quantum of the open system.
    * server deadline: $t_n + q$
- If the application is preemptively scheduled but predictable,
  - server type: Total bandwidth server
  - replenishment rule: Same as the rule for unpredictable applications except q is equal to 0 and t_n is the next event time.

(b) Server maintenance rules

FIGURE 12–11   (*continued*)

Predictable Applications.   You recall that there are three types of predictable applications: cyclically scheduled applications, nonpreemptively scheduled applications, and priority-driven, preemptively scheduled applications that have known next event times. The server used to execute a cyclically scheduled application is a constant utilization server. For the purpose of server maintenance, the workload presented to the server appears to be a single thread. The thread is ready for execution at the beginning of each frame (i.e., at times 0, f, $2f$, and so on). The execution time of this thread is $\tilde{u} f$. Hence, the OS scheduler replenishes the server budget at the beginning of the frames. Each time, the OS scheduler gives the server $\tilde{u} f$ units of budget and sets the deadline of the server accordingly. When the application becomes idle, the OS reclaims the remaining budget. (This emulates the case where the virtual slow processor idles during parts of some frames.)

Similarly, each nonpreemptively scheduled real-time application is executed by a constant utilization server. The OS treats the application as a single aperiodic task and replenishes the budget of the server according to the rules given in Section 7.4.2. If the server is schedulable, it emulates a slow processor of speed $\tilde{u}$ in the following sense for both types of applications. If we compare the schedule of the application in the open system with its schedule on a slow processor of speed $\tilde{u}$, (1) scheduling decisions are made at the same time and (2) every thread completes at the same time or sooner in the open system.

Each preemptively scheduled application is executed by a server that is similar to a total bandwidth server.[23] The rules for maintaining the server of a predictable preemptive application are motived by the example on priority inversion due to budget over replenishment that was described in Section 7.9.2. Whenever the OS scheduler gets ready to replenish the server budget, say at time t, it queries the server scheduler for the next event time t'. It gives the server $\tilde{u}(t' - t)$ units of budget; the new deadline of the server is t'. This way, if a new thread with a higher priority is released at the next event time t', the OS scheduler will be able to give a new chunk of budget to the server for the execution of the new thread.

Unpredictable Applications. When periodic tasks in a preemptively scheduled application have release-time jitters or sporadic tasks, it is impossible for the server scheduler to compute an accurate estimate of the next event time. In the extreme when nothing is known about the release times of some threads, the OS scheduler simply maintains the server in the same way as the server S_0 for nonreal-time applications. In other words, it replenishes the server budget periodically, q units of time apart, giving the server $\tilde{u}q$ units of budget each time. We call this design parameter of the open system the *scheduling quantum*. We will discuss shortly the effect of the scheduling quantum on scheduling overhead and processor utilization.

When it is possible for the server scheduler to provide the OS scheduler with a lower bound $\hat{t}$ to the next event time, the OS scheduler sets the server deadline at $\hat{t} + q$ and sets the server budget to $\tilde{u}(\hat{t} + q - t)$ where t is the current time. Since the actual next event time t' (i.e., the next context switch) is never more than q time units earlier than the current server deadline, should a higher-priority thread be released at t', it is delayed by at most q units of time. In other words, the duration of a priority inversion due to overreplenishment of server budget is never more than q units of time.

12.5.4 Sufficient Schedulability Condition and Acceptance Test

Again, the OS scheduler subjects the application to an acceptance test whenever an application $\mathbf{T}_k$ requests to execute in the real-time mode. The required capacity of the application is s_k, and in the open system, it is scheduled by its server scheduler according to algorithm Σ_k. Deng, *et al.* [DLZS] showed that the following conditions together constitute a sufficient condition for the application $\mathbf{T}_k$ to be schedulable when executed in the open system according to algorithm Σ_k.

---

[23]Unlike a total bandwidth server, the server of a preemptively scheduled application is not always work conserving. When the next event is the release of a thread with a higher priority than the thread currently at the head of the server queue, the OS server waits until the current server deadline to replenish the server budget, even if the executing thread completes before the deadline. As a consequence, every thread may be blocked once by a nonpreemptable section in another application. In contrast, in a one-level priority-driven system, a thread can be blocked only if it is released while some lower-priority thread is in a nonpreemptable section.

1. The size $\tilde{u}_k$ of the server S_k used to execute $\mathbf{T}_k$ is equal to s_k, if $\mathbf{T}_k$ is predictable, or $\tilde{u}_k = s_k \delta_{k,\min}/(\delta_{k,\min} - q)$ if $\mathbf{T}_k$ is unpredictable, where $\delta_{k,\min}$ is the shortest relative deadline of all threads in $\mathbf{T}_k$ whose release times or resource acquisition times are unknown.

2. The total size of all servers in the open system is no more than $1 - \max_{\text{all } j}(B_j/D_{\min,j})$ where the max function is over all real-time applications $\mathbf{T}_j$'s in the system, B_j is the maximum execution time of nonpreemptable sections of all applications other than $\mathbf{T}_j$, and $D_{\min,j}$ is the shortest relative deadline of all threads in $\mathbf{T}_j$.

3. In the interval $(t, d - q)$ from any budget replenishment time t of S_k to q time units before the corresponding server deadline d, where $q \geq 0$ and $d - q > t$, there would be no context switch among the threads in $\mathbf{T}_k$ if $\mathbf{T}_k$ were to execute alone on a slow processor of speed s_k.

Figure 12–11(c) summarizes the acceptance test that the OS scheduler subjects each application to and the choice of server size that the scheduler makes when admitting a new real-time application. The rationale behind them are conditions 1 and 2 stated above: The OS scheduler makes sure that these conditions are met. Similarly, the replenishment rules in Figure 12–11(b) are such that condition 3 is satisfied for all types of real-time applications.

Information provided by requesting application T:

- required capacity s and scheduling algorithm Σ;
- maximum execution time B of all nonpreemptable sections;
- existence of aperiodic/sporadic tasks, if any;
- the shortest relative deadline δ of all threads with release-time jitters;
- the shortest relative deadline $D_{\min}$ if the application is priority driven or the shortest length of time between consecutive timer events if the application is time driven.

Information maintained by the OS scheduler:

- the total size U_t of all servers in the system, and
- the above parameters provided by existing real-time application.

Step 1: Choose the size u of the server for the new application as follows:

- $u = s$ if $\mathbf{T}$ is predictable, or
- $u = s\delta/(\delta - q)$ if $\mathbf{T}$ is unpredictable.

Step 2: Acceptance test and admission:

- If $U_t + u + \max_{all\,j}(B_j/D_{\min,j}) > 1$, reject $\mathbf{T}$;
- Else, admit $\mathbf{T}$:
  - increase U_t by u,
  - create a server S of the chosen size for $\mathbf{T}$, and
  - set budget and deadline of S to 0.

(c) Acceptance test and choice of server size

FIGURE 12–11 (*continued*)

12.5.5 Scheduling Overhead and Processor Utilization

Deng *et al.* [DLZS] simulated systems with different workloads for the purpose of determining the scheduling overhead of the two-level priority-driven scheme. Specifically, they compare the numbers of context switches and queue insertion/deletion operations incurred in systems using the two-level scheme with the corresponding numbers in a closed system using a one-level priority-driven scheduler.

Their simulation results show that scheduling overhead of the open system depends critically on the scheduling quantum. This design parameter can be set to 0 when all real-time applications are predictable. In this case, the scheduling overhead of the open system is essentially the same as that of a closed system. (The number of context switches are the same. There are more queues to maintain but all the queues are shorter.) When some real-time applications are nonpredictable, we must choose a nonzero scheduling quantum. The scheduling overhead of the open system is significantly higher than that of the closed system only when the scheduling quantum is small.

We note that the smaller the minimum relative deadline, the smaller the scheduling quantum must be. Even when the minimum relative deadlines of all applications are large, we may still want to use a small scheduling quantum. The reason is that the size of the server for each nonpredictable application required to meet the schedulability condition 1 grows with the scheduling quantum. A larger server than the required capacity of the applications means a lower processor utilization for real-time applications. In short, in order to accommodate nonpredictable applications with large release-times jitters and small relative deadlines, some processor bandwidth (on the order of 30 percent) is not available for real-time applications. This bandwidth is either wasted as scheduling overhead, when the scheduling quantum is small, or set aside for the sake of compensating blocking time in nonpredictable applications, when the scheduling quantum is large. The latter is better because the extra processor bandwidth over the required capacity of the real-time application will be used by server S_0 for nonreal-time applications.

12.5.6 Service Provider Structure and Real-Time API Functions

In the open system, services such as network and file access are implemented as special-purpose user-level server applications. As stated earlier, the OS scheduler creates a passive server to execute each service provider. Each SSP has a daemon thread, which is created when the service provider is admitted into the system. Its responsibilities are (1) to create work threads in the address space of the service provider in response to requests for service from clients, and (2) to process incoming data to identify the receiving thread and to notify that thread. The daemon thread is suspended immediately after it is created. When the daemon thread wakes up to run, the passive server executes it using the server's own budget.

Scheduling of Work Threads   When a client application T_k requests service from an SSP, it sends a budget and a deadline for consuming the budget along with its request to the service provider. The parameters of the work thread created to service the client include its budget and deadline, which are equal to the respective values given by the request. The scheduler of the passive server schedules its daemon thread and all the work threads on the EDF basis, and the OS scheduler schedules the passive server according to the deadline of the thread at the head of the server's ready queue.

The passive server also has a suspend queue. Whenever the budget of the passive server is exhausted but the executing thread remains incomplete, it is removed from the server's ready queue and inserted in the suspend queue. When the requesting application sends more budget, the scheduler of the passive server reactivates the work thread, setting its budget and deadline accordingly and moving it back to the ready queue. When the thread completes, any unused budget is returned to the requesting application.

API Functions for Invocation of System Services. A real-time client application requests service by sending the service provider one of two Real-Time Application Programming Interface (RTAPI) calls: *send_data( )* and *recv_data( )*. The former is called when a client application requests the service provider to accepts its data (e.g., to send a message or write a file.) When called at time t by an application $\mathbf{T}_k$, the function *send_data( )* first invokes the server scheduler of server S_k to transfer its budget and deadline to the passive server of the service provider. The call wakes up the daemon thread of the service provider. When this thread executes, it creates a work thread, as described in the previous paragraphs. In the meantime, the calling thread within the client application is blocked until the work thread completes.

A client application calls *recv_data( )* to request a service provider to process incoming data on its behalf. Similar to *send_data( )*, *recv_data( )* also causes a transfer of budget to the passive server of the system service provider. If the data to be received are not available at the time, the call effectively freezes the client application, since the server of the application has no budget to execute and the service provider cannot execute on behalf of the application as the data are not available. To circumvent this problem, the client application first calls *wait_data( )* to wait for the data. If the data are available, *wait_data( )* returns immediately. Otherwise, the thread calling *wait_data( )* is blocked. Unlike *send_data( )* and *recv_data( )*, *wait_data( )* does not transfer budget to service provider. Hence, when the calling thread is blocked, the server of the application can still execute other threads in the client application. When incoming data arrive, the daemon thread processes the data just to identify the receiver of the incoming data and, after the receiver is identified, wakes up the thread that called *wait_data( )* if the thread exists, and *wait_data( )* returns. The client application then calls *recv_data( )* to transfer to the service provider the budget needed by the SSP process and receive the incoming data.

In effect, a call of the *send_data( )* or *recv_data( )* function causes a transfer of budget from the server of the client application to the passive server of service provider. Because this transfer does not violate any of the schedulability conditions stated above, the client remains schedulable. The schedulability of other applications is not affected by the execution of the service provider.

Other Real-Time API Functions. In addition to the real-time API functions for communication between real-time applications and system service providers, the open system also needs to provide API functions for the creation, admission, and termination of real-time applications. As an example, the prototype system described in [DLZS] provides a function called *register_application( )*. A real-time application calls this function to specify for the operating system its required capacity, as well as its choice of real-time scheduling algorithm and resource-access protocol among the ones supported by the system.

The prototype supports periodic and aperiodic tasks. A real-time application calls a create periodic task function to create a periodic task of the specified phase, period, and relative deadline, as well as informing the operating system of the resources the periodic task will require and the maximum length of time the task will hold these resources. Similarly, it calls a create aperiodic task function to create an aperiodic task that will execute in response to a specified list of events. After creating and initializing all its tasks, an application then calls *start_application( )* to request admission into the open system.

The prototype also provides API functions for use by SSPs in their interaction with client applications. Examples of these functions are *add_thread_budget( )*, which replenishes the budget of the specified thread in response to the *add_budget( )* request.

12.6 CAPABILITIES OF COMMERCIAL REAL-TIME OPERATING SYSTEMS

This section describes several real-time operating systems that run on common processors and have sizable user bases. They are LynxOS [Bunn], pSOSystem [Moto], QNX [QNX], VRTX [Ment] and VxWorks [Wind]. In many respects, these operating systems are similar. Below is a summary of their commonalities; with few exceptions, you can replace the noun "the operating system" in the summary by the name of any of them.

- *Conformance to Standards*: The operating system is compliant or partially compliant to the Real-Time POSIX API standard, so you have preemptive fixed-priority scheduling, standard synchronization primitives, and so on, but the operating system may support only threads or processes (i.e., not both) and may implement only a subset of the standard functions. The operating system also has its own set of API functions, which may differ significantly from the corresponding POSIX functions and, in the cases where they are similar, may have more features. Some of the operating systems also provide AT&T System V and BSD system call interfaces (e.g., LynxOS) and Willows Win32 Library (e.g., QNX). (You can find information on Willows Library from http://www.willows.com.)

- *Modularity and Scalability*: The kernel is small, and the operating system configurable. In particular, the operating system can be scaled down to fit with the application in ROM in small embedded systems. By adding optional components to the kernel, the operating system can be configured to provide I/O, file, and networking services.

- *Speed and Efficiency*: Most of these operating systems are microkernel systems. Unlike microkernel systems of old, which usually have higher run-time overhead than monolithic operating systems, these microkernel operating systems have low overhead. In some, sending a message to a system service provider incurs no context switch. Important timing figures such as context-switch time, interrupt latency, semaphore get/release latency, and so on, are typically small (i.e., one to a few microseconds).

- *System Calls*: Nonpreemptable portions of kernel functions necessary for mutual exclusion are highly optimized and made as short and deterministic as possible.

- *Split Interrupt Handling*: Similarly, the nonpreemptable portion of interrupt handling and the execution times of immediate interrupt handling routines are kept small. The bulk of the work done to handle each interrupt is scheduled and executed at an appropriate priority.

- *Scheduling*: All real-time operating systems offer at least 32 priority levels, which is the minimum number required to be Real-Time POSIX compliant; most offer 128 or 256 (or 255). They all offer the choice between FIFO or round-robin policies for scheduling equal-priority threads. They allow you to change thread priorities at run time, but none provides adequate support for EDF scheduling and good hook for user-level bandwidth-preserving servers and slack stealers.

- *Priority Inversion Control*: The operating system provides priority inheritance but may allow you to disable it to save the overhead of this mechanism if you choose to use a resource access-control scheme that does not need priority inheritance. The system may also provide ceiling-priority protocol.

- *Clock and Timer Resolution*: The operating system may provide a nominal timer resolution down to nanoseconds. However, even on the fastest processor today, the operating system takes about a microsecond to process a timer interrupt, so you should not expect to be able to release a thread periodically with a period down to microseconds or precision and granularity in time down to tens and hundreds of nanoseconds.

- *Memory Management*: The operating system may provide virtual-to-physical address mapping but does not do paging. The operating system may not offer memory protection. Even when it does, it provides the user with the choice among multiple levels of memory protection, ranging from no protection to private virtual memory.

- *Networking*: The operating system can be configured to support TCP/IP, streams, and so on.

The remainder of the section highlights some distinguishing features of the operating systems listed above, especially those features not mentioned in the above summary. The fact that we say that an operating system has a feature but do not mention the same feature in our discussion on another operating system does not imply that the other operating system does not have the same or similar features! The section refrains from giving you a table of features and performance data on the operating systems described here. Such information will most likely to be out-of-date by the time this book reaches you. The best source of up-to-date information on any operating system is the home page provided by the vendor. There you are also likely to find a good tutorial on basic operating system primitives in general.

12.6.1   LynxOS

LynxOS 3.0 moves from the monolithic architecture of earlier versions to a microkernel design. The microkernel is 28 kilobytes in size and provides the essential services in scheduling, interrupt dispatch, and synchronization. Other services are provided by kernel lightweight service modules, called Kernel Plug-Ins (KPIs). By adding KPIs to the microkernel, the system can be configured to support I/O and file systems, TCP/IP, streams, sockets, and so on, and functions as a multipurpose UNIX operating system as earlier versions do.

Unlike single-threaded system service providers in traditional microkernel systems, KPIs are multithreaded. Each KPI can create as many threads to execute its routines as needed. LynxOS says that there is no context switch when sending a message (e.g., RFS) to a KPI, and inter-KPI communication takes only a few instructions [Bunn].

LynxOS can be configured as a self-hosted system. In such a system, embedded applications are developed on the same system on which they are to be deployed and run.[24] This means that the operating system must also support tools such as compilers, debuggers, and performance profilers and allow them to run on the same platform as embedded applications. Protecting the operating system and critical applications from these possibly untrustworthy applications is essential. Moreover, their memory demands are large. For this reason, LynxOS not only provides memory protection through hardware Memory Management Units (MMUs) but also offers optional demand paging; we have already described this feature in Section 12.3.3.

In LynxOS, application threads (and processes) make I/O requests to the I/O system via system calls such as *open( )*, *read( )*, *write( )*, *select( )*, and *close( )* that resemble the corresponding UNIX system calls. Each I/O request is sent directly by the kernel to a device driver for the respective I/O device. LynxOS device drivers follow the split interrupt handling strategy. Each driver contains an interrupt handler and a kernel thread. The former carries out the first step of interrupt handling at an interrupt request priority. The latter is a thread that shares the same address space with the kernel but is separate from the kernel. If the interrupt handler does not complete the processing of an interrupt, it sets an asynchronous system trap to interrupt the kernel. When the kernel can respond to the (software) interrupt (i.e., when the kernel is in a preemptable state), it schedules an instance of the kernel thread at the priority of the thread which opened the interrupting device. When the kernel thread executes, it continues interrupt handling and reenables the interrupt when it completes. LynxOS calls this mechanism priority tracking. (LynxOS holds a patent for this scheme.) Section 12.1.1 gave more details.

12.6.2 pSOSystem

Again, pSOSystem is an object-oriented operating system. Like the other operating systems described in this section, it is modular. pSOS+ is a preemptive, multitasking kernel that runs on a single microprocessor, while pSOS+m is a distributed multiprocessor kernel. pSOS+m has the same API functions as pSOS+, as well as functions for interprocessor communication and synchronization. The most recent release offers a POSIX real-time extension-compliant layer. Additional optional components provide a TCP/IP protocol stack and target and host-based debugging tools.

The classes of pSOSystem objects include tasks, memory regions and partitions, message queues, and semaphores. Each object has a node of residence, which is the processor on which the system call that created the object was made. An object may be global or local. A global object (a task or a resource) can be accessed from any processor in the system, while a local object can be accessed only by tasks on its local processor. A remote node with respect to any object is a processor other than its node of residence. You may have notice that this is how the MPCP model views a static multiprocessor system. In Section 9.1.3, we called the node of residence of a task (object) its local processor and the node of a residence of a resource (e.g., a semaphore) its synchronization processor.

---

[24]The opposite is a cross-development environment, where the host environment is separated from the target embedded systems. Embedded applications are written and compiled in the host environment and then moved to the target system to run and to be debugged and tested.

The basic unit of execution is a task, which has its own virtual environment.[25] pSOS+ provides each task with the choice of either preemptive priority-driven or time-driven scheduling. The application developer can also choose to run user tasks in either user or supervisory mode. pSOSystem 2.5 offers, in addition to priority inheritance, priority-ceiling protocol.

In Section 12.1.2, we said that in most modern operating systems, the processor jumps to the kernel when an interrupt occurs. pSOSystem is an exception. Device drivers are outside the kernel and can be loaded and removed at run time. When an interrupt occurs, the processor jumps directly to the interrupt service routine pointed to by the vector table. The intention is not only to gain some speed, but also to give the application developer complete control over interrupt handling.

pSOSystem allocates to tasks memory regions. A memory region is a physically contiguous block of memory. Like all objects, it may be local (i.e., strictly in local memory) or global (i.e., in a systemwide accessible part of the memory). The operating system creates a memory region in response to a call from an application. A memory region may be divided into either fixed-size buffers or variable-size segments.

12.6.3   QNX/Neutrino

QNX is one of the few multiprocessor operating systems suitable for real-time applications that requires high-end, networked SMP machines with gigabytes of physical memory. Its microkernel provides essential thread and real-time services. Other operating system services are provided by optional components called resource managers. For example, in the recent version, called Neutrino, the microkernel supports only threads. A process manager is needed to support processes that are memory-protected from each other, and the process manager is optional. Because optional components can be excluded at run time, the operating system can be scaled down to a small size. (The QNX 4.x microkernel is 12 kilobytes in size.)

QNX is a message-passing operating system; messages are the basic means of interprocess communication among all threads. Section 12.3.1 already talked about its message-based priority inheritance feature. This is the basic mechanism for priority tracking: Messages are delivered in priority order and the service provider executes at the priority of the highest priority clients waiting for service.

QNX implements POSIX message queues outside the kernel but implements QNX's message passing within the kernel. QNX messages are sent and received over channels and connections. When a service provider thread wants to receive messages, it first creates a channel. The channel is named within the service provider by a small integer identifier. To request service from a service provider, a client thread first attaches to the service provider's channel. This attachment is called a connection to the channel. Within the client, this connection is mapped directly to a file descriptor. The client can then send its RFS messages over the connection, in other words, directly to the file descriptor.

---

[25]The most well-known application of pSoSystem is Iridium, the system of communication satellites. The version of pSOSystem used in Iridium takes 400 microseconds to context switch among tasks, while the application is required to run 125 thread repetitions in each 90-millisecond L-Band interval. A two-level scheme is used to keep the overhead of context switches among threads low. The operating system schedules a small number (two or three) of scheduler tasks. When a scheduler runs, it polls threads.

While POSIX messages are queued and the senders are not blocked, QNX's message send and receive functions are blocking. A thread that calls the QNX send function *MsgSendv( )* is blocked until the receiving thread executes a receive *MsgReceivev( )*, processes the message, and then executes a *MsgReply( )*. Similarly, a thread that executes a *MsgReceive( )* is blocked if there is no pending message waiting on the channel and becomes unblocked when another thread executes a *MsgSend( )*. The blocking and synchronous nature of message passing eliminates the need of data queueing and makes a separate call by the client to wait for response unnecessary. Each message is copied directly to the receiving thread's address space without intermediate buffering. Hence, the speed of message passing is limited only by the hardware speed. You recall that the thread used to process a message inherits the priority of the sender. Therefore, for the purpose of schedulability analysis, we can treat the client and the server as if they were a single thread with their combined execution time.

Neutrino also supports fixed-size, nonblocking messages. These messages are called pulses. QNX's own event notification mechanism, as well as some of the POSIX and real-time signals, use pulses. Like QNX messages, pulses are received over channels.

In addition to thread-level synchronization primitives, Neutrino provides atomic operations for adding and subtracting a value, setting and clearing a bit, and complementing a bit. Using these operations, we can minimize the need for disabling interrupts and preemptions for the purpose of ensuring atomicity.

12.6.4   VRTX

VRTX has two multitasking kernels: VRTXsa and VRTXmc. VRTXsa is designed for performance. It has a POSIX-compliant library, provides priority inheritance, and supports multiprocessing. Its system calls are deterministic and preemptable. In particular, VRTXsa 5.0 is compliant to POSIX real-time extensions. It is for medium and large real-time applications. VRTXmc, on the other hand, is optimized for power consumption and ROM and RAM sizes. It provides only basic functions and is intended for applications such as cellular phones and other small handheld devices. For such applications, the kernel typically requires only 4-8 kilobytes of ROM and 1 kilobyte of RAM.

Most noteworthy about VRTX is that it is the first commercial real-time operating system certified by the Federal Aviation Agency (FAA) for mission- and life-critical systems, such as avionics. (VRTX is compliant to the FAA RTCS/DO-178B level A standard. This is a standard for software on board aircraft, and level A is for software whose failure would cause or contribute to a catastrophic failure of the aircraft. The process of compliance certification involves 100 percent code coverage in testing.) VRTX is used for the avionics on board Boeing MD-11 aircraft.

Rather than providing users with a variety of optional components, VRTX provides hooks for extensibility. For example, the TCB of a new task created by *TCREATE( )* is extended to include application-specific information. An application can also add system calls.

Like the other operating systems described here, VRTX also has its own API functions. An example is mailboxes, which can be used to transfer one long word of data at a time (as opposed to queues for transferring multiple long words of data).

VRTX allocates memory in fixed-size blocks. For efficiency, free pool may be divided into noncontiguous partitions with different size blocks.

12.6.5 VxWorks

A man on the street may not know VxWorks by name but most likely knows one of its applications, as it was the operating system used on Mars Pathfinder, which NASA sent to Mars in 1997. You recall that after Pathfinder landed on Mars and started to respond to ground commands and take science and engineering data, its computer repeatedly reset itself. This frequent reset made worldwide news daily. Fortunately, JPL and VxWorks were able to pinpoint the problem. This was done with the aid of a trace generation and logging tool and extensive instrumentation of major services (such as pipe, message queues, and interrupt handling), which were used during debugging and testing and were left in the system. They fixed the problem on the ground and thus saved the day for Pathfinder. According to Glenn Reeves, the Mars Pathfinder flight software cognizant engineer [Reev],[26] the cause was the classical uncontrolled priority inversion problem. Although VxWorks provides priority inheritance, the mechanism was disabled. The prolonged blocking experienced by a high-priority task caused it to miss its deadline, and the computer was reset as a consequence. The fix was, of course, to enable priority inheritance.

Before moving on, we want make a couple of parenthetical remarks on lessons learned from this incident. First, we cannot rely on testing to determine whether tasks can complete in time and how often a task may be late. (The computer reset behavior was observed only once during the months of testing on the ground. It was deemed infrequent enough to not warrant concern before Pathfinder left the ground.) Second, it is good practice to leave the instrumentation code added for debugging and testing purposes in the deployed system. System and software engineering experts can give you numerous reasons for doing so, not just so that you can use it to debug the system after it is deployed.

Back to VxWorks, the Pathfinder incident highlights the fact that VxWorks allows us to disable major function such as memory protection and priority inheritance. You can specify what options are to be enabled and what options are to be disabled via global configuration parameters. In the case of Pathfinder, the global configuration variable is the one that specifies whether priority inheritance is enabled for mutual exclusion semaphores. Once this option is set, priority inheritance is enabled or disabled as specified for all mutual exclusion semaphores created afterwards.

---

[26]Just in case the Web page cited here is no longer available when you look for it, here is a brief description of the problem. Pathfinder used a single computer to control both the cruise and lander parts. The CPU connected via a VME bus with interfaces to the radio, the camera, and a MIL-STD-1553 bus. The 1553 bus in turn connected to the flight controller and monitoring devices, as well as an instrument, called ASI/MET, for meteorological science. The tasks of interest were the bus scheduler, the data distributor and the ASI/MET task.

The bus scheduler was the highest priority task in the system. It executed periodically to set up transactions on the 1553 bus. During each period, data acquisition and compression took place and the ASI/MET task executed. In the midst of each period, the data distributor was awakened to distribute data. Its deadline was the beginning of the next scheduling period when the scheduling task began to execute; the scheduling task reset the computer whenever it found the data distributor incomplete at the time.

The data distributor was the high-priority task involved in uncontrolled priority-inversion, and the ASI/MET was the low-priority task, while data acquisition and compression tasks has medium priorities. Specifically, the data distributor and ASI/MET shared a mutual exclusion semaphore, which is a binary semaphore that can have priority inheritance. However, the priority inheritance option was disabled at the time, so while the data distributor was blocked by ASI/MET, the medium priority tasks could execute, prolong the duration of priority inversion, and prevent the data distributor from completing on time. This was what happened in Pathfinder on Mars.

VxWorks is a monolithic system. It is not a UNIX system but provides most interface functions defined by POSIX real-time extensions. As we mentioned earlier, an operating system's own API function may have more features than the corresponding POSIX function. An example is the timeout feature of Wind semaphores, the operating system's own semaphores. A parameter of the take-semaphore *semTake( )* function is the amount time the calling task is willing to wait for the semaphore. The value of this parameter can be NO_WAIT, WAIT_FOREVER, or a positive timeout value. Indeed, many VxWorks API functions (e.g., message queues) have the timeout feature. Another feature of Wind semaphores is *deletion safety*, that is, the prevention of a task from being deleted while it is in a critical section. A task can prevent itself from being accidentally deleted while it is holding a semaphore by specifying SEM_DELETE_SAFE in its take-semaphore call.

A VxWorks feature that was mentioned earlier is preemption lock. The operating system also provides similar functions [i.e., *intLock( )* and *intUnlock( )*] which a task can call to enable and disable interrupts. These functions makes the user-level implementation of the NPCS protocol easy.

While VxWorks is not a multiprocessor operating system, it provides shared-memory multiprocessing support as an option. Specifically, VxMP provides three types of shared-memory objects: shared binary and counting semaphores, shared message queues, and shared-memory partitions. They can be used for synchronization and communication among tasks in static multiprocessor systems.

VxWorks virtual memory exemplifies the kind of memory management options typically found in modern real-time operating systems. In a system with an MMU, the basic memory management provides virtual-to-physical address mapping. It allows you add new mappings and make portions of the memory noncacheable. (An example where this capability is needed is when we add memory boards to enlarge the shared memory for interprocessor communication. We want the portions of memory that are accessed by multiple processors and DMA devices to be noncacheable, that is, disallow any CPU to copy these portions into its data cache. This way, you do not have to maintain cache consistency manually or turn off caching globally.) Full-level memory management, including protection of text segments and the exception vector table and interfaces to the MMU, is provided by VxVMI, which is an optional component. By default, all tasks use a common context at system initiation time. A task can create a private virtual memory for the sake of protection by calling VxVMI functions to create a new virtual memory and update the address translation table. Thus an application can control access to its data or code as needed.

Finally, while LynxOS is a self-host system, the Tornado environment for VxWorks is a cross-development environment. Tornado provides an extensive set of development and performance monitoring and analysis tools. These memory-demanding tools reside on a host machine, separate from embedded applications, and therefore do not create the necessity of memory protection and paging/swapping as in LynxOS. However, host resident tools cannot access symbol tables on the target machine. For the purpose of creating a system that can be dynamically configured at run time, you must use the target-resident shell for development and you can configure module loader and unloader, symbol tables, and some debugging tools into VxWorks.

12.7 PREDICTABILITY OF GENERAL-PURPOSE OPERATING SYSTEMS

Sometimes, we may choose to run real-time applications on a general-purpose operating system despite its shortcomings. Reasons for this choice include the timing requirements of our applications are not hard, the general-purpose operating system costs less, there is a large user base, and so on. This section assumes that the choice of using a general-purpose operating system has already been made. As application developers, we must be fully aware of the sources of unpredictability. By adopting an application software architecture that minimizes the use of problematic features of the operating system and a scheduling and resource access-control strategy that keeps the effect of priority inversion in check, we may achieve sufficient predictability despite the operating system.

Rather than talking about general-purpose operating systems in general, we focus here on the two most widely used ones, Windows NT [Solo, Hart] and Linux [CaDM]. Windows NT (NT for short) is the most popular, and there is a growing trend to use it for real-time computing. This section discusses in turn each of the shortcomings of NT from a real-time computing point of view and describes approaches to partially overcome the shortcomings. Even more than NT, Linux is unsuitable for real-time applications. However, unlike NT, which we must live with as it is, we are free to modify Linux. This section describes existing real-time extensions of Linux for hard and soft real-time applications.

12.7.1 Windows NT Operating System

Windows NT provides many features (e.g., threads, priority interrupt, and events) that are suitable for real-time applications. Its actual timer and clock resolutions are sufficiently fine for all but the most time-stringent applications. However, its large memory footprint rules out its use whenever size is a consideration. Even when its size is not a problem, its weak support for real-time scheduling and resource-access control and unpredictable interrupt handling and interprocess communication mechanisms can be problematic. It is essential for time-critical applications to avoid system services that can introduce unpredictable and prolonged blocking. By keeping processor utilization sufficiently low and providing priority-inversion control at the user level, these applications can get sufficient predictability out of NT.

Scheduling.   The scheduling mechanisms provided by Windows NT are designed for good average performance of time-shared applications. We should not be surprised to find them less than ideal for real-time applications.

Limited Priority Levels.   Windows NT provides only 32 thread priorities. The lowest 16 levels (i.e., 0–15) are for threads of time-shared applications. The operating system may boost the priority and adjust the time slice (i.e., scheduling quantum) of a thread running at one of these priority levels in order to speed up the progress of the thread. Levels 16–31 are real-time priorities. The operating system never adjusts the priorities of threads running at these levels.

The small number of system priority levels by itself is not a serious problem, even for applications that should ideally be scheduled at a large number of distinct priorities, if we do not need to keep the processor utilization high. You recall that we can compensate for a small number of available priority levels by keeping the processor (sufficiently) lightly loaded. As an example, suppose that we assign priorities to threads according to the rate-monotonic algorithm and use the constant-ratio mapping scheme described in Section 6.8.4 to map the assigned priorities to system priority levels. Lehoczky *et al.* [LeSh] showed that if we keep the processor load from exceeding 1/2, we can map at least 4098 assigned thread priorities to the 16 available system priority levels.[27] (You can find the schedulable utilization of a rate-monotonic system as a function of mapping ratio in Section 6.8.4.)

Many kernel-mode system threads execute at real-time priority level 16. They should affect only real-time threads with priority 16. However, higher-priority real-time threads may delay system threads. This means that in the presence of real-time applications, memory managers, local and network file systems, and so on, may not work well.

Jobs, Job Scheduling Classes, and FIFO Policy.[28]   Another problem with Windows NT 4.0 is that it does not support FIFO with equal priority. As we will see shortly, the lack of FIFO scheduling capability is more problematic than an insufficient number of priority levels. In this respect, NT 5.0 offers a significant improvement over NT 4.0, as it is possible to choose the FIFO option on NT 5.0.

To explain, we note that NT 5.0 introduces the concepts of jobs and scheduling classes. A job may contain multiple processes but each process can belong to only one job. In an SMP system, we can statically configure the system by setting a limit-affinity flag of each job and, thus, bind all the processes in the job to a processor. Other features of the new job objects include the ability to set limits of a job object that control all processes in the job. Examples are user-mode execution time and memory usage limits on a per job or per process basis. A process (or a job) is terminated when the system finds that the process has accumulated more user-mode execution time than its previously set limit. A job containing periodic threads can periodically reset its own execution time limits and thus turns its execution-time usage limit into an execution rate limit. NT 5.0 simply terminates an offending job (or process) when it exceeds any of its usage limits, rather than putting job in the background, so the per job execution time and memory limit feature cannot be used as it is to implement the CPU reservation scheme described in Section 12.4.

Like NT 4.0, NT 5.0 also offers different priority classes. Time-critical processes should be in the real-time priority class. As stated earlier, on NT 5.0, all 16 real-time priority levels are available to a user thread in the real-time priority class. In addition to priority classes, NT 5.0 offers nine job scheduling classes; class 9 is for real-time applications. Whether all processes in a job belong to the same job scheduling class depends on whether the scheduling class limit is enabled or disabled. When this flag to set to enabled, all processes in the job use the same scheduling class.

---

[27]A small complication is that in Windows NT 4.0, the API function *SetThreadPriority( )* allows a user thread to specify only 7 out of the 16 real-time priority levels. However, a kernel thread can set the priority of any real-time thread to any of the 16 levels. Hence, we need to provide the priority mapping function in a device driver. We set the priority of a thread by calling this function instead of *SetThreadPriority( )*. This kluge will not be necessary in NT 5.0 (also called Windows 2000) since all 16 real-time priority levels are available to user-level real-time threads.

[28]Here, the term job is overloaded: What NT 5.0 calls a job is not what we have meant by a job throughout the book.

A combination of parameters allow us to choose either the FIFO or round-robin policy (within equal priority) for a process, and hence all threads in it. The operating system schedules all processes according to the round-robin policy by default. However, a real-time process (i.e., a process of real-time priority class) in a job whose scheduling class has value 9 and scheduling class limit enabled is scheduled according to the FIFO policy. In other words, we choose the FIFO option for a process by putting the process in the real-time priority class, giving the scheduling class of the job containing the process a value 9, and enabling the scheduling class limits for the job.

Resource Access Control.   NT does not support priority inheritance. There are two ways to control priority inversion in a uniprocessor system without the help of this mechanism. All of them are at the user level and do not completely control priority inversion.

User-Level NPCS.   The simplest way to overcome the lack of priority inheritance is to use the NPCS protocol described in Section 8.3. You recall that according to this protocol, a thread executes nonpreemptively when it holds any resource (i.e., a lock, a mutex object, or a semaphore). In the case of reader/writer locks and mutexes, it is simple to implement an approximate version of this protocol as a library function. The function assumes that priority level 31 is reserved for exclusive use by threads in their nonpreemptable sections. When a thread calls the NPCS function to request a resource, the function stores the thread's current priority and sets the priority to 31 and then grants the resource to the thread. The function restores the thread's priority when the thread no longer holds any resource.

We say that this is an approximate implementation of the NPCS protocol because setting the thread priority to 31 is not the same as making the thread nonpreemptive. The user-level protocol cannot enforce the exclusive use of priority level 31 for the purpose of emulating nonpreemption. Threads that do not use this library may have priority 31. In NT 4.0, these threads are scheduled on the round-robin basis with the thread that is holding a lock. They can delay its progress. Moreover, this delay is theoretically unbounded.

In contrast, this user-level NPCS protocol is effective in a uniprocessor system running NT 5.0 when threads under the control of the protocol are scheduled on the FIFO basis. At the time when a thread's priority is raised to 31, no other thread with priority 31 is ready for execution. Since the thread is scheduled on the FIFO basis, after its priority is raised to 31, no other thread can preempt it until it releases all the resources it holds.

Ceiling Priority Protocol.   An alternative is the Ceiling-Priority Protocol (CPP) described in Section 8.6. You recall that the CPP requires prior information on the resources required by each thread. Each resource has a priority ceiling, which was defined in Section 8.5 for single-unit resources and Section 8.9 for multiple-unit resources. According to the CPP, a thread holding any resource executes at the highest priority ceiling of all the resources it holds.

To implement this protocol on a uniprocessor running NT 4.0, we need to restrict real-time threads to have even priority levels (i.e., 16, 18, . . . , 30). (The reason for this restriction is again that NT 4.0 does not support FIFO among equal-priority policy.) If the highest priority of all threads requiring a resource is $2k$, then the ceiling-priority of the resource is $2k + 1$. (The ceiling priority of a resource with multiple units can be defined analogously.) Like the NPCS protocol, the user-level CCP cannot prevent unbounded priority inversion if there are threads that have priorities higher than 16 and are not under its control

Again, we do not have this problem with NT 5.0. We can use all 16 real-time priorities. By scheduling all threads under the control of CCP according to the FIFO policy, the protocol keeps the duration of priority inversion among them bounded.

Deferred Procedure Calls.   Interrupt handling is done in two steps in Windows NT. As in good real-time operating systems, each interrupt service routine executed in the immediate step is short. So interrupt latency in NT is comparable to the latencies of real-time operating systems.

Unpredictability arising from interrupt handling is introduced in the second step. NT device drivers are written such that an interrupt service routine queues a procedure, called a Deferred Procedure Call (DPC), to handle the second step of interrupt handling. DPCs are executed in FIFO order at a priority lower than all the hardware interrupt priorities but higher than the priority of the scheduler/dispatcher. Consequently, a higher-priority thread can be blocked by DPCs queued in response to interrupts caused by lower-priority threads. This blocking time can be significant since the execution times of some DPCs can be quite large (e.g., 1 millisecond or more). Worst yet, the blocking time is unbounded.

However, it is possible to do priority tracking within NT. We do so by using a kernel thread to execute the DPC function. In other words, rather than having the Internet Service Routine (ISR) part of a device driver queue a DPC, it wakes up a kernel mode thread to execute the DPC function. This is similar to how the second step of interrupt handling is done in LynxOS. Specifically, the initialization routine (i.e., DriverEntry routine), the DPC function, and ISR of a device driver should be as follows.

- The initialization routine creates a kernel mode thread and sets the priority of the thread at a level specified by the device driver. The thread blocks waiting to be signaled by the ISR and, when signaled, it will execute the function provided by the device driver.
- The function provided by the driver does the remaining part of interrupt handling when executed by the kernel thread.
- When the interrupt service routine runs, it wakes up the kernel thread after servicing the device.

A question that remains is, what priority should the device driver thread have? The correct priority of the thread may remain unknown until the thread has executed for a while. (For example, suppose that when an incoming message causes an interrupt, the network driver thread is to have the priority of the thread that will receive the message. The receiving thread is not identified until the message header is processed.) A way is to give the driver thread a high priority, say 30, initially. (We assume that priority 31 is used exclusively to emulate preemption lock.) When it is awaked and executes, it sets its own priority to the priority of the thread which caused the interrupt as soon as it identifies that thread. (This scheme was suggested by Gallmeister [Gall] as a way to emulate priority inheritance by message passing.)

Asynchronous Procedure Calls and LPC Mechanism. In Section 12.3.2 we described briefly NT events and Asynchronous Procedure Calls (APCs), which serve the same purpose as signals in UNIX systems. Events are synchronous. Like Real-Time POSIX signals, events are queued and hence will not be lost if not handled immediately. Unlike Real-Time POSIX signals, however, they are delivered in FIFO order and do not carry data. APCs complement events to provide asynchronous services to applications as well as the kernel. Each (kernel or user) thread has its own APC queue, which enqueues the APCs that will be executed by the thread. When called to do so, the kernel inserts an APC in the queue of the specified thread and requests a software interrupt at the APC priority level, which is lower than the priority of the dispatcher (i.e., the scheduler) but higher than the priorities of normal threads. When the thread runs, it executes the enqueued APC. Since a thread is at the APC priority level while it is executing an APC, the thread is nonpreemptable by other threads during this time and may block higher-priority threads. Therefore, it is important that the execution times of APCs be kept as small as possible.

Another source of unpredictability in Windows NT is Local Procedure Calls (LPCs). This is an example of incorrect prioritization. LPCs provide the interprocess communication mechanism by which environment subsystem Dynamic Link Libraries (DLLs) pass requests to subsystem service providers. It is also used by remote procedure calls between processes on the same machine, as well as by the WinLogin process and security reference monitor.

Specifically, the LPC mechanism provides three schemes to communicate data across address space boundaries. Short messages are sent over an LPC connection when the sending process or thread makes a LPC call which specifies the buffer containing the message. The message is copied into the kernel space and from there into the address space of the receiving process. The other schemes make use of shared memory sections and are for exchanges of long messages between the sender and receiver.

Since the LPC queue is FIFO ordered, priority inversion can occur when a thread sends a request over an LPC connection to a service provider. Furthermore, without priority tracking, a service provider thread which was created to service a request from a high-priority thread may execute at a nonreal-time or low real-time priority.

We can avoid this kind of priority inversion only by avoiding the use of the LPC mechanism. In NT 4.0, the Win32 API functions that use LPC to communicate with subsystem service providers are (1) console (text) window support, (2) process and thread creation and termination, (3) network drive letter mapping, and (4) creation of temporary files. This means that a time-critical application should not write to the console, create and delete threads, and create temporary files. A multimode application must create and initialize threads that may run in all modes at initialization time. This restriction not only further increases the memory demand of the system but also reduces the configurability of the system.

12.7.2 Real-Time Extensions of Linux Operating Systems

The adoption of Linux has increased steadily in recent years as the operating system becomes increasingly more stable, its performance improves, and more and more Linux applications become available. The remainder of this section describes two extensions that enable applications with firm or hard real-time requirements to run on Linux. As you will see shortly, these extensions fall far short of making Linux compliant to POSIX real-time extensions. More seriously, applications written to run on these extensions are not portable to standard UNIX machines or other commercial real-time operating systems.

Important Features.   Like NT, Linux also has many shortcomings when used for real-time applications. One of the most serious arises from the disabling of interrupts by Linux subsystems when they are in critical sections. While most device drivers disable interrupts for a few microseconds, the disk subsystem may disable interrupts for as long as a few hundred microseconds at a time. The predictability of the system is seriously damaged when clock interrupts can be blocked for such a long time. The solution to this problem is to rewrite all the offending drivers to make their nonpreemptable sections as short as possible, as they are in real-time operating systems. Neither extension described below attacked this problem head on; rather, one tries to live with it, while the other avoids it.

Scheduling.   Linux provides individual processes with the choices among *SCHED_FIFO, SCHED_RR*, or *SCHED_OTHER* policies. Processes using the *SCHED_FIFO* and *SCHED_RR* policies are scheduled on a fixed-priority basis; these are real-time processes. Processes using *SCHED_OTHER* are scheduled on the time-sharing basis; they execute at priorities lower than real-time processes.

There are 100 priority levels altogether. You can determine the maximum and minimum priorities associated with a scheduling policy using the primitives *sched_get_priority_min( )* and *sched_get_priority_max( )*. You can also find the size of the time slices given to processes scheduled according to the round-robin policy using *sched_rr_get_interval( )*. Since you have the source, you can also change these parameters.

Clock and Timer Resolutions.   Like NT, Linux updates the system clock and checks for timer expirations periodically, and the period is 10 milliseconds on most hardware platforms. [In Linux, each clock interrupt period is called a *jiffy*, and time is expressed in terms of (the number of) *jiffies*.] Consequently, the actual resolution of Linux timers is 10 milliseconds.

To improve the clock resolution on Pentium processors, the kernel reads and stores the time stamp counter at each clock interrupt. In response to a *gettimeofday* call, it reads the counter again and calculates from the difference in the two readings the number of microseconds that have elapsed from the time of the previous timer interrupt to the current time. In this way, it returns the current time to the caller in terms of *jiffies* and the number of microseconds into the current *jiffy*.

In addition to reading the time stamp counter at each clock interrupt, the timer interrupt service routine checks the timer queue to determine whether any timer has expired and, for each expired timer found, queues the timer function that is to be executed upon the expiration of that timer. The timer functions thus queued are executed just before the kernel returns control to the application. Timer error can be large and unpredictable because of the delay thus introduced by the kernel and possibly large execution times of the timer functions.

Threads.   Until recently, Linux did not offer a thread library. Rather, it offers only the low-level system call *clone( )*. Using this system call, one can create a process that shares the address space of its parent process, as well as the other parts of the parent's context (e.g., open file descriptors, message managers, and signal handlers) as specified by the call.

Recently, X. Leroy developed LinuxThreads (http://pauillac.inria˜xleroy/linuxthreads/). Each thread provided by this thread library is a UNIX process that is created using the *clone( )* system call. These threads are scheduled by the kernel scheduler just like UNIX processes.

LinuxThread provides most of the POSIX thread extension API functions and conforms to the standard except for signal handling.[29] In particular, LinuxThreads uses signals SIGUSR1 and SIGUSR2 for its own purpose. As a consequence, these signals are no longer available to applications. Since Linux does not support POSIX real-time extensions, there is no signal for application-defined use! Moreover, signals are not queued and may not be delivered in priority order.

The major advantage of the one-thread-per process model of LinuxThreads is that it simplifies the implementation of the thread library and increases its robustness. A disadvantage is that context switches on mutex and condition operations must go through the kernel. Fortunately, context switches in the Linux kernel are efficient.

UTIME High-Resolution Time Service.   UTIME [HSPN] is a high-resolution time service designed to provide microsecond clock and timer granularity in Linux. With UTIME, system calls that have time parameters, such as *select* and *poll*, can specify time down to microsecond granularity.

To provide microsecond resolution, UTIME makes use of both the hardware clock and the Pentium time stamp counter. Rather than having the clock device programmed to interrupt periodically, UTIME programs the clock to interrupt in one-shot mode. At any time, the next timer interrupt will occur at the earliest of all future timer expiration times. Since the kernel responds as soon as a timer expires, the actual timer resolution is only limited by the length of time the kernel takes to service a timer interrupt, which is a few microseconds with UTIME.

Since the clock device no longer interrupts periodically, UTIME uses the Pentium time stamp counter to maintain the software clock. When the system is booted, the clock is programmed to interrupt periodically. During initialization, UTIME reads and stores the time stamp counter periodically and calculates the length of a *jiffy* in term of the number of time stamp cycles in a *jiffy* and the number of time stamp cycles in a second. Having thus calibrated the time stamp counter with respect to the clock and obtained the numbers of cycles per *jiffy* and cycles per second, UTIME then reprograms the clock to run in one-shot mode.

Hereafter, whenever a timer interrupt occurs, the interrupt service routine first updates the software clock based on the time stamp counter readings obtained at the current time and at the previous timer interrupt. UTIME provides time in terms of *jiffies*, as well as *jiffies_u*, which give the number of microseconds that have elapsed since the beginning of the current *jiffy*. It then queues the timer functions that are to be executed at the current timer interrupt, finds the next timer expiration time from the timer queue, and sets the clock to interrupt at that time. Because of the extra work to update the time and set the timer, the execution time of the

---

[29]According to POSIX, an asynchronous signal, for example, one that is sent via *kill( )* or a tty interface, is intended for the entire process, not only a thread within the process. If the thread to which the signal is sent is blocking the signal, the signal is nevertheless handled immediately as long as some thread within the same process is not blocking the signal. In other words, any thread within the process that is not blocking the signal can handle the signal. This feature is not implemented in LinuxThreads. (It is not straightforward to implement this feature within LinuxThread because each thread is a process and has its own process ID.) When such a signal is sent to a Linux thread which is blocking the signal, the signal is queued and is handled only when the thread unblocks the signal.

timer interrupt service routine in Linux with UTIME is several times larger than in standard Linux.

If a jiffy has elapsed since the last timer interrupt, the kernel executes the standard Linux heartbeat maintenance code, including decrementing the remaining quantum of the running process. As in standard Linux, the execution of timer functions is postponed until the kernel completes all these chores and gets ready to return control to the application.

KURT, Kansas University Real-Time System.   KURT [HSPN] makes use of UTIME and extends Linux for real-time applications. It is designed for firm real-time applications that can tolerate a few missed deadlines.

Real-Time Modes and Processes.   KURT differentiates real-time processes from normal Linux processes. It has three operation modes: focused mode, normal mode, and mixed mode. Only real-time processes can run when the system is in focused mode. Applications with stringent real-time requirements should run in this mode.

All processes run as in standard Linux when the system is in normal mode. The system starts in this mode. In the mixed mode, nonreal-time processes run in the background of real-time processes.

Time-Driven Scheduling of Real-Time Processes.   In the KURT model, a real-time application consists of periodic and nonperiodic processes. The invocation times (i.e., the release times) of all events (i.e., jobs or threads) in all these processes are known. Each process starts as a nonreal-time process. To run in one of the real-time modes (i.e., focused or mixed modes) as a real-time process, a process first registers itself with the system using a KURT system call for this purpose, while it declares its parameters and chooses a scheduling policy. (To return to be a nonreal-time process, it unregisters.) After all processes in the real-time application have registered, the system can then be switched to one of real-time modes.

Mode switch is done under the control of an executive process. There is at least one executive process. After all processes that are to run in a real-time mode have registered, the executive process computes a schedule of all events based on the invocation times of all events declared by real-time processes. Having thus prepared real-time processes to run, the executive process calls *switch_to_rt( )* to switch the system into one of the real-time modes: *SCHED_KURT_PROCS* for the focused mode and *SCHED_KURT_ALL* for the mixed mode. Once in a real-time mode, events in real-time processes are scheduled according to the precomputed schedule in the time-driven manner. (KURT says that they are explicitly scheduled.)

KURT Components.   The KURT system consists of a core (i.e., a kernel) and real-time modules called RTMods. The core contains the KURT time-driven scheduler. It schedules all real-time events. Real-Time Modules are standard Linux kernel modules that run in the same address space as the Linux kernel. Each module provides functionality and is loadable. The only builtin real-time module is *Process RTMod*. This module provides the user processes with system calls for registering and unregistering KURT real-time processes, as well as a system call that suspends the calling process until the next time it is to be scheduled.

Source of Unpredictability.   In Chapter 5, we assumed that the schedule table fits and resides in memory. In contrast, KURT allows large schedule files that fit only partially in memory and have to be read into memory from time to time. Moreover, KURT makes no change in the disk device driver to minimize the length of time the driver may block timer interrupts and to correctly prioritize file system processing. Consequently, KURT does not provide sufficient predictability for hard real-time applications even when they run in the focus mode.

RT Linux.   RT Linux [Bara] is designed to provide hard real-time performance in Linux. It assumes that the application system can be divided into two parts. The real-time part runs on the RT kernel, while the nonreal-time part runs on Linux. The parts communicate via FIFO buffers that are pinned down in memory in the kernel space. These FIFO buffers are called RT-FIFOs. They appear to Linux user processes as devices. Reads and writes to RT-FIFOs by real-time tasks are nonblocking and atomic.

RT Linux eliminates the problem of Linux kernel blocking clock interrupts by replacing hardware interrupts by software emulated interrupts. Rather than letting Linux interface interrupt control hardware directly, the RT kernel sits between the hardware and the Linux kernel. Thus, the RT kernel intersects and attends to all interrupts. If an interrupt is to cause a real-time task to run, the RT kernel preempts Linux if Linux is running at the time and lets the real-time task run. In this way, the RT kernel puts Linux kernel and user processes in the background of real-time tasks.

If an interrupt is intended for Linux, the RT kernel relays it to the Linux kernel. To emulate disabled interrupt for Linux, the RT kernel provides a flag. This flag is set when Linux enables interrupts and is reset when Linux disables interrupts. The RT kernel checks this flag and the interrupt mask whenever an interrupt occurs. It immediately relays the interrupt to the Linux kernel only if the flag is set. For as long as the flag is reset, RT kernel queues all pending interrupts to be handled by Linux and passes them to Linux when Linux enables interrupts again.

The real-time part of the application system is written as one or more loadable kernel modules. In essence, all real-time tasks run in the kernel space. Tasks in each module may have their scheduler; the current version provides a rate-monotonic scheduler and an EDF scheduler.

12.8 SUMMARY

This chapter gave an overview of several commercial and widely used operating systems. It also described operating system services that should be provided but are not by these systems.

12.8.1 Commercial Operating Systems

The real-time operating systems described in Section 12.6 provide either all or most of the Real-Time POSIX API functions. (It is no wonder many students in real-time systems classes at Illinois said "they are practically the same" after hearing fellow students' presentations on these systems.) The systems typically offer their own API functions. Some of them are better than the standard functions either in functionality or in performance or both. Nevertheless, you may not want to use system-specific functions for the sake of portability.

Best Features.   Section 12.6 emphasized implementation features that are important for real-time applications. Examples of best practices discussed in the section include priority tracking in interrupt handling (Section 12.6.1), support for the MPCP model (Section 12.6.2), message-based priority inheritance (Section 12.6.3), hooks for extensions in the user level (Section 12.6.4), shared-memory multiprocessing support (Section 12.6.5), and modularity and ability to disable unneeded mechanisms.

Performance Information.   The chapter gave you no help in selecting an operating system for your applications. In particular, it presented no performance data. The best source of performance information, as well as distinguishing features, is the vendor's own home page. In addition to context-switch time, operating system vendors typically provide data on interrupt latency and dispatch latency of their own systems. Interrupt latency is the time the system takes to start the execution of an immediate interrupt routine. (It was defined more precisely in Section 12.1.2.) Dispatch latency is the length of time between the completion of an immediate interrupt service routine to the start of the thread released as a result of the interrupt. Both delays are measured in the absence of higher-priority interrupts, as they should be. The published data usually include both the vendor's system and close competitors', so by looking at such data provided by several vendors, you can get a reasonably good sense of how biased the data are.

Many other performance figures are also important. They include the amounts of time the system takes to block and deliver a signal, to grant semaphores and mutexes, and so on, as well as performance of file and networking systems. Such data are usually not published. If you ask, the vendor may give you some, but without similar data on competing systems for comparison. For this reason, you may need to measure candidate systems yourself, and you can find what and how to measure in [Gall]. (A point made by Gallmeister is that determinism is important for hard real-time applications. We have stressed here that determinism is not necessary; predictability is. The algorithms described in earlier chapters allow us to predict the real-time performance of the application system as long as the operating system allows us to bound the time and resources it spends and to prioritize our jobs.)

General-Purpose Operating Systems.   Section 12.7 discussed some of the reasons that Windows NT and Linux are not ideal for real-time applications. The most recent version of NT, NT 5.0 (Windows 2000), provides user threads with 16 real-time priority levels and the FIFO with equal-priority policy. It can deliver reasonably predictable performance under the conditions discussed in Section 12.6.1.

Like deferred procedure calls in NT, Linux interrupt handlers may prevent the scheduler from carrying out its activities in a timely fashion. KURT and RTLinux are Linux extensions designed to allow real-time applications to run with Linux applications. Section 12.7.2 described these extensions. The major drawback of the extensions is their nonstandard API.

12.8.2 Desirable Operating System Primitives

Several services and mechanisms can significantly simplify the implementation of user-level schedulers and resource managers. Section 12.2.2 described ones that are simple to implement within any operating system, have lower overhead, and do not introduce backward-compatibility problems. They are not provided by existing real-time operating systems and, hopefully, will be provided by future versions.

Dynamic Priority Scheduling.   EDF scheduling was considered less desirable than fixed-priority schemes because its implementation was thought to be more complex. More importantly, it is unstable under overloads. However, the total bandwidth and weighted fair-queueing algorithms can effectively keep individual tasks from interfering each other. They provide one of the best approaches to scheduling soft real-time tasks with hard real-time tasks. An operating system can easily support EDF scheduling (and therefore these bandwidth-preserving server algorithms) without high overhead in the same framework as fixed-priority scheduling.

Busy Interval Tracking.   None of the existing operating systems provides busy interval tracking service. Without the operating system's help, it is impossible for a user thread to determine the beginning and end of busy intervals of the system, or threads with priorities above a specified level, without undue complexity and overhead. In contrast, it is simple for the kernel to track of busy intervals and export the information on their endpoints. This information is needed by many algorithms for scheduling aperiodic tasks, synchronizing end-to-end tasks, and so on. Figure 12–7 shows a way for the kernel to provide this service.

Correct Interval Timers.   The interval timers provided by many operating systems may underestimate the amount of time a thread has executed. If such a timer is used to monitor the budget (or slack) consumption of a bandwidth-preserving server (or a slack stealer), the underestimation may cause periodic tasks to miss deadlines.

Support for Server Threads.   The mechanism for round-robin scheduling can be naturally extended to support user-level bandwidth-preserving servers or slack stealers. Also needed is an API function for setting the time slice (scheduling quantum) of a thread.

*12.8.3   Resource Reservation and Open Environment

Section 12.4 presented the resource reservation and scheduling mechanisms of Real-Time Mach and NT/RK resource kernel. While some experimental operating systems support resource reservation, usage monitoring, and enforcement, most commercial operating systems still do not.

Most operating systems (even those that support multiple scheduling policies) schedule all applications according to the same scheduling algorithm at any given time. Whether each application can meet its timing requirements is determined by a global schedulability analysis based on parameters of every task in the system. Section 12.5 presented an architecture of an open system in which each application can be scheduled in a way best suited for the application and the schedulability of the application determined independently of other applications that may run with it on the same hardware platform.

EXERCISES

12.1 The following pseudocode shows a way to detect and handle overruns of a timed loop. During each iteration, k functions, names *function_1* through *function_k* are executed. Each iteration is never supposed to take more than MAX_TIME units of time. At the start, a watchdog timer is set using *wdTimerSet( )*. The arguments include the ID of the timer and the delay to the expiration time. When the timer expires, the kernel interrupts the timed loop and invokes the overrun handler, named by the third argument, and passes to the handler the name of the function being executed when overrun occurs.

onTime: *wdTimerSet* (myTimerId, MAX_TIME, overRunHandler, function_name)
    Call *function_1( )*
    Call *function_2( )*
    . . . .
    . . . .
    Call *function_k( )*
    goto onTime

Discuss how promptly the overrun handler can respond and what factors affect its response.

12.2 If the *timer_sleep( )* function allows only the specification of a time interval for the calling thread to sleep, a periodic task can be implemented as follows.

timer_sleep (firstReleaseTime - *clock*);
nextReleaseTime = firstReleaseTime
do forever
    nextReleaseTime = nextReleaseTime + period;
    statements in the program of the thread
    timer_sleep (nextReleaseTime - *clock*);
enddo;

where the value of *clock* is equal to the current time and firstReleaseTime is the delay to the first release time of the thread.

(a) Discuss the factor(s) that may introduce release-time jitters and how large the release-time jitter can be?

(b) If the thread overruns, nextReleaseTime may be earlier than the current time and the argument of the timer_sleep function is negative. What should be the semantic of the function?

12.3 Consider two timer system calls: *timer_sleep( )* and *timer_notify( )*. Among the parameters of the former is a time instant; the call puts the calling thread to sleep until the time instant. Among the parameters of the latter are a time instant and a thread ID (or handle). At the specified time instant, the kernel signals the thread thus identified by the call. Using these timer system calls, rewrite the pseudocode of the cyclic executive in Figure 5-10 so it can steal the slack in each frame to improve the response times of aperiodic tasks. State your assumptions on the implementation of periodic and aperiodic tasks.

12.4 In an operating system, the resolution of the system clock and timers is x. The processor time the scheduler takes to service each timer event is e, and a context switch to the kernel takes no more than CS units of time. Suppose that the kernel executes and services timer events once every y units of time.

(a) In this part, we want to know how the actual timer resolution depends on these system parameters.

    i. Suppose that x and y are large (i.e., in order of milliseconds) compared with e and CS (e.g., in order of microseconds). What is the actual timer resolution?

    ii. Suppose that x and y are comparable with e and CS. What is the actual timer resolution?

(b) We expect that the lengths of intervals returned to a user thread which repeatedly calls *timer_sleep* (z) to deviate from the nominal interval length z. Measurements of many real-time operating systems have found that the maximum deviation can be as large as 20 percent of the nominal value even when there is only one user thread. It was also observed that an abnormally long interval is typically followed by an abnormally short interval, which may in turn be followed by a long interval. Give an explanation of why the lengths of consecutive intervals are correlated.

(c) Suppose that the number of timer events serviced by the kernel at each clock tick is never greater than l. Derive a formula expressing the error in the time intervals returned by the kernel. You may assume that there are no external interrupts or exceptions of higher priorities while the kernel is servicing the timer calls.

12.5 In the literature you may have seen measurement data on response times of POSIX real-time extension timer system calls *nanosleep( )* and *timer_settime( )* in some UNIX operating systems.

(a) Suppose that an operating system does tick scheduling with a 10-millisecond tick size. It has been reported that the calling thread may be suspended for almost 20 milliseconds when it calls nanosleep(0.01) or nanosleep (0.005) to be suspended for 10 or 5 milliseconds, respectively, even when there is no other thread in the system. Moreover, for all requested interval lengths that are multiples of 10 milliseconds, the inaccuracy in the suspension interval is approximately 10 milliseconds. Explain why we expect this behavior.

(b) Consider an operating system in which each timer event causes a context switch to the kernel, which processes the event as soon as possible. Suppose that the time required to complete this work is e and the context switch time is CS.

    i. Suppose that during a time interval when there is only one user thread, the thread repeatedly calls nanosleep(t) i times. Estimate the error in the requested interval length as a function of e, CS, t, and i for the cases where $t > e + CS$ and $t < e + CS$.

    ii. Suppose there are two threads in the system. Each repeatedly calls nanosleep(t) i times, and suppose that when two timer events occur at the same time, the one belonging to the higher-priority threads is processed first. Discusses the inaccuracy of the timers of the threads.

12.6 As stated in Section 12.2.1 implementation 1 in Figure 12–5(a) neglected the fact that a SIGALRM could have arrived before the thread calls *sigwaitinfo( )* to wait for the signal again. In that case, the signal would be blocked. In a Real-Time POSIX compliant system, the system keeps track of this by incrementing the overrun count of the times. By examining the overrun count, the thread can determine the number of times the timer has expired while it is executing. Rewrite the pseudocode so the thread will be released the correct number of times within any time interval. Make sure that the interrelease time is never less than 100.

12.7 In Section 12.2.2. it was stated that on a K-bit CPU, the scheduler makes at most $\Omega/2K - 1 + \log_2 K$ comparisons to find the highest priority nonempty queue among Ω fixed-priority queues. Describe in detail how this operation is done. (*Hint*: Consider the use of a bit vector containing 1 bit per priority queue to keep the empty/nonempty status of the queues.)

12.8 An application consisting of 11 periodic threads with relative deadlines 1, 2, 5, 6, 12, 19, 21, 27, 45, 75, and 150 is scheduled on EDF basis. Suppose that the operating system uses the queue structure described in Figure 12–6 and supports four distinct relative deadlines, that is, $\Omega' = 4$. Find a mapping from the relative deadlines of the threads to four relative deadlines supported by the system. What is the schedulable utilization of the system?

12.9 An operating system provides 256 fixed priorities to threads in the system, but only 32 priorities levels for their messages exchanged through message queues. Suppose that each sending thread chooses the priority of its messages by mapping the 256 thread priority levels to 32 message priority levels. Compare the uniform mapping and constant ratio mapping schemes. Which one is better and why? Here, we measure the performance of a mapping scheme by the average number of messages in each message queue found to have an identical priority; the fewer, the better.

12.10 The pseudocode description in Figure 12–8 makes the following assumptions. Give a brief argument to explain why these assumptions are true when there is only one processor and threads never self-suspend,

  (a) Immediately before it is denied a lock and becomes blocked, the priority of a thread is higher than all the ready and blocked threads in the system. (For this reason, there is no need to check whether the priority of each thread in the blocking chain is indeed lower than the newly blocked thread.)

  (b) If within one critical section while a thread *TH* is holding a resource *R* it has inherited more than one priority through the resource, the priority it inherits later is higher. (Because of this, the IL of a thread *TH* contains only one record on each resource *R* through which the thread inherits a higher priority than its assigned priority.)

12.11 The pseudocode of *restore_pr( )* in Figure 12–8 does not detail how the new priority of a thread is computed after the thread releases a resource. Give a pseudocode description of this computation.

12.12 Modify the pseudocode implementations of periodic threads in Figure 12–5 to add rule 1 of the release-guard protocol. Assume that the synchronization notification from the predecessor task is in the form of an incoming message.

12.13 Rather than making the kernel bigger, a seemingly better alternative is to implement the stack-based priority ceiling and ceiling-priority protocols at the user level.

  (a) Design a user-level resource manager that intersects lock requests from user threads and allocates resources to threads according to one of these protocols. You may need to extend to basic kernel for this purpose. In that case, describe and justify your extensions.

  (b) Are the stack-based and ceiling-priority versions easier to implement than the basic priority-ceiling protocol? Explain your answer.

12.14 In Section 12.2.2 we described the *restore_pr( )* function for restoring priority of a thread after the thread releases a resource *R* through which it has inherited a higher priority than its assigned priority. That function uses a circular link list to store the Inheritance Log (IL). The computation of the new priority π_r of the thread requires the scan of the entire list. A way to simplify this computation is keep IL as a stack. Every time a thread inherits a new priority through a resource *R*, *inherit_pr( )* pushes a record (*R*, current priority) on IL.

  (a) Describe in psuedo code the new *restore_pr( )*.

  (b) Discuss the pros and cons of these two data structures.

12.15 To deliver a per process signal to a process containing a large number of threads, some of which may have blocked the signal, the operating system must scan the signal masks of all threads to find one that does not block the signal. If it finds none, it queues the signal until some thread in the process unblocks the signal. The overhead of this search is undesirable. How can this overhead be minimized?

POSIX Thread and Real-Time Extensions

This appendix presents a brief overview of the thread and real-time extensions of the POSIX (Portable Operating System Interface) standard 1003.1 [IEEE90b, Zlot, IEEE98]. Throughout this chapter, we referred to these extensions collectively as Real-Time POSIX. You can find detailed descriptions of thread and real-time extensions, as well as how to program using them, in [Bute] and [Gall].

POSIX is an API standard. Applications that conform to the standard are portable at the source code level across operating systems that conform to the standard. An operating systems is said to conform or compliant to the standard if it provides all the interface functions required by the standard.[30] An application is said to conform if it uses only the required functions to access operating system services.

POSIX 1003.1 defines the basic functions of a Unix operating system, including process management, device and file system I/O, and basic IPC and time services. All modern, general-purpose operating systems support this standard. The real-time (1003.1b) and thread (1003.1c) extensions of POSIX 1003.1 define a subset of POSIX interface functions that are particularly suitable for multithreaded real-time applications. Specifically, 1003.1c extends 1003.1 to include the creation of threads and management of their execution. Real-time extensions defined by 1003.1b include prioritized scheduling, enhanced signals, IPC primitives, high-resolution timer, memory locking, synchronized I/O, asynchronous I/O, and contiguous files. Previous sections of this chapter described some of these functions: Specifically, Sections 12.2.2 described prioritized scheduling, Section 12.3.1 described message passing, and Section 12.3.2 described real-time signals.

Threads. The POSIX API is based on the UNIX process model (i.e., a single thread of control per process). This model is incompatible to the thread model of real-time applications. As we have seen earlier, an embedded application may have only one process but

---

[30]A compliant operating system may provide additional functions provided that the unrequired functions do not conflict with the required functions.

have multiple threads of control. POSIX thread extension assumes that threads are the basic units of concurrency. Among the interface functions defined by POSIX 1003.1c are those for creating, initializing, and destroying threads; managing thread resources; and scheduling their executions.

There are also functions for setting and reading attributes of a thread, as well as functions for initializing and destroying the object used by the system to maintain all attributes of each thread. Priority and scheduling policy are examples of thread attributes, as well as its stack size and address.

The thread extension also redefines the semantics of basic POSIX process management functions [i.e., *fork( )*, *exec( )*, *wait( )*, *exit( )*] so that they can be used by multithreaded processes. Take *fork( )* as an example. This function creates a duplicate process with its own address space. The new process inherits all the threads in the parent process. Among the threads in the child process, only the thread that called *fork( )* is active. The states of the other threads are undefined.

Similarly, the thread extension defines the rules for signals targeted at the thread and process levels. For example, a signal is ignored if a thread in a multithreaded process ignores the signal. On the other hand, signal mask is maintained at the thread level. Therefore, a thread can mask signals independently of other threads in the same process. An unignored signal targeted at a thread is blocked only when that thread blocks it. An unignored signal targeted to a process is delivered to any thread that is not blocking the signal.

This chapter assumes that threads are handled by the kernel. This is true for most of the operating systems described here. Threads may also be handled by library functions. Linux thread library is an example.

Clocks and Timers.   Clock and timer interface functions make time visible to the application threads. POSIX real-time extensions assume that the system may have more than one clock. The function *clock_settime(clock_id, *timeval)* allows a thread to set the value of a specified clock, and the function *clock_gettime(clock_id, *timeval)* allows a thread to read the time measured by the specified clock. Rather than only three timers in Unix, there can be 32 timers per process. Section 12.2 gave examples illustrating the use of functions that a thread can call to create, set, cancel and destroy its timers. In addition, there are functions for getting the resolution of a clock and time remaining of a timer.

The data structures used by timer interface functions allows for nanosecond resolution. However, timer resolution supported by most operating systems is far more coarse for reasons discussed in Section 12.2.

The system keeps an overrun count for each timer. When an overrun of the timer occurs (i.e., when the SIGALRM signal delivered upon an expiration of the timer is blocked), the system increments the overrun count. The *timer_getoverrun( )* function gives the overrun count for a timer and allows the application to keep track of timer expirations reliably.

Scheduling Interface.   Real-Time POSIX requires a compliant operating system to support fixed priority scheduling with at least 32 priority levels. Priority levels are numbered so that the larger the number, the higher the priority.

A thread (process) may choose the scheduling policy or policies for itself and other threads (process). Specifically, a thread may (1) set and get its own priority and priorities of other threads and (2) choose among FIFO (*SCHED_FIFO*), round-robin (*SCHED_RR*), and implementation-specific (*SCHED_OTHER*) policies.

In principle, a Real-Time POSIX compliant system can support the EDF algorithm and other dynamic priority algorithms, since a user-level scheduler can use functions such as *pthread_att_setschedparam(*att, param)* to set the priority of a thread according to the deadline of the thread or some other attribute. However, the additional system calls at the release of each thread to get the current time and set thread priority adds considerable amount of scheduling overhead, making the implementation of a EDF scheduler expensive and the responsiveness of the scheduler poor.

Since threads may make independent choices of scheduling policies and priorities, it is possible for different threads within the same process to be scheduled according to different scheduling policies. The standard does not restrict the priority levels used by different scheduling policies within a system. Rather, whether different scheduling policies have overlapping priority levels is the choice of each implementation. In most real-time operating systems, the ranges of priority levels completely overlap. So, at any priority level, some threads may be scheduled according to the FIFO policy and some according to the round-robin policy.

Synchronization.   Synchronization facilities provide semaphores, mutexes and condition variables. POSIX semaphores are special objects. Once such an object is created and opened, the semaphore it provides allows processes to synchronize with each other. POSIX semaphores are simple and have very low overhead, especially when implemented in shared memory. However, since priority inversion is uncontrolled, it is not ideal for real-time applications.[31]

In contrast, Real-time POSIX mutexes support both Priority Inheritance and Ceiling Priority protocols. (Ceiling Priority Protocol is called Ceiling Protection Protocol in Real-Time POSIX terms.) Specifically which protocol a mutex object supports depends on whether the protocol attribute of the mutex is set to *POSIX_PTHREAD_PRIO_INHERIT* or *POSIX_PTHREAD_PRIO_-PROTECT*. (A thread sets this attribute by calling the function *pthread_mutexattr_setprotocol ( )* after it creates the mutex.) In the latter case, the mutex has a priority ceiling: When a thread with current priority $\pi(t)$ locks the mutex, it executes at the priority ceiling of the mutex. An operating system can use the priority-inheritance mechanisms described in Section 12.3.1 to support priority inheritance through mutexes.

Condition variables allow a thread to lock a mutex depending on one or more conditions being true. This is done by associating the mutex with a condition variable which defines the waited-for condition. (In general, a condition may be defined by a Boolean expression of several condition variables.) When the thread locks the mutex and finds the condition not true, it releases the mutex and returns to wait for the condition to become true. When we say that the system supports condition variables, we mean that it makes the thread's release of the mutex and return to wait for the specified condition atomic. When another thread makes the

---

[31] Some semaphores are named, while those for synchronizing shared memory accesses are typically unnamed. In the case of named semaphores, ceiling priority protocol can be implemented at the user level in the manner described in Section 12.6.1.

condition true, the waiting thread is waken up to lock the mutex again and proceed to enter the critical section guarded by the mutex.

Interprocess Communication, Event Notification, and Software Interrupt.   Real-Time POSIX improves predictability in interprocess communication by providing the application with control over message passing. As discussed in Section 12.3.1, Real-Time POSIX messages are prioritized, just like threads, and they are dequeued in priority order. Send and receive are nonblocking. Moreover, receive notification makes it unnecessary for a receiver to check for the arrival of a message to an empty queue.

Section 12.3.2 discussed the Real-Time POSIX signal facility for multithreaded real-time applications. Signals are primarily for event notification and software interrupt. POSIX provides only two application-defined signals. POSIX signals are delivered in FIFO order, are not queued, and cannot pass data. In contrast, Real-Time POSIX provides at least eight application-defined signals, are delivered in priority order, and can carry data. Moreover, blocked signals are queued.

Shared Memory and Memory Locking.   Real-Time POSIX compliant systems support shared memory, in addition to file mapping (i.e., *mmap*, using which an application can map any file into its own address space and then access file as if it were in memory.) In such a system, a process can create a shared memory object that is accessible by other processes.

Real-time application in a Real-Time POSIX compliant system that supports virtual memory can control memory residency of their code and data using functions *mlockall* and *mlock*. The former tells the operating system to lock the entire memory; the latter tells the operating system to lock the specified range of address space of a process in memory.

Synchronized I/O.   POSIX real-time extension provides the application with more control over file operations, specifically, over when data in the file are actually written to the disk and file state information stored on the disk updated. For performance sake, most operating systems hold output data to disk in a buffer cache. In response to a write, the system moves the output data blocks to its own buffer. If the system receives a request to read the blocks before it flushes them to the disk (i.e., writes the buffer to disk and frees the buffer space), it can respond to the request without accessing the disk. The output data is safely stored on disk only when the buffer is flushed. The system flushes the buffer when the buffer is full or when the user requests the buffer be flushed. (The Unix system call for this purpose is called *sync*.)

The Real-Time POSIX file synchronization facility is called synchronized I/O. If available (i.e., if *_POSIX_SYNCHRONIZED_IO* in *<unistd.h>* is not defined as -1), synchronized I/O supports two levels of file synchronization: data integrity and file integrity. Data integrity is maintained when output data blocks are safely stored on disk. File integrity of a file is maintained when both data in the file and state information on the file are stored on disk. An application (e.g., a transaction to update a disk-resident database or a checkpointing process) can maintain data and file integrity to a great extent by calling the Real-Time POSIX synchronized I/O system calls *fdatasync* and *fsync*, respectively.

However, data (or file) can be inconsistent temporarily even when the application calls *fdatasync* (or *fsync*) immediately after each write. (Because the application can be preempted after a write but before the corresponding *fdatasync*, the duration of inconsistency can be arbitrarily long.) This may not be tolerable for some applications (e.g., a checkpointing process). For applications which require immediate file synchronization, POSIX real-time extension provides three file descriptor flags: *O_DSYNC*, *O_SYNC*, and *O_RSYNC*. By setting one or more of these flags, the application tells the operating system to synchronize I/O immediately following each write (and read) operation.[32] Specifically, when file descriptor flag *O_DSYNC* is set, the operating system flushes the data and state information immediately after each write. When the flag *O_SYNC* is set, the operating system also updates inode, in addition to flushing data and state information, after each write. The most stringent flag is *O_RSYNC*. When this flag is set, the operating system carries out the synchronization operation immediately following each read as well as each write.

Asynchronous I/O.   Real-Time POSIX provides the asynchronous I/O (AIO) capability so that I/O operations can be carried out concurrently with computations. (For example, a thread may send a video frame after compressing it. The thread can compress the subsequent frame concurrently with the output of the compressed frame.) The functions for asynchronous read and write are *aio_read( )* and *aio_write( )*, respectively. One of their arguments is a pointer (or array of pointers) to an AIO control block, which is called *aiocb* (or an array of *aiocb*s). This data structure specifies the I/O operation requested by the system call. Its elements include the descriptor of the file to be read or written, the address of buffer to read to or write from, the number of bytes, and the notification signal to be delivered upon completion.

A thread or process that uses one of the real-time scheduling policies (i.e., *SCHED_RR* or *SCHED_FIFO*) can prioritize its I/O request, and the priority of the request is specified by the *aio_reqprio* element in the *aiocb* of the request. A Real-Time POSIX compliant operating system orders asynchronous I/O requests with respect to themselves according to their specified priorities. In order to safeguard incorrect prioritization, the priority *aio_reqprio* of an I/O request gives the number of priority levels by which the request priority is lower than the current priority of the caller. Therefore, the standard prevents a caller from requesting an asynchronuous I/O of a priority higher than its own current priority.

A thread or process can suspend itself to wait for the completion of an asynchronous I/O operation by calling the *aio_suspend( )*. This function provided by the POSIX real-time extension has a two-fold advantage over *sigsuspend( )*. First, we note that at any time, multiple asynchronous I/O operations requested by the caller may be outstanding; any of them may complete first and causes the delivery of a notification signal. *aio_suspend( )* enables the caller to wait for the signal that notifies the completion of a specific operation. In contrast, the caller of *sigsuspend( )* may be awaken by the notification signal of any outstanding asynchronous I/O operation. Second, like the real-time signal *sigwaitinfo( )*, *aio_suspend( )* is a synchronous wait function. When the waited-for signal is delivered, *aio_ suspend( )* returns without having to wait for a signal handler to complete.

---

[32]Gallmeister [Gall] warned that a file may still not be written to disk platter when it is written to the disk by the operating system. The reason is that the disk may have internal cache and output data blocks may be held there temporarily.

Real-Time files.   Real-time applications typically prefer preallocation of fixed-size files in order to avoid the unpredictable delay introduced by dynamic allocation. Moreover, they often access files sequentially. For this access pattern, seek time is minimized (and repeated setting of DMA devices eliminated) when each file consists of contiguous disk blocks. POSIX real-time extension allows the applications to provide advisories to the operating system; that file allocation should be optimized for sequential access is an example. Since the system is not required to follow advisories, applications have only limited control on file layouts.

Bibliography

Below is a list of references cited in text. It is far from comprehensive. The references point to places where you can find in-depth information on various topics. Whenever there are several publications on a topic, the bibliography usually cites the most recent one(s) and in more easily found pubications. The reason for this choice is that more recent publications provide pointers to earlier work but not the other way around.

[AbMo]   Abbott, R., and H. Garcia-Molina, "Scheduling real-time transactions: a performance evaluation," *Proceedings of the 14th Very Large Data Bases*, 1988.

[ABTR]   Audsley, N., A. Burns, K. Tindell, M. Richardson, and A. Wellings, "Applying a new scheduling theory to static priority preemptive scheduling," *Software Engineering Journal*, vol. 5, no. 5, pp. 284–292, 1993.

[ACZD]   Agrawal, G., B. Chen, W. Zhao, and S. Davari, "Guaranteeing synchronous message deadlines with the timed token medium access control protocol," *IEEE Transactions on Computers*, vol. 43, no. 3, pp. 327–339, March 1994.

[AMMM]   Aydin, H., P. Mejia-Alvarez, R. Melhem, D. Mosse, "EDF, LLF, and PFair policies are also optimal for reward-based scheduling," *Proceedings of IEEE Real-Time Systems Symposium*, December 1999.

[AMWH]   Arnold, R., F. Mueller, D. Whalley, and M. Harmon, "Bounding worst-case instruction cache performance," *Proceedings of IEEE Real-Time Systems Symposium*, December 1994.

[AnRJ]   Anderson, J., S. Ramamurthy, and K. Jeffay, "Real-time computing with lock-free objects," *ACM Transactions on Computer Systems*, vol. 15, no. 6, pp. 388–395, May 1997.

[ANSI]   ANSI Standard X3.139, FDDI Token Ring Medium Access Control, 1987.

[AKRS]   Aras, C. M., J. F. Kurose, D. S. Reeves, and H. Schulzrinne, "Real-time communication in packet-switched networks," *Proceedings of the IEEE*, vol. 82, no. 1, January 1994.

[AsWi]   Astrom, K. J., and B. Wittenmark, *Computer-Controlled Systems*, Chap 1, 3rd Edition, Prentice Hall, Upper Saddle River, NJ, 1997.

[AsWZ]   van As, H., J. Wong, and P. Zafiropoulo, "Fairness, priority and predictability of the DQDB MAC protocol under heavy load," *Proceedings of International Zurich Seminar*, March 1990.

[BaHR]   Baruah, B., R. Howell, and L. Rosier, "Feasibility problems for recurring tasks on one processor," *Theoretical Computer Science*, Vo. 118, No. 1, pp.3–20, 1993.

[Bake]   Baker, T. P., "Notes on [LiLa]," unpublished notes.

[Bake91] Baker, T. P., "A stack-based resource allocation policy for real-time processes," *IEEE Real-Time Systems Symposium*, 1991.

[BaOz] Balakrishnan, S., and F. Ozguner, "A priority-driven flow control mechanism for real-time traffic in multiprocessor networks," *IEEE Transactions on Parallel and Distributed Systems*, vol. 9, no. 7, July 1998.

[Bara] Barabanov, M., "A Linux-based real-time operating system," M.S. thesis, Computer Science, New Mexico Institute of Mining and Technology, Socorro, NM, June 1997.

[BaSh] Baker, T. P., and A. Shaw, "The cyclic executive model and Ada," *Proceedings of IEEE Real-Time Systems Symposium*, pp. 120–129, December 1988.

[BCGM] Baruah, S., D. Chen, S. Gorinsky, and A. Mok, "Generalized multiframe tasks," *Real-Time Systems Journal*, July 1999.

[BeBu] Bernat, G., and A. Burns, "Combining (n m) hard deadlines and dual priority scheduling," *Proceedings of IEEE Symposium on Real-Time Systems*, December 1997.

[Bett] Bettati, R., "End-to-end scheduling to meet deadlines in distributed systems," Ph.D. thesis, Department of Computer Science, University of Illinois at Urbana-Champaign, 1994.

[BKMM] Baruah, S., G. Koren, D. Mao, B. Mishra, A. Raghunathan, L. Roser, D. Shasha, and F. Wang, "On the competitiveness of on-line real-time task scheduling," *Proceedings of IEEE Real-Time Systems Symposium*, pp. 106–115, December 1991.

[Blas] Blaswicz, J., "Selected topics in scheduling theory," *Annals of Discrete Mathematica*, vol. 31, 1987.

[BLOS] Burchard, A., J. Liebeherr, Y. Oh, and S. H. Son, "New strategies for assigning real-time tasks to mulatiprocessor systems," *IEEE Transactions on Computers*, vol. 44, no. 12, pp. 1429–1442, December 1996.

[BoDe] Boddy, M., and T. Dean, "Solving time-dependent planning problems," *Proceedings of International Joint Conference on Artificial Intelligence*, August 1989.

[Bogl] Bogler, P. L., *Radar Principles with Applications to Tracking Systems*, John Wiley and Sons, 1990.

[BuDW] Buneman, P., S. Davidson, and A. Watters, "A semantics for complex objects and approximate queries," *Proceedings of the Seventh Symposium on the Principles of database Systems*, March 1988.

[Bunn] Bunnell, M., "Galaxy White Paper," http://www.lynx.com/lynx_directory/galaxy/galwhite.html.

[Bute] Betenhof, D. R., *Programming with POSIX Threads*, Addison-Wesley Longman, 1997.

[BZBH] Braden, R., L. Zhang, S. Berson, S. Herzog, and A. Jamin, "Resource ReSerVation protocol (RSVP)—version 1, functional specification," Proposed Standard, RFC 2205, September 1997.

[CaDM] Card, R., E. Dumas, and F. Mevel, *The Linux Kernel book*, John Wiley and Sons, 1997.

[ChAZ] Chen, B., G. Agrawal, and W. Zhao, "Optimal synchronous capability allocation for hard real-time communications with timed token protocols," *Proceedings of IEEE Real-Time Systems Symposium*, pp. 198–207, December 1992.

[Chen] Chen, M. I., "Schedulability analysis of resource access control protocols in real-time systems," Ph.D. thesis, Technical Report No. UIUCDCS-R-91-1705, Department of Computer Science, University of Illinois, August 1991.

[Cheo] Cheong, I., "Heuristic algorithms for scheduling error-cumulative, periodic jobs," Ph.D. thesis, Department of Computer Science, University of Illinois, January 1993.

[ChCh] Chetto, H., and M. Chetto, "Some results of the earliest deadline scheduling algorithm," *IEEE Transactions on Software Engineering*, vol. 15, no. 10, pp. 1261–1269, October 1989.

[ChLi]   Chen, M. I., and K. J. Lin, "Dynamic priority ceilings: A concurrency control protocol for real-time systems," *Real-Time Systems Journal*, vol 2, no. 4, pp. 325–346, December 1990.

[ChLL]   Chung, J. Y., J. W. S. Liu and K. J. Lin, "Scheduling periodic jobs that allows imprecise results," *IEEE Transactions of Computers*, vol.19, no.9, pp. 1156–1173, September 1990.

[Clar88]   Clark, D., "The design philosophy of the DARPA Internet protocols," *Proceedings of ACM SIGCOMM*, August 1988.

[Clar90]   Clark, R. K., "Scheduling dependent real-time activities," Ph.D. thesis, CMU-CS-90-155, Department of Computer Science, Carnegie-Mellon University, August 1990.

[ClSZ]   Clark, R. K., S. Shenker, and L. Zhang, "Supporting real-time applications in an integrated service packet network: Architecture and mechanisms," *Proceedings of ACM SIGCOMM*, 1992.

[CoGa]   Coffman, E. G and M. R. Garey, "Proof of the 4/3 conjecture for preemptive vs nonpreemptive two processor scheduling," *Journal of ACM*, vol. 40, no. 5, November 1993.

[CoGJ]   Coffman, E. G., Jr., M. R. Garey, and D. S. Johnson, "Approximation algorithms for bin-packing—a survey," *Analysis and Design of Algorithms in Combinatorial Optimization*, G. Ausiello and M. Lucertini, Eds., Springer-Verlag, pp. 147–172, 1981. Also, "Approximation algorithms for bin-packing—an updated survey," 1984.

[Cohe76]   Cohen, D., Specifications for the Network Voice Protocol, RFC 741, ISI/RR 7539, USC/Information Sciences Institute, March 1976.

[Cohe96]   Cohen, N. H., *Ada as a Second Language*, McGraw-Hill, 1996.

[CoSt]   Comer, D. E. and D. L. Stevens, *Internetworking with TCP/IP*, vol. 1. Prentice Hall, 1999.

[Crow]   Crowley, C., *Operating Systems*, pp. 293–294, Irwin, 1997

[Cruz]   Cruz, R., "A calculus for network delay, part I: network elements in isolation," *IEEE Transactions on Information Theory*, vol. 37, no. 1. pp. 114–121, 1991.

[DaAo]   Dally, W. and H. Aoki, "Deadlock free adaptive routing in multicomputer networks using virtual channels," *IEEE Transactions on Parallel and Distributed Systems*, vol. 4, 1993.

[DaSe]   Dally, W. and C. L. Seitz, "Deadlock free message routing in multiprocessor interconnection networks," *IEEE Transactions on Computers*, vol. 36, 1987.

[DaTB]   Davis, R. I., K. W. Tindell, and A. Burns, "Scheduling slack time in fixed priority preemptive systems," *Proceedings of IEEE Real-Time Systems Symposium*, pp. 222–231, December 1993.

[DaWe]   Davis, R. I., and A. J. Wellings, "Dual priority scheduling," *Proceedings of IEEE Real-Time Systems Symposium*, December 1995.

[DeKS]   Demers, A., S. Keshav, and S. Shenker, "Analysis and simulation of a fair queueing algorithm," *Proceedings of ACM Sigcomm*, pp. 1–12, 1989, and *Journal of Internetworking Research and Experience*, October 1990.

[DeKT]   Dey, J. K., J. Kurose, and D. Towsley, "On-line scheduling policies for a class of IRIS (Increasing Reward with Increasing Service) real-time tasks," *IEEE Transactions on Computers*, vol. 45, no.7, July 1996.

[DeLS]   Deng, Z., J. W. S. Liu, and J. Sun, "A Scheme for Scheduling Hard Real-Time Applications in Open System Environment," *Proceedings of 9th Euromicro Workshop on Real-Time Systems*, pp. 191–199, June 1997.

[DhLi]   Dhall, S. K., and C. L. Liu, "On a Real-Time Scheduling Problem," *Operations Research*, vol. 26, no. 1, pp. 127–140, February 1978.

[DLZS]   Deng, Z., J. W. S. Liu, L. Zhang, M. Seri, and A. Frei, "An open environment for real-time applications," *Real-Time Systems Journal* vol. 16, no. 2/3, pp.155–186, May 1999.

[DoEl]   Doyle, L., and J. Elzey, "Successful use of rate-monotonic theory on a forbidable real-time system," *Proceedings of IEEE Real-Time Systems Symposium*, pp. 74–77, December 1993.

[DrHo]   Driscoll, K., and K. Hoyme, "The airplane information management system: An integrated real-time flight-deck control system," *Proceedings of IEEE Real-Time Systems Symposium*, pp. 267–270, December 1992.

[Duat]   Duato, J., "On the design of deadlock free adaptive routing algorithms for multicomputers: Theoretical aspects," *Proceedings of the Second European Conference on Distributed Memory Computing*, Springer-Verlag, 1991.

[EaLZ]   Eager, D. L., E. D. Lazowska, and J. Zahorjan, "Adaptive load sharing in homogeneous distributed systems," *IEEE Transactions on Software Engineering*, vol. SE-12, no. 5, May 1986.

[Elli]   Ellis, J. R., "A new approach to ensuring deterministic processing in a integrated avionics software systems," *Proceedings of IEEE NAECON*, 1985.

[FeLi]   Feng, W., and J. W. S. Liu, "Algorithms for scheduling real-time tasks with input error and end-to-end deadlines," *IEEE Transactions on Software Engineering*, vol. 23, no. 2, February 1997.

[FeRU]   Felperin, S., P. Raghavan, and E. Upfal, "A theory of wormhole routing in parallel computers," *IEEE Transactions on Computers*, vol. 45, no. 6, June 1996.

[FeVe]   Ferrari, D., and D. Verma, "A scheme for real-time channel establishment in wide-area networks," *IEEE Journal on Selected Areas in Communications*, vol 8, no. 3, April 1990.

[FiPa]   Figuera, N. R. and J. Pasquale, "An upper bound on delay for virtual clock service discipline," *IEEE Transactions on Networking*, Vol. 3, No. 4, pp. 309–408, August 1995.

[Fren]   French, S., *Sequencing and scheduling: An introduction to the mathematics of the job-shop*, John Wiley and Sons, 1982.

[FrPW]   Franklin, G. F., J. D. Powell, and M. L. Workman, *Digital control of dynamic systems*, 3rd ed., Addison-Wesley, 1998.

[GaBa]   Ghazalie, T. M., and T. P. Baker, "Aperiodic servers in deadline scheduling environment," *Real-Time Systems Journal*, vol. 9, no. 1, pp. 31–68, 1995.

[GaJo77]   Garey, M. R., and D. S. Johnson, "Two processor scheduling with start time and deadlines," *SIAM Journal of Computing*, vol. 6, 1997.

[GaJo79]   Garey, M. R., and D. S. Johnson, *Computers and Intractability: A Guide to the Theory of NP-Completeness*, W. H. Freeman, 1979.

[GaJS]   Garey, M. R., D. S. Johnson, and R. Sethi, "The complexity of flow-shop and job-shop scheduling," *Math. Oper. Res.*, vol. 1, 1976.

[Gall]   Gallmeister, B. O., *POSIX.4: Programming for the Real World*, O'Reilly & Associates, Inc., 1995.

[GiMW]   Gill, P. E., W. Murray, M. H. Wright, *Practical Optimization*, Academic Press, 1981.

[Gold]   Goldberg, A. V., "Processor efficient implementation of a maximum flow algorithm," *Information Processing Letter*, vol.38, pp.179–185, May 1991.

[Gole]   Golestani, S., "A framing strategy for congestion management," *IEEE Journal on Selected Areas in Communications*, vol. 9, no. 7, pp. 1064–1077, September 1991.

[Grah]   Graham, R. L., "Bounds on multiprocessing timing anomalies," *SIAM Journal of Applied Mathematics*, vol. 17, no. 2, March 1969.

[GrZi]   Grass, J., and S. Zilberstein, "Value driven information gathering," *Proceedings of AAAI Workshop on Building Resource-Bounded Reasoning Systems*, 1997.

[GuGH] Gutierrez, J. C. P., J. J. G. Garcia, and M. G. Harbour, "On the schedulability analysis for distributed hard real-time systems," *Proceedings of Euromicro Workshop on Real-Time Systems*, pp. 136–143, June 1997.

[Ha]   Ha, R., "Validating timing constraints in multiprocessor and distributed sytems," Ph.D. thesis, Department of Computer Science, University of Illinois at Urbana-Champaign, 1995.

[HaCL] Haritsa, J. R., M. J. Carey, and M. Livny, "On being optimistic about real-time constraints," *Proceedings of ACM Symposium of Principles of Database Systems*, 1999.

[HaKL] Harbour, M. G., M. H. Klien, and J. P. Lehoczky, "Fixed priority scheduling of periodic tasks with varying execution priorities," *Proceedings of IEEE Real-Time Systems Symposium*, pp. 116–128, December, 1991.

[HaLH] Han, C. C., K. J. Lin, and C. J. Hou, "Distance constrained scheduling and its applications to real-time systems," *IEEE Transactions on Computers*, July 1996.

[Han]   Han, C. C., "A better schedulability test," *Proceedings of Real-Time Systems Symposium*, December 1997.

[HaRa] Hamdaoui, M. and P. Ramanathan, "A dynamic priority assignment technique for streams with (m, k)-firm deadlines," *IEEE Transactions on Computers*, vol 44, no. 12, December 1995.

[Hart] Hart, J. M., *Win32 System Programming*, Addison-Wesley, 1997.

[HaSH] Han, C. C., K. G. Shin, and C. J. Hou, "Synchronous bandwidth allocation for real-time communications with the timed token MAC protocol," *IEEE Transactions on Computers*, 1997.

[Have] Havender, J. W., "Avoiding deadlock in multitasking systems," *IBM Systems Journal*, vol 7, no. 2, pp. 74–84, 1968.

[Heit] Heitmeyer, C., ed., *Formal Method for Real-Time Computing*, John Wiley and Sons, May 1996.

[HeWh] Healy, C., and D. Whalley, "Tighter timing predictions by automatic detection and exploitation of value-dependent constraints," *Proceedings of IEEE Real-Time Technology and Applications Symposium*, June 1999.

[HoJC] Hong, D., T. Johnson, and C. Chakravarthy, "Real-time database scheduling: A cost conscious approach," *Proceedings of ACM International Conference on Management of Data*, 1993.

[HoLW] Ho, K. I. J., J. Y. T. Leung, and W. D. Wei, "Scheduling imprecise computation tasks with 0/1 constraints," Technical Report, Department of Computer Science and Engineering, University of Nebraska, 1992.

[HoRa] Homayoun, N., and P. Ramanathan, "Dynamic priority scheduling of periodic and aperiodic tasks in hard real-time systems," *Real-Time Systems Journal*, vol 6, no. 2, pp. 207–232, 1994.

[HoZi] Horvitz, R. and S. Zilberstein, eds., Flexible Computations in Intelligent Systems: Results, Issues, and Opportunities, Workshop of AAAI, November 1996.

[HSPN] Hill, R., B. Srinivasan, S. Pather, and D. Niehaus, "Temporal Resolution and Real-Time Extensions to Linux," Technical Report ITTC-FY98-TR-11510-03, Department of Electrical and Computer Sciences, University of Kansas, June 1998.

[HuFL] Hull, D., W. Feng and J. W. S. Liu, "Enhancing the performance and dependability of hard real-time systems," *IEEE Computer Performance and Dependability Symposium*, Erlangen, Germany, April 1995.

[HuLi] Huang, N. F., and H. I. Liu, "A study of isochronous channel reuse in DQDB metropolitan area networks," *IEEE/ACM Transactions on Networking*, vol. 6, no. 4, August 1998.

[IEEE85]   IEEE/ANSI Standard 802.4, Token Passing Bus Access Method and Physical Layer Specifications, IEEE, New York, 1985.

[IEEE89]   IEEE Standard 802.5, *Token Ring Access Method and Physical Layer Specification*, IEEE, New York, 1989.

[IEEE90a]   IEEE Standard 802.6, DQDB MAN, Medium Access Control and Physical Layer Protocol Documents P802.6/D12, 1990.

[IEEE90b]   IEEE, Portable Operating System Interface (POSIX)—Part 1: System Application Program Interface (API).

[IEEE98]   IEEE Standard 1003.13, POSIX Real-Time Profiles; also ISO/IEC standard 9945-1 (1996).

[Inte]   *PSOSystem Systems Concepts*, Integrated Systems, Inc., November 1996.

[ISO93]   ISO International Standard 11898, Road Vehicles—Interchange of Digital Information—Controller Area Network (CAN) for High Speed Communications, 1993.

[ISO94]   ISO International Standard 13818-2, MPEG-2, Information Technology—Generic Coding of Moving Pictures and Associated Audio Information—Part 2: Video," 1994.

[JoPa]   Joseph, M. and P. K. Pandya, "Finding response times in real-time systems," *Comp. Journal*, vol. 29, no. 5, 1986.

[KaGa93]   Kao, B., and H. Garcia-Molina, "Deadline assignment in distributed soft real-time systems," *Proceedings of 13th IEEE International Conference on Distributed Computing Systems*, pp. 428–437, 1993.

[KaGa94]   Kao, B., and H. Garcia-Molina, "Subtask deadline assignment for complex distributed soft real-time tasks," *Proceedings of 14th IEEE International Conference on Distributed Computing Systems*, pp. 172–181, 1994.

[KaGS]   Kang, D. I., R. Gerber, and M. Saksena, "Performance-based design of distributed real-time systems," *Proceedings of IEEE Real-Time Technology and Application Symposium*, June 1997.

[KaKK]   Kalmanek, C. R., H. Kanakia, and S. Keshav, "Rate controlled servers for very high speed networks," *Proceedings of IEEE Global Telecommunications Conference*, December 1999.

[KaMZ]   Kamat, S., N. Malcolm, and W. Zhao, "Performance evaluation of a bandwidth allocation scheme for guaranteeing synchronous message with arbitrary deadlines in an FDDI network," *Proceedings of IEEE Real-Time Systems Symposium*, pp. 34–43, December 1993.

[KeLi70]   Kernighan, B. W., and S. Lin, "An efficient heuristic procedure for partitioning graphs," *Bell Systems Technical Journal*, vol. 49, no. 2, 1970.

[KeLi91]   Kenny, K. B. and K. J. Lin, "Building flexible real-time systems using the FLEX language," *IEEE Computer*, May 1991.

[KhSZ]   Khanna, S., M. Sebree, and J. Zolnowsky, "Real-time scheduling in SunOS 5.0," *Proceedings of USENIX Workshop on Unix*, 1992.

[KiMH]   Kim, S.-K., S. L. Min, and R. Ha, "Efficient worst-case timing analysis of data caching," *Proceedings of IEEE Real-Time Technology and Applications Symposium*, June 1996.

[KiTo]   Kim, B. and D. Towsley, "Dynamic flow control protocols for packet-switching multiplexers serving real-time multipacket messages," *IEEE Transactions on Communications*, vol. 34, no. 4, April 1986.

[Klie]   Klienrock, L. *Queueing Systems: Vol.2, Computer Applications*, John Wiley & Sons, 1976.

[KoPa]   Kochanski, R. J., and J. L. Paige, "SAFENET—the standard and its applications," *IEEE LCS*, vol. 2, no.1, pp.46–51, February 1991.

[Kope]   Kopetz, H., "Event-triggered versus time-triggered real-time systems," *Proceedings of International Workshop on Operating Systems of the 90s and Beyond*, Vol. 563 of *Lecture*

Notes in Computer Science, ed. by A. Karshmer and J. Nehmer, pp. 87–101, Springer-Verlag, 1991.

[Korf]   Korf, R. E., "Real-time heuristic search," *Artificial Intelligence*, vol. 42, no. 2, 1990.

[KoSp]   Korth, H. F., and G. D. Speegle, "Formal model of correctness without serializability," *Proceedings of ACM SIGMOD Conference on Management of Data*, 1988.

[KRPO]   Klien, M. H., T. Ralya, B. Pollak, R. Obenza, and M. G. Harbour, *A Practitioner's Handbook for Real-Time Analysis*, Kluwer Academic Publishers, 1993.

[KuMo91] Kuo, T. W. and A. K. Mok, "Load adjustment in adaptive real-time systems," *Proceedings of IEEE Real-Time Systems Symposium*, December 1991.

[KuMo93] Kuo, T. W. and A. K. Mok, "SSP: a semantic-based protocol for real-time data access," *Proceedings of IEEE Real-Time Systems Symposium*, December 1993.

[Kuo]   Kuo, T. W., "Real-Time Database—semantics and resource scheduling," Ph.D. Thesis, University of Texas at Austin, 1994.

[LBJR]   Lim, S. S., Y. H. Bae, G. T. Jang, B. D. Rhee, S. L. Min, C. Y. Park, H. Shin, K. Park, and C. S. Kim, "An accurate worst-case timing analysis for RISC processors," *Proceedings of IEEE Real-Time Systems Symposium*, December 1994.

[Leho]   Lehoczky, J. P., "Fixed priority scheduling of periodic task sets with arbitrary deadlines," *Proceedings of the IEEE Real-Time Systems Symposium*, December 1990.

[Leig]   Leigh, J. R., *Applied Control Theory*, 2nd ed., Peter Peregrinus Ltd., 1987.

[LeRa]   Lehoczky, J. P., and S. Ramos-Thuel, "An optimal algoririthm for scheduling soft-aperiodic tasks in fixed priority preemptive systems," *Proceedings of the IEEE Real-Time Systems Symposium*, pp. 110–123, December 1992.

[LeSD]   Lehoczky, J. P., L. Sha, and Y. Ding, "The rate-monotonic scheduling algorithm: Exact characterization and average case behavior," *Proceedings of Real-Time Systems Symposium*, pp. 166–171, December 1989.

[LeSh]   Lehoczky, J. P., and L. Sha, "Performance of real-time bus scheduling algorithms," *ACM Performance Evaluation Review*, vol. 14, May 1986.

[LeSo]   Lee, J., and S. H. Son, "Using dynamic adjustment of serialization order for real-time database systems," *Proceedings of IEEE Real-Time Systems Symposium*, December 1993.

[LeSS]   Lehoczky, J. P., L. Sha, and J. K. Strosnider, "Enhanced aperiodic responsiveness in hard real-time environments," *Proceedings of IEEE Real-Time Systems Symposium*, pp. 261–270, 1987.

[LeWh]   Leung, J. Y. T., and J. Whitehead, 'On the complexity of fixed-priority scheduling of periodic real-time tasks," *Performance Evaluation*, vol. 2, pp. 37–250, 1982.

[LiHa]   Liu, J. W. S, and R. Ha, "Efficient methods for validating real-time constraints," in *Principles of Real-Time Systems*, ed. S. H. Son, pp. 199–224, Prentice Hall, 1994.

[LiLa]   Liu, C. L. and Layland, "Scheduling algorithms for multiprogramming in a hard real-time environment," *J. Assoc. Comput. Mach.*, vol. 20, pp. 46–61, 1973.

[LiLK]   Lin, K. J., J. W. S. Liu and K. Kenny, "FLEX: A language for programming flexible real-time systems," pp. 251–290, in *Foundations of Real-Time Computing: Formal Methods and Specifications*, ed. A. M. Van Tilborg and G. M. Koob, Kluwer Academic Publishers, 1991.

[LiMu]   Li, J. P., and M. Mutka, "Priority based real-time communication for large scale wormhole networks," *Proceedings of International Parallel Processing Symposium*, August 1994.

[LiMW]   Li, Y.-T. S., S. Malik, and A. Wolf, "Cache modeling for real-time software: beyond direct mapped-instruction cache," *Proceedings of IEEE Real-Time Systems Symposium*, December 1996.

[Liou]   Liou, M., "Overview of the px64 kbits/sec video coding standard," *Communications of the ACM*, vol.34, no.4, pp.59–63, April 1991.

[LiSt]   Livingston, M., and Q. F. Stout, "Embeddings in hypercubes," *Mathematical and Computational Modeling*, vol. 11, pp. 222-227, 1988.

[LLRD]   Liu, J. W. S., C. L. Liu, J. L. Redondo, Z. Deng, T. S. Tia, R. Bettati, J. Sun, A. Silberman, M. Storch, and D. Hull, "PERTS: a prototyping environment for real-time systems," *International Journal of Software Engineering and Knowledge Engineering*, vol.6, no.2, pp. 161–177, June 1996.

[LLSB]   Liu, J. W. S., K. J. Lin, W. K. Shih, R. Bettati, and J.Y. Chung, "Imprecise Computations," *IEEE Proceedings*, vol. 82, pp. 1–12, January 1994.

[LLSC]   Liu, J. W. S., K. J. Lin, W. K. Shih, J. Y. Chung, A. Yu, and W. Zhao, "Algorithms for scheduling imprecise computations," *IEEE Computer*, May 1991.

[Lock86]   Locke, C. D., "Best-effort decision making for real-time scheduling," Ph.D. Thesis, CMU-CS-86-134, Department of Computer Science, Carnegie-Mellon University, May 1986.

[Lock96]   Locke, C. D., lecture notes at Workshop on Real-Time Data Bases, Newport Beach, CA, March 1996.

[LoVM]   Locke, C. D., D. R. Vogel, and T. J. Mesler, "Building a predictable avionics platform in ada: A case study," *Proceedings of IEEE Real-Time Systems Symposium*, 1997.

[LSLH]   Lam, K., S. H. Son, V. Lee, and S. Hung, "Using separate algorithms to process read-only transactions in real-time systems," *Proceedings of the IEEE Real-Time Systems Symposium*, December 1998.

[LSST]   Lehoczky, J. P., L. Sha, J. K. Strosnider, and H. Tokuda, "Fixed priority scheduling theory for hard real-time systems," in *Foundations of Real-Time Computing, Part 1: Scheduling and Resource Management*, ed. A. M. van Tilborg and G. M. Koob, Kluwer Academic Publishers, 1991.

[McEl]   McElhone, C., "Adapting and Evaluating Algorithms for Dynamic Schedulability Testing," Technical report YCS 225, Department of Computer Science, Univerity of York, England, 1994.

[Ment]   Mentor Graphics, *VRTX Real-Time Operating System*.

[MeST]   Mercer, C. W., S. Savage, and H. Tokuda, "Processor capacity reserve: Operating system support for multimedia applications," *Proceedings of the IEEE International Conference on Multimedia Computing and Systems*, May 1994.

[MMOP]   Montz, B., D. Mosberger, S. W. O'Malley, L. L. Peterson, T. A. Proebsting, "Scout: A communications-oriented operating system," *Hot OS*, May 1995.

[MoCh]   Mok, A. K.-L., and D. Chen, "A multiframe model for real-time tasks," *Proceedings of IEEE Real-Time Systems Symposium*, December 1996.

[MoJR]   Molano, A., K. Juvva and R. Rajkumar, "Real-time filesystems: Guaranteeing timing constraints for disk accesses in RT-Mach," *Proceedings of the IEEE Real-Time Systems Symposium*, December 1997

[Mok]   Mok, A. K.-L., "Fundamental design problems of distributed systems for hard real-time environment," Ph.D. thesis, MIT, 1983.

[MoPe]   Mosberger, D. and L. L. Peterson, "Making path explicit in the Scout operating system," *Proceedings of OSDI'96*, October 1996.

[Moto]   *pSOS+*™*/68K Real-Time Executive, User's Manual*, Motorola, Inc.

[MoMW]   Molini, J. J., S. K. Maimon, and P. H. Watson, "Real-time system scenarios", *Proceedings of IEEE 11th Real-Time Systems Symposium*, December 1990.

[MPEG]   MPEG, Coding of Moving Pictures and Associated Audio for Digital Storage Media at up to about 1.5 Mbits/sec, MPEG 91/185, 1991.

[Naka]   Nakazato, H., "Issues on synchronizating and scheduling tasks in real-time database systems," Ph.D. thesis, Technical Report No. UIUCDCS-R-93-1786, Department of Computer Science, University of Illinois, January 1993.

[NiFB]   Nichols, B., J. Farrell, and D. Buttlar, *Pthread Programming: Using POSIX Threads*, O'Reilly & Associates, Inc., February 1996.

[PaGa93]   Parekh, A. K., and R. G. Gallager, "A generalized processor sharing approach to flow control in integrated service networks: the single-node case," *IEEE/ACM Transactions on Networking*, vol. 1, no. 3, June 1993.

[PaGa94]   Parekh, A. K., and R. G. Gallager, "A generalized processor sharing approach to flow control in integrated service networks: the multiple-node case," *IEEE/ACM Transactions on Networking*, vol. 2, no. 2, April 1994.

[PaLC]   Pakin, S., M. Lauria, and A. Chien, "High performance messaging on workstations: Illinois Fast Messages (FM) for Myrinet," *Supercomputing'95*, San Diego, California.

[PeSh]   Peng, D., and K. Shin, "Static allocation of periodic tasks with precedence constraints in distributed real-time systems," *Proceedings of International Conference on Distributed Computing Systems*, 1989.

[Phil]   Philp, I. R., "Scheduling real-time messages in packet-switched networks," Ph.D. thesis, Technical Report No. UIUCDCS-R-96-1977, Department of Computer Science, University of Illinois, October 1996.

[QNX]   *QNX Operating System, System Architecture* and *Neutrino System Architecture Guide*, QNX Software Systems Ltd, 1999.

[Rama]   Ramanathan, P., "Overload management in real-time control application using (m, k)-firm guarantee," *IEEE Transactions on Parallel and Distributed Systems*, vol. 10, no. 6, June 1999.

[Reev]   Reevve, G. E., "What really happened on mars," http://research.microsoft.com/ mbj/Mars_Pathfinder/Mars_Pathfinder.html, 1997.

[ReHS]   Rexford, J., J. Hall, and K. G. Shin, "A router architecture for real-time point-to-point networks," *Proceedings of International Symposium on Computer Architectures*, May 1996.

[RKMO]   Rajkumar, R., J. Kanaka, A. Molano, and S. Oikawa, "Resource kernels: A resource-centric approach to real-time systems," *Proceedings of the SPIE/ACM Conference on Multimedia Computing and Networking*, January 1998.

[OhBa]   Oh, D. I. and T. P. Baker, "Utilization bounds for n-processor rate-monotone scheduling with static processor assignment," Technical Report, Department of Computer Science, Florida State University, 1996.

[SAJB]   Stoica, I., H. Abdel-Wahab, K. Jeffay, S. Baruah, J. Gehrke, and C. Plaxton, "A proportional share resource allocation algorithm for real-time, time-shared systems," *Proceedings of IEEE Real-Time Systems Symposium*, pp.288–299, 1996.

[SaKK]   Saran, H., S. Keshav, and C. R. Kamanek, "A scheduling discipline and admission control policy for Xunet 2," *Multimedia Systems*, vol. 2, 1994.

[SCFJ]   Schulzrine, H., S. L. Casner, R. Frederick, and V. Jacobson, RTP: A Transport Protocol for Real-Time Applications, Internet Engineering Task Force, Audio/Video Transport Working Group, Internet Draft, August 1999.

[ScZh]   Schwan, K., and H. Zhou, "Dynamic scheduling of hard real-time tasks and real-time threads," *IEEE Transactions on Software Engineering*, vol. 18, no. 8, pp. 736–748, August 1992.

[SeJo]   Sevcik, K. C., and M. J. Johnson, "Cycle time properties of the FDDI token ring protocol," *IEEE Transactions on Software Engereering*, vol. 13, no. 3, pp. 376–385, 1987.

[Shan]   Shannon, C. E., "Communication in presence of noise," *Proceedings of IRE*, vol. 37, 1949.

[ShLC]   Shih, W. K., J. W. S. Liu, and J. Y. Chung, "Algorithms for scheduling tasks to minimize total error," *SIAM Journal of Computing*, vol. 20, no. 3, June 1991.

[ShLi95] Shih, W. K., and J. W. S. Liu, "Minimization of the maximum error of imprecise computations." *IEEE Transactions on Computers*, March 1995.

[ShLi96] Shih, W. K., and J. W. S. Liu, "On-line scheduling of imprecise tasks to minimum total error," *SIAM Journal of Computing*, vol. 25, no. 5, October 1996.

[ShRL88] Sha, L., R. Rajkumar, and J. P. Lehoczky, "Real-time synchronization protocol for multi-processors," *Proceedings of IEEE Real-Time Systems Symposium*, 1988.

[ShRL90] Sha, L., R. Rajkumar, and J. P. Lehoczky, "Priority inheritance protocols: An approach to real-time synchronization," *IEEE Transactions on Computers*, vol. 39, 1990.

[ShSS]   Sha, L., S. S. Sathaye, and J. K. Strosnider, "Analysis of dual-link networks for real-time applcations," *IEEE Transactions on Computers*, vol. 46, no. 1, January 1997.

[SiGa]   Silberschatz, A., and P. B. Galvin, *Operating Systems Concepts*, Addison-Wesley, 1997.

[SKNL]   Skillman, T. L., W. Kohn, D. Nguyen, C. Ling, and D. Dodhiawala, "Class of hierarchical controllers and their blackboard implementations," *Journal of Guidance, Control and Dynamics*, vol. 13, no. 1, January 1990.

[SoLi]   Song, X., and J. W. S. Liu, "Maintaining temporal consistency: Pessimistic vs optimistic concurrency control," *IEEE Transactions on Knowledge and Data Engineering*, October 1995.

[Solo]   Solomon, D. A., *Inside Windows NT*, 2nd ed., Microsoft Press, 1998.

[SpBu]   Spuri, M., and G. Buttazzo, "Scheduling aperiodic tasks in dynamic priority systems," *Real-Time Systems Journal*, vol. 10, pp. 179–210, 1996.

[SpSL]   Sprunt, B, L. Sha, and J. P. Lehoczky, "Aperiodic task scheduling for hard real-time systems," *Real-Time Systems Journal*, vol 1, no. 1, pp. 27–60, 1989.

[SRLR]   Sha, L., R. Rajkumar, J. Lehoczky, and R. Ramamritham, "Mode change protocols for priority-driven preemptive scheduling," *Real-Time Systems Journal*, vol. 1., 1989.

[SRSC]   Sha, L., R. Rajkumar, S. H. Son, and C. H. Chang, "A real-time locking protocol," *IEEE Transactions on Computers*, vol. 40, no. 7, July 1991.

[Stal]   Stalling, W., *Data and Computer Communications*, 5th ed., Prentice Hall, 1997.

[StLS]   Strosnider, J. K., J. P. Lehoczky, and L. Sha, "The deferrable server algorithm for enhanced aperiodic responsiveness in hard real-time environments," *IEEE Transactions on Computers*, to appear.

[StML]   Strosnider, J. K., T. Marchok, and J. P. Lehoczky, "Advanced real-time scheduling using the IEEE 802.5 token ring," *Proceedings of IEEE Real-Time Systems Symposium*, pp. 42–52, 1988.

[StNa]   Steinmetz, R., and K. Nahrstedt, *Multimedia: Computing, Communications and Applications*, Prentice Hall, 1995.

[StTo]   Savage, S. and H. Tokuda, "Real-Time Mach timers: Exporting time to the user," *Proceedings of the 3rd USENIX Mach Symposium*, April 1993.

[StVa96] Stiliadis, D., and A. Varma, "Latency-rate servers: a general model for analysis of traffic scheduling algorithms," *Proceedings of Infocom*, 1996.

[StVa98a] Stiliadis, D., and A. Varma, "Rate-proportional servers: a design methodology for fair queueing algorithms," *IEEE/ACM Transactions on Networking*, Vol. 6, No. 2, April 1998.

[StVa98b]   Stiliadis, D., and A. Varma, "Efficient fair queueing algorithm for packet-switched networks," *IEEE/ACM Transactions on Networking*, vol. 6, no. 2, April 1998.

[SuLi]   Sun, J., and J. W. S. Liu, "End-to-end synchronization protocols of fixed priority periodic tasks," *Proceedings of the 16th IEEE International Conference on Distributed Computing Systems*, Hong Kong, June 1996.

[Sun]   Sun, J., "Fixed priority scheduling of end-to-end periodic tasks," Ph.D. thesis, Department of Computer Science, University of Illinois at Urbana-Champaign, 1997.

[SuTa]   Suzuki, J., and M. Taka, "Missing packet recovery techniques for low-bit-rate coded speech," *IEEE Journal on Selected Areas in Communications*, vol.7, no.5, June 1989.

[TaWo]   Tanenbaum, A., and A. Woodhull, *Operating Systems: Design and Implementation*, Prentice Hall, 1996.

[Tia]   Tia, T. S., "Utilizing slack time for aperiodic and sporadic requests scheduling in real-time systems," Ph.D. thesis, Technical report No. UIUCDCS-R-95-1906, Department of Computer Science, University of Illinois at Urbana-Champaign, April 1995.

[TiBW]   Tindell, K., A. Burns, and A. Wellings, "Allocating real-time tasks: An NP-hard problem made easy," *Real-Time Systems Journal*, vol.4, no.2, May 1992.

[TiCl]   Tindell, K. and J. Clark, "Holistic schedulability analysis for distributed hard real-time systems," *Microprocessing and Microprogramming*, vol. 50, no. 2/3, pp. 117–134, April 1994.

[TiLi]   Tia, T. S. and J. W. S. Liu, "Task and resource assignment in distributed real-time systems," *the International Journal of Mini and Microcomputers*, vol. 17, no. 1, pp. 18–25, November 1995.

[Topo]   Topolcic, C., Experimental Internet Stream Protocol: Version 2 (ST-II), Internet RFC 1190, October 1990.

[ToNR]   Tokuda, H., T. Nakajima, and P. Rao, "Real-Time Mach: Towards a predictable real-time system," *Proceedings of the USENIX Workshop on Mach*, October 1990.

[Turn]   Turner, K. S., "New directions in communications," *IEEE Communication Magazine*, vol. 24, no. 10, pp. 8–15, October 1986.

[VaKo]   Van Tilborg, A. M., and G. M. Koob, *Foundations of Real-Time Computing: Formal Methods and Specifications*, ed. A. M. Van Tilborg and G. M. Koob, Kluwer Academic Publishers, 1991.

[VeZF]   Verma, D. C., H. Zhang, and D. Ferrari, "Delay jitter control for real-time communication in packet switching network," *Proceedings of Tricomm'91*, pp. 35–46, April 1991.

[VrLi]   Vrbsky, S., and J. W. S. Liu, "APPROXIMATE: a query processor that produced monotonically improving approximate answers," *IEEE Transactions on Knowledge and Data Engineering*, vol. 5, no. 6, December 1993.

[Wind]   *VxWorks Programmer's Guide*, WindRiver System, Inc., 1997.

[WoOn]   Woods, J., and S. O'Neil, "Sub-banded coding of images," *IEEE Transactions on Acoustic Speech Signal Communications*, vol. 34, pp.1278–1288, October 1986.

[Xu]   Xu, J., "Multiprocessor scheduling of processes with release times, deadlines, precedence, and exclusion relation," vol. 19, no. 2, pp. 139–154, February, 1993.

[XuPa]   Xu, J., and D. L. Parnas, "On satisfing timing constraints in hard real-time systems," *IEEE Transactions on Software Engineering*, vol. 19, no. 1, pp. 70–84, January 1993.

[ZDES]   Zhang, L., S. Deering, D. Estrin, S. Shenker, and D. Zappala, "RSVP: A new resource reservation protocol," *IEEE Network Magazine*, September 1993.

[Zhan]   Zhang, L., "VirtualClock: a new traffic control algorithm for packet switching networks," *Proceedings of ACM SIGCOMM*, 1990. Also, "A new architecture for packet switched network protocols," Ph.D. thesis, Massachusetts Institute of Technology, July 1989.

[ZhFe]   Zhang, H and D. Ferrari, "Rate-Controlled Static-Priority Queueing," Technical Report TR-92-003, Computer Science Division, University of California at Berkeley, February 1992.

[ZhKe]   Zhang, H. and S. Keshav, "Comparison of rate-based service disciplines," *Proceedings of ACM SIGCOMM*, 1991.

[ZiRu]   Zilberstein, S., and S. J. Russell, "Anytime sensing, planning and action: a practical model for robot control," *Proceedings of International Joint Conference on Artificial Inteligence*, 1993.

[ZLDP]   Zhang, L., J. W. S. Liu, Z. Deng and I. Philp, "A two-level scheme for scheduling periodic messages on Myrinet in an open real-time environment," *Proceedings of IEEE Real-Time Systems Symposium*, December 1999.

[Zlot]   Zlotnick, F., *The POSIX.1 Standard: A Programmer's Guide*, Benjamin Cummings, 1991.

Index